MOON HANDBOOKS®

NICARAGUA

SECOND EDITION

RANDY WOOD & JOSHUA BERMAN

© JOSHUA BERMAN

AVALON TRAVEL

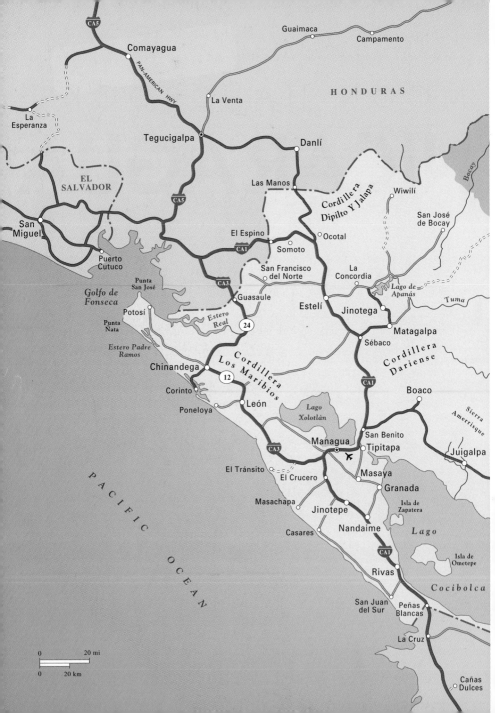

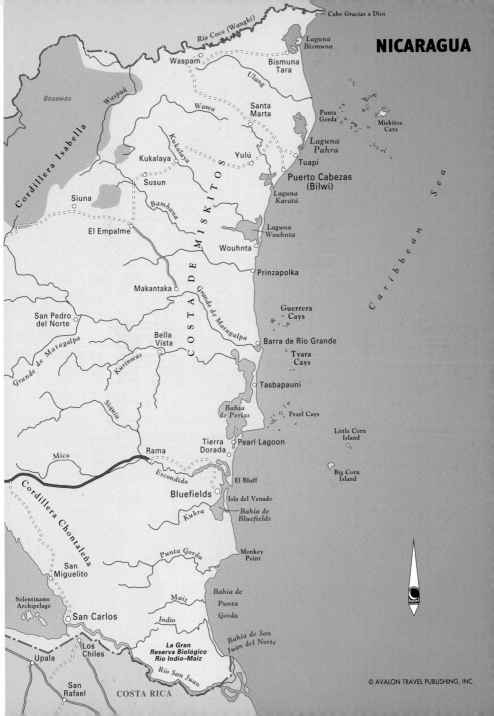

CONTENTS

Discover Nicaragua

Explore Nicaragua

MAPS

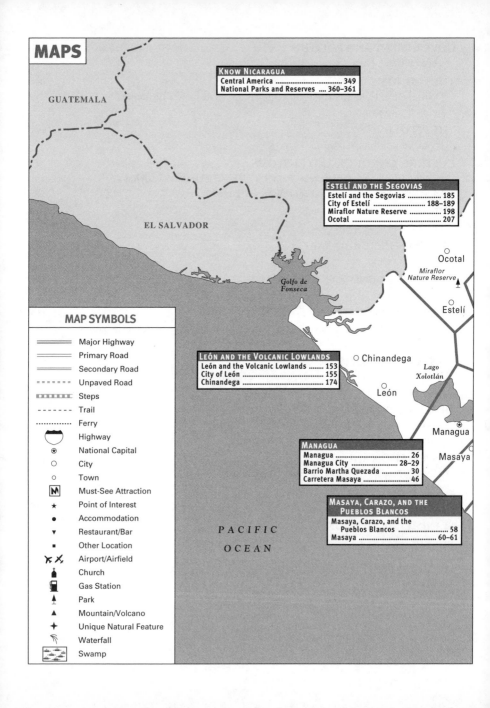

GUATEMALA

EL SALVADOR

Ocotal

Miraflor Nature Reserve

Estelí

Golfo de Fonseca

MAP SYMBOLS

===== Major Highway
===== Primary Road
===== Secondary Road
------- Unpaved Road
▢▢▢▢▢ Steps
- - - - - Trail
.... Ferry
⬭ Highway
⊛ National Capital
○ City
○ Town
Ⓜ Must-See Attraction
★ Point of Interest
● Accommodation
▼ Restaurant/Bar
■ Other Location
✕ ✕ Airport/Airfield
⛪ Church
🛢 Gas Station
⬥ Park
▲ Mountain/Volcano
✛ Unique Natural Feature
🗈 Waterfall
🚢 Swamp

○ Chinandega

Lago Xolotlán

León

⊛ Managua

Masaya

PACIFIC

OCEAN

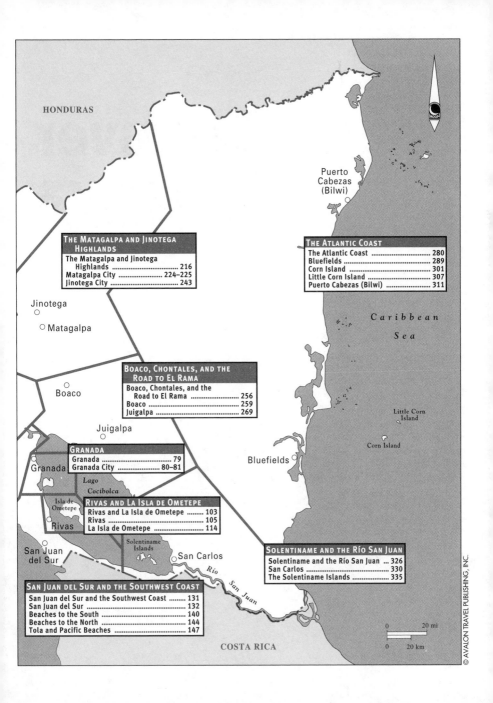

HONDURAS

Puerto
Cabezas
(Bilwi)

Jinotega

Matagalpa

Caribbean

Sea

Boaco

Little Corn
Island

Juigalpa

Corn Island

Bluefields

Granada

Lago
Cocibolca

Isla de
Ometepe

Rivas

Solentiname
Islands

San Juan
del Sur

San Carlos

Río
San
Juan

COSTA RICA

0   20 mi

0   20 km

© AVALON TRAVEL PUBLISHING, INC.

Discover Nicaragua

Fiery and molten under its shifting skin, peaceful and vast on the surface of its great lakes, Nicaragua is at once inspiring, frustrating, and as deeply relaxing as a low-slung hammock. Here you'll find all manner of adventures, be they the kind with vines, monkeys, and machetes, or the type of unsought intercultural epiphanies that brand our souls for life.

Nicaragua, the black sheep of Central America, is sorely misunderstood in the world. Since disappearing from the headlines in the early 1990s, life in Nicaragua has moved steadily forward, leaving behind in the rest of the world's minds only the olive-clad images of the war-torn 1980s. But this is not a nation of perpetual crisis! The revolution and ensuing civil war that ended in 1990 now make up one more chapter in the nation's tumultuous history, and their recent memory adds grit to the reality of today's Nicaragua.

Nicaraguans—nearly six million of 'em—are fiercely proud of their heritage. Everything that makes them Nicaraguan—from the geology and history of their land to their poetry and music—distinguishes them from their Central American neighbors. Nicaraguans survive amidst the day-to-day struggle that is life in the Developing World and they do so with a vitality and an ability to enjoy life in a way more prosperous societies seem to have forgotten.

Nicaragua's toddler tourism industry continues to stretch and improve, nourished by a recent investment boom and a steady increase in visitors, and it is this freshness that makes touring Nicaragua such a powerful, rewarding, and challenging experience. Canned tourist programs are few and far between, and a trip here means spending time among Nicaraguans, whose charm, strong opinions, and casual hospitality are probably their nation's greatest attraction. They will show you that there is more to do and see in Nicaragua than you'll ever have time for—even if you make this your home for several years.

While Nicaragua has never failed to attract visitors, the majority have been less than traditional tourists—people from all over the world have come here to work, write, study, paint, and volunteer. Increasingly, they are also coming to relax on Nicaragua's beaches, hike her jungles, float her rivers, and explore her countryside.

If you are only passing through Nicaragua, you may never know what you missed. But then, if you were merely passing through, you wouldn't be holding this book in your hands, preparing to immerse yourself deep within this geologically and culturally vibrant landscape.

Moon Handbooks Nicaragua features abundant destinations where it is entirely possible that the reader will be the only foreign traveler in town. This extraordinary opportunity carries unique cultural (and logistical) challenges. Consequently, this book will be most appreciated by travelers who find this lack of established infrastructure inspiring and exhilarating, rather than a shortcoming. Visitors who rise to Nicaragua's challenges find themselves changed by the experience.

So pack a little extra patience and the brightest color film you can find—and welcome to Nicaragua. The Land of Lakes and Volcanoes. The Heart of America.

Nicaragua has amazing powers to lead you to places and experiences you never could have arranged. Sticking to a tightly planned itinerary means you'll allow common unavoidables, like lost luggage and flat tires, to wear you down. Do not be afraid to wander, linger, and be drawn deep into the countryside. In the words of Joseph Conrad, "In the tropics one must before everything keep calm."

Where to begin? Nicaragua south of Managua is more developed for travelers, offering a huge variety of enticing destinations and sights. North of Managua is less explored, and with a handful of exceptions, is less comfortable, more amenable to adventure and excitement, and wholly wild. Ideally, your trip should take in a little of both. While you can spend a full week on the Pacific beaches, why go home without a taste of a volcano, a walk through a coffee plantation, or an afternoon in a quiet mountain pueblo? The immense landscape will inspire you to pick and choose from tropical forests, the dry highlands, and the humid coasts. No matter where you go, we encourage you to take the time to get to know the people—a great reason to visit Nicaragua regardless of the landscape.

You can easily spend several days each in the streets of colonial Granada, the slopes of La Isla de Ometepe, or the rum-and-sun beach town of San Juan del Sur; a full week or more if you combine all three. Work your way up the Pacific coast to student-filled León and the dry agricultural mecca of Chinandega, from either of which you can visit remote volcanoes and visit beaches you'll probably have all to yourself.

Or venture uphill into rolling green mountains that hide plantations of coffee, cold streams, and hillsides of family farms. Estelí boasts revolutionary murals and the lush forest of Miraflor and Tisey; Matagalpa has two proud cathedrals and long views from the mountains around town; Jinotega is the gateway to the untrodden, as most of Nicaragua's landmass still lies farther afield to the east.

Much of Nicaragua's early history revolves around the San Juan River, and if you've got the time, you can visit the artist colony in the Solentiname archipelago, float the river in a small boat, or hike into tropical jungle around Los Guatuzos.

The Atlantic coast may as well be a country unto itself, so isolated has it been throughout Nicaragua's history; today, only a one-hour flight from Managua will deliver you to fresh seafood, Caribbean isles, long stretches of deserted shoreline, and a whole lot of reggae.

Following, we've outlined some regional routes to serve as general launching pads for your own adventures. You can choose to explore just a portion of a route or combine several. Be creative.

WHEN TO GO

Generally speaking, the most luscious months—when everything is still green from the rains and the days are often sunny and dry—are December, January, and February. June, July, and August are nice as well, with cooler temperatures and few crowds. April and May are the hottest, driest months, prone to intense dust and clouds of smoke caused by farmers burning their fields in preparation for planting; September–November are the wettest months, and also hurricane season, when you can expect periodic tropical depressions or worse.

Located between 11 and 15 degrees north latitude, Nicaragua has a tropical climate. Temperatures range from 27°C to 32°C (81°F to 90°F) during the rainy season, and from 30°C to 35°C (86°F to 95°F) in the dry season, but regionally vary remarkably: In the mountains of Matagalpa and Jinotega, the temperature can be 10°C cooler, while in León and Matagalpa, they can be 10°C warmer, making ordinary travelers feel like glazed chickens roasting over the coals. Nicaragua's *invierno* (winter, or rainy season) lasts from approximately May to October, and *verano* (summer, or dry season) lasts from November to April—rain during these months may mean just a quick shower each afternoon, or it may go on for days. As you travel east toward the Atlantic coast or down the Río San Juan, the rainy season grows longer and wetter until the dry season only lasts the month of April.

Travelers can witness *fiestas patronales* (saint's day parties) throughout the year in various cities and villages, but several are worth planning your trip around: the fiestas in Diriamba around January 19th, the **Palo de Mayo** on the Atlantic coast (throughout the month of May), the **Crab Soup Festival** on Corn Island (August 27–28), and the **Fiesta del Toro Venado** in Masaya (last Sunday of October).

WHAT TO TAKE

"Take everything," her colleagues had advised Margaret Kochamma in concerned voices, "you never know," which was their way of saying to a colleague traveling to the Heart of Darkness that: (a) Anything Can Happen To Anyone. So (b) It's Best to be Prepared.

Arundhati Roy

While you obviously can't take *everything*, a well-prepared backpack is still important. Everything you bring to Nicaragua should be sturdy and, ideally, water-resistant, especially if you intend to explore the Atlantic coast or any part of Nicaragua in the rainy season. Choose a good bag not so large you'll be uncomfortable carrying it for long distances or riding with it on your lap in the bus, and secure its zippers with small padlocks. Take a small daypack or shoulder bag as well.

CLOTHING

Your clothing should be light and breathable in this warm, tropical country, but in the mountains outside Matagalpa, Jinotega, and Estelí, you will appreciate something a bit warmer, like a flannel shirt. Don't forget a shade hat that preferably covers the back of your neck: You'll use it during the entire trip to keep the sun off. It's not necessary to come to Nicaragua dressed for safari or wilderness (although Nicas laugh themselves silly watching gringos get off the plane dressed to hunt elephants). It is, however, very important to look clean. Having a neat personal appearance is important to all Latin Americans. Most travelers to Nicaragua are surprised to see how well-dressed even the poorest Nicaraguans are. Old, faded, or torn clothing is tolerated, but you'll find being well-groomed will open a lot more doors. In the countryside, Nicaraguan men typically don't wear shorts. Jeans travel well, but you will probably find them hot in places like León and Chinandega; khakis are lighter and dry faster. Roads are rough, even in cities, so good walking shoes will ease your trip considerably, since you'll be walking more often than you expect. You'll be hard-pressed to find shoes larger than a men's 10.5 (European 42) for sale in Nicaragua. Take a pair of shower-sandals with you, or better yet, buy a pair of rubber *chinelas* anywhere in Nicaragua for about $1.

A lightweight, breathable raincoat and/or umbrella will serve you well. A small flashlight or headlamp is indispensable for walking at night on uneven streets and for those late-night potty runs in your hospedaje, and an alarm clock will facilitate catching early-morning buses. If you wear glasses, bring along a little repair kit. The smallest keychain-type compass will be invaluable for finding your way around, as directions in this book typically refer to compass directions (finding the hotel three blocks north of the park is a lot easier if you know which direction north is).

PAPERWORK

Make a photocopy of the pages in your passport that have your photo and information. When you get the passport stamped in the airport, it's a good idea to make a photocopy of that page as well, and store the copies somewhere other than in your passport. This will facilitate things greatly if your passport ever gets lost or stolen. Also consider taking a copy of your health/medevac insurance policy, an international phone card for calling home, and a small Spanish dictionary and phrase book. Also bring a couple of photos of home to show Nica hosts and friends, who will invariably be interested.

MISCELLANY

Bring a small first-aid kit (see the Health and Safety section for suggestions), plenty of plastic bags and zip-locs for protections from both rain and boat travel, and a cheap set of ear plugs for the occasional early-morning rooster or karaoke concert. Don't worry if you forget reading material—most hotels and lodges have a selection of abandoned or traded English-language books.

MANAGUA

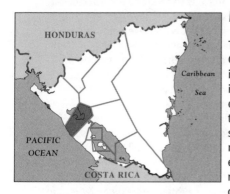

The most chaotic and elusive of the Central American capitals, Managua is tenaciously making itself interesting to passers-through and the various *internacionalistas* who make it their adopted home. You can easily see its cadre of attractions in a quick morning, but it's more fun on a weekend, when you can enjoy its vibrant nightlife as well. Though you could conceivably pass through Nicaragua without visiting Managua at all, its central location makes it an important transport hub and the place to go for services not available elsewhere.

MASAYA, CARAZO, AND THE PUEBLOS BLANCOS

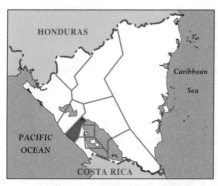

An hour south of the capital, Masaya and the dozens of villages that comprise the Pueblos Blancos are known for their residents' artistic passion and creativity. Start with a trip to Volcán Masaya, where you can peer down into Nicaragua's fiery volcanic entrails, then visit the shaded stalls of Masaya's craft markets in Masaya. Spend a lazy afternoon driving around the charismatic Pueblos Blancos and have lunch at the lip of an ancient volcanic crater, overlooking its azure lagoon. You could easily spend two full days in this region, as Volcán Masaya and the crafts market will occupy the better part of day, and the Pueblos another full day, particularly if you're constrained to public transportation. The Pueblos make a nice diversion for those spending a longer time in Managua, as these highlands are markedly cooler than the nearby capital.

GRANADA

The most picturesque and comfortable of Nicaragua's colonial cities, Granada has been charming travelers with its red-tiled roofs, breezy lakeshore, and drowsy tropical lifestyle since the days of the Spanish, who made the city their Atlantic port (via Lake Cocibolca and the Río San Juan). Today, Granada is without doubt Nicaragua's best-adapted city to the needs of the foreign traveler.

Many use Granada as a tranquil base from which to explore Masaya and the Pueblos, the 365 *isletas* right offshore, the Island of Zapatera, and the pristine cloud forests of nearby Volcán Mombacho. You're also striking distance from Laguna de Apoyo, where you can cool your heels in a "bottomless" volcanic lake or enjoy fresh fish at a shoreside restaurant.

RIVAS AND LA ISLA DE OMETEPE

An administrative city with a vibrant colonial history, Rivas will likely be a stop on your way to one of the undisputed crown jewels of Nicaraguan adventure travel: La Isla de Ometepe. The twin volcanic peaks of Ometepe—one hot and active, one dormant and forested—are irresistible for peak baggers; but if sweating up trails isn't your cup of island-grown coffee, you'll still enjoy the myriad swimming holes, lagoons, and waterfalls, or just kicking back at one of several extraordinary hostel getaways, rife with pre-Columbian petroglyphs, barnyard animals, and farm-fresh food.

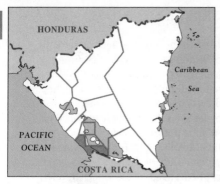

SAN JUAN DEL SUR AND THE SOUTHWEST COAST

Nicaragua's favorite beach town and a frequent stop for northbound travelers anxious to escape the Costa Rican hordes, San Juan del Sur offers a fun, tranquil setting and an increasing number of quality restaurants and accommodations. The Pacific coastline extends over the horizon in both directions from this historic bay, and the adventurous traveler can easily launch excursions to the innumerable beaches and point breaks of the Pacific shore. This is important habitat for some of Nicaragua's more exotic wildlife, including the Paslama turtle, thousands of which beach themselves once a year to reproduce. Witnessing the hatching, when millions of young turtles crawl out from their eggs and enter the ocean, is breathtaking.

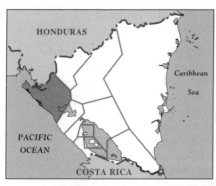

LEÓN AND THE VOLCANIC LOWLANDS

Both León and Chinandega are colonial cities in the hot arid lowlands of Nicaragua's Pacific northwest. Both towns nestle at the feet of the Maribio volcanoes, an uninterrupted chain of hills that defines this corner of the country—both by their presence on the horizon and by their occasional geological burps and shudders. León offers an entirely different energy and attitude than are found in Granada, and its importance as a political and economic center over the past four centuries has bequeathed it a rich history. Stop in at the imposing, baroque cathedral, the largest in Central America, or wander the indigenous Subtiava neighborhood, with a magnificent church of its own. From León and Chinandega, you can climb every one of the varied and unique Maribio volcanoes. In addition to swimming beaches near León, there are a number of remote and rarely visited protected areas throughout the Cosigüina Peninsula, including mangrove swamps, estuaries, and several turtle-nesting beaches. Most travelers stroll León's streets, maybe walk up Cerro Negro, and move on after only two days in the region, but these passers-through have only seen the tip of the, er, volcano, as there is plenty to occupy an active traveler for a week or more.

ESTELÍ AND THE SEGOVIAS

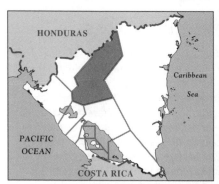

Nicaragua's mountainous north is easily accessible by comfortable public transportation, so you don't have to go too far off the beaten track to find adventure in cowboy country. These peaks are some of the oldest lands in Central America, and they boast a variety of hardwood forests, pine-covered hills, and stony river valleys in an unforgettable landscape of contrasts. Just as exciting are this region's people, whose hard lifestyle makes them gritty and resilient. Spend a day at Estanzuela's gorgeous waterfall and wildlife reserve, or head into the hills for a weekend in Miraflor, valuable habitat for some of Nicaragua's most exotic birdlife and an important orchid-raising area. Press farther northward to the historic towns of the Segovias—dry as dust but alive with local history, legends, and mystery.

THE MATAGALPA AND JINOTEGA HIGHLANDS

This is coffee country, Nicaragua's rugged interior where traditional "tourist" destinations taper off and the free-spirited traveler finds a land of undeveloped adventure. Countless green valleys and steep mountain peaks define the landscape, and the mountain country's hard working, sometimes aloof residents define its character. You can find lots of undeveloped hikes here: to peaks, waterfalls, and more. But you can just as easily spend a weekend in an eco-lodge or butterfly farm, tour coffee plantations, or just hang around small towns getting to know the locals; various village guest programs can put you in their very homes. Everyone's got a war story in these mountains, and hearing some of them will add texture to your travels. Depending on how deep into the wilderness you're interested in venturing, and how much you will rely on the infrequent transportation, you could spend 3–4 days or more exploring this region.

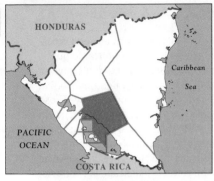

BOACO, CHONTALES, AND THE ROAD TO EL RAMA

The broad, golden hillsides along the east side of Lake Cocibolca fold upward into the rocky precipices of the Amerrisque mountains, former stomping grounds of the Chontal people during pre-Columbian times. Today, the lowlands run thick with cattle ranches that produce the lion's share of Nicaragua's cheese and milk. Uphill from the ranches, the roads dwindle to rutted tracks and Nicaragua's prehistory comes back to life, in the form of totem-like statues the Chontal left behind. Most travelers pass through this area at 100 kph on buses bound for El Rama and the Atlantic coast, but spending a night in Juigalpa or Boaco is enlightening, and may lead you on to the area's hot springs, petroglyphs, and horseback treks. From here, you can find guides to take you up into the Amerrisques and beyond, and explore a wild wild west that hasn't lost its edge.

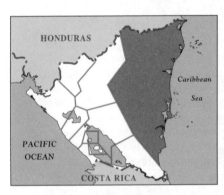

THE ATLANTIC COAST

The swampy, tropical coast of Nicaragua's Atlantic shore is humid year-round and offers up a Caribbean experience like no other. This Caribbean is gritty, muddy, and full of raw, unbridled energy quite different from any Cancún-tainted visions you may harbor. From Bluefields, you can explore the delightful Laguna de Perlas ("Pearl Lagoon") and the sandy desert islands of the Pearl Cays, but offshore lies buried treasure. Both Corn Island and Little Corn Island are little-visited Caribbean gems as gorgeous below the waterline as above. When you get tired of the kilometers of coral reef that surround the islands, settle in for a deep bowl of crab soup, a steaming lobster, or some grilled fish plucked fresh from the sea. Little Corn has no roads and no vehicles, so the only sound you hear should be the Caribbean wind in the trees. The Atlantic coast, especially the northeast Miskito communities of Bilwi and the Río Coco, could easily be a separate trip because it is culturally and geographically so divergent from the rest of Nicaragua. Those flying out to the Corn Islands will find 3–5 days to be sufficient.

SOLENTINAME AND THE RÍO SAN JUAN

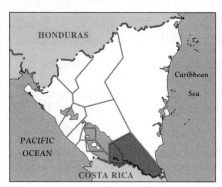

HONDURAS

Caribbean Sea

PACIFIC OCEAN

COSTA RICA

Life moves slowly along the broad river that drains the enormous Lake Cocibolca. This gorgeous, verdant lowland is Nicaragua's wettest, and its remoteness means you'll spend more time and more money getting around. The Spanish fort at El Castillo has watched over the river traffic since the 17th century and was the stage for an important and dramatic chapter in Nicaragua's history. Both downstream and along the southern shore of Cocibolca, wildlife reserves and cultural curiosities characterize this region. The Solentiname archipelago isn't easy to get to, but once there, you'll be rewarded with an up-close look at the birthplace of liberation theology and a thriving colony of painters whose works have gone on to populate museums around the world. Explore the wilds of Los Guatuzos, important habitat for monkeys, birds, and a whole lot of amphibians. Or set sail downstream for the most forgotten corner in the nation: Greytown, full of the bones of English sailors and home to more ghosts than residents.

Like other countries in the region, Nicaragua has its own carved-out tourist route through its principal attractions (a.k.a. "gringo trail"), offering the chance to travel in the company of fellow vagabonds, but always with easy access to off-beat side trips. The Granada–Ometepe–San Juan del Sur circuit can be done in about one week; save another week for tackling the northwestern lowlands and a third for the Atlantic coast or Río San Juan.

Wherever you head, Granada is a good place to ease into things, with colorful surroundings, wonderful cuisine, and more creature comforts than elsewhere in the country.

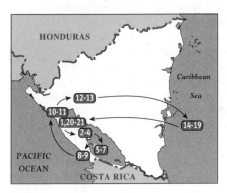

Zipping through Cutirre's canopy on the slopes of Volcán Mombacho.

DAY 1

Arrive in the afternoon at Managua's International Airport. Transfer to a hotel in town, catch a performance, enjoy some of the local restaurants, and above all, get accustomed to the heat, and relax after your flight.

DAYS 2–3

Hop a bus to Granada and spend at least two or three days there. Tour the city the first day, visiting museums and enjoying the languid waterfront. Your second day, paddle to the nearby *isletas* or go hiking on Volcán Mombacho, whose heights above the city make for a cool day.

DAY 4

Using Granada as your base, make a full-day trip to the city of Masaya and its local active volcano.

Start early at Volcán Masaya National Park, then browse the handicrafts in the Old Market. Return to Granada that evening.

DAYS 5–7

Pack up and head south. Catch the boat at San Jorge to Ometepe. Spend 2–3 days exploring the island's unique getaways, or arrange a guide to take you to the top of one of the volcanoes for more adventurous travel.

DAYS 8–9

Catch the boat back to San Jorge and bus it south through Rivas to the beach at San Juan del Sur. Spend at least one night there, but tag on a few more if the surf's up or the turtles are laying.

DAYS 10–11

Catch the early express bus to Managua. Transfer directly to León. It's been a long trip, so relax, walk around the hot town, check out a few museums, and save time for ice cream in the park.

~~DAYS 12–13~~

Catch a ride to Matagalpa, then continue east to the village of San Ramón. It will take you the better

part of a day to get here, so enjoy the afternoon and that plate of *gallo pinto* waiting for you in the mountains. Spend the next two days hiking to the mines and touring a coffee farm or two.

DAYS 14–19

Return to Managua and take the afternoon flight to Corn Island. Spend two days on Corn Island and two days on Little Corn, soaking up sun, fresh lobster, island vibes, and perhaps a dive on the reef.

DAY 20

Take the morning flight back to Managua to see a few more of the city's sights before last-minute shopping at the Mercado Roberto Huembes.

DAY 21

Adios, jodido! Feliz viaje!

Granadinos treasure their city's bright, colorful architecture.

The Path of Sandino

Whether or not you agree with the politics of today's Sandinistas, there is no doubt that the man, Augusto Cesar Sandino—his ideals, actions, and legacy— left an indelible footprint on Nicaraguan history, culture, and politics. Step back in time and learn more about why this is so.

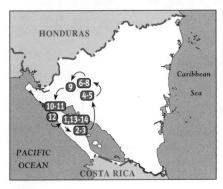

where you'll visit the small museum and birth house of Carlos Amador Fonseca, founder of the Frente Sandinista de Liberación Nacional (FSLN). Explore the city and pay a visit to one of various regional coffee cooperatives, struggling success stories of the revolution's agrarian reform. Also, seek out the grave of U.S. volunteer Benjamin Lin-

DAY 1

Arrive at Managua's International Airport. Transfer to **Masaya** (turn right at the silhouette of Sandino) and check in to your modest hotel.

DAY 2

Take a bus to **Niquinohomo**, birthplace of Sandino. Visit the humble home where he was born the bastard son of a poor servant and her rich employer. There is now a library and mini-museum here, and be sure to snap a pic of the bronze statue at the town's entrance.

DAY 3

Back in Masaya, visit the **gallery of heroes and martyrs** in the town hall; also walk through the **Monimbó neighborhood,** site of the famous uprising in 1979, and, 50 years before, the place where an impressionable young Sandino witnessed occupation by U.S. Marines.

DAYS 4–5

Go north, to *la montaña*. Take a bus to Matagalpa,

statue of Augusto Cesar Sandino in Niquinohomo

der, killed by the Contras while helping villagers construct a small hydroelectric project.

DAY 6
Travel to Jinotega, then hop a bus for San Rafael del Norte, occasional secret base of Sandino's troops and hometown of his sweetheart. Visit the small Sandino museum here, the church where he and Blanca Aráuz wed, and enjoy the cool climate of Nicaragua's highlands—*guerilla* country.

DAYS 7–8
Take the short ride to the Miraflor Nature Reserve and arrange a homestay with one of the families in the cooperative, some of whom have living grandparents with memories of Sandino.

DAY 9
Pop down to Estelí, where you'll spend the morning visiting another gallery of heroes and martyrs, then north again to Ocotál, site of many a battle between Sandino and U.S. troops.

DAY 10
It will take most of your day to get to León, so enjoy those celebratory beers while sitting in the Puerto Café Benjamin Linder, a restaurant-bar-Internet joint that supports local disabled children in honor of the young namesake martyr's ideals.

DAY 11
Explore the museums and historical murals of León; as you walk the streets, note the exuberance (and leftist graffiti) of the student population. It was this same youthful Leonese spirit that demanded reform from the Somoza regime.

DAY 12
Hit the beach at Las Peñitas, where you can relax

Orchid lovers should not miss the Miraflor Nature Reserve.

and read some of the books about Sandino that you picked up in León's bookstores.

DAYS 13–14
The circle is completed as you return to Managua and, after dropping off your bags in your hotel, head straight for the massive Sandino silhouette on the lip of the Tiscapa Crater. Contemplate the war relics there as you look out over Managua, then walk toward the lakefront, passing the alleged spot of Sandino's assassination. Make your way to Carlos Fonseca's eternal flame, and end at the Peace Memorial.

Volcano hopping, anyone? Pack some sturdy boots and hike one or all of the more than a dozen ascents detailed in this book. Nicaragua's Maribio and Dirian mountain ranges contain both dormant and active cones, each one completely unique in scenery, difficulty, vegetation, and length. A few of these hikes have established, well-blazed trails (Mombacho and Masaya Parks are notable exceptions), many don't. In undeveloped-for-tourism areas, "hiking" means turning off the pavement, taking a poor dirt road to an even poorer one, and then entering the country's vast network of mule- and footpaths that have connected rural communities for centuries. You'll share the road with horses, cattle, and families walking to and from their fields. You'll discover small adobe chapels, hidden shrines to the Virgin Mary, and cool watering holes, all on your way to or from another crater. Of course, you should always, when possible, hire a local guide, as a way to both support the community and to not get lost, both respectable goals.

Following is a quickie week-long jaunt up a couple of favorites, but after seeing the long chain of gas-streaming peaks stretching off into the horizon, you'll realize that this is only the beginning.

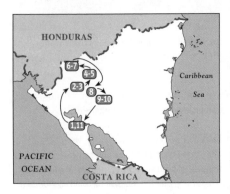

Climbing one of the many volcanoes from accessible León.

DAY 1

Arrive at Managua International Airport and transfer to Granada.

DAY 2

After enjoying the specter of Volcán Mombacho looming over the colonial streets, get a ride to its summit and walk the various ridge trails around its jungled craters; the wonderful loops make a good warm-up for what's to come.

DAY 3

Spend the morning at Volcán Masaya's gaping crater, only an hour from Granada and guaran-

One way to get down: "volcano surfing" on Cerro Negro

teed to impress. On the way back, enjoy a swim in the Laguna de Apoyo, an unspoiled crater lake, easily accessed by bus from Masaya.

DAY 4

Transfer to León and find someone to take you to Cerro Negro, a relatively short but stout and rewarding hike.

DAY 5

Rest up on the beach at Las Peñitas and paddle out to Isla Juan Venado.

DAY 6

Today's the big day. Hook back up with your guides in León and set out early to tackle Momotombo, a 1,300-meter, eight-hour round-trip on horseback and foot. Celebrate with a fancy dinner in León that night.

DAY 7

Back to Managua, back to work, or just back to the beach.

DIVING AND SNORKELING

Snorkeling is best off the Corn Islands and various cays. Diving is a relatively new pastime, with only three shops in the whole country: one in San Juan del Sur and one on each of the Corn Islands. The latter two share a combined 12 kilometers of reef. The shop on Little Corn (www.divelittlecorn.com) has newer equipment, and the reef there was less affected by recent hurricanes. Both islands' reef systems feature a stunning diversity of wildlife, including rays, eels, angels, groupers, sharks, and enormous pools of African pompano. Both shops offer PADI certifications for about $250, plus a range of packages for all skill levels. Although the diving off the Corn Islands is impressive, the most spectacular and undoubtedly world-class site is found nearly 25 difficult kilometers farther out to sea around a sea mount called Blowing Rock.

Nicaragua's Pacific side offers diving too, particularly in the south near San Juan del Sur, but conditions are predictably unpredictable (visibility can change from 1 to 20 meters from day to day). There are rock reefs here (no coral formations) inhabited by large fish, including colorful wrasses, parrotfish, snappers, and huge surgeonfish. Once abundant, shark populations have thinned severely due to overfishing. The best Pacific diving in Nicaragua is between December and April during periods of clear, cold water upwelling associated with the strong offshore winds. Visibility is significantly poorer during the rainy season (June–November) due to sediment from the rivers, which enrich coastal water and provoke algal blooms.

For freshwater diving, Nicaragua offers the volcanic crater lakes of Apoyo (near Masaya) and Xiloá (near Managua). The diving in both lakes is part of ongoing biological research of the endemic cichlid fish

The quietest way to explore Granada's *isletas* is by kayak.

species, and experienced divers can rent tanks from the folks at the Proyecto Ecólogico in Laguna de Apoyo. Apoyo has better visibility, but Xiloá has more colorful fish, and is especially interesting during the peak breeding season in November and December. There are still at least 10 undescribed fish species in the freshwater crater lakes, but hurry, as they are being decimated by the tilapia.

SURFING

The year-round offshore breezes generated by the vast, blustery surface of Lago Cocibolca collide with incoming Pacific swells to create ideal conditions. Surfer-type characters have been prowling the southwest coast for nearly a decade now, and there's still plenty of gaps in the lineup for a skilled rider like yourself. Check the San Juan del Sur chapter for more information on exclusive surf charters and how to go it on your own.

KAYAKING AND CANOEING

So much water, so few boats. Some of the country's most incredible paddle-accessible attractions are serviced by few and small fleets of open, non-motorized free craft. That's because the demand to glide through Granada's maze of *isletas,* Ometepe's Río Istian, or the mangrove estuary at Padre Ramos is still surprisingly low, considering the extraordinary outdoor opportunities offered by these, and other, places in Nicaragua. In many cases, you'll have to be creative to find ways to float the endless lakes, rivers, estuaries, archipelagos, and coastlines of Nicaragua that gave the country its name. Any water-bordering community will likely have small boats the owners use for fishing or transport. Ask for a *canoa, panga,* or *botecita,* and see what shows up. Dugout canoes are common throughout the country, and you can ask to rent one along the Río San Juan and other areas.

For the glory-seeking paddler, Nicaragua is the place to make the cover of an extreme sports rag: the 700-kilometer stretch of the Río Coco from Wiwilí to the Caribbean at Cabo Gracias a Dios has (as far as we know) only been navigated end to end by pirates, guerilla soldiers, and indigenous boaters. There may be some hairy portages around some of the legendary waterfalls, and rumor has it that no one has ever even published a photograph of the falls between Raiti and San Carlos.

SPORT FISHING

Sportfishing trips are available out of San Juan del Sur, the Corn Islands, an increasing number of Pacific beach towns, and along the Río San Juan. Saltwater sportfishing on the Pacific coast is focused primarily on *hurel* (jacks), *pargo* (snapper), and *pez gallo* (roosterfish) inshore and bonito, *pez vela* (sailfish), and *dorado* (mahimahi) offshore. All commonly reach sizes in excess of 50 pounds.

In addition to casting for kingfish, amber jack, red snapper, and barracuda off the Corn Islands, bonefishing in the flats around Little Corn Island is exciting, but you'll have to have some idea of what you are doing, as experienced guides are limited.

There are freshwater fish to be caught in Lake Apanás and El Dorado in Jinotega, and of course, in Lake Cocibolca and down the Río San Juan. The giant freshwater bull sharks and sawfish are all but gone, but mammoth *sábalos* (tarpon), bigger than your mother and carrying up to 50 pounds of meat, are still abundant, as are *robalos, guapote,* and the basin's newest resident, tilapia. The introduction of the tilapia has had a disastrous effect: One study shows that diseases introduced by tilapia have resulted in a 50-percent decline in Lake Cocibolca's total biomass and another reports that the foreign fish have eliminated all aquatic vegetation in the Laguna de Apoyo.

Nicaragua north of Managua is offbeat and little-traveled, and gives the creative traveler lots of opportunities. *Pueblo*-hopping through the Segovia mountains and participating in the *Ruta de Café* will immerse you in an authentic and sublime world you won't soon forget. Each town has a swimming hole, local hike, or archeological site that will beckon you further. Go! Alternate legs include passing through San Juan de Limay and the back roads to León; or from Jinotega, looping through Yalí to Condega. This sample itinerary will give you a taste of what to expect:

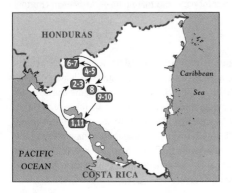

DAY 6

Stop in for lunch at one of the quiet northern agricultural towns, like Condega, or Palacagüina; press on to Ocotal, and spend the evening roaming the park and city center.

DAY 7

Day trips galore await from Ocotal—seek out the ruins, or head northeast to Jalapa if you have the time. Otherwise, check out the humble church and exhibits in the Ocotal *casa de cultura* and hop an express bus back to Estelí.

DAY 1

From Managua, head north to Estelí and spend the day walking the streets of this bustling commercial center, viewing the murals and markets, and enjoying cool weather.

DAYS 2–3

Take an early-morning bus to the Estanzuela waterfall; stay in a cabin on the Tisey Reserve, from where you can arrange hikes, horseback expeditions, and farm tours. Return to Estelí at the end of day three.

DAYS 4–5

From Estelí, go east and up, into the Miraflor Reserve, where you can experience a rural homestay, photograph orchids, and try to spot elusive wildlife. Even if you don't find any quetzals or ocelots, the locals will regale you with legends and ghost stories. Spend the night, return in the morning, and grab a bus north.

DAY 8

Leave Estelí in the morning and make your way through Sébaco to Matagalpa. Enjoy the city for the day, maybe even take a quick hike up Cerro Apante.

DAY 9

Here's your chance to visit a coffee plantation and witness the process that brings us that magical beverage. You can go rural if you like, staying in San Ramón or further afield, or choose the relatively upscale accommodations at Selva Negra.

DAY 10

Enjoy a beautiful, fun-filled day of monkeys in the trees, hearty country dining, and a guided tour through the farm.

DAY 11

Return to Managua, hopefully with a few pounds of freshly roasted coffee in your pack.

The watery "Golden Route" through southern Lake Cocibolca and down the Río San Juan is tougher to access than it was when boat service was more frequent, so you'll need a minimum of 7–10 days to get there, get around, and get back. Once you reach San Carlos (by boat, bus, or small plane), public boat transportation is regular and cheap, but limited to a handful of boats per week. As a result, unless you really drop a lot of cash to hire your own personal boat and driver, you may find yourself stranded on one of 36 Solentiname islands for three days, with nothing to do but go fishing or bird- and crocodile-watching in a dugout canoe—we can think of worse things. The Río San Juan is unquestionably worth a visit, especially the photogenic fort and river town at El Castillo.

Note that air and boat schedules require careful timing on this trip, so we've constructed one possible way to coordinate the logistics, which should help get you started in the region. Because schedules can change, be prepared for the worst and bring something to read while you're waiting for the next boat.

DAY 1: TUESDAY

Fly from Managua to San Carlos in the early morning. If you really want the full-blown adventure, take the slow boat from Granada on Monday, not Tuesday: You'll arrive Tuesday morning. Poke around San Carlos until the afternoon, when the boat leaves for Solentiname.

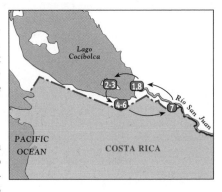

DAYS 2–3: WEDNESDAY–THURSDAY

Enjoy this island artist colony set in a unique area of profound natural splendor. You can hire boats to take you among the islands, enjoy scarlet sunsets, and absorb the intense tranquility of the archipelago. Return to San Carlos Thursday morning to catch the boat to Los Guatuzos. If you'd rather go directly and bypass San Carlos, strike a deal with a local Solentiname boat-owner.

DAYS 4–6: FRIDAY–SATURDAY

Hike and explore the fascinating tropical landscape of the Los Guatuzos reserve. A two-day stay will give you a taste for the reserve, but real outdoors enthusiasts will probably prefer to stay until the next boat (Tuesday, unless you make other arrangements). Arrival in San Carlos on Saturday means you are just in time to catch a boat downstream.

Cast away and start your adventure down the mighty Río San Juan, bound for El Castillo.

DAY 7: SUNDAY

Start your day off in El Castillo early, so you can hear the sky fill with birds. Visit the old Spanish fort or rent a horse for a bush trip.

DAY 8 AND BEYOND

Most travelers return to San Carlos for a flight to Managua at this point, but if the downstream horizon is beckoning, then keep on floating, and happy trails.

Explore Nicaragua

Managua

Sun-baked and sweltering, Managua is a place of contradictions and challenges. Less a city that *is* than a city that *was,* it has a history that lurks around every corner; less an urban center than an enormous conglomerate of nondescript neighborhoods, modern-day Managua is what a city looks like when everything has gone wrong. Managua is not an easy place to get to know, but you will be rewarded for your efforts, for there is much to experience in this intense, clamorous capital, and spending time among its 1.5 million inhabitants is essential for anyone who hopes to understand the country. The sweating taxi driver negotiating his Russian-made cab down unnamed streets; the university student clamoring for a bigger education budget; the slick, young entrepreneur touting his new theme-bar in the *zona rosa;* the seamstress in the free-trade zone demanding fair treatment—these are the people struggling to shape the new Managua into a more livable city.

Managua is the economic, political, academic, and transportation heart of Nicaragua and, financed by the wave of nouveau riche Nicaraguans

PALACIO NACIONAL

Must-Sees

Look for **M** to find the sights and activities you can't miss and **M** for the best dining and lodging.

Managua

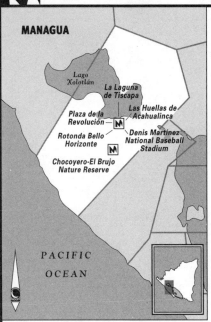

Zip high above Managua at Tiscapa Crater's canopy tour.

M Plaza de la Revolución: Still the cultural heart of Nicaragua's capital, Nicaragua's old downtown also features the lakefront Malecón and old Cathedral ruins (page 32).

M La Laguna de Tiscapa: Just one of the area's many volcanic lakes but the only one you can zip over while tethered to a steel cable; or just enjoy the view (page 34).

M Las Huellas de Acahualinca: This glimpse of Managua's mysterious past is haunting for the questions it raises, not the ones it answers (page 36).

M Rotonda Bello Horizonte: A brightly lit, noisy cluster of open-air restaurants where barrel-chested mariachi crooners will sing you love songs for tips. (page 37).

M Denis Martínez National Baseball Stadium: If in town during baseball season, order some peanuts and beer and root for the home team, *El Boer* (page 42).

M Chocoyero–El Brujo Nature Reserve: Located just south of Managua, in a gorgeous patch of protected hillsides and ravines, this community-based tourism venture offers some wonderful day hikes (page 52).

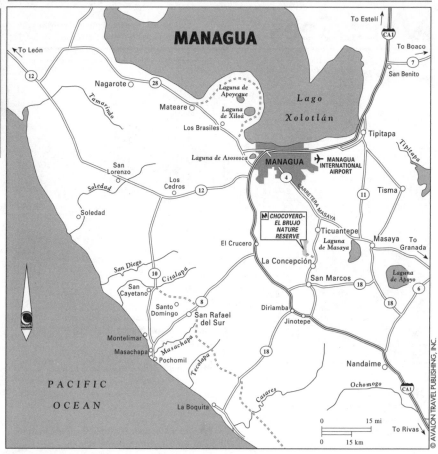

MANAGUA

To León

To Estelí

To Boaco

San Benito

Nagarote

Mateare

Los Brasiles

Laguna de Apoyeque

Laguna de Xiloá

Lago Xolotlán

Tipitapa

Laguna de Asososca

MANAGUA

MANAGUA INTERNATIONAL AIRPORT

Tisma

San Lorenzo

Los Cedros

Tamarindo

Soledad

Soledad

CHOCOYERO-EL BRUJO NATURE RESERVE

Ticuantepe

Laguna de Masaya

Masaya

To Granada

El Crucero

La Concepción

San Marcos

Laguna de Apoyo

San Diego

Citalapa

San Cayetano

Santo Domingo

San Rafael del Sur

Diriamba

Jinotepe

Montelimar

Masachapa

Masachapa

Pochomil

Tecolapa

Nandaime

PACIFIC OCEAN

Casares

Ochomogo

La Boquita

To Rivas

0   15 mi

0   15 km

© AVALON TRAVEL PUBLISHING, INC.

(a.k.a. Nicas Ricas) returning from self-imposed exile in Miami, its reconstruction has accelerated. Since the mid-1990s, tens of kilometers of roads have been repaved, several luxury hotels completed, and a new cross-city bypass built.

Today, as Managua stretches inexorably southward, its layout reflects its violent history: The ruins of old Managua remain at the water's edge—from there, in all directions, spread hundreds of shapeless, characterless *barrios* (neighborhoods) that rose from the rubble after each new natural or manmade disaster. Along Carretera Masaya, pricey shops, clubs, and restaurants continue sprouting up to

service the new neighborhood developments of the wealthy.

PLANNING YOUR TIME

Managua has no obvious city center but can be broken down into a few regions of particular interest to the traveler: **Carretera Masaya,** where the lion's share of the restaurants, bars, and discos are found, **Barrio Martha Quezada,** the neighborhood with all the international bus stations and a long tradition of budget accommodations, and **El Malecón** and nearby Plaza de la Revolución, where you can wander amongst the ruins of

Old Managua's grandstand was one of the few structures to survive the earthquake of 1972.

the old city while looking at all the new government buildings.

Many travelers are unable to avoid at least a short visit to Managua, usually to switch buses or do errands. If you have a few extra hours, visit the sites at the waterfront or check the view from the Sandino statue on the Tiscapa Crater, both of which can be accomplished in a few hours. But to experience what Managua means to its inhabitants, it's best to spend a night as well, and enjoy some of the best clubs, bars, and restaurants in the nation. Additionally, there are wonderful day or overnight trips to be had to the reserves south of the city and to the Pacific beaches only an hour to the west.

HISTORY

Nestled in a shifting bed of volcanic debris and ash, pockmarked by crater lakes, and riven with tectonic faults, Managua's very geology speaks of destruction and rebirth. This is a city grown out of rubble and shaped since prehistory by desperation and tragedy. Once a dusty tropical village of fishermen whose ferocity astounded the Spanish con-

quistadores, Managua has in recent history been broken, burned, and bombed a half-dozen times, suffering just as often at the hands of nature as the hands of humankind. Still, it continues to shake off the dust and recreate itself.

Inhabited since 4000 B.C., Mana-huac (the big water vessel) was home to the Nahuatl at about the time of Christ. They later defended themselves against the Spanish so viciously that the latter retaliated by razing the city; the land remained abandoned another 300 years. By the mid-1800s, it was again a prosperous fishing village, while both León and Granada rivaled for political control of the nation. To ease tensions, the Conservatives and Liberals reached a compromise and declared Managua the new capital, in blissful ignorance of the seismic faults that lay beneath it. That mistake became horrifyingly apparent in 1931, when an earthquake of 5.6 on the Richter scale leveled Managua, still a small municipality of 10 square city blocks, and killed more than 1,000 people. For five years, Managuans rebuilt their city, only to see it consumed by flames in the Fire of 1936.

Again, they rebuilt.

© RANDY WOOD

Managua

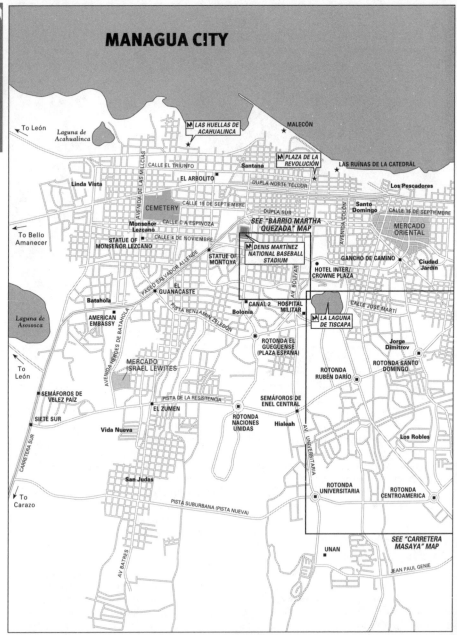

MANAGUA CITY

To León

Laguna de
Acahualinca

MALECÓN

LAS HUELLAS DE
ACAHUALINCA

PLAZA DE LA
REVOLUCIÓN

LAS RUÍNAS DE LA CATEDRÁL

CALLE EL TRIUNFO

Santana

Los Pescadores

Linda Vista

EL ARBOLITO

DUPLA NORTE TELCOR

Santo
Domingo

CALLE 15 DE SEPTIEMBRE

CEMETERY

CALLE 15 DE SEPTIEMBRE

DUPLA SUR

MERCADO
ORIENTAL

Monseñor
Lezcano

CALLE C A ESPINOZA

SEE "BARRIO MARTHA
QUEZADA" MAP

STATUE OF
MONSEÑOR LEZCANO

CALLE 4 DE NOVIEMBRE

DENIS MARTÍNEZ
NATIONAL BASEBALL
STADIUM

GANCHO DE CAMINO

Ciudad
Jardin

To Bello
Amanecer

STATUE OF
MONTOYA

HOTEL INTER/
CROWNE PLAZA

EL
GUANACASTE

Batahola

CANAL 2

HOSPITAL
MILITAR

CALLE JOSÉ MARTÍ

Laguna de
Asososca

AMERICAN
EMBASSY

Bolonia

LA LAGUNA
DE TISCAPA

ROTONDA EL
GÜEGÜENSE
(PLAZA ESPAÑA)

Jorge
Dimitrov

To León

MERCADO
ISRAEL LEWITES

ROTONDA SANTO
DOMINGO

ROTONDA
RUBÉN DARÍO

SEMÁFOROS DE
VELEZ PAÍZ

PISTA DE LA RESISTENCIA

SEMÁFOROS DE
ENEL CENTRAL

SIETE SUR

EL ZUMEN

Vida Nueva

ROTONDA
NACIONES
UNIDAS

Hialeah

Los Robles

To
Carazo

San Judas

ROTONDA
UNIVERSITARIA

ROTONDA
CENTROAMERICA

PISTA SUBURBANA (PISTA NUEVA)

SEE "CARRETERA
MASAYA" MAP

UNAN

JEAN PAUL GENIE

Managua

Lago Xolotlán

Domitila
Lugo

CARRETERA NORTE

To Airport
and Tipitapa

CA1

IMMIGRATION

ROTONDA BELLO
HORIZONTE

PISTA LARREYNAGA

SEMÁFOROS DE
LA TENDERÍ

STATUE OF
LA VIRGEN

MAYOREO
BUS
TERMINAL

CALLE 14 DE SEPTIEMBRE

EL EDÉN

EL BY-PASS

Bello
Horizonte

SEMÁFOROS DE
RUBENIA

Las Americas

PISTA PORTEZUELO

(CENTROAMERICA)

MERCADO
HUEMBES

Altamira

La Fuente

Colonia
Centroamerica

Renée
Shick

Villa
Venezuela

ROTONDA JEAN
PAUL GENIE

CARRETERA MASAYA

0   1 mi

0   1 km

MOON

To Masaya

© AVALON TRAVEL PUBLISHING, INC.

DENIS MARTÍNEZ NATIONAL BASEBALL STADIUM

BARRIO MARTHA QUEZADA

To Malecón

0   200 yds
0   200 m

CALLE JULIO BUITRAGO

BANPRO · LA CASA CASTILLO

GUESTHOUSE SANTOS · ANEXO DE LA QUINTANA LOS MANGOS · HOSPEDAJE MEZA · ANTOJITOS CHINOS

CALLE 27 DE MAYO

NATIONAL ARBORETUM · To Airport

CYBER CENTER BANISA · LA QUINTANA · LAS ANCLAS · JARDÍN DE ITALIA

HOSPEDAJE EL DORADO · FRITANGA · EL MOLINITO · LA CASA AZUL · LA SUISSE PANADERÍA

EL VIAJERO

AV. BOLÍVAR

PLAZA INTER MALL

HOTEL LOS FELIPE · TICABUS · CASA VANEGAS · CAFETÍN TONALLI

TOURISM OFFICE

MYRNAS · THE SHANNON PUB

MÁGICA ROMA

HOTEL CROWNE PLAZA

LA CURVA
To Laguna de Tiscapa

LICORERÍA LA CHOCOYA · EL CHANGON · BAR LA LOMA

To Hotel Europeo

To Plaza España

BOLONIA

© AVALON TRAVEL PUBLISHING, INC.

By the late 1960s, Managua was the most modern capital in Central America, home to nearly half a million inhabitants and a modern center with two skyscrapers. But 27 minutes past midnight on December 23, 1972, an earthquake of 6.3 on the Richter scale suddenly and completely laid waste to the five square miles of the city. In the aftermath, Christmas decorations still hung in tatters from the rubble. 10,000 people lost their lives, 50,000 homes were destroyed, and the city's entire infrastructure was reduced to wreckage. Managua was without water, sewers, and electricity, hospitals lay in ruins, and the roads were choked with debris.

This was a disaster from which Managua has never quite recovered, as little of the initial ma-

terial aid arrived at its intended destination. President Anastasio Somoza Debayle, consumed by avarice, saw to it that the aid money channeled through the "emergency committee" under his control ended up in his personal bank accounts. For Nicaraguans who'd lost everything, being forced to purchase donated relief items from the National Guard was the last straw: The revolution would fully erupt only seven years later.

The final battles of the Sandinistas' triumph stained most of the city with blood; Somoza liberally bombed the *barrios* of Riguera and El Dorado. Afterwards, Managua stagnated under the Sandinista government, whose disintegrating economy left little for reconstruction, and again under the cash-strapped Chamorro government,

FOLLOWING DIRECTIONS

Locating addresses in Managua is unlike any system you've ever seen, but with a few tips, some basic vocabulary, and a couple of examples, you and your cab driver will master it in no time. Street names and house numbers are few and far between, and where they do exist, they are ignored. Addresses in Managua begin with a landmark (either existing or historical), which is then followed by a listing of how many *cuadras* (blocks) should be traveled and in which direction. Remember this: North is *al lago* (toward the lake); east is *arriba* (up, referring to the sunrise); south is *al sur* (to the south); and west is *abajo* (down, where the sun sets).

Some other key phrases to know are *contiguo a* (next door to), *frente a* (across from), *casa esquinera* (corner house), and *a mano derecha/izquierda* (on the right/left-hand side). Also note that *varas* are often used to measure distances of less than one block; this is an old colonial measurement just shy of a meter.

Directions throughout this chapter are given in English for consistency's sake, but always beginning with the landmark exactly as it is referred to in Spanish. By studying the following examples, you should be able to find your way around with few hassles.

De la Plaza España, tres cuadras abajo, tres c. al lago, casa esquinera.
From Plaza España, three blocks west, three north, corner house.

De donde fue el Sandy's, 200 varas arriba, frente al gran hotel.
From where Sandy's used to be, 200 meters to the east, across from the big hotel.

De los semáforos El Dorado, dos cuadras al sur, una c. arriba, casa lila.
From the El Dorado traffic light, two blocks south, one east, purple house.

Reparto San Juan, de la UNIVAL, 50 varitas al lago, edificio de cinco pisos.
In the San Juan neighborhood, just 50 meters north of the UNIVAL, five-story building.

---

which finally set the stage for the current wave of reconstruction.

SAFETY IN THE CITY

Managua is less dangerous than other Central American capitals, but the best way to stay out of trouble is to avoid areas where you'll find it. Rough *barrios* include Renée Schick, Jorgé Dimitrov, La Fuente, San Judas, Villa Venezuela, Batahola, Las Americas, Bello Amanecer, Vida Nueva, Los Pescadores, Domitila Lugo, Santana, and Hialeah. The walk between the *hospedajes* (hostels) of Barrio Martha Quezada and the Plaza Inter/Hotel Crowne Royale should be avoided after dark, as this neighborhood is home to increasingly braver knife-bearing teenagers. Also, watch yourself in crowds, particularly those of the Mercado Oriental, urban buses, and sporting, music, or political events.

The safest and cleanest neighborhoods are Los Robles, Altamira, San Juan, and Bolonia, all offering more upscale accommodation and bed-and-breakfasts.

SIGHTS

Managua's touristic significance is limited at best, but if you appreciate Managua's history, you'll enjoy a walk around some of the crumbling historical sites. Most of Managua's buildings and sights can be visited in a single morning's walk. To truly appreciate the somewhat decrepit monuments and buildings, it helps to ask locals about the way Managua was in the good old days. Most will be glad to tell you stories.

© RANDY WOOD

The ruins of Managua's old cathedral still haunt the breezy lakeshore.

Plaza de la Revolución

In pre-Sandinista days, **Plaza de la Revolución** was known as Plaza de la República. Today, it still forms a "city center" of sorts, around which are located many of the historical sights of Managua. It is best visited early in the morning, when the breeze off the lake is cool, the trees are full of birds, and the streets are safer.

Catedral Santiago de los Caballeros had barely been completed when the earthquake of 1931 struck. It survived that one, but was significantly weakened in 1972, still standing, but unusable. **Las Ruinas de la Catedrál Vieja** (as they're known now) have remained a standing testament to the earthquake and are Managua's most captivating tourist attraction. Even though it's been closed due to the danger of falling concrete, you can still peer in and appreciate its ravaged, sunlit interior. Across the street, heading toward the lake, the brightly-painted **Casa Presidencial** is the office of the president and was built in 1999 amid protests over the lavish expenditure.

The Palacio Nacional de Cultura houses Nicaragua's National Museum but at various times has also housed the Ministry of Housing, the treasury, the comptroller-general, and the National Congress. Sandinista commandos raided the building in 1978 and held the entire Congress hostage, winning international recognition and the liberation of several political prisoners. In addition to the national library, several murals and the Institute of Culture can be found here. Just behind it, the parking garage–looking framework was a building under construction when the 1972 earthquake hit.

El Centro Cultural de Managua is housed in the first two floors of what was once a much taller Gran Hotel, Managua's principal lodging before 1972. Now a green two-story building with murals on the outside, its first floor offers to the public a café as well as a battery of art exhibits, concerts, puppet shows, and dances. The second floor holds studios of prominent Nicaraguan artists and the city's only (secret) public bathrooms. The hallways are lined with striking black-and-white photographs of old Managua, pre- and post-earthquake. Handicraft fairs are held here the first Saturday of each month. Carved into the southeast corner of the building is **La Cavanga,** a bar built in the style of 1950s Managua, where you can catch live acoustic music on weekend nights. Sneak up to the roof to see how the upper floors of the old hotel were never replaced, yet another monument to the earthquake. At the building's western end is the old Cinema Gonzalez, reincarnated as a Coca-Cola–sponsored evangelical church.

President Alemán received much international criticism for building the **Fuente Audiovisual** instead of advancing the reconstruction after Hurricane Mitch. The sound-and-light show happens twice every evening to the dancing of the fountain waters, 6–7:15 P.M. and 9–10 P.M.

Set in the small green space of the Parque Central are several monuments of historical significance. An eternal flame guards the **Tomb of Comandante Carlos Fonseca,** father of the Sandinista revolution. Buried across from him is Santos Lopez, a member of General Sandino's "crazy little army" in the 1930s, who helped train latter-day Sandinistas in the general's ideology and the art of guerrilla warfare. The historical frieze that circles the **Templo de la Música,** a brightly painted gazebo, highlights the arrival of Columbus, Rafael Herrera fighting pirates, independence from Spain, Andrés Castro fighting William Walker, and more. It's just as interesting for the antics of the sparrows that inhabit its arches.

The **Plaza de la Cultura República de Guatemala** is a small park dedicated to Guatemalan author Miguel Angel Asturias Rosales, winner of the Nobel Prize in literature in 1967 for his colorful writings about national individuality and Native American traditions. He wrote frequently of the tyranny of dictators, the beauty and hostility of nature, and the struggle against domination by U.S. trusts, themes with which the Sandinista government felt much empathy.

West of the Parque Central is the former Palacio de Telecomunicaciones (ENITEL). Across the street are two colonial-style homes that also withstood the earthquake—not much else did in this neighborhood, including a *discoteca* (dance club) on the same block that collapsed and killed nearly everyone inside.

Parque Rubén Darío, dominated by a stark, white marble statue, is adjacent to the Parque Central and honors Nicaragua's most-beloved poet. Built in 1933, it was restored in 1998 with the help of the Texaco Corporation (whose logo is displayed a little too prominently on the statue's base). At the water's edge and replete with marble and brass, **El Teatro Rubén Darío** was designed by the same architects that created New York's Metropolitan Opera House. It too survived the earthquake and remains a classy place to take in a performance of dance, theater, or music. The second-floor balcony offers a wonderful view of the lake, and the crowds give you a glimpse of Managua's privileged aristocracy. Check the newspaper for performances or call tel. 505/266-3630 or 505/228-4021 for upcoming events.

Just west of the theater, the decrepit little park in memory of **Samora Moises Machel** honors the leader of the guerrilla movement that brought independence to Mozambique, a nation whose history of attempted socialism, counterrevolution, and democracy parallels Nicaragua's.

The Plaza de la Fé (Faith Plaza) was built during Alemán's administration in tribute to Pope John Paul II, who made his second visit to Nicaragua in 1996. Spartan, clean, and ringed with white cast-iron benches, it boasts the only public trash cans in the city, while just to the west, hungry gangs of children pick through uncontained piles of garbage in empty lots. Managua's northern limit is defined by the blustery shoreline of Lake Xolotlán, which you can admire from the Malecón, a public walkway along the water's edge lined with food and drink stands. The brass statue of Simón Bolívar, hero of the Latin American liberation movement greets you as you arrive (even if he is facing the wrong way).

Just south of these sights are **Los Escombros,** the grass-lined ruins of old downtown Managua, where no one dares build, and where Managua's poorest squat in the crumbling hulks of what the earthquake didn't pull completely to the ground. Not a safe area at any time of day. Pass through instead to the lighthouse-esque and disturbingly apocalyptic **Monumento de la Paz,** designed to oversee a new era of peace. Beneath the concrete are buried the destroyed remains of thousands and thousands of weapons from the Contra war, many of which—including a tank—can be seen protruding through the cement. It is representative of the great strides President Chamorro took during her presidency to ensure Nicaragua's days of violence and war would be relegated to the past.

The imposing, Hulk-like statue of **El Guerrillero sin Nombre** (The Nameless Guerrilla Soldier) grasps a pick-ax in one hand and an AK-47 in the disproportionately muscular other. This is an important city landmark and a symbol of the revolution's aspirations, inscribed with one of Sandino's most treasured quotations: "Only the laborers and farmers will go to the end." More recently, the Liberal government countered with a different statue honoring the worker.

Across from the new *cancillería* (foreign affairs) building, where the old Iglesia de San Antonio used to stand, is the **monument to victims of the earthquake of 1972.** This touching statue, constructed in 1994, was the brainchild of journalist Aldo Palacios. It portrays a man standing amidst the wreckage of his home and is inscribed with the poem, "Requiem a una Ciudad Muerta," by Pedro Rafael Gutierrez.

Avenida Bolívar

One of the few Managua streets known by name, Bolívar runs south from the Nameless Guerrilla statue, past several lesser-known historical sites. One block south of the Guerrellero sin Nombre, the southwest corner with a lone wooden telephone pole marks the site of journalist Pedro Joaquin Chamorro's assassination as he drove to his office on January 10, 1978. Whether the drive-by was paid for by Tachito or his business partner in the infamous blood-bank business was never determined, but Chamorro's death helped spark the revolution. Look for a concrete monument directly behind the telephone pole. Continuing south, you'll pass some government buildings and basketball courts before coming to the **National Arboretum** (Open Monday–Saturday, 8 A.M.–5 P.M., $.50) on your left, home to more than 180 species of trees found in Nicaragua. It is practically unvisited except by local school groups and is especially attractive in March, when the fragrant *sacuanjoche* (Nicaragua's national flower) blooms brightly; the scarlet flowers of the *malinche* tree blossom from May through August. The trees are planted atop the remnants of Somoza's

Hormiguero (Anthill), a military base belonging to the National Guard and destroyed in 1972 by the earthquake. Popular legend has it that this was the site where, on February 21, 1934, General Sandino was ambushed and assassinated after meeting with President Sacasa at his home on the Tiscapa Crater. Watch for ghosts.

La Laguna de Tiscapa

Continuing south on Avenida Bolívar, pass the Plaza Inter mall on your left, then turn left behind the Crowne Plaza Hotel to find the **Parque Historica,** a breezy spot overlooking a volcanic lagoon and the rest of the city. The twin-towered monument halfway up the road is the **Monumento Roosevelt,** which delineated the southern terminus of the city pre-earthquake. Twenty meters farther up the hill is the statue of justice, sardonically decapitated ages ago. The statue of Sandino atop the crater lip is one of Managua's most recognizable symbols and is protected by the military: The Sandinistas erected it atop the wreckage of Somoza's presidential mansion. Just up the hill but closed to the public rests Las Masmorras, a barbarous prison in which Somoza tortured many political prisoners, including Daniel Ortega.

The Laguna de Tiscapa, once a treasured swimming hole of pristine waters, was defiled in the 1980s when it began receiving untreated sewage from nearby neighborhoods. That hasn't kept the mayor's office from trying to exploit its potential for tourism. Try out the **zip lines** (a.k.a. canopy tour) that send you rocketing over the crater on three cable-connected platforms (8 A.M.–4:30 P.M. Mon.–Sat., $10 for foreigners, $6 for Nicas). As canopy tours go, Managua's is cheaper than elsewhere with no sacrifice in safety, but the waters below are sketchy, so concentrate instead on the broad panoramas around you—some of the best in the capital—and keep your speed up. When historical figure Comandante Tomás Borge tried the lines, he got stuck halfway across like an old sock, to the delight of crowds that jeered, "Cut the cable!" On the northeast side of Laguna Tiscapa, just two blocks from the Ministerio de Gobernación, is the site of the old U.S. Embassy, leveled during the earthquake.

Managua's escombros are full of ghosts.

Elsewhere in Managua

At the center of an immense field of young co-conut trees along the Carretera Masaya is the new cathedral, **Catedral de la Inmaculadá Concepción de María,** constructed just two years after the conclusion of the civil war. Commissioned by American Thomas Monahan and designed by Mexican architect Ricardo Legorretta, this dynamic and open cathedral houses the Dutch bells of the old cathedral. Playing on the soaring forms of Spanish colonial architecture and using colors and materials of the Latin culture, the new cathedral is home to the pulpit of Nicaragua's famous and controversial Cardinal Miguel Obando y Bravo. Mass is celebrated Tuesday–Saturday at noon and 6 P.M. and Sunday at 11 A.M. and 6 P.M.

In the amphitheater of **La Tribuna** (from Hotel Crowne Plaza, a few blocks north to the traffic circle, and one block east), 19th-century Presidents Chamorro and Zelaya oversaw grand ceremonies; damage from the 1972 earthquake was never repaired. Check it out on your way next door to La Barracuda for a swim (see the Public Swimming Pools section). Hardcore history fans will appreciate the **monument to Bill Stewart** (one block west and two blocks south of the semáforo El Dorado), the U.S. journalist for ABC-TV whose death at the hands of the National Guard was captured by his cameraman and destroyed U.S. support for Somoza's faltering regime. A few blocks south in the same neighborhood, the **Iglesia de los Angeles** is a living monument to the revolution, painted on all sides in bright murals that tell the story of Nicaragua. Beautiful on its own, it can be better appreciated with a guide: Contact Solentiname Tours (tel. 505/270-9981, zerger@ibw.com.ni) for an expert who will lead you through the story.

Just west of the petroleum refinery on the road leading west out of town is **La Cuesta del Plomo** (accessible from ruta bus 183), the ravine where Somoza was allegedly fond of making folks "disappear." Families whose loved ones didn't come home after a few days would go to this hillside to search for their bodies. Off in the distance in Lake Managua is La Isla del Amor (Island of Love), the small island where the dictator used to take his lovers to a personal cottage in the days before auto-hotels made the whole thing easier.

Las Huellas de Acahualinca

This modest and recently remodeled museum at the northwest end of the city (tel. 505/266-5774, open 8 A.M.–5 P.M. Mon.–Sat., $2), showcases 6,000-year-old traces of civilization. The prehistoric footprints were found in the last century, four meters below the ground surface. Debate rages as to whether they represent humans fleeing a volcanic eruption or just heading to the lake to fish. Charter a taxi to take you there and back (about $5 for an hour), or take buses 102 or 159 (102 runs past Barrio Martha Quezada).

Museums

Located in the Palacio de Cultura, **El Museo Nacional de Nicaragua** (tel. 505/222-2905, open 7:30 A.M.–4:30 P.M. Mon.–Fri., 9 A.M.–5 P.M. Sun., $1) highlights natural history, as well as pre-Columbian ceramics and statues from all over Nicaragua's territories.

UNAN, the national university, hosts **El Museo Geologico de la UNAN-Managua** (Colonia Miguel Bonilla #258, tel. 505/270-3983, open 8 A.M.–4:30 P.M. Mon.–Fri.), whose exhibits of rocks, fossils, and mineral finds were gathered by students both in Nicaragua and abroad. Call before arriving.

Art Galleries

More a cultural center than a museum, **Códice** (Colonial Los Robles *segundada etapa,* house #15, tel. 505/267-2635, open 9 A.M.–7 P.M., sometimes later, Mon.–Sat.) displays changing exhibitions of sculpture, paintings, and ceramics, all set around a lovely courtyard. There are often musical performances here in the evenings, and the patio is a peaceful corner in which to enjoy a light lunch and a drink.

Galería de Los Tres Mundos (Los Robles, two blocks north of the French restaurant La Marseillaise, open 8 A.M.–5 P.M. Mon.–Fri.) is the home base for Padre Ernesto Cardenal, displaying not only many of his sculptures, but also a selection of paintings and balsa work from the Solentiname Islands. This is also the center for Nicaragua's writers association, and some of the country's most famed poets and authors can be found bustling around the gallery and few offices. Los Tres Mundos is run by a foundation of the same name that offers painting classes and has a small library and bookstore.

Galería Añil (Bolonia, from Canal 2 TV, one block west, 10 meters south, tel. 505/266-5445, open 8 A.M.–5 P.M. Mon.–Fri., 8 A.M.–12 P.M. Sat.) boasts works from more than 40 Latin American painters and sculptors. **El Museo Galería Genesis** (located one block east and 75 meters south of the old Sandy's, #22, open 9 A.M.–7 P.M. Mon.–Sat.) specializes in contemporary and primitivist art. Visit **Galería Epikentro** (from Plaza España, four blocks north, 75 meters west, open 9 A.M.–6 P.M. Mon.–Fri., 9 A.M.–4 P.M. Sat.) for more contemporary and primitivist Nicaraguan art, sculpture, and frequent book readings by local authors.

Galería Praxis (from the Bolonia Optica Nicaragüense one block west, one block north, tel. 505/266-3563) has drawings, paintings, sculpture, and a small café. **Galería Pléyades** (Blvd. Villa Fontana #40, tel. 505/278-1350, open 8:30 A.M.–6 P.M. Mon.–Fri., 9 A.M.–1 P.M. Sat.) is actually a private home that displays several genres of Nicaraguan art around a graceful patio.

El Águila (Km 6 on the Carretera Sur, tel. 505/265-0524, open 9 A.M.–5:30 P.M. Mon.–Sat.) is the home and studio of celebrated and accessible artist Hugo Palma. **Galería Solentiname** (Barrio Edgard Munguía Transfer, 600 meters south of the UNAN, tel. 505/277-0939, open 9 A.M.–5 P.M. Mon.–Sat.) is set in the home of Doña Elena Pineda, a native Solentinameña who has done a great job of promoting the works of painters from the famous archipelago.

ENTERTAINMENT AND EVENTS

Although dingy pool halls and cheap dives litter every corner of the city, travelers will want to stick to a few main areas for sampling the nightlife: The first is found along Carretera Masaya from the new Cathedral to the Rotonda Centroamerica (and if you have a car, a bit beyond). This area is known as Managua's *zona rosa* (hot spot) and most new restaurants, casinos, and discos are being developed in this area. Another center of activity is the region immediately surrounding Hotel Crowne Plaza and Plaza Inter mall, with several decent bars and upscale restaurants.

Plan your evening with the help of www.2night.com or www.bacanalnica.com, which list events and parties in the city.

Rotonda Bello Horizonte

Traveling east across Managua, you'll run into this dazzling traffic circle crowded on all sides by restaurants, fast-food joints, and a pizzeria, all of which serve as the battle ground for competing bands of big-hatted, deep-voiced mariachis. It's a fun scene whether or not you appreciate the greasy food. You'll likely be the only foreigner among jovial crowds of Nicas.

Discotecas

Wondering how young Nicas manage to eat so much fried food and still stay thin? Dancing is one of the most popular forms of recreation in Managua, so even if you're a wallflower, go out and nurse a beer while watching Managuans of all ages dressed to the nines at their exuberant best. Better yet, get out there and shake your moneymaker. Venues range from enormous and open to intimate and mysterious. Thursdays and Fridays are the warm-up for Saturday night, which goes until sunrise.

The line forms early at **XS (Excess)**; dance to salsa, merengue, and *reggaetón salseado*, or relax with rum served by the bottle in several different indoor and outdoor settings. Ignore the cheesy Native American theme of **El Chamán** and focus on the tightly-packed dance floor. Huge among

"Awake, sweet love of my life..." Managua's mariachi crooners

the college crowd and right next door to both Metrocentro and many Carretera Masaya restaurants, this is a good place to finish your evening.

When you've had enough salsa and merengue, go island-style—Managua's Costeño crowd is right at home in **Island Taste** (Km 6 Carretera Norte). Go on a Thursday, when there's enough elbow room to enjoy the Garífuna, *soka,* and reggae vibes—Fridays and Saturdays, the place is typically too full to turn around, much less dance.

Bars and Clubs

Located stumbling distance from the *hospedajes* in Barrio Martha Quezada, **M The Shannon Pub** (from TicaBus, one block east, half-block south) is ground zero for beer-swilling, dart-chucking expatriates and Nicas alike—owned by "don Miguel," an affable, longtime Irish expat who, when the stars are properly aligned between Managua and Dublin, is the only vendor of Guinness draft cans in the country. Open daily for breakfast and from 3 P.M.–closing, the Shannon Pub offers a unique and tasty selection of bar food (from *tostones y queso* to corn beef and cabbage), plus national beers, imported whiskey, and a satellite jukebox.

Not far away, **M El Changon** (two blocks south and 15 meters west of the Crowne Plaza Hotel, open from 7 P.M. Wed.–Sat.) is named for Cuban witchcraft, and has a scruffy, bohemian atmosphere, a soundtrack that includes reggae, rap, and rhumba, and a cozy, open-air dance floor that doubles as a stage for local rock bands. Just around the corner, on the hilly road that goes past the Plaza Inter, both **Bar La Loma** (tucked discretely behind the Escuela de Manejo La Profesional) and **La Curva** are popular. Several other bars just downhill of El Changon change name annually and make good backups if the alcohol content in your bloodstream drops (one of them is open 24-hours).

One of the most atmospheric bars in the city, **La Cavanga** (The Heartbreak) hosts live music on weekends in one of the few buildings not razed by the '72 earthquake. Take a trip back to 1950s Managua at the bottom of a tall glass of icy rum with a twist of lime.

Along Carretera Masaya: Your best bet is to take a cab to Plaza Coconut Grove, which hosts several (ever-changing) bars, most of which fall out of favor after a year. Also look for **Club Paraíso and La Cantina,** and **Acqua,** whose Thursday ladies' nights are hot. **Z-bar ("Zeta bar"),** a few hundred meters north of the Rotonda Metrocentro has an overpriced and sub-par disco inside, but the outdoor sitting area is a great place to chill out over a cold Victoria with friends. South of town in one of Managua's new posh strips, **Hipa-Hipa** remains popular in spite of bad service and selective bouncers—if you make the cut, you'll bump elbows with cell phone–toting Miami Boys and their *fresa* companions (strawberries, as Managua's young glamour girls are affectionately known).

Dexter's Club (one block south of the Rotonda Bello Horizonte) is a low-key Caribbean-culture hangout. You'll hear it before you see it.

Gay Bars

The first openly gay bar in Nicaragua was Locos, now under new management as **Miami** (Estatua de Montoya one block south, one block west) with the same atmosphere as before. **Tabu** (Entrada del Hospital Militar, three blocks north, one west, 10 yards north, tel. 505/851-7495) is newer and cooler, and the dancing lasts until earlier in the morning. The following options are located in slightly sketchier neighborhoods, so use caution: **Le Bistro** (puente el Eden, 2.5 blocks north on the right side by the hardware store) and **Galanes** (Ciudad Jardin, main road in front of the Mariscada).

Live Music

Managua's music scene, at once homey and refined, is alive and well—as long as you know where to look. The following nightclubs specialize in live performances:

Instead of trying to book themselves gigs around town, the legendary Mejía Godoy brothers (Carlos and Luis Enrique) simply built their own club. **M Casa de los Mejía Godoy** (from Shell Plaza del Sol two block south, tel. 505/270-4928 or 505/278-4913, fmejiago@cablenet.com.ni) is also a foundation that sponsors projects around the country to help battered women and youth at risk.

NICARAGUAN FOLK MUSIC AND THE HOUSE OF MEJÍA GODOY

In the wide, vast—and incredibly loud—sea of music flowing through Nicaragua's living rooms, bars, vehicles, and airwaves, music of true Nicaraguan roots is not the easiest to hear. However, once you get to know the distinctive 6/8 rhythms, the sound of the marimba, and the melodies that every single Nicaraguan knows by heart, you'll realize just how much Nicaraguan music is woven into its society.

Only a few musical remnants of Nicaragua's indigenous societies survived the conquistadores; these precious acts of dance, costume, and distinctive melodies are best observed today during the *fiestas patronales* of Masaya, Diriamba, and the various pueblos dotting the hills between them. These pre-Colombian fragments were further enriched by the different cultures they encountered along the way. Much of this influence was Spanish, and at some point, the African marimba traveled up the Río San Juan, landed in Granada, and found its home among the *folkloricos* of Carazo and Masaya.

Things are different in the northern hills of Nicaragua, where Carlos Mejía Godoy was born in 1943. The music there, he explains, is composed of *campesino* versions of the waltz, polka, and mazurka. Born and taught to play the accordion and guitar in Somoto, Carlos Mejía is neither the "father" nor "inventor" of Nicaraguan folk music, as some would have it. In fact, he is only one in a line of multiple generations of songwriting Nicaraguans. However, his love and passion for Nicaraguan culture, combined with his sheer talent as a musician, songwriter, and performer, have made Carlos Mejía and his long catalog of songs central in any discussion (or jam session) involving Nicaraguan music.

Don Carlos says he wishes he had two lives: one to learn all there is to be learned about Nicaraguan culture and a second to perform and use that knowledge. To most observers (and fans), it would appear he has done an adequate job at squeezing both

into the one life he was given. Not only did he join the Sandinista Revolution in 1973 and proceed to compose its soundtrack, but throughout his life, Carlos Mejía has delved deeply into the *campo*, always in search of the regionally distinct riches of his country's cultural fabric. His songs are vibrant, colorful celebrations of everything Nicaraguan—from its geography, food, and wildlife, to praise for the town gossip and shoe-shine boy.

When asked about the Nicaraguita flower that inspired him to write the most famous song in the country's history ("Nicaragua, Nicaraguita"), Carlos Mejía quoted a passage entitled "La Flor Escogida" (The Chosen Flower) by Profesor Carlos A. Bravo. In that passage, the rare variety of *sacuanjoche* (Nicaragua's national flower) is described as *"roja incendida, un clarinazo, listada de oro"* (burning red, a trumpet blast, with golden rays). Carlos Mejía called this "such a beautiful thing," and one is not sure if he was speaking of the flower or the lyrical words describing it—perhaps for him, there is no distinction between the two.

Pick up some of Carlos Mejía's music and learn his lyrics before you leave, but don't stop your discovery there. Carlos's brother Luis Enrique is a world-renowned salsa king, and they can both be found performing at their club in Managua, **La Casa de los Mejía Godoy.**

Other respected Nica folksters include Nandaimeño Camilo Zapata, the granddaddy of them all; also seek out Tino Lopez, Justo Santos, Otto de la Rocha, Norma Elena Madea, and the duo Guardabarranco. In addition, every town in Nicaragua has multiple generations of pluckers and crooners, many of whom are a wealth of knowledge and all too willing to sing (or teach) you some songs.

An excellent guide (in Spanish) to Nicaraguan music can be found at www.musicanica.com.

Both brothers perform here regularly, Carlos on Thursday and Saturday, with or without his band Los de Palacagüina. Friday is Latin rhythm night with salsa king Luis Enrique, and Sunday features other Nicaraguan or international performers. Both brothers are born showmen and present a theatrical mix of stories, bawdy jokes, and famous songs. The club is expensive by Nica standards, but well worth it. Buy tickets the afternoon of the performance for $8–15; shows are Wednesday through Sundays only and start at 9 P.M.

The breezy, outdoor terrace of **La Ruta Maya** (150 meters east of the Estatua de Montoya, tel. 505/268-0698, open Thurs.–Sat., $4–6.) is a pleasant place to appreciate a wide variety of performers from singer-songwriters to reggae and everything in between. Also look for acoustic performances at the Shannon Pub and Changon.

Casinos

Casinos are the latest, um, crapshoot in the Managua entertainment scene; glassy, gaudy, government-sponsored **Pharaoh Casino** (Carretera Masaya) is rivaled by **Star City Casino** (across from the Princess Hotel), which is better-appointed and far louder. A younger crowd frequents the **Las Vegas** if they're unable to get into the **Hollywood** strip club adjacent.

Movies

Since the late 1990s, Managua's cinemas have been modern and viciously air-conditioned, and show most new Hollywood releases, often no more than a few weeks after being released in the States. English-language movies (with the exception of animated children's flicks) are presented with Spanish subtitles. If you need to get away from it all, check show times in the newspaper or the *Revista Cinematográfica* (a weekly bulletin distributed at most gas stations and some hotels and restaurants). Shows change every Thursday and will set you back about $3.

Located in the Metrocentro Mall, **Cinemark** (tel. 505/271-9037 or 505/271-9000) is a six-screen multiplex right above the food court. The **Cinema Plaza Inter** (tel. 505/222-5090 or 505/222-5122) is on the third floor of the Plaza Inter mall. Although it is conveniently located a

few blocks east of Barrio Martha Quezada, where you'll probably be staying, numerous foreigners have been mugged making the walk—take a cab.

Theater and Dance

Managua's finest theater, **El Teatro Nacional Rubén Darío** (at the Malecón, tel. 505/266-3630 or 505/228-4021) hosts top-name international acts. Check the newspaper for performances or call. **La Escuela Nacional de Teatro** (Palacio Nacional de Cultura, tel. 505/222-4449) is primarily a teaching facility that presents performances on weekends by students and small professional troupes from all over Latin America; call for a list of events, as they're not always published. The **Sala De Teatro Justo Rufino Garay** (from the Estatua Montoya three blocks west and 20 meters north, next to Parque Las Palmas, tel. 505/266-3714) is better frequented and offers similar fare on weekends only; a calendar of events is often available at supermarkets and Texaco stations.

Located across from the UCA, **La Academia de Danza** (tel. 505/277-5557) has frequent performances and concerts. The students deliver professional and talented renditions of traditional, folk, modern jazz, Brazilian, and ballet; call or drop by for a schedule of events, or if you're in town for the long haul, consider taking one of their dance classes to prepare you for the club scene.

SPECIAL EVENTS

Las Fiestas Patronales each August are when Managua celebrates its patron saint Santo Domingo and are the highlight of the calendar year. On the first of the month, the saint is brought down from a small church in the hilly neighborhood of Santo Domingo and on the 10th he is returned. On both those dates, and for much of the time in between, Managua celebrates. Expect parades, horse shows, unlimited quantities of beer and rum, and a lot of fun and colors. INTUR sponsors a series of events during this time, like Las Noches Agostinas, featuring cultural presentations and live music throughout the capital.

Now a holiday celebrated throughout the country, July 19, 1979 marked the final victory against Somoza during the Sandinista revolution.

Waiting for the saint: a youngster paints himself in motor oil for the arrival of Managua's Santo Domingo.

July 19th celebrations are especially exciting in Managua, with parades and presentations in Plaza de la Fé. The parades used to take place in Plaza de la Revolución, until Alemán filled it with his musical fountain.

SHOPPING
Markets
For a gorgeous selection of arts and crafts in a pleasant atmosphere, visit **Mama Delfina** (Enitel Villa Fontana, one block north, tel. 505/267-8288), which collects the work of artisans from all over the country. It also boasts a little café on a breezy second-floor balcony where you can mull over your purchases with a tall glass of icy cacao.

Mercado Huembes is full of the exuberance, color, and life that so typifies Nicaragua. Huembes is the most tourist-friendly of the markets in Managua. Massive and cacophonous, Huembes offers fruits, vegetables, meat, cheese, flowers, cigars, clothes, shoes, and the best arts and crafts section this side of Masaya. Open every day from

around 7:30 A.M. to around 5 P.M., Huembes is also a major bus terminal (see the Getting There By Bus section).

The sprawling labyrinth of Mercado Oriental, on the other hand, is a confusing maze of legal and illegal commerce—from plastic furniture to haircuts, aircraft parts to an illegal abortion—that has slowly consumed more than 30 city blocks. If you can't find it in the Oriental, you can't find it in Nicaragua. But once you've found it, will you find your way out again? Mercado Oriental is more menace than joyride: Someone gets robbed here every seven minutes, and travelers should avoid it.

If you are in Managua during the first few weeks of December, be sure to catch the massive **IMPYME** crafts fair on Avenida Bolívar—arts, crafts, and food from all over the country, plus a two-week carnival.

Malls
The two U.S.-style malls built in 1998 and 1999 (Plaza Inter and Metrocentro) have notably dissimilar personalities: While Metrocentro hosts

© TOMÁS STARGARDTER

the typical bevy of Cartier, LaCoste, and Chanel counters, Plaza Inter has made a go at cheaper-quality imported goods from Asia (the Plaza is wholly owned by Taiwanese investors). The Centro Comercial de Managua is a pleasant open-air strip mall built in the Somoza era, offering a good selection of books, clothing, fabric, and sporting goods, plus two banks, an Internet café, and a post office— not a bad place to get some errands out of the way if malls aren't your cup of tea. Just north of the National Cathedral, La Galería is a high-end shopping complex. Try the DISNISA for a great selection of imported wines and liquor.

Bookstores

Air-conditioned and well-stocked, **Hispamer** (Reparto Tiscapa, just east of the UCA, tel. 505/278-1210) is the largest bookstore in the city. In the Centro Comercial, there are several small, but interesting bookstores compete for your attention, including **Librería El Güegüense** (tel. 505/278-7399 or 505/278-5285), one of the better choices for books about Nicaragua and foreign-language dictionaries, and **Librería Rigoberto López Pérez** (tel. 505/277-2240), named for the poet who, for love of his country, assassinated Anastasio Somoza García. The latter features a wide selection and friendly atmosphere.

Musical Instruments

Purchase musical instruments, guitar strings, and accessories at one of the two stalls in the artisan section of the Roberto Huembes Market, or at one of two modern music stories in Altamira; they are practically across the street from each other, located just north of the Farmacia Quinta Avenida.

SPORTS AND RECREATION

Denis Martínez National Baseball Stadium

A.k.a. *El Estadio Nacional,* this landmark is a proper metaphor for Managua: partially destroyed and rebuilt after the earthquake to something less than its original grandeur, originally named after Anastasio Somoza García, then renamed by the Sandinistas after that man's assassin, then renamed again, this time after

Nicaragua's native son baseball hero. Catch Managuans at their baseball-lovin' finest as you help them root for the home team, *Boer,* (whose logo is blatantly ripped off from the Cleveland Indians). Seats behind home plate cost less than $2.

Public Swimming Pools

Escuela Club de Natación La Barracuda (one block east of the semáforo Plaza Inter, tel. 505/222-7044, $1 per visit, $15 per month) is a clean swimming pool that once belonged to the army. The **UNI** has a medium-size pool open to the public (tel. 505/267-0274, $1.50/hour). But the best pool in the city for relaxing in is at the **Hotel Best Western Las Mercedes** (across the street from the airport, tel. 505/263-1011 or 505/263-1028, open 9 A.M.–5 P.M. daily). Your $10 entrance fee can be applied to sandwiches and beer. The pool at the five-star **Hotel Camino Real** (Carretera Norte, tel. 505/263-1381, $10 daily) is a close second. Poolside barbecues on Sundays cost an additional $18 and are not usually worth the extra money.

Golf

It's no surprise that Nicaragua's wave of Miami-raised nouveax riche would get around to re-opening the country's old-time exclusive country clubs, notably the 18 holes at Nejapa Country Club (tel. 505/266-9652), located between Veracruz and Sabana Grande. The course hosts events, such as the "Amigos de la Zona Franca" tournament, and you can get a round in. There's also Club Terraza in the Villa Fontana area. Although there's no doubt that the names on the club roster make up the family history of the country, not all rich people can get in. When asked who would not be allowed in, one Club Terraza official said, "those who have been accused of corruption, even if the judicial system finds him innocent," making a less-than-subtle reference to Arnoldo Alemán.

ACCOMMODATIONS

Under $10: Barrio Martha Quezada

It should be readily apparent why Barrio Martha Quezada is called Gringolandia: The approximately 12 square blocks north and west of the

COLLEGE TOWN

Nicaragua's next generation of leaders attends more than 30 Managuan universities, the three biggest of which are **La Universidad de Centroamerica** ("La UCA", rhymes with "hookah"), **La Universidad Nacional Autónoma de Nicaragua** ("La UNAN"), and **La Universidad Nicaragüense de Ingeniería** ("La UNI"). Visiting the courtyards, soda shops, cafés, and bars on campus provides a great opportunity to mingle with up-and-coming revolutionaries and neo-liberal capitalists alike. Find out about the latest student strike, sit-in, or tire-burning session in the fight for six percent of the national budget, cheaper tuition, and of course, a classless society without corruption, war, or unfair wages. The intersection in front of the UCA and UNI is a regular hotspot during student strife, and a huge social scene otherwise. It is also a transportation hub, with minivans departing the city daily for nearby destinations.

TicaBus terminal are cluttered with budget accommodations and basic services that cater to the backpacker set (re: Internet, phones, bakeries, and bars). This neighborhood borders with a few dangerous blocks to the east, where youthful thieves sometimes prey on foreigners, so local businesses pay for additional security patrols (listen for the guy with the whistle).

With its cheap rates ($4 pp), vast common space, and famed organic funkiness, **Ⓜ Guesthouse Santos** (located from TicaBus, one block north and 1.5 blocks west, tel. 505/222-3713) remains a sound anchor on the backpacker trail; surrounding its two-story open-air lounge and ever-present assemblage of barefoot *cheles* zoned-out to CNN are a messy heap of 30 quasi-secure, rainbow-painted rooms without right angles and under improvement for the last 30 years. Mattresses are firm, private bathrooms are, um, post-modern, and many basic services are close at hand. Ask Don Santos about the time Daniel Ortega and Yasser Arafat met in the *sala*.

A half block east, **La Quintana** (tel. 505/254-5487 or 505/254-5492, $5 s) is smaller than

Santos, with clean, shared bathrooms and an irascible proprietress who shuts the door at 11 P.M. and doesn't open it until morning (argue with her and see what happens); try to get a front room with a window for ventilation. Laundry service available.

The owner of **Hospedaje El Dorado** (tel. 505/222-6012, $5 s) chooses her guests very carefully, so it's one of the safest places—if you make the cut, that is. You are given a key to the gate for late-night entry; laundry service available. **La Casa Castillo** (tel. 505/222-2265, $5 s) has six rooms with private baths. It's cleaner than most but sometimes hot; concentrate on how good those real box-spring mattresses feel instead.

There are a dozen other options in this neighborhood, usually consisting of simple, nondescript breeze-block rooms with rudimentary bathroom facilities. **Casa Vanegas** (tel. 505/222-4043, $6 s) is just that—the Vanegas family's house. They'll make you feel at home in your own room with private bath. Others—Casa Meza, El Viajero, and El Molinito—are more rustic than necessary and cater to a Central American clientele. Worst of all is the *hospedaje* inside the TicaBus station, which might serve in a pinch but is otherwise overpriced at $10 per person for penitentiary-like rooms and shared baths.

$10–25

Ⓜ Hotel Los Felipe (one block west of TicaBus, tel. 505/222-6501, $15/20/25 s/d/t), though more expensive than the other options in this neighborhood, is easily the best of the low-priced hotels. Rooms are clean and safe and have cable TV and phone; Internet, parking, pool, a shady patio area under a thatched roof, laundry service, and private baths are also available. Another classy, comfortable option among the neighborhood riff-raff is **Hospedaje Jardín de Italia** (one block north of the Shannon Pub), whose handful of rooms are clean and feature real beds, private bathrooms, TV, and air-conditioning; $10 pp with fan (price doubles during high season or if you turn on the a/c). This is a pleasant, bright space with hammocks and Internet.

$25–50

If you find yourself complaining too loudly about Managua, try upgrading your accommodations. Once you leave the Barrio Martha Quezada, prices rise sharply but so do the quality of the rooms, every one of which in this section includes air-conditioning, hot water, direct telephone lines, and often room service and/or breakfast.

Located in the Bolonia neighborhood, **M Hotel Europeo** (75 meters west of Canal 2, tel. 505/268-4930 or 505/268-4933, europeo @ibw.com.ni, www.hoteleuropeo.com.ni, $33.50 s, $41 d, $48.50 t) is easy to recommend: eleven clean, quiet, and beautifully furnished rooms, plus continental breakfast, a small pool, laundry service, and cable TV. **La Casona** (north corner Canal 2, half a block west, Bolonia, tel. 505/266-1685, info@estancialacasona.com, www .estancialacasona.com, $36 s, $48 d) is a pleasant, comfortable, and clean family-run place with more than 10 years of experience. At about the same level of amenities, **Casa San Juan** (Reparto San Juan Calle Esperanza 560, tel. 505/278-3220, sanjuan@cablenet.com.ni, paginasamarillas.com/casasanjuan.htm) is basic but quiet and close to the universities.

Posada de Maria La Gorda (Reparto El Carmen, tel. 505/268-2455 or 505/268-2456) is accustomed to the international set and provides Internet, laundry, and cable TV; $35–60 plus special group rates. **Maracas Inn** (one block north and one west of the Hospital Militar, tel. 505/266-8612 or 505/266-8982, $55–80) has 30 clean, well-kept rooms and offers breakfast, fax, laundry service, taxi service to the airport, and parking.

M Hotel El Ritzo (from the Lacmiel, three blocks east, 25 meters south, tel. 505/277-5616, hotelritzo@alianza.com.ni, www.hotelritzo.com.ni, $55 d) is not only tastefully decorated, quiet, and gorgeous, but is the only hotel worth considering within walking distance of the many restaurants and discos of the Carretera Masaya area.

A convenient place to stay if you have an early flight—and a nice hotel to boot—the **Best Western Las Mercedes** (tel. 505/263-1011, $52 d) is directly across from the airport. Decompress on the last night before your flight in a decent restaurant or with the mixed bag of travelers and diplomats lounging by the pool.

$50–100

In the Los Robles area just west of Carretera Masaya, **Hotel Los Robles** (in front of Restaurante La Marseillaise, tel. 505/267-3008, info@hotel losrobles.com, www.hotellosrobles.com, $85 d) is a charming yet professional hotel with a tropical feel, consisting of quiet rooms set around a garden courtyard, gym, pool, and restaurant services, wireless Internet, a/c, cable TV in all the rooms, and a business center; their breakfast buffet is splendid.

Situated in a shady, peaceful neighborhood, **Hotel Casa Real** (Rotonda Rubén Darío two blocks west, two blocks south, half a block east, tel. 505/278-3838, info@hcasareal.com, www.hcasa real.com, from $65) boasts a trilingual staff, a small pool, and an excellent menu.

Hotel Real Bolonia (from Plaza España 1.5 blocks north, across from the German Embassy, tel. 505/266-8133, hotelreal@hotelreal.com.ni, $75) features 14 rooms adorned with antiques, paintings, and sculpture, all set around a large garden.

La Posada del Angel (Hospital Militar three blocks west, 20 meters north, across from the Iglesia San Francisco, tel. 505/266-1347 or 505/266-1483, $65) has a long-standing reputation for excellent customer service; rooms have hot water, minibar, laundry service, cable TV, and strongbox.

Another good quality bed-and-breakfast in a safe, central neighborhood is **Hotel Brandt** (Reparto San Juan, from the north side of Hercules gym one block east, tel. 505/270-2114, 505/270-2115, or 505/270-2116, fax 505/278-8128, bbbho@cablenet.com.ni, www.brandtshotel.com.ni, $55/70 s/d), with excellent facilities and service.

Over $100

Managua's increasing number of premium hotels cater to discerning business travels and offer five-star service, airport shuttles, pools, dry cleaning, concierge, business centers, top-notch restaurants, hundreds of rooms, and mostly central locations.

A Managua landmark since before the revolution, the pyramidal Hotel Intercontinental Managua has changed hands and is now the **Hotel Crowne Plaza** (tel. 505/228-3530, managua@interconti.com). The **Intercontinental Metrocentro** (adjacent to the Metrocentro mall, tel. 505/271-9483) is one of Managua's best-situated hotels, with convenient access to the Metrocentro mall and the many restaurants that line Carretera Masaya. Two blocks south, the **Hotel Princess** (Carretera Masaya, tel. 505/270-5045) is of the same caliber.

The **Holiday Inn** (Pista Juan Paul II, tel. 505/270-4515, holidayinn@tmx.com.ni) is the least conveniently situated of the premium hotels, but its interior is lovely and its service excellent. On Carretera Norte and a quick ride from the airport, the **Camino Real** (U.S. or Canada toll-free tel. 800/948-3770, caminoreal@centralamerica.com, $120) has 116 first-rate rooms and is a popular conference center.

Long-Term Accommodations

If you don't mind the grunge, you can surely work out some kind of long-term rate at any of the cheap *hospedajes* for around $150 a month. That's about the least you'd pay for your own safe apartment in Managua, and entire houses can be found for rent for as low as $300.

For a fully serviced guesthouse, $500 per month is the going rate. **Los Cedros** (Km 13, Carretera Sur, across from the Iglesia Monte Tabor, tel. 505/265-8340) has 30 furnished rooms with bath, terrace, kitchen, pool, and plenty of green space. Next to Las Cazuelas restaurant and across from Guesthouse Santos, **Hotel/Apartamentos Los Cisneros** (tel. 505/222-3535) rents small, fully furnished apartments that include refrigerator, private phone, and parking facilities. Otherwise, dip into your expense account and check in at **Los Robles** (one block west, two blocks south of the Hotel Inter Metrocentro, tel. 505/278-6334), which has 12 safe rooms at $1,300 per month with maid service, cable TV, fridge, kitchen, and a/c. If you're content living outside the city limits, several excellent long-term options line the far reaches of Carretera Masaya. **Hotel Campo Real** (Km 12.5, tel. 505/279-7067, camporeal@ideay.net.ni, www.hotelcampo real.com) is one of many places with all the amenities that will make you feel at home.

FOOD

Every year, Managua produces dozens of new restaurants; some stick around, others fold within the year when the jet set moves on to something newer and trendier.

Street Food, a.k.a. Fritangas

Barrio Martha Quezada is littered with cheap eateries and street-side grills, notably the *fritanga* one block west and half a block north of TicaBus—open nights from about 6– 9 P.M. Or try **La Racachaca** (from the Plaza España, 1.5 km west), a 10-minute taxi ride from Martha Quezada and easily the most famous *fritanga* in Managua; your cab driver will know where it is because he probably eats there himself.

Fast Food, Nica Style

Pollo Campero and **Tip-Top** chicken chains are all over the city and offer fried chicken, sandwiches, and more, for about $3–4. Or try local hamburger joints **Hamburlooca** and **Quickburger** (across the street from the UNI). For a closer look at the capital, get local at the Rotonda Bello Horizonte: There are several fried chicken places as well as **Pizzería Los Idolos.**

Breakfast

There are numerous bakeries scattered throughout Barrio Martha Quezada, notably **Cafetín Tonalli** (2.5 blocks south of Cine Cabrera), a unique women's cooperative that produces extraordinarily good breads and cakes, and sells juices, cheese, coffee, and more (Swiss training!). Take out or eat in their enclosed outdoor patio. One block west of TicaBus, **Café Myrna** (open 6 A.M.–lunch, $3.50 for a full meal) offers a full Nica breakfast menu, plus pancakes, huevos rancheros, fresh coffee, and tall, blended fruit drinks in a pleasant atmosphere. A block and a half east of the Calle 27 traffic light, look for the colorful storefront of **Frutilandia** (open 7 A.M.–5 P.M. Mon.–Sat.), where you'll find a fresh, delicious menu of fruit smoothies, shakes, and simple meals.

Managua

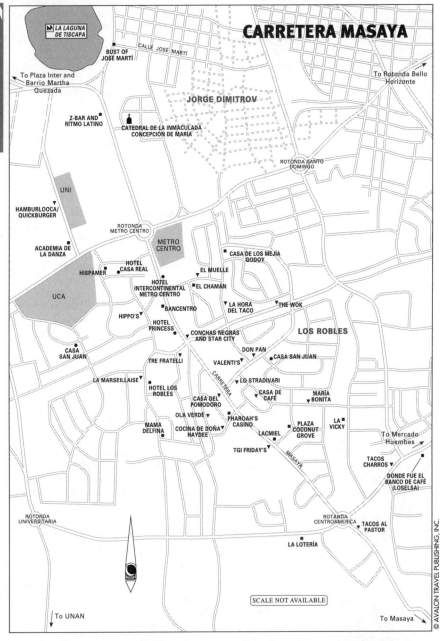

CARRETERA MASAYA

LA LAGUNA DE TISCAPA

BUST OF JOSÉ MARTÍ

CALLE JOSÉ MARTÍ

To Plaza Inter and Barrio Martha Quezada

To Rotonda Bello Horizonte

JORGE DIMITROV

Z-BAR AND RITMO LATINO

CATEDRAL DE LA INMACULADA CONCEPCIÓN DE MARÍA

ROTONDA SANTO DOMINGO

UNI

HAMBURLOOCA/ QUICKBURGER

ROTONDA METRO CENTRO

ACADEMIA DE LA DANZA

METRO CENTRO

CASA DE LOS MEJÍA GODOY

HOTEL CASA REAL

HISPAMER

EL MUELLE

HOTEL INTERCONTINENTAL METRO CENTRO

EL CHAMÁN

UCA

BANCENTRO

LA HORA DEL TACO

THE WOK

HIPPO'S

HOTEL PRINCESS

CONCHAS NEGRAS AND STAR CITY

LOS ROBLES

CASA SAN JUAN

DON PAN

CASA SAN JUAN

TRE FRATELLI

VALENTI'S

LA MARSEILLAISE

CARRETERA

LO STRADIVARI

HOTEL LOS ROBLES

CASA DE CAFÉ

MARÍA BONITA

CASA DEL POMODORO

OLA VERDE

PHAROAH'S CASINO

PLAZA COCONUT GROVE

LA VICKY

To Mercado Huembes

MAMA DELFINA

COCINA DE DOÑA HAYDEE

LACMIEL

MASAYA

TGI FRIDAY'S

TACOS CHARROS

DONDE FUE EL BANCO DE CAFÉ (LOSELSA)

ROTONDA UNIVERSITARIA

ROTONDA CENTROAMERICA

TACOS AL PASTOR

MOON

LA LOTERÍA

SCALE NOT AVAILABLE

To UNAN

To Masaya

© AVALON TRAVEL PUBLISHING, INC.

Fritanga food: backyard barbecue meets a pot of boiling oil.

Cafés and Coffee Shops

Managua's premier classy coffee shop is **La Casa de Café** (a landmark in the Los Robles neighborhood, and smaller venues in the MetroCentro Mall and airport) with pricey meals, key lime pie, strawberry muffins, and juice drinks all served on a gorgeous, second-story open terrace overlooking the street. Everything's good except occasionally, believe it or not, the coffee. A mini-me version of the same establishment occupies the slot next to the cinema in the Metrocentro mall. Better java comes from **Don Pan** (across from Pizzeria Valentis), which also serves sandwiches and baked goods. If you're visiting the sights, check out the **Palacio Nacional de Cultura's** café, offering pastries, coffee, tea, and more.

Vegetarian and Healthy Food

Naturaleza (two blocks west, one north from the Hospital Bautista, tel. 505/222-6944) is the only holistic, new age, organic food store in the city. It's small but packed with soy products, vit-

amins, natural body care and medicines, candles, and incense.

Ananda (half a block east of the Estatua Montoya, tel. 505/228-4140, open 7 A.M.–9 P.M.) is Managua's original vegetarian option, with whole foods and fresh fruit juices.

The newest upscale sensation is **Ola Verde** (behind Pharoah's Casino; follow the road to the end and turn right, tel. 505/270-3048 www.olaverde.info, open from 9 A.M., breakfast starts at around $4, lunch around $6), offering fresh juices, salads, soups, hummus, and *babaganoush*—a pleasant menu of changing vegetarian and chicken dishes. Ola Verde also has a small shop of natural products and is a popular meeting spot for foreigners.

Traditional Nicaraguan

La Cocina de Doña Haydee (one block west of Casino Pharoah) serves Nicaragua's best specialties in a clean, quiet atmosphere; you could get the same food at a good *fritanga* for a fourth of

Managua

the price, but if you'd rather avoid street food, this is your place. Specialties include *vaho, indio viejo,* and *nacatamales,* each a different Nicaraguan dish of corn, meat, and vegetables. **Mi Pueblo** (Carretera sur Km 9) is on the southwestern side of town and is worth the trip for lunch to check out one of the best views in town, bar none.

Steak and Burgers

La Plancha (from the Semáforos Plaza del Café 150 meters to the east) is home to some of the best meat in town. Ask for the *parrillada* rack or just go for the grill, *a la plancha,* about $10–12 a plate. Perhaps the best-known steak place in the city, **El Churrasco** is located right on the Rotonda El Güegüense. **Los Ranchos** isn't cheap (about $15 per entrée), but they've served a fantastic steak au poivre since the days of Somoza (Carretera Sur Km 3, tel. 505/266-0526, open noon–3 P.M., 6–11 P.M.).

Eskimo (next door to the Fábrica Eskimo, tel. 505/266-9701) serves a varied menu of meats, fish, and shellfish, all in the $6–9 range; the *pollo en vino* is a popular choice. If the Nica beef is too tough for you, **Hippo's Bar and Grill** (from the old Sandy's, one block west) sells $5 burgers made of USDA-approved, genetically enhanced, imported gringo ground beef—plus a polished bar with all kinds of treats. **T.G.I.Fridays** (Carretera Masaya Km 5) is just like in the States with burgers, chicken, sandwiches, pasta dishes, and bouncy waiters in dippy costumes; about $20 a person by the time you've ordered drinks.

Spanish

El Mesón Español y Barra La Tasca (Bolonia Mansión Teodolinda 350 meters south, tel. 505/266-8561) boasts fantastic paella and shellfish for about $20.

Mexican

⋈ La Hora del Taco (Monte de los Olivos, one block north, tel. 505/277-5074, $5 and up) serves traditional, reasonably priced Mexican food; the fajitas are a favorite. **Tacos Charros** (Colonia Centroamérica, tel. 505/278-2337) is the cheapest place to eat tacos, enchiladas, and the like, all for around $3. **María Bonita** (1.5 blocks west

of Distribuidora Vicky, tel. 505/270-4326) is another favorite, offering dinner in an open, romantic atmosphere for about $6, and a traditional and European breakfast bar Monday–Saturday 6:45–10 A.M. for $3. Stop in at **Tacos al Pastor** on your way to the Alhambra movie theater. It's a small but charming restaurant that also sells beautiful pottery; dishes run about $3.

Seafood

Start at **El Muelle** (one block east of the Hotel Intercontinental Metrocentro, $6–8), easily some of the best seafood in Managua. In a recent poll, 4 out of 5 wealthy married old men and their 18-year-old girlfriends preferred **Conchas Negras** (across the street from the Hotel Princess). Start with the *ceviche* and a Corona.

Asian

You'll need a cab to get to **The Wok** (a short hop down the bypass in front of Hotel Princess). Dishes start at $6. But **Ming Court** (adjacent to the Plaza Inter and Hotel Crowne Plaza) is top of the line, and easily the best and most expensive Chinese food in the country; dishes from $8–10.

Italian

The faithful standby for travelers who can't stand to see another red bean, Italian restaurants abound in Managua; in fact, there are more than the city can possibly support, so look for this category to thin out. **La Casa del Pomodoro** (Carretera Masaya Km 4, a block from Pizzería Valentis) is a big favorite, serving large portions of quality food; their $5 calzones will fill you up for two days. **Mágica Roma** (Hotel Crowne Plaza one block west) serves up more elegant fare. It's run by a war-era photojournalist whose photos you can appreciate while you dig into dishes prepared by a real Italian, about $8 per plate. **Tre Fratelli** (on Carretera Masaya) sports a modern bar, indoor and outdoor seating, and a high-end menu that includes the Italian classic Fiorentina steak. Expect to pay upwards of $10 per plate for dinner, but the executive lunch goes for about $6, or just enjoy happy hour from 6–9. And the best value for your money, **Valenti's**

Pizza (Colonial Los Robles, two blocks east of Lacmiel, tel. 505/277-5744) serves inexpensive pizza and beer in a festive atmosphere. Across the street from Valenti's, **Lo Stradivari** is a step up in price and quality. Try their fresh pesto and their cannelloni.

French

For those who appreciate being surrounded by wonderful art while they wait for their five-star meal, **La Marseillaise** (Calle Principal Los Robles, tel. 505/277-0224) predates the war and is one of the most expensive—and best—restaurants in town. They serve classic French cuisine, including delicious fillets of meat and fish, and stunning desserts, in a gorgeous building.

INFORMATION AND SERVICES

The daily newspaper will keep you *al tanto* (up to date) in terms of events and festivals. INTUR, the government tourism institute (tel. 505/222-3333, www.intur.gob.ni), staff a kiosk in the airport and an office near the Plaza Inter mall, where they sell maps, distribute local guides and listings, and offers a visitor's desk for tourists, open 8:30 A.M.–2 P.M. Mon.–Fri.

Emergency

Dial 118 for police, 115 or 120 for the fire dept., and 128 for the Red Cross ambulance. There are several hospitals in Managua; the most modern is the private **Hospital Vivian Pellas** (outside of Managua on the highway to Masaya), built in 2004. For less serious ailments and stomach disorders, Hospital Bautista (tel. 505/249-7070, Barrio Largaespada, near the main fire station) is accustomed to dealing with foreigners.

Libraries

A rarity in a nation that reads few books, Managua's public library, **Biblioteca Dr. Roberto Incer Barquero** (behind the bank at km 7 Carretera Sur, tel. 505/265-0500 ext. 465, open 8:30 A.M.–4:30 P.M. Mon.–Fri.) was built in 1999 and houses a notable collection of newspapers from the war years. The old National Library is located in the Palacio de Cultura down

by the waterfront. INHCA is a remarkable collection of historical and cultural resources housed within the UCA; accessing them requires a library card obtainable from the director by paying a $10 fee.

Banks

The banks that survived the liquidity crises of 2000–2001 are leaner and meaner these days, and compete fiercely for your dollars. Banking hours in Managua are 8 A.M.–4 P.M. Monday–Friday, and 8 A.M.–noon on Saturday. Along Carretera Masaya, you'll find the Banco de América Central (BAC, owned by the wealthy Pellas family), Banco Caley Dagnal, Banco de Finanzas (BDF), and Banic. For travelers staying in Barrio Martha Quezada, the nearest bank is the Banco de Nicaragua (Banic) Sucursal Bolonia. Several other nearby banks are clustered around Plaza España, including BAC and Banco Uno. You'll find shorter lines at Multicambios, on the south side of Plaza España. Additionally, there's a BDF conveniently located in front of the Hotel Inter.

Mail, Fax, and Phone

The Palacio de Comunicaciones, located across the plaza near the ruins of the old cathedral, contains the central office of both Correos de Nicaragua and ENITEL, with full mail, fax, telex, express courier, and phone services. In the *palacio,* the *oficina de filatelia* sells stamps from previous editions beginning in 1991 (Nicaragua is well known among philatelists for having the most beautiful postage stamps in Central America), plus postcards and greeting cards (open 8 A.M.–5 P.M. Mon.–Fri., 8 A.M.–1 P.M. Sat.). More compact, easier post offices to deal with are found in the Centro Comercial, Altamira, and the airport.

For packages, **DHL** (tel. 505/228-4081) is located in front of the Hotel Intercontinental, and on Carretera Masaya near the Hotel Princess. **Federal Express** has been operating in Nicaragua since 2000. Find it on Carretera Masaya near Subway, and in Ofiplaza El Retiro Ste. 515 (150 meters south of Rotonda Los Periodistas, tel. 505/278-4500).

Internet

You can hardly throw a *rosquilla* in Managua without hitting an Internet café offering Internet phone calls ("voice over IP"), and the better hotels have a machine or two you can use on-premises. If you're sleeping in Barrio Martha Quezada, Cyber Center Banisa, located two blocks south of the stadium, is your best bet, or try the place next door to Shannon Pub. Otherwise, head toward the university area, across from the main UCA gates, where there are a half dozen Internet joints, all with the cheapest rates in the city, usually open till 9 P.M. during the week. Macintosh addicts can get their fix (or get their own Macs fixed) at the **iMac Center** (tel. 505/270-5918, open 8 A.M.–5 P.M.,) tucked behind the UCA, a few doors down from HISPAMER bookstore.

Supermarkets

The many branches of La Colonial and La Union not only stock their modern aisles with national and imported foodstuffs, they also sell clothing, sandals, books, CDs, cosmetics, and more. The easiest to reach from Barrio Martha Quezada is just up the road at Plaza España (8 A.M.–7 P.M. Mon.–Fri., 8 A.M.–5 P.M. Sat., 9 A.M.–3 P.M. Sun.). If you're in the Carretera Masaya area, you're better off at the La Colonial on the Rotonda Centroamerica. Visit Costco Familiar (located across the street from Valenti's Pizza, open 9 A.M.–10 P.M. Mon.–Sat., 9 A.M.–3 P.M. Sun.) for gourmet goodies, alcohol, and imported bulk items, including dark European beers (and crappy U.S. ones), shiitake mushrooms, chewing tobacco, and specialty olive oils and cheeses. There are several other supermarkets around the city, but most travelers will find what they need at one of the many smaller "mini-supers" and *pulperías* that populate the neighborhoods.

Photography Supplies

Just about all supermarkets sell print film, but for more complex needs like Ektachrome, slide- or B/W film, head over to **Kodak Express Profesional** (behind the CompuMax in the Colónia Centroamérica). **Konica** (across from the McDonald's at Plaza España) will process your film

and also sells their own brand of slide film. For expensive black-and-white processing by hand, go to the **Galería Mexico,** (Altamira, across from María Bonita, tel. 505/278-1058). The quality of film processing varies wildly, even within the same store. Digital-camera users looking for a place to download their images are still mostly out of luck: Few cyber-cafés will be able to deal with your chip, smartcard, or similar hardware unless you bring your own software and smooth-talk the owner.

Laundry and Dry Cleaning

If you're roughing it, you'll have noticed most *hospedajes* have a *lavandero* (cement-ridged washboard). Buy a slug of bar soap ($.30) at the local *pulpería,* roll up your sleeves, and scrub away like everybody else. Most *hospedajes* have someone who will wash and iron your foul travel clothes for a reasonable fee as well. Otherwise, try one of the **Dryclean USA** locations. The most convenient branch is located at the Plaza Bolonia right behind Santa Fé Steakhouse.

Travel Agents

Many travel agents operate just southeast of the Plaza España and are a short cab ride from Barrio Martha Quezada. **Viajes Atlantida** (one block east and a half block north of Plaza España, tel. 505/266-4050 or 505/266-8720) is a renowned agency and the official representative for American Express in Nicaragua. **Turismo Joven** (8:30 A.M.–5:30 P.M. Mon.–Fri., 8:30 A.M.–12 P.M. Sat., tel. 505/222-2619) is the local representative for STA, the student travel association, and offers students discounted airfare. Close to Barrio Martha Quezada, **Viajes MTOM** (adjacent to Optica Nicaragüense, tel. 505/266-8717) is quite professional.

Classes/Studying Opportunities

You can join classes in Latin dancing any time at **La Academia Nicaragüense de la Danza** (50 meters north of the UCA gates, tel. 505/277-5557). If you think you'll be in Managua long-term, you or your children can learn horseback riding on the beautiful facilities of **Escuela de Equitación Haras de Albanta** (Km

13 Carretera Vieja a León, 500 meters north of the Entrada Chiquilistagua, tel. 505/883-8899 or 505/882-0369).

GETTING AROUND

Managua's characterless and amorphous neighborhoods, congested streets, and perplexing system of directions confound and fatigue even the most experienced travelers. You will inevitably wind up using taxis to get around for meals and entertainment, and the addresses given in this book are written with that in mind (please see the Following Directions special topic). If you plan on staying for a more extended period, learning the *ruta*, or *urbano* bus system will save you a lot of coin, as taxi fares add up quickly. Also, when walking Managua's rutted streets, be extra careful that you don't fall into one of the thousands of uncovered, anklebreaking manholes, sometimes up to three meters deep and popularly disparaged as "gringo traps." Should you fall into one, you will surely be swept into the depths of hell or into the waters of Lake Xolotlán (same thing, really). Step carefully.

Taxis

Not to fear, Managua's 14,000 taxis will find you before you find them—odds are, if you even approach the edge of the street, taxis will circle you like vultures, beeping for your attention (extra beeps if you're particularly attractive). Taxis won't take you anywhere in Managua for less than about $1, and crossing the city usually costs no more than $5, although the ride to and from the airport is becoming increasingly expensive for foreigners, costing $7–15, depending on your haggling abilities.

Managua taxis have no meters, so settle on a price before getting in the vehicle! This is a subtle art: Begin by leaning into the passenger seat window and giving your directions to the *taxista*. After he responds with an offer, the negotiations never go back and forth more than twice, and once you've accepted a price, don't gripe about it (remember as you argue over the equivalent of a couple of nickels that these guys scrape by to support their families by driving 12 hours a day, six or seven days a week). Each additional person

raises the fare, and what you pay depends ultimately on how well you bargain. Start off strong by first asking someone at your hotel, restaurant, etc. how much you should pay before you step to the curb to bargain.

GETTING THERE AND AWAY

For detailed information on traveling between Managua and other countries, see the Getting There and Away section in the Know chapter, and for travel to points around the country, please refer to the same section in each regional chapter. Four main bus terminals link Managua to the towns and cities of Nicaragua's farthest corners. In general, buses depart approximately every hour, 5 A.M.–5 P.M.

To Points North and East

Buses to Estelí, Matagalpa, Ocotal, Jinotega, Boaco, Juigalpa, El Rama, and San Carlos operate out of the **Mercado Mayoreo** bus terminal on the eastern edge of town. From the other end of Managua (i.e., Barrio Martha Quezada), you can take the 102 *ruta* bus to get there, but plan up to an additional hour's travel through Managua's heart; a taxi is much quicker and should cost no more than $3 for a solo traveler.

Expresos del Norte services the entire north of Nicaragua with express buses. Their fleet includes a few Scania luxury buses (a rare treat), and they have a posted schedule, ticket window, and office where you can call to check on times (tel. 505/233-4729).

To Points West and Northwest

Buses to León, Chinandega, and Carazo depart from the **Israel Lewites** terminal (named for a Jewish-Nicaraguan martyr of the revolution but occasionally referred to by its post-Sandinista name, El Boer). The terminal is surrounded on all sides by a chaotic fruit market by the same name; watch your belongings and expect a slightly more aggressive crowd of *buseros*.

To Points South

Buses to Carazo, Masaya, Granada, Rivas, Ometepe, the border at Peñas Blancas, and San Juan del Sur depart from **Mercado Roberto Huembes** in south-central Managua. The taxi ride from Barrio Martha Quezada should cost no more than $2 a person. Before you get to Huembes, be sure to specify *parada de los buses* (bus stop) to your driver, as opposed to *el mercado de artesanía* (crafts market), located on the opposite side of the same market. This is a very busy terminal, serving thousands of commuters from points south, and its porters and bus-assistants will swarm you as you get out of your taxi.

Also, a once-makeshift bus lot across from **La UCA** has become a permanent and very convenient resource for anyone looking for fast, express minibus service to Carazo (Jinotepe and

Diriamba), Masaya, and Granada. You'll be surprised how many passengers they can cram into these little vans. Service starts around 6 A.M. and runs as late as 9 P.M. You can also get Carazo expresses at Mercado Israel, from *el portón rojo* (the big red door).

Hitchhiking

Because many of Managua's most marginal neighborhoods are located on the city's fringes, trying to hitch your way out of the capital means putting yourself at personal risk and is thus discouraged. There are also so many buses, minivans, and taxis that no one is likely to stop for you.

Near Managua

CHOCOYERO–EL BRUJO NATURE RESERVE

Less than 28 kilometers away from downtown Managua is a little pocket of wilderness so vibrant with wildlife you'll forget the capital is literally just over the horizon. In addition to having well-kept hiking trails, Chocoyero–El Brujo (tel. 505/278-3772 or 505/279-9774, cnd@cablenet .com.ni) is also one of few places in Nicaragua that encourages tent camping, making it a great place to spend an evening in the wild.

Chocoyero is a 41-square-kilometer protected area within one of Managua's most important water supplies (which gives nearly 20 million gallons of water per day—20 percent of the city's consumption). In the midst of moist hardwood forest and pineapple farms are two 25-meter waterfalls separated by a rocky knife-edge. One of the falls dumps all of its water straight into the ground, magically disappearing into the earth instead of forming a river—or so thought the natives. For this, they assumed the waters were enchanted and named the cascade El Brujo (the warlock). The other fall, Chocoyero, was named because of the incredible number of *chocoyos* (parakeets) that inhabit the adjacent cliff walls.

Chocoyero–El Brujo is a bird-watcher's paradise, though you'll likely bump into some other

creatures as well. In addition to the five kinds of *chocoyo* that inhabit the valley, there are 113 other bird species (including several owls), 49 species of mammals, and 21 species of reptiles and amphibians. Sharp-eyed travelers may even spot small cat species, like *tigrillos* and *gatos de monte*, and you'll likely hear the monkeys in the treetops—both howlers and capuchins.

Chocoyero–El Brujo's infrastructure consists of a rustic, wooden base camp where guides will meet you and walk you the remaining way to the falls. The entrance fee for foreigners is $3.50; guides, available on weekends, charge a nominal fee ($2–5 for a group of 12, usually). The best time to see the *chocoyos* is around 4 P.M., when the flocks are returning to their cliff nests after a long day at the office. . . er, forest. They leave the nests at around 5:30 A.M., so to witness their departure, you'll need to arrive the previous day and spend the night. You can rent two-person tents on the premises for $11 each, or set up your own. This is a safe, pretty, and easily-accessible area in which to camp for a night. It will cost you $3.50 per person to do so, and you can rent one of 6 tents (2–3 persons per tent) for $4 per night. If you call ahead and make a reservation, they'll even cook simple, traditional Nica fare for you, $2.50–$3 per meal. The Reserve is actively promoting low-ropes courses, envirocamps, and more to local schools and church groups.

Getting There

Easiest is to charter a sturdy taxi from Managua with a group to take you all the way there. Otherwise, take any bus leaving Managua's Huembes terminal bound for La Concepción (called La Concha for short); buses leave Managua every 15 minutes. Get off at kilometer 21.5, where you'll see a wooden sign for the park entrance, then stretch out for a good, long walk. The dirt road that travels seven kilometers southwest to the reserve will lead you down a series of volcanic ridges and across a broad valley to the falls. It's an easy two-hour walk, passing through fields of pineapples, bananas, and coffee. Halfway down the road, you'll find a small community where you can rent bikes or horses to take you the rest of the way in (horse $1 per hour, guide $1 per hour, bicycle $.50 per hour). There also may be some buses from Ticuantepe that take you all the way in—ask around.

MONTIBELLI WILDLIFE RESERVE

A 162-hectare private reserve on the road to Chocoyero–El Brujo, Montibelli offers a campground set within the biological corridor between Chocoyero–El Brujo, Montibelli, and Volcán Masaya National Park. Montibelli has a two-hour loop trail, views of the Masaya Volcano, tent areas, a small restaurant with Sunday barbecues, guided tours, bird-watching, and recurrent butterfly festivals. It is accessed by turning off the Ticuantepe–La Concha Highway at Km 19; from there, it's a 2.5-km walk to the facilities, known locally as the Casa Blanca. Take any bus to La Concha and get off at the dirt road at Km 19 on the north side of the highway—or better yet, arrange for transport by contacting Claudia Belli in Managua (tel. 505/270-4287, info@montibelli.com, www.montibelli.com).

THE LAGUNAS OF XILOÁ AND APOYEQUE

Less than a half hour from the capital on the highway to León, the Peninsula de Chiltepe protrudes into the southwestern shore of Lake Xolotlán, cradling two ancient volcanic cones drowned in clean rainwater. Part of the Maribios chain, the twin crater lagoons of Xiloá and Apoyeque are a fun daytrip if you find yourself in Managua for more than a weekend and anxious for some greenery.

Legend says the **Xiloá** lagoon was formed when an indigenous princess of the same name, spurned by her Spanish lover, went down to the lake's edge to cry. She cried so much that the valley began to fill with tears, and the lagoon formed around her.

Broader and more easily accessed, Xiloá was a popular swimming hole for decades, but former Minister of Tourism director Herty Lewites took the initiative to develop the site more completely, with thatched-roof *ranchónes*, concrete pads, parking areas, and lunch stands. In 1998, Hurricane Mitch submerged the facilities under a meter of water. Rather forgotten, the lagoon will probably be deserted except for yourself and the occasional marine biologist, scuba diving to study the lake's endemic species.

Apoyeque still bears much of its original cone shape—the lagoon is enclosed in steep crater walls that form the highest part of the Chiltepe Peninsula. The Nicaraguan military occasionally uses it for training special forces in the art of rappelling, and a radio tower perches on the southwest lip of the crater. In 2001, Apoyeque was the epicenter of a series of seismic tremors. The rest of the peninsula and the lower slopes of the two volcanic peaks are lush cattle farms, many owned by the Seminole tribe of Florida, which has invested heavily in the area.

Buses leave Managua's Israel Lewites market infrequently and go directly to the water at Xiloá. It's easier to take any León-bound bus from the same market, get off at the top of the road to Xiloá, and walk (30 minutes). Pay $.25 per person ($1 per vehicle) to enter the park facilities at the water's edge. Getting to Apoyeque is more of an undertaking and should be treated as a challenging hike to the local swimming hole. Take the road from Mateare, which you can walk or hitch down until you reach the access road for the radio antenna. That road will lead you to the ridge, from where you'll have to painstakingly and carefully make your way into the crater.

From Xiloá, a well-marked but little-used dirt road circles the entire peninsula (28 km), coming out in Mateare. The road passes by several cattle ranches as you circumnavigate the two craters. The view from the northeastern side of the peninsula is particularly beautiful in the late afternoon when the sky fills with colors.

PACIFIC BEACHES

Roughly 65 kilometers due west of the capital are a handful of easy-to-reach beaches, with facilities ranging from low-key *hospedajes* to all-out, all-inclusive resorts.

Pochomíl

Pochomíl is one town whose name is not Nahuatl. Farmers in the early 20th century used the word *pocho* to mean money. At the time, the lands now known as Pochomíl were called *La Quijada* (the jaw). But when Felipe Gutierrez, a farmer from a few kilometers south, moved in and started an ambitious farm on which he raised ducks and goats, he named it Pocho-Mil, in reference to the thousands of *córdobas* he hoped to earn.

Wealthy Managuan politicians are quickly buying up Pochomíl's gorgeous sandy coastline and building beach homes. Competition among hotel and restaurant owners is particularly fierce—as you get off the bus expect to be assaulted by employees of a dozen restaurants all trying to drag you into their establishments to eat and drink. No one place is any better than another—you can expect palm-thatch huts built on the sand and a menu of fried fish and cold beer no matter where you go. Travelers driving their own vehicles will pay a $1 entrance fee.

Accommodations

Hotel and restaurant rates fluctuate wildly according to the calendar. Semana Santa and Christmas are the most expensive time of year to visit, followed by random peaks during the dry season. In the wet season, prices become significantly more flexible. Any month of the year, traveling with a group gives you significant leverage to bargain for a good deal. In addition to what's listed here, at press time, a new Marriott resort compound was under construction.

One of the longest-established places on the beach, **Hotel Altamar** (tel. 505/269-9204, $11 per room with private bath, $9 per room with

© RANDY WOOD

Pacific beach resort

shared bath) has 15 rooms along a long corridor that leads down to a patio restaurant and beach. Rooms generally hold three travelers. Its restaurant, situated at the top of a long stairway to the beach, is good, if a bit lethargic, and enjoys a great view of the Pacific. Rent a shady hut or a hammock for the day down on the beach for better access to the water.

All the way down the road at the north end of the beach is the luxury **Hotel Villa del Mar** (tel. 505/269-0426, $35 d with private bath and a/c). Originally one of Herty Lewites's creations, it slowly deteriorated through the 1990s until the Universidad Americana (UAM) bought and renovated it. It now serves as part of the university curriculum for students studying tourism and business administration. Besides the beautiful beach, there is a swimming pool, kiddie pool, wood-paneled conference room, palm-thatch huts set on a grassy lawn, and a fancy open-air restaurant serving three meals a day. Visit Villa del Mar for the day; the $7 entrance fee can be applied to meals and beverages served on the premises.

Next door to Villa del Mar is the more humble **Hotel Cabañas del Mar** (tel. 505/269-0433, $18 d or $25 t with private bath and a/c) trimmed in bamboo. They serve a full menu of traditional food and some vegetarian dishes.

Access **Hotel Mar Azul** (tel. 505/885-9539, $17) by going straight over the dune at the traffic circle, and then down 20 meters of dirt road. This is the establishment with which you'll most likely be able to work out a bargain, but the simple, concrete rooms are ascetic and bleak.

Getting There and Away

Buses leave Managua for Pochomíl every 30 minutes all day until about 5 P.M. The last bus from Pochomíl back to Managua departs at 5:30 P.M. from the cul-de-sac.

BEACHES NEAR POCHOMIL

Montelimar Beach

Somoza knew what he was doing when he picked this spot to build his personal beach paradise, and **Barceló Resorts** (tel. 505/269-6769 or 505/269-6752, U.S. and Canada toll-free 800 /227-2356, playamontelimar@barcelo.com, $112–144 a couple, huge discounts in the off-season) knew what they were doing when they turned it into Nicaragua's premier resort in the 1990s. In between, the Sandinistas used it as a military base. This is an all-inclusive, five-star luxury resort, and the price includes 24 hours of unlimited feasting, drinking, swimming, and playing. The Montelimar compound is enormous, with multiple beachside bars, sports, and a co-ed, spunky crew of "animators" to help you have a good time. The 290 rooms (including 56 beachside bungalows) are first rate, with private bath, a/c, TV, strongbox, and minibar. It also has facilities for groups and conventions, plus airport shuttles, shopping, on-site casino, travel agency, etc. Any bus to Pochomíl will also get you to Montelimar, and there are various tour operators that arrange for transfers from Managua airport or hotels.

Los Cardones Ecolodge

Although it shares the same Pacific shoreline as Montelimar, one of Nicaragua's fanciest resorts, **Los Cardones** (Take the Carreterra Masachapa to Km 49, then drive 15 Km on the Playa San Diego Road until you hit the beach, tel. 505/618-7314, info@loscardones.com, www.loscardones.com) offers a completely different experience. Set on five acres of organically managed land, Los Cardones rents simple but elegant bungalows with solar hot water and soft beds at water's edge, $36 s/d (discounts for advance reservation, reserve from May to November, numerous inclusive packages available). Their inspired and creative menu involves lots of fresh fish, and their commitment to both the local community and the ecosystem is admirable. Rent surf or boogie boards for the waves, collect shells on the beach, or hike out to see the pre-Columbian petroglyphs. Their yoga center will be ready soon. They'll send a car to Managua for you; or to get there by bus, take the bus to San Cayetano from Mercado Israel Lewites in Managua (leaves every 45 minutes from 4 A.M. to 9 P.M.) and get off at "California." Then walk or hitch 15 kilometers toward the ocean and follow the signs.

Masaya, Carazo, and the Pueblos Blancos

The City of Flowers, as Rubén Darío christened Masaya a century ago (he was talking about the girls, not the flora), is the epicenter of a thriving community of artisans and craftspeople who work in leather, pottery, fabric, oil paint, and much more. That's not to say you won't find inspired handicrafts elsewhere in the nation, but the intensity of the creativity and passion of Masayan artists far exceeds that of their compatriots, and the diversity and originality of their creations re-

flects that. Tourism officials have attempted to fortify this image of Masaya by refurbishing the square city block of the Old Market. A visit inside the castle-like walls of the market is a safe, colorful, pleasant experience—especially when there is folk dancing and music on one of the stages.

In the hills surrounding Masaya, dozens of small, picturesque towns perch on a cool, breezy *meseta* (elevated flatland) punctuated by enormous, azure crater lakes and the nation's most accessible active

© RANDY WOOD

Must-Sees

Look for **M** to find the sights and activities you can't miss and **M** for the best dining and lodging.

Bargain for treasure in the open air market.

© JOSHUA BERMAN

M El Malecón: Take a stroll along the crater's lip, which marks Masaya's western edge, and enjoy the view of the lagoon below (page 59).

M National Handicrafts Market: The immense variety of goods available in Masaya's market will tempt you to fill your luggage with handmade treasures (page 60).

M Coyotepe: The dungeons of this hilltop fort are just as impressive as the wide, 360-degree vista from the battlements (page 67).

M Volcán Masaya National Park: Peer into the gates of hell, wherein dwell demon parakeets—

then visit the gift shop of this popular national park (page 67).

M The Catarina Mirador: This crater's lip patio terrace, with one of the best panoramas in Nicaragua, often offers live marimba music to accompany your beverage (page 69).

M San Juan de Oriente: At this potter's paradise, you can browse through thousands of hand-crafted ceramic pieces (as well as paintings and other crafts), or talk your way into the workshop and watch how it's done (page 70).

MASAYA, CARAZO, AND THE PUEBLOS BLANCOS

volcano. Here the lifestyle is unhurried—even by Nicaraguan standards—and the curious traveler can admire not just the evocative and inspiring landscape but many beautiful handicrafts, each one the specialty of one of the Pueblos Blancos.

PLANNING YOUR TIME

While most tourists shop for an hour or two before returning to Granada or Managua, allow extra time to walk to the cliff-top lookout point near the baseball stadium, where you'll also find the hammock factories (a 15-minute level walk from the Old Market). Don't forget to save half a day for peering into the angry maw of Volcán Masaya and visiting its curious museum and hiking trails; the views and history of the Coyotepe fortress are also worth an hour of your time. Allow a full day to explore the surrounding pueblos, best done in a rented car or chartered taxi, though bus transport is frequent enough to facilitate village-hopping across the *meseta*. While the majority of visitors remain based out of nearby cities, consider spending the night in Masaya, especially during one of the city's colorful festivals.

Masaya

Masaya's Old Market, ground zero for elaborate handicrafts, is so pleasant, many visitors choose not to stray outside its limits and depart Masaya unaware of the intense and chaotic city that surrounds it. This is unfortunate, as the city of Masaya is far more than the merchandise displayed on the walls of the market. It spreads over a tropical plain only 234 meters above sea level and nestles against the slopes of a volcano; at its western edge, paths carved by the Chorotegas plummet steeply down to the Laguna de Masaya, around which 20 Chorotega villages once clustered. These people were called Darianes and first sparred with the Spanish in 1529. Masaya was officially founded as a city in 1819 and has prospered ever since.

The 85,000 souls that call Masaya their home are proud of their Chorotegan roots and bellicose history. Several centuries of rebellion and uprising—first against the Spaniards and later against William Walker's forces in 1856, the U.S. Marines in 1912, and in a number of ferocious battles against the National Guard during the revolution, earned them a reputation as fierce fighters.

Masaya is less picturesque than Granada but better steeped in culture and national pride. Masayans are a creative, festive people with many unique customs, including their solemn, mysterious funeral processions, in which crowds of mourners slowly parade the coffin (drawn by a pair of white, elegantly costumed horses) from the deceased's home to the church, and then to one of 15 cemeteries. Take a horse-drawn carriage to the breezy *malecón*, 100 meters above the crater lake; go to a baseball game with 8,000 cheering fans; tour the family-run hammock factories; sit in the shade of one of 11 parks; or stay and relax amidst the sights and smells of the market all day. You won't regret an afternoon—or more—here.

ORIENTATION AND GETTING AROUND

Masaya sits due south of the Managua–Granada Carretera along the east side of the Laguna de Masaya. The street that runs north along the plaza's east side is the Calle Central, and as you travel it toward the Carretera, it becomes increasingly commercial, essentially making up Masaya's main street. One block east of the southeast corner of the park, you'll find the stone walls of the Mercado Viejo (Old Market). Walking six blocks west of the central park will take you to the hammock factories, baseball stadium, and *malecón;* traveling due south leads you to Barrio Monimbó; going five blocks north will put you in the heart of the Barrio San Jerónimo around the church of the same name, situated at the famous *siete esquinas* (seven corners) intersection. The heart of Masaya is easily walkable, but several hundred taxis, buses, horse-drawn carriages, and more exotic forms of transport will help you get out to farther extremes like the *malecón* or the highway.

SIGHTS AND ATTRACTIONS

The central plaza is officially called **Parque 17 de Octubre,** named for a battle against the Guardia in 1977. There are plenty of bullet holes to prove it, plus two imposing command towers immediately to the west. The church in the northeast corner is La Parroquia La Asunción. The unremarkable, triangular **Plaza de Monimbó** park on the southern side of Masaya comes to life every afternoon at around 3 P.M. as the throbbing social and commercial heart of the Barrio Monimbó, a particularly indigenous-rooted, Sandinista neighborhood. It's a stirring scene, with lots of food, smiles, and bustle.

El Malecón

High above the blue waters of Laguna de Masaya, the windswept malecón is a beautiful promenade with long views to the north and west. It shares its space with the baseball stadium parking lot, making for the most scenic tailgate party you'll ever likely experience.

Museo y Galería Héroes y Mártires

A tribute to those Masayans who fought against the National Guard during the many street battles of the revolution, the collection of guns and photos of the fallen (and some of their personal effects) is eclipsed by the unexploded napalm bomb Somoza dropped on the city in '77. Located inside the Alcaldía, 1.5 blocks north of the park, open 8 A.M.–5 P.M. Mon.–Fri., donation requested.

ENTERTAINMENT AND EVENTS

Every Thursday from 5–11 P.M., **Jueves de Verbena** consists of dance, theater, art expos, music, and more, all presented in the Old Market on one of several stages. If "touristy" things aren't your cup of tea, shake it up with the locals at the most popular local bar in town, **La Rhonda,** on the south side of the park, with beer, lots of space, good appetizers—in the words of one Masayan native, "The three Bs: *bueno, bonito, y barato*" (good, nice, and cheap).

If you're here on a weekend during the season (January–May), be sure to catch the local baseball team and pride of the city, San Fernando. They play ball in the **Estadio Roberto Clemente,** named for the Puerto Rico–born Pittsburgh Pirate who died in a plane crash delivering aid to Nicaraguan earthquake victims in 1973.

Clubs and Nightlife

Although a long trek from the city center, **Cocojambo** is one of Nicaragua's—not just Masaya's—best discos. In the same area, the private **Club Social** occasionally books a big music act and opens its doors to the public. More centrally located but a big step down in atmosphere, the **Delfín Azul** gets exciting on Saturday nights. Get snooty in a "private" room at the back. Managua-based **Pharaoh Casino** has a branch in Masaya, on the main drag with a clean, cool room of slots, roulette, and cards (open 11 A.M.–3 A.M. every day, tel. 505/522-5222).

SHOPPING
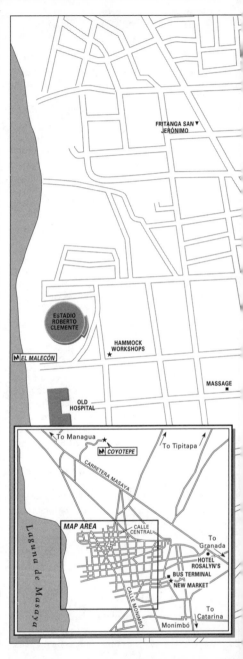 National Handicrafts Market

Shopping is, ostensibly, the reason anyone comes to Masaya. All roads lead first to the Mercado Viejo, built in 1891, destroyed by fires in 1966 and 1978, and most recently refurbished in 1997—this

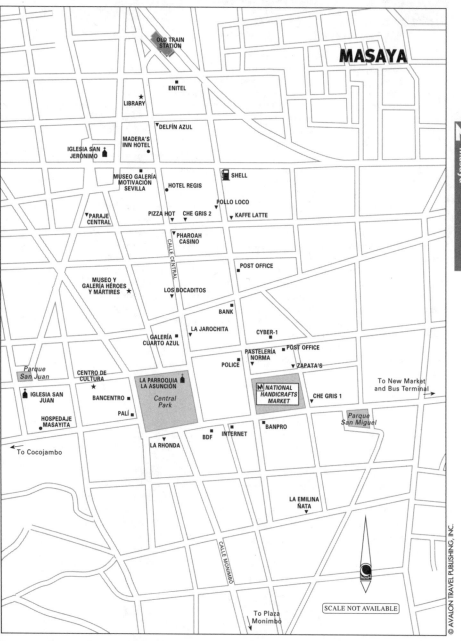

MASAYA

OLD TRAIN STATION

ENITEL

★ LIBRARY

DELFÍN AZUL

MADERA'S INN HOTEL

IGLESIA SAN JERÓNIMO

MUSEO GALERÍA MOTIVACIÓN SEVILLA

HOTEL REGIS

SHELL

POLLO LOCO

PIZZA HOT   CHE GRIS 2

KAFFE LATTE

PARAJE CENTRAL

PHAROAH CASINO

CALLE CENTRAL

POST OFFICE

MUSEO Y GALERÍA HÉROES Y MÁRTIRES ★

LOS BOCADITOS

BANK

LA JAROCHITA

CYBER-1

GALERÍA CUARTO AZUL

PASTELERÍA NORMA

POST OFFICE

POLICE

ZAPATA'S

Parque San Juan

CENTRO DE CULTURA ★

LA PARROQUIA LA ASUNCIÓN

NATIONAL HANDICRAFTS MARKET

CHE GRIS 1

To New Market and Bus Terminal

IGLESIA SAN JUAN

BANCENTRO

Central Park

Parque San Miguel

HOSPEDAJE MASAYITA

PALÍ

BANPRO

To Cocojambo

LA RHONDA

BDF   INTERNET

LA EMILINA ÑATA

CALLE MONIMBÓ

MOON

To Plaza Monimbó

SCALE NOT AVAILABLE

© AVALON TRAVEL PUBLISHING, INC.

Masaya

YEAR-ROUND FIESTA TOWN:
A GUIDE TO MASAYA'S PARTIES

Masayans celebrate all year long, observing various religious, historical, and indigenous rites with a wild collage of marimba music, traditional costume, poetry, painting, food, drink, and age-old customs. Many of the dances are family traditions, in which a certain role—and its accompanying mask and costume—is passed down from generation to generation. The costumes are a key element of the festivals and are often elaborate and gorgeous.

A few weeks before Easter, the celebration of **San Lázaro** features believers promenading with their ornately costumed pets, to thank the patron saint for keeping the household animals in good health.

The fiestas only get weirder.

In the **Festival of the Cross,** celebrated in May, people exchange thousands of palm-thatch crosses in honor of La Señora de la Asunción. The virgin icon is carried to Monimbó in remembrance of the miracle that occurred there during the last eruption of Volcán Masaya's Santiago Crater, in which the virgin saved the city from the hot ashes.

September–December are the peak fiesta months in Masaya, when nearly every weekend is colored by festivities. Things get started with the official **fiestas patronales** on September 20, in honor of the Patron Saint Jerónimo, and last essentially three months. Before the end of the celebration, however, is the extravagant and good-spirited **Fiesta del Toro Venado,** on the last Sunday of October. It's like American Halloween, but instead of ghosts and goblins Masayans don disguises that poke fun at their favorite politicians, clergy, and other public figures.

Held on the penultimate Friday of October, the **Fiesta de los Agüisotes** (Fiesta of the Bad Omens) is a nod to Nicaragua's darker side: Folks dress up as scary figures from local legends, such as the *chancha bruja,* the *mocuana,* and the *arre chavalo* (a headless priest from León).

The patron-saint celebration ends the first Sun-

day of December with the **Procesión de San Jerónimo.** This is perhaps the most stunning of Masaya's fiestas, as the statue of the city's patron saint is paraded through the streets amidst a sea of flowers. Look for the *Baile de las Inditas* (Dance of the Little Indian Girls), *Baile de Negras* (Dance of the Black Women), and the *Baile de Fantasía* (Dance of Fantasy). Every Sunday from September through December features a folk dance of some sort, a competition between rival troops, or even dancers that go from house to house performing short dances to marimba music.

In mid-January, the **Festival of San Sebastian** explodes with life and energy in the indigenous Monimbó *barrio* (neighborhood). The celebration's highlight is the *Baile de Chinegro de Mozote y Verga,* in which participants engage in a mock battle, hitting each other with big sticks and finally coming together in a peace ritual. The *tunkún* drum (a Mayan instrument) beats out the rhythm of the dance, along with a whistle called a *pífano.* At the end of the ritual, everybody screams together:

"¡*Viva San Sebastian!*" (Long live San Sabastian!)

"¡*Viva el Mayordomo!*" (Long live the Master of the Parade!)

"¡*Viva Santa Marta Vencedera!*" (Long live Saint Martha the Conqueror!)

La Novena del Niño Dios is an interesting December ritual in which small children are given pots, pans, whistles, and firecrackers and are sent into the streets at 5 A.M. to noisily call all the other children together for the 6 A.M. mass in celebration of the Christ-child's birth.

Pieces and parcels of Masaya's festivals are found in the various *fiestas patronales* of the many surrounding pueblos, each of which present their own peculiar twist to the events. In mid-June, for example, San Juan de Oriente's party involves "warriors" dancing through the streets and whipping each other with stiffened bull penises.

time in a successful attempt to convert it into a destination for foreign tourists. Also known as the Mercado Nacionál de Artesanías, the Old Market is safe, open, and comfortable—as opposed to the new market, or the Mercado Municipal, located at the main bus station about a half kilometer to the east. This is the real deal, with a low, hot, tin roof, cramped aisles, and everything from hammocks to underwear to raw beef livers for sale. The new market has an impressive artesanía section as well, but lower prices contrast with noticeably more flies and pickpockets. If your Spanish skills are up to it, you've got more bargaining power at the Old Market: Some *córdoba*-pinchers choose to browse at the new market, and then walk east to find the same item in the old one for a lower price.

Art Gallery
Esperanza Sevilla ("Hope," she explains, referring to her first name, "the last thing we lose in life") exhibits the work of a selection of Nicaraguan painters, including primitivist pieces, volcanic rocks, and a beautiful selection of greeting cards, at **Museo Galería Motivación Sevilla** (just off the main street and right behind the Iglesia San Jerónimo, tel. 505/860-4466, esp-sevilla@yahoo.com). On the main street half a block north of the Central Park, the **Galería Cuarto Azul** exhibits art and sculpture and is run by the artists themselves.

Hammock Workshops
Masaya hammocks are handmade by the thousands, for sale in local markets and for export alike. The most obvious place to purchase one is in either of the markets. However, if you'd like to get closer to the source, visit one of the many *fábricas de hamacas* in Masaya, most of which are clustered on the same block near the southwest edge of town, across from the old hospital on the road to the *malecón* and baseball stadium. There you'll find at least a half-dozen family businesses, with Mom, Dad, Grandpa, and Junior all casually weaving away on their front porches. Some of these factories have storefront shops that accept credit cards, and they will gladly show you how their wares are produced. It takes roughly two full days for three people to make a

Sergio Zepeda makes custom guitars in the same workshop that his father and grandfather used.

single hammock, which in turn, sells for around $30. Prices vary widely, according to style, size, and quality. Happy hangin'.

Handmade Guitars
Sergio Zepeda is a third-generation luthier at **Guitarras Zepeda** (200 meters west of the Unión Fenosa, tel. 505/883-0260, guitarraszepeda @yahoo.com), making quality, custom-fitted guitars in the same home and workshop as his grandfather did. His best quality guitars go for $150, with Cocobolo Rosewood back and sides and imported Red Cedar or spruce tops; cheapest are $59 all-cedar guitars, custom paint jobs, etc. Two weeks to order.

ACCOMMODATIONS
Apart from the 17(!) sex hotels along the highway outside town, Masaya's hotel options are limited but adequate for anyone curious about the nightlife here.

Masaya

HANDICRAFTS AND ARTESANÍA: WHAT TO BUY

The Nicaraguan peoples' natural creativity combined with overt necessity have bequeathed the nation a rich diversity of handicrafts as beautiful as they are practical, as rich in function as they are in form. If you're interested in shopping, the city of Masaya and surrounding pueblos present the nation's best opportunity to admire—and acquire—elaborate and gorgeous pottery, intricately woven hammocks, wood carvings, ceramic miniatures, leatherwork, and embroidered *guayaberas*. Here's a brief guide to some of what you'll find.

Start with **hammocks.** You may kick yourself later if you arrive home without one of these gorgeous pieces of art tucked under your arm. Nicaraguans are big fans of their hammocks, and with good reason. They're well made and very reasonably priced: around $30, depending on size and quantity. Hammock-weaving is a family craft passed down through generations. Each one takes 2–3 days to assemble from cotton cords, sometimes produced locally. Check the weave and the quality of the cord—stiffer cord tends to last longer and tighter weaves tend to be more comfortable. Though you can find good hammocks in the exterior of the Roberto Huembes market in Managua, Masaya is the heart of Nicaragua's home-crafted hammock industry, and visiting the many family "factories" is as easy as walking up to the porch and saying "*Buenos días.*"

The **soapstone** sculptors of San Juan de Limay, Estelí, produce intricate, delicately-polished figurines inspired by animals, Rubenesque women, and pre-Columbian designs. The smaller pieces are simple to transport home, but at Masaya, you can have larger pieces well packed and shipped home for you. You'll see iguanas, parrots, frogs, oxen, wagons, and more, plus ornately carved nativity scenes and chess sets, all carefully rendered in the salmon and ivory hues natural to the Limay soapstone.

Nicaraguan **pottery** is an art form first practiced in pre-Columbian times, with designs that have continued uninterrupted into the present. Today's potters produce all manner of vases, bowls, urns, pots, and more in rich earthy hues, some delicately etched, some left crude. You can also find fantastic mobiles and wind chimes consisting of clay birds, bells, or ornamental shapes, like stars and planets. The trick is getting them home with you after your trip.

The carpenters and craftspeople of the small towns around Masaya turn out gorgeous **wooden furniture** for themselves, not you (OK, maybe you, too). It is not uncommon to see a dirt-poor *campesino* shack graced with a set of beautifully crafted rocking chairs of stained wood

Under $10

M **Hotel Regis** (on Calle Central, 3.5 blocks north of the church on the main plaza, tel. 505/522-2300, $3.50 s) has a dozen neat, clean rooms (including some for groups and families), with shared bath and fan, and a respectable breakfast for $2. The couple that runs the place is friendly, knowledgeable about things to do in the area, and speaks some English—however, they are strict about running a clean shop, look down on partying, and close their doors at 10 P.M. Otherwise, get a barebones room at **Hospedaje Masayita** (two blocks west of the central park, tel. 505/605-1995).

$10–25

M **Madera's Inn Hotel** (2 blocks south of the fire station, tel. 505/522-5825, hmaderas@ibw.com .ni, from $10 with fan and shared bath to $25 with private bath and a/c) offers a dozen rooms on two floors set around a beautifully furnished common room, Internet, and friendly service. The rest of your options are on the highway: **Rosalyn's** (toward Granada next to the Pepsi distributor, tel. 505/522-7328, $15 and up) or **Hotel Volcán Masaya,** (toward Managua, Km 23 next to the national park entrance, tel. 505/522-5825, $10 d and up).

© JOOST GUTTINGER

and woven rattan. Rocking chairs called *abuelitas* (grandmothers) or *mecedoras* are sturdy and comfortable, and if you ask, they'll gladly disassemble them and condense them into well-wrapped airline-suitable packages.

The **basketwork** you'll find around the country is an extension of the bamboo baskets you see stacked up with produce in the countryside markets. Nueva Segovia and the northeast Miskito regions of Nicaragua, however, produce curious baskets and urns from bundles of wrapped pine needles that have been bound into long coils, then wound in concentric coils. Look for them in Ocotal and the markets in Managua.

The first **primitivist paintings** from the Solentiname archipelago came into the world spotlight in the 1960s as an offshoot of Ernesto Cardenal's Liberation Theology movement on the islands. Minimalist and vibrant, the paintings typically portray romanticized and meticulously detailed scenes of tropical Latin America: markets, oxen, proud, tall trees laden with tropical fruit, and skies full of toucans and parrots. Not only are the paintings easy to appreciate and enjoy, but they are instantly recognized the world over as an art form unique to Nicaragua.

Looking for a gift that doesn't last long? Nicaragua produces a broad, sinful selection of ephemeral pleasures, including fine **cigars,** smooth **rum,** and rich **coffee.** Nicaragua's hand-rolled cigars start with Cuban seed and the good earth around Estelí. Find them for sale in Huembes market in Managua as well as the Old Market in Masaya. Gringos: Just because you can buy Cuban Cohibas, it doesn't mean you can bring them home to the States, whether they are real or counterfeit! Do your part to comment on the U.S. embargo by lighting one up beachside in Nicaragua. And even though your liver tells you otherwise, customs will limit you to six liter-sized bottles of rum at the airport.

FOOD

If you just need some nourishment to sustain your unbridled shopping binge, close options are the **Pastelería Norma** (20 meters north of the Old Market) for baked goods, juices, and snacks; and **Che Gris** (on the east side of the Old Market) for heavy plates of Nicaraguan classics. Off the northeast corner of the Old Market, don't miss a fish taco and beer session at **Zapata's,** a low-key corner Mexican joint, incredibly cheap ($1/taco) and fun.

Otherwise, countless small eateries line both sides of the main street from the central park all the way up to the old train station, and are a great chance to find out why Masayans refer to themselves as *come-yucas* (yucca eaters). If you're spending the night in Masaya, then sink your teeth into some juicy, greasy, fried treasures at one of three lively *fritangas:* **Fritanga Alvarez** (across from the entrance to Santa Rosa), **Fritanga San Jerónimo** (a few blocks west of the church with the same name), or at *La Emilina Ñata en el Barrio Loco,* or "Flat-nose Emilina's in Neighborhood Crazy." Open every day from 5 P.M. or til its world-famous grilled beef runs out.

INFORMATION

The INTUR office is located within the Old Market, open business hours (closed for lunch, tel. 505/522-7615). They might be able to answer specific questions about the area or upcoming events.

SERVICES

Hospital Hilario Sanchez Vásquez (on the highway toward Granada, tel. 505/522-2778) is the biggest facility in town. The large, blue police station (tel. 505/522-4222 or 505/522-2521) is half a block north of the Old Market across from Norma's bakery. Besides the multiple ATMs within the Old Market, two convenient **banks** are within stone's throw of the Old Market: Bancentro on the west side of the Central Park, and a BDF one block north of the Old Market. Western Union is located by the old train station. Several cheap and crowded **Internet** places line the south side of the central park. Both Correos de Nicaragua and a DHL Worldwide Express are available inside the Old Market compound to facilitate sending gifts immediately. The ENITEL phone office is a block south of the old train station.

Massage and Natural Medicine

Overextend your credit line? Certified acupressure and reflexologist **Patricia Cuadra** (half a block west of the Iglesia San Juan, tel. 505/522-2893) will open up your body's energy paths and magically relieve muscular tension for under $10! Reiki Tibetan chakra alignment costs the same for an extra hour. **Medicina Natural** (located half a block southwest of the Plaza de Monimbó, tel. 505/522-3122) sells herbal meds and a treatment called the "Bio-energetic Method."

GETTING THERE AND AWAY

"Masaya! Masaya! Masaya!" It's almost difficult not to travel to Masaya. Nearly every southbound bus leaving Managua from Roberto Huembes passes the city, which is right on the highway, only 27 kilometers from Managua. The most efficient way to go is to take any of the Masaya- or Granada-bound *expresos* from the UCA. They leave regularly 7 A.M.–9:30 P.M., arriving in Masaya's Parque San Miguel; from there, they depart for Managua 6 A.M.–8 P.M. The ride costs under $1. There is also *expreso* service between Masaya's Plaza de Monimbó and Mercado Oriental in Managua, first leaving Masaya at 3 A.M. and running through 7 P.M. Ordinary bus service leaves and arrives at the main terminal in the parking lot of the Mercado Nuevo.

Near Masaya

 COYOTEPE

The battlements of this fort (open 8:30 A.M.–5 P.M., 365 days a year, $.75) overlook the city of Masaya from an isolated hill on the southeast side of the highway. Take a cab, or hike up the road—the view alone of Masaya, its lagoon and volcano, both great lakes, and the far-reaching surrounding countryside is worth it; that's before you even descend into the dungeons. Built at the turn of the 20th century, this site witnessed a fierce battle between national troops and U.S. Marines in 1912. Somoza rehabilitated it as a prison in which particularly cruel treatment was de rigeur, so the Sandinistas made sure not to spare it during the revolution.

Today, Coyotepe is in the hands of another group of uniformed menfolk who should not be underestimated: Nicaraguan Boy Scout troops will accompany you through the pitch-black underground prison facilities in exchange for a small fee (for special attention, or at least a smile, greet your guide with the three-finger Scout salute and their motto in Spanish: "Siempre Listo"—"Always Prepared").

VOLCÁN MASAYA NATIONAL PARK

An easy and unforgettable day trip from Managua, Masaya, or Granada, Volcán Masaya National Park (carretera Masaya, tel. 505/522-5415, open 9 A.M.–4:45 P.M. seven days a week, $4

Masaya

"Siempre listo!" Boy Scouts manage the Coyotepe fortress.

© RANDY WOOD

admission) is one of the most visibly active volcanoes in the country, featuring several naked,
gaping craters and a constant stream of sulfurous
gas, visible from as far away as the airport in
Managua. From one of its craters, you can often
glimpse incandescent rock and magma—but at
only 632 meters above sea level, Volcán Masaya
looks more like a vulgar wound in the earth's
surface than a classic volcanic cone (for that, just
glance north toward Momotombo). The crater
and its unique environs boast a visitor center,
nature museum, hiking trails, and a road all the
way to the dramatic abyss, which the Spaniards
declared to be the very gates of hell.

Volcán Masaya was called Popogatepe (mountain that burns) by the Chorotegas, who feared it
and explained eruptions as displays of anger to be
appeased with sacrifices, often human. In the
early 1500s, Father Francisco Bobadilla placed a
cross at the crater lip in order to exorcise the
devil within. Not long afterward, though, it occurred to the Spanish that the volcano might
contain gold instead of the devil, and—hell forgotten—both Friar Blas del Castillo and Gonzalo
Fernandez de Oviedo lowered themselves into
the crater on ropes with the intention of mining
the molten lava. They unearthed neither the
devil nor gold.

Several volcanoes and craters make up the
bulk of the park, including Volcán Nindirí, which
last erupted in 1670, and Volcán Masaya, which
blew its top in 1772.

The relatively new Santiago Crater was formed
between the other two in 1852. It is inhabited
by a curious species of parakeet that lives con-
tentedly in the crater walls, oblivious to the toxic
gases and in defiance of what science says should
be inhospitable conditions. You might see these
chocoyos del cráter (crater parakeets) from the
parking area along the crater's edge. In April
2000, the Santiago crater burped up a single
boulder, which crushed an Italian tourist's car
in the parking lot.

Information and Services

The exhibits at the **Visitor's Interpretation Center** and museum improve continually and include three-dimensional dioramas of Nicaragua

LA LAGUNA DE MASAYA

The still waters of the Laguna de Masaya belie
the violent origin of the lake. Long before the
first Chorotegans settled in 20 small villages
around its perimeter, the Laguna was one of Volcán Masaya's gaping throats, choked off long ago
by shifting channels of magma beneath the surface
of the earth and abandoned to slowly fill up with
rain water. These days, the most impressive views
of the Laguna are from the 100-meter-high vantage points of the malecón in the city of Masaya,
or from the restaurants that line Carretera Masaya.
It's one of Nicaragua's bigger crater lakes: 8.5
square kilometers set at the foot Volcán Masaya
and 73 meters deep in the center. While several
trails, some of which were made by the Chorotegas themselves, lead the intrepid hiker down to the
water's edge, the lake water receives some of
Masaya's municipal sewage, so it's no swimming
hole. Dip your heels in nearby Laguna de Apoyo
instead (see Granada chapter).

and Central America, models of active volcanoes, and remnants of indigenous sacrifice urns
and musical instruments found deep in the volcano's caves; there is also a display of old litho-
graphs and paintings of the volcano as the
Spaniards saw it.

There are several guided tours worth considering, none of which cost more than $2 and all of
which support the protection of the park. They
will surely open a new perspective of the volcano
for you, especially if you speak some Spanish. Of
special interest is the walk to the Tzinancanos-
toc Bat Cave, a passageway melted out of solid
rock. Make sure to buy tickets for any guided
tours you want to take while you're at the visitor
center before proceeding up to the crater's edge.
Tours leave from the lip of the Santiago crater,
not the visitor center, and you can't purchase tickets from the guides.

The park also contains several hiking trails
through a veritable moonscape of lava formations
and scrubby vegetation. Consider spending a day
here, as the hikes are well worth the time and
offer good opportunities to cross paths with some

of the park's wildlife, including coyotes, deer, iguanas, and monkeys. The Coyote Trail will lead you east to the shore of the Laguna de Masaya. If planning to hike, bring plenty of water and adequate protection from the sun, as there are no shade trees.

NINDIRÍ

Situated just north of the highway between the entrance to the national park and the city of Masaya, Nindirí was the most important and densely populated of the indigenous settlements in the area—up to 1,500 years before the arrival of the Spanish. In Chorotega, its name means Hill of the Small Pig, and its principal attraction is the 1000-artifact collection in the **Museo Tenderí,** named after a local cacique and celebrating pre-Columbian culture. Also, ask around about the Cailagua site, with petroglyphs overlooking the Laguna de Masaya. During the last week of July, the festival for patron saint Santa Ana employs many of the ancient dance, costume, and music rituals popular to the whole Masaya and Carazo region.

The Pueblos Blancos

Escaping the heat of the lakeside lowlands is as easy as a 40-minute bus ride to the Pueblos Blancos and Carazo. A dozen curious towns stand shoulder to shoulder in the breezy hillsides just south of Managua. The "White Villages" are named for the purity and color of their churches. They enjoy relative isolation 500 meters above sea level, separated to the north by the Sierras de Managua, to the east by the slopes of Volcán Masaya, to the south by the Laguna de Apoyo and Volcán Mombacho, and to the west by the dry, desolate decline toward the Pacific Ocean. These towns are picturesque and languid, easily visited in a day or weekend.

The names of the various villages sound most poetic when sung consecutively by bus *ayudantes,* hanging out the open door as they trawl the terminal at Huembes: "Masatepe!Catarina!Niquinohomo!Nandasmo!Piodoce!Masatepe!" Each town proudly claims some unique treasure to set it apart from the rest—bamboo craftwork, black magic, folk dances, Sandino's birthplace, crater lakes, wicker chairs, beaches, and renowned festivals. Visiting the pueblos makes an easy day trip, but to really take advantage, book a room in San Marcos, Catarina, or Jinotepe, and take some time. Whether you are touring furniture workshops, coffee plantations, or outdoor plant nurseries, you'll find plenty to do.

ORIENTATION AND GETTING AROUND

Renting a car is the best way to visit the Pueblos, but you can get around just as easily with the *expreso* minivan system. No more than 10 or 12 kilometers separate any two towns, all of which are easily accessed from Masaya, Granada, and Managua.

Buses to the Pueblos Blancos leave from Huembes, continue south on the Carretera Masaya, and then turn west into the hills at various points, depending on the route. Be sure to tell your *ayudante* the town where you'd like to get off and have him tell you when you are there. The Carazo buses—to Jinotepe and Diriamba—travel via Carretera Sur and leave from the Mercado Israel Lewites and from a lot across from the UCA.

◪ THE CATARINA MIRADOR

This hillside pueblo clings to the verdant lip of the spectacular Laguna de Apoyo crater lake. The Mirador is a blustery cliff-side walkway and restaurant complex at the edge of the crater with one of the best panoramas in Nicaragua. Look for the red tiled roofs of Granada, broad Lake Cocibolca behind, and on a clear day, the twin volcanic peaks of Ometepe. The view at the Mirador is only one reason people visit Catarina;

Masaya

© RANDY WOOD

The art of bamboo basket weaving is passed from parent to child.

lush, ornamental plant nurseries and the shops of local artisans and basket makers lining Catarina's streets are the others. The Catarina shopping spree begins before you even turn into the entrance to the town, and continues up past the church and along the final hill to the entrance of the Mirador. There you'll only be asked to pay an *entrada* if you have a vehicle ($.75).

The *laguna* is a first-class swimming hole (despite the requisite monster legends), and a network of tough foot paths link the Mirador to the waterside. But a better access route is via direct bus service between the *laguna* itself and Masaya or Managua (see the section on Laguna de Apoyo in the Granada chapter).

Hotel Jaaris (tel. 505/558-0020, $8 s) and **Hospedaje Euro,** both one block west (i.e. downhill) from the Catarina church, offer simple but clean accommodations.

SAN JUAN DE ORIENTE

San Juan potters turn out splendid and attractive ceramic vases, pots, plates, and more, in both a proud celebration of pre-Columbian

styles and more modern inspirations. Shop at one of the small cooperatives along the entrance to town, or in the many tiny displays in people's homes as you walk through the narrow streets.

DIRIÁ AND DIRIOMO

Named for the indigenous Dirian people and their leader, Diriangén (the famed rebel cacique and martyr whose spilled blood at the hands of the conquistadores is immortalized in Carlos Mejía Godoy's anthem, "Nicaragua Nicaragüita"), Diriá and Diriomo face each other on both sides of the highway. Both towns are known for their unique celebrations throughout the year, mixing elements of pre-Columbian, Catholic, and bizarre regional customs (like the "dicking" festival in which participants smack each other with dried-out bull penises, sometimes practiced in San Juan de Oriente as well). Diriá, on the east, boasts a *mirador* smaller and less-frequented than the more famous one at Catarina, as well as additional trails down to the Laguna de Apoyo. Across the highway,

Diriomo is renowned for its sorcery: The intrepid traveler looking for a love potion or revenge should seek out one of the pueblo's *brujos* (or at least read the book *Sofía de los Presagios;* see the Further Study section).

NIQUINOHOMO

The Valley of the Warriors to the Nahuatl people lived up to its name when Augusto César Sandino was born there at the turn of the 20th century. Sandino's childhood home off the northwest corner of the park has been restored as a library and museum. A 4,000-pound, solid bronze statue of the man, with the famous hat and bandolier of bullets around his waist, stands at attention at the east side of town. Niquinohomo also boasts a 320-year-old church with an impressive red tile roof. The cemetery on the opposite end of town is worth a look, with many brightly painted tombs and ornaments. Although the town is also famous for its *brujas* and *brujos* (witches), the mayor's office deny that such creatures are found here. "Go to Diriomo," they say.

MASATEPE

Masatepe (Nahuatl for place of the deer) is a quiet pueblo of about 12,000 that explodes in revelry the first Sunday of every June for its famous Hípica (horse parade). Stick around after the festivities for a steaming bowl of Masatepe's culinary claim to fame—*sopa de mondongo* (cow tripe soup), served hot in front of the town's gorgeous, architecturally unique church. The *hípica* is just one part of the *fiestas patronales* in honor of la Santísima Trinidad, the black Christ icon a Chorotegan found in the trunk of a tree during the years of the Spanish colony. Find other meals in the Bar Sarapao or Eskimo shop on the north side of the park.

Outside of the city, both sides of the highway are lined with the workshops of the extraordinarily talented Masatepe carpenters, whose gorgeous, handcrafted hardwood and rattan furniture is prized throughout the country. You'll wish you could fit more of it in your luggage (a set of chairs and a coffee table go for about $100), but console yourself with a gorgeous hardwood rocking chair, which they'll disassemble and pack down to airline-acceptable size for you for a small fee.

If driving to Masatepe from the south, save time for a meal at  **Mi Teruño Masatepino** (on the east side of the road, just north of the turnoff for Pio XII and Nandasmo), a delicious open-air restaurant featuring Nicaragua's traditional country cuisine.

SAN MARCOS

San Marcos is sort of the hub of the Pueblos Blancos and hosts Nicaragua's best (and most expensive) university, the **Ave Maria College of the Americas** (three blocks south of the park, www.avemaria.edu.ni), a Catholic, bilingual, four-year liberal arts university with about 400 students and a sister campus in Ann Arbor, Michigan. Its modern facilities belonged to the

Salesmen go door to door in the pueblos.

University of Mobile (Alabama) before 1998. Ave Maria is one of the beneficiaries of Catholic conservative and Domino Pizza founder, Thomas Monaghan. San Marcos has experienced a boom in development since the establishment of a new *zona franca* (free trade zone) on the outskirts of town. While visiting, don't miss the town's photogenic church and town square.

Food and Services

The **Chat House** Internet café and restaurant is one block north and half a block east of the park; and **King Pizza** is three blocks east of the park on the road east to Masatepe. **La Casona** (near the park) is new, clean, and pleasantly-appointed: Stop in for tacos, burgers, and sand-wiches. The owner, Frank, speaks English, Spanish, and Italian, and serves breakfast, lunch, and dinner, and accepts credit cards. The **Kablenet Café,** offering Internet service and simple snacks, is 1.5 blocks south of the park's southeast corner.

Bancentro is across the street from the park's northwest corner.

Accomodations

The Casa Blanca (two blocks east of the church's southeast corner, tel. 505/535-2727 or 505/432-2720, $35 s/d) has 16 spiffy, simple rooms with private bath and is the nicest hotel in town. Ask about the Spanish intensive courses they offer.

Carazo and the Pacific Beaches

The Pan-American Highway runs along the western edge of the Pueblos plateau, through the towns of Diriamba, Dolores, Jinotepe, and Nandaime before continuing south through Rivas to the border. Called collectively Carazo, they are commercial centers more prominent than the rest of the Pueblos Blancos. From Diriamba, a road snakes downhill through tropical dry forest (more "dry" than "tropical," really) to a handful of beach towns. The area is notable for the costumes, dancing, and music of its festivals, unique in Nicaragua for their preservation of pre-colonial Nicaraguan culture. Carazo is also considered the soccer capital in a country where baseball is normally king. Diriamba houses Nicaragua's national soccer team, and its weekend games are a lot of fun.

DIRIAMBA

While the map suggests that this pueblo is no more than a small suburb of Jinotepe, Diriamba is most definitely a town with its own flavor. Its **Fiesta of San Sebastian** in the third week of January is an annual religious, theatrical, folklore celebration uninterrupted since colonial days. Featuring both pagan and Catholic elements, it is without rival in Nicaragua. Diriamba's prominent **clock tower** is unique but is more useful for giving directions than telling the time. If you're in Diriamba any time other than the festival, enjoy the **Museo Ecológico de Tropico Seco** (tel. 505/422-2129, open Mon.–Fri.), which displays much of the region's natural history. The MARENA office here ministers some of the local turtle-nesting refuges.

Accommodations and Food

Things get tight around the fiestas in January so plan ahead. **Hospedaje Diriangén** (one block east, .5 block south of the Shell, tel. 505/422-2428, $7 s with private bath and fan), is clean enough and safe. The **Casa Hotel Diriamba** (one block east of the clock tower, 505/523-2523, $7 s, $11 d) is more central. Out on the boulevard heading out of town, **Jardín and Vivero Tortuga Verde** (tel. 505/422-2948, rodalsa@ibw.com.ni, $40 s) has reinvented itself as a bed-and-breakfast. There are very few rooms, but they're clean and set amidst a beautiful garden filled with statues. The main road on either side of the clock tower offers several cheap options for meals.

Getting There and Away

Right next to the clock tower, a fleet of *interlocales* run to and from Jinotepe for about $.25,

THE FESTIVAL OF SAINT SEBASTIÁN

Every pueblo's *fiestas patronales* have something that make them unique, but Diriamba's celebration of the Holy Martyr San Sebastian stands above the rest as Nicaragua's most authentic connection to its indigenous roots. Many of the dances, songs, and costumes are true to traditions that predate the arrival of the Spanish by hundreds of years. But this is no nostalgia act—indeed, the integration of pre-Columbian ritual with Catholicism and the telling of modern history is as fascinating as the colors, costumes, and music.

This celebration is actually three fiestas for the price of one, since icons of San Santiago of Jinotepe, San Marcos (of San Marcos), and San Sebastian of Diriamba have been observed together since the three of them first traveled from Spain, landing at nearby Casares beach. The icons are still believed to have the special bond they formed during their journey, and they get together to celebrate this three times a year during the fiesta of each of their towns. Santiago and Marcos meet up at the *tope* (end of the road) in Dolores on (or around) January 19, where they are danced around the village to a bombardment of cheers and homemade fireworks. The next day, they reunite with their pal, Sebastian, in Diriamba, where the town has been partying for four days in preparation.

The following day is the peak of activities, the actual *Día de Santo*, marked by special masses and (increasingly) groups of tourists that come to view the long, raucous procession, famous for its theatrical dances and costumes. The following are the most important acts: **The Dance of Toro Huaco** is entirely of indigenous ancestry and features peacock-feather hats and a multi-generation snake dance, with the youngest children bringing up the rear and an old man with a special tambourine and whistle up front. **El Gùegùense,** also called the **Macho Ratón,** is recognizable for its masks and costumes depicting burdened-down donkeys and the faces of Spanish conquistadores. The Gùegùense (from the old word *gùegùe*, which means something like grumpy old man) is a hardhanded social satire with cleverly vulgar undertones that depicts the indigenous peoples' first impression of the Spanish—it has been called the oldest comedy act on the continent. The

© JOSHUA BERMAN

Masaya

El Gigante dance depicts the biblical story of David and Goliath, and **La Danza de las Inditas** is a group act, recognizable by the white cotton costumes and the sound of the marimba. Most of the dancers are carrying out a family tradition that has been kept for dozens of generations, and each usually has a grandma-led support team on the sidelines to make sure their costumes and performances are kept in order.

A true believer will tell you that Diriamba's fiesta begins not on January 19, but on February 2 of the previous year, when the official *fiesteros* apply for roles in the upcoming celebration; they then begin more than 11 months of preparation, all of which is seen as a display of faith and thanks to their beloved San Sebastian. Those that don't show their devotion by dancing or playing music do so by carrying the icons or fulfilling promises to walk a certain number of blocks on their knees, sometimes until bloody.

Bring plenty of film, and be sure to try the official beverage of the festival: *chicha con genibre,* a ginger-tinted, slightly fermented cornmeal drink. Most of the masks and costumes in the productions are also for sale, as are action figures depicting the various dance characters.

6 A.M.–9 P.M. daily. Walk east and take your first left to find *microbus expresos* to Managua's Israel Market and the UCA for $1, 5 A.M.–7 P.M. A little farther east at the first *caseta* (booth) on the left, you can ask about all the buses that pass from Jinotepe (Managua: 4:30 A.M.–6 P.M.; Masaya: 5 A.M.–6 P.M.).

JINOTEPE

Jinotepe ("Xilotepetl" or "Field of Baby Corn") is a sometimes-sleepy, sometimes-bustling villa of 27,000 set around **La Iglesia Parroquial de Santiago** (built in 1860) and a lively park shaded by the canopy of several immense hardwood trees. It's a peaceful little place, considering its geology: Jinotepe's feet nestle into a deep bed of ash from Volcán Masaya and it's surrounded on three sides by tectonic faults. Jinotepe's student population, thanks to a branch of UNAN, helps to keep things youthful and lively, and its outdoor market is fun. Jinotepe is accessible and full of surprises: Walk around and enjoy the small-town ambience without hurry. Don't miss the beautiful two-block-long **mural** on the nursing school (three blocks west of the park's northwest corner) and the towering **statue of Pope John Paul II** in front of the church (his back is turned to the marketplace).

Accommodations

Hospedaje Masaya (.5 block north of the park's northwest corner, $4 s) offers simple accommodations. Otherwise, head to the **Hotel Casa Grande** (from the park one block north and two west, tel. 505/532-2741 or 505/412-3284, casagrande@nicarao.org.ni, $35 s/d, $55 suite) for fancy digs with in-room telephone, TV, private bath, hot water, and fan; laundry and ironing service, guard for your car, restaurant and bar, and Internet are available as well. They can also organize a trip to their facilities at Huehuete Beach and are experienced at dealing with large groups and conferences.

Food

The park is a pleasant, shady place to relax: Try a *cacao con leche* (chocolate milk-ish) in the kiosk under the shade trees. For more substantial fare, try **Buen Provecho** (1.5 blocks north of the cathedral) or **Buffet Santa Ana** (two blocks north, .5 block west of the cathedral), two good lunch buffets. But the best meal in town is certainly **M Pizzería Coliseo** (open 12:30–9 P.M. Tues.–Sun., $5 and up), a legitimate Italian restaurant. Fausto has been preparing delicious Italian pizzas and pasta for more than 20 years. In the three blocks north of the church, you'll find several other eateries, and of course, the Hotel Casa Grande has an upscale dining room of its own.

Services

Enitel, Correos, and the Alcaldía (mayor's office; note Sandino paintings inside and out) are all on the north side of the main plaza. Find both the BDF and Bancentro banks a block north of the cathedral, as well as the Western Union (tel. 505/532-0301). Two supermarkets, Super Santiago and Palí (open 8 A.M.–8 P.M.) are in the market area. Film is widely available—check the Kodak Express across from the Palí. Loads of dinky bookstores line this university town. Start with Librería Santiago (two blocks north of the church, 8 A.M.–6 P.M.).

Getting There and Away

Sleek, comfortable minibuses leave from across from the UCA in Managua until 10 P.M. From Jinotepe, buses leave from the COOTRAUS terminal—a dirt lot along the Pan-American Highway directly north of the park. Ordinary buses leave there regularly: for Managua (4:30 A.M.–6 P.M.), Masaya (5 A.M.–6 P.M.), Nandaime (6 A.M.–6 P.M.), and Rivas (5:40 A.M.–3 P.M.). Microbuses to Managua leave from the unofficial Sapasmapa terminal on the south side of the Instituto Alejandro, 4:45 A.M.–7:30 P.M., ($.75). If you're heading to Managua, this is your best bet. Otherwise, hang around the park and wait for the minibuses that head to the UCA (hint: Listen for "Managuamanaguamanagua!"). *Interlocales* to Diriamba and San Marcos queue up on the street in front of the Super Santiago—only the front one will load passengers, departing when the van is full. If you are traveling to Costa

Rica, TicaBus coaches pass by the local office bound for San José every morning at 8 A.M.; purchase tickets in advance.

NEAR JINOTEPE
Hertylandia
Six kilometers outside Jinotepe on the road to San Marcos, **Hertylandia** (tel. 505/532-308-183 or 505/412-2156, open 9 A.M.–5 P.M. Wed.–Sun., $12) is Nicaragua's only amusement park. Built in the 1990s by Sandinista venture capitalist Herty Lewites (who later went on to become Managua's mayor from 2000–2004), the place is a bit wimpy and run-down but still good for cooling off in water rides, bumper boats, video arcades, and a motocross track.

CARAZO BEACHES
La Boquita and Casares aren't the most glorious beaches in the country, but there is no denying the grandeur of the Pacific Ocean. This stretch of coastline is home to several small fishing communities, ready to serve you fresh seafood and a bottle of cold Victoria, which turns golden in the setting sun (or the rising sun, depending on what kind of night you have in mind). On a big swell, the surf is up at both places. Located within a few kilometers of each other, La Boquita and Casares also boast interesting rock formations and beachcombing. Note that this area is very popular during Semana Santa, New Year's Day, and several other national holidays. Make reservations at the hotels, or at the very least, expect a drunken mob scene during the aforementioned busy times, especially at La Boquita, where thieves and gang-bangers looking for trouble are not unheard of.

La Boquita
Easily accessed by public transport all day long, La Boquita is a beach complex primarily for Nicaraguans on family outings. There is a $1 entrance fee to enter with your own vehicle, and you can expect representatives of the dozen or so rancho restaurants to try to corner your business in the parking lot. Take a gander before

making a commitment; you may very well wish to rent some shade under one of the rancho roofs, where you can also order drinks and food.

To make a night of it (highly recommended if you're into drawn-out, beautiful sunsets), the **Hotel Palmas del Mar** (tel. 505/552-8715 or 505/887-1336, pglo@tmx.com.ni, $40 for a/c, cable TV, and private bath,) is the mainstay of the town. The creation of a Frenchman, Palmas del Mar is a fancy place with swimming pools, good restaurant service, and 22 rooms. Special package deal: $40 per person includes three meals and room—a good deal, given that most dishes on the menu run about $12 each.

Immediately adjacent to Palmas del Mar is Hospedaje El Pelícano, a dilapidated dive of bare, wooden rooms for $11 each. If you continue walking down to the estuary past a row of several restaurants, you'll find **Hospedaje Suleyka** (tel. 505/552-8717, $14), with six small, bare rooms at the side of a restaurant. Better than the *hospedaje* is the restaurant and store, where you can buy bathing suits, suntan lotion, sandals, and more.

Casares
More oriented toward catching and selling fish than hosting beachgoers, Casares is uncomfortably short on shade. However, it's also short on crowds, and its long, wide beach is great for watching the boats coming in and out. On the drive between La Boquita and Casares, seek out El Pozo del Padre, a self-contained rocky bathtub that's loads of fun at high tide. The only place to stay in Casares is **Hotel Lupita,** offering 16 rooms with private baths, a/c, and a small pool for $40.

La Maquina
This is one of the "private wild reserves" protected by MARENA and managed by the landowners—it is located on the north side of the road between Diriamba and the coast, identifiable by a rather inconspicuous sign. The main attraction is a popular waterfall and shallow bathing area on the river when you first enter, but there is much more to the park than that, including forested areas, short hiking trails, and picnic facilities.

Río Escalante-Chacocente

One of two Pacific-shore beaches where the paslama turtle lays its eggs (La Flor is the other, please see that section in San Juan del Sur chapter for important information on viewing the turtles), this is a protected wildlife area. The beach provides habitat for numerous other species as well, including white-tailed deer, reptiles, and several types of flora. Getting to Chacocente isn't easy, which, for the sake of the turtles, is just as well. There's one bus a day from Diriamba, and one bus back. There's no way to make a day trip out of it, as both buses leave at the crack of dawn, and Chacocente has no facilities for travelers. The ecological management of the beach prohibits camping during the nesting season.

Getting There and Away

La Boquita and Casares are about 35 kilometers due west of Diriamba. Public transportation leaves from the main market, on the highway east of the clock tower. Express microbuses leave every 20 minutes for the 40-minute, $.75 ride to La Boquita 6:20 A.M.–6 P.M. Regular buses take 1.5 hours and leave between 6:40 A.M. and 6:30 P.M.—they like to turn off their engines and coast the last part. From La Boquita the first bus leaves at 5 A.M., the last one back from the beach at 6 P.M.

Masaya

Granada

Granada is at once both the oldest city on the continent and the most developed tourist destination in Nicaragua. Some consider this "colonial jewel" to be the future of Nicaraguan tourism, the vanguard of what could be. True, if one is holding up Antigua, Guatemala as the archetype—i.e., the backpacker mecca model, where there are more foreign-run Internet cafés and hostels than actual native residents. But Granada's charm won't be taken over any time soon—too many of the distinctive buildings are the private homes of well-off, proud Nicaraguans who wouldn't think of giving up their family's place in the city (even if a few of their neighbors have done so). And there is good reason for Granada's recent tourism boom. It is a fascinating city—full of bright colors, violent history, lake breezes, and the sounds (and smells) of horse-drawn carriages.

Granada is the place to meet other vagabonds with whom you can swap stories over a few liters of Victoria in the tropical shadow of Volcán Mombacho. This is also your base camp for boat trips through the Isletas and canopy tours in the Mombacho cloud forest. There's even a ship to Ometepe and the Río San Juan—but hold your horses, bucko, and check into one of the funky *hospedajes* for a couple of nights. Take in some Granada before going back to the wilds of Nicaragua. Nowhere else in the country will you find such an array of excellent restaurants set against a rainbow of architecture. This is less a city

Must-Sees

Look for **M** to find the sights and activities you can't miss and **M** for the best dining and lodging.

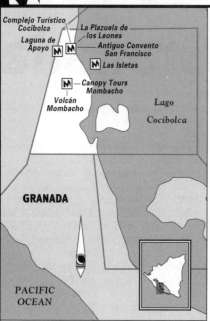

Complejo Turístico Cocibolca
Laguna de Apoyo **M** **M** La Plazuela de los Leones
Antiguo Convento San Francisco
M Las Isletas
M — Canopy Tours Mombacho
Volcán Mombacho
Lago Cocibolca

GRANADA

PACIFIC OCEAN

Even cloudy days can seem tranquil and picturesque in the Laguna de Apoyo, seen here from the restaurant Norome.

M Antiguo Convento San Francisco: The towering stone statues displayed in one of the Convento's many courtyards are a stunning glimpse into the nation's pre-Colombian past (page 83).

M La Plazuela de los Leones: Witness to centuries of Granada's most exciting events, the Plazeula is Granada's cultural epicenter, bursting with art, music, historical works, and, of course, Internet access (page 84).

M Complejo Turístico Cocibolca: Less a tourist center than a broad shoulder of a park, its leafy canopy and fresh lake breeze set the tone for languid, breathless tropical afternoons. The panoramic backdrop—broad, magnificent Lake Cocibolca—is unmatched in Nicaragua (page 86).

M Las Isletas: Spend a lazy day swimming, picnicking, and relaxing among the hundreds of gorgeous islands that comprise Las Isletas (page 94).

M Laguna de Apoyo: This volcanic crater lake just might be Nicaragua's prettiest swimming hole, but you can just as easily enjoy lunch alongside this "bottomless" beauty (page 95).

M Volcán Mombacho: More than a gorgeous background for your Granada photographs, this is a first-class set of hiking trails, an eco-lodge, a canopy tour, and a lot more (page 98).

M Canopy Tours Mombacho: Fifteen platforms, a hanging bridge, and lots of excitement await you from the treetops on the slopes of Mombacho. Plus, you'll enjoy one of the best views in town—if you can keep your eyes open, that is (page 99).

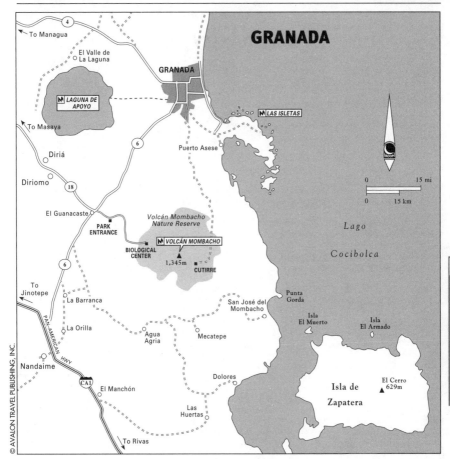

GRANADA

To Managua
To Masaya
To Jinotepe
To Rivas

El Valle de La Laguna
GRANADA
LAGUNA DE APOYO
Diriá
Diriomo
El Guanacaste
PARK ENTRANCE
Volcán Mombacho Nature Reserve
BIOLOGICAL CENTER
VOLCÁN MOMBACHO
1,345m
CUTIRRE
La Barranca
La Orilla
Agua Agria
Mecatepe
Nandaime
El Manchón
Las Huertas
Dolores
San José del Mombacho
Puerto Asese
LAS ISLETAS
Punta Gorda
Isla El Muerto
Isla El Armado
Isla de Zapatera
El Cerro 629m

Lago Cocibolca

0   15 mi
0   15 km

PAN-AMERICAN HWY

© AVALON TRAVEL PUBLISHING, INC.

Granada

than a large, relaxed colonial town, where most evenings find the people out on the sidewalks, talking and laughing. Walk the streets, tour the churches, then enjoy a free concert in the park; there is much to love about Granada.

PLANNING YOUR TIME

Granada is the city about which travelers most like to write home, so take the time to explore its bright streets as well as the destinations that surround the city—much of what Nicaragua has to offer is an easy day trip from here. At the very least, plan on a day and a night in Granada to

enjoy the lakeshore, the cafés, and the club scene at night. Add an additional day for a hike in the cloud forest of Mombacho and/or some canopy tours, another day for a hike down into the crater lake of Laguna de Apoyo, and maybe some time to visit Volcán Masaya and the artisan markets of Masaya and Catarina.

HISTORY

Granada's history is as long as the history of colonial Nicaragua itself. Granada was founded by Francisco Hernández de Córdoba on the edge of the warm waters of Lake Cocibolca,

Granada

GRANADA CITY

BASEBALL STADIUM

RAILROAD MUSEUM

Parque Sandino

ESSO TIGER MARKET

LA INMACULADA

CALLE

BODAN

← To Managua

BUDGET

AVENIDA

AVENIDA

GUZMAN

CALLE

NICABUS

CALLE

CERVANTES

ATRAVESADA

PHARMACY ROW

AV

POST OFFICE

HOTEL CASA SAN FRANCISCO

To Charly's Bar

CASA DE LOS ALEMANES

CALLE

MISTER PIZZA

TELE PIZZA

CALLE DR. SILVIO CUADRA SAENZ

INTERNET

KODAK

ELENA ARELLANO

THE BEARDED MONKEY

CALLE

OLD HOSPITAL

BANCENTRO

LA PLAZUELA DE LOS LEONES

CASA DE LOS LEONES

EL TERCER OJO

LA FÁBRICA

CINEMA

HOTEL COLONIAL

CAFÉ DEC'ARTE

EL CLUB

ENITEL

CAFÉ NUIT

HOTEL ALHAMBRA

TACOS LORY

TU BODEGUITA

TICABUS

Aduana

POSADA DON ALFREDO

MANSIÓN MUSEO DE GRANADA

BANPRO

Parque Colón

HOSPEDAJE CENTRAL

Arroyo

CALLE

CONSULADO

CATHEDRAL

EL ZAQUAN

MOMBOTOUR

IGLESIA LA MERCED

DRAGON DORADO

AL PICCOLO MONDO

INTUR

XALTEVA

ALCALDÍA

LA GRAN FRANCIA

DOÑA ELBA CIGAR FACTORY

IGLESIA XALTEVA

Parque Xalteva

CALLE

REAL

SUPER LACAYO

NICA BUFFET

MANAGUA BUSES

HOSTAL SAN ANGEL

CALLE EL TAMARINDO

AVENIDA

CALLE

MORAZAN

RESTAURANTE EL MEDITERRANEO

LA HOYADA

HOSTEL OASIS

TAZA BLANCA

QUERUBE'S

CALLE

LA CONCEPCIÓN

CALLE

14 DE SEPTIEMBRE

BARRICADA

MARKET

CALLE VEGA

LA CEIBA

PALÍ

SHELL PALMIRA

BUSES SOUTH

To Nandaime

CALLE

Arroyo Zacateligüe

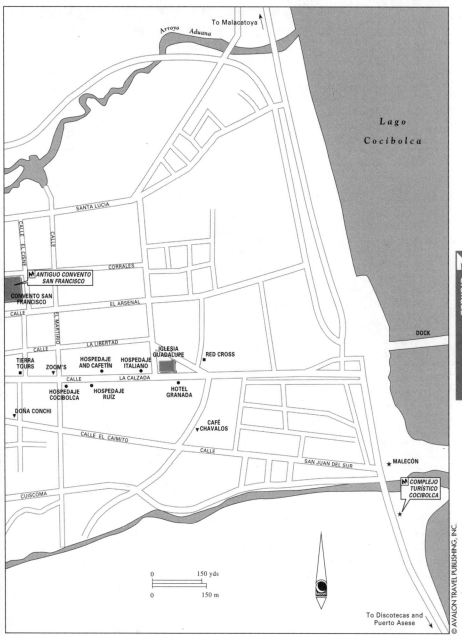

M
Granada

GREY-EYED MAN OF DESTINY

In the 21st century, responsible travelers take great pains to integrate into the culture of the foreign land they are visiting, learn the language, and be sensitive to the customs of their host country. One hundred and fifty years ago, none of that was necessary. That meant a self-styled adventurer like William Walker could assemble a mercenary band, fight on behalf of a Nicaraguan political faction, then declare himself president and burn, loot, and pillage at whim.

The year was 1853, and Nicaragua's Liberals and Conservatives were once again at each other's throats in a fierce competition for political power. The Liberals saw a chance to beat the Conservatives once and for all with some hired foreign guns and invited American adventurer, white supremacist, and filibuster William Walker to join them in the battle in Nicaragua. He accepted, and within the year, they realized they'd created a monster.

Walker, the self-proclaimed "Grey-eyed Man of Destiny" from Nashville, Tennessee arrived with a band of 300 thug mercenaries he'd rounded up in the tough neighborhoods of San Francisco and promptly led the Liberals to a rousing victory over the Conservatives. But he had no intentions of going home. Two years later, he usurped power, arranged for elections that he rigged to his advantage, and declared himself the president of Nicaragua. His goal was to make Nicaragua a slave state loyal to the American South's nascent confederacy.

The United States, at the brink of civil war, officially recognized Walker as president of Nicaragua. Walker reinstituted slavery and declared English the official language of the country. But Walker did what no Nicaraguan leader has been able to accomplish since: He united the people. In a rare moment of fear-inspired solidarity, the Nicaraguans temporarily forgot their differences, banded together, and with the help of the other Central American nations and some financing from Cornelius Vanderbilt (who had lost his steamship company to Walker), defeated Walker at the Battle of San Jacinto on September 14, 1856, now a national holiday. Not long afterward, he was captured and executed by a rifle squad in Honduras. The Liberals fell into disgrace, and the Conservatives effectively ruled the nation for the next 30 years.

The scars Walker wrought on the nation run deep. As he and his men fled Granada, they paused long enough to burn the city to the ground and plant a sign that proclaimed "Here was Granada." You can still see scorch marks on some buildings in the city. On the highway leading north from Managua to Estelí, you'll find a statue commemorating the victory over Walker's troops by a mobilized populace at San Jacinto. And deep inside every Nicaraguan is a secret distaste for loud, bold Americans with ambitious plans and a confident gait. William Walker's own account, *La Guerra de Nicaragua*, tells his fascinating story in no uncertain terms. Just be careful who sees you reading it.

nestled against the indigenous community of Xalteva, and despite its tradition of being repeatedly destroyed and rebuilt, if Córdoba were to rise from the grave today and walk the streets of his city, he would find it relatively familiar. A trade city, Granada soon became the home of an affluent Spanish merchant class, largely of Veracruz, Cartagena, and La Habana origin. From its beginnings, Granada was a symbol of Spanish opulence, an unsubtle show of mercantile success in the New World. Combined with its vulnerability as a port town, this made Granada a popular target for other powers. The English especially enjoyed sending their fiercest buccaneers up the Río San Juan to sack and burn the city, humiliating the Spaniards before returning to their homeland with gold and treasures.

Because of its population of old-money, landowning families, Granada has always been the seat of the Conservative party (and still is, even though they only won 3 percent of the vote in the last presidential election). As such, Granada was the capital of Nicaragua several times, always vying with the Liberals of León for control of the country.

It was the Liberals who first called upon United States filibuster William Walker to launch what was perhaps the worst attack against Granada, even by pirate standards. Walker was eventually driven from the area, but not before burning it to the ground and burying a symbolic coffin in the central plaza under a wooden sign that read, "*Aquí fue Granada*" ("Here was Granada").

Since then (in true Nicaraguan form), Granada has risen from its own ashes, existing today as both a "living museum" and a modern, industry- and tourism-based city.

ORIENTATION AND GETTING AROUND

Granada has several easy landmarks, starting with the central, tree-lined plaza (known alternately as the Parque Central and Parque Colón) and the cathedral on its east side. Calle Calzada extends east along the north side of the cathedral and runs straight to the municipal dock. A number of *hospedajes* and hotels are clustered along this street. You can also orient yourself to the ever-present peak of Volcán Mombacho, rising to the south of the city. Walking west from the main plaza, you'll come to the Xalteva neighborhood and eventually the cemetery and road to Nandaime. There are many services and a number of attractions along the Calle Atravesada, which runs north-south, one block west of the plaza. Taxis are numerous and cheap, and of course, there are the horse-drawn carriages, which you can always find on the western side of the plaza (prices vary). Where horse-drawn carriages are concerned, do your part for animal rights by patronizing those drivers who seem to be treating their horse well— you can go one step further by admonishing the owners of sick, skeletal horses with a simple, "muy flaco" ("too skinny"), accompanied by a disgusted shake of the head.

© JOSHUA BERMAN

Enjoy the sights—and smells—of Granada from one of many horse-drawn carriages.

SIGHTS

Lace up your comfy shoes, fill up a water bottle, and slip on your shades—this town was made for walkin'. There's really no other way to get a feel for Granada than to strut its varied streets, ideally early or late in the day with a camera in hand. You'll want to use color film, as there are more shades of yellow and orange paint here than Vincent van Gogh ever dreamed of. Be sure to break away from the main plaza and its environs, as the twisting, narrow streets to the north and west are chock full of Granada.

Antiguo Convento San Francisco

A dozen airy galleries set around landscaped courtyards exhibit dioramas of the Chorotega and Nahautl peoples, interpreting how they lived, fought, celebrated, and more. But the **Convento San Francisco** (two blocks north and one east of the main cathedral, tel. 505/552-5535, 8:30 A.M.– 5:30 P.M. Mon.–Fri., 8 A.M.—5 P.M. weekends, $2) is most remarkable for its open-air collection of 30 towering alter-ego statues, collected a century

© JOSHUA BERMAN

in Granada's central park, a statue honoring all mothers

ago from nearby Zapatera Island. The carved basalt shows human forms with the heads of jaguars, birds, and other animals whose spirits were thought to flow through the soul of humans—a rare look into the cosmology of Nicaragua's pre-Columbian peoples. The museum also enjoys stunning photo-ops of Granada's rooftops, the lake, and Mombacho. The towering, sky-blue convent was first built by Franciscan monks in 1529 and was burned to the ground by pirate Henry Morgan 150 years later. Since then it has housed William Walker's troops, U.S. Marines, a contingent of engineers surveying a possible canal route in the 1920s, and the National University.

You can find a smaller version of the exhibits at the private collection of the **Mansion Museo de Granada** (1.5 blocks west of the park, open Tues.–Fri., $2 entrance).

The **Fortaleza de la Pólvora** (at the terminus of Calle Xalteva, next to a deep gully) was built in 1748 to secure Granada's gunpowder supply from invading pirates. Its medieval ar-

chitecture speaks of simplicity and strength: five squat towers and one heavily guarded gate with two oaken doors. In the 20th century, both the city government and later Somoza's National Guard used La Pólvora as a military garrison, and later, a jail. These days it's a museum of arms. Climb the towers for a breath of wind and a good perspective of the skyline.

La Plazuela de los Leones

The pedestrian space guarded by the cannon off the northeast corner of the main plaza is where Henry Morgan set 18 cannons during his sacking of the city, and where, a century later, William Walker was sworn in as President of Nicaragua. On the *plazuela's* eastern side, you'll find the well-known **Casa de los Leones** whose interior has been transformed into an international cultural center (tel. 505/552-4176 or 505/552-6437, c3mundos@tmx.com.ni, www.tmx.com.ni/c3 mundos, open 7 A.M.–6 P.M. daily). Don Diego de Montiel, governor of Costa Rica, built the Casa de los Leones in 1720. William Walker did not miss the opportunity to burn this place as well and left nothing standing but the portal bearing the Montiel family crest (still visible). The unique, neoclassical colonnade facade was the result of the building's reconstruction. In 1987, the historical monument became the headquarters of the Casa de los Tres Mundos Foundation, whose lofty mission is "to foster an understanding of universal and human values among people of all religions and political persuasions, as well as providing new economic opportunities for the Nicaraguan People." As such, the Casa houses an art and music school, museum, historical archive, library, concert hall, literary café, bookstore, and exhibition space, and regularly hosts resident artists from around the world. Visiting artists exhibit their work, teach classes, and donate a piece of art created during their stay.

Walking Tours

Granada is best appreciated by walking its streets. Start before breakfast to beat the heat and traffic, or hire a horse and carriage from the park. Here are suggested routes:

One of Granada's original streets, **Calle Atravesada** crosses north-south from the old train station to the tin-roofed, bustling chaos of the municipal market. The railroad station was built in 1886 and renovated (with help from the Spanish) into a railroad museum, now sadly closed for lack of funding. The walk south takes you past a number of grandiose, aristocratic homes, representative of the lifestyle of Granada's wealthy—past and present.

Calle Real Xalteva or just "La Xalteva," is the second principal street of the city. Walking west from the south side of the plaza, you'll come across the **Iglesia la Merced,** which throughout the 1940s inspired renowned Nicaraguan poets like Pablo Antonio Cuadra, Joaquín Cuadra, and Ernesto Cardenal. A few blocks farther west brings you to the **Iglesia Xalteva** and the stone-tower park across the street. At its western end, the 10-meter-high arched stone walls known as **Los Muros de Xalteva** were erected by the Spaniards in the mid-1700s to separate the Spanish settlements from those of the locals. Continuing west on La Xalteva, the street eventually ends at the Fortaleza de la Pólvora.

© MARILYN WOOD

La Plazuela de los Leones, Granada

If nothing else convinces you of Granada's historic wealth, head immediately to the **cemetery** on the southwest corner of the city grid. There, enormous marble tombs—bigger than the homes of most Nicaraguans elsewhere—shelter the cold bones of several centuries of Granada's elite. Note the column-lined Capilla de Animas and the replica of the Magdalena de Paris, both built between 1876 and 1922. The Granada cemetery supposedly houses the bones of five Nicaraguan presidents.

Parque Colón at the center of town is the epicenter for Granada's more interesting buildings. The colonial yellow building at the southwest corner of the park belongs to the wealthy Pellas family, Nicaragua's version of the Rockefellers. Cross the park to the magnificent cathedral, at whose flank you'll find the **Cruz del Siglo** (Century Cross), inaugurated January 1, 1900. Entombed in its cement are coins, pieces of art, and a gilded bottle from the 19th century. From there, head east along the Calle la Calzada, which takes you to the 17th-century Iglesia de Guadalupe (Convento San Francisco), first built in 1626 and most recently refurbished in 1945. Continuing along the palm-lined boulevard, you'll reach the **muelle and malecón** (dock and quay) on the water's edge. Turn right and pass through "the rooks" (a pair of statues) to enter the Complejo Turístico Cocibolca.

Ⓜ Complejo Turístico Cocibolca

The Tourist Complex is the whole lakeshore, where the afternoon breeze is fresh and clean, and the sidewalks fill with clamoring hot-dog and *chicharrón* vendors. The *complejo* is less a tourist center than a broad shoulder of a park, but its leafy canopy and fresh lake breeze set the tone for languid, breathless tropical afternoons, and the panoramic backdrop—broad, magnificent Lake Cocibolca—is unmatched in Nicaragua.

ENTERTAINMENT AND EVENTS

Hopefully, the **Noches de Serenatas** will be reinstated soon, a free concert series held on Friday nights on the plaza in front of the Casa de Leones. If not, definitely check the events listing there for other concerts, often by visiting international musicians, and ranging from jazz to strings to ambient jungle sounds. One block west of the plaza, **El Teatro Karawala** offers mainstream movies, good for rainy evenings; word is they'll soon turn into a luxurious four-screen multiplex.

Bars

You'll always find something going on at the various hostels around town, see Accommodations section for more. Ⓜ **El Tercer Ojo** (one block north and 1.5 blocks east of the park) is the scene of a lively happy hour from 5–7 P.M. A block east, **Zoom's** is unpretentious and cheap; open from noon, 7 days a week. Trendier and hipper, Ⓜ **La Fábrica** (1.5 blocks west of the plaza's northwest corner) draws a lively, mixed crowd from as far away as Managua due to its cavernous interior, unique cocktails, great food, and occasionally local Nica grunge bands. Across the street, **Café Nuit** is one of the city's most beautiful bars, with a sculpted garden. It attracts mostly locals and often has live music. On the next corner, you'll find **El Club,** a popular upscale bar with frequent special bashes and theme parties.

Discos

Granada does less dancing than other Nicaraguan cities, so the disco scene is a little wanting. The only in-city disco is **Kwai's Pub,** where neither the food nor the atmosphere is thrilling. Countless others line both sides of the Complejo Turístico Cocibolca. **Cesar's,** just south of the gate, is one of the most entertaining places to dance, and a bit farther into the park, **Pantera** is just as good and hosts the occasional live band. Do not walk to or from the disco strip at night, even in a group, and especially after drinking. The stretch of road between the water's edge and the city center is a notorious hangout for young, nervous, and knife-wielding would-be crooks.

SHOPPING

Granada's mercantile tradition extends into the present. The municipal market is located one block south of the plaza, and the chaotic bustle spills out onto the shops and sidewalks of Calle Atravesada. For a less frantic experience, stick to the gift shops on the west side of the park adjacent to Hotel

Alhambra or visit **El Tiangue** gift shop in Hotel La Gran Francia (southwest corner of the park, tel. 505/552-6000). Antique lovers will adore **Casa de Antiguedades** (tel. 505/874-2034, harold sandino@hotmail.com) a block north of the park on Calle Arsenal. Walking east from there, you'll find several more upscale *artesanía* shops.

This is *guayabera* country, and there are several places to buy the elegant Latin shirts, the best (and most expensive) being **Guayabera Nora,** right around the corner from the Bearded Monkey.

Tobacco grown in the cool hills around Masatepe, and often blended with northern Nicaraguan leaves, fill the **Doña Elba Cigar Factory,** (located one block west of the Iglesia Xalteva, open 7 A.M.–7 P.M.). Named after the owner's mother, the rolling factory produces some 3,000 cigars daily. There's also a well-stocked cigar shop right on the north side of the park.

The **Maverick Reading Lounge** (.5 block west of the Plaza de la Independencia's north end) is a souvenir shop/café/used-book exchange run by a friendly Canadian who is very plugged into the Granada expat scene—a wealth of information.

SPORTS AND RECREATION

Catch a lively game of baseball at Granada's baseball stadium, or just enjoy the crowd as you watch the home team, **Los Tiburones,** do their thing.

ACCOMMODATIONS

Granada offers a tremendous number and variety of accommodations, growing quickly. Calle Calzada ("Hospedaje Row") is the easiest street to find lodging, though very good options are scattered elsewhere throughout the city. Hoteliers in Granada pay close attention to their competition, so prices fluctuate both up and down through the course of the year.

Under $10

Airy dorm-style rooms centered around a wooden bar and open colonial courtyard give **The Bearded Monkey** (across from the fire station, tel. 505/552-4028, thebeardedmonkey@yahoo.com, www.thebeardedmonkey.com, $3 dorm bed, $5 s)

the kind of friendly, communal space that draws the backpacker crowd. They've got the right idea: a great menu, cool music, Internet, footlocker and bike rentals, a selective book trade, and they change dollars and American traveler's checks.

Hostel Oasis (one block north, one block east of the market, tel. 505/552-8005 or 505 /552-8006 www.nicaraguahostel.com, $6 dorm bed, $10 s, $15 d, $22 with private bath) opened in 2002 and quickly became a favorite. Oasis offers free Internet sessions and international calls to attract those clients that haven't heard about the quiet swimming pool set in the center of its cool indoor patio, free coffee, book trade-in, DVD rental, and lockers.

Hospedaje Central (located 1.5 blocks east of the central park, on Calle Calzada, tel. 505/552-7044) is more fun than tidy; its bar is popular, where happy hour seems to go on all day in a cloud of clove-cigarette smoke. More than 80 beds here mean you'll have no trouble finding a place to sleep, although the cheaper 14-bed dorm ($4 pp) fills quickly, so you'll likely end up in one of the darker but private rooms ($13/16 s/d). The *hospedaje* also offers food, computers, a tour desk, and laundry.

As you walk east along this strip, you'll find several quiet places run by Nicaraguan families, including **Hospedaje Cocibolca** ($6/12 s/d, breakfast served 7–11 A.M. for additional charge). **Hostal San Angel** (a half block south of the park's southeast corner, tel. 505/552-6373, $9 with private bath and mosquito net) is more like a homestay.

$25–50

The beautiful 176-year-old home that was converted into **Posada Don Alfredo** (two blocks west of the plaza, tel. 505/552-4455, alfredpaul baganz@hotmail.com, $25–35) boasts seven enormous, airy rooms around a lush, open-air garden and patio, and all include private bath, hot water, and TV, plus bike and kayak rental. Says Don Alfredo: "I am German so hotel is very clean." Nearby, **El Club** (3 blocks west of the NW corner of the park, 552-4245, www.elclub-nicaragua.com, $35 s/d) has a modern look, cozy little rooms, and the city's longest (and sometimes loudest) bar.

Spotless, well-run, and modern, **Hospedaje Italiano** (.5 block west of Convento de Guadalupe, tel. 505/552-7047, $25/32 s/d) offers a range of amenities: remote-controlled a/c, private bath, and TV for $25/30/40 s/d/t.

Over $50

Granada has the best assortment of upscale hotels in the nation, each striving to offer a unique colonial experience that doesn't skimp on the amenities. In this range you get hot water, a/c, private baths, cable TV, and a whole lot of class. This is all certainly true at **Casa San Francisco** (kitty corner to the Convento San Francisco, tel. 505/552-8235, csfgranada@yahoo.com, www.casasanfrancisco.com), a charming colonial cluster of 13 beautifully decorated rooms that range from $40–55, breakfast included, small pool, quiet and central neighborhood, run by a few well-traveled ex–Peace Corps Volunteers. You'll also find a great (and cheap) on-site restaurant and bar, small gardens, and fountains.

 **Hotel Alhambra** (on the west side of the park, tel. 505/552-4486, fax 505/552-2035, hotalam@tmx.com.ni, from $50d with a/c, TV, private bath, telephone, hot water, and access to the pool) was one of Granada's first luxury hotels. Built around a gorgeous landscaped patio, its location across from the park is the best in town. **Hotel Colonial** (20 meters west of the park's northwest corner, tel. 505/552-7299, hotel-colonial@nicaragua-vacations.com, www.nicaragua-vacations.com, $50s/$65d) hosts up to 50 guests in rooms surrounding an outdoor patio, pool, and bar. Unfortunately, most of the lower-priced rooms at **Hotel Casona de los Estrada** do not match its grand, magnificent entrance, but the $79 double sure comes close. On the north side of Casa de los Leones (tel. 505/552-7393) is a 6-room refurbished colonial guesthouse whose hardwood charm extends from the simple rooms to the elegant garden-side bar.

One of Granada's first buildings (having withstood even the fire that consumed the rest of the city in the days of William Walker) has been delicately and passionately restored and

La Gran Francia is luxurious and tasteful.

VOLUNTEERING IN GRANADA

There are numerous opportunities in Granada to get involved—both short- and long-term. If you're serious about finding somewhere to volunteer, look into the options below, or for local guidance, seek out Donna Tabor either by email (ugogirl@tmx.com.ni), or by asking around at one of the projects listed below. Donna first came to Granada in the mid-1990s as a Peace Corps Volunteer, and has since been active in supporting the city's underprivileged youths (see Café Chavalos in the food section of this chapter). Another good resource, whom you can contact before your trip, is Birgit Cory, who lives in San Francisco in between her frequent expeditions to Nicaragua, both leading trips and working with the street kids of Granada (US tel. 415/333-4104, birgitlein@hotmail.com).

Escuela Yo Puedo (I Can School) is a learning center for children who are denied formal education because of family restrictions that force them to work in the streets, usually shining shoes or selling candy. The school is run by U.S.-based nonprofit Building New Hope (5464 Upsal St., Pittsburgh, PA 15206, U.S. tel. 412/647-5245, www.buildingnewhope.org), which welcomes volunteers who wish to spend time, play games, and read to the children. You'll need some basic Spanish skills and the ability to commit to several months working daily with the kids; contact Donna Tabor to learn more, visit the website, and feel free to send a tax-deductible donation to support the project.

Cristo Sana a los Niños is located near the park, and is a home for boys from dysfunctional families. Residents agree to leave their glue jar

outside, and in exchange, receive room, board, and schooling, including a computer project and art class. Talk to Sister Marfía Mercedes about volunteering here in the afternoon—having a special skill helps. **Hogar Madre Albertina** (tel. 505/552 7661, from Colegio Padre Misieri, two blocks north) is a desperately under-funded orphanage for girls where residents typically have nothing to do except watch television all day. Volunteers are welcome to read to the girls, play games with them, or take them on day trips; in Granada, ask around for a copy of an activity guide to help you with ideas. They're also looking for computer and English instructors, for both the girls and the sisters in charge.

La Harmonía is an Italian-run organization for disabled children around the corner from the Casa de los Leones. If your Spanish is good, visiting medical missionaries are always looking for translators, or just come spend time doing crafts projects with the kids.

La Esperanza Granada (www.la-esperanza-granada.org) accepts volunteers to participate in various community-education and health projects in several small villages outside the city. A one-month minimum commitment is required, but periodically there are short-term projects available; intermediate Spanish is desirable. There is no fee to volunteer, and inexpensive accommodations are available at their new volunteer house ($2–3 per day), at local hostels, or a homestay option can be arranged to practice Spanish and participate in cultural exchange. The office is found in the Hospedaje Central.

reopened as **ꟽ La Gran Francia** (southeast corner of the park, tel. 505/552-6000, www.lagranfrancia.com, rooms and suites from $85 with breakfast). A careful blend of neoclassical and colonial elements in hardwoods, wrought iron, and porcelain characterize every detail—down to the hand-painted sinks. Its 21 rooms, some with balconies, are set around a courtyard and pool. Or for a bit more, try the Duke's Suite, named after an 18th-century mystery man—one of the few accommodations in Granada with a Jacuzzi tub.

FOOD

Breakfast

It's tough to beat the bottomless cup of coffee and meals at **Nica Buffet** (1 block south and .5 block west of the southwestern corner of the park, open every day 6–11:30 A.M.). The huge menu features pancakes, biscuits and gravy, eggs and bacon, and omelets, and it's not expensive; you'll find similar fare at **Kathy's Waffle Hut,** located across from the Convento San Francisco.

Or try the orange-infused French toast (or anything else from the creative breakfast menu) at **Casa San Francisco,** kitty corner to the Convento San Francisco, open daily from 6:30 A.M.

Nica

Besides the endless *chancho con yuca* (pork with boiled yucca) in the park, cheap eats can be found during the evenings at the *fritangas* on Calle Calzada, down by the lake. The **Taza Blanca** (one block north, half a block west of the market) has tacos, sandwiches, and light lunches for about $2, as does nearby **Querubes** (lunch buffet only) in the market. Off the southeast corner of the park, find **Don Dafa's** for a cheap ($3) lunch buffet.

For lip-smacking, upscale Nicaraguan dishes and steaks, don't miss **El Zaquan,** located behind the main Cathedral—your nose should lead you to the meat-covered open flame grill and dishes like *churrasco jalapeño* for around $8.50; open daily noon–3 P.M., and from 6 P.M. to closing.

Mexican

Casa San Francisco (open daily 6:30 A.M.–10 P.M.) has a very reasonable and delicious menu of Mexican treats and margaritas, from $2 burritos to $6 fajitas, plus other items, like the "Thai burger." *Buen provecho.* The Bearded Monkey serves a proper, fat burrito, possibly the best in town.

Vegetarian

Café DecArte (two blocks east of the park, open after 11 A.M.) serves up soups, sandwiches, and delights, like "Thai Peanut Salad," along with quiche, milkshakes, and fresh pita bread ($3–6). And both **The Bearded Monkey** and **Hotel Central** offer veggie chili and other cheap options (about $2).

Pizza

Locals and backpackers rave about the prices at **Telepizza** (new location 1.5 blocks east of Bancentro, tel. 505/552-4219, open 10 A.M.–10 P.M. daily), with large pies from $5 and delivery available. Their gigantic $2 stuffed calzones may be one of the best deals in town. Also popular is **Mr. Pizza,** right around the corner, across from Convento San Francisco. And the only real, thin-crust, wood-fire oven pizza can be had at **Don Luca's** (on Calle Calzada, east of the cathedral).

European

The upscale and elegant **El Arcángel** restaurant on the ground floor of La Gran Francia features excellently-prepared fusion cuisine, a blend of Latin-American ingredients with international inspiration; prices run from $8 a plate. Or start with drinks at the bar on the second-floor balcony. **El Tercer Ojo** (from the park, one block north, 1.5 blocks east, open 10 A.M.–midnight Tues.–Sun., happy hour 5–7 P.M.) has the same idea but isn't as fancy. Enjoy gorgonzola pasta and other delicacies in a gauzy atmosphere of candles, tiki torches, and soothing music.

Charly's Bar and Restaurant (located four blocks west of the old hospital mansion on the edge of town, tel. 505/552-2942, open 11 A.M.–3 P.M. and 6–11 P.M. Mon.–Fri., 11 A.M.–11 P.M. Sat. and Sun., closed Tues.) is a German-style rancho serving schnitzel, sauerkraut, and draft beer in a big, crystal boot—don't worry, they'll pay for your taxi if you eat there.

Doña Conchi (located two blocks east of the cathedral on Calle Caimito, tel. 505/552-7376, closed Tuesdays) offers a taste of her native Spain in the most intimate atmosphere in Granada; dinner by candlelight under the stars, surrounded by a dramatically lit, lush garden patio. Everything is delicious, especially the large, fresh dinner salads and pitchers of sangria. Don't forget to ask to hear the story about the centuries-old bullet holes in the wall. One door west, **El Mediterraneo** (tel. 505/552-6764, closed Mondays) is another elegant Spanish restaurant set in an airy garden patio adorned with colorful artwork.

INFORMATION AND TOUR SERVICES

The local **INTUR** office (southeast corner of the plaza, tel. 505/552-6858) is open 8 A.M.–noon, 2–5 P.M. Monday–Friday. It has a good selection of local brochures and maps. There is a gorgeous intro, but limited information at Granada's homepage: **www.granada.com.ni.** MARENA (tel.

505/552-4560) has jurisdiction over the three protected regions in the area—Volcén Mombacho, Isla de Zapatera, and the Laguna de Apoyo. Its office on the north side of Granada is open 7 A.M.–2 P.M. Monday–Friday.

You used to have to either pay $25 per person for local tours or do it on your own. **Tierra Tours** (from the main cathedral, two blocks west on Calle Calzada, tel. 505/862-9580, alvaroab@ibw.com.ni) offers a creative menu of half-day, full-day, and overnight trips in the Granada area for a fraction of the price of other Granada tour ops, especially if you can pull a small group together. In addition to local tours of Granada, Masaya, and Catarina, Tierra offers various kayaking, camping, hiking, and swimming trips to destinations that include Volcán Mombacho, the Isletas de Granada, Laguna de Apoyo, and Isla de Ometepe. Ask about the overnight cabins and tent platforms at the nearby Butterfly Reserve.

Mombotours (near the BDF, tel. 505/884-8992, www.mombotours.com) has awesome kayak tours of Las Isletas, as well as bike tours /rentals and canopy trips.

Servitur (tel. 505/838-7820 or 505/552-2955, orvind@hotmail.com) is connected to the Hotel Alhambra, offering travel agent services and a variety of local trips in the Granada area, including a horse-drawn-carriage city tour and fishing trips. Right around the corner, **Amigo Tours** (tel. 505/552-4080, bernal@amigotours.net, www.amigotours.net) is connected to the lobby of the Hotel Colonial; on the more expensive, air-conditioned side of things, Amigo specializes in area tours, national airline bookings, car rentals, and transfers to and from Costa Rica.

SERVICES
Emergency
The biggest hospital, **Bernardino Díaz Ochoa,** is a few kilometers out of town, on the road toward Managua (tel. 505/552-2207 or 505/552-2719). On the same highway, a bit closer to town is the **Hospital Privado Cocibolca** (tel. 505/552-2907 or 505/552-4092). For minor treatments, the section of Calle Atravesada just south of the bridge is occupied by more than a dozen clinics, blood

A local Nica woman carries her wares back from the market.

labs, and pharmacies. The **National Police station** is located on the highway to Nandaime, tel. 505/552-4712, and 75 meters west of the cinema, tel. 505/552-2977 or 505/552-2929.

Groceries
The two major supermarkets are the **Palí** (on Calle Atravesada just south of the market) and **Lacayo** (west of the park on Calle Xalteva), with an ATM and great wine selection.

Phones and Mail
The main **ENITEL** building is right off the plaza's northeast corner, and the **post office** (open 8:30 A.M.–5 P.M. Mon.–Fri.) is just north of the Casa de los Alemanes.

Internet
Internet cafés throughout the city usually offer service for $1–1.25/hour and Internet phone service for around $.10/minute. Start at a couple

Granada

A sign of the times on Granada's Plazuela de los Leones.

of places across the street from Hotel Colonial, open till 10 P.M. **K@blenet** (just east of Super Lacayo) is the cheapest and plushest Internet option. Closer to the center of town is **Café-mail** (just north of Bancentro on the west side of the street, open 8:30 A.M.—10 P.M. daily); snazziest is the **Cafémail** in the Casa de los Leones (open 7 A.M.–10 P.M.),offering a kind of coffee-bar experience.

Banks
Banco de America Central is on the southwest corner of the plaza, and Banpro and Bancentro are on Calle Atravesada, just a few blocks away. There are street money changers out in full force along this same section of Atravesada and ATMs in both the Banpro and the Esso station.

Laundry
Mapache Laundry Service (next to Tierra Tours, Calle La Calzada) offers quality service and personal attention as they wash your clothes in their handful of modern machines; delivery and pick-up service, $3 per six pounds, open 7 A.M.é5 P.M. Mon.–Sat. There's another laundry place (from the middle of the central park, 1.5 blocks west, tel. 505/552-6532) that also offers pickup/delivery service, about $4/load.

Rentals: Cars and Bikes
The **Budget** office is located in the Shell Guapinol gas station on the road to Managua (tel. 505/552-2323, open 8 A.M.–6:30 P.M. daily). Cars rent from $19–100 a day, and they can make you an offer on a cheap rented cell phone while you're there.

On the south side of the cathedral (Calle El Caimito, $3/hour, $6 for 5 hours, or $9/day) you can rent a brand-new mountain bike.

Film
Granada is one of the most photogenic cities in Nicaragua; if you can't wait till you get home to see those bright street shots, the **Kodak** shop (tel. 505/552-5455, open 8 A.M.–6 P.M. daily) is on Calle Atravesada, just north of the Bancentro.

Haircuts
Granada has particularly famous old-style barber shops, where skilled craftsmen—all wearing stiff, white *guayaberas*—will give you the perfect cut for a buck. Pay another $1 for a straight-edged shave, nose-hair cut, and face massage. Try the **"007"** just west of the plaza's southwest corner.

GETTING THERE AND AWAY
By Plane
Nature Air flies prospective real estate moguls and impatient tourists between San José, Costa Rica and Granada on Wednesdays, Fridays, and Sundays ($120 one way). Not a bad option if you want to miss Managua: Check out www.nature air.com for details.

By Bus to Other Points in Nicaragua

There are four places to catch a bus out of town. Managua-bound *expresos* (COGRAN, 1.5 blocks south of the plaza's southwest corner, tel. 505 /552-2954) leave every 15–20 minutes, 5:45 A.M.– 8 P.M. Monday–Friday, until 7 P.M. Saturday, and until 6 P.M. Sunday. Another fleet of minivans leaves from the Parque Sandino, on the north side of Granada near the old railroad station, with regular departures 5 A.M.–7:30 P.M. Both services travel to la UCA in Managua. From there, the same vehicles leave for Granada every 15 minutes, from 5:50 A.M.–8p.m.

Regular bus service to Rivas, Nandaime, and Jinotepe works out of the Shell Palmira, on Granada's south side, just past the Palé supermarket. The first bus to Rivas leaves at 5:45 A.M. and takes 1.5 hours; service continues at random intervals until the last one at 3:10 P.M. Nandaime buses leave every 20 minutes. Jinotepe *expresos* take a mere 45 minutes compared to the nearly two-hour *ordinario* trip through the pueblos. Around the corner, behind the Palé, is the bus terminal with service to Masaya (although any Managua-bound *expreso* will let you off in Masaya as well).

By Bus to Costa Rica and Panamá

Avenida Arrellano, on the west end of Granada, is part of the San José– and Panama City–bound routes for Central American bus lines. The three offices are all located on the east side of the street, and reservations should be made at least two days in advance. The TicaBus terminal (tel. 505/552-4301) is half a block south of the Old Hospital; be there at 6:15 A.M. for the 7 A.M. bus. TransNica (tel. 505/552-6619) is three long blocks south of the Old Hospital, on the corner of Calle Xalteva; three daily south-bounders leave at 6:30 A.M., 8 A.M., and 11 A.M.; be there a half-hour before departure.

By Boat

The old ferry departs Granada's municipal dock Monday and Thursday at 2 P.M., arriving in San Carlos around 3 A.M. When weather permits, the boat stops at Altagracia before cutting across to the eastern lakeshore and a port call in San Miguelito. The trip costs about $4 each way and returns from San Carlos at 2 P.M. on Tuesdays and Fridays. The boat can get crowded and uncomfortable at times, especially around Semana Santa when the lake turns *bravo* (rough) and the weather is hot. Get to the port early and be aggressive to stake your territory. During the rest of the year, the ride is usually *tranquilo*, and you may even be able to get some sleep on the deck.

The *M/N Mozorola* (tel. 505/552-8764 or 505/884-9548) makes the four-hour cruise to Altagracia, Ometepe (depending on the wind) twice a week, leaving Granada every Wednesday and Saturday at 11 A.M. (returns from Altagracia Tuesday and Friday at 11 A.M.). Adverse weather conditions can cause the cancellation of the trip, but it's otherwise a great ride past the Isletas and the Island of Zapatera.

Near Granada

■ LAS ISLETAS

This 365-island archipelago was formed when Volcán Mombacho erupted some 20,000 years ago, hurling its top half into the nearby lake in giant masses of rock, ash, and lava. Today, the islands are inhabited by a few hundred *campesinos* and an ever-increasing number of wealthy Nicaraguans and foreigners who continue to buy up the *isletas* for their garish vacation homes. Apart from the natural beauty of the *isletas,* the Fortín de San Pablo is a Spanish fort that was largely unsuccessful in preventing pirate attacks on Granada. The islanders themselves are interesting and friendly, maintaining a rural life unique in Nicaragua. The children paddle dugout canoes or rowboats to school from an early age, and their folks get along by fishing and subsistence farming.

Visiting the Isletas

Your trip begins at either Cabañas Amarillo or Puerto Asese, both a 7-minute drive south of town at the end of the waterfront road (about $1 via taxi). The latter is more popular, the former provides more shade and wider views—as well as the only kayak tours (fork left at the Asese sign). At the docks, you'll find a restaurant, snack bars, and a whole bunch of boats looking for your business. Choose a *lanchero* (boatman) and don't expect to haggle over prices, as gasoline is expensive. You'll pay about $8 a person for a half-hour tour. Beef up your visit by asking to visit an island where a family can serve you lunch—or pull up and "refuel" at one of the mellow island bars before continuing your tour. You can also take a dip in the lake water or have your *lanchero* bring you to the island cemetery or old fort. A better deal is to be dropped off at one of the deserted islets and then picked up later in the afternoon. Take along provisions and make a lazy afternoon of it.

Riding the *lanchas* is far from ideal if you want a wilderness experience in the isletas—the motors spew smoke and scare the birds away and keep

Las Isletas once comprised the top of the volcano looming close by.

you far up out of the water. Much more enjoyable is the sound of birdsong as your paddle cuts through the water; sign up for one of several **kayak tours** in the *Mombotour* office in Granada (near the BDF, tel. 505/884-8992, www.island kayaksnicaragua.com). Learn how to sea kayak (intro, advanced, and Eskimo-roll classes), then take a tour of the islands and old fort. The intro class, which includes all equipment, transportation, and tour of the Fortín San Pablo, costs $34 a person and lasts three hours. Special bird-watching paddles run $20–30; Nica guides are available and for the full petroleum-free experience, try the bike-kayak combo tour.

Accommodations

Hotel Isleta La Ceiba (Managua office tel. 505/266-1237, nlr@nicaraolake.com.ni, www .nicaraolake.com.ni) has 10 rooms with a/c, fan, private bath, pool, hot water—on your own desert island. They've got a fleet of boats to play around in, plus plenty of games including volleyball, billiards, and futbolón—also boat and fishing trips and a new three-platform canopy tour. The price of $50 per person includes taxes, one night of lodging, three meals, and transportation to and from the Club Náutico Cocibolca in Granada (a 15-minute boat ride).

PARQUE NACIONAL ARCHIPIÉLAGO ZAPATERA

Officially declared a national park by the Sandinistas in 1983, the Zapatera Archipelago is still struggling for the financial resources to protect and manage its many riches. About 34 kilometers south of Granada, Zapatera is an extinct volcano surrounded by Isla el Muerto and other islets, all of which comprise 45 square kilometers of land, and are home to some 500 residents. These islands were of enormous importance to indigenous peoples, who used them primarily as a vast burial ground and sacrifice spot. The sites of La Punta de las Figuras and Zonzapote are particularly rich in artifacts and have a network of caves that have never been researched. Also seek out the petroglyphs carved into the bedrock beaches of Isla el Muerto. An impressive selection of Zapatera's

formidable stone idols is on display in the Convento San Francisco, but the islands' remaining archaeological treasures remain relatively unstudied and unprotected—and continue to disappear.

Zapatera is a natural wonder, rising 629 meters above sea level and boasting virgin forest and a great deal of wildlife on its upper slopes. The archipelago is home to parrots, toucans, herons, and other waterfowl, plus white-tailed deer, an alleged population of jaguars, and a rich fishery off its shores.

However, despite a 1,000-page MARENA document describing its management, protection of Zapatera's treasures has been completely ineffective. Because only one park ranger visits the islands a couple times per month, inhabitants and visitors continually violate regulations by littering, robbing archaeological pieces, and illegally hunting the islands' wildlife. Its forests are being illegally harvested at an unprecedented rate.

Access the park from Granada's Puerto Asese, or if you can swing it, from the lakeshore in a borrowed dugout canoe. If you've got a tent, this is a great place to put it to use; just be sure you're not on the land of anyone who cares. There are no facilities on Zapatera, so be well prepared.

⋈ LAGUNA DE APOYO

Nicaragua's cleanest, bluest, and deepest swimming hole is this 48-square-kilometer body of water trapped inside the crater of the Apoyo Volcano. The deepest measured point (200 meters) is the lowest point in all of Central America. Its shores are easily accessible, and a remarkably small number of tourist facilities (and luxurious private homes) have been constructed at the water's edge. The volcano still has some underwater thermal vents and experiences the occasional seismic tremor, but for the most part, it's considered dormant and its walls are thickly vegetated with green forest and a chaotic network of trails, most of which exists as a protected nature reserve.

The earthquake in 2000 originated under the town of Catarina (which sits atop the western lip of the crater) and actually caused the water of the lake to slosh from side to side, starting a rumor that it was boiling. There are several fish species

© JOSHUA BERMAN

Laguna de Apoyo is one of Nicaragua's best swimming holes; potential dippers sun themselves at the Monkey Hut dock.

endemic to the lake—products of the forces of evolution in an isolated habitat. Scientists at the Proyecto Ecologico are at work describing some of the remaining "undiscovered" species here and offer scuba tours to view their subjects.

Hiking in the forests of the crater walls, you may observe species of toucans, hummingbirds, blue jays, howler and white-face monkeys, and rare butterflies. As you explore, be sure to wave a friendly greeting when passing the Lugareños (as residents of the local small communities are known). To fit in, pronounce your "Adios" as a long, drawn out, "Adiooooh." No need to be as cordial to the monkeys, who may fling their feces at you if you get too close.

Food and Accommodations

The road from above reaches the bottom and forms a T. Turn right and continue two kilometers to Norome. Turn left and you'll pass the Monkey Hut gate. Continuing a bit further, the road dips next to the water where you'll find Restaurante Los Ranchitos, with simple Nica food served by the humble Doña Chepita. Across the road, on the uphill side, don't miss the large-roofed transvestite-friendly bar with a hot cross-dressing scene on weekends.

The Monkey Hut is a relaxing retreat on a beautiful, terraced piece of land at the water's edge, with a fully equipped kitchen and a small selection of rooms. Soft drinks, water, and beer can be purchased at the hut— all other supplies need to be packed in. Dorm beds and hammocks go for $9, a handful of private, simple rooms, with shared bath and fan for $15/20 s/d. Day trippers are welcome: To use the kayaks, tubes, basketball court, and shaded lakeside area costs $4 per day. For reservations and weekly/monthly rates, contact the Bearded Monkey (tel. 505/552-4028) in Granada.

The **Proyecto Ecologico** (tel. 505/868-0841 or 505/882-3992, eco-nic@guegue.com.ni, www.guegue.com.ni/eco-nic) is a not-for-profit research station, Spanish school (since 1992), *hospedaje*, and backpacker getaway. For the Spanish school, you can stay with local families or in the Proyecto's dormitory (see Spanish Schools in the Know Nicaragua section). Not surprisingly, the staff at the Proyecto know lots about the surrounding flora and fauna—ask about the lake's endemic fish. The Proyecto also has simple backpacker rooms for $5, and six simple rooms with shared bath and fan for $16/19 s/d, breakfast included. Enjoy great, home-cooked meals served on a *tranquilo* wooden deck ($3 lunches and dinners). Also offered: fishing and motorboat trips, kayaks, and the chance to participate in one of several volunteer reforestation brigades each year.

Right next door, **Los Clarineros Hospedaje** (tel. 505/522-6215 or 505/887-5952) has four rooms with balconies facing the water: two singles for $13 a night and two for couples at $15, or rent a cabin for $30; credit cards accepted.

One of Nicaragua's newer class acts, **Norome Resort and Villas** (tel. 505/883-9093, info@noromevillas.com, www.noromevillas.com; Granada office on the southeast corner of the central park, tel. 505/552-2552) is an upscale, full-service resort with 109 tasteful rooms in 48 Caribbean-style villas, built up the crater's wall and nestled comfortably into the surrounding forest. Private bath with bathtubs, a/c, TV/DVD, and kitchenettes cost from $45 d. The restaurant and bar perched over the water are stunning and the food is excellent (meals $4–9); listen to the waves lap below and the monkeys howl in the forest behind you as you enjoy your meal or write to Mom on your laptop using Norome's wireless Internet service. The hotel boasts a full stock of plastic kayaks and sailboats (all non-motorized), also massages, Jacuzzi, pool, and access to hiking trails. Day visitors are welcome, $7 minimum at bar or restaurant.

Services

Public services at the bottom of the crater are limited to whatever is provided by the restaurants and accommodations; best to do some shopping in your base city and come prepared. As for tours, low-key, locally guided excursions can be arranged by calling **Bismarck** in Masaya at tel. 505/862-0777; ask about bird-watching, hiking, biking, swimming, horseback riding, and

camping trips. Also check with **Tierra Tours** in Granada; ask about their butterfly farm and overnight trip near the east side of the *laguna*.

Getting There and Away

It's about a 20-minute ride from either Masaya or Granada, and about an hour from the airport in Managua. There are two paved roads to take you up and over the crater lip and down to the water's edge; one originates on the Masaya–Granada Highway, the other on the Masaya–Catarina road. They join just before passing through the village of Valle de Laguna, where you'll turn right at the T and then make a quick left to begin your descent (pay a $1 entrance fee if driving). The paved road winds downward and ends exactly at the gate to former president Alemén's vacation home (hmm).

Most visitors split the $7 taxi fee from either Granada or Masaya, or else take the cheap transportation provided from the Bearded Monkey in Granada. Buses (under $1) leave the main Masaya market terminal at 10:30 A.M. and 3:10 P.M. for *baja al plan* (the bottom of the *laguna*); buses leave for Valle de Laguna (the town) hourly 5:30 A.M.–6 P.M. (from Valle, it's about a half-hour walk to the bottom of the crater). Leaving Laguna de Apoyo, there are three buses: 6 A.M., 11:10 A.M., and 4:40 P.M. (3 P.M. on Sunday is the last bus).

Hiking from Granada

All that's separating you and a dip in the deep waters of the Laguna de Apoyo is an easy 2.5-hour round-trip hike due west from Granada's cemetery. Simply go to the northeast corner of the cemetery and start walking the dirt road that borders it on the north side. Keep walking (or biking) as straight as possible whenever there is a fork in the road, and feel free to ask the Nicas living along the road if you are on the right track. They all know the trail, using it to water their cattle or sometimes to do laundry. Eventually, the rutted road will curve to the south and you will come to a crossroads. Turn right across a fenced-in field, which you will cross until you hit the lip of the crater. The descent is pretty obvious but treacherous after a rain, since it is torn

Granada

Mombacho's well-kept trails lead you around the forested rims of several defunct and overgrown craters.

up by the cows. At the bottom, you'll find an isolated beach (of sorts). There are no services here—just cool swimming and a bunch of birds. The walk is mostly level, but not very shaded until you hit the crater.

◼ VOLCÁN MOMBACHO

This is the big daddy with the blown top that serves as the perfectly exotic backdrop for your photos of Granada's cathedrals and tile roofs, and it is definitely worth a visit. Every bit of cool, misty, Volcán Mombacho's cloud forest higher than 850 meters above sea level is officially protected as a nature reserve. This equals about 700 hectares of park, rising to a peak elevation of 1,345 meters, and comprising an incredibly rich, concentrated island of flora and fauna. Thanks to the Fundación Cocibolca, the reserve is accessible and boasts the best-designed and maintained hiking trails in the nation.

Overgrown with hundreds of orchid and bromeliad species, tree ferns, and old-growth cloud and dwarf forests, Mombacho also boasts three species of monkeys, 168 observed birds (49 of which are migratory), 30 species of reptiles, 60 mammals (including at least one very secretive big cat), and 10 amphibians. The flanks of the volcano, 21 percent of which remains forested, are composed of privately owned coffee plantations and cattle ranches. Maintaining the forest canopy is another crucial objective of Fundación Cocibolca, since this is where more than 90 percent of Mombacho's 1,000 howler monkeys reside (the monkeys travel in 100 different troops, and venture into the actual reserve only to forage).

There is a short (half-hour) trail through the coffee farm at the bottom of the volcano, where you wait for your ride up. Once on top, there are two main trails to choose from. Sendero el Cráter, which encircles the forest-lined crater, and features a moss-lined tunnel, several lookouts, and a spur trail to the fumaroles (holes in the ground venting hot sulfurous air). The fumaroles area is an open, grassy part of the volcano with blazing wildflowers and an incredible view of Granada and her Isletas. The whole loop, including the spur, is 1.5 kilometers, with a few ups and downs, and takes a casual hour to walk. The Sendero la Puma is considerably more challenging—it is a four-kilometer loop with several difficult climbs that lead to breathtaking viewpoints. It begins at a turnoff from the fumaroles trail, and you should allow a minimum of three hours to complete it (and lots of water). Well-trained, knowledgeable local guides (some with English) are available for $5 for the Sendero el Cráter (per group, plus tip) and $10 for the Sendero la Puma. Note, because of the altitude and the clouds, the visibility from these trails may be much diminished on bad-weather days.

The reserve is closed on Mondays (for maintenance), and usually restricts Tuesdays and Wednesdays to organized groups. From Thursday to Sunday, all are welcome. The entrance fee ($7.50 for foreigners, $5 for Nicas and residents, $4 for students and children) includes admission to the reserve, transport to and from

© JOSHUA BERMAN

Granada and all 365 *isletas* are visible from the slopes of Volcán Mombacho.

Granada

the top of the volcano, and insurance. If you've got the time and the strong legs, feel free to hike all the way up the steep road yourself. Allow a couple hours (and lots of water) to reach the top.

Volcán Mombacho Biological Center

Located at the base of one of Mombacho's 14 communications antennas, on a small plateau called Plan de las Flores at 1,150 meters, the research station is also an interpretive center, *hospedaje, cafetín,* ranger station, and conference center. The center was completed in 2000 and is still growing. There are drinks and snacks here, including a *corriente* (standard) dish for $3.50. As of press time, there are 10 dormitory beds in a loft above the interpretive center. It costs $25 to rent out the whole *albergue,* (hostel) which sleeps up to 10 people. A package deal is available, which includes dinner, a guided night hike (on which you can search for the famous red-eyed frog and Mombacho salamander), and breakfast; or pitch a tent for $15 and buy meals on the side. For more information on updated prices and pack-

ages, contact the Biological Station at tel. 505/552-5858, or Fundación Cocibolca (in Managua) at tel. 505/278-3224 or 505/277-1681, fcocibol@ibw.com.ni.

Canopy Tours Mombacho

Put yourself on belay at the **Mombacho Canopy Tour** (tel. 505/888-2566 or 505/852-9483, gloriamaria@cablenet.com.ni, $25 pp, less for Nicas), located up the road from the parking lot, just before the road passes through the El Progreso coffee mill. They've got a 1,500-meter course involving 15 platforms and a 25-meter-long hanging bridge. Many tour operators offer a full-day Mombacho package that involves a visit to the reserve followed by a canopy tour on the way down, or you can set this up yourself by calling Fundación Cocibolca (tel. 505/248-8234).

On the opposite (east) face of Volcán Mombacho, cloud-forest coffee farm meets canopy tour at the Cutirre Farm. **Mombotour** (on the west side of the Iglesia La Mercéd in Granada, tel. 505/552-4548 or 860-2890, mombotur@tmx.com.ni, $15–30 pp) offers a range of half-day trips, involving some combination of high-ropes canopy tour, horseback ride, bird-watching hike, and coffee-farm tour. Trips include transportation to and from Granada, plus an optional lunch buffet for $7.50. The 15-kilometer ride to the Cutirre Farm takes longer than you'd expect. The road turns into a river during the wet season, but the trip is worth it; once you arrive, the views from the lodge are spectacular, looking straight out at Isla de Zapatera, and behind it, the cone of Volcán Concepción. There is also a small but attractive insect museum, with a full butterfly farm in the works. Bird-watchers can take a walk through the plantation with guides experienced in spotting any of the 43 species observed here.

The canopy tour, suspended from 14 of the giant shade trees on the coffee farm, is a professional, safe system of 17 platforms, a hanging bridge, and 13 horizontal zip lines, ending with a 23-meter rappel from a massive ceiba tree. Show up at Mombotour's Granada office to arrange your trip, which leaves at either 10 A.M. or 2 P.M. (arrive one hour prior), returning you to Granada about three hours later.

Getting There

Although the majority of Mombacho's visitors arrive as part of a tour package, it is entirely possible to visit the reserve on your own, and it makes a perfect day trip from Managua, Granada, or Masaya. You'll start by taking a bus (or express minivan) headed for Nandaime or Rivas (or, from Granada, to Carazo as well), getting off at the Empalme el Guanacaste. This is a large intersection, and the road up to the parking lot and official reserve entrance is located 1.5 kilometers toward the mountain—look for the signs. The walk to the parking lot is a solid half-hour trek, mostly uphill and in the sun. Water and snacks are available at the parking lot—be sure to drink lots before and during this first leg of your journey. Once you arrive at the parking lot, you'll pay the entrance fee and then board one of the foundation's vehicles to make the half-hour, six-kilometer climb up to the Biological Station. The lumbering troop transports depart at 8:30 A.M., 10 A.M., 1 P.M., and 3 P.M. Thursday–Sunday, and return shortly after each climb up the hill (last bus down is 6 P.M.). In your own 4WD vehicle, you'll be asked to pay $13 in addition to your entrance fee. The park is closed Mondays and open by reservation only on Tuesdays.

Rivas and La Isla de Ometepe

South of Managua, the land crumples suddenly into the impressive and windblown peak of Las Nubes (934 meters) and then falls slowly to the south until it spills into the verdant and lush plains that form the southwestern part of Nicaragua. Here Lake Cocibolca presses the land into a narrow belt that barely separates the lake from the Pacific Ocean. It's possible that, millions of years ago, it didn't separate them at all: There is geological evidence that suggests Lake Cocibolca once flowed across this slim margin of land to the west, emptying into the Pacific near the fishing community of Brito, instead of down the Río San Juan and into the Atlantic Ocean as it does today.

The isthmus of Rivas is laden with history and ghosts. Although known as the land of Nicarao, the area was first inhabited by the Kiribisis tribe, who were pushed aside by the more powerful Chorotegas. The Nicaraos came afterward and had lived in the area seven or eight generations when the Spanish arrived. Rivas is the

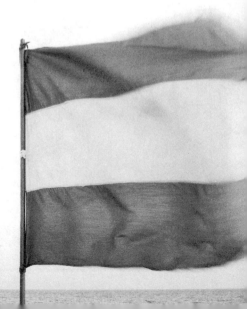

Must-Sees

Look for **M** to find the sights and activities you can't miss and **N** for the best dining and lodging.

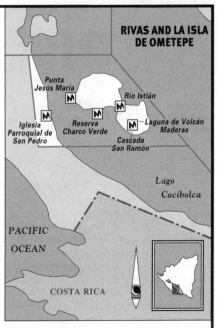

M Iglesia Parroquial de San Pedro: This old church has changed very little since the days when thousands of gold-rush passengers rode by it in horse-drawn carriages (page 104).

M Punta Jesús María: Usually visited as a day trip from Moyogalpa, this is a unique sand-spit beach experience where you can mingle with the locals and drink a cold one in Concepción's shadow (page 120).

M Reserva Charco Verde: The beaches, short trails, abundant vegetation, and friendly accommodations make this a pleasant retreat (page 120).

M Laguna de Volcán Maderas: This full-day mud bath of a hiking expedition will reward you with deep jungle and howling monkeys (page 123).

M Río Istián: Paddling a kayak through these still waters is breathtaking, especially early in the morning or during sunset (page 125).

M Cascada San Ramón: The trail to this 56-meter waterfall is well marked and well worth it (page 126).

RIVAS AND LA ISLA DE OMETEPE

Punta Jesús María

Río Istián

Iglesia Parroquial de San Pedro

Reserva Charco Verde

Laguna de Volcán Maderas

Cascada San Ramón

Lago Cocibolca

PACIFIC OCEAN

COSTA RICA

Volcán Maderas as seen across the isthmus from "The Pirate's Treasure."

© JOSHUA BERMAN

Rivas and La Isla Ometepe

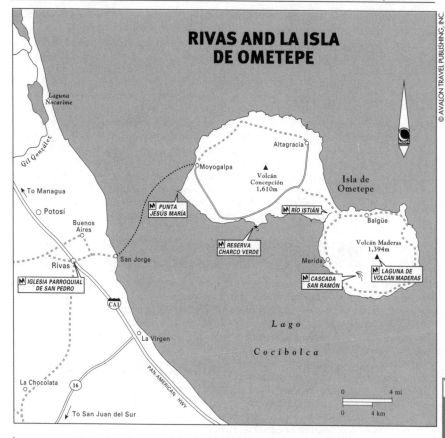

RIVAS AND LA ISLA DE OMETEPE

© AVALON TRAVEL PUBLISHING, INC.

Laguna Nocarine

Gil Gonzalez

To Managua

Potosí

Buenos Aires

Rivas

M IGLESIA PARROQUIAL DE SAN PEDRO

San Jorge

M PUNTA JESÚS MARÍA

Moyogalpa

Volcán Concepción 1,610m

Altagracia

M RÍO ISTIÁN

Isla de Ometepe

Balgüe

Volcán Maderas 1,394m

M RESERVA CHARCO VERDE

Merida

M CASCADA SAN RAMÓN

M LAGUNA DE VOLCÁN MADERAS

CA1

La Virgen

Lago

Cocibolca

La Chocolata

16

PAN-AMERICAN HWY

To San Juan del Sur

0   4 mi

0   4 km

largest community in the area, a peaceful colonial city of some 45,000 traders and farmers set around a stately white cathedral.

During the California gold rush, hundreds of thousands of passengers sailing between New York and California touched terra firma for the only time in their 30-day passage here, traveling in horse-drawn carts between San Jorge and San Juan del Sur before boarding ships for California. About the same time, William Walker tasted defeat at the hands of armed locals around the colonial farm of El Mesón, now a historical and archaeological museum in the city of Rivas. Nearly a hundred years later, many of the battles in 1978 and 1979 were fought on the wealthy lands south of the capital, and young Sandinista troops

suffered a major setback in Nandaime before they were to eventually claim their victory.

The twin-peaked Isla de Ometepe rises out of the waters of Lake Cocibolca just east of Rivas and patiently awaits inquisitive travelers. An intensely volcanic island still steeped in tradition and mystery, Ometepe is the ancestral home of the Nahuatl people and the birthplace of modern Nicaragua. Legend has it the warrior chief Nicarao lies buried somewhere along Ometepe's tree-lined coast.

This southwestern part of the country does not suffer the same intense, grinding poverty so obvious in the parched lands of the north and west. It rains more in the south, and the rivers flow nearly year-round. The soils on Lake Cocibolca's western shore are rich, productive, and deep volcanic. Cattle graze lazily here in immense, lucrative ranches and sugarcane fields drape the valleys south from the foot of Mombacho, one of Nicaragua's most picturesque volcano peaks.

PLANNING YOUR TIME

It's a rare traveler who plans more than a few hours in Rivas or San Jorge, but that may be all the more reason to spend some time in either of those towns. There's no denying, however, that the main area attraction is La Isla de Ometepe, whose twin volcanoes are visible from nearly anywhere in the area. Although it is feasible to travel to and from the island in a single day (you'd have to hire a vehicle to drive you around Concepción and take you to a couple of the sites), you'll be missing out—big time. In fact, you ought to allow a day of travel on each end of your Ometepe adventure, plus a minimum of two or three nights on the island. Moyogalpa or Altagracia make good bases for hitting local beaches and climbing Concepción, but most visitors come here to enjoy the tranquility of one of the several isolated accommodations dotting the shores and slopes of both volcanoes. If hiking's your game, allow a full day to climb each volcano and a full day of rest after each trek. Schedule in a kayak trip, waterfall walk, and a horseback ride, and you've spent one wonderful week that you will certainly want to write home about.

Rivas

The bastion city of southern Nicaragua, Rivas is an important center of commerce and trade with plenty of old-world charm—and none of the tourism development of nearby Granada. Few travelers make this a destination, but the beach crew at San Juan del Sur pops up frequently to get cash, visit a doctor or pharmacy, check email, and buy groceries or bus tickets to points north or south. Rivas is also the site of a Costa Rican consulate, in case you have immigration issues.

At 45,000 people, Rivas is just big enough to be fun, and just small enough to be friendly. It's often hot because of its low altitude, but just as often a cool lake breeze sweeps through town from nearby Lake Cocibolca. Rivas is known as Ciudad de los Mangos due to the abnormally high number of mango trees in and around the city, and the swarms of chatty *chocoyos* (parakeets) that live in the town park are big aficionados of the fruit. Their calls fill the skies around sunset.

Rivas was known as Valle de la Ermita de San Sebastián until 1717, when a delegation of pious villagers traveled to Guatemala, the capital of the republic at that time, to request their little town be declared a villa with the name of La Pura y Limpia Concepción de Nuestra Señora la Virgen María. The villagers were given an audience by Capitán General del Reino Francisco Rodríguez de Rivas,

who agreed to make the change. To thank him, the villagers decided to modify the name to La Villa de la Pura y Limpia Concepción de Rivas de Nicaragua. Thankfully for travelers and mapmakers, that name was considerably shortened.

ATTRACTIONS AND SIGHTS
M Iglesia Parroquial de San Pedro

Rivas's church looks well-worn and well-loved. Built in the 18th century, the Church of San Pedro has witnessed the California gold rush, William Walker, and the Sandinista Revolution. As you scan its old walls, remember that every single passenger that made the trip across Nicaragua in the days of Cornelius Vanderbilt's steamship line passed by this ancient old monument. It is today, as always, a peaceful place to seek refuge; mass is held evenings around 6 P.M.

Other Churches and Museums

Four blocks west of the park at the town's center, the **Iglesia de San Francisco** was built in 1778 and was the first convent of the Franciscan friars. A beautiful statue out front commemorates the devotion of the friars to both God and their work. When they began construction of the nearby Bancentro, an underground tunnel was discovered

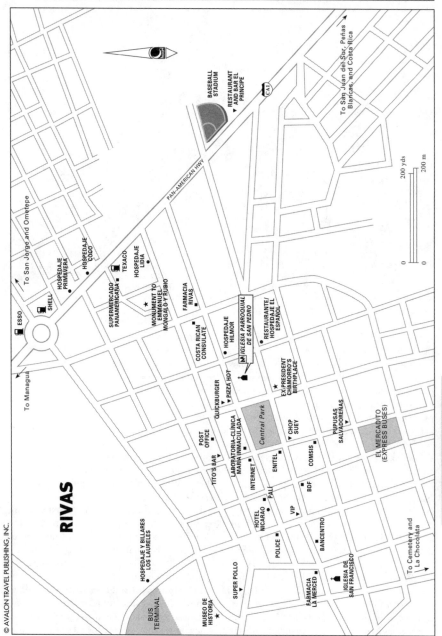

Rivas and La Isla Ometepe

Rivas' cathedral witnessed the Gold Rush.

that linked the Iglesia San Francisco with the plaza (the open area adjacent to the central park's north side); the tunnel passes beneath the library (one door east of Bancentro). Little is known of the tunnel, except it was probably dug at the same time the church was, meaning it was in place and probably used during the Battle of Rivas, when the plaza was the site of a military barracks.

The Rivenses claim "nationalism began in Rivas." Though the expression makes reference to Rivas's defeat of William Walker, Rivas was also the birthplace of several former presidents of Nicaragua, including Máximo Jérez (Liberal, governed from June 8, 1818 to August 12, 1881), Adén Cárdenas (Conservative, governed from March 1, 1883 to March 1, 1887), and most recently, Violeta Barrios de Chamorro (Coalition, governed from April 25, 1990 to January 10, 1997). Chamorro's childhood home is located across the street from the Iglesia de San Pedro's south side. There are also several direct descendants of William Walker living in Rivas.

Rivas has its own history museum: the **Museo de Historia y Antropología de Rivas,** set on the western side of town in a 200-year-old house that was once part of a cacao and indigo plantation. On June 29, 1855, the Casa Hacienda Santa Úrsula, as the building was known in its former incarnation, was the scene of a heroic battle in which William Walker and his men were defeated. The Battle of Rivas, as it became known, was one of the first manifestations of Nicaragua's growing sense of nationalism in the late 19th century. The museum has a healthy collection of pre-Columbian pottery and domestic utensils, like kerosene lamps, silverware, and tools, from the mid-19th century. Several old maps of the region are also on display, and, of course, the entire building itself is a museum piece, in the style of mid-17th-century Mediterranean farmhouses. The museum is open rather irregular hours but generally follows an 8 A.M.–4:30 P.M. schedule. Foreign travelers pay $1 to enter; the museum sells several books.

The **Monument to Emmanuel Mongalo y Rubio** marks the final resting place of a young Rivas teacher who lived here in the mid-1800s. Mongalo y Rubio gained his fame during the Battle of Rivas by setting fire to the Mesón (the museum building) where Walker and his men had sought refuge; as they abandoned the blazing building, they were captured or shot.

Another museum piece in its own right, the **Biblioteca Pública de Rivas**, next to Bancentro, is considered one of the oldest buildings in Nicaragua still standing. It dates back to at least the early 17th century. Among its various incarnations, the *biblioteca* (library) was a secondary school founded in 1872 by Máximo Jérez and El Colegio de la Inmaculada Concepción. Still easily visible in the building is a hole caused by a stray shot during the Battle of Rivas.

At the southeast end of town not far from the road to La Chocolata, the Rivas cemetery is set on a little hill with a nice view of town and the surrounding hillsides. It's worth visiting in the late afternoon, as Rivas sunsets are often blazing washes of red and orange, thanks to the humidity in the air from Lake Cocibolca.

ENTERTAINMENT AND EVENTS

The **Restaurante y Disco El Principe** (next to the baseball stadium on the highway to the border) is the most popular and laid-back night spot. Or check out the **V.I.P.,** where Rivas's in-crowd goes to drink at tables set in an indoor-outdoor garden atmosphere; clientele generally have cell phones and great hair. At **Tito's Bar** the atmosphere is casual and friendly, and the beer is ice cold. Tito's has a small dance floor and a couple of pool tables. But if shooting pool is your bag, there are better tables at **Billares Los Laureles,** where games cost about $1 each. Alternate Saturday nights in the town plaza (across from the park) are **Noches Rivenses,** typically presentations of dance, music, and theater.

SPORTS AND RECREATION

No one enjoys baseball as much as Rivenses; at last count, there were 138 officially registered baseball teams and more than 3,900 registered players in the municipality, with stadiums in every town in the area. Attending a Sunday-afternoon game in the town's impressive stadium on the highway is a great way to experience Rivas and the energy of its

people; tickets are $1, and in lieu of chili dogs, there are plenty of *vigorón* (fried pork and yucca) and enchiladas in the grandstand. Ironically, even with all the community support, Rivas's national pro team had to drop out of the 2002 national championship race for lack of funds. Blame the mayor, who sold stadium lighting donated by Japan to the team in León.

ACCOMMODATIONS
Under $10
For budget travelers, **Hospedaje Lidia** (just east of the park, $5 a night per person for shared bath, $9.50 per couple) is the most popular and has a dozen clean rooms; the ones with private bath are reserved for groups of three or four travelers and cost $14. At the northeast and southeast corners of the church are two more options: **Hospedaje Hilmor** has beds from $3 s. **Restaurante/Hospedaje El Español** ($18 d) is a pleasant corner place with a friendly and atmospheric bar and smoking room in the front *sala*. In the back are four simple rooms. Each pair of rooms shares a bath. Along the highway, outside of town are several unremarkable and inexpensive places to stay, and many travelers prefer to spend the night in nearby San Jorge (see that section for more details).

$25–50
Hotel Cacique Nicarao (a block west of the park, tel. 505/564-3234, $35 s/$45 d/$55 t plus tax with cable TV, a/c, and a guarded parking lot) is an upscale, modern hotel complete with front desk, attentive staff, and plush rooms.

FOOD

Across the street from the Iglesia San Pedro is **Pizza Hot,** (closed Mondays) serving slices only New Yorkers won't agree with, and the outdoor tables are a nice place to catch up on your journal and people-watching. There's a **Quickburger** next door with $1 burgers, open seven days.

On the southwest corner of the park is **Chop Suey,** a Chinese place that isn't far off the mark, though all the dishes have been subtly adapted to suit the Nicaraguan palate; $4–6 a plate. Fried, baked, broiled, breaded, and roasted chicken are found in **Pollo Dorado** (closest to the center of town) and **Super Pollo,** near the market.

Possibly the lowest-price alternative in town is  **Pupusas Salvadoreñas,** (located across from El Mercadito, only open evenings) where tasty, authentic Salvadoran meat, cheese, or bean *pupusas* (greasy, stuffed pancakes) are served hot off the grill with salad, $2. Also open only in the evenings, there are several *fritangas* in the plaza, notably **La Gitana** (the gypsy), who shows up in her pickup truck around 11 P.M. and serves the meanest *gallo pinto* in town.

The best upscale restaurant is in the **Hotel Cacique Nicarao,** which—besides its traditional menu of well-prepared foods—is one of the only places in Nicaragua where you can get buffalo wings with hot sauce. Most of the bars listed previously have reasonable food as well.

Along the Highway

Near the southern limits of the city of Rivas there are several high-priced options that do a good business with truckers, travelers, and business people heading through on their way to the border. Highly recommended is **La Estancia** on the east side of the highway, with a sort of "farm ranch meets barn" feel to it; well-prepared chicken or beef dishes go for $6, and fresh shrimp dishes are $10 and up. Happily, they take credit cards. Almost directly across the highway is **El Mariscazo,** a word that is difficult to translate directly, but means something like "A huge slap in the face with seafood." It's a good option for fish, shrimp, and lobster, all of which run in the $10–13 range, and none of which you'll be smacked with.

SERVICES

There are several well-stocked pharmacies in town if you're looking for suntan lotion, aloe, painkillers, or medication. The biggest and best is right across from the park on the side of the plaza, **Laboratorio-Clínica María Inmaculada** (open 8 A.M.–4:30 P.M. Mon.–Fri. and

Rivas market

until noon on Sat.); in addition to the pharmacy, a well-respected doctor is available for consults 2–4 P.M. Monday–Friday. They've also got professional massage therapists. Another well-stocked pharmacy is the **Farmacia Rivas** (two blocks east of the park at the intersection of the boulevard, tel. 505/563-4292).

The **ENITEL** office is a block west of the park, open 7 A.M.–9:40 P.M. daily. The **post office** (north and west of the park) has fax service and is open 7:30 A.M.–4:30 P.M. Monday–Friday and 7:30 A.M.–noon Saturday.

Of the many Internet joints in town, the most popular is on the northwest corner of the park, and is open and airy. Find others just west of the park.

Banks

There are several banks in town including BDF, Bancentro, Banpro, and BAC, all of which operate essentially on a schedule of 8:30 A.M.–4:30 P.M. Monday–Friday, 8:30 A.M.–noon Saturday. Because BAC owns the credit card company Credomatic, you can take advances against your credit cards there, for—amazingly—no fee.

The Costa Rican Consulate in Rivas offers help with immigration issues for Costa Rica–bound travelers. It's located a block east and north of the cathedral, open 7 A.M.–5 P.M. Monday–Friday and 7 A.M.–noon Saturday.

GETTING THERE AND AWAY

Buses leave Managua's Roberto Huembes terminal for Rivas every 30 minutes. Several express buses depart in the early morning before 8 A.M. Express buses to San Juan del Sur and the border at Peñas Blancas will let you off on the highway at Rivas. They leave Huembes at 5 A.M., 8 A.M., 9:30 A.M., and 3:30 P.M.

Regular buses leave from the market on the northwest side of Rivas: every hour for Jinotepe and Granada, every 25 minutes for Nandaime, Diriomo, Diriá, Catarina, Masaya, and Managua. The last bus for Managua leaves from the Texaco station on the highway at 6 P.M. Four daily buses go to Belén and six for Las Salinas (9 A.M., 11 A.M., 12:40 P.M., 2:30 P.M., 4 P.M., and 4:30 P.M.). A better way to reach Carazo destinations is to take one of the express minibuses, which leave from El Mercadito on the other end of town about once every hour.

To and From Costa Rica

Service to Peñas Blancas and the border begins at 5 A.M. and continues every 30–45 minutes. The last bus leaves Rivas at 5:30 P.M. (the ride takes less than an hour and costs less than a dollar). On the highway in the Supermercado Panamericana (next to the Texaco station), you can buy tickets for the TicaBus, which passes by Rivas each morning bound for Costa Rica between 7 and 8 A.M., and between 3 and 4 P.M. every afternoon bound for Managua. Buy your tickets the day before ($10–12 to San José, Costa Rica).

Taxis to San Jorge and
San Juan del Sur

To San Jorge, a taxi should cost you no more than $.80 per person, whether you take it from

OMETEPE FERRIES FROM SAN JORGE

San Jorge–Moyogalpa

9 A.M.	Karen María
9:30 A.M.	Reyna del Sur
10:30 A.M.	Ferry Ometepe
11:30 A.M.	Señora del Lago
12:30 P.M.	Santa Marta
1:30 P.M.	Reyna del Sur
2:30 P.M.	Ferry Ometepe
3:30 P.M.	Reyna del Sur
4:30 P.M.	Señora del Lago
5:30 P.M.	Ferry Ometepe

Moyogalpa–San Jorge

5:30 A.M.	Karen María
6 A.M.	Señora del Lago
6:30 A.M.	Santa Marta
6:45 A.M.	Ferry Ometepe
7 A.M.	Reyna del Sur
11 A.M.	Reyna del Sur
11:30 A.M.	Karen María
12:30 P.M.	Ferry Ometepe
1:30 P.M.	Señora del Lago
4 P.M.	Ferry Ometepe

These times are subject to change. For the most up-to-date schedule, or to be sure that your boat is running, call Ometepe Tours at tel. 505/563-4779.

Rivas and La Isla Ometepe

the traffic circle or from Rivas. Ignore any taxi driver that tries to charge your foreign-looking self $2 or more. Taxis from Rivas to San Juan del Sur cost around $8 per person, or $1 if it's a *colectivo*, but you'll have to share.

Near Rivas

NANDAIME

Just south of where the highways from Granada and Carazo join to continue on to Rivas and the border, you'll pass by the mid-size city of Nandaime, located on the Pan-American Highway in the shadow of Volcán Mombacho. This is a humble, unassuming pueblo with the most basic of traveler's amenities, a small-town tranquility, and a passion for music. Nandaime's most famous son is Camilo Zapata, a key founder of the Nicaraguan folk style, who composed the song, "El Nandaimeño." Nandaime is also home to three "philharmonic orchestras." Before you run out to rent a tux, though, you should probably know that these are *chichera* groups, ragtag bands composed of a bass drum, a snare, cymbals, a sousaphone, and loud, clashing brass found in parades and bull-rings. Chichera music is happy, loud, and scrappy.

Domitila Wildlife Reserve

Just south of Nandaime, Domitila (tel. 505/881-1786, domitilareser@yahoo.com, www.domitila .org) is a private wildlife reserve, consisting of 230 hectares of tropical dry forest and lakeshore, with tree nurseries, hiking trails, and a ton of wildlife. Domitila is eco-savvy and uses composting toilets and its own wastewater treatment facility. You'll find comfortable, private cabins built on the premises, complete restaurant service, and facilities for groups of up to 25 researchers, scientists, or travelers. The $45 per person rate includes three meals per day and bed in the dorm, $65 pp for private room; $5 pp for day use, gourmet lunch for $10. Call and arrange a wildlife tour ($20 pp); bird-watching, butterfly tours, horseback riding, and luxury trips to the island of Zapatera, where hot meals are prepared

© RANDY WOOD

Usually more crowded, the rancho at Domitila is frequented by scientists and tourists alike.

Cruz de España

and served to you on-site, are also available. Call at least 24 hours in advance to make reservations. The entrance is located five kilometers south of Nandaime (km 72) on the road to Rivas; turn off the highway onto a dusty dirt road, which will lead you 10 kilometers past the Lagunas de Mecatepe to Domitila.

SAN JORGE

The tiny lakeside port of San Jorge is your access point to La Isla de Ometepe, and as such, most travelers breeze straight through it on the way to catch a boat to the island. If you have time to kill before your ferry departs, there's no reason to spend it dockside sitting on your luggage and waiting. Some travelers even find this a pleasant village in which to spend a night, especially with its new pleasant, cheap accommodations aimed at backpackers. A traditional village with a strong Catholic spirit, San Jorge is primarily a town that survives on the cultivation of plantains, its principal crop. Nearby Popoyuapa, true to its

Nahuatl-sounding name, cultivates cacao, the tree whose seed is used to produce cocoa and eventually chocolate, and which was once used by the Nicarao people as a form of currency.

Be advised that at certain, unpredictable times of the year, a southern wind brings plagues of small white gnats, which swarm the lakeside in San Jorge and eastern shores of Ometepe. *Chayules,* as they are known, don't bite or sting, but are relentless and always seem to wind up in your mouth, making the beach less than enjoyable.

Sights

Halfway down the long road to town, you'll pass under **La Cruz de España,** a graceful concrete arch that suspends a stone cross directly over San Jorge's main drag. This main street runs through town down to the water's edge and the docks. The monument commemorates October 12, 1523, the day Spanish conquistador Gil González Dávila and indigenous cacique Nicarao-Calli first met and exchanged words.

Rivas and La Isla Ometepe

The cross is supposedly built over the very point where the meeting took place.

Across the street from the base of the arch is a mural commemorating the same event, with the words attributed to Nicarao, "*Saben los Españoles del diluvio, quien movía las estrellas el sol y la luna. Dónde estaba el alma. Cómo Jesús siendo hombre es Dios y su madre virgen pariendo y para qué tan pocos hombres querían tanto oro.*" ("The Spanish know about the flood, who moved the stars, the sun, and the moon. Where the soul was found. How Jesus, a man, is God and his virgin mother giving birth, and why so few men wanted so much gold.") Many believe that the Spanish went on to refer to Nicaragua as "The Land of Nicarao," which over time evolved into the modern word "Nicaragua."

Even if you just cruise through San Jorge in a taxi, keep an eye out for the squat **Iglesia de las Mercedes,** one of Central America's earliest churches. Built around the year 1575, it was renovated and repainted a bright yellow in 2001. Most tourists keep their bathing suits packed until they get to Ometepe, but San Jorge's kilometer-long beach is hugely popular among Nicaraguans, who flock there during Semana Santa to enjoy the lake and the awesome view of twin-peaked Ometepe on the horizon.

San Jorge celebrates its *fiestas patronales* in honor of San Jorge every year on April 19–23 (the date changes to accommodate Semana Santa when necessary). Expect the beach to be packed. San Jorge usually has a parade or two during the celebrations, and there are performances of traditional dances, including *Las Yeguitas* (the dance of the little mares) and **Los Enmascarados** (the dance of the masked ones).

Accommodations and Food

If you missed the last boat to La Isla and don't feel like backtracking to Rivas, book one of the rooms at **M Hotel Las Hamacas** ($10 d for private bath and fan, $15 with a/c), no more than 100 meters west of the dock. Also consider **Hotel Restaurant Azteca** (from the dock, go two blocks past the castle, make a right, and go two more blocks, tel. 505/879-9512, 46 dorm beds for $2 pp). It's run by an adorable French Canadian–Swiss couple who will serve you a $3 meal or put you up in the huge dorm. There is a bit of privacy plus a pool, private rooms and Internet, pleasant common areas, locker rental, and nighttime guards to keep you safe.

You won't go hungry in San Jorge's numerous food-and-drink joints lining the beachfront, but neither will the menu have any surprises: chicken, beef, fish, french fries, and maybe a burger or simple sandwich.

Getting There

Take any southbound bus from Managua's Huembes Terminal to Rivas and get off at the traffic circle on the highway at Rivas. From there to the dock at San Jorge is four kilometers, accessible by Rivas buses once an hour ($.25); they pass the traffic circle approximately 20 minutes after the hour. Unless you happen to be there right at that moment, however (or are traveling on an extraordinarily tight budget), take a taxi to San Jorge for $1 per person—ignore anyone who tries charging more. There is one Managua–San Jorge express, departing Huembes at 9 A.M., arriving in San Jorge at 10:50 A.M. The same bus departs San Jorge evenings at 5 P.M., arriving in Managua at 10:50 P.M.

La Isla de Ometepe

The island of Ometepe is Nicaragüense to the core and yet completely insulated from the rest of the country (and the rest of the world) by the choppy waters of Lake Cocibolca. Singer-songwriter Luis Enrique Mejía Godoy called this "an oasis of peace," and the name has stuck. Not even the violence of the 1970s and 1980s reached the island. Proud locals refer to the rest of Nicaragua as "over there." Story has it that in 1957, as Volcán Concepción rumbled and threatened to erupt, the government ordered the islanders to evacuate Ometepe; they soundly refused, claiming they preferred to die on their island than live anywhere else.

Ometepe is awash in myths and legends, some of which date back to the days of the Nahuatl. Long before the Spanish arrived, the islanders considered Ometepe sacred ground, inhabited by gods of great power, and today a palpable sense of mystery and magic permeates day-to-day life.

Ometepe's allure attracts Nicaraguans from other regions of the country in addition to foreign stragglers, and a visit here is a sensory experience unlike any other. At night, the slopes of the volcanoes echo with the deep roar of howler monkeys, and by day the air is filled with the sharp cry of the thousands of parakeets and *hurracas* (bright blue jays that scold you from the treetops). Retaining much of its original forest, Ometepe represents what Nicaragua may have been like in 1522 when Gil González Dávila first set eyes on it: broadleaf trees, clean lake water, and fresh air, all under the towering presence of Concepción and Maderas, two immense volcanoes that make up the bulk of the island.

Nicaragua's pre-Columbian history may have begun on and around Ometepe. Legend has it that the Nahuatl people in what's now Mexico, under pressure from the more powerful Aztecs, followed the Central American isthmus southward

© RANDY WOOD

the Port at Moyogalpa, Ometepe

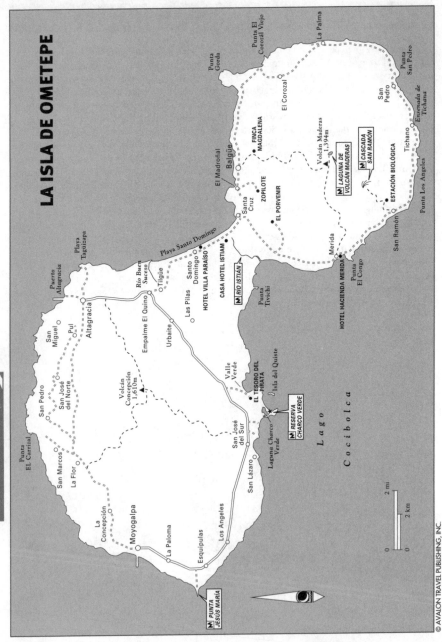

LA ISLA DE OMETEPE

A LOVE STORY—THE LEGEND OF OMETEPE AND ZAPATERA

It is said that long ago, neither Lake Cocibolca nor the islands existed. In their place was a broad green valley called Caopol, inhabited by animals that lived in thick forest. Not a single human lived in the forested valley, but the Chorotega, Chontales, Nagrandando, and Niquirano tribes all inhabited the edges of the valley, where they fought battles between tribes.

In the Niquirano tribe, there was a lovely Indian maiden by the name of Ometepetl, who caught the eye of the young Nagrandan warrior named Nagrando. He fell deeply in love with her, and she with him. Their love remained a secret because the Niquiranos and Nagrandans were sworn enemies. The day Ometepetl's father learned of the illicit romance, he grew furious and swore he would chase Nagrando to his death, rather than see his daughter marry a Nagrandan. Ometepetl and Nagrando fled to the valley where they hid in the forest to escape the fury of Ometepetl's father. There they decided the only way they'd ever be able to have peace would be to die together. Ometepetl and Nagrando slit their wrists with a sharp blade and died in each others' arms.

Ometeptl, as death overcame her, leaned backwards, and her breasts swelled. The sadness that overwhelmed the valley caused the sky to darken and an intense rain to fall. The valley began to flood, and her breasts became the twin peaks of Concepción and Maderas. Nagrando grew into an island as well, the volcanic island of Zapatera, located halfway between the lands of the Nagrandan people and his love Ometepetl. Ometepetl's father and the men who accompanied him in the search to kill Nagrando all perished in the flood. They became the Isletas de Granada and the Solentiname archipelago.

in search of a new home, guided by a vision of two volcanoes in the middle of a broad lake. When they saw Ometepe (Nahuatl for two hills), they knew their exodus had come to an end. Today, Ometepe is a mosaic of small farms of deep, rich soil that produce plantains, avocados, beef, milk, coffee, and honey. Its two principal towns, Moyogalpa and Altagracia, are lazy commercial centers, port towns, and transportation hubs.

You can hardly miss them: The centerpieces of the island are the twin Cenozoic volcanic peaks of Volcán Concepción and Volcán Maderas. The island of Ometepe has been called the edge of the tropics, and the dividing line between tropical and dry falls right between the two volcanoes. Maderas is an extinct volcano whose crater is filled with a shallow lagoon. The slopes of Maderas are lined with more tropical and humid species, including cloud forest at the top.

Concepción is an active volcano whose slopes are covered with tropical dry forest species like *guacimo* and *guanacaste*. In 1880, Concepción began to tremble, each day more violently until

December 8, when it erupted with such force that lava and smoke flowed out of the crater for nearly a year. It was this eruption that created some of its more distinctive features visible today, like the Lava de Urbaite, Peña Bruja (a broad cliff visible from Altagracia), and Peña de San Marcos. Concepción erupted again in 1883, launching large rocks from the crater, and again in 1889 and 1902. This last eruption produced so much ash that it ruined crops in Rivas. Concepción is still active, and has erupted in the past century in 1907, 1921, 1924, and most recently in 1957.

Today, Ometepe's 38,000 residents work primarily in agriculture: As your bus lumbers around the island, you'll see them gathering plantains, rice, tobacco, sorghum, sugar cane, corn, and coffee.

MOYOGALPA

Moyogalpa (which, to the chagrin of local tourism promoters, is Nahuatl for Place of the Mosquitoes—don't worry, bugs usually aren't bad at all here) is Ometepe's principal port town

Rivas and La Isla Ometepe

Volcán Concepción

and major commercial center. While many tourists pass straight through Moyogalpa, the town also makes a good base for your travels, especially with the hugely popular scene at the Hospedaje Central.

Sights

A good place to start your exploring is the **Fundación Entre Volcanes,** located across the street from the Moyogalpa ENITEL office. This small NGO is involved in several community projects across the island and may be able to help you find ways to volunteer your time while on the island. They also have some representative handicrafts of the region on display.

At the top of the hill, Moyogalpa's **Catholic church** is a charming place to visit, with a bell tower just high enough over the tree line to afford you a great view of the town, coastline, and lake. In front of the church is a park with two statues: a Native American with a spear, and a boy urinating—the islanders definitely maintain a sense of humor.

La Sala de Artesanía (or *El Museo*) located to-

ward the top of main street, has a small but interesting collection of pre-Columbian artifacts found on the island over the years. Owner and amateur historian Herman García and his wife Ligia are very knowledgeable about island history and lore, and *artesanía* in general, including which communities on Ometepe you can visit to see the artisans at work. Naturally, much of what you see on display is for sale.

Ometepe farmers raise a lot of cattle and produce enormous quantities of meat and cheese. Visit COPROLAC to arrange a tour of the cheese-processing facilities; speak with Moises Ghittis or Lisimack Amador, located on the west side of the cemetery in La Quinta. Both Ghittis and Amador are friendly types who may show you around their own farms as well, if you're lucky. Saul Cuadra raises bees and harvests honey. Look him up (he lives in front of the mayor's office) if you're interested in apiculture and would like to visit the bee farm; he doesn't travel out to the farm every day, so be flexible and be sure to pay him fairly for his effort.

There's a small pool hall on main street, the **J&M,** where you can go to meet the locals. Next door, the **Rancho Viejo** is a popular place to drink and relax, and the Disco Johnny Bar is the place to shake it on weekends.

The town of Moyogalpa celebrates its patron saint, Santa Ana, June 23–26. The Baile de las Initas is performed in much the same way as the indigenous dance it replaced, with traditional costumes and the resonant sound of the marimba.

Shopping

In addition to more than 200 museum pieces that represent the indigenous peoples of Ometepe, the Sala Arqueologica (one block west of the park, closed on Saturday and Sunday) sells examples of local handicrafts, including something called the hickory fruit style. Many of the museum pieces were found by the owner of the museum, Ligia González de García, on her own farm.

Beaches and Hikes

Besides the challenging hike to the top of Volcán Concepción (see Hiking the Volcanoes of Ometepe special topic), there are many other

HIKING THE VOLCANOES

The volcanoes that form the island of Ometepe are an irresistible temptation for visitors to the island, many of whom climb one or both while visiting. *Please* hire a local guide! Over the past several years, these tranquil volcanoes have played witness to a handful of tragic incidents involving lost, injured, and dead hikers—don't join the crowd! In fact, it's highly likely you will be required by law to hike the volcanoes with a guide. It's a small compromise to make, as the two peaks—nearly the same height, but radically different in personality—are well worth the trouble.

Climbing **Volcán Concepción** (1,610 meters) is popular among travelers who like physical duress—it's not an easy climb, particularly the last third of the way, which is treeless and rocky. However, those who reach the summit are rewarded with the unique thrill of knowing they're perched at the razor's edge of the maw of an active volcano (in the middle of an island in the middle of a lake in the middle of Central America). You will be buffeted by a cold lake wind all the way up the slope until the moment you reach the crater lip, when the blast of hot sulfurous air rushing out of the bowels of the earth will strike your face. It's that mixing of hot and cold air that forms the almost permanent cloud cover at the top of the volcano. Should you reach the top during one of the few days a year when the clouds clear, you will be rewarded with an unparalleled view of the island, the lake, and the volcano's stony interior. Keep in mind: Volcán Concepción is an active volcano that nearly erupted in 1957.

There are several guides in Moyogalpa and Altagracia, and almost all the hotels have their own guides as well. Berman Gómez at the Hotel Ometepetl is highly recommended (he was trained in Costa Rica in guide services and travels with first-aid supplies and a radio). You can hire a guide for $10–20 per group of five people.

Most travelers hike Concepción by way of the towns La Concha or La Flor, and there is an eastern approach from Altagracia that takes you through an impressive amount of monkey-inhabited forest before hitting the exposed section.

The hike is not to be underestimated—you'll get an idea of the severity of the volcano's surface just by admiring its steep cone shape as you cross the lake. (Concepción is one of the most perfectly cone-shaped volcanoes in Central America; Momotombo is another.) Allow a full day for the hike, five hours up and four hours down. Take plenty of water, sun protection, and good shoes and socks to protect your feet.

Volcán Maderas (1,394 meters) is the more frequently hiked of the two Ometepe volcanoes. There's a trail starting at the Finca Magdalena that leads to the crater lip, then down into the crater to a mist-swept turquoise lake straight out of Tolkien. The final descent down to the crater lake requires a rope descent and should not be attempted without proper safety equipment—make sure your guide packs this. The trail, unfortunately, has seen better days. Lack of appropriate maintenance has made a mud pit out of much of the upper stretch. Allow four hours to go up and two or three to come back down, and count on spending an hour at the crater lake (59 minutes of which you'll spend deciding whether or not to jump in the icy, mushy-bottom *laguna*). If you're not staying at the Finca Magdalena, you must pay a trail fee to enter and pass through the coffee plantations. You'll pass a petroglyph or two on the way up.

The other ascent leaves from Merida and, after a rigorously steep three-hour start, includes more time in the upper reaches, which one tourist called "the enchanted, magical" part of the hike. The Hotel Hacienda Merida offers this excursion, including transport back from Magdalena if you choose to descend the other side.

treks you can take along the slopes of the volcano without actually climbing to the crater's edge. Take with you a healthy sense of curiosity and enough Spanish to talk your way from farm to farm. The people of Ometepe are friendly and welcoming enough to let you traipse through their land in search of adventure, but remember that how you behave while "trespassing" will determine how the travelers who follow you will be received.

From Moyogalpa to the north, travel along the beach to the community known as Barrio de los Pescadores. Señor Augusto Rodríguez will take you out on fishing and boat tours—talk to him about a trip around the south side of Ometepe to the tiny Isla de Quiste, where you can camp. In the same town, Carlos Loco is a local painter who has done some impressive paintings of Ometepe. From Barrio de los Pescadores, follow the path closest to the beach, which will lead you through hardwood forest, farms, and clusters of bamboo huts. Three kilometers past the little lagoon of Charco Pelota, you'll find the farm of César Mora; ask for permission to cut through, then follow the path up to the main road and cross it; walk back down the road toward Moyogalpa. An interesting side trip is the farm of Oscar Mora, which you'll reach via a small path on your left as you head back to town. From his farm, the view of the island is unforgettable, and his farm has other paths you can explore by asking his family for permission.

Accommodations

The nicest places on Ometepe are at Santo Domingo beach across the island, but Moyogalpa has a relatively large selection of budget beds. **Hotel Restaurant La Bahía** (located across from the Shell Station, tel. 505/841-2482, $4 pp) offers second-story rooms with tons of light and air, and a view of Concepción from the back porch. **Hotelito Ali** (tel. 505/569-4196) has nine rooms set around an ample garden patio for $5 pp with private bath. Ali also has a decent restaurant that serves breakfast, lunch, and dinner. Hospedaje Central is located six blocks from the dock, just ask around and you'll end up there; all the rest of Moyogalpa's hotels are main drag that you find by getting off the boat on the walking uphill.

Without a doubt, the most popular budget option is **M Hospedaje Central** (tel. 505/569-4262, hospedajecentralometepe@hotmail.com, 17 dorm beds for $2 each, $8/10/12 s/d/t with clean beds, private baths, and fans), spawned from its sister digs in Granada and the first place most backpackers turn for the familiar funkiness of which they are so fond; take a place in the 17-bed dormitory or camp outside for less. The bar/comedor has a world-music soundtrack and a satellite TV and movie lounge, plus plenty of hammocks. Services include a washing machine, book exchange, and tour arrangements. Artists are welcome to add to the organic murals and may even receive free lodging; and, of course, they've got the only espresso machine in Moyogalpa.

Treat yourself at **Hotel Ometepetl** (tel. 505/569-4278, $25 d with a/c and private bath). Service is professional and the staff is experienced at arranging tours, finding guides, and renting vehicles. They have a gift shop on site.

Bananas and plantains are two of Ometepe's principal exports.

VOLUNTEERING IN OMETEPE

Where else but the "Oasis of Peace" would you expect to find so much good work going on? Opportunities include participation in long-standing solidarity partnerships, lending a hand at one of various orphanages, sustainable agriculture work, and research projects.

Learn more about the **Bainbridge–Ometepe Sisters Island Association** (www.bosia.org), and start by buying a bag of fair trade–, organic-, shade-certified coffee, grown at Finca Magdalena—profits are sent back to Nicaragua in the form of development projects around the town of Balgüe.

There are several projects on the island that lend a hand to street kids and glue sniffers from around Nicaragua; a high level of Spanish is recommended, as this can be frustrating, difficult work (and equally rewarding, of course). One is the residential center of **Sí a la Vida** (www.asalv.org), an organization that welcomes international volunteers who can expect to, according to their website, work directly with the kids in sports, arts, handicrafts, and tutoring, as well as specialized services like health care, construction, and agriculture. Volunteers also accompany Nicaraguan staff in the streets and markets of Managua. (To volunteer, contact Bob and Millie Royce, U.S. tel. 206/842-8517, bomiki@bainbridge.net). There's also the **Quincho Barrilete** chapter in the town of San José del Sur, known to accept volunteers.

In the community of San Lázaro, just to the east of Punta Jesús María, is the **Nuestros Pequeños Hermanos** (NPH, www.nphamigos.org) orphanage, run by Our Little Brothers and Sisters, who provide "a Christian family environment based on unconditional acceptance and love, sharing, working and responsibility." Adopt a godchild, come for a visit, or visit their website to apply to their volunteer program.

In the community of Santa Cruz, you'll find the **Fundación Entre Volcánes** (tel. 505/569-4118), which runs projects all over Maderas and may well be in your time frame, should you get tired of just snoozing on the beach and want to lend a hand. Contact Raúl Mayorga or Martín Juarez for details—Raúl works in Moyogalpa (two blocks south and one block east of the Shell station, tel. 505/882-5562) and Martín is based out of the town of Los Angeles (Ometepe, not California).

The Ometepe Biological Field Station in San Ramón collaborates with the Washington, D.C.–based **Smithsonian Institution Migratory Bird Center** in their "Bridging the Americas" educational program for school children of both Nicaragua and the United States. To volunteer, send a brigade, support financially, or to donate educational equipment, like field guides and binoculars, contact Mary Deinlein at the National Zoo (U.S. tel. 202/673-4908), or Alvaro Molina in Nicaragua (tel. 505/453-0875, merida@ibw.com.ni), or visit their website, www.lasuerte.org. Alvaro can also get you involved with local schools in the town of Merida—feel free to bring supplies down for local teachers.

The rooms at **Hotel Casa Familiar** ($10 pp with a/c) are clean and the beds comfy.

Food

All the aforementioned accommodations serve food, the nicest of which can be found at the restaurant at Ometepetl, with meals about $5. **La Casa Familiar** is popular for basic Nica fare, like chicken, steak, fish, and sandwiches. In addition to standard backpacker lunches and dinners (spaghetti, burritos, etc.), **Hospedaje Central** serves a large breakfast—important if you're off to hike the big hill. Doña Esperanza Jimenez, a half-block east of the park, serves huge, inexpensive meals.

M Los Ranchitos (4 blocks up the hill from the dock, then 0.5 block south, tel. 505/569-4112, open daily 7 A.M.–9 P.M.) is a favorite among locals and Peace Corps Volunteers with a huge menu and surprisingly good pizza (large pie for only $6). Los Ranchitos also has rooms for rent and taxi service.

Services
The ENITEL office is located 1.5 blocks east of the main street, closed on Sundays. The Moyogalpa hospital (tel. 505/569-4247) is three blocks east of the park along the highway out of town. For Internet, go to the Arcia Cyber Café, which is air-conditioned and open daily from 8 A.M.– 9 P.M., or continue up the main street and use one of the computers at the Museo. The nearest cash machine is in Rivas and the only place that accepts traveler's checks is Hotel Ometepetl (minus 10 percent).

Getting Away
Buses leave from the dock, travel straight up the hill along the main street, stop at the park, then head east out of town (except for the rare few that turn left, passing through La Flor and San Marcos on their way to Altagracia). The bus schedule changes from week to week, but in general, there's a bus to meet every boat. For the most up-to-date schedule, ask around the dock, or look for a posting in the tour offices or Hospedaje Central. On Sundays, it's safe to assume there is no bus service at all—not completely true, but you're better off believing it: buses are few and far between.

NEAR MOYOGALPA
San Marcos
Just northeast of Moyogalpa along the "back way around the island" is the small community of San Marcos, home to a women's group that makes and sells ceramic pieces, including authentic replicas of pre-Columbian art. Ask around in town for the *taller de artesanía*.

ℳ Punta Jesús María
The long, sandy peninsula of Punta Jesús María is lovely for swimming and absorbing a bit of island tranquility. At the end of the sandy spit, a small recreational center complete with run-down playground and coolers of cold beer await you. This is a good place to catch a sunset or kill

THE LEGEND OF CHICO LARGO

Over the years, this famous legend has taken two forms. In the first version, an old man by the name of Chico Largo lives in the wetlands of Charco Verde. There he appears to people at night and offers to make a deal with them: wealth and prosperity during the entirety of their lives, in exchange for their souls, which upon death, he converts into cattle. Many of the cows on the island, then, are the souls of Ometepe's previous generation, which opted for a life of decadence instead of hard work.

In the second version, the cacique Nicarao is buried with his throne made of solid gold along the edge of the Charco Verde. In this version, Chico Largo is a descendant of Nicarao and roams the area guarding and protecting Nicarao's tomb. Chico Largo, since he is already guarding the tomb, has now taken it upon himself to guard the forest, animals, and fish as well, and is the primary protector of Ometepe's wildlife.

an afternoon relaxing and soaking your bones. Talk with the owner, Joaquín Salazar, about setting up your tent on the beach and spending the night with the crickets and the lapping of the lake washing up on the sandy shore. He's usually agreeable about camping if you've been buying beer from him. Otherwise, make friends and hitch a ride. Taxis from Moyogalpa charge about $7 each way.

ℳ Reserva Charco Verde
At Charco Verde you can swim in the lake to the call of monkeys in the trees and watch colorful birds whiz over your head. This is still a relatively wild area, with enough tall trees remaining to house some very exciting wildlife. The entire area has been cordoned off to prevent development, leaving this cove an oasis of peace to be shared by you and the monkeys (who, incidentally, do their own part by throwing excrement at intruders from the trees—seriously).

There are three places to stay in this area, each owned by a different Rivera brother or sister.

The beach at Charco Verde is one of Nicaragua's more beautiful.

They all offer boat trips along the shoreline to fish or to reach Isla de Quiste, and rent horses. They have a cattle farm just up the beach—ask if you can visit and milk some cows. **Hospedaje Charco Verde** ($18 per room or $5 pp—strange but true) is right next to the reserve with easy trail access. At **La Posada de Chico Largo** (tel. 505/886-4069 or 505/830-7608, chicolargo @yahoo.com, $4 dorm beds or $5 pp for room with private bath), you can eat three great meals and enjoy the pleasant company of the owners, who are great folks in spite of their nickname, "Los Diablos." For starters, ask about La Mirador del Diablo trail.

Up the beach a way (toward Moyogalpa), Rubén Riveras runs a family-style guesthouse on the beach called **Hotel Finca Venecia;** eight cabins (3–5 beds each) run for $25–50 and there are four rooms for $5 pp. It's one km to the nearest stretch of beach but the hammock pavilion is quiet and pacific and access to Charco Verde is easy. Rubén rents horses and bikes for exploring the island. The restaurant serves well-prepared pasta, chicken, fish, and beef dishes. From his place, it's an easy walk along the shore into the reserve of Charco Verde and to Playa Balcón. A

voluntary contribution is requested to maintain the reserve—$1–2 is appropriate.

Isla de Quiste

An island off of an island, Quiste means cyst in Spanish, probably in reference to its small size. It's overgrown and vacant, and a scant 100 meters long—a perfect place to pitch a tent and camp. To get there, all you need to do is make arrangements with someone with a small boat. In Charco Verde, Rubén Riveras has a motorboat and will make trips out to the island. He'll drop you off on the island and pick you up again later (or the next day) for about $15, depending on the number of travelers. But you can also try to strike a deal with any of the locals in the small communities to the north of Moyogalpa, like Barrio de los Pescadores.

Valle Verde and El Tesoro del Pirata

The pirate's treasure is, in this case, an isolated retreat on a wide, black-sand beach in-between the two volcanoes of La Isla. Reach the cove by hiking through the Charco Verde Reserve or by getting off the bus at the entrance just beyond the community of San José del Sur, then walking 15 minutes or so from the highway, following the

Rivas and La Isla Ometepe

signs. **El Tesoro** (tel. 505/832-2429, $25d/$30t for cabaña with a/c and private bath, camping for $2 pp) is located on the backside of the volcano, so you may hear the monkeys as you sit at the beachside restaurant and eat some of the best fish on the island. And that cabin price drops quickly if you show up with friends. Rent a tent for $6 if you need one. The views are fine, so is the swimming and boating. Enjoy!

ALTAGRACIA

The second largest community on Ometepe, and an important island port, Altagracia is more picturesque than Moyogalpa, but a little harder to get to. In 2000, *National Geographic* filmed a documentary about vampire bats here—and while there are indeed many vampire bats, they are a threat only to the local chickens, which the bats like to suck dry by hanging from the chickens' nerveless feet.

Sights and Entertainment

Altagracia's *fiestas patronales,* in celebration of San Diego, are held November 12–18. In addition to the traditional festivities common to other Nicaraguan towns, the Baile de las Ramas (Dance of the Branches) is a major component of the celebration. The dancers tear off smaller branches of the guanacaste tree, and hold them to their heads while dancing to imitate the worker *zompopo* ants carrying leaves off to the ant hills. Though the Spanish colonials claimed it was in honor of their successful fight against the ants, the locals claim it is an ancient dance in honor of gods that long predated the Spanish.

El Museo Ometepe (open 9 A.M.–5 P.M. daily, travelers pay $1) has a few exhibits of the flora, fauna, and archaeology of Ometepe, including statues and ceramic pieces unearthed around the island.

Accommodations

Altagracia's three lodgings are located within a block of each other, so feel free to walk around and compare before settling in. **M Hotel Central** (tel. 505/552-8770, $4 pp for a private bath and fan, $7 pp for a more private cabin out back) is a favorite, boasting a nicely furnished reading room, small gardens, and friendly staff. The owner of Central, Oscar Flores, is related to the owners of the two fancy hotels in Playa Santo Domingo and he'll be glad to drive you out there for a small fee.

Hotel Castillo (tel. 505/552-8744, $3 pp for room with shared bath, $4 private bath) offers similar services. The pleasant wooden deck at **Hotel Don Kencho** (tel. 505/552-8774, $6 s with private bath) overlooks the street.

Services

You'll find decent local information and a computer at the **Camara de Turismo** in the park. The **ENITEL** phone office and the post office are found diagonally across from the park on the same corner as the Museo Ometepe. The **Casa Cural,** located on the south side of the park, has six computers and Internet service Monday–Friday. There's also one computer at **Tienda Fashion,** a block south of the park. You'll have no privacy there, as the computer is located in the middle of the store, but it's open late and on weekends. Check out the crafts while you're waiting.

The small **Centro de Salud** (on the southeast corner of the park, tel. 505/552-6089) can treat patients 24 hours a day, but for serious injuries you should find a way to get to the hospital at Moyogalpa (get the owner of your hotel to take you in a vehicle).

NEAR ALTAGRACIA

From the park, walk east down a sandy road about 30 minutes to the bay of Playa Tagüizapa, a fine sandy beach for swimming. You can pick up supplies in town for a picnic and make a lazy day of it.

Located three kilometers north of the town of Altagracia, the port has boat service between Granada and San Carlos (Río San Juan). The road that leads to the port is shady and makes a nice, short walk—allow about 45 minutes each way. On the way, you'll pass Playa Paso Real, an out-of-the-way bathing beach you'll likely have all to yourself. If you're heading to the port to catch the boat to Granada or San Carlos, it's worth your while to speak with the owner of Hotel

Central. They offer pickup truck service to the port, so you don't have to carry all your luggage that far. Be aware that when the water is too rough, the boat may not show up at Altagracia, preferring to hug the eastern shore of the lake.

PLAYA SANTO DOMINGO

The narrow wedge of land that connects the volcanoes of Concepción and Maderas is a strip of rich volcanic soil that washed down from the slopes and joined the two islands. The swampy river that meanders through the center of the isthmus is the Istián, and paddling its waters, with a volcano on either side, you can be breathtaking (see the section on Merida). There is also the nearby Ojo de Agua, which makes a popular hike and dip.

Playa Santo Domingo is a several-kilometer-long stretch of black sand on the northern part of the Isthmus Istián, offering Ometepe's most upscale accommodations, relatively speaking. The swimming can be nice, but with the near-constant onshore breeze, the water is usually choppy.

Rent a charming stone cabin at **Villa Paraíso** (tel. 505/563-4675, ometepe@hotelvillaparaiso.com, www.hotelvillaparaiso.com, $20 per couple with private bath and a/c, $55 for suites with a/c, fridge, satellite TV, and hot water, $12 s/$18 d for small, simple rooms upstairs). The breezy water front restaurant is fabulous. Call early for reservations as the place fills up quickly, especially on weekends and holidays. Right next door, **Hotel Finca Santo Domingo** (tel. 505/552-8761) offers a handful of boxy cement rooms for $15–30, some with a/c.

Just two kilometers farther down the beach is the far more comfortably priced (and just as good) **Casa Hotel Istiam** (tel. 505/868-8682, $8 pp for rooms with private bath, $5 pp for rooms with shared bath), which faces a cleaner beach and a broader horizon, including a spectacular view of Volcán Maderas, than the previous two places; you can camp here as well. There is one $20 double with a/c and private bath, and friendly service and a good restaurant cinch the deal. Make reservations while in Moyogalpa at Hotel Ometepetl.

 LAGUNA DE VOLCÁN MADERAS

After crossing the isthmus, you'll come to a fork in the road near the settlement of Santa Cruz. Turning left takes you to a pair of backpacker-oriented settlements, both extremely rustic.

A ten-minute walk up the trail from the village of El Madroñal leads to **La Finca Ecologica El Zopilote** ($3 pp, tents available for camping), a hillside cluster of creative thatch huts and platforms run by a few peace-loving Italians and their pack of hounds. A couple of private, stilted rooms go for $10 a couple. Meals are not provided, but there is an open-air kitchen where you can fix your own meals; the compound also has compost toilets, an artisan's workshop, and a clay oven for bread and pizza. Ask about their full-moon celebrations, Maya sweat lodge, or just enjoy the permaculture plantation throughout the grounds.

Just uphill from the town of Balgüe is the famed **Finca Magdalena** (tel. 505/880-2041, info@fincamagdalena.com, www.fincamagdalena .com), a coffee cooperative established in the

© JOSHUA BERMAN

Playa Santo Domingo stretches between Ometepe's twin peaks.

Rivas and La Isla Ometepe

© RANDY WOOD

Volcán Maderas

1980s on land confiscated from the Maltodano family. The Finca Magdalena, besides being a working coffee plantation involving 27 families, also offers a lodge and guesthouse and immediate access to the attractions of Volcán Maderas. Magdalena has been a must-see stop on the Central America backpacker trail for a decade; its barnlike, second-story dormitory offers beds for less than $2, or get a partitioned, more secure stall for $5 d or even a private hut for $15. Campsites are available. Everyone showers in the same bracing cold water piped directly from a spring up the slope.

Their new satellite Internet connection may be a precursor to linking a good part of Ometepe via wireless Ethernet—but don't get so caught up checking your email that you forget to watch the moon set over the silhouette of Concepción while eating fresh farm cooking hot from the wood stove ($1–3). Be sure to take home some fresh honey or roasted coffee as a souvenir—it's a good way to help support the farm.

Local guides can take you the rest of the way up the volcano and are very likely mandatory after a pair of hikers got lost and eventually died up on the mountain. While the hike to the crater is thrilling, it's also a grueling mud-slog year-round. Easier hikes take you to the pre-Columbian petroglyphs scattered throughout the grounds (you won't find them on your own). Horseback rides and coffee tours are also available—contact them about volunteer and work opportunities.

To get to the Finca Magdalena, take the bus to Balgüe and follow signs up the hill. From the road, it's a 20-minute walk up the road to the farm (it's easier if you arrive before dark). Five daily buses depart the dock in Moyogalpa, the last at 3:30 P.M.

On the road toward San Ramón, keep an eye out for the left-hand entrance to the **Albergue Ecológico El Porvenir** (tel. 505/552-8770, $4 pp, shared bath), a wonderful hillside retreat with modern buildings, incredible views, and a full menu of food and activities. See the owners of Hotel Central in Altagracia or Hotel Villa Paraíso for more information about transport and booking.

Merida

Some 250 families get by on Maderas's southwestern shore, mostly by fishing and growing basic grains and *platanos*. Merida was the site of a Somoza coffee hacienda before the revolution, and the ruins of the old mill and dock are now home to

Hotel Hacienda Merida (tel. 505/868-8973, merida@ibw.com.ni, www.lasuerte.org, $3–4 pp for basic, clean dorm beds, $6 pp for a room with private bath, camping for $1.50 pp), a quiet, lakeside compound whose friendly atmosphere and scarlet sunsets budget travelers are raving about. Busy yourself here with myriad activities—biking, hiking, fishing, paddling, horseback riding, and a fair amount of card playing and chess; windsurfing is coming soon. The menu is filled with wonderful Nicaraguan dishes, and the buffets ($3.50) are excellent—listen for that bell, Pavlov. Internet available. The Nicaraguan owner, Alvaro Molina, speaks perfect English and is a walking guidebook for Ometepe and beyond—he has also collected a great resource library for travelers and naturalists. Keep an eye out for his minivan in Granada and/or Peñas Blancas, which will whisk you straight to his boat at San Jorge, then take you to the Finca without having to endure the wretched bus ride across Ometepe.

Río Istián

The kayak ride from Merida to Río Istián is not to be missed, especially early in the morning or during the sunset. If the wind is up, it can be a difficult trip to get there (allow 1–2 hours of hard paddling), but as you enter the still waters of the marshy isthmus choked with all sorts of trees and birds under the reflection of the volcanic peaks, you will agree it was worth it. Bring plenty of water. The shorter paddle to Isla el Congo, just offshore, is nice as well, but beware the vicious spider monkeys!

A rigorous and none-too-obvious trail leads up to Maderas's crater lagoon and down the other side from Merida; hire a guide and get an early morning start. The Hotel Hacienda Merida offers this excursion, including transport back from Magdalena.

Two daily buses leave Moyogalpa for Merida at 8 A.M., 2:30 and 4:30 P.M., returning at 4 A.M.,

Paddling the Río Istián provides gorgeous views of both of Ometepe's volcanoes.

Rivas and La Isla Ometepe

8:30 A.M., and 3 P.M. The trip takes a bone-crunching 2.5 hours.

Ⓜ Cascada San Ramón

Four kilometers up the road from Merida, the tiny village of San Ramón is home to a biological station frequented by student groups and researchers from all over the world and, of late, tourists as well. The **Estación Biológica de Ometepe** (tel. 505/563-0875, ometepe@ibw.com.ni, from $10 pp for shared bath, to a $50 suite with TV, massive bed, and Jacuzzi) has a huge kitchen, as the staff here are accustomed to accommodating large groups. Researchers use the station's kayaks and small boats to explore the Río Istián.

The most popular attraction by far is the stunning 56-meter waterfall on the south slope of Maderas, visible at the end of a 2–3 hour hike up from the lake (a $2 pp fee is charged at the gate below, free for station guests). The signs say it is a three-kilometer trail, but that's probably an underestimation. You can drive your four-wheel drive vehicle part way up to the water tank for an extra few dollars; from there, it's less than an hour walk to the falls. Those kilometers are straight up hill, mind you, so don't overestimate your hiking prowess.

The sole bus to San Ramón leaves Moyogalpa at 8 A.M., returning daily at 2:30 P.M.

The East Coast of Maderas

The lonely east coast of Maderas is one of the most isolated spots in Nicaragua, connected tentatively by a poor excuse for a road that bears no buses. The locals are not used to receiving guests. This is good territory for a hike, as you circumnavigate the entire volcano (allow 12 hours for this lovely death march), or do it on one of Hotel Hacienda Merida's mountain bikes in about six hours. The coast of Tichana hides lots of unexplored secrets, including caves full of paintings, as well as some petroglyphs near Corozal.

GETTING AROUND OMETEPE

Buses leave Moyogalpa from the port, pass through the town park at the top of the hill, then head counterclockwise around the island to Altagracia (one or two go the other direction). From

The moss-adorned San Ramón waterfall is well worth the hike up.

Altagracia, buses depart for Moyogalpa and for the small towns of Maderas (San Ramón, Merida, Balgüe, and Santo Domingo). If you board a bus in Moyogalpa that's heading to Maderas, remember you'll pass through Altagracia first, where you'll spend 30 minutes waiting for more passengers before continuing on to Maderas. From Moyogalpa to Altagracia it's approximately one hour, and from Altagracia to Balgüe it's another hour. The island is bigger than you think.

On Sunday, the entire transportation system breaks down. Buses, which are scheduled infrequently anyway, may or may not run according to the whims of the driver. Ask a lot of questions if you want to travel by bus on Sundays.

Your best bet to cross the island is to either arrange a transfer with your hotel or *finca* beforehand, or to chip in with some friends and hire one of the many taxis that will mob you when you get off the ferry. The other option is to bring your own four-wheel drive vehicle (non-4WDs will be useless here). The *Ferry Ometepe* is the only vessel that accepts vehicles, though space is extremely limited and it's not cheap. If you're interested in taking your vehicle across with you, call 505/459-4284 at least 72 hours in advance, and then again the day before your trip to remind them of your reservation (more than one reservation has gotten lost). The price for transport of your vehicle will be $28 including all taxes, plus your passenger fare.

Rental Cars and Taxis

Likewise, you can rent vehicles while on Ometepe, but they're not cheap either. Check out Hotel Ometepetl's "fleet," usually a late-model Toyota or Suzuki Samurai; about $35 per 12 hours. Or hire a taxi in Moyogalpa. The representatives of taxi cooperatives usually linger at the port to drum up business as each boat arrives—don't worry, they'll find you. A taxi from Moyogalpa to the beach resort of Santo Domingo is around $15, though you have more leverage if you're traveling in a group.

ORGANIZED TOURS

The first operation you'll find is located near the ferry dock in San Jorge: **Ometepe Tours** (tel. 505/563-4779, or in Moyogalpa tel. 505/569-4242, maquipi1@hotmail.com, www.ometepe-tours.com.ni, $65 plus meals and boat fare) will arrange package tours of the island, including guides, vehicles, and hotel reservations. By the time your boat crosses the waters of Cocibolca, the arrangements will be made, and one of four Ometepe Tour vehicles will pick you up at the dock. It doesn't get much easier than that. This Nicaraguan family is friendly and honest and also provides the only day trip of Ometepe, leaving San Jorge at 9:30 A.M., then driving a relaxing five-hour loop around Concepción with well-planned visits to the sites, after which they'll have you back in San Jorge by 5 P.M., so you can hurry back to your hotel in San Juan del Sur.

After disembarking in Moyogalpa, you'll quickly find a few more tour-guide options, including **Ometepe Ecotours** (tel. 505/569-4244, hugonava@ibw.com.ni), **Ometepe Travel** (tel. 505/887-0191, discoverometepe@hotmail.com), and **Exploring Ometepe** (tel. 505/895-5521,

exploringometepe@hotmail.com); the last is home to locally famous guide, Berman Gómez (tel. 505/836-8360). All of these operations are reputable and offer fairly creative trips, but take some time to check out their literature before deciding which best suits your needs.

Most accommodations around the island will help to arrange tours as well, getting you up both volcanoes or on a number of hikes or horseback rides.

GETTING THERE AND AWAY

There are a handful of old, wooden (but safe) boats that ply the waters between San Jorge and the port at Moyogalpa, all of which you may share with boxes, bananas, cattle, and crowds of locals back from doing errands in Rivas and Managua. The *Ferry Ometepe* is a steel boat with radar and life jackets. One-way costs $2.

Lake Cocibolca can get rough when the wind is high. At those times, choosing a larger vessel may make all the difference between a leisurely ride and a tumultuous barf-fest. Avoid the rough seas by traveling early morning and late evening; the nicest ride is on the roof of the Ferry, where you'll avoid the crowds and enjoy the wide horizon. If you are prone to motion sickness, try to get a seat toward the center of the ship, where the pendulum motion will be less noticeable, and when the nausea comes on, fix your sight on the horizon.

Note that the various vessels are independently owned and, unfortunately, few will offer you honest information about the others, so if you're told, "The next boat doesn't leave for four hours," keep asking. Ometepe Tours (office near the port—look for the monkeys—tel. 505/563-4773) will give you good information.

From Granada and Onward to San Carlos

Though Granada was once the principal link with Ometepe, San Jorge has now surpassed it in importance. Even so, the stubborn old *Mozorola* (tel. 552-8764) makes the four-hour cruise twice a week, leaving Granada every Wednesday and Saturday at 11 A.M. and departing Ometepe (Altagracia) every Tuesday and Friday at 11 A.M.

ferry to Ometepe

Adverse weather conditions may cause the cancellation of the trip, but otherwise it's a great sail past the Isletas and along the coast of the island of Zapatera.

The *EPN* (Empresa Portuario de Nicaragua) ferry leaves Granada on Mondays and Thursdays at 3 P.M., arriving in Altagracia between 7 and 8 P.M. The ship continues onward to San Miguelito and San Carlos, arriving at 4–5 A.M. You can usually stay on the boat until the Río San Juan boats begin operating at 6 or 7 A.M. A first-class ticket costs a couple dollars more and earns you more room to hang a hammock.

On the return trip, the ferry leaves San Carlos on Tuesdays and Fridays at 2 P.M., passes Altagracia at 11 P.M., and arrives in Granada at 4 A.M. The price for a one-way passage between Granada and Ometepe is $3, but when seas are high, the ship will skip Ometepe altogether, preferring to hold tight to the lee shore of the lake.

San Juan del Sur and the Southwest Coast

Once a quiet fishing village in a forgotten corner of the country, San Juan del Sur is now Nicaragua's primary Pacific coast destination for both national and foreign tourists. Many of the pueblo's 18,000 residents still make a go at fishing, but most are putting their money on the steady stream of big-spending visitors that, after having been predicted for more than a decade, is finally here. Everyone and their mother is developing a new shuttle service, bar, surf camp, or *hospedaje*—but not to worry, it's all happening at a leisurely pace and, besides random annoying bursts of fireworks, San Juan is still a quiet village.

San Juan's principal resource is its perfect, protected harbor and its crescent beach, open to the setting sun and protected by El Indio (The Indian), whose silhouetted face hides in the rocky cliffs on the north end of the bay. Surf's up, but so is foreign investment. Fortunately in San Juan del Sur, business and pleasure mix easily, usually over

Must-Sees

Look for **M** to find the sights and activities you can't miss and **M** for the best dining and lodging.

M Sunset: Feel the earth turn downward, man, while sitting on San Juan del Sur's public beach; surfboard optional (page 131).

M Da Flyin Frog: This 17-platform canopy tour offers a lively forest and views of the ocean (page 132).

M La Flor Wildlife Refuge: Even if you miss the spectacular nighttime turtle-nesting events, a simple walk along this protected beach and up the forested river is remarkable (page 142).

M Bahía Majagual: There is a daily water taxi from San Juan's beach to this beauteous bay, but why not spend a night or two at the beachfront campground or hostel (page 144).

the beach at Bahía Majagual

© JOSHUA BERMAN

M Playa Gigante: Somewhere around here, a wave is arching around the point with no one around to ride it (page 146).

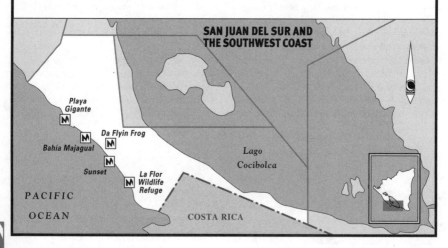

SAN JUAN DEL SUR AND
THE SOUTHWEST COAST

Playa
Gigante
M

Da Flyin Frog
M

Bahía Majagual

M

Sunset

La Flor
M Wildlife
Refuge

PACIFIC

OCEAN

COSTA RICA

Lago
Cocibolca

San Juan del Sur

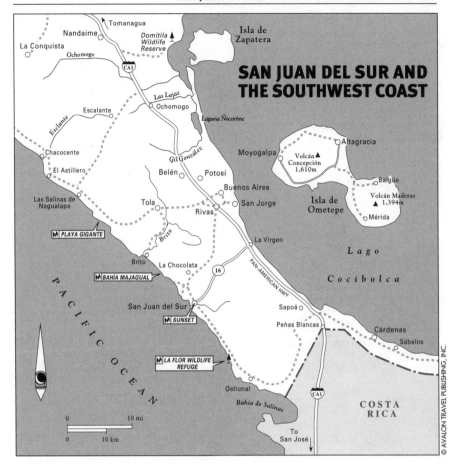

SAN JUAN DEL SUR AND THE SOUTHWEST COAST

© AVALON TRAVEL PUBLISHING, INC.

heaping plates of seafood, pasta, and fresh snapper. You're sure to cross paths with the land sharks, property pimps, and the frenzied flock of checkbook-toting prospectors madly scouring the coastline for a piece of the pie. Only in Granada is the interest more ravenous. Don't let the frenzy sour your mood. The beach is clean and mellow, and the evenings are rum-soaked and starry.

PLANNING YOUR TIME

To fully appreciate the San Juan del Sur area, a minimum of three days is required: one day in town, one beach trip north to Bajia Majagual or Playa Madera, and one south to Remanso, La Flor Wildlife Reserve, or the village of Ostional; plan an extra half-day for a canopy tour or sailing excursion. Also, if you're the type who can't get enough sunsets and fresh-fish dinners, you won't want to leave so quickly, and neither will surfers, especially when the swell's up.

SIGHTS AND SPORTS
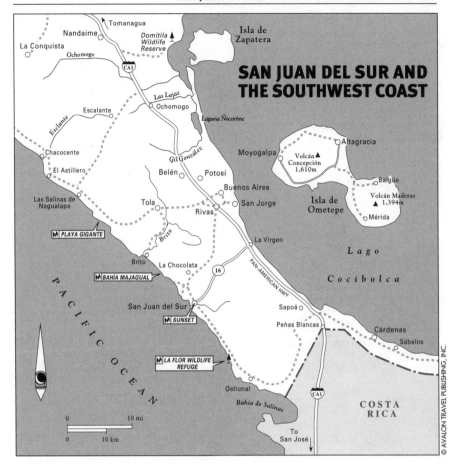 Sunset

The main show in town is the crimson tropical sunsets over the languid harbor waves, sometimes lasting for hours if conditions are right; make

San Juan del Sur

SAN JUAN DEL SUR

Río San Juan del Sur

OTANGANI BEACH

RESTAURANTE ROCAMAR

PIZZERÍA RISTORANTE 'O SOLE MIO

Bahía San Juan del Sur

RICARDO'S BAR

BEACHFRONT

MARIE'S

IGUANA BAR
RESTAURANTE EL TIMÓN

RD

BIG WAVE DAVE'S

CON-RAY

CYBER LEO'S

HOTEL BEACH FUN

HOTEL CASA BLANCA

HOTEL COSTA AZUL

CENTRAL

HOTEL ESTRELLA

JOXI

CALLE

HOTEL COLONIAL

MARKET ST

CASA ORO

RESTAURANTE EL GLOBO

HOTEL GRAN OCEANO

REBECCA'S INN

BANK

ALCALDÍA

FREDERICA'S B&B

PIZZERÍA SAN JUAN

TEXACO

To La Virgen

16

To Ostional

DIVE SHOP

HEALTH CLINIC

HOSTAL LA MARIMBA

HOTEL ROYAL CHATEAU

HOSPEDAJE NICARAGUA

MARKET/ BUS STOP

HOSPEDAJE ELIZABETH

LA FOGATA

LIBRARY

PELICAN EYES PIEDRAS Y OLAS RESORT

HOTEL VILLA ISABELLA

Central Park

CHURCH

TOWN DOCK

CASA DE CULTURA/ NICARAGUA SPANISH SCHOOL

WATER TANK

DOÑA ROSA SILVA'S SPANISH SCHOOL

RICHARD MORALES TAXI SERVICE

ENITEL/ POST OFFICE

POLICE

SCALE NOT AVAILABLE

© AVALON TRAVEL PUBLISHING, INC.

sure you're on the beach with a cocktail in hand, or bobbing in the surf, watching the silhouetted fishing boats and waiting for the next set to roll in.

 Da Flyin Frog Canopy Tour

The newest canopy tour in the country and arguably the best, **Da Flyin Frog** (tel. 505/611-6214, tiguacal@ibw.com.ni, $25 pp) is a popular 17-platform, two-kilometer ride through the trees with stunning views of the sea; located just outside town on the mayor's cattle ranch on the Chocolata road, closed Mondays.

Hikes from Town

As the property around San Juan del Sur gets chopped up, bought, and sold, the new influx of property owners may have mixed reactions to hikers cutting across their plots. Be sensitive to this and always ask permission when possible.

The **lighthouse** is easily reachable (two hours round-trip) and offers fantastic views up the coast and south to Costa Rica. Walk south to the town port, go through the main gate, then through a smaller one next to the new building. Follow the trail up the hill, past an angry herd of goats, and through one of the last local pelican nesting areas (tread lightly); fork right and continue to the lighthouse—turning left brings you to the ruins of the old fort.

For a viewpoint from the **antennas,** take a bus toward Rivas and ask the driver to let you off at Bocas de las Montañas. From there, head up through the trees and pastures to the breezy and beautiful *mirador* (lookout)—an hour each way.

There are some 1,700-year-old **petroglyphs** accessible via a 1.5-hour countryside walk beginning east of the Texaco station. Take a left (north), pass the school, and walk right through a gate after about 500 meters; find the farmhouse and ask permission to cut through. Consider asking for a local guide. If not, follow the water pipes and the river until you find the stone. Continue upstream to reach the waterfalls, impressive only during the rainy season—wear good shoes and long pants to avoid being stung by the nettle-like *pica-pica* plant.

Some of the closer beaches, north and south of town, make for good day hikes as well, as does rock-hopping the northern curve of the bay and around the point—mind the tides and bring drinking water to counter the sun exposure you'll experience.

Surfing

He moved on to Nicaragua, where the surf apparently hadn't dropped below head-high since prehistoric times.

Allan C. Weisbecker

Surfing is a personal and spiritual pursuit considered more an art form than a sport by its true followers. Nevertheless, the modern world is one in which 17-year-old kids are paid $100,000 a year to surf, and magazines cover their lives as though they were rock stars. There is ferocious competition worldwide for the best waves and Nicaragua is one of the last countries on the planet to be overrun by this phenomenon, despite plentiful Pacific beaches and the incredible phenomenon of nearly year-round offshore winds.

Many of the beaches listed further in this chapter (and many more that are not mentioned) have world-class surf breaks, which the dedicated

will have little trouble finding. But forget about San Juan del Sur proper, whose bay is mostly calm, save the occasional, perfect waist- or shoulder-high swell when the winds are right. For more detailed information, check out online surf reports for Nicaragua, or seek out local knowledge from the folks listed below. Many of the best breaks are only accessible by boat, so pull a group together to pitch in for the diesel.

See local shredders Byron and Kervin López in their shop, **Arena Caliente,** next to the market. They run trips for as little as $20 a person, rent and sell boards, take boat trips to local breaks, and provide car rides to Madera for $6 pp. Also, track down local characters Chelo, Geo, or "El Rana" (The Frog), a.k.a. Alberto Granada, for beach tours by boat.

Dale Dagger (tel. 505/568-2492, ddagger@ibw.com.ni, www.nicasurf.com) has been scouting breaks for more than a decade, ever since he shipwrecked on the shore nearby. Find him in his shop on the east end of town and ask about booking a trip on his boat, *La Masayita*—the coolest excursion in town. For rates, visit his website. He'll book your trip from home with week-long packages based either in local upscale hotels or in one of his rustic lodges on an isolated beach up the coast.

For more information, see the surf camp and charter services in the Tola section in this chapter.

Fishing, Sailing, and Diving

Try your hand hooking sailfish, shark, snappers, tuna, or anything else that takes a bite. Ask around town for Superfly, or book a trip with Richard of Ricardo's Bar ($350 gets you six hours, food, alcohol, and, maybe, a big one). Anyone else with a boat probably has something to offer as well, including all the surf and dive shops and a number of hotels, including El Pacifico. Geo is good for customized fishing trips or cruises, just ask around in front of Hotel Estrella to find him.

Take Chris Berry's *Pelican Eyes* for an all-day jaunt (find him in his hotel, Piedras y Olas, or tel. 505/568-2110, pelican@ibw.com.ni), lunch on a deserted beach, and an open bar all day; $60 pp for day cruises or surf charters. As for diving, this is not the Caribbean, but when conditions

San Juan del Sur

Catch of the day: San Juan del Sur fishermen haul a load of dorados to market.

are right, there's a great wreck dive ($60 for two tanks) and certification courses are offered ($240 open water) out of the dive shop just west of the Texaco station (tel. 505/867-8194, fidellop@hotmail.com, www.abucear.com).

SHOPPING

During weekends, holidays, and cruise-ship arrivals, there are numerous street vendors from all over selling clothes, hammocks, jewelry, and other artesanía. **El Papagayo Artesanía** is a French-owned shop with goods from around the world, open 9 A.M.–7 P.M.

ENTERTAINMENT AND EVENTS

Like any tropical beach town, San Juan del Sur's party is mellow and year-round, but the excitement spikes during Christmas, New Year's, and Semana Santa. During these times, the town is flooded with visitors, many of them young, well-off Nicaraguans who pack the many street and beach parties. During the rest of the year, the town's only disco, **Otangani Beach,** is open Thursday–Sunday, and **Ricardo's** offers a "movie night" Mondays and Thursdays. In the town center, look for the neon glow of **Conray's Bar,** a lively spot with drinks and *bocas,* (appetizers) open from 6 P.M. to late-night.

The *fiestas patronales* takes place June 16–24, but you may find the events of July 17 even more interesting—the Procesión de la Virgen del Carmen is a celebration of the Patron Saint of Fishermen. Locals parade the icon through town, and finally to the docks where waiting boats take her (and most of the townspeople) for a lap around the bay. September 2 is the commemoration of the tidal wave of 1992, a 60-foot monster that swept across main street, destroying many structures (and whole villages, like El Tránsito, farther up the coast).

VOLUNTEERING IN SAN JUAN DEL SUR

Fortunately for the community, the environment, and the children of San Juan del Sur, a growing number of expats and tourists arrive with a genuine desire to give something back to this beautiful corner of the country. Following is some information on a few of those efforts and how you can contribute. Note that some of the projects listed below are supported by 501(c)(3) organizations in the United States, making your donation tax deductible.

There are several opportunities to **teach English** in San Juan del Sur, either at the school near the park (El Centro Escolar, contact La Directora, Anna Louisa Mora Mune) or at the Women's Center (Casa de las Mujeres, located behind the Texaco station, contact Mayra); ask about volunteering in exchange for a free or reduced-price homestay with a family. Teaching materials are available in the town library, where you can ask about further teaching opportunities.

A. Jean Brugger and Chris Berry created the **Fundación A. Jean Brugger** (tel. 505/568-2110, ajbfund@ibw.com.ni, www.sanjuandelsur.org.ni/community/brugger) in 2000 to support the education and training of the promising young people

Donate your time, money or books to San Juan's lending library, across from the Catholic Church.

of San Juan del Sur. The Foundation provides scholarships, uniforms, school supplies, and job training for dedicated area students. It also supports anti-litter campaigns and, since Pelican Eyes Piedras y

Olas Hotel underwrites most administrative costs, nearly 100 percent of your donation goes to helping the students. Monetary donations are always needed and materials, such as school supplies and children's socks, are appreciated as well. In addition, the foundation maintains a 10-acre nature preserve on the hillside behind Piedras y Olas, which, hopefully, will soon accommodate hikers.

The local book-lending project has been a smashing success in a country largely devoid of lending libraries. The **San Juan del Sur Biblioteca Movil** is located across the street from the park and, besides offering books and reading space to San Juaneños, brings books to young and old in outlying communities. The project was founded by Jane Mirandette (janem101@aol.com), the proprietress of Hotel Villa Isabella and is supported by a U.S.-based nonprofit organization, the Hester J. Hodgdon Libraries for All Program. Besides helping monetarily, tourists can volunteer at the library, teaching English, organizing books, or reading to youngsters, and books in Spanish are always welcome. If you can't bring them to Nicaragua, you can send Spanish-language books to a storage space at: 1716 Del Norte Blvd., Loveland, CO, 80538 (visiting Coloradans who bring a suitcase of books from Loveland get a free night in Jane's hotel).

San Juan del Sur has no fewer than five sister cities around the world: two in Germany, one in Spain, one in Norway, and one in Massachusetts. The **Newton–San Juan del Sur Sister City Project** (david.gullettte@simmons.edu, www.newtonsanjuan.org) sends brigades down twice a year (medical, dental, optical, construction, teaching English, etc.) and also directly supports the library project. To make a tax-deductible contribution, send a check to Treasurer Fiora Houghteling, 15 Bullough Park, Newton, MA 02460. The local contact in San Juan is Rosa Elena Bello at the Servicios Medicos Comunales (rosaebel@ibw.com.ni).

The **Pangea Partnership** (www. pangeapartnership.org) offers a unique program to provide workshops in sustainable development construction techniques, like straw-bale houses, for mixed groups of Nicaraguan students and foreigners. Workshops typically run 10–14 days; be prepared to roll up your sleeves and sweat.

© JOSHUA BERMAN

San Juan del Sur

ACCOMMODATIONS

San Juan lodging runs the gamut from grungy hostels to luxury hotels. Nearly all the cheapest *hospedajes* are on the main street, are Nicaraguan-owned, and are usually extensions of someone's home. There are two principal streets; your bus or taxi will let you off on the one with the market, which runs perpendicular to the beach and is lined with a dozen *hospedajes*. The beachfront road has a few nicer hotels and most of San Juan's restaurants and bars. The sole disco is at the northern terminus of the beach road.

Under $10

Dozens of family-run, cheap *hospedajes* compete to be your pillow; feel free to walk the streets and compare before settling down for the night. One of the first places you'll come to as you enter town is **M Hostal La Marimba** (tel. 505/568-2491, lamarimba@mercadeo.com, $5 for a bunk or $15 for a double with private bath), a spotless, safe cluster of five rooms with shared kitchen and BBQ space, and excellent attention from Lilly, your host.

At the east end of market street, **Elizabeth's** (tel. 505/568-2270) is a tucked-away two-story affair, with 19 tiny, wood-floor rooms starting at $5 for shared bath, or $12 for the newer rooms with private bath. Elizabeth is a sweetheart, and the atmosphere is usually pretty quiet.

You'll find a few more similar places as you walk toward the beach, including **Hospedaje La Fogata,** which has been around for 40 years and has the biggest open-air common space of them all. The 11 rooms and three toilet stalls are nothing special, and the space is a bit gloomy, but Jennifer is a native San Juaneña with a wealth of local knowledge and history, and rooms are only $4. Turn right at the next corner for **Hotel Beach Fun** (formerly Casa 28, tel. 505/568-2441, $3.50 shared bath, $7 pp private bath), an 18-year-old *hospedaje* in a 90-year-old building. The 16 rooms are run-down, but the open courtyard is nice and so are the owners. **Hotel Costa Azul** (tel. 505/568-4294, $7 pp for the seven rooms, or $20 d for a/c and TV) also looks *tranquilo* and clean, although you'll be sharing

your common space with customers of the in-house Internet café.

Where the market street reaches the sea, you'll find **Hotel Estrella** on your left (tel. 505/568-2210, hotelestrella1929@hotmail.com), reportedly the first hotel in San Juan del Sur, constructed in 1929. Less glamorous than in its glory years, Estrella is still the only place in town where you get an oceanfront balcony for $5 a person. Drawbacks include having to walk downstairs to use the bathroom and the bats, unless you're into that sort of thing.

Casa Oro (rockettom@hotmail.com) is a dorm-style youth hostel in a big, old, wooden building just west of the central park; $5 a night gets you a bunk bed, access to the kitchen, and a hammock by the garden, $6 pp for a private room.

$10–25

Well recommended is the welcoming feeling at **Rebecca's Inn** (tel. 505/600-7512, martha _urcuyo@yahoo.es), run by Martha, who grew up in this house and can tell you about the local lore in English; $13–15 for doubles, kitchen use, and parking.

The small space of **Casa Internacional Joxi** (tel. 505/568-2483, casajoxi@ibw.com.ni) is efficiently developed into two floors, with a great balcony and 12 rooms starting at $15/30 s/d (a/c, TV, shared or private bath). Joxi has always been a bargain and well liked, but recent management changes have led to several complaints regarding surly service and staff, including one involving an unsolved theft.

$25–50

On your left as you roll into town (before turning right onto the market street toward the ocean) is the Nicaraguan-owned 20-room **Royal Chateau Hotel** (tel. 505/568-2551, $35 with a/c, private bath, TV, $25 without a/c). Right across from the beach, the **Hotel Casa Blanca** (tel. 505/568-2135, casablanca@ibw.com.ni, $46/50 s/d plus tax) is first-rate, with a small pool, parking, laundry, breakfast, and 24-hour security.

Hotel Colonial (a half block from the park, tel. 505/568-2227, $44s), has 12 cramped rooms with private bath, TV, a/c, and continental breakfast.

Right around the corner, **Hotel Gran Océano** (tel. 505/568-2219, $40/44/50 s/d/t) offers similar rows of small rooms with the same amenities as the Colonial. **Hotel El Pacifico** (tel. 505/568-2557, pacifico@ibw.com.ni, rooms from $35–55, including breakfast) is located across the river in the Barrio El Talanguera, well-removed from the hustle and bustle of the city. Get there via the Chocolata road turnoff at the gas station before entering San Juan. Rooms are basic and comfortable, with wood floors, a/c, private bath, parking, pool, restaurant, and bar. Ask about their fishing/beach trips.

$50–$100

Across from the water, **Frederica's B & B** (tel. 505/568-2489, rapido1@ibw.com.ni) has a pair of lovely, fully equipped doubles for $50, or $55 with a/c. The popular  **Hotel Villa Isabella** (tel. 505/568-2568, jane101@aol.com, www.sanjuandelsur.org.ni/isabella, $65 for a queen bed with private bath, a/c, TV/VCR, and a full breakfast) is a spotless, sparkling white 13-room bed-and-breakfast on the east side of town, a two-minute walk to the beach. Isabella also offers four spacious condos: $95 for one bedroom, $150 for two; discounts available throughout the year. You'll also find a small pool, business services, handicapped access, and a huge selection of free movies and DVDs. Their signature breakfast is not meager continental affair: You'll get homemade waffles, cinnamon rolls, banana pancakes, eggs your way, fresh fruit, and great coffee.

Over $100

Pelican Eyes Piedras y Olas (tel. 505/568-2511, www.piedrasyolas.com, pelican@ibw.com.ni) has raised the bar in San Juan del Sur and Nicaragua. This compound of straw-bale and adobe villas built into the hillside on the east end of town is one of the most creative and gorgeous upscale accommodations in the country, complete with a top-notch bar, restaurant, and infinity pool overlooking the ocean. The 15 rooms range from $90–135 for a double, full breakfast included,

© JOSHUA BERMAN

The pool, bar, and restaurant at Pelican Eyes Piedras y Olas Resort share the same magnificent tableau of the bay.

San Juan del Sur

plus tax; rooms include a/c, TV, kitchenette, and lovely outdoor decks, and are built against a 10-acre nature reserve.

FOOD AND BARS
Cheap and Local
Eat three *corriente* meals a day at one of the counters inside the municipal market—under $2 a meal. Evenings, try one of the *fritangas* across from Hospedaje Elizabeth's, or walk to the southwest corner of the park for **Asados Vilma,** a.k.a. The Chicken Lady, with grilled meat dishes and mountains of *gallo pinto* from $2.

Nearly every *hospedaje* and hotel, and some of the beach restaurants make a variety of breakfasts, usually for $2–3. Start with the Iguana, which serves a formidable, bacon-and-egg breakfast all day long from 7:30 A.M. Iguana also has Internet service, bar, restaurant, and boogie-board rentals.

Seafood and Típico
A long row of virtually identical thatched-roof Nicaraguan ranchos lines the middle part of the beach. Most of these restaurants have excellent seafood, with fish dishes from $4 and shrimp and lobster dishes from $9–12. Of note is the seafood soup at **Rocamar,** located at the north end of the beach road. **Marie's** maintains a reputation for fine cuisine, with wonderful pasta and veggie dishes, in addition to seafood. This can be a fun, cozy bar as well, open every evening except Monday.

N Ricardo's Bar (tel. 505/568-2502, ricardosbar@yahoo.com) serves European dishes, burgers, and tasty appetizers, like a shrimp quesadilla that is out of this world. Come for the food, stay for the drinks—or vice-versa. Ricardo's book exchange, beach chairs, and movie nights (Monday and Thurday) are well-appreciated, and the bar is renowned for having possibly the best bar service in the country. Its proprietors, Marie and Richard, are a wealth of knowledge if you are looking for something to do besides damage your credit card (and liver) by swilling tequila sunrises all afternoon.

Another mellow bar with great food, including a monster Philly cheese steak, is **Big Wave Dave's,** open early for breakfast and serving bar food, drinks, and darts all day long, meals from $4. For the late-night bar scene, be sure to sample the mayhem at **Las Flores,** down the block from the market; they also rent rooms and the proprietress, Mache, is great for local knowledge and gossip.

Italian
Walking north on the beach road, you'll find the **N Pizzería Ristorante O Sole Mio** (tel. 505/568-2101, open 5:30–9:30 P.M. Tues.–Fri., 11:30 A.M.–10 P.M. weekends), with its authentic pizza and Italian dishes, imported wine, and a seafood pasta to die for. Meals, including pizza, start at $5. Open since 1997, O Sole Mio closes during the week in the off season. **Pizzería San Juan** (open from 5 P.M. daily) is run by another Italian expat and is centrally located right off the park's southwest corner. Don Maurizio's homemade pastas are delicious, especially when smothered in lobster sauce and served with wine from the homeland. Check out his fantastic pizza, sold by the slice or at $7 a pie.

Fine Dining
In a class of its own, **Bar y Restaurante La Cascada** (tel. 505/568-2511) offers tables set above the village with a prime view of the ocean and sunset at the Pelican Eyes Piedras y Olas Hotel. The cuisine at La Cascada is exquisite and expensive—entrées like lamb, seafood risotto, and curries run from $11–20, or try the parmesan-crusted baked mahi mahi over herb spaetzle for $18. Also open for breakfast and lunch, with burgers and salads for $7; enjoy the pool and wireless Internet as you sip from an extensive tropical-drink menu.

INFORMATION AND SERVICES

From home, start your exploration at www.sanjuandelsur.org.ni. Many of the businesses listed in this chapter can be found on this local network of Web pages and they post updated rates. There is still no one official point for tourism information in San Juan del Sur (the nearest INTUR office is in Rivas), but there are many local efforts to stay on top of the quickly developing scene—Marie at

CRUISE SHIPS

In 1998, the Holland America Line added San Juan del Sur as a port of call on several of their cruises. The announcement sparked hope in the people of San Juan del Sur, who began preparing their sleepy town to receive the thousands of cruise ship passengers scheduled to disembark.

After several years of regular biweekly stops, whether or not *los cruceros* have benefited San Juan del Sur depends entirely on whom you ask. The well-to-do Careli Tour company, which enjoys a monopoly on the buses and guides who whisk most of the passengers straight from the dock in San Juan to day trips in Granada or Masaya, isn't complaining. These passengers never set foot in San Juan proper, and the few hundred who decide to remain in town do not spend money in restaurants or hotels. A few bars have made a good business catering to partying crewmembers, but the passengers themselves don't do much drinking. The *ciclo*-taxis and their drivers that cart passengers to and from the dock are all imported from Rivas and few of the crafts vendors that display along the tree-lined beachfront strip are Nicaraguan. In fact, the majority of San Juaneños have not gained a dime from the arrival of the cruise ships and would only notice their absence by the lack of tinted-window bus convoys rumbling past their doors every two weeks.

Concerned Holland America passengers should attempt to leave some dollars behind for someone other than their tour guides, whether in San Juan del Sur or in other Nicaraguan cities they visit.

Ricardo's bar has even put together her own local guide and map, or check the bulletin board at the Casa de Cultura and at various *hospedajes*.

Nearly all of the nicer hotels (and restaurants) accept major credit cards. There's finally a bank in town, Banco de Finanzas, located in the ENITEL building at the south end of the beach road near the post office. The couple of pharmacies in town have limited supplies, and the Centro de Salud provides free consults 8 A.M.–7 P.M. Monday–Saturday, 8 A.M.–noon Sunday; the dentist is there Thursday mornings, the gynecologist Saturdays. However, for any serious medical concerns, plan a trip to Rivas, as the Centro is typically understaffed and crowded.

Internet

San Juan's handful of Internet cafés are more expensive than other places in Nicaragua but are plentiful and easy to find. There's one at Hotel Costa Azul and another up the block at Leo's, both good options.

Other Services

Most of the nicer hotels provide laundry service, and the cheaper ones can probably scrub your clothes as well. If you'd rather go to an independent *lavandería* (laundromat) with modern machines, you'll find one between Hotel Villa Isabella and Royal Chateau, charging a steep $4.50 per load (wash, dry, fold). For short- or long-term storage of vehicles and large equipment (surfboard, etc.), contact Mike at Hotel Villa Isabella for one of his "Sano y Salvo" garages.

GETTING AROUND

You won't need a taxi to get around town (you'll only see them trolling for passengers to Rivas), but make use of the open *ciclo*-taxis (three-wheeled bicycle taxis), a fun way to cruise up and down the beach road.

To travel up and down the coast, you'll need a sturdy car, sturdy legs, or a decent mountain bike. You can rent bikes in town at Elizabeth's, Joxi, or Fogata. Taxi drivers lounge around the market and can take you up and down the coast. Ask around your hotel or favorite bar about turtle tours and water taxis. Reliable, friendly private taxi services include Richard Morales (located three blocks south of Hotel Villa Isabella, tel. 505/882-8268) and Juan Carlos Selva (tel.

505/866-6174 or 505/568-2564) who both charge between $40 and $60 a day, and can do airport, Masaya, and coast trips, or anything else you desire.

GETTING THERE AND AWAY

The direct trip to San Juan del Sur from Managua takes 2–2.5 hours in your own vehicle or express bus from Roberto Huembes terminal. The most comfortable way to make the trip is the 4 P.M. *lujo* (luxury) bus, but there are also direct expresses leaving at 9 A.M., 9:30 A.M., and 10 A.M., and sometimes early evening as well (about $3). Slow, crowded, *ordinario* service to Rivas is plentiful and operates from 5 A.M.– 5 P.M. You can just as easily take an express bus to Rivas and take a taxi the final stretch to the beach. Beware! The guys at Huembes can be extremely aggressive—they will grab your bags out of the taxi you arrive in and push you onto a slow Rivas bus, all the while lying to you that it is going directly to San Juan and then demanding a tip. Ask the other passengers to be sure.

Private taxis from Rivas to San Juan del Sur cost $7 and take 20 minutes; better yet hop in a *colectivo* taxi, which will pack in as many passengers as it can but only charges $.75 for the 26-kilometer ride. Express buses departing from San Juan del Sur to Managua leave from the corner in front of the market at 5 A.M. (this is the nicer *lujo* bus), 5:30 A.M., 6:30 A.M., and 3:30 P.M. *Ordinarios* to Rivas and Managua leave every hour from 5 A.M. to 5 P.M. You can also catch a *colectivo* taxi to Rivas from 4 A.M. to about 3 or 4 P.M.

To and From Costa Rica

From the Costa Rican border at Peñas Blancas, buses for Rivas leave every half-hour. Get off at **Empalme la Virgen** and flag a bus, taxi, or ride going to San Juan from Rivas. The beach is 18

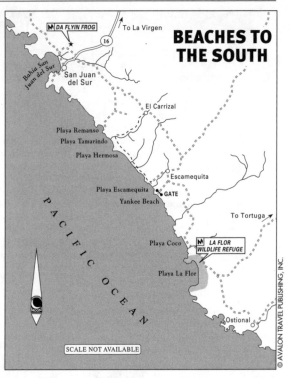

BEACHES TO THE SOUTH

SCALE NOT AVAILABLE

© AVALON TRAVEL PUBLISHING, INC.

kilometers due west of La Virgen; taxis from the border to San Juan charge $11–20.

To the border at Peñas Blancas, get a ride to La Virgen in a bus or taxi, then catch a lift south; the first Rivas–Peñas Blancas bus passes at 7:30 A.M. Or book a ticket at the new TicaBus Agency, one block west of the Texaco (tel. 505/834-3425).

BEACHES TO THE SOUTH

A number of remarkable beaches are accessible by driving (or walking or biking) the road to Ostional (see the bus schedule in Ostional section for access to all of the following). You'll first pass through Barrio Las Delicias, which includes the sports stadium, cemetery, and friendly suburban folks, and leads you to a fork in the road known as "El Container." Go right here and walk another kilometer to **Playa Remanso.** There are no services here, so be prepared with water and food. In

¿PURA VIDA? NICARAGUAN RELATION WITH COSTA RICA

The tense relationship between these incongruous Central American neighbors parallels the relation between the United States and Mexico: namely, a massive flood of desperate immigrants crosses the border into a more prosperous and stable nation and is subsequently accused of driving down wages, taking all the jobs, and straining social services without paying taxes. As the immigrants are darker skinned and easy to distinguish, they're easy to blame.

Some estimates put the number of Nicaraguans living in Costa Rica at more than a million, but with the constant flux and large percentage of illegals, no one knows for sure. The real number might be half that. But many Ticos are sure of one thing: Nicaraguans are "lazy, no-good, poor, and dirty." Oh yeah, they're "Indios," to boot.

Nicaraguans, for their part, generally mistrust the Ticos and don't appreciate their arrogance. "The truth is," wrote none other than Carlos Fonseca, founder of the FSLN, from exile in San Jose in 1960, "that it doesn't even seem to be located next to Nicaragua—it is so totally different. . . And even though this country is different from Nicaragua, and I am longing for a different Nicaragua, Costa Rica doesn't appeal to me, and I wouldn't want the Nicaragua of the future to be anything like Costa Rica. Here it seems like history has stopped and everything has been the same for a thousand years and will be the same for a thousand more. On the other hand, one can live peacefully here and it's the best vacation spot in the world. That's no good for me because I'm not looking for a peaceful life, and I'm not on vacation."

Costa Rica is obviously a wealthier, more stable country. In his 1985 travelogue, *So Far From God,* Patrick Marnham called Costa Rica "the most European of the countries of the isthmus." To keep it that way, the Costa Rican economy is wholly dependent on low-cost Nicaraguan laborers for harvesting their sugar cane and coffee and filling the ranks of the construction workforce in the urban centers. In an effort to control immigration, Costa Rican officials conduct regular round-ups of illegal aliens, returning as many as 150 to Nicaragua daily. As you travel south into Costa Rica, you can expect patrolmen to stop and search your bus several times for illegals.

Costa Rica continues to press for a resolution to Nicaraguan immigration issues. Too much blustery rhetoric from Managua regarding other issues, like the sovereignty of the Río San Juan, may tempt the Ticos to crack down even more on illegal immigrants, something Managua would very much like to avoid. Even today, Nicaraguan immigrants have reported irregular and inhumane incarceration by Tico authorities, often for weeks at a time without formal charges (and sometimes without daylight, toilets, or sufficient food).

Cultural tensions predate these immigration issues; in fact, only 50 years ago, Ticos used to emigrate to Nicaragua to work on the cattle farms. Early-19th-century border squabbles divided competing Spanish governors. Later, after helping to defeat William Walker's army in Rivas, Tico soldiers stuck around in a full-scale occupation of southern Nicaragua, withdrawing only after being granted the Guanacaste Peninsula in an 1858 treaty. During the 1980s, U.S.-backed Contra forces illegally based operations in Costa Rica, prompting an irritated Costa Rican President Oscar Arias Sanchez to help negotiate an end to Nicaragua's conflict.

Much of Nicaraguan tourism is direct spillover from the decidedly more trammeled lands of Costa Rica; you can now book a direct flight from Liberia to Granada, and hundreds of travelers pour over the border at Peñas Blancas every day. Ask any one of these intrepid visitors, and they too will tell you how different the two countries are.

© JOSHUA BERMAN

Yankee Beach has great surf, but difficult access.

addition to its consistent but mediocre beach break for surfing, Remanso has a long, interesting shore that is fascinating to explore at low tide—look for bat caves, tide pools, blow holes, and plenty of wildlife.

Walking 30 minutes farther south, you'll hit **Playa Tamarindo. Playa Hermosa** is either an hour beach hike from the parking lot at Remanso or by walking the 20-minute trail from the bus stop at El Carizal, farther down the road toward Ostional.

A bit farther, access to Yankee Beach was prohibited at press time. A sure way to get in and surf Yankee is to stay at **Cabinas Amaure's,** a rustic $25-a-night affair on the hill back from the beach: Look for the signs or ask for Neil and Amaure in town.

Playa El Coco

Playa El Coco is a jewel of a beach, great for swimming and fishing, and easy access to the turtles at La Flor. **Parque Marítimo El Coco** (18 kilometers south of San Juan, tel. 505/892-0124, parquemaritimo@playaelcoco.com.ni, www.playaelcoco.com.ni) is a compound on the wide beach with a popular restaurant called **Puesta del Sol** (open 8 A.M.–8 P.M. daily, sometimes closes early) with meals from $7. There are also 16 various fully equipped bungalows and houses for rent; prices range from $48 a night into the hundreds of dollars—weekend packages are very reasonable with a group of people. Houses have a/c, satellite TV, hot water, and kitchen, and sleep up to eight people for $150 a day. You should come prepared with supplies, but there is an on-site mini-super, plus bike rental, Internet access, and a new conference facility.

M La Flor Wildlife Refuge

One of the two Pacific turtle nesting beaches in Nicaragua, the park is co-managed by Fundación Cocibolca, an NGO that is attempting to involve the local community in decision-making processes. Foreigners pay $10 pp to enter, another $20 per group for camping (bring your own gear). Some just come to lounge on the beach, swim with the turtles who are waiting to come up and lay at night, or walk down to the river for a wealth of wildlife. Most, however, try to catch one of the nighttime *arribadas,* or mass

San Juan del Sur

TURTLES

The Olive Ridley, or Paslama, sea turtle *(Lepidochelys olivacea)* is an endangered species well-known for its massive synchronous nesting emergences. These seasonal occurrences, called *arribadas,* occur several times during each lunar cycle in the July–February nesting season and, at their peak (August–October), result in as many as 20,000 females nesting and laying eggs on a single beach.

In Nicaragua, the two beaches that receive the most turtles are **Playa Chacocente** and **Playa La Flor,** both on the southwestern Pacific coast. Playa La Flor, located about 15 kilometers north of the Costa Rican border and 18 kilometers southeast of San Juan del Sur, is a 1.6-kilometer-long beach that has been protected as part of a wildlife preserve. However, some 4,000 people in nine nearby communities have long derived some form of income from the turtle-egg harvest. During the nesting season, government officials work with local community leaders to allow for a semi-controlled harvest of 10–20 percent of the total eggs deposited on the beach. Despite this management strategy, hatchings have been less successful every year. Fly larvae, beetles, coyotes, opossums, raccoons, skunks, coatimundi, feral dogs, pigs, and humans all prey on Olive Ridley sea turtles in one form or another. High tides and beach erosion sweep away other eggs, and once they emerge from their shells, they are pounced on by crabs, frigate birds, caracara, vultures, and coyotes before they can reach the sea. Once in the water, they must still battle a host of predatory fish.

In general, females lay two clutches of eggs per season and remain near shore for approximately one month. The mean clutch size of the females differs from beach to beach but averages about 100 eggs; incubation takes from 45 to 55 days, depending on the temperature, humidity, and organic content of the sand.

The *arribadas* and hatching events both occur during the night and witnessing these phenomena is an unforgettable experience. Tourism can protect the turtles, as it provides an incentive to continue protection efforts. However, you can just as easily harass, injure, or frighten the turtles if you're not careful. Don't count on park rangers to tell you what's acceptable; use your common sense to respect this inspiring natural process and *please* pay close attention to the following rules during your expedition to the beaches of La Flor or Chacocente:

Turtle Viewing Etiquete

1. Do not take use your camera's flash when taking pictures of turtles coming out of the sea, digging a nest, or going back to the ocean—the light can scare them back into the ocean without laying their eggs. The only time that you can take a picture of them is when they are laying eggs; the flash will not disturb them as much, as they enter a semi-trance state.

2. Keep your flashlight use as minimal as possible; use a red filter over the lens or color it with a temporary red marker. If the moon is out, use its light instead.

3. Do not dig out any nests that are being laid or are hatching.

4. Do not eat sea turtle eggs, whether on the beach or in a restaurant. Despite their undeserved reputation as an aphrodisiac, the raw eggs may carry harmful organisms and their consumption supports a black market that incentivizes poaching.

5. Do not touch, attempt to lift, turn, or ride turtles.

6. Do not interfere with any research being performed on the beach (i.e. freeing hatchlings from nest boxes, etc.).

7. If camping, place your tents beyond the vegetation line so as not to disturb the nesting turtles.

Thanks to Shaya Honarvar, Department of Bioscience & Biotechnology, Drexel University.

nesting events (see the Turtles special topic).

Ostional

This picturesque bay and community at the extreme southwestern tip of Nicaragua is a fishing town, not a tourist destination, so feel free to chat with the mellow villagers or strike up a deal for a boat ride, fishing trip, or traditional meal cooked in someone's home. Buses from Rivas pass through the San Juan del Sur market at 1 P.M., 4 P.M., and 5 P.M. They leave the center of Ostional at 5 A.M., 7:30 A.M., and 4 P.M. The ride takes about two hours to cover the relatively short distance, so settle back onto your hard seat to enjoy the scenery as it bumps by.

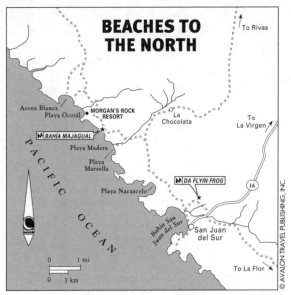

BEACHES TO THE NORTH

© AVALON TRAVEL PUBLISHING, INC.

BEACHES TO THE NORTH

By land, these beaches are all accessed via the road to Chocolata, just east of the Texaco station (much of this road served as the old railroad grade back in the day). **Playa Nacascolo** (a.k.a. Navy Beach) and **El Torre** are only reachable by walking through fields and asking directions. Seven kilometers in, turn left at Chocolata to a fork in the road: Left goes to Marsella and Madera, right to Majagual.

Playa Marsella

This pleasant, breezy beach provides good snorkeling around the rocks (watch the currents). The resort at Marsella (tel. 505/850-0300, www.nicaragualand.com) is perched way above the beach; cliff-top cabins have incredible views at about $50 a couple. Or just come to enjoy the restaurant and its spectacular vista.

Playa Madera

One of the most consistent and easy-to-access surf breaks from San Juan, Madera boasts a fast, hollow beach break, best on incoming tides. At present, there's a simple wooden bunk house with a kitchen offering cheap lodging, but word on the beach is that they may get booted soon by the real landowners. There's a parking spot right at the top of the beach and a more established campground a short walk away at Matilda's, which is at the northern part of the beach, also accessible by driving to Majagual. **Matilda's** (tel. 505/862-5727) is a friendly and lovely little site, right on the beach, and they'll rent you a tent, sleeping pad, and place to pitch it for only $3 pp, less with your own gear; cooking facilities are available, as are a few private rooms with bath and fan for $20 d, plus a bunks for $5 in the small dorm. Keep an eye out for an up-and-coming area eco-venture and "jungle beach retreat" at www.experiencenicaragua.com. To get to and from Madera, see the Majagual section below.

Bahía Majagual

Hidden at the end of 12 rough kilometers from San Juan del Sur, this is one of the most beautiful beaches on this coast—no joke—and home to a low-key budget getaway once frequented by high-ranking Sandinista officials; a few

Playa Ocotal, as seen from the exlusive Morgan's Rock Hacienda & EcoLodge.

Generalísimos are still holding onto nearby pieces of property. **Bahia Majagual Eco-Lodge** (tel. 505/886-0439, majagual@ibw.com.ni, www.sanjuandelsur.org.ni/majagual) is a backpacker beach compound, very popular with Central America vagabonds from around the world, as well as picnicking Nicaraguans. Stay in one of the 32 dorm beds for $5 pp, or one of four private rooms with their own bathrooms for $24 d. Lots of activities and equipment are available, including horseback rides, fishing and snorkel gear, and boogie and surf boards (it's a quick walk to the break at Madera). Camp out for $2 pp, or reserve a protected hammock for $4 (BYO mosquito net). There is a full-service kitchen and bar serving great fish, great *gallo pinto* (rice and beans), and horrid coffee. They also offer book exchange and laundry service, and satellite Internet will soon be available. The nighttime scene varies from a mellow campfire to an all-out beach disco. Remember, only the room prices are listed above, everything else costs extra, plus a service charge and tax—bring plenty of cash and keep an eye on your tab as it's easy to spend more than you planned on. Ma-jagual accepts córdobas, dollars, and traveler's checks, but no credit cards (yet).

Majagual encourages day visitors and makes it easy with various options. By bus from Rivas, head toward the Chocolata road (19 km west of Rivas) and walk 5 km west. You can walk more easily from San Juan del Sur (7 km). A private taxi costs around $10.

Two water taxis—Rana and Geo—leave from the beach at San Juan del Sur across from Hotel Estrella and depart Majagual at 5 P.M.; round trip is $7 pp.

Morgan's Rock

Continuing north along the coast, Playa Ocotál is the home of a much-hyped high-end eco-lodge that is at the vanguard of Nicaragua's upscale tourism market. One can hope, anyway, that future resort development throughout the country will attain the quality and environmental responsibility of **Morgan's Rock Hacienda & Eco Lodge** (tel. 506/296-9442, info@morgansrock.com, www .morgansrock.com). This remarkable and exclusive resort is part of a 1,000-hectare reforestation project and an 800-hectare private nature reserve,

San Juan del Sur

and its 15 elegant hardwood cabins are built into a bluff above the crashing surf on the beach below. As few trees were cut as possible during the development, so you'll have to walk a 110-meter-long suspension bridge through a lush canopy to reach your cabin, which is the most luxurious and beautiful tree house your childhood fantasies ever dreamed up. The structures—as well as the main lodge, which features a gorgeous infinity pool—were designed with all local materials and feature ingenious architecture and attention to detail. Check out the photo tour on the website if you don't believe us.

You're on vacation here, so no phones or Internet, but there's plenty to do: Activities include sunrise kayak tours of the estuary, tree-planting excursions, and tours of their shrimp farm and sugar mill, where they brew their own Morgan's Rum. In fact, more than 70 local workers are employed to grow and produce much of the restaurant's vegetables, dairy products, herbs, and other needs. How much, you ask? A cool $400 per couple per night gets you a cabin, three meals, and all the drinks you'd like to consume. The facilities and services are for guests only, so sorry, no day trippers.

Tola and Pacific Beaches

Ten kilometers west of Rivas is the agricultural community of Tola, gateway to the steadily improving shore road and a string of lonely, beautiful beaches that make up 30 kilometers of Pacific shoreline. Until very recently, you would have been the only foreigner on any of these beaches, but the word is out and land prices are rising. Still, there are few tourist facilities and only a few isolated lot developments. A nine-hole golf course at Playa Iguana may be open by the time you read this, as well as other projects, but until then, the beaches west of Tola are still an adventure and, incidentally, home to some of Nicaragua's most closely-guarded surf secrets.

TOLA

Tola is famous in Nicaragua as the subject of a common expression: *"Te dejó esperando como la novia de Tola."* (He left you waiting like the bride of Tola.) It refers to the real-life soap-opera story of a young woman named Hillary, who, on the day of her wedding, was left standing at the altar at Belén while the groom, Salvador Cruz, married his former lover, Juanita.

There are a few decent eateries in town, the most popular of which, **El Naranjito,** has tables around a central courtyard, beer by the bottle or pitcher and, naturally, lots of rum (discount on food if you buy a bottle). **La Esquina** is better known for the owner, Marta Palma. It usually hosts a rowdier crowd, and the *fritanga* is yummy. If you'd rather leave the bar brawls behind, have your dinner at **Lumby's,** a block toward the school on the same street as La Esquina; you can super-size that enchilada by ordering *doble carne* (double meat) for $.35 more—feel your arteries clogging as you chew.

Operating since September 2001, **Esperanza del Futuro** (tel. 505/563-0482), a community-development program run by Doña Loida (an influential Sandinista leader, elected Mayor in 2004), aims to provide better education to people in rural areas. There is a library, a set of classrooms, a sewing co-op, and planted crops, and they give classes in guitar, agriculture, herbal medicine, and computers. Many travelers have stayed and worked with Doña Loida, from a week or two to as long as six months. They'll help arrange cheap room and board. Esperanza del Futuro is located on the road that leads from the park to the baseball field/basketball court, about 100 meters past the baseball field.

PLAYA GIGANTE

Gigante is the first beach you come to after Tola and is named after the Punta Pie de Gigante (The Giant's Foot). This is a beautiful crescent beach well off the beaten track. The community of Gigante consists of a few dozen poor homes and about 500 locals. At the beach, there are a

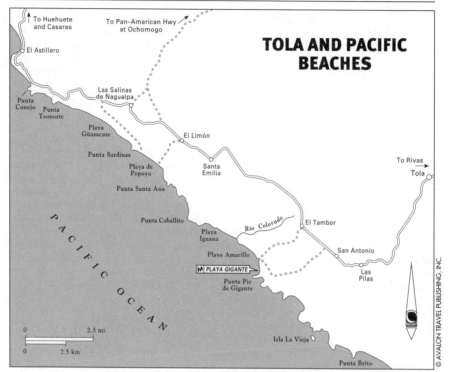

few traditional food shacks (and one place to play pool), usually owned by folks from Tola. From February through May (especially on Sundays), you have a great chance of buying fresh whole fish right off the boat, which the local folks will cook up just for you with rice, salad, and plantains for under $3. During Semana Santa, the food gets even better, and more plentiful; poke around.

To get to Gigante, take the La Salinas bus from Tola or Rivas and get off at either of the two entrances to the beach (the second one is a bit easier to follow). If you are not traveling by car, you'll need to walk or bike about seven kilometers to the beach on a hilly dirt road. Look for Rivas–Tola–Gigante buses, leaving around 8 A.M. and returning late in the afternoon to Tola and Rivas. Travelers pay one price (under $1) and go on the same bus both ways. During Semana Santa, the buses run daily and the beach

gets crowded with people from all over Rivas. At this time, many locals set up camp under the trees and spend the week at the beach sleeping in hammocks or under black plastic tarps. Also during Semana Santa, expect to see daily cockfights and a lot of phenomenally drunk Nicaraguan men, every year several of whom overestimate their swimming prowess and drown.

LAS SALINAS DE NAGUALAPA

Another quiet and poor beachfront community, Las Salinas has a lovely beach, with several waves popular among surfers, and a place to stay. Check out **La Tica,** a simple and pleasant restaurant/*hospedaje* where the owners are friendly and helpful; rooms cost about $2 pp.

Las Salinas's hot springs are worth exploring if you get sick of the beach. Ask at La Tica for directions or take the road next to the school east (away from the water) about four kilometers past cow fields. The hot springs are natural but have been cemented. There's one pool for swimming, for which you pay around $.25. The local women are big fans of the hot springs for scrubbing clothes and have washboards set up.

GUASACATE AND POPOYO

Guasacate is one of Nicaragua's better beaches but remains virtually unvisited and undeveloped. It's a huge stretch of sand with access to the famed Popoyo break. Hopefully, the recent construction of wealthy private homes won't complicate the development and use of the beach for the public. The entrance to Guasacate is located 5–8 kilometers down the first left-hand road after crossing a bridge in Las Salinas. It's paved the whole way. The nearby *aguas termales* (hot springs) cost a few cords to get in.

Guasacate is also home to **Popoyo Surf Lodge,** (www.surfnicaragua.com, surfnicinc1@hotmail .com) run by a Florida native known throughout Las Salinas as J.J. (or Jota-Jota) and his wife, Kim. Popoyo has a range of accommodations, from simple rooms to units with private bathrooms, a/c, and tile floors. The restaurant serves three square veggie-friendly meals and lots of fresh fish; reservations and packages available through Waveriders. "Mama" Gloria Mendoza's Tiltin' Hilton, (a.k.a. **Casa/Bar Mendoza**) also offers basic lodging, including hammocks for $2, camping $3 pp, and a few small, cleanish rooms; three meals a day $2–4. **Surfing Martinez,** in a smaller building across the street, has $2 hammocks and dark, sandy, tiled rooms, all

with shared bath, for $5 pp; shared showers are. . . simple.

Also in the neighborhood, located about 300 meters from the beach, is **Surfari Charters** (tel. 505/874-7173, www.surfaricharters.com, surfari charters@hotmail.com). They specialize in all-inclusive surf trips, so check their website for more information (or just to see some really amazing surf pics).

At least one bus a day leaves Roberto Huembes in Managua bound for El Astillero via Ochomogo (not Tola). From San Juan del Sur or Costa Rica, you'll be driving through Rivas and Tola, following the signs to Rancho Santana, then continuing past this development's gates until you reach Las Salinas. Buses depart Rivas about every hour. A taxi to Guasacate from Astillero costs $7, from Rivas $30. The road to the beach will take you past several austere salt flats, from which the nearby town of Las Salinas gets its name.

EL ASTILLERO AND BEACHES TO THE NORTH

Most of the little deserted beaches in the 10-kilometer strip between Las Salinas and Astillero don't even have names. El Astillero itself is a fishing village full of small boats and is, in fact, the first safe boat anchorage north of Gigante. North of El Astillero, the road turns inland away from the coast. Accessing the beach anywhere along this area requires a boat and a lot of dedication. Ask around in El Astillero. There are plenty of underemployed sailors and fishermen that would be glad to strike a deal with you if you're interested in exploring the coastline.

Peñas Blancas and the Border with Costa Rica

Peñas Blancas is the official border crossing into Costa Rica. Since 1999, the border post has undergone massive construction and renovation, making it a nicer—and better organized—post than even Costa Rica's (although the Ticos have a cafeteria on their side, something still lacking on the Nica side of the border). A major effort is underway, with financing from the United States, to make the border crossing a bottleneck and entrapment point for drug traffickers headed north. Many of the buildings you see in the compound are drug-inspection points for the dozens of tractor-trailers that cross the border every day. Needless to say, this is one place you don't want to be smuggling furs. Sniffing dogs are common.

Border hassles can last anywhere from one to ten hours! The longest waits happen at times when the hundreds of thousands of Nicaraguans living across the border are traveling to and from their country—this happens a week before and after Christmas, Easter, and also any Nicaraguan election. The best time of day to cross is during the afternoon. More commonly, you can squeeze through in under an hour.

HOURS AND FEES

The border post is getting ready to switch to a 24-hour service, but assume that the "overtime" annoyance fees will still be charged if you show up before 8 A.M., during lunch, or after 5 P.M.

Travelers exiting Nicaragua pay $2 at the border during normal hours and $4 during overtime hours. Travelers entering Nicaragua pay $7 during normal hours and $9 during overtime hours. Everyone traveling to the border on an international bus service like TicaBus or TransNica will be forced to pay $1 to the town government of Cárdenas before reaching the border—"just because."

Inside the Customs and Immigration building, find a branch of Bancentro, which can help you change money if necessary. It's open 8 A.M.–8 P.M. (i.e., whenever the border is open).

Travelers driving their own vehicles north from the border will be forced to pass their vehicles through a dubious "sterilization process" in which the exterior of the vehicle is sprayed with some mystery liquid that kills certain porcine and bovine diseases; it costs $1 and takes five minutes unless the line is long. Roll up the windows.

PAPERWORK

Just a passport and some cash is all that's required of North American and European travelers, but don't forget to get stamped on both sides! Failing to do so can get you into serious trouble when you try to leave the country. To enter Costa Rica, Nicaraguan citizens must have acquired a Costa Rican visa from the consulate either in Rivas or Managua. Upon entering Nicaragua, most North American and European travelers are granted a 90-day visa, with the exception of Canadian and Japanese citizens, who for some reason are only given 30 days.

By law, folks entering Costa Rica must have a ticket to leave the country. They usually don't check, as long as you're dressed like you have money. If they do, you lose your place in line and go to the table outside, where Transport Dendu will sell you an open-ended ticket from San Jose to Managua for $7.

ENTERING NICARAGUA WITH YOUR VEHICLE

If you are driving your own vehicle, the process to enter Nicaragua from Costa Rica is lengthy, but usually not too difficult. Rental vehicles, however, cannot cross the border. You must present the vehicle's title (*Titulo de la Propiedad*), as well as your own driver's license and passport. Get proper stamps from Hacienda (Timbres de Hacienda), and a property certificate from Hacienda. Also make sure you have a current tag and Tico insurance; all of this can be taken care of in Liberia. You will be given a temporary (30-day) permit to drive in Nicaragua that will cost you $10—should you lose the permit, you will be fined $100.

San Juan del Sur

GETTING THERE AND AWAY

International bus services like TicaBus, TransNica, and NicaBus are popular ways to get across the border easily and comfortably, the best service being the new TransNica Plus, since you travel with 30 instead of 55 passengers. In many cases, the bus has a "helper" who collects your passports and money and waits in line for you. The disadvantage is that the bus won't pull away from the border post until every single traveler has had their papers processed, which can be time-consuming in some cases (waits up to four hours are not unheard of). More confident travelers like to take a Nicaraguan bus to the border, walk across to Costa Rica, and take a Costa Rican bus to San José, which is often faster. Express buses from Managua to Peñas Blancas depart Mercado Huembes at 5 A.M., 8 A.M., 9:30 A.M., and 3:30 P.M. Buses and microbuses leave the market in Rivas every 30–45 minutes. On the Costa Rican side, the last bus leaves the border bound for San José at 10 P.M. (about a six-hour ride).

CONTINUING INTO COSTA RICA

After crossing the border, you've got two choices. One, buy a ticket to San Jose from the TransNica booth across from customs ($6 pp, ride takes 6–8 hours, departures daily at 5:15 A.M., 7:30 A.M., 9:30 A.M. direct, 10:45 A.M., noon, 1:30 P.M. direct, 3:30 P.M., and 6 P.M.). Or, get a Liberia–Pulmitan bus to Liberia ($1.50 pp, two hours, last bus at 5:30 P.M.).

If you go to Liberia, 14 daily buses go to San Jose ($4, 3–5 hours) and leave every 20 minutes to the Nicoya Peninsula and its beaches. Liberia, the capital of Guanacaste, is also a good base for Santa Rosa National Park, where William Walker and crew were resoundingly defeated, and Rincon de la Vieja National Park, with impressive volcanoes. In fact, Guanacaste used to belong to Nicaragua and some say it still feels connected, or at least socially and physically independent of Costa Rica proper. Many locals still have family in Nicaragua, and this is the only department with its own flag. If you want to spend the night, try **Hotel Liberia** (tel. 506/666-0161, www .hotelliberia.com, $5 pp with shared bath, $9 pp with private bath and really nice room). They provide lots of local information to set you on your way.

Getting to Monteverde from Liberia is a pain; the whole trip takes at least six hours and costs around $8 total. Take the 9:30 A.M. bus to Cañas, then connect with the first bus to Tilaran, where you wait for the 2:30 P.M. bus to Monteverde.

León and the Volcanic Lowlands

The northwestern plains of Nicaragua comprise the most populated, agriculturally fertile, and swelteringly hot corner of the country. The centerpiece of the landscape—a massive chain of active volcanoes that stretches northwest from Lake Xolotlán all the way to the Gulf of Fonseca—is striking, especially when one or more of them is trailing gases and ash into the white-hot sky. The long Pacific coastline of the region boasts white- and black-sand beaches, mangrove habitat, and hundreds of kilometers of bird-filled estuaries.

The region's two major cities include colonial León, whose narrow streets are lined with cathedrals and universities, and whose coffee shops and cafés are filled with the buzz of politics. León's 500 years of political history have been punctuated throughout the centuries with the staccato call of uprising, resistance, and war—and confrontations with Mother Nature date back to the city's founding. A half-hour north along the line of hulking volcanoes is the city of Chinandega, agribusiness capital of the country.

Must-Sees

Look for **M** to find the sights and activities you can't miss and **M** for the best dining and lodging.

M Museums: Begin your art immersion at the **Casa de Cultura** and then continue around the corner at the fabulous **Centro de Arte Fundación Ortiz-Gurdián** (page 160).

M Las Ruínas de León Viejo: Hire a local guide to show you some of these fascinating recent excavations (page 169).

M Los Hervideros de San Jacinto: Steam, sulphur, and pits of boiling mud. It's like visiting hell, except a gleeful ten-year-old is leading you around. The Hervideros are a very real look at Nicaragua's volcanic underside (page 170).

M Poneloya and Las Peñitas Beaches: Relaxing and peaceful accommodations at the ocean's edge, all with easy access to the impressive Isla Juan Venado (page 171).

M Padre Ramos Wetlands Reserve: If you're into isolated beaches and protected bird-filled estuaries, the bouncy trip north is worth it (page 181).

HONDURAS

Golfo de Fonseca

M Padre Ramos Wetlands Reserve

Los Hervideros de San Jacinto **M**

Museums **M**

Poneloya and Las **M** Peñitas Beaches

Las Ruínas de **M** León Viejo

PACIFIC

OCEAN

Lago Xolotlán

LEÓN AND THE VOLCANIC LOWLANDS

The Maribio Volcanoes stretch north from the top of Cerro Negro.

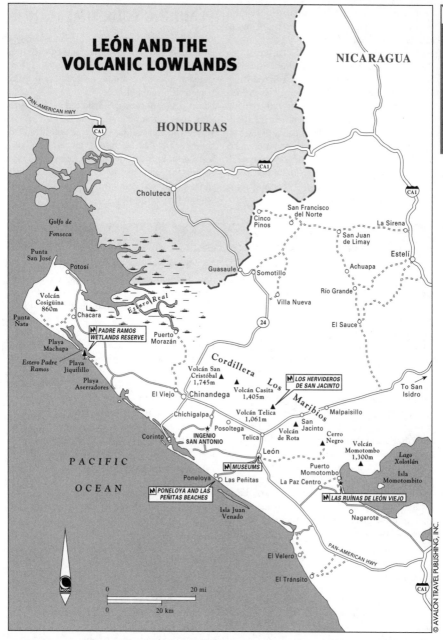

León

LEÓN AND THE VOLCANIC LOWLANDS

NICARAGUA

HONDURAS

PAN-AMERICAN HWY

CA1

CA1

CA1

Choluteca

Golfo de
Fonseca

San Francisco
del Norte

Cinco
Pinos

La Sirena

San Juan
de Limay

Estelí

Punta
San José

Potosí

Guasaule

Somotillo

Achuapa

Volcán
Cosigüina
860m

La
Chacara

Estero Real

Río Grande

Punta
Nata

Villa Nueva

El Sauce

PADRE RAMOS
WETLANDS RESERVE

Puerto
Morazán

24

Playa
Machapa

Cordillera

Estero Padre
Ramos

Playa
Jiquilillo

Volcán San
Cristóbal
1,745m

LOS HERVIDEROS
DE SAN JACINTO

Playa
Aserradores

El Viejo

Chinandega

Volcán Casita
1,405m

Los

To San
Isidro

Maribios

Chichigalpa

Volcán Telica
1,061m

Malpaisillo

Corinto

Posoltega

INGENIO
SAN ANTONIO

Telica

San
Jacinto

Volcán
de Rota

Cerro
Negro

Volcán
Momotombo
1,300m

Lago
Xolotlán

PACIFIC

León

MUSEUMS

Puerto
Momotombo

Isla
Momotombito

OCEAN

Poneloya

Las Peñitas

La Paz Centro

PONELOYA AND LAS
PEÑITAS BEACHES

LAS RUÍNAS DE LEÓN VIEJO

Isla Juan
Venado

Nagarote

PAN-AMERICAN HWY

El Velero

El Tránsito

CA1

MOON

0   20 mi

0   20 km

© AVALON TRAVEL PUBLISHING, INC.

Tension seeps out of the land here in the form of boiling mud pits, geothermal vents, and the occasional trembling of a volcano. The Leoneses and Chinandeganos know well that life can be short and violent, and it should thus be lived intensely. León and Chinandega suffered more than most during Hurricane Mitch, during which more than two meters of rain fell in three days. Nowhere else in Nicaragua was the destruction as intense, and the still-visible landslide at Las Casitas is a silent reminder of the worst of it. As you ride from Managua to Chinandega, bear in mind that every single bridge along that route was washed away in October 1998, and some weren't rebuilt until years later.

PLANNING YOUR TIME

León is one of the few destinations in Nicaragua with more tourist sights than you can see in a single day. Plan on two to three days to explore the city, and allow another three days for day trips to the ruins of León Viejo and a volcano climb. Then, of course, you'll need at least three more days to rest up on the beach at Las Peñitas, where you can paddle along the wildlife-filled shores of Isla Juan Venado by morning and observe nesting turtles at night. The more adventurous will want to add in another three days to visit the reserves in far-off Padre Ramos and Volcán Cosigüina.

City of León

The principal dusty, mellow metropolis of the low-lying Nicaraguan northwest, León remains little frequented while, just 100 kilometers across the plains, its ancient political rival, Granada, bustles with tourists and foreign investors. Granada's gorgeous lakefront property may have something to do with that, but León once had that too—the Spaniards built the first city of León along the shore of Lake Xolotlán, moving only when Volcán Momotombo shook the ground beneath their feet. Still, modern Leoneses are justifiably proud in their own right. Traditionally designed colonial homes and a plethora of grand churches and cathedrals stand shoulder to shoulder along León's streets, awash in a tropical torpor that keeps things to a casual hum; indeed, León throbs with a sense of vibrancy and enthusiasm that's Nicaraguan to the bone. If you can beat the heat, León has a great deal to offer the casual traveler, including numerous museums and sights within the city limits and a host of day trips within an hour of your hotel door.

HISTORY

Today's León is the city's second incarnation. The short-lived first attempt was the Spanish settlement that Francisco Hernández de Córdoba founded next to the indigenous village of Imabite on the shore of Lake Xolotlán in 1524. The Spanish were less than hospitable to the neighboring native people, whom they forced into slavery and often punished with death at the jaws of attack dogs. The old city was abandoned in 1610 when Volcán Momotombo erupted. The Spanish relocated their city to León's present location alongside the already existing indigenous village of Subtiava. As the centuries passed and both populations expanded, Subtiava found itself—for better or worse—a *barrio* (neighborhood) of Spanish León.

Before 1852, León was the capital of Nicaragua several times, always under the leadership of Liberal governments. León has also, since colonial times, been both a university town and a hotbed of leftist thought. That predisposition for radical ideas proved to be fertile ground for Sandinista support. The Leoneses contributed greatly to the revolution from its earliest days in the 1960s, and as a result, Somoza punished them dearly, in one case by torching the central market.

In September 1978, Sandinista forces attacked key locations in León, including the installations of the National Guard at the famous XXI building, and were soundly beaten. Somoza retaliated with fury, using the air force to bomb the populations of both León and Chinandega. He also tortured and executed anyone suspected of

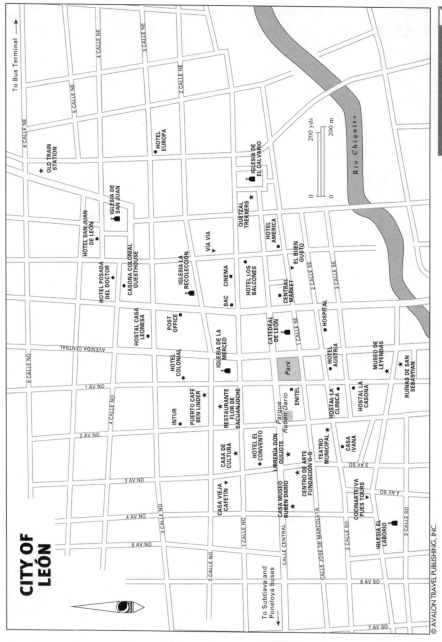

CITY OF LEÓN

To Bus Terminal →

Old Train Station

Hotel Europa

Hotel San Juan de León

Iglesia de San Juan

Casona Colonial Guesthouse

Hotel Posada del Doctor

Iglesia La Recolección

Via Via

Iglesia de El Calvario

Quetzal Trekkers

Hotel America

El Buen Gusto

Hotel Los Balcones

BAC   Cinema

Central Market

Hostal Casa Leonesa

Post Office

Iglesia de La Merced

Hospital

Catedral de León

Hotel Colonial

Hotel Austria

Museo de Leyendas

Ruinas de San Sebastián

Intur

Puerto Café Ben Linder

Restaurante Flor de Sacuanjoche

Entel

Hostal La Clínica

Hostal La Casona

Parque Rubén Darío

Casa de Cultura

Hotel El Convento

Librería Don Quijote

Teatro Municipal

Casa Ivana

Casa Vieja Cafetín

Centro de Arte Fundación V-G

Casa Museo Rubén Darío

Cocinarte/Va Pues Tours

Iglesia El Laborio

To Subtiava and Poneloya buses →

Río Chiquito

Park

Parque Rubén Darío

Avenida Central

6 Calle NE
5 Calle NE
4 Calle NE
3 Calle NE
2 Calle NE

6 Calle NO
1 Av NO
4 Calle NO
2 Av NO
3 Av NO
4 Av NO
5 Av NO

2 Calle NO
3 Calle NO

1 Av NO

Calle Central
Calle José de Marcoleta
1 Calle SO
2 Calle SO
3 Calle SO

3 Av SO
4 Av SO
6 Av SO
7 Av SO

1 Calle SE
2 Calle SE
3 Calle SE

0   200 yds

0   200 m

© AVALON TRAVEL PUBLISHING, INC.

N

León

HIKING THE MARIBIO VOLCANOES

Nicaragua has been called "a violent expanse of volcanic strength," and there is nowhere better to feel that force than on the hot, baked slopes of its mountains of fire. Start early and bring a minimum of three liters of water per person.

Momotombo, 1,300 meters, eight hours round-trip
The quintessential cone-shaped volcano, Momotombo rises up from the shores of Lago Xolotlán in a particularly menacing posture—and history has proven that the menace is real. Momotombo is climbable, but it's not easy, especially when you hit the loose volcanic gravel that comprises the upper half of the cone. Your triumphant reward will be one of the best views possible of Lago Xolotlán without use of an airplane. From the Ruínas de León Viejo, head out of town to the main highway and turn right (north) along the highway. Follow that to the geothermal plant, where you'll have to convince the guard to let you through to hike. They're sensitive about people traipsing across their installation, so honor whatever promises you make.

Telica, 1,061 meters, 4–5 hours round-trip
Despite its tendency to spew ash over its namesake town, Volcán Telica makes for a good climb.

Take a bus from León to Telica, then follow the road to the community of La Quimera and keep going until the road disappears beneath your feet and becomes the volcano. Alternatively, access the volcano from Santa Clara, the town adjacent to the Hervideros de San Jacinto.

Cerro Negro, 675 meters, three hours round-trip
This is the most frequently active volcano in the chain (its last eruption was August 1999). The lowest and youngest of the Maribios, Cerro Negro rises like a black-sand pimple from the landscape, completely free of vegetation and scorching hot when there is no cloud cover. A road takes you to the base; from there, follow the makeshift "trail," part of which will have you fighting gravity on the loose rocks, stepping up, sliding back; repeat. The trail loops around the steaming crater—if the wind blows the gases across your path, move fast to get out of it. Going down is easy—bring a beater snowboard for the quickest and most stylish descent, or rent a stainless steel–plated ride and protective gear from Va Pues Tours. There are a number of approaches; the most common heads due east from León, near the town of Lechecuago. Leave as early in the morning as humanly possible.

---

sympathizing with the Sandinistas. León lost many sons and brothers, and the bullet holes still adorn many buildings today.

By mid-1979, a weakened and militarily strained Somoza was unable to stop Sandinista troops as they entered León on June 2 and "liberated" it two days later. By the 17th, Somoza's last bastion of support in the city, the barracks of the National Guard, had been abandoned. The city of León has been largely Sandinista ever since, voting for the FSLN in the last three presidential elections.

SIGHTS

The **Parque Rubén Darío,** a block west of the central park, is a tribute to four famous Nicaraguan writers, all sons of León: Azarías H. Pallais (1884–1954), Salomon de la Selva (1893–1959), Alfonzo Cortéz (1893–1969), and, of course, the beloved Rubén Darío (1867–1916).

León's **Old Train Station,** built in 1884, was Nicaragua's first and most majestic. It survived a fire in 1956 that left only the outer walls standing and was subsequently rebuilt. A rowdy market has taken over the old building, but the grandeur of days of yore still resonate in the rafters.

El Fortín de Acosasco sits on a low, grassy hill just south of the city. Conservative president Sacasa built it in 1889 to keep an eye on the Liberals that would overthrow him four years later. The fort was later abandoned until Anastasio Somoza took interest and rehabilitated it. El Fortín has since served as both a military base and jail, and is presently abandoned once again. From the Subtiava church, it's an easy 45-minute walk: Go one block east and head due south out of town

La Casita, 1,405 meters, eight hours round-trip Access can be very difficult because of property issues (see San Cristóbal below). Near the top of the climb, the guides will lead you into the saddle between La Casita and Cristóbal and then to the peak of La Casita itself. There are some radio towers here, and the terminus of an access road damaged during the landslide. Though it's also possible to hike to the top along the slide itself, it's a treeless, sun-baked hike, not to mention possibly disrespectful to the thousands who remain buried beneath it. Although not as tall, La Casita offers a better view of Managua and the lake than Cristóbal does.

San Cristóbal, 1,745 meters, eight hours round-trip This is the granddaddy of volcano hikes in the Pacific region, long but the grade is moderate and even easy compared to some of the hikes listed previously. You'll need a guide to help you wend your way through the myriad fields, farms, and fences that obstruct the path upward (and which change every planting season). Find your guide in Chichigalpa. Enrique Reyes and his brothers are experienced at leading trips up San Cristóbal, and can be found in the Barrio Pellisco

Occidental, across from the Escuela Hector García (tel. 505/885-9154). If they're not around, finding a guide in Chichigalpa is easy. Horses cost $2 a day, and you should pay the guides at least $8 per group.

Cosigüina, 860 meters, six hours round-trip to edge of crater, 11 hours round-trip to crater lake Literally, a walk in the woods and then you're at the vegetation-carpeted crater lip with crazy views. Start walking from Potosi, or rent horses ($2 per day). Head back along the road toward the community of La Chacara, where the slope of Cosigüina is most amenable for climbing. From the edge of the crater, you can see across the Gulf of Fonseca into El Salvador. There are competing claims about whether one can descend to the crater lake without the use of ropes. If you intend to descend the approximately 300 meters down to the crater lake, you should take 30 meters of good rope with you (you can purchase it in El Viejo or Chinandega) and consider a guide from La Chacara. Luís Mejía Castro in El Viejo knows the Reserva Natural and its volcano intimately (from the Cine Imperial, two blocks west, tel. 505/886-5477).

and up the hill along the shady dirt road. The view of the city from the fort is worth the walk.

On September 21, 1956, the poet-student Rigoberto López Pérez disguised himself as a waiter to gain access to the ballroom of León's **Old Social Club.** There, he fatally shot Anastasio Somoza García, marking what some say was the beginning of the long end of the dictatorship. The National Guard killed López immediately, making him a much-revered martyr to the cause of the revolution. This event is portrayed by the black-and-white tiled floor and pistol in the mural found in the **Park of Heroes and Martyrs,** a block north of the cathedral.

Murals

León is home to several noteworthy murals, most of them products of the 1980s. Across from the north side of the cathedral is a long, horizontal

piece, painted with help from a German organization and telling the history of a proud and turbulent nation. Starting on the left with the arrival of the Nahuatl people, the mural traces the planned interoceanic canal, the exploits of William Walker, Sandino's battle with the U.S. Marines, the revolution of 1979, and the happy ending of a fertile, peaceful Nicaragua; flanking a doorway across the street, Sandino steps on Uncle Sam's and Somoza's heads. One block to the west is another pointedly political mural: the CIA, in the form of a thick serpent, coils through the Sandinistas' agrarian reform, literacy campaign, and construction efforts, to strike at a Nicaraguan hand at the ballot box.

Also keep an eye out for more modern murals, like the intricate, anti-corruption beast on the basketball court, and for bold, left-leaning graffiti; at the time of this update, one wall in the central

A WALKING TOUR OF CHURCHES AND RUINS

La Catedral de León is the largest cathedral in Central America and the modern city's focal point. One (probably apocryphal) story claims the architect accidentally switched two sets of plans while on the ship from Spain, and the larger of the two cathedrals, originally intended for Lima, Peru, was built in Nicaragua. The cathedral was constructed in 1747 at the request of Archbishop Isidoro Bullón y Figueroa and inaugurated in 1860 as a basilica by Pope Pius XI. It's an imposing and majestic baroque structure whose grandeur is magnified by the open space of the park in front of it. You can observe elements of late Gothic and neoclassic architecture, primarily from inside. Check out the paintings of the stations of the cross and the 12 apostles. The **Tomb of Rubén Darío** is a notable element of the cathedral—look for the golden statue of a lion. The cathedral holds the mortal remains of the musician José de la Cruz Mena and several religious figures. Look for the famous *Cristo de Pedrarias,* a painting that once hung in the cathedral of León Viejo. The particularly beautiful **Patio de los Príncipes** is a small courtyard of Andalusian design, with a fountain in the center and colorful beds of flowers. Ask in the INTUR office about **rooftop tours.** The conglomerate of white towers and domes that form the roof of the Catedral de León is fascinating in its own right—and the view of the city and nearby volcanoes is unsurpassed.

North and East from the Central Park
Iglesia de la Merced is 1.5 blocks north of the main cathedral is the church considered most representative of León in the 1700s. It was originally built in 1762 by the Mercedarian monks, the first order of monks to arrive in Nicaragua during the years of the conquest. It is essentially baroque in style but has neoclassical elements in the front and colonial on the south. It faces a small but lovely park popular amongst León's skate boarders. Particularly attractive is the church's side bell tower.

Passing the Iglesia de la Merced and walking two blocks east along 2 Calle NE, you'll find the yellow **Iglesia de la Recolección** on the north side. This church has the most perfect baroque style of the León churches and a massive, functional bell tower. It was built in 1786 by Bishop Juan Félix de Villegas and is the only church in León constructed using carved stone.

From the Iglesia de la Recolección, continue one more block and turn north. Walk two blocks until you reach the picturesque **Iglesia de San Juan.** The old train station is a block farther north from the east side of the church. Built from 1625 to 1650 and rebuilt in the 1700s, the Iglesia de San Juan's architecture is a modern interpretation of neoclassicism. This neighborhood of León will give you a good feel for what León was like in the 1700s: church, park, small houses of adobe using traditional *taquezal* construction techniques, and the nearby market.

Walking four blocks south down the same road, you'll find the **Iglesia del Calvario** on your left side. It is set at the top of broad steps on a small hill overlooking one of León's narrow streets. Renovated in the late 1990s, El Calvario was built 200 years previous in a generally baroque style, but with neoclassical ornamentation in the front that reflects the increasing French influence in Spain in the 18th century. Inside are two famous statues known as El Buen y el Mal Ladrón (The Good and the Bad Thief).

South and West from the Central Park
La Iglesia y Convento de San Francisco, three blocks west of the park on the north side, and across the street from the Casa Museo Rubén Darío, contains two of the most beautiful altars of colonial Nicaragua. The church was built in 1639 by Fray Pedro de Zuñiga and rebuilt and modified several times afterwards, notably in the mid-1980s to restore the damage done to it during the revolution. Its small, tree-lined courtyard is a pleasant place to escape from the hot sun and relax.

© JOSHUA BERMAN

One of León's numerous colonial cathedrals.

Turning and walking a block south, you come to the unassuming **Iglesia de San Juan de Dios,** built in 1620 as a chapel for León's first hospital (now gone). Its simplicity and colonial style reflect the wishes of Felipe II when he designed it in 1573.

Two blocks farther south and one short block to the west is the **Iglesia del Laborío,** a graceful, rural-feeling church in the old mixed neighborhood of El Laborío. This church, one of León's earliest, formed the nucleus of the working-class neighborhood that provided labor to León's wealthy

class in the 17th century. The street from Laborío east to the Ruínas de la Ermita de San Sebastián is known as **Calle la Españolita** and was one of the first streets built in León.

The **Ruínas de la Ermita de San Sebastián** consist of the shattered remnants of the outer walls, and inexplicably, the intact bell tower. The Ermita was built in 1742 on a site long used by the indigenous people for worship of their own gods. It suffered major damage in 1979 during Somoza's bombardment of León. El Museo de Tradiciones y Leyendas is across the street.

León

plaza screams death for Bush, the "imperial invader," and another nearby calls Sharon an "assassin, coward, and clone of Hitler."

M Museums

Nowhere else in Central America will you find such an eclectic assortment of museums than in León. Covering the political, natural, and all things cultural, they're sure to intrigue.

La Casa de Cultura is a must-see while in León. It is an old colonial home complete with swimming pool, and home to a collection of artwork that includes a disparaging painting of Ronald Reagan and Henry Kissinger. Light lunches and snacks are available. Or try your hand at chess against León's local club (open 8 A.M.–noon and 1:30–6 P.M. Mon.–Fri., and the occasional Sat. and Sun., tel. 505/311-2116).

Inside a 200-year-old building across from the Parque Rubén Darío, the **Museo Alfonso Cortéz** houses many of the personal belongings of Nicaragua's beloved metaphysical poet, including some of his poems as originally written in

the margins of newspapers. It's generally open 8 A.M.–5 P.M. Monday–Friday; donations accepted.

Of Nicaragua's estimated 250,000 insect species, only 1 percent have been labeled or studied; that's still a lot of bugs remaining. The **Museo Entomológico** (tel. 505/311-6586, jmmaes@ibw.com.ni) is related to the UNAN and houses the best collection of national insect life in the country. The museum is generally not open to the public, but if you've got some kind of insect credentials, special visits can be arranged.

La Casa de Rubén Darío (tel. 505/311-2388) is a glimpse into León in the 19th century. Nicaragua's favorite son lived here with the aunt and uncle who raised him until the age of 14. Fellow poet Alfonso Cortéz later inhabited the same house at a time when he went insane (the room he inhabited still has the iron bars he bent in an effort to escape his confinement). Darío's bed and the rest of the furnishings of the museum are typical of middle-class León in the late 19th century, as is the building itself, built from adobe

Red tile is still the rage in León.

RUBÉN DARÍO (1867–1916)

Poet, journalist, diplomat, and favorite son of Nicaragua, Rubén Darío has become the icon for all that's artistic or cultural in Nicaragua. Born Felíx Rubén Garcia Sarmiento in 1867 in the quiet agricultural town of San Pedro de Metapa (now Ciudad Darío), Darío hardly knew his parents. He was raised instead by an aunt and uncle, Colonel Félix Ramírez Madregil and Bernarda Sarmiento, in the colonial city of León. Darío was a fast learner who was already able to read at the age of three. He studied in the Jesuit school Iglesia de la Recolección in León and began composing poetry at the age of 11. In 1882, he was sent to El Salvador by friends who wanted to dissuade him from marrying Rosario Murillo. There he met, befriended, and was inspired by the renowned poet Francisco Gavidia. In 1884, he returned to Nicaragua to work in the National Library of Managua.

Darío departed for Chile in 1886, where he worked as a journalist for the newspaper *La Nación*. His epic poem about the glories of Chile won first prize in a contest sponsored by a Chilean millionaire. His breakthrough came with the publication of *Azul* in 1888, in which Darío introduced a profound change in the aesthetic conception of Spanish American literature. The stories in *Azul* revealed Darío's encounter with Prussian literature and exotic themes of a fantastic world: fauns, gnomes, fairies, nymphs, swans, azure lakes, and grand parks and castles. He was influenced by many, but his style was unique, playing off elements of the naturalism and symbolism movements of the era.

In 1893, he was named ambassador of Colombia to Argentina. He moved to Buenos Aires, a cosmopolitan city that suited him well. His friends there were the educated and elite, and he continued to publish his writings while the Latin American modernist literature movement began to organize under his influence.

In 1898, Darío resumed writing for *La Nación* in Europe. In 1910, he published what is largely considered to be his finest work: "Poema de Otoño." He was director and founder of the international publication, *Magazine,* while in France. In 1905, Darío published one of his best, and last, works: "Cantos de Vida y Desesperación," in which he introspectively re-embraces his Latin roots and examines themes of the passage of time, the suffering of a youth gone by, the pain of the loss of physical pleasure, the tiredness of life, man and his inevitable destiny, and the North American advance into Latin America during that period.

Shortly thereafter, in 1908, he became ambassador of Nicaragua to Spain. He remained in Europe until 1916, when, with his health failing, he returned to Nicaragua where he received a hero's welcome. Darío passed away in León on February 16th. One of his most quoted phrases is: "*Si la patria es pequeña, uno grande la sueña*" ("If one's nation is small, one makes it large through dreams").

with a clay-tile and cane roof. On display are original copies of his most famous works translated into several languages and copies of a magazine he published in Paris. The silver crucifix given him by Mexican poet Amado Nervos, correspondence from when Darío was the consul to Argentina and ambassador to Spain, and period coins and currency are also displayed; open 8 A.M.–noon and 2–5 P.M. Tuesday–Saturday, 8 A.M.–noon Sunday; donations of $1–2 are accepted for the upkeep of the building.

A block west of the Parque Casa de Rubén Darío, the **Centro de Arte Fundación Ortiz-Gurdián,** taking up two buildings on opposite sides of the street, is said to have the best collection of international artwork in Nicaragua, with an emphasis on images of colonial America (open 11:30 A.M.–6:30 P.M. Tue.–Sun.).

El Museo de Tradiciones y Leyendas (in Barrio Laborío, open 8 A.M.–noon, 2–5 P.M. daily, admission $.50) is the result of one strong-willed woman's wish to maintain Nicaragua's precious

León

legends for the generations that followed her. Inside are figures she sewed herself, representing Nicaragua's favorite folk tales: the golden crab, La Carreta Nagua, the pig-witch, and La Mocuana. Equally interesting is the building itself, the former XXI jail and base of the 12th Company of Somoza's National Guard.

Built in 1921, the **XXI** saw nearly 60 years of brutal torture. The mango tree that now shades this museum was planted by a prisoner and watered from the same well that was used for electric shock and head-dunking sessions. There is a solemn photograph collection of young, Sandinista heroes and martyrs at **La Galería,** 1.5 blocks west of the central park. Unfortunately, León's most famous grassroots tribute to the revolution, Luís Manuel Toruño's Museo Insurreccional, was shut down after several decades of displaying his fascinating collection of clutter from one of the most important historical events of the century. Ask around just in case the charismatic, toe-ringed cobbler springs up somewhere else.

El Barrio Subtiava

Subtiava (Maribio for Land of the Big Men), though now a neighborhood of León, was once an indigenous settlement of its own; and to some degree, it still is. Subtiava retains its cultural identity and has a small local government, although it is presided over by the León municipality. Leoneses claim they can recognize who's from Subtiava by their facial features and skin tone, but to the casual traveler, it may be impossible to tell the difference. There are several things of interest here, besides the thrill of walking through the streets of a village predating Columbus; notably, several ruins. Just about any of the microbuses that circulate through León will take you to Subtiava if you're not up for the 12-block walk.

La Catedral de Subtiava is second only to the Catedral de León in size and is the keystone of the community. Construction began in 1698 and finished 12 years later. The cathedral is beautiful in its aged simplicity and has many stories to tell. In one, the indigenous inhabitants of Subtiava were uninterested in the Spanish attempts to convert them to Christianity and kept worshiping their own gods. In an effort to at least get the locals into the church, the Spanish carved a wooden image of the sun, representing the local god, and mounted it on the ceiling of the church. This persuaded the locals to attend, but not to worship the god of the Spanish. It was a compromise that left everyone satisfied, even if, during a church service, the Spanish and the locals were simultaneously worshiping different gods. The sun is still there, beautifully crafted and mounted on the high interior ceiling of the cathedral. The cathedral's immense wooden columns bear testament to the kind of forest that surrounded León 300 years ago; think about that while you sweat. Next to the cathedral to the southwest is the Casa Cural, home to the local Catholic priest. The building predates the Cathedral of Subtiava by 160 years (though it was rebuilt in 1743).

THE LEGEND OF ADIACT AND THE TAMARIND TREE

Several competing versions of this tale have been passed down over three centuries of Nicaraguan history. When Subtiava was still a rebellious Native American village and the Spanish were trying to subdue its inhabitants, victory appeared in the form of a young woman named Xochilt Acalt (Flower of the Sugar Cane). Her father was Adiact, the cacique of the Subtiava people and a ferocious warrior renowned for his victories in battle with the Spanish. But legend goes Xochilt fell in love with a young Spanish soldier. Some say the Spanish took advantage of the love affair to capture and hang Adiact; others say that when he learned of the illicit relationship, he hung himself in shame. Xochilt Acalt disappeared from town, and legend has it she too committed suicide (though some say she banished herself to Poneloya, where another tribe took her in). Either way, everyone agrees that the 300-year-old tamarind tree that still stands proudly in the center of Subtiava is where Adiact was hanged. To modern Subtiavans, the tree still represents the rebelliousness of the indigenous people and is a source of much community pride.

Across the street from the cathedral on the north side is the **Museo Adiact** (open 8 A.M.– noon, 2–5 P.M. Mon.–Fri., 8 A.M.–noon Sat.; pay a voluntary donation on your way in—$1 or $2 is appropriate), a run-down but captivating museum that houses many of the area's archaeological treasures. Sadly, some of the better idols and statues were stolen in the late 1980s and sold to foreign museums.

Five blocks east of the cathedral's southern side is a small park dedicated to the last cacique of Subtiava, Adiact, and his daughter, Xochilt Acalt. From the Cathedral of Subtiava, three blocks south and two blocks west is **El Tamarindón,** an enormous tamarind tree from whose branches the Spanish hung Adiact. Now a small park has been made around the base of the old tree.

There are two sets of ruins in Subtiava, **Las Ruínas de Veracruz** and **Las Ruínas de Santiago.** Both are easily found and unguarded (i.e., no fee). The church at Veracruz was Subtiava's first, built sometime around 1560 and abandoned due to its small size in the late 1700s. The eruption of Volcán Cosigüina in 1835 caused its subsequent collapse. The church at Santiago, constructed in the early 1600s, is significant because its small square bell tower is still intact. Veracruz is located one block west of the cathedral, set in high weeds; Santiago is one block north of the cathedral on the other side of Calle Central (look for a small sign).

ENTERTAINMENT AND EVENTS

Bars and Discos

Las Ruinas (Calle Central, one block west of the park, tel. 505/311-4767) is a cavernous disco popular among the young crowd. **Dilectus** (south of the city center on the highway, tel. 505/311-5439) is the fanciest and most expensive disco in town, with a fun crowd and well-mixed music; it's also an upscale and attractive restaurant with occasional live music and karaoke. Thursday is mariachi night and Friday is teen night; entrance fee is $2, but budget in for a taxi-ride home at the end of the night. Across from Parque La Merced, **Don Señor** is the favorite hangout of the college crowd and internationals; open Tuesday–Saturday

from 4 P.M., Saturdays are best for dancing. Watch the sun set from the **Mirador** bar and restaurant upstairs, and keep an eye out for break-dancing battles on the basketball court below.

Various bars and cafés advertise weekly live music. Check **Vía Vía's** open mic, and the acoustic shows at Jala de Jarra, Puerto Café Benjamin Linder, Restaurante Flor de Sacuanjoche, and CocinArte. Bar/restaurant **Tequetzal** (half a block west of the central park) hosts live music on Thursday nights, and La Raza, Leon's most popular band, plays regularly, often on Fridays at Don Senor's.

Don't miss León's answer to London's double-decker bus or San Francisco's trolleys: **El Bus Pelón** (the bald-headed bus) runs half-hour rides around the city, weekends only, from about 5 P.M.–10 P.M., sometimes featuring live chichero music. Line up at the southwest corner of the central park. The ride, which is popular with local Leoneses, only costs a few *córdobas* and is a great chance to watch the sun set and mingle with locals.

Cinemas, Theater, Dance

León's **cinema** is in the Plaza Siglo Nuevo (from the cathedral, one block north, one block east, tel. 505/311-7080). Look for the *cartelera* (schedule) at shops around the city for show times or call; tickets cost $3. **El Teatro Municipal José de la Cruz Mena** (one block south of the southwest corner of the central park, tel. 505/311-1788, atjcmena@ibw.com.ni) is the cultural heart of the city, open to the public for half-hour theater tours during the day with all kinds of event going on at night; stop by to find out what's playing, as some big-name performers prefer a gig in León to Managua.

Special Events

Ask the INTUR office in León about events during the time you plan to be in town. June 1st is the celebration of Somoza's defeat in León and August 14th is **La Gritería Chiquita,** when devout Catholics celebrate being spared from Cerro Negro's frequent eruptions. León celebrates its *fiestas patronales* on September 24th and the weeks surrounding it.

sawdust paintings during Semana Santa in León

León's **Semana Santa** celebrations are acclaimed throughout Nicaragua as the nation's most lively. In addition to tons of food and drink (and the best *nacatamales*—Nicaraguan tamales—in the country), beds of sawdust are laid out in the streets and ornately painted to show brightly colored religious scenes. When the festivities end, they are swept away. Semana Santa is a week of Catholic masses, parties, and lots of trips to the beach.

SHOPPING

The market immediately behind the cathedral is León's central clearinghouse for fruits and vegetables, but you won't find much in the way of artesanía. Being a university town, León has many interesting bookstores; the best is **Librería Don Quijote** (two blocks west of the park, open 8 A.M.–7 P.M. Mon.–Sat., until early afternoon Sun.), with an interesting selection of new and used books including many old Sandinista titles. **La Galería** (1.5 blocks west of the central park) calls itself a "Bazar [sic] de Artesanía," and sells various types of art. More local crafts can be found at **Papaturo's Gift and Gallery** inside the Ben Linder Café, including organic coffee roasted on site, ceramics from San Juan de Oriente, some soapstone, and local children's art.

SPORTS AND RECREATION

León has earned more baseball championship documents than any other city in Nicaragua; catch a game during the season (January–May). Go swimming at the Hotel San Cristóbal pool (on the bypass highway) for the price of lunch and drinks (on the expensive side). Or find the Metro-Spa in Reparto Fatima and play some racquetball.

ACCOMMODATIONS
Under $10

Some budget options (less than $4) surround the bus terminal where most travelers arrive in León, but they're universally dismal and in a neighborhood that can be dangerous at night. Luckily, there are numerous centrally located places, starting with **Casa Ivana** (across from the Teatro Municipal's south side, tel. 505/311-4423, $7 d, secure parking available), featuring seven clean, quiet, safe rooms with private baths along a long garden in a family house. Around the corner, there are two more small, low-key hostel-type accommodations across the street from each other, two blocks south of the central park: **La Clinica** (tel. 505/311-2031) has a handful of cozy/cramped (depending on your attitude) rooms for under $4, with fan, food, and laundry available. **La Casona** (tel. 505/311-5282) has $3 dorm beds and rooms with private bath, fan, and corrugated zinc roof for $7/9.50 s/d. Also check **Parador de Oviedo** (a.k.a. *sin nombre*, or without name, since Parador de Oviedo is apparently not 100-percent official; tel. 505/311-6750), in the quiet neighborhood across the street from the Iglesia el Calvario, with a dorm room for under $4 and a few additional rooms. They offer laundry service and breakfast.

Vía Vía (75 meters south of the Servicio Agrícola Gurdián, tel. 505/311-6142, www.viaviacafe.com), León's popular and cavernous hostel, offers dorm beds for $3, hammocks and mattresses for a bit less, and two private rooms for $8/10 s/d. The dorm is for sound sleepers only, as it shares a three-quarter wall with a bar whose gringo clientele may keep you up at night. Vía Vía also offers local tours, yoga, salsa, Spanish classes, and a book exchange.

$10–25

ℕ Casona Colonial Guesthouse (tel. 505/311-3178, located half a block west of the Parque San Juan) $10 d with private bath, hot water, and a fan is quite possibly the best bargain in León, complete with high ceilings, flower-filled courtyard, and beautiful wooden furniture. They give you a key so you can come and go at any hour, and there's a TV in the courtyard. Breakfast is available for $2, or try the cafetín next door. **Hotel America** (one block east of the market, tel. 505/311-5533, $10 s, $15 d with private bath and fan) is a large and high-ceilinged old hotel whose black-and-white tiled floors date back to the days of Somoza. Breakfast is available for $2.50, or try the bakery across the street for cheap fresh pastries.

Hotel Colonial (tel. 505/311-2279, 2.5 blocks north of the northwest corner of the park) is in a gorgeous, historical building, but its "upscale" rooms are rundown and overpriced; the cheaper rooms ($15) are worth a look, especially for groups.

$25–50

In the center of León, **Hotel Austria** (from the cathedral, one block south and half a block west, tel. 505/311-1206 or 505/311-7178, haustria @ibw.com.ni, www.hotelaustria.com.ni, $36 /50 s/d plus tax) offers 17 immaculate, modern rooms with a/c, TV, phones, and hot water; and

it includes continental breakfast and guarded parking for your vehicle. The hotel features an on-site restaurant and comfortable space for relaxing or group meetings.

In a converted colonial home, the **Hostal Casa Leonesa** (from the cathedral, three blocks north and half a block east, tel. 505/311-0551, cleonesa @ibw.com.ni, www.lacasaleonesa.com, $35/45 s/d) has nine gorgeous rooms around a small pool and garden, each with a/c, TV, hot water, and phone. The beautiful common space makes you feel like León royalty.

Hotel San Juan de León (tel. 505/311-0547, hsanjuan@ibw.com.ni, www.sanjuandeleon.com .ni) has 22 smallish rooms on two floors surrounding a tasteful courtyard and kitchen for guests' use. Rooms with private bath and fan are $25 d, ten bucks more for a/c; breakfast included, TVs in rooms. Around the corner, the same hotel owner kicks things up a notch at **Hotel Posada del Doctor** (tel. 505/311-4343, www.posadadeldoctor.com, one block west of Parque San Juan) $30 d for private bath, TV, fan, and continental breakfast, $40 for a/c., with 10 lovely rooms around a very bright and pleasant garden.

Grand Hotel (one block south of the old train station, tel. 505/311-1327, www.grandhoteldeleon.com, $30 for TV and private bath, $35 with a/c) is less regal than its name implies; it's more like a standard U.S. motel. Its 17 clean, predictable, and secure rooms are ideal for motorists passing through. Located on a bustling market street across from the southwest side of the bus terminal, you won't want to wander the streets around the Grand at night. The imposing, well-kept 30-room compound of **Hotel Europa** (tel. 505/311-6040, heuropa@ibw.com.ni, $25 d with fan, $35 with a/c, TV, hot water) has been around since the 1960s, when it catered to the train crowd. Recently remodeled and clean, it offers a restaurant, lounge areas, and guarded parking for your vehicle.

$50–100

Expect old, wooden, colonial stateliness in the 20 rooms at **ℕ Hotel Los Balcones** (three blocks east of the cathedral, $52 d with TV, a/c, hot water). Upstairs rooms enjoy a small balcony.

León

Hotel El Convento ((tel. 505/311-7053, informacion@hotelelconvento.com.ni, www.hotelelconvento.com.ni, next door to the San Francisco Church, a few blocks west of the central park), $69 s, $87 d including bathtubs and continental breakfast $69 s, $87 d including bathtubs and continental breakfast offers luxurious grandeur within its walls, several of which were reconstructed from stones used in the convent's original 1639 construction. From the beautiful centerpiece garden and fountain that greet you as you enter to long, cool corridors adorned with art and antiques, El Convento offers all the amenities you would expect in this class, plus business services, a ballroom, restaurant, and local tours for its guests.

Long-term Lodging

There are many cheap student rooms advertised around town, which serve well for budget travelers and volunteers who have decided to stop and stay a while, either for work or service. The house known as **El Encuentro** (located at the Quetzal Trekkers office, 1.5 blocks east of Iglesia la Recoleccion, $75/month per person, $100/month for couples) is popular with this crowd.

FOOD

León has never been known for exotic or elegant cuisine, although a few Euro-oriented options are beginning to pop onto the scene. For the most part, however, what you'll find here caters to a largely student crowd—i.e., *típica* (traditional plates), burgers, and pizza, as well as traditional chicken, steak, and seafood dishes, often in open-air corner café-restaurants.

Cheap Comida Típica

Enjoy a substantial traditional breakfast in the picturesque Hotel Colonial for about $2.50, and have lunch for under $2 at **Comedor Lucía** (across from Vía Vía). The best finger-lickin' *fritanga* in town is no doubt **El Buen Gusto** (a couple blocks east of the Catedral's south side); mix and match from their sidewalk smorgasbord and hubcap grill between 10 A.M. and 10 P.M., closed Sundays.

N Restaurante Taquezal (half a block west of

© JOSHUA BERMAN

Hotel El Convento is León's new upscale digs, set in the city's center.

the central park's southern end) has a pleasant atmosphere and a varied menu; typical dishes cost $5–9. Try the "Nicaccino": cappuccino with a shot of Nicaraguan rum.

Restaurante Flor de Sacuanjoche serves lots of meat, seafood, and veggie options, including salads, "soysage," and veggie burgers. They also do a good business in another vegetarian favorite: liquor. Meals run $4–6, open daily 10 A.M.–midnight. **Payita's,** a pleasant, outdoor corner café in the middle of all the university action, offers burgers, hot dogs, or *comida corriente* (plate of the day) from $2 and up.

Cafés

Right in front of the cathedral, **El Sesteo** is a trendy, high-priced, open-air corner spot and the international crowd's favorite place to sip cappuccino or eat their famous *churrasco* (steak, about $7). It's open daily 8 A.M.–9:30 P.M. **N Puerto Café Benjamin Linder** is a restaurant, coffee shop, bar, Internet café, and craft store, whose profits help support a local group of disabled children. The shop is a tribute to the only U.S. citizen killed in the Contra war (see the Matagalpa chapter). A beautiful indoor mural depicts his life in Nicaragua; enjoy it while ordering from their creative, veggie-friendly food and coffee menu (also lots of sandwiches, snacks and bar food, with special $2 lunches). Open 11:30 A.M.–11:30 P.M. Monday–Saturday. The vegetarian restaurant and coffee shop at **CocinArte** (across from the north side of La Iglesia el Laborío, tel. 505/611-8784) also promises alternative cinema, a crafts shop and a comfortable reading and lounging space, plus creative and low-priced veggie eats.

International

Enjoy pizza and authentic Lebanese dishes at **Restaurante Italian Pizza** (located a half block north of the cathedral, delivery: tel. 505/311-0657, open 9 A.M.–9 P.M.). The pizza at **Hollywood Pizza** (located in the movie theater complex, tel. 505/311-0636, open 11:30 A.M.–9:30 P.M. Mon.–Fri., later on weekends) is less exciting but the a/c is wintry. They too deliver. More pizza and Italian cuisine can be had at the **Mediterraneo** (half block north of the Iglesia Guadelupe, open at 4 P.M. Tues.–Fri., at 11 A.M. weekends).

There are two options for Mexican cantina food (meals $4–7) and *cervezas:* **Jala de Jarra** (on the corner north of the Teatro Municipal, open 11 A.M.–11 P.M. Mon.–Sat., later on Saturday) is the nicer of the two, with heavy medieval furniture, including thick, wood tables and benches on the sidewalk. The other, **Guadalajara** (across from Puerto Café Benjamin Linder, tel. 505/311-6748) is louder, simpler, and will home-deliver food from its long Mexican menu.

For dark-lit, slightly mysterious ambience, slink into either the **Casa Vieja Cafetín** (one block north of Hotel El Convento entrance) or **Allante Bar Café** (across from the Teatro Municipal), both with standard surf, turf, and barfood menus, both open Monday–Saturday for dinner. Or try the **Matchico "Jazz Bar Café"** (2.5 blocks north of the Cathedral) for a French-based, pre-Columbian theme menu.

INFORMATION AND TOUR SERVICES

The official **INTUR** office (from the central park, one block west and 2.5 north, tel. 505/311-3682) has brochures, postcards, and updated bus schedules; a more centrally located **Information Office** (a few meters north of the Cathedral, tel. 505/311-3992) also offers mounds of brochures, plus a gang of eager UNAN students waiting to help you with local information and maps. Both offices open Monday–Saturday during normal business hours, including a two-hour lunch break. Also check in the Casa de Cultura for local tour services or visit **www.leononline.net.**

Several tour operators provide transport and guides to all the nearby sites, including León Viejo, San Jacinto Hot Springs, Isla Juan Venado, and volcano expeditions. **Va Pues Tours** (in their adjoining vegetarian restaurant and art center, Cocinarte, across from the north side of Iglesia Laboría, tel. 505/611-8784, info@vapues.com, www.vapues .com) offers reasonably priced trips to all these places and then some—ask about their steel-plated snowboards for shreddin' up Cerro Negro or their overnight turtle-viewing trips with a local biologist; many volcano trips and a rum factory tour as well. Also recommended are **Journey Nicaragua's** Rigo Sampson (tel. 505/311-3306 or 505/868-1569, rsampson@ibw.com.ni) and Flavio Parajón (tel. 505/311-4381, fparajon2003@yahoo.es).

Quetzal Trekkers (1.5 blocks east of Iglesia la Recolección, leon@quetzaltrekkers.com, www .quetzaltrekkers.com) is a highly-recommended non-profit trip organizer that specializes in longer volcano trips, including hiking and overnight options; profits go to helping street kids here and in Xela, Guatemala, where they were first formed. They accept short-term volunteers to help with their operations.

For information about local reserves, visit the office of **Universitárea Protegida** (a block west of the municipal theater, tel. 505/880-9011UÁP, www.eii.org/uap), a non-profit that places university students in rural protected areas to do research on plants and animals. You'll find info about the program, plus maps, contacts in local areas, and a book exchange.

SERVICES

Banks

Bancentro is only a block north of the cathedral, and most of the other banks are within a block east and north of there. There is a cluster of three ATMs one block east of the cathedral, in the BAC, la Union Supermarket, and Plaza Siglo Nuevo (movie theater complex).

Medical

The hospital is in the center of León, one block south of the Cathedral; you're probably better off in one of the two private clinics with emergency rooms that face each other on the block west of Café Puerto Benjamin Linder, Policlinica la Fraternidad (tel. 505/311-1403) and Policlinica Occidental (tel. 505/311-2722), but weekends and after normal business hours, they may not have a doctor on site.

Internet

Droves of tourists and students in León have inspired a plethora of options in all directions from the park. The most air-conditioned and agreeable option is **CompuService** (across from Policlinica la Fraternidad, open 8 A.M.–9:30 P.M. Mon.–Sat., 9 A.M.–6 P.M. Sun.), with all kinds of fast services, including docks for laptops and cold beers from the restaurant next door. If they are full, walk west to the corner and half a block north and look for **CyberFast** (on the left across from INTUR), offering a/c, cheap rates, and a generous seven-day schedule. Another excellent, spacious, and cooled option is **Club en Conexion** (from the cathedral, three blocks north, half block east, open 7:30 A.M.–9:30 P.M. Mon.–Fri., till 7 P.M. Sat.).

Mail, Phones, and Other Services

The **Correos** (three blocks north of the back side of the main cathedral, open 8 A.M.–5 P.M. Mon.–Fri., 8 A.M.–noon Sat.) deals with faxes as well as mail. **Agencia de Viajes Premier** (across from the Rubén Darío park, tel. 505/311-5535) is León's only authorized UPS agent. **ENITEL** (on the west side of the central park) is open 8 A.M.–9 P.M. daily, but public phones are every-where, and you can call as well from many Internet cafés.

Of the several huge supermarkets, the most central is **La Union** (a block east of the cathedral, open 7:30 A.M.–8 P.M. Mon.–Sat., 8 A.M.–6 P.M. Sun.).

Travel Agents and Tickets

Viajes Mundiales (from the cathedral, three blocks north, half a block east, tel. 505/311-6263 or 505/311-5920, viajesmu@ibw.com.ni, open 8 A.M.–noon and 2–6 P.M. Mon.–Fri., until 1 P.M. Sat.) is a full international agency and official representative of major airlines. Two blocks west, you'll find an authorized **TransNica** agency (tel. 505/311-5219) with bus service to Costa Rica, Honduras, and El Salvador. **Agencia de Viajes Premier** (by the Iglesia San Juan, tel. 505/311-5535) is the authorized agent for La Costeña airline tickets, to plan your flight to the Atlantic coast.

Opportunities to Volunteer and Study

Ask about ongoing projects supported by Puerto Café Benjamin Linder and the Casa de Cultura. Even if language barriers prevent you from working directly with Nicaraguan street kids, you can still help out by volunteering for Quetzal Trekkers, whose proceeds go to local projects.

If you're going to be in León for more than a brief visit, consider taking a class at the Casa de Cultura (tel. 505/311-2116), which offers classes in guitar, drawing and painting, tae kwon do, dance (folk and modern), "mental relaxation," and more. At Modas Carolina (two blocks east of the cathedral, tel. 505/311-1462), Marlene Sánchez gives sewing and clothes-making classes; two hours per day, mornings, afternoons, or Saturdays. Vía Vía offers dancing and yoga classes.

GETTING THERE AND AWAY

The main bus station (La Terminal) is in the northeast corner of town, where you'll find transportation to all parts except Poneloya and Las Peñitas (buses to these beaches depart from their own terminal at the Mercadito Subtiava). Big yellow buses and small, white *interlocales* depart regularly for Managua, Chinandega, and points along the Telica–San Isidro highway. There are also daily expresses to Estelí and Matagalpa (5 A.M. and 8:40 A.M.). Buses for Managua run from 4 A.M. till about 7 P.M.

Hitchhiking to Managua is easiest from the StarMart parking lot at the *salida* (exit from Leon). There you can corner drivers stopping to fill up on gas and hot dogs. Across the intersection is the road north to Chinandega and the border, but if you want to go east to Estelí or Matagalpa, you'll want to make it a couple kilometers north at the *empalme* (turn-off) for San Isidro.

ORIENTATION AND GETTING AROUND

León is laid out in the traditional colonial grid system with the central park and cathedral at the center. The main bus station and market are located nearly a kilometer northeast of the park, and Barrio Subtiava is 12 blocks due west. Within the city, taxis charge $.50 during the day and $1 at night. Small city buses and converted pickup trucks also crisscross León and charge about $.15; ask about your destination before getting on.

Near León

SOUTH OF LEÓN

N Las Ruínas de León Viejo

The small town of La Paz Centro is a pueblo of artisans who make handicrafts with locally found clay. Their *fiestas patronales* are September 10th (San Nicolás de Tolentino). Near the center of town, a small Casa de Cultura sells local artwork.

La Paz Centro is your gateway to the sleepy ruins of Spain's first settlement in Nicaragua, found in Puerto Momotombo. This well-developed historical site is an easy and worthy day trip from León. Francisco Hernández de Córdoba founded the first León in 1524 and Pedrarias Dávila governed it. Dávila had Hernández de Córdoba decapitated in the town square two years later. In 1610, Volcán Momotombo erupted, burying the site under ash. But León may have already been abandoned, after a series of earthquakes convinced the settlers to look elsewhere for a place to call home. (Momotombo has erupted several times since then, most recently in 1905.)

Dr. Carlos Tünnerman and a team from the National University (UNAN) first uncovered the ruins in 1966. In 2000, archeologists uncovered the remains of both Córdoba and Dávila and placed them in an on-site mausoleum. León Viejo is now a World Heritage Site. The Nicaraguan Culture Institution has completed some fascinating excavations of the site and has trained many local guides to take you around, most of whom are friendly, enthusiastic, and speak passable English. Entrance is $2, plus a small fee to take photographs or video.

The site is open seven days a week, with tour guides from 8 A.M.–5 P.M. Catch a bus from León to catch either an 8 A.M. or 11 A.M. connection in La Paz Centro; last return bus from the ruins is 3 P.M. Contact tel. 505/222-2905, ext. 112 for the Palacio Nacional de la Cultura in Managua, or tel. 505/886-2087 for the park center at the ruins.

Volcán Momotombo and Momotombito Island

Volcán Momotombo is the most challenging Pacific volcano to climb (see Hiking the Maribio Volcanoes special topic); its little brother, the island of Momotombito, is an excellent adventure in the waiting. Long-extinct Momotombito was once a pre-Columbian religious sanctuary, when the islet was called Cocobolo. Today, it is an uninhabited natural reserve of tropical dry forest, but getting there isn't easy. Your best bet is to pay someone with a small boat in the town of Puerto Momotombo to row you the 25 kilometers along the north shore of Lake Managua to the island (better yet—take turns and work off some of that *gallo pinto*). While the small town of El Cardón, on the other side of Volcán Momotombo, is closer, the town itself is difficult to get to from the

the ruins of León Viejo

highway. Should you decide to camp on the island, bring your own water and supplies to last you at least two days, and don't pay your boatman until he returns to take you off the island. Remember, the lake is horrendously polluted.

Nagarote

About halfway between Managua and León, the historic village of Nagarote (Chorotega for the road of the Nagarands) is representative of Nicaragua's small agricultural and cattle villages. Its claim to fame is an enormous old genícero tree said to date back to the time of Columbus and whose broad branches shade the markets. Find the genícero and a statue of Diriangén two blocks north and one block west from the central park. The Casa de Cultura is located one block south of the tree. Nagarote is also renowned for its *quesillos,* a snack of mozzarella-like string cheese, sour cream, and onions wrapped in a hot, soft tortilla.

Nagarote also makes a good jumping-off point for some interesting hikes through the Cordillera del Pacífico, the range of mountains that runs alongside the highway to León. Walk southeast out of town and pass the Colonia Agrícola Presidente Schick. The road will take you up into a relatively wooded and uninhabited area of pretty mountain valleys, and eventually to a good view of the lake. From there, start your descent to the highway and catch a bus to León or Managua. Use INETER quad maps Nagarote and Mateare.

NORTH OF LEÓN

ⓜ Los Hervideros de San Jacinto

On the southeast flank of 1,060-meter Volcán Telica, Los Hervideros de San Jacinto are a nest of boiling mud pits and thermal vents fueled by the underground geothermal activity. They make a great day trip from León. To get there, take a bus bound for Estelí, San Isidro, or Malpaisillo and get off at the town of San Jacinto (approximately 25 kilometers from León). The entrance is marked by an enormous arch and a posse of women and children selling "artifacts" from the hot springs.

The young boys will offer to guide you around for $.20, a good deal considering the danger of falling into a scalding mud bath. There are community-based tourism projects and trail improvements in the works, as well as a new hotel.

El Sauce and Achuapa

In the foothills of the Segovia Mountains, to the north and east of León, El Sauce (rhymes with wow-say) was once the eastern terminus of the railroad that carried Nicaraguan coffee down to Corinto. In the 1800s, caravans of mules lumbered into town, laden with thousands of pounds of coffee beans. El Sauce has since faded into a sleepy cowboy village whose pride and joy is a breathtaking colonial church built in 1750 in tribute to the patron saint, el Cristo Negro de Esquipulas (the Black Christ). El Sauce celebrates its *fiestas patronales* on January 18th and causes a massive pilgrimage from all over Nicaragua to view the Black Christ icon. Perhaps the fame of El Sauce's Cristo Negro is due in part to access provided the town by the Sauce–León–Corinto branch of the Nicaragua National Railroad, which carried cattle, coffee, and passengers between 1932 and 1993.

El Sauce is off the beaten track but makes a good first stop on forays into the wilds of Achuapa, San Juan de Limay, and Estelí. There are a couple places to eat, and several *hospedajes:* try Hotel El Viajero, tel. 505/319-2325, $3 per night.

WEST OF LEÓN

Poneloya and Las Peñitas Beaches

Only a 20-minute drive from León, Poneloya is the most popular beach in the area and has been a playground of the wealthy for generations. Nearby, less-visited and pristine Las Peñitas beach has recently become a popular destination for foreign travelers who wish to explore Isla Juan Venado Wildlife Reserve. Both beach towns together house fewer than 3,000 people, until Semana Santa, when hotels at both beaches swell to capacity. Be sure to make reservations at least a month in advance; also expect prices to be double what is listed below.

The road from León splits when it reaches the coast, the right fork placing you in Poneloya where you'll find two hotels. **Hotel Lacayo** (tel. 505/886-7369, $5 pp, shared bath), with its sagging cots and your own dilapidated balcony overlooking the ocean), is a massive, breezy beachfront barn on stilts that continues to defy gravity after 70 years of hosting beachgoers. Don't mind the bats; they eat mosquitoes. Across the street, **Hotel La Posada** (tel. 505/317-377, in León tel. 505/311-4812, $20 t) has 19 concrete rooms with private bath, fan, and a/c. It's simple but essentially clean.

Traveling several kilometers south (the left fork from León) will bring you to a series of accommodations that make up Las Peñitas, presented here in the order you'll find them. **Hostal La Montaña** (tel. 505/882-9816, $35 d with private bath and a/c) is a good, romantic getaway, with four nice rooms, a bar, and restaurant. **Hotel Suyapa Beach** (tel. 505/885-8345, frobertoreyes@yahoo.com, $29 and up with a/c and private bath) is a modern, well-kept hotel/restaurant with 22 rooms and hosts vacationers and conference-attendees around its small pool. Continuing south, **Mi Casita** (tel. 505/852-9766, $13 d with shared bath, $17 private bath) offers five brightly painted rooms with soft beds, fan, and the sound of the surf.

Newcomer **Hotelito El Oasis** (tel. 505/839-5344, patrick426@caramail.com, $15 t) is reasonably priced, spacious, and has rooms with fan and private bath; enjoy the small rancho and hammock area, and a reasonably priced menu. At the end of the road, you'll find **La Barca de Oro** (tel. 505/895-8881, tortuga@ibw.com.ni, four rooms at $14 t with fan, mosquito net, and private bath); there is also one room with shared bath $10 s/d, and the "honeymoon suite" with a/c costs $25. La Barca looks directly out to the northern tip of Isla Juan Venado, only 100 meters away across a protected lagoon. They can help you arrange all kinds of local (and inland) excursions. You can also rent kayaks or hire locals to give a massage or pedicure at this popular backpacker getaway.

Buses for Poneloya leave every half-hour from the Subtiava Mercadito, from early in the morning until 6 P.M. They stop first Poneloya, idling for ten minutes, then continue to Las Peñitas; the trip to the end of the road at Barca de Oro can take up to an hour. You'll save a lot of time and pay a bit more (about $7, not bad if you have three or four people) with a taxi from León. The last bus back to León leaves Barca de Oro at 6:40 P.M.

Isla Juan Venado Wildlife Reserve

The 21-kilometer strip of tropical dry forest, mangroves, and inland estuary south of Las Peñitas provides habitat for hundreds of species of migratory birds, as well as crocodiles and other wetland creatures, and is also an important nesting beach for sea turtles. The park is named for a man who, in colonial times, made his living hunting deer on the island and selling the meat in the market of Subtiava.

Many León-based tour operators run trips to Isla Juan Venado, but you can just as easily strike a deal with one of the many boatmen in Las Peñitas to explore the endless riverine channels. Arrange your trip at least one day in advance, especially if you plan on a sunrise excursion, when you'll see the most wildlife (late afternoons are good, too). Take sun protection and lots of water. You'll need to purchase tickets ($2 pp) at a two-story house 100 meters down the beach from Barca de Oro; the money goes to a women's group that keeps the beaches clean.

You can also access the reserve from the rustic community of Salinas Grandes on the south side of the island, where you can rent kayaks and stay in beachfront ranchos at Rigo's Guest House (tel. 505/311-3306 or 505/868-1569, rsampson @ibw.com.ni).

El Velero and El Transito Beach Communities

South from León, the gorgeous two-kilometer stretch of white-sand beach known as **El Velero** (the sailboat) is occupied mostly by summer homes for wealthy Leoneses. The limited options for travelers are not cheap and have fallen into total disrepair. Buses for Puerto Sandino and El Velero leave from the station at León.

Upon entering the hamlet, look for the administration office, where you can rent one of a half-dozen state-run cabins. Prices run from $25 a night for bunk beds and a fan to $50 for an air-conditioned cabin with two double beds. To make it worth your while, bring several friends

volcanic rock formations on the beach at El Transito

and a cooler full of food, as each cabin contains a fridge and a gas stove. The few restaurants that exist in El Velero are sketchy and not always open.

A quiet fishing community 60 kilometers from Managua along the old highway to León, **El Tránsito** was devastated by the tidal wave of 1991. The town was rebuilt shortly afterward with extensive help from the Spanish; you can see the new town on the hills above the old one, which was at the shoreline. The swimming here can be a bit tricky, as there's a strong undertow that will pull you north along the cove. A safer bet is to walk south along the shoreline to see the rock formations and popular swimming holes behind them. These rocks run parallel to the shoreline and buttress the full blow of waves. If you're swimming in one of the several pools there, you can count on an occasional saltwater shower, often with no warning at all. Ten minutes' walk north along the shoreline takes you to the wreckage of El Balneario, an old abandoned vacation spot. Enjoy cheap, cold beer and fresh fish on the south end of the village. Buses leave Managua every afternoon from Israel Lewites at 11:15 A.M., 12:40 P.M., and 2 P.M. Buses leave El Transito every day at 5 A.M., 6 A.M., and 7 A.M.

Chinandega

Besides the full-grown alligators in the central park, there are few tourist attractions per se in the city of Chinandega. Nevertheless, this regional capital makes a perfect base camp for volcano and beach expeditions, and provides a chance to see Nicaraguans coping with the hottest, driest part of their country.

The same threatening volcanoes that loom over the city of Chinandega and its surrounding plains are also responsible for the high fertility of the soil. This attracted the Nahuatl, who called their new home Chinamilt (close to cane).

Chinandega suffers the same poverty as the rest of the nation, but Chinandega also boasts a prosperous community of old and new money, based primarily in sugar, bananas, peanuts, sesame, soy, and shrimp. Cotton used to be the number-one cash crop in the 1960s, but the deforestation and agro-chemicals essential to its production caused monumental environmental damage, like poisoned aquifers and toxic soil, still affecting life to this day. The agricultural ac-

tivity of the region and proximity to the northern borders and Port of Corinto make Chinandega Nicaragua's most important agribusiness center.

Did we mention that it's hot in Chinandega? It's so hot in Chinandega, you can expect to break a sweat while you're in the shower. *This* is what it feels like to be a rotisserie chicken. You'd be wise to drink at least a liter of water on the ride up because you'll sweat it all out before you can walk to the park to see the alligators. Pick your spirits up with a self-guided tour of Chinandega's colonial churches and central market, and then find an air-conditioned spot to eat some ice cream.

ENTERTAINMENT AND RECREATION

For a classy dancing experience, the **M Dilectus disco** (located just east of town on the road to León) is one of the nation's finest. If you prefer a looser, younger crowd and still want air-conditioning, try **Montserat** on the highway to

San Cristobal lords over the scorching streets of Chinandega, occasionally powdering them with a layer of gray-white ash.

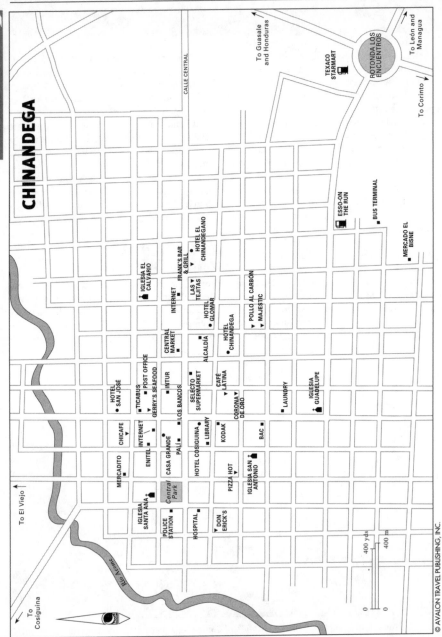

CHINANDEGA

To El Viejo

To Cosiguina

Río Acome

To Guasale
and Honduras

To León and
Managua

To Corinto

ROTONDA LOS
ENCUENTROS

TEXACO
STARMART

CALLE CENTRAL

ESSO-ON
THE RUN

BUS TERMINAL

MERCADO EL
BISNE

IGLESIA EL
CALVARIO

FRANK'S BAR
& GRILL

HOTEL EL
CHINANDEGANO

INTERNET

LAS
TEJITAS

HOTEL
GLOMAR

POLLO AL CARBÓN

MAJESTIC

CENTRAL
MARKET

ALCALDIA

HOTEL
CHINANDEGA

POST OFFICE

TICABUS

GERRY'S SEAFOOD

HOTEL
SAN JOSÉ

INTUR

LOS BANCOS

SELECTO
SUPERMARKET

CAFÉ
LATINA

CORONA
DE ORO

LAUNDRY

IGLESIA
GUADELUPE

MERCADITO

CHICAFE

INTERNET

ENITEL

PALÍ

CASA GRANDE

HOTEL COSIGUINA

LIBRARY

KODAK

BAC

IGLESIA
SANTA ANA

Central
Park

PIZZA HOT

IGLESIA SAN
ANTONIO

POLICE
STATION

HOSPITAL

DON
ERICK'S

400 yds

400 m

0

0

© AVALON TRAVEL PUBLISHING, INC.

Guasale. **La Terraza** (on the road to El Corinto) is very pleasant, with dancing on the weekend, decent food, and a clean swimming pool! Your next step down is an outdoor rancho-style disco called **El Bosque** (on the highway north), or give your feet a break and drink $2 pitchers of Victoria in the outdoor central park kiosk. There is a great air-conditioned bar at the Hotel El Chinandegano.

If you really enjoy sweating, join in a pickup basketball game at the courts by the park. If watching **baseball** is more your style, catch Team Chinandega in season (the stadium is located west across the river, on the road to El Viejo). You'll find a clean public swimming pool at the Instituto San Luis (on the east end of town, open Fri.–Sun., $1.50 for the whole day), complete with high dive, cheap beer, and a hot dog and burger stand. There are also plenty of waves to surf up and down the entire coast and zero surfers. This means the waves are yours alone, but so are the equipment, logistics, and responsibility.

SHOPPING

Buy crafts and homemade wine at **Chicafe,** where your purchase will support the efforts of several local women's craft cooperatives. The three markets (Bisne, Central, and the Mercadito) are dark and deep and are all surrounded by several square blocks of additional retail action—whip out some moist *córdobas* and go nuts. The **Kodak** store (two blocks east and one south of the central park) has an impressive stock of photo and computer supplies (and extreme air-conditioning). Chinandega has two fully-stocked **supermarkets:** El Palí in front of the park, and El Selecto, 3.5 blocks farther east.

ACCOMMODATIONS

Under $10

At less than $5 a night, **Hotel Chinandega** is the best dump in town: centrally located, 15 rooms, relatively clean, and only slightly depressing and dingy.

$10–25

Hotel Glomar (across from the alcaldía, tel. 505 /341-2562, 13 rooms, $10 s, $13 d for fan and shared bath, $17 s and $22 d for private bath and a/c) is clean enough. Find similar accommodations in the **Casa Grande** (tel. 505/341-0325, $15 s and $15 d with fan, $25 with TV and a/c); there's free laundry service, and the friendly owner, Don Alvaro, can help organize volcano expeditions.

$25–50

The Hotel San José (tel. 505/341-2723, movalles @starband.com, $25 s and $35 d with private bath, TV, a/c, breakfast) has eight beautifully decorated and well-kept rooms in a converted home. **Hotel El Chinandegano** (tel. 505/341-4800, hchinandegano@radionetinc.com, $25 s/d with a/c, private bath, breakfast, phone) has 10 quality rooms, professional service, laundry, parking, and lovely, bird-filled common spaces.

The plushest digs in the city center are at **Hotel Cosigüina** (located half a block south of esquina de los bancos, corner of the banks, tel. 505/341-3636, www.hotelcosiguina.com, $30 s and $40 d with a/c, hot water, private bath, phone). They also rent cars, have Internet service, and serve food and drinks in El Cráter Sports Bar and Fumaroles Restaurant, both decent.

FOOD

You won't go hungry in Chinandega, with everything from the *comida corriente* in any of the markets (meals for less than $2) to a host of expensive restaurants. Located on the Calle Central, seven blocks east of the park, **Las Tejitas** may have been the best *fritanga* in Nicaragua; so say the stream of regular clients, including several generations of locally placed Peace Corps volunteers. Sit outside on the sidewalk and enjoy a heaping plate of juicy roasted chicken, *gallo pinto, tajadas,* (fried plantain chips) and any number of deep-fried delicacies, all for under $3, drink included; open evenings. For just a couple *córdobas* more, eat in the air-conditioned comfort of Don Erick's buffet and bar (three blocks west of the Kodak), with fantastic food and service.

A welcome addition to Chinandega is the relaxed, tasteful **Chicafe** (half a block west of the Almacen Quinonez, open 8 A.M.–6 P.M. Mon.–Sat.). Enjoy a coffee menu, fruit smoothies, snack foods, and homemade wine and sangria, plus treats like French toast and peanut butter and jelly sandwiches. Chicafe is run by a local NGO that supports several women's cooperatives and children projects.

Check **Gerry's Seafood Restaurant y Marisquiería** (on main drag, north of bank corner, open 10 A.M.–10:30 P.M. Mon.–Sat.) for good ceviche ($3) and fish dishes from $4.50. Hotel Cosigüina has a quaint rancho in the back called **El Crater,** with meals from $8. At **Frank's Bar and Grill** (open 11 A.M.–10:30 P.M. daily) you'll find fine wines from around the world and a fine dining ambience, with meals from $8–10.

Many fancier restaurants abound along the highways in and out of town, and gringo fare is plentiful, including a Jerry's Subs and Pizza in the StarMart and all kinds of junk food and sandwiches at On the Run. **Hamburlooca** (tel. 505/341-3264) will delivery great and greasy burgers to your hotel.

INFORMATION AND SERVICES

INTUR (tel. 505/341-1935, chinandega@intur .gob.ni) maintains an office in the Centro Comercial Chinandega, tucked back by the FedEx and Costa Rican Consulate. They can recommend local businesses and guides. INETER sells detailed area maps and topo maps out of its office west of town, across the river. The police take up the entire block along the west side of the central park, and the hospital is right across the street to the south. Money changers work the streets near the central market, and most of Chinandega's banks are clustered on *la esquina de los bancos,* two blocks east of the park.

The post office is three blocks east of the park and 1.5 north. Also, the TicaBus agent will send FedEx packages via their Managua office. The ENITEL phone office is one block east of the park—look for the giant red and white tower. ATMs can be found at Banco America Central (el BAC), as well as at Starmart and On the Run. Get your laundry done just north of the Iglesia Guadelupe.

Internet

Chinandega's abundant Internet options are in constant flux, though you'll want to seek out the ones with air-conditioning. Check the big one four blocks east of the corner of banks, or Café Latino, one block east and half a block south from Kodak.

Consulates

The Consulate of El Salvador is two blocks north of *la esquina de los bancos,* (tel. 505/341-2049, open 8 A.M.–2 P.M. Mon.–Fri.; when applying for a visa, leave your passport before 11 A.M.). The Honduras Consulate is across from ENITEL (tel. 505/341-0949, open 8:30 A.M.–4:30 P.M. Mon.–Fri.). The Costa Rica Consulate is located half a block north from BANPRO (tel. 505/341-1584, open 8:30 A.M.–5 P.M. Mon.–Fri., until noon Sat.).

GETTING THERE AND AWAY

The main bus station is at Bisne Market, just past Rotonda los Encuentros. From La Rotonda, highways run north to Somotillo and the border with Honduras at Guasale (this is easily the most deteriorated stretch of the entire Nicaraguan highway system, a real bonecrusher), east to León and Managua, south to Corinto, and west into Chinandega. A second bus station located at the Mercadito (just north of the central park) provides service to El Viejo, Jiquilillo, Potosi, Cosigüina, and Puerto Morazán.

Car rentals starting at $35 a day are available at the Avis office in the Hotel Cosigüina and Budget in Hostal Las Mañanitas. Local buses, expresses ($1.85) and microbuses ($2.20), run regularly between Chinandega and Managua's Israel (Boer) Market, beginning at 4:30 A.M. and ending around 8 P.M. Service to and from León is even more frequent and hitching in any direction from La Rotonda is a cinch.

Those traveling north into Honduras or El Salvador can buy tickets in the TicaBus office. Prices are the same as from Managua, and you'll need to be in front of the StarMart no later than 6 A.M. to catch your ride, although "sometimes the bus comes later." The first TicaBus that passes (en route from Managua) will take you to Tegucigalpa and the second to San Salvador and Guatemala. Be advised: Any foreigner who enters El Salvador must be carrying a visa. Get yours at the Salvadoran Consulate (across the street from TicaBus) for $30.

ORIENTATION AND GETTING AROUND

Chinandega's two hubs of activity are the area surrounding the Mercado Bisne (from the English word "business"), and the town center, or simply, *el centro*. The Mercadito is located two blocks north of the central park, and the Central Market a few blocks east of the park, along the Calle Central. La Rotonda los Encuentros and the Texaco StarMart are both important reference points you'll pass on your way into town. Everything is walkable, but—*ay caramba*—is it hot! Taxis are plentiful and cost $.40 within city limits; *ruta* buses are $.10.

Near Chinandega

EL VIEJO

Only a few kilometers west of Chinandega, El Viejo is a cheerful farming town of some 35,000 El Viejanos, as they like to be called. Less service-oriented than its big neighbor, El Viejo can still launch you on your next adventure. El Viejo is much older than Chinandega. Originally an indigenous community called Texoatega, for the fierce cacique who once ruled it, the town was renamed for the old Spaniard who arrived in 1562 carrying a sacred image of the Virgin Mary. According to legend, when the Spaniard tried to sail back to Spain, the Virgin created a hurricane so that she would be returned to her new home in Nicaragua. The old man complied, and the image soon became the most important Virgin Mary in the country. Her fame has lasted through the centuries, and in 1996 the Pope himself recognized her when he came to declare El Viejo's church a Basilica Minor. The church is impressive and worth your time to visit.

Buses arrive half a block north of the basilica, across the street from the market where you'll find the cheapest eats. Buses (called *interlocales*) back to Chinandega leave from behind the basilica and run until about 11 P.M.

Entertainment and Accommodations

Nightlife in El Viejo is exciting and sometimes downright rowdy. Local volunteers say it's all "beer and bark" though, and everyone makes up and shakes hands the next day. Just south of the basilica is **Texoatega,** a nightclub whose fame spreads as far as León. It has clean, good food and service, with a huge variety of music (check out mariachi night on Thursdays). **Los Coquitos,** on the same block, is home to boxing matches and super cheap pitchers of beer. **La Piscina,** two blocks north of the basilica and half a block east, serves great meals and appetizers, and opens the dance floor Thursday–Saturday. Their *piscina* (swimming pool) is reportedly drained and cleaned once a week and costs $.75 to use all day. An outdoor movie theater, one block south of ENITEL and behind the hardware store, shows a daily double feature for under $.50. The first flick is for the whole family and the second is. . . um. . . for adult, single men only.

El Viejo's *fiestas patronales* fall the week of December 6, with firework-spitting bulls every night and culminating in the *Lava la Plata,* when the nation's president often shows up to help "wash the church silver." Until recently, the only places to stay were in "hotels of love." Now, Casa de Huesped La Estancia, two blocks north of the basilica, has six simple rooms with shared bath for $3.75 a night.

CHICHIGALPA

Set in the middle of hundreds of square kilometers of sugarcane, Chichigalpa's **Ingenio San Antonio** is Nicaragua's largest and most powerful sugar refinery, and more importantly, the Compañía Licorera, Nicaragua's alcohol monopoly and

THE TRAGEDY OF VOLCÁN CASITAS

On October 30, 1998, the quiet municipality of Posoltega (whose Nahuatl name, Posoli-tecatl, means neighbor of the boiling place) was catapulted into a horrendous sort of fame as the site of one of the worst naturally caused disasters in Nicaragua's history. After Hurricane Mitch dropped two meters of rain in just three days, the southwest flank of Volcán Casitas transformed into a gigantic wave of mud and rock more than three meters high and nearly 1.5 kilometers wide. The communities of El Porvenir and Rolando Rodríguez were instantly consumed by the very soil on which they were built. Some 2,500 people immediately lost their lives. Those who were not buried lived through the horror of losing nearly everything and everyone in their lives. Immediate relief efforts were held up by the politics of President Alemán, who stalled help to the Sandinista leadership of Posoltega.

A survivor told one Witness for Peace volunteer, "You should have seen how the children, the little ones, fought to survive. People were pulling themselves up out of the mud naked, completely covered in mud. They looked like monsters in a horror movie. All you could see were their eyes. Children didn't even recognize their own parents. For days we could hear the ones who were still half-buried crying for help."

Today, the slide is still clearly visible from the León-Chinandega highway. International efforts helped construct several new communities for survivors, despite reports of disappearing relief funds reminiscent of Somoza's post-earthquake "emergency committee." The new suburban communities, however, provided no means of production for a people accustomed to living off the land. Many were psychologically devastated and eventually made their way illegally to search for work in Costa Rica.

The entire slide area has been declared a national monument, and a memorial plaque personally delivered by U.S. President Bill Clinton can be visited in the Peace Park on the highway, near the turnoff for Posoltega.

source of all the Toña, Victoria, Flor de Caña, and Ron Plata you've been drinking. The two companies belong to the wealthy Pellas family, who founded the sugar refinery in 1890 and have produced sugar and liquor ever since, (except between 1988 and 1992 when the Sandinista government briefly expropriated it (the Chamorro government subsequently returned it).

As alcohol is a mainstay of Nicaraguan culture and legend, the refineries and distilleries have been important parts of Nicaraguan life for more than a century. If you're interested in seeing how the cane is crushed, processed, and distilled, arrange for a tour of the Flor de Caña distillery by calling the plant in advance (try asking for Simón Pedro Pereira) and requesting a guided tour, tel. 505/343-2344. At the moment, there is no charge for the tour, but neither are there free samples.

CORINTO

The barrier island and economically important port town of Corinto lies 20 kilometers southwest of Chinandega. Because of its shipping activity and beaches (one of which boasts a giant shipwreck reminiscent of *Planet of the Apes*), Corinto is fairly well developed for tourists with a small range of simple hotels and seaside restaurants. Corinto's 20,000 inhabitants live on 49 square kilometers of island, connected to the rest of Nicaragua by two small bridges.

The Spanish first made use of the harbor in the 1500s, but didn't completely conquer the region until 1633, when an armada of 26 ships, 500 Spaniards, 227 horses, and 2,000 slaves arrived, swiftly defeating Texoatega's troops and taking many of them as additional slaves. The original port, placed at El Realejo (which still exists as a faint shadow of its former self), was transferred closer to the ocean at Corinto in 1858 after mangroves and sediment had choked the waterways.

Even when Corinto's first dock was built in 1875—then nothing more than a wooden pier jutting into the harbor—Corinto was a vital link in Nicaragua's transport and shipping facilities. Nicaragua's railroads transported coffee from El Sauce to Corinto, from where ships took it to the United States and elsewhere. A railroad constructed during Zelaya's presidency further expanded the port and its strategic significance.

In 1912, nearly 3,000 U.S. Marines landed in Corinto in response to Benjamin Zeledón's revolution, beginning what would be a 20-year occupation of Nicaragua. In October 1983, CIA operatives stole into the harbor under cover of night, where they mined the harbor and blew up several oil tanks on the docks. The economic and psychological damage strained an already suffering Sandinista goverment, but the "covert" operation, when publicized later, earned the Reagan administration international condemnation and enraged U.S. citizens who, before Corinto, had not known what their government was up to in Nicaragua.

From 2000–2001, the Alemán administration revitalized the port and dredged the harbor with project financing from the World Bank in order to increase export production. Today, Corinto remains what it has been since the days the Spanish landed with their horses and slaves: a vibrant coastal community with all the headaches and spice of a port town.

Sights and Entertainment

Besides soaking up the sun and rum at Playa Paso Caballo, the curious traveler will want to take a look at the beached oil tanker, a short walk up the coast. The ship washed up here sometime in the 1980s after it caught fire (nothing to do with the war) and its owners decided to salvage what they could and let the rest drift to shore and burn. Both the beach and the tanker are located on the northern tip of the island, and all buses from Chinandega pass by here before continuing to the center of town. Be careful, as the rip currents are notoriously strong. Paso

Caballo fills up on Sundays and holidays, during which times you should keep a good eye on your stuff—in fact, keep an eye on your stuff all year round. Several ranchos on the beach provide shade, food, and alcohol.

In town, what was once the **Old Railroad Terminal and Customs House** is now a museum in tribute to the old train, well worth a visit. Two discos, Ali Baba and Centauro, are on the road between town and the northern beaches.

Festivals

If you are in the neighborhood around the weekend that falls closest to May 3, don't miss the **Féria Gastronómica del Mar** (Seafood Festival), where you can try more than 100 different Corinteña recipes with fresh fish, shrimp, and other local delicacies. The festival takes place in the central park, Saturday and Sunday 10 A.M.–3 P.M.

Accommodations, Food, and Services

The family-run **Hospedaje Vargas,** (about a block west of the Texaco station where buses arrive, tel. 505/882-0187, $4.50 s for shared bath, $6 s for private bath) is simple and has fans in all 10 of its rooms. **Hospedaje Luvy** (1.5 blocks west of the central park, tel. 505/342-2637, $5 s, $6 d with fan, shared bath) is similar. All 10 rooms in the **Hotel Central** (tel. 505/342-2637, $30 s, $40 d, with a/c, private bath, cable TV) enjoy a view of the industrial container loaders of Corinto's docks.

As always, your best bargain is the *comida corriente* in the town market. Otherwise, numerous cafetíns dot the town, and a row of restaurants flank the town beach. **Restaurante Costa Azul** and **El Peruano** have typical dishes and seafood starting at $5. They are both very pleasant, breezy, open-air ranchos with views of the harbor and islands. Also consider **New Orleans** (one block east of the mini-supermarket), with free crab soup for serious drinkers. It's run by a recently returned Nica who has brought a little culture back from his old home in the French Quarter.

The best restaurant in town got nudged out of the main plaza and can now be found toward Playa Paso Caballo on the main road to Chinandega, near the bridge (from which you can jump into the water)—it's called **El Español** and the owner makes a mean sangria. **Corinto Online** (half a block north of the park) will connect you to Internet for $2.50 per hour. Getting to and from Corinto is a snap from Chinandega's Bisne Market, or by hitching from the Rotonda.

PUERTO MORAZÁN

Accessed by bus from Chinandega, Puerto Morazán is the gateway to the magnificent and sinuous Estero Real, whose mangrove estuary provides habitat for countless marine species and birds. Morazán was built at water level, so it's no surprise that during Hurricane Mitch it flooded so severely only the church steeple appeared over the surface of the water. Shortly after Mitch, the community rebuilt itself on its original site, in spite of plans to relocate the community to higher ground.

Morazán is extraordinarily poor, but this was not always the case. During World War II, Morazán's port, railway terminus, and customs office saw the movement of tons of cargo bound for European and North American destinations. When the war ended, so did Morazán's brief period of prosperity, and when Volcán Chonco erupted, damaging the railroad tracks, the final nail was put in Morazán's coffin.

The estuary itself is gorgeous, even if its "protected" status has been largely ignored by MARENA officials and the shrimp industry. Take a bus from El Viejo and pay someone to take you out into the estuary to bird-watch. You won't be disappointed by the extraordinary variety of wildlife, nor by the amazing view of Volcán Cosigüina.

COSIGÜINA PENINSULA AND BEACHES

Nicaragua's northwest corner is a magnificent volcanic knuckle jutting out into the Golfo de Fonseca. The scenery is stunning, the beaches isolated, and the people strongly rooted in their indigenous past. All buses to the area leave from Chinandega's Mercadito and make stops in El Viejo before continuing on. Many of the following spots only have bus service once a day, which means you'll be making an overnight trip if you don't have your own wheels. Bring a hammock, flashlight, food, and plenty of water. El Viejo's nuns know the area well—find them for additional information on any of the following.

Reserva Natural Volcán Cosigüina

Not only does this nationally protected reserve provide incredible views from the volcano's rim, but the dense vegetation inside the crater is the haunt of the only scarlet macaw population this side of the Segovia Mountains (for information about macaw research and restoration work, visit the UAP office in Leon). Hiking or horseback riding to the rim is not to be missed (see Hiking the Maribio Volcanoes special topic). Your journey begins in the poverty-stricken town of Potosí, former trading port with El Salvador until the Contras blew it up (the El Salvador–Nicaragua ferry was nearly reconstructed in Potosí recently, but plans shifted the project to Corinto). Of note is the three-day festival around May 19 on Meanguera, an El Salvadoran island that allows for unchecked passport access during the fiesta. You can reach Potosí at the end of a miserable 3.5-hour bus ride down "the crappiest road ever." Six buses leave daily and cost $1.50 each way. Fifteen kilometers past Potosí in the community of El Rosario, the park's official ranger station, run by a non-profit organization called LIDER, sits below the volcano and is the best place to begin your exploring. There you will find helpful rangers, horses (5$/day) and tents (3$/day) to rent, and bunk beds if you want to stay the night ($3). To organize a trip to Cosigüina, contact the LIDER office in El Viejo at tel. 505/344-2381.

Hiking the Cliffs at Punta Ñata

One bus a day leaves Chinandega at 12:10 P.M. for the 3.5-hour ride to the town of Punta ñata. It is worth the time and hassle! Five-hundred-meter cliffs preside over the Pacific Ocean and the Farallones Islands (formed by Cosigüina's last eruption). Find a guide in Punta to show you the hike and how to climb down the cliffs.

Beaches

Los Aserradores is quiet and desolate, and the

waves are more subdued than elsewhere on the coast. Santa Maria del Mar is a favorite. The bus leaves Chinandega at 12:30 P.M. and returns the next day at 5 A.M.

Mechapa is one of the longest, shallowest stretches of pure beach in Nicaragua, rumored to be 20 kilometers in length. Buses leave Chinandega at 1:40 P.M. and return at 4 P.M. Buses to Punta San José, on the tippy tip of the peninsula, depart at 9:30 A.M. and 1:10 P.M., returning for Chinandega at 2:30 P.M. and 5 P.M.

Less than a one-hour bus ride out of El Viejo, Jiquilillo Beach makes for a beautiful, solitary day trip all year except during Semana Santa, when the place is a madhouse. Relatively deserted, undeveloped, and absolutely beautiful, this is a beach like no other. Long gone is the town that once stood here, demolished by the 1992 tsunami. Six buses make the daily roundtrip, starting at 6 A.M. If you miss the last bus back at 3 P.M., you can book a simple room at Hospedaje Los Zorros and keep partying. Rent one of the four or five ranchos for about $3 each a day; they serve decent food and rum and Cokes. In between hammock naps, check out the fishermen harvesting larvae for nearby shrimp farms.

La Marina Puesta del Sol Resort and Spa

Surrounded by abject poverty on all sides, this incongruous $10-million luxury development, located less than an hour's drive from Chinandega at Playa Los Aserradores, targets the yacht, or "cruiser" community. Expect five-star services and prices (tel. 505/276-0323 or 505/883-0781, www.marinapuestadelsol.com).

Padre Ramos Wetlands Reserve

The bus to Jiquilillo continues up the coast, past Hospedaje Los Zorros, and arrives at the end of the road in the community of Padre Ramos. A simple fishing village of some 150 dispersed families, Padre Ramos is the gateway to the neighboring protected wetlands, and consequently the site of several grassroots tourism projects. The estuary is a decidedly mellower place to swim than the ocean and is home to

all the wildlife—especially birds—you could hope to see (for info about ongoing bird research in the reserve, stop by the UAP office in Leon). Check out the visitor's center when you arrive to ask about fishing and boat trips into the wetlands. In Padre Ramos, you'll want to pay a visit to **Elli's Rancho** (next to the visitor's center) to sample one of her enormous fish dishes for under $4 a plate; alternately, dine at the traditional rancho restaurant on the water's edge. You can get a quick boat ride to the community of Venecia across the estuary, where you'll find long stretches of utterly deserted beach. The entire area is a breeding ground for sea turtles, who come to lay and hatch between November and January. If you want to spend a few days in Padre Ramos, stay at **La Tortuga Boluda** ($3 pp), a family-run hostel behind the school, just 50 meters from the beach and 100 from the estuary. Simply tell the bus driver to let you off in front of Doña Reyna's house and she and her seven granddaughters will make you feel like you are part of the family. Your few-day stay here might turn into weeks.

HONDURAN BORDER AT EL GUASAULE

Located about 1.5 hours north of Chinandega on the Pan-American Highway, El Guasaule is the principal Pacific-side border crossing with Honduras. It is six kilometers beyond the town of Somotillo, where you'll find a large number of trucker and traveler services. At the actual border, there is a Bancentro branch and some basic food services. Reach the migration office at Guasaule at tel. 505/346-2208.

Hours and Fees

El Guasaule is open 24 hours, and there are always heavy truck traffic and road repair problems on the Nicaraguan side. It costs $2 to leave Nicaragua and $7 to enter the country. Just a passport and some cash is all that's required of North American and European travelers, with the notable exception of El Salvador—United States citizens must purchase a visa for $30 (available at the consulate in Chinandega or during your trip, bring cash), even

León

if you are only passing through the tiny country on your way to Guatemala.

Crossing the Border with Your Vehicle
If you are driving your own vehicle, the process to enter Nicaragua is lengthy, but usually not difficult. You must present the vehicle's title, as well as your own driver's license and passport. You will be given a temporary (30-day) permit to drive in Nicaragua, which will cost you

$10—should you lose the permit, you will be fined $100.

Getting There and Away
There are numerous and regular buses traveling between the Bisne Terminal and El Guasaule, and the main international bus lines (TicaBus, etc.) heading to Honduras and El Salvador pass through Chinandega on their way to the border.

Estelí and the Segovias

O, the beauty of the mountains at Estelí. They sprang from the earth in improbable contorted forms, in shapes "plenty of fantasy," as the old tobacco map had put it.

Salman Rushdie

The ride north from Managua begins by lifting you out of the sultry Pacific lowlands and into the Sébaco Valley, lush with rice and sorghum fields. From there, the highway struggles upward to the city of Estelí ("Diamond of the Segovias"), then continues through mountains and valleys dotted with peaceful rural villages whose strong, hardy inhabitants are proud to call themselves Norteños and who brag loudly about the beauty of their women, landscape, and music. Most get along by subsistence farming and ranching, but tobacco and coffee also carpet these hills, and some communities boast talented artisans in pottery, leather, and stone. The curious and unrushed traveler will not regret breaking away from the Pan-American Highway and going deep into the countryside.

© RANDY WOOD

Must-Sees

Look for **M** to find the sights and activities you can't miss and **M** for the best dining and lodging.

M Custom cowboy boots: They're custom-made from high quality leather, so don't leave Estelí without a pair for long rides into the wild or just dancing, northern style (page 191).

M Salto Estanzuela and the Tisey Reserve: Visit Estelí's premier swimming hole and eco-lodge, where you can hike, ride horses, or just jump in for a swim (page 196).

M Miraflor Nature Reserve: The best place in Nicaragua to get back to nature and spot the elusive quetzal or other exotic wildlife (page 199).

M San Juan de Limay: Rumble over the mountain pass and down into the valley to seek out one of the famous soapstone workshops (page 205).

M Iglesia de Nuestra Señora de la Asunción: Ocotal's church has seen it all, and even withstood the world's first air-raid bombing in the 1930s (page 206).

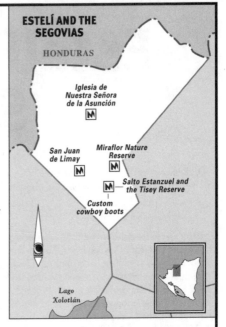

ESTELÍ AND THE SEGOVIAS

HONDURAS

Iglesia de Nuestra Señora de la Asunción M

San Juan de Limay

Miraflor Nature Reserve M

Salto Estanzuel and the Tisey Reserve M

Custom cowboy boots M

Lago Xolotlán

Travel in style with a custom pair of kickers.

Estelí

ESTELÍ AND THE
SEGOVIAS

HONDURAS

Teotecacinte

Jalapa

Murra

Las Manos
Cerro Mogotón
Cordillera Dipilto y Jalapa
Santa Clara   Ciudad Sandino
Santa
María
San Fernando   Susucayan
Macuelizo   Ocotal   Ciudad Antigua
**IGLESIA DE
NUESTRA SEÑORA
DE LA ASUNCIÓN**
Quilalí
Totogalpa
San Juan
del Río Coco
Telpaneca
Somoto
PAN-AMERICAN HIGHWAY
Palacagüina   Río Coco
Yalagüina
El Espino   Ducualí Grande
CA1
Pueblo Nuevo
San Sebastián de Yalí
Las Sabanas   Condega
CA1
**MIRAFLOR
NATURE RESERVE**
Cinco Pinos   San José de
Cusmapa   San Rafael
del Norte
La
Concordia
San Francisco
del Norte
**SAN JUAN
DE LIMAY**   La Sirena

Jinotega
**CUSTOM
COWBOY BOOTS**
Somotillo   Achuapa   Estelí   To Matagalpa
**SALTO ESTANZUELA
AND THE TISEY RESERVE**   Santa Cruz
Villa Nueva   To Matagalpa
Río Grande   La Trinidad   San Isidro
San Nicolas
El Sauce   Sébaco
0   10 mi
CA1
0   10 km
To Chinandega
To Léon   To Managua
To Léon

© AVALON TRAVEL PUBLISHING, INC.

PLANNING YOUR TIME

The north country is rich in mystery and charm, and underneath its gentle exterior of pine trees and carefully tended fields, you will find the ruins of ancient cities, deep pools fed by cascades of cool mountain water, and rugged communities of farmers. If you can't wander the hills for 4–5 days, then spend at least a day and night in the city of Estelí, where you'll meet rugged Norteños, sample fine cigars, and admire the town's inspiring collection of murals. With more time and flexibility, the bird-watcher, hiker, historian, and wanderer will find much to captivate his or her interests in the Segovias. Start with a visit to the Estanzuela waterfall, the lodge and trails at Tisey, or the stunning broadleaf forest reserve of Miraflor, where pervasive orchids and the rush of wind through the treetops will refresh your senses from the aching heat of the Nicaraguan lowlands. Get a feel for the agricultural lifestyle by passing a lazy afternoon in any of the small northern towns off the Panamerican highway—like Condega, La Trinidad, or Pueblo Nuevo—or rise with the morning sun in the stark border towns of Ocotal or Somoto. The truly curious can go deeper still, in long loops eastward into the sandy pine-covered hills of the Segovias, with visits to the lonely frontier towns of Jalapa and Quilalí, or to Cusmapa, the highest town in Nicaragua.

HISTORY

Upon the Spanish arrival to this part of the isthmus, the Nahuatl cacique Mixcoatl, or Snake of the Clouds, ruled the countryside. The Spanish conquistador Francisco Hernández de Córdoba personally founded the city of Segovia on the banks of the Río Coco where it met the Jícaro, and the first settlers began exploring for veins of gold in the nearby hillsides. Both the ferocity of the natives' attacks on the Spanish and the proximity of better sources of gold led the Spanish to abandon this early settlement and move farther north along the Río Coco. The Xicaque, Miskito, and Zambo tribes attacked the new settlement with growing ferocity, however, strengthened and emboldened by shiny new firearms from the British. What the natives started, English pirate Henry Morgan finished in 1654, when he sailed all the way up the Río Coco, guns blazing, and reduced the city to rubble. The Spanish packed up shop and moved west to the present village of Ciudad Antigua, which became the capital of the Segovia region. There was no respite here either, though, and while some settlers bravely duked it out with the natives, others looked for a quieter lifestyle farther south in the broad valley of Estelí. Not until the early 19th century did the little village of Ocotal begin to assume any importance, when the Catholics transferred valuable religious artifacts to the new church of Nuestra Señora de la Asunción. The faithful followed the relics westward, and Ocotál began to grow.

Until 20 years ago, violence and hardship continued to plague the region. In the early 1930s, General Sandino and his men were firmly entrenched in the mountains north of Ocotal, and the American government, intent on capturing him, sent in the Marines. The gringos remained based in Ocotal while they scoured the countryside around Cerro Guambuco and built the country's first airstrip in Somoto, from which they launched strikes on the city of Ocotal, the first city in the history of the world to experience an air raid. During the 1980s, much of the conflict between Sandinistas and Contras took place in the same area, punishing outpost towns like Jalapa fiercely.

These days, military conflict has been relegated to distant memory, and the new danger is ecological: The notorious pine bark beetle swelled to crisis populations in the late 1990s, chewing through the thick stands of Ocote pine trees more quickly and efficiently than axe-wielding *campesinos* had been able to do.

City of Estelí

Spread across a broad, flat valley 800 meters above sea level, Estelí is an unassuming city whose 110,000 merchants, ranchers, artists, and cigar rollers are prouder than most. In Nahuatl, Estelí means the river of blood, an apt moniker for an area so thoroughly saturated with Sandinista rebels in the days that led up to Somoza's overthrow (Somoza did not hesitate to carpet bomb this city: Ask locals where to find *"la bomba,"* a relic from the air strikes), and Contra rebels thereafter. These days, most Estelianos live a bucolic life of farming and commerce, and the city of Estelí is the undisputed capital of that lifestyle.

ORIENTATION AND GETTING AROUND

Buses to Estelí will deposit you in one of the two bus terminals on the east side of the highway, and express buses bound farther north will drop you off at the nearby Shell Esquipulas. In either case, pro-

ceed in the same way: Take a cab to the central park ($.50) to start your exploration. Estelí is quite possibly the only city in the country to take the trouble to name avenues (north-south) and streets (east-west). Still, the Nicaraguan penchant for giving directions in terms of landmarks and number of blocks completely overrides the best of intentions.

The two avenues that border the park, and one additional avenue on either side, make up the bulk of the commercial district. Avenida Central, on the west side of the park, hosts the greatest number of businesses and restaurants. Estelí is a long city; you can cut short the walking by hopping a cab for the fixed price of $.30/$.60 anywhere in the city (except La Casita restaurant on the south side of town). *Urbano* buses run a big loop around the city, including up and down the main avenues.

Since 2002, Estelí has experienced a mini-surge of gang violence that has angered the residents and raised the tension on city streets at night. You're essentially safe in Estelí, but exercise

Boy Scout parade in Estelí

Estelí

CITY OF ESTELÍ

To Jinotega

To Miraflor

DISCO TABU ▸

To Somoto, Ocotal, and Honduras

TEXACO STARMART

UCA MIRAFLOR ★

SOCCER STADIUM

Río Estelí

REPOSTERÍA ESPAÑA ▾

CAFÉ-NET ■

INTERNET ■

ARTESENÍA LA ESQUINA ▾

CAFÉ BAR VUELA VUELA ▾

LIBRERÍA RUBÉN DARÍO ■

ALCALDÍA ■

INTERNET ■

CENTRO CULTURAL JUVENTUS ▾

HOTEL EL MESÓN ■

PIZZA HOT ▾

HOTEL LOS ARCOS ●

DON PAN ▾

CATHEDRAL ✝

Central Park

CINEMA ■

5 NE

4 NE

3 NE

2 NE

1 NE

WHITE HOUSE PIZZA ▾

HOTEL EL CHICO ●

SHELL

To El Sauce

Estelí

HOTEL ALAMEDA

SHELL ESQUIPULAS

COTRAN NORTE

To Hospital and Managua

PAN-AMERICAN HIGHWAY

CA1

CALLE TRANSVERSAL

1 SE
2 SE
3 SE
4 SE
5 SE
6 SE
7 SE
8 SE
9 SE
10 SE
11 SE

HOTEL PANORAMA

To COTRAN Sur

PHONE OFFICE

QUICKBURGER

ARTESENÍA NICARAGUENSE

BUFFET LAS DOÑAS

HOTEL MODERNO

HOTEL SACUANJOCHE

HOSPEDAJE SAN FRANCISCO

Parque Infantil

HOSPEDAJE CHEPITO

LA CASA DE CULTURA

POST OFFICE

LA ESQUINA DE LOS BANCOS

GRAN VÍA

LIBRARY

COMEDOR PINAREÑO

CAFETÍN EL RECANTO

CASA HOTEL NICARAO

BANGENTRO

PALÍ

LECHE AGRIA

ROSTICERIA ESPECIAL

PETRONIC

AVENIDA PRINCIPAL

AVENIDA 1 SO

PENSIÓN JUÁREZ

SUPER EL HOGAR

HOTEL ESTELÍ

HOSPEDAJE FAMILIAR

SUPER LAS SEGOVIAS

RINCÓN LEGAL

FUNARTE

NICA CIGARS

MARKET

To Baseball Stadium

200 yds
200 m
0
0

© AVALON TRAVEL PUBLISHING, INC.

THE CHILDREN'S MURAL WORKSHOP

In 1987, in response to a request for help from community leaders in the struggling Barrio Batahola in Managua, three former art students began teaching mural workshops to children. The program was a success and two years later, the three muralists passed their roles on to other youth in Managua and moved to Estelí to continue their program. The idea was to empower the people while at the same time reclaiming Nicaraguan culture and promoting the participation of children in society. They found that painting murals was an empowering achievement for the participants, and the creation of the murals was invariably tied to further community activities and social work (and lots of pretty pictures to look at).

Today, the mural project is known as the **Fundación de Apoyo al Arte Creador Infantíl** (FUNARTE), a nonprofit, nongovernmental organization run by a group of young adults who grew up through the original mural workshops. They offer weekly painting workshops to hundreds of Esteliano children for free and give special workshops for imprisoned teenagers and children with disabilities. The murals depict their history, culture, and the daily reality in which they live.

There are well over 100 murals in Estelí, the majority of which were painted by participants of FUNARTE's workshops. The murals are best viewed and photographed in the late afternoon sun, as many of the best are on west-facing walls. The paintings are everywhere, but take special note of those on the Alcaldía (mayor's office), Casa de Cultura, and in and around the Parque Infantíl (nine blocks south of the main plaza). Also, be sure to get a good look at the long, horizontal mural on the wall of the army base along the Pan-American Highway, just south of the main bus station.

To visit FUNARTE's headquarters (tel. 505/713-6100, muralism@ibw.com.ni), walk four blocks south from the southwest corner of the plaza, then two west to reach the main workshop, itself covered in powerful paintings; continue another block west, turn right past the mural depicting the book *The Little Prince,* and make your next left to arrive at the offices and classroom.

more care here than elsewhere, and keep an eye out for harmless but annoying "Jimmy Loco," a one-armed, purple-faced septuagenarian with a penchant for harassing blondes.

SIGHTS

El Parque Central

Estelí's central **park** is a hub of mellow activity and a magnet for local characters. Buy an ice cream cone, kick back on a bench, and watch it all swirl by. The **Iglesia de San Francisco** was built in layers starting in 1823. It began as nothing more than a humble adobe chapel with a straw roof. Rebuilt in 1889 to a grander scale and given a roof of clay tiles with a baroque facade, the church was later redesigned as a modern building, with stately columns, a neoclassic facade, and twin bell towers topped with crosses. Estelí's real attractions lie outside the city.

La Galería de Héroes y Mártires

La Galería (half block south of the church, tel. 505/713-3753, emayorga70@yahoo.com, open 9 A.M.–4 P.M. Mon.–Sat.; voluntary fee) is only one of the accomplishments of the Association of Mothers of Heroes and Martyrs of Estelí, a support group of some 300 women who lost children during the battle against Somoza's National Guard. The gallery itself is a single room in what was once one of Somoza's jails, filled with memorabilia from the days of the revolution—photos of Estelí as an urban battleground, quotes from Sandino and Che Guevara, and displays of weaponry and shell casings. Most touching are the portraits of young men and women killed in action, sometimes accompanied by uniforms and other personal effects.

Connected to the Galería, you'll find the less powerful, but still interesting **Museo de Historia y Arqueología** (open 9 A.M.–noon Mon.–Fri., closed weekends and Wed.), with a small display of petroglyphs, artifacts, and a series of obligatory revolutionary photos.

La Casa de Cultura

Still in the same building, but on the south side, the Casa de Cultura is easily recognized by its giant vertical murals announcing the activities within: Dance, Painting, Music. Offering a series of classes to the general public, the Casa often has a display of local artists in its spacious lobby. The entire block used to belong to a prominent Esteliano family before being confiscated by the Sandinistas.

Estelí Cigar Factory

Out of the private-label Estelí Cigar Factory (tel. 505/713-5688, etelici@ibw.com.ni) come more than 60 brands of *puros* (cigars) for export to the United States and Europe, the most popular of which are Cinco Vegas, Cupido, and Badge of Honor. Don Kiki, the owner and master roller, of Cuban and Eastern European descent (a "Jewbano," he says), is a portly, amiable craftsman, who may even give you a tour of his establishment if you call ahead to make an appointment. Hop a bus northbound and get off near El Rancho de Pancho.

Empresa Nica Cigars, (around the corner from the COTRAN Sur, tel. 505/713-2230) is another non–free trade company, which means they are permitted to sell to local markets—visiting tourists. They will also allow curious visitors to come inside and take pictures of their rollers. You'll smell the tobacco from blocks away.

ENTERTAINMENT AND EVENTS

Cinemas

Estelí's old movie theater on the main plaza is back in business, showing mostly Hollywood fare Thursday–Sunday ($1.50). The seats are packed in pretty tight, but look for the "gringo row" if you've got long legs.

Bars and Discos

The self-declared "most flavorful and culturally minded bar in town," the **Rincón Legal** (on the north side of the park) is the brainchild of Frankie Legal, who built a joint where Cubans and Nicas

can celebrate their common culture of revolution and music; this is the place to be for the wandering European *gauche.*

Tabu is Estelí's best disco. Thursday is ladies' night; says one local resident: "Lots of pretty young women, lots of ugly old men." Also very popular, **El Rancho de Pancho** (a few kilometers north of Estelí on the Pan-American Highway) is especially lively on Saturday, but get there early, as El Rancho is jam-packed by 10 P.M.

Estelí's *fiestas patronales* take place around October 12 and most years include a famous *hípica* (show-horse) parade.

SHOPPING

Provided you're not interested in fruits and vegetables (in which case you want the *Mercado*), the entire length of Avenida Principal is lined with boutiques whose shop girls might whistle at you to entice you into the store.

 Custom Cowboy Boots

Estelí is the place to buy handmade **leather goods** like belts, saddles, and cowboy boots:

© RANDY WOOD

Estelí leather workers make more than custom cowboy boots.

SMOKIN' NICARAGUA

There is history in that cigar you're smoking—stories hidden among the tightly packed folds of tobacco and along the delicate veins of its wrapper leaf. As you light the *puro* in your hand and watch it turn into ash and smoke, take a sip of rum and ponder the unique legacy of the Estelí cigar industry.

It all began with the 1959 Cuban revolution, when capitalist Cuban cigar lords found their businesses liquidated into the new socialism. These artisans of the finest cigars in the world quickly gathered secret caches of the precious tobacco seeds their families had been cultivating for centuries and fled to Miami. From there, it was only a couple of years before they discovered Nicaragua. One grower told *Cigar Aficionado* magazine that Cuba and Nicaragua "have the most fertile dirt in the world for tobacco. It's almost like God said, 'I'm going to pick these two countries and I'm going to use them for tobacco.'"

And so the core of the old Cuban cigar aristocracy moved to Estelí and, with their precious seeds from the homeland, began turning out world-renowned cigars once again. They endured another popular revolution in 1979, the ensuing civil war and land redistribution, and then survived the cigar boom and bust of the 1990s, followed by the waters of Hurricane Mitch that tore through their fields in 1998. But the business is sunk deep into the rich soil, and the handful of familial cigar dynasties that first came to Nicaragua 30 years ago are still here, and still rolling world-class cigars.

Most of the tobacco fields and giant wooden drying barns are found across the Estelí valley as it runs north away from the city, as well as in many upper reaches all the way to Jalapa. In Estelí there are about 10 serious cigar producers, a few of which will let travelers in their doors for an informal tour and perhaps a taste test. Most businesses are *zona franca* (free-trade zone), however, which prohibits them from selling their product within Nicaragua. Don Orlando Padrón, head of Cubanica Cigars,

keeps the doors to his Estelí factory shut for another reason: to protect the secrets that produce one of the most internationally acclaimed cigars in the world, *El Padrón*.

Some of the other heavy hitters are Latin Tobacco, Estelí Cigar, Tabacalera Perdomo (formerly Nick's Cigars), Plasencia, and Nicaraguan American Tobacco (NATSA). Their facilities are scattered across Estelí, and their degree of hospitality varies. Don

Much of Nicaragua's tobacco was brought to the Estelí Valley from Cuba.

Kiki, of Estelí Cigars, sometimes gives casual tours, maybe even a cup of Cuban coffee and a smoke.

Cigar-making is a proud family tradition here and elsewhere in the world, and there's no denying the craftsmanship of a fine cigar. But as the blunt you're smoking burns lower, and the heat of the cherry seeps into the leaf between your fingers, consider the yang side. Organic tobacco is grown in Nicaragua, but barely; most production employs massive quantities of chemicals, which invariably find their way into the earth, the water, or the lungs, hands, and feet of the workers. Tobacco handlers often absorb the toxic elements of the leaf, and although at least several of Estelí's factories have impressive, airy environments for their workers, conditions for the rollers are often no better than the worst sweatshops. And the history burns on.

Find them all along the southern half of Avenida 1 S.O. A pair of quality cowhide boots (or deerskin or snakeskin, the latter of which might get confiscated at your home customs office) goes for about $45 and takes a week when custom fit to your foot. Order a pair on your way north and pick 'em up on the way back to Managua. **Guitarras y Requintas el Arte** (located adjacent to INISER, tel. 505/713-7555) sells handmade guitars, mandolins, and *guitarrones* (the bass guitar used by mariachis) out of a tiny barber shop for around $90–120; the floor is littered with wood shavings and hair clippings.

Artesanía

Two shops—**Artesanía La Esquina** (one block north of the cathedral, tel. 505/713-2229) and **Artesanía Nicaragüense** (one block south of the cathedral, tel. 505/713-4456)—each have a huge selection of Nicaraguan arts and crafts from all over the country. In general, prices are cheaper in the Managua and Masaya markets, but for locally produced items, like soapstone carvings and Ducualí pottery, these are good places to shop. Plans are in the works for a government-sponsored crafts market in the Hospital Viejo building on Avenida Principal.

Bookstores

Tiny **Librería Leonel Rugama** (on the Ave. Principal, across from the Kodak) is run by the famous poet-martyr's parents. Rugama's dramatic death at the hands of Somoza's National Guard is legendary: Cornered in a building in Managua, the young soldier single-handedly held off a contingent of guardsmen while Carlos Fonseca escaped through the sewers. Ordered to his knees by the Guardia, he was commanded, *"Rindase, Sandinista!"* ("Surrender, Sandinista!"). Rugama retorted, famously, *"Que se rinda tu madre!"* ("Let your mother surrender!") before he was shot.

ACCOMMODATIONS

Estelí is a big believer in tourism, and hotels have multiplied as fast as the bed bugs (just kidding). Here are some tips:

Under $10

Estelí's least expensive lodging is on the south side of town by the Parque Infantíl. **Hospedaje Chepito** (one block south of the *parque,* tel. 505/713-6388, $4.50 s with shared bath) is a favorite with the backpacker set. At about the same level of comfort, but far safer, **Hospedaje Sacuanjoche** (2.5 blocks south of Enitel, tel. 505/713-2862) is family-run and peaceful. A bit closer to the action, **Hospedaje Familiar** (half block north of Super Las Segovias next to the Tip-Top distributor, tel. 505/713-3666, $5–13, private bath, TV) is run by Edith Valenzuela Lopez, a tried-and-true Sandinista with more than 33 years of hosting *internacionalistas.*

$10–25

A few doors north of Hospedaje Familiar, **M Hotel Estelí** (tel. 505/713-2902, $6–15, private bath, TV, and parking) has 13 rooms on two stories, including several nice, furnished doubles and matrimonials.

The eight rooms at **Hotel El Mesón,** (one block north of the cathedral, tel. 505/713-2655, $12/17 s/d, private bath, hot water, and fan, add $9 more for a/c) are quiet and clean, and the hot water makes January mornings a lot more bearable. They have parking, a bar and restaurant, a travel agency, and car rental, and will change traveler's checks. Not far away, **Hotel Moderno,** (one block east of the park and two south, tel. 505/713-2378, fax 505/713-4315, $20/25 s/d.) consists of 11 rooms—all with private bath, hot water, TV, and fan—surrounding a shaded courtyard, conference room, bar, and restaurant.

$25–50

The gorgeous **Hotel Los Arcos/Café Vuela Vuela** (one block north of the cathedral, $30–60 with all the amenities) is run by a Spanish development organization in a charming colonial edifice. All profits go toward development activities like their schools, continuing education programs, and street children. If you're more interested in a relaxing evening than a night in town, **M Hotel Cualitlán** (from COTRAN Sur, 2 blocks south, 4 east, and 1 north, tel. 505/713-2446, $30 s $40 d) is a walled-in guest-house compound unlike any other in Estelí. It boasts a verdant sitting area with a tree-canopy roof, soothing music, and a creative menu geared to the international traveler. Choose one of several delightfully appointed *cabañas*—something like Swiss chalets—set around the lush tropical courtyard, all with hot water and cable TV.

Long-Term Housing

All of the Spanish schools (see Spanish Language Schools in the Know Nicaragua chapter) have networks of families accustomed to housing foreigners for a weekly or monthly rate. Doña Edith at the **Hospedaje Familiar** offers extended room-and-board deals, starting at $150 a month. For house and apartment rentals, call Bienes Raices Gomez at tel. 505/713-3835.

FOOD

The Esteliano diet is hardy, not elegant, and the limited dining options serve mostly thick steaks, fried chicken, and bowls of soup big enough to drown in. The nicest restaurants are found in the town's upscale hotels and on the blocks around the park. Some notable eateries include **Comedor Pinareño** (one block south of the park, $2–7), with its Cuban menu and selection of fine cigars. **La Gran Vía** (just south of the *esquinas de los bancos,* closed Sun.) serves Chinese meals from $4.50. **Leche Agria** (2.5 blocks south of *la esquina de los bancos*) serves excellent *quesillos,* (cheese and tortilla snack) juices, and cheeses. **Comedor Popular La Soya** (on the Ave. Principal, 2.5 blocks south of the park), true to its name, serves soy-based meals and soy-milk drinks.

Bakeries and Coffee Shops

The menu is simple, healthy, and homegrown at **La Casita** (across from La Barranca, south entrance, open 7 A.M. to 7 P.M. Tues.–Sat., 9 A.M.–7 P.M. Sun., and 1–7 P.M. Mon., closed first Mon. of every month, tel. 505/713-4917, casita@sdnnic.org.ni). Yogurt, home-baked breads, fresh cheeses, vegetables, granola, juices, and coffee drinks are all served in a pleasant garden atmosphere along the shore of a babbling brook.

But regardless of the menu, La Casita is one of the most pleasant places in town. It is located on the Pan-American Highway, a few kilometers south of the city. Take an *urbano* bus to the new hospital, then walk south around the bend in the road; or hail a taxi for about $1.50—it's well worth the trip. In addition to featuring wonderful food and mellow music, La Casita sells local crafts and plants, including herbs, ornamentals, and much much more. The owner is a Scotsman named David Thomson who, after many years of experience teaching natural resource management in Nicaraguan development programs, concluded that imposing new technology on a people is less effective than simply providing an alternative by being an example. Thus, when he was asked by a Danish NGO to travel to the village of Siuna to demonstrate his unique bread oven, he politely refused. But when a women's organization from that remote town displayed an interest in organizing a trip to his *finca* in Estelí, he was more than happy to show them how to construct such an oven in their own pueblo. La Casita is truly an example of good management of natural resources and a development paradigm whose goal is sustainability, not growth. Enjoy the philosophy, or just the great breakfasts.

Juventus Centro Cultural (two blocks west of the central park's southwest corner, open 9 A.M.–6 P.M. Mon.–Sat.), is situated on top of the hill that drops down to the river, making for great panoramas of the mountains to the west as you enjoy *licuados* (fruit shakes), granola, open-face Swiss and Brie sandwiches, and hot drinks. There is an excellent Spanish bakery, **Repostería España,** 3.5 blocks north of the central park, and a German one, **Repostería Alemán,** behind the cathedral.

INFORMATION

INTUR's tiny, tucked-away office in the back of the Hospital Viejo (open 7 A.M.–2 P.M. Mon.–Fri., tel. 505/713-6799) was useless to the tourist at last check, but stop in and see if they're offering any services. The public library, a corner building covered with murals, is one block west and one south of the park (open 8 A.M.–noon and 2–5 P.M. Mon.–Fri., tel. 505/713-7021).

Guide Services

Most of Estelí's Spanish schools offer eco-tours and day trips to surrounding sites in addition to, or as part of, their language classes. UCA Miraflor has transportation and tours of Miraflor and access to a network of local guides.

SERVICES

Emergencies

El Hospital Regional de Estelí (tel. 505/713-6300), was donated by the Spanish government in the mid-1990s and is located just south of the city. Ave. Principal has many private clinics—offering both Western and Eastern medicine. **La Policía Nacional** (tel. 505/713-2615) is located on the main highway, toward the northern exit.

Banks and Exchange

La esquina de los bancos, home to at least three respectable banks, is one block west and one block south of the park; **Bancentro** is 2.5 blocks south on Avenida Principal. The travel agency in Hotel Mesón changes traveler's checks, as do most of the banks, and there is a cash machine in the StarMart. Don't worry, the black-market money changers will find you on the main avenue.

Mail and Phones

The post office is open 7 A.M.–8 P.M. The **Farmacia Corea** (a block north of the main market, tel. 505/713-2609) offers mail and package service, as well as money transfers. **DHL Worldwide Express** is one block west of the park, and a half-block north, in the same office as Careli Viajes (tel. 505/713-7077). ENITEL (one block south of the church and half a block east, tel. 505/713-2222) is open 8 A.M.–8 P.M. Monday–Friday and 8 A.M.–5 P.M. Saturday.

Travel Services and Car Rental

Agencia de Viajes Tisey (in Hotel El Mesón, tel. 505/713-3099, fax 505/713-4029, barlan @ibw.com.ni) is a modern and professional agency that deals with airlines and Budget rental cars.

NATURAL MEDICINE IN ESTELÍ

Knowledge of folk medicine and the use of natural plants and herbs in curing all types of ailments is common throughout all of Nicaragua, especially in rural areas where natural meds are cheaper and more available than modern drugs. However, nowhere in the country is the use of natural medicine as well institutionalized as it is in Estelí.

There are several organizations devoted solely to the production, marketing, and selling of natural medicines. The two most prominent are CECALLI and ISNAYA. The former maintains a nursery and nature museum at its gardens south of Estelí, right next door to the La Casita café. They sell their herbs, teas, and other natural products in a store on the Avenida Principal, 1.5 blocks north of the plaza.

Managed by the Centro Nacional de la Medicina Popular Tradicional, ISNAYA maintains a beautiful farm called El Cortijo, located near La Sirena, eight kilometers north of Estelí on the Pan-American Highway. They also run several stores and a lab and packaging plant in the city of Estelí. Check with ISNAYA's offices (from the park, three blocks south, 1.5 to the west, tel. 505/713-4841) if you are interested in living and working on the farm for an extended period.

Internet

The most convenient cyber café is **Soluciones Computarizadas** (off the northwest corner of the park), but there are several additional cafés north of there, such as **PCnet** (1.5 blocks north of the park). Cyber cafés are typically open 8 A.M.–9 P.M. Monday–Saturday, 8 A.M.–6 P.M. Sunday.

Special Courses

Estelí provides considerable opportunities to learn a new skill, if you're going to be in town awhile. **La Casa de Cultura** (tel. 505/713-3021) offers daily classes in folk dancing, theater, guitar, keyboard, and painting. Right next door, the **Association of Mothers of Heroes and Martyrs** will school you in *"piñata and pastry making."*

The **Colegio Musica de Estelí** (two blocks north of the park) offers classes in guitar and keyboard. Ask Doña Edith in the Hospedaje Familiar about classes in yoga and eastern medicine.

GETTING THERE AND AWAY

Both express and ordinary buses for Estelí leave from Managua's Mayoreo Terminal, located in the northeast corner of the capital. Seven *expresos* per day pass Esteí bound for Managua, making stops along the highway. Fourteen buses go directly to Estelí from Somoto, the last one leaving at 5 P.M.

From Estelí, buses leave the COTRAN Norte (North) at regular intervals for Ocotal, Somoto, and points north from 4 A.M. until 5 P.M., and

COTRAN Sur (South) for Managua, Matagalpa, León, and Yalí. There are 28 express buses to Managua daily from 3:30 A.M. until 6 P.M., 26 buses to Matagalpa (5:15 A.M.–4:50 P.M.), and one express bus to León (6:45 A.M.), plus a few daily microbuses to León (they leave when they fill up, and competition is fierce).

The large amount of long-distance traffic running up and down the Pan-American Highway makes hitchhiking from Estelí a breeze. To go south toward Managua, take an *urbano* bus or taxi to the southern exit. Across the street from the Petronic gas station is a good spot because vehicles have to slow down to climb the small hill. For points north, go to the StarMart parking lot.

Near Estelí

SALTO ESTANZUELA AND THE TISEY RESERVE

El Salto Estanzuela is the region's most famous swimming hole, a gorgeous 15-meter, rainy-season-only cascade that plunges into a cold, shady pool, all smothered in colorful native flora and fauna. It's just southwest of the city. Swim behind the falls for a refreshingly cool perspective on Nicaragua.

A bit farther down the same road, **Reserva Tisey,** a reserve co-managed by the Nature Conservancy, boasts a rustic eco-lodge, fields of organic vegetables, a network of hiking trails, and trips on horseback, not to mention the best panoramic view in the entire nation, hands down. From the top of Tisey on a clear day, you can make out the Pacific coastal plain and the entire chain of volcanic peaks from Cosigüina to Lake Managua and Momotombo, the Estelí valley, and north to the mountains of the Segovias on the horizon.

Start your adventure by settling in at **Eco-Posada Tisey** (505/713-6213 or 836-6021, $4 for communal living, $9.50 for a double bed and some privacy, $1 per meal). They will find you guides, rent horses, or show you around the organic farm that stocks most of Managua's supermarkets with fresh veggies. There's more to see there than you'll likely have time for, so plan a few

days at least. One trail climbs to a lookout (1,300 meters) where you'll enjoy the phenomenal view and the falls (no horses in the swimming pool, y'-hear?). The folks at the Posada can show you some of the reserve's other highlights, like the septuagenarian sculptor who picked up hammer and chisel to absorb some of his nervous energy when he quit drinking, or the bat cave, local hangout for more than 10,000 winged friends (hint: bring a hat). Closer to the lodge, taste fresh cheeses and vegetables, or visit the farming community of La Garnacha.

Getting There

You can hike to the waterfall from the highway. The road to Estanzuela leaves the Pan-American just south of the new hospital and is sandwiched between two *pulperías* (markets) where you can stock up for the journey. This is the terminus of the *urbano* bus routes, or take a taxi from the city center for about $.50. The five kilometer walk should take between 60 and 90 minutes each way. It's an easy hike, but with lots of ups-and-downs. Otherwise, hop a bus for the 20-minute ride (buses leave COTRAN Sur at 6:30 A.M. or 1:30 P.M.). Before you reach the hamlet of Estanzuela, for which the waterfall is named, look for a gated road on your right; it's at the bottom of a

© JOSHUA BERMAN

Esteli

La Trinidad

hill, just after the first two dilapidated wooden homes of the village. Head downward for about 10 minutes until the track veers steeply down to the left. Before it turns to the right again, take the path in front of you straight down to the falls, which you should now be able to hear.

LA TRINIDAD

Just as the Pan-American Highway begins its curvy climb north into Nicaragua's mountains, a mid-size pueblo straddles the road and monitors your entrance into the north country. It would be easy to stay on the bus as you pass through La Trinidad toward Estelí, only 22 kilometers farther north, but it would be just as easy to get off at the Texaco station and wander up to the park, where few tourists have ever set foot.

La Trinidad, named for the three hills that cradle it gently in their arms, is a festive town of bread bakers, bus drivers, musicians, and cowboys. Its unhurried and friendly populace can often be found hanging out in the lush park, a well-tended central plaza—green even in the height of the dry season—and home to Kameleón, La Trinidad's pet tree sloth, who lives untethered in the park's canopy. The Catholic church, although decidedly ugly and non-colonial, may be worth a visit during mass to hear the dueling mariachi choirs.

"La Trini" is also famous (or infamous, depending on who you're talking to) for being an island of anti-*Sandinismo* in a zone of strong FSLN support. This fact stems from the handful of resident landowning families who used to control much of the Sébaco Valley to the south before losing the land in massive confiscations in the early 1980s. The Contras mounted a major military offensive in 1986 to take a stretch of the Pan-American Highway through La Trinidad. They were outgunned by Sandinista military in helicopter gun ships. The failed maneuver was nevertheless instrumental in making clear that the Contras had the support of many local citizens, who in La Trinidad kept the guerrilla soldiers well fed during the battles.

The rip-roaring *fiestas patronales,* celebrating La Virgen de Candelaria and Jésus de Caridad, occur during the last week of January and roll raucously into the first week of February, with a famous *hípica* (show horse) parade that attracts riders from all over Central America.

MIRAFLOR NATURE RESERVE

© AVALON TRAVEL PUBLISHING, INC.

Hikes

Walk one block south and two west of the park to begin a half-hour climb up to the old Spanish cross and stunning views of La Trinidad, the Sébaco Valley, and the rising hills in all other directions. Another beautiful countryside hike can be had by walking westward up the river valley road to the shady Rosario shrine—allow about an hour each way. The hill to the east of the highway is the legendary Mocuana, with its caves of witches, gold, snakes, and a tunnel to Sébaco, if you believe everything you hear. La Trinidad's homegrown fiesta band, Los Mokuanes, have been playing their *embrujo musical* (musical witchcraft) all over Central America (and occa-sionally in the United States) for more than 30 years.

Food

La Trinidad offers delicious, typical, and cheap food without the hype. Don Juan's **Las Sopas,** on the southern outskirts of town, is a popular stopover for Pan-American commuters and truck drivers, with an open-air patio, a pathetic attempt at a zoo, and a fantastic menu of local soups—in-cluding *sopa de huevos de toro* (bull balls soup), ox tail, and chicken soup. To fit in with your fellow lunchers, squeeze in plenty of lime, and down a shot of Extra Lite rum after every couple of spoon-fuls (tell the bus driver to let you off here, or take a taxi from the town's center).

ⓜ MIRAFLOR NATURE RESERVE

More than a trip into Estelí's misty mountains, a visit to Miraflor is a trip backward in time. Perhaps this is what Costa Rica's Monteverde was like 40 years ago before it was populated with four-star resorts and laced with splinter-free wooden walkways. Miraflor is unabashedly rustic, natural, and unpretentious. Declared a protected natural reserve in 1990, this rudimentary tourist infrastructure was developed by locals, with their own sweat and labor and in the absence of any external help.

Miraflor as an entity is totally unique even if, as an entity, it's a little vague. There's no town, per se, or even a real center. Rather, the 5,000 Mirafloreños live dispersed throughout the 206 square kilometers of the reserve in a geographically dispersed but socially united community. The Miraflor Reserve is privately owned, cooperatively managed in many parts, and almost entirely self-funded by associations of small-scale producers. Most notable among these is the UCA Miraflor (or in full: the *Union de Cooperativas Agropecuarias Héroes y Mártires de Miraflor*—not to be confused with the University of Central America), an association of 14 small farmer cooperatives and 120 families living within the protected area. UCA Miraflor is primarily an agricultural credit and loan institution, but has also tackled issues and begun programs, such as community health and education, organic agriculture and diversification of crops, cooperative coffee production, gender and youth groups, and conflict resolution. Tourism, Miraflor's greatest potential, was just an afterthought.

Sights and Attractions

Miraflor has something for everyone—nature lovers, hikers, social justice workers, organic farmers, artists, horse lovers, orchid fanatics, birders, and entomologists—each of whom will find their own personal heaven here. You can certainly visit parts of Miraflor in a day trip from Estelí, but read on and consider experiencing the unique accommodations.

It should be noted that every attraction in Miraflor is privately owned, often by poor *campesinos*. Your financial support is the driving force that will lead to the continued preservation of these magnificent forests, because, "hey, this would be a great place to chop down the trees and plant some beans."

Fauna: 236 distinct bird species belonging to 46 different families inhabit or fly through these mountains—that's nearly 40 percent of all bird species in the country, including four species of the elusive quetzal (*Pharomachrus mocinno*), toucans, the ranchero (*Procnias tricaruntulata*), with its three dangling chins, and the Nicaraguan national bird, the guardabarranco. Miraflor is also one of your best chances to spot coyotes, sloths, deer, howler monkeys, or one of six different feline species, not to mention raccoons, skunks, armadillos, and exotic rodents.

Orchids: Miraflor is one of the richest and most unexplored orchid viewing regions anywhere. Among the more than 300 identified species is an enormous colony of *Cattleya skinniri* (the national flower of Costa Rica), not to mention scads of bromeliads and a museum of other orchids from throughout the reserve.

Hikes and Adventure: Short hikes are possible through any of the hundreds of pockets of forest, but ask your guide to take you on one of the more adventurous trips. Although difficult to access, the 60-meter waterfall at *La Chorrera* is one of the wildest spots in the reserve. **The Caves of Apaguis** were dug in pre-Columbian times by gem seekers and have been occupied ever since by *duendes* (dwarves), as any local will inform you. The mature cloud forest of **Bosque Los Volcancitos** is Miraflor's highest point at 1,484 meters and is known habitat for howler monkeys and quetzals. If the monkeys don't snatch away your binoculars, expect fantastic views from El Tayacán, Cerro Yeluca, Cerro El Aguila, La Coyotera, and Ocote Calzado. Furthermore, the forests are replete with mysteries, such as the *casa antigua,* a 1,200-year-old foundation in the Tayacán area, surrounded by dozens of other unearthed *montículos* (mounds). Archeologists haven't even begun to investigate the rest of them.

Progressive Agriculture: If you enjoy inspired agriculture and alternative farming practices, the

Estelí

SWAMP THINGS: LEGENDS OF THE MIRAFLOR LAGOON

La Laguna de Miraflor is, compared to other *lagunas* (lakes) in the country, a mere puddle, whose marshy banks are crowded with vegetation and birdsong. Its fame lies not in its grandeur, but in its myth. There are at least five legends surrounding the lagoon, stories passed down over the years that have smothered the 10-hectare body of water in a shroud of mystery as thick as the white clouds sweeping over its surface.

The most famous of these legends is the **Ramo de Flores:** Every Thursday of *Semana Santa* (Holy Week), a cluster of beautiful flowers rises to the surface of the lagoon and circulates around and around. The flowers, say some, are bringing a message to the people that they should unite. The name Miraflor (flower view) comes from this legend, and variations tell of a tiny dancing prince in the middle of the flowers and dwarfs bearing the flowers to give to local girls.

Also well-known is the story of the **Ciudad Perdida** (The Lost City). Only the oldest of Mirafloreños know of the secret entrance, but everyone knows of the vast fields of exotic fruit-bearing trees in the city at the bottom of the lagoon (which, by the way, has been measured at 27 meters deep, plus three meters of sediment). One can eat all they want when in the city, but if they try bringing the fruit back to the surface world, they will not be allowed to pass.

Every now and then, the water of the lagoon turns jet black; evidence, say some, of the giant **black serpent** that lives in the water and occasionally stirs up the sediment on the bottom. The snake may or may not have something to do with the lagoon's vengeful nature, punishing anyone who speaks disrespectfully of it or disbelieves its power. One unfortunate young man did so "recently" while swimming in the middle—he had barely spoken his blasphemy when a whirlpool formed, sucked him under, and then spit him back up, whereupon he apologized profusely and pledged his eternal respect for the enchanted waters.

Just across the road, the **Laguna de Lodo,** or Lagoon of Mud, has its share of legends as well. The mud pond is half the size of its counterpart and lies above the subterranean river that feeds the main lagoon. One day, a local *leñador* (lumberjack) was working near the Laguna de Lodo and dropped his axe into the mud, which promptly swallowed it up. He cried and cried and cried, until his axe finally rose to the surface. . . with a head and blade of shining gold.

© RANDY WOOD

Myth, mystery, and a lost city lie beneath the surface of Miraflor's lagoon.

© ERICKA BRICEÑO

Miraflor offers both cultural and natural attractions, including wildflowers galore.

campesinos at Miraflor will gladly show you their cutting-edge lifestyle, including organic compost, natural pest management, watershed protection, live fences, crop diversification, soil management, reforestation, worm farming, and environmental education. In addition, Miraflor's small-scale, fair trade, organic coffee cooperatives and cupping lab (in Cebollál) are among the nation's finest.

Accommodations and Food

Start with a call or visit to the UCA-Miraflor office in Estelí (from the Esso station, two blocks north, one west, half north, tel. 505/713-2971, miraflor@ibw.com.ni, www.miraflor-uca.com, open 8 A.M.–12:30 P.M. and 2–5 P.M. Mon.–Fri.). The building faces the Pan-American and has a well-marked corner store of natural agricultural supplies, but the office entrance is located on the other side, facing away from the highway. They will present your options and help arrange lodging, taking care to distribute guests fairly among the various families who have agreed to host guests. Expect to pay between $10 and $15 per person per night, with all meals included.

Campesino Homes: These families have been trained in the subtle art of entertaining picky travelers, and their homes, while clean and well-maintained, are primitive. Accommodations better resemble Appalachian-trail huts than guesthouses.

Cabins: Although there are numerous guesthouse cabins throughout the reserve, and the UCA will tell you all about them, the following are the most well-known and professionally run operations to date: Doña Corina Picado's **Posada La Soñada** (Estelí phone number weekdays only, tel. 505/713-6333) offers several cabins of cut pine, each furnished with bunk beds, candles, and an overarching sense of peace and quiet, best experienced with a hot cup of locally grown *manzanilla* (chamomile) tea, sitting on the porch and watching the clouds roll through the forest in her backyard. Doña Corina is an experienced and well-traveled cook wise in the arts of the delicate traveler's taste buds. Also ask about Doña Maribel Gonzales's **Las Perlas de Miraflor** ($12 per person per night includes three meals), lovely accommodations with very reasonably priced tours and horseback rides.

Just down the road, hidden in its own clump of cloud forest and coffee, is the **Finca Lindos Ojos** (tel. 505/713-4041, kahrin@ibw.com.ni, $25 per

Estelí

Estelí

person per weekend, $10 day trips), run by a German couple in Estelí and boasting two queen-size beds for couples. The farm produces organic coffee and vegetables and has a solar panel and generator for the water pump and lights. Lindos Ojos is affiliated with the UCA, but handles its own business. Ask about package trips that include meals, guided hikes, and organic agriculture demonstrations.

What to Bring
At 1,400 wonderful meters above sea level, Miraflor is a remote, cloud-covered, and sometimes downright chilly paradise. Go prepared for inclement weather (perhaps by picking up a sweatshirt at one of Estelí's millions of used-clothing stores) and bring your own bottled water if you're concerned about that sort of thing. Also, a flashlight or some candles will be helpful on that midnight walk to the latrine.

Getting There and Away
At press time, a contractor had finally agreed to repair the wretched dirt road to Miraflor, so let's hope the work is done by the time you read this, but be prepared for bumps, dust, and mud, anyway. There are four buses a day from Estelí: one from COTRAN Sur at 6 A.M., the others from COTRAN Norte at noon, 2:15 P.M., and 3:40 P.M. With the exception of the 2:15, which drops you off at the doorstep of Posada La Soñada, the other three buses drop you off at La Rampla bus stop, a quick 10-minute walk from the Posada. The UCA office may also be able to arrange transport.

Returning to Estelí, a bus from Yalí passes by La Rampla at 7 A.M., 11 A.M., and 4 P.M. Hitching in this remote area of the Estelí countryside is very difficult, as there are not many rides.

CONDEGA
The 9,000 inhabitants of the so-called *Tierra de los Alfareros* (Land of the Potters) eke out a living raising cattle or corn and beans as did the Nahuatl centuries before them. Truckloads of pre-Columbian pottery have been dug out of area cornfields, and the tradition lives on today with a women's cooperative in Ducualí Grande that produces pottery in much the same way.

Before the revolution, only three *terratenientes* (landowners) owned all the land from Condega to Yalí. Condegans roundly supported the Sandinistas, which led to lots of harassment from Somoza's National Guard (Sandinista Omar Cabezas—see Suggested Reading—hid out for months with his troops in the mountains outside of Condega, reportedly in a cave near El Naranjo). In 1979, the Sandinista government confiscated those properties and redistributed them to the locals, and Condega has voted Sandinista ever since.

Contra soldiers found easy pickings in the unprotected farms of the Canta Gallo Mountains east of Condega, where several major skirmishes took place during the 1980s. Most locals can tell you some of the horror stories. More recently, Hurricane Mitch destroyed more than 200 houses and two of the three local industries (a cigar box factory and a tannery). The waters of the Río Estelí rose to a point only two blocks east of the park. Stand at that point and look east toward the river to appreciate the scale of the flooding (or ask David Silva at Tenería Expisa on the west side of the highway to show you his photo album of the hurricane).

Condega's sister city in the United States is Bend, Oregon; contact Timoteo Jeffries, coordinator of the **Bend-Condega Friendship Project** (tjeffries77@yahoo.com).

Sights
"In Condega, we don't have an airport, but we've got a plane," locals will tell you, referring to the famous **airplane park** on a hillside at the edge of town. Toward the end of his grip on power, Somoza took to strafing the northern hillsides with his air force. When, on April 7, 1979, the Sandinistas downed one of his planes, it was considered a major victory and huge morale booster. Follow the dirt road behind the cemetery up the hill 100 meters to the top.

Founded in 1977, the **Casa de Cultura** occupies the former command post of the National Guard. One of its elements, a public library, enjoyed widespread community support during the Sandinista years, when each family donated a book to the room. The Casa offers classes in sewing and guitar playing and operates a fascinating **musical instrument workshop** where you can order a custom-made guitar, *guitarrón,* or violin. Among other attractions, the **Julio Cesár Salgado museum** (open 9 A.M.–5 P.M. weekdays, reading room open 1–5 P.M. weekdays), named after the town's first archaeologist, has a fascinating collection of pre-Columbian ceramic work that local farmers have unearthed in the cornfields around town. Take in a ballgame weekends at the **ballfield** just north of town, and don't miss the *fiestas patronales* on May 15th, traditionally the first day of the rainy season—a big deal in this rain-starved region.

A couple of blocks north of the town square and half block toward the river (east) is a **cigar factory,** where you can ask to see the process and buy really fresh *puros* at a great price.

There are several pharmacies in town, but **Ramón Zavala,** owner of the Farmacia Santa Martha one block east of the park, is worth visiting regardless of whether you need medicine. He runs a lively business in traditional and herbal medicines, homemade stogies, and farm goods. His stories of the Contra attacks east of Condega are riveting.

To reach the famous pottery cooperative, **Taller de Cerámica Ducualí Grande,** take a bus north about two kilometers and get off where a large concrete sign points west to the workshop. Follow that road one full kilometer across the bridge and through the community of Ducualí Grande. Turn left when you see the small church, and look for the white sign on the right side. The workshop was founded in the 1980s with the help of a Spanish volunteer, and the 13 workers still proudly turn out charming ceramic pieces, using the simplest of wheels and firing the pieces in a wood stove; prices run from $1–7.

Hikes near Condega

Get a feel for the arid countryside outside Condega on one of several simple hikes based out of Condega. Stock up in town and leave early in the morning for these hikes, all of which take a full day of walking.

Plaicí Loop: From Condega, walk or bus one kilometer to the baseball stadium. Hike 8.5 kilometers east along the road to Yalí, then turn south toward Plaicí (Nahuatl for Valley of Fear). You can also catch a Yalí bus (one leaves approximately every hour from the park at Condega). Hiking south through Plaicí, ask for directions to get to San Ramón, which is located along the highway (total distance 20 kilometers).

Venecia Coffee Farms: Venecia is a relatively new town, created to house the local coffee workers when the land was made a coffee cooperative. As a stand-out Sandinista position, it was attacked by the Contras relentlessly, who burned it mostly to the ground in the mid-1980s. The city has plans to establish an eco-tourism park called Canto Gallo, with established trails between San Jerónimo and Venecia, including huts, family hosts, and opportunities to work on the coffee *fincas.* Until then, you're on your own: From Condega take the early-morning bus (5 A.M.) east to the coffee cooperative of Venecia (45 minutes). There are several small trails starting in Venecia that wind down and around the hillside through pine trees and coffee fields. The view is fantastic and the air is cool compared to Condega. There are neither lodging facilities nor restaurants in Venecia (but ask about staying with a family), so travel prepared to take the last bus from Venecia back to Condega at 5 P.M.

San Andrés: From Condega, take any of the buses heading to Yalí/La Rica, and get off at Empalme El Hato (12 kilometers, 45 minutes). Follow that dirt road straight through El Hato and Sialcuna northwest to the small cattle town of San Andrés. The road will take you through a pine forest down to the edge of the Río Coco (total distance 25 kilometers). The hilltop of Cerro Sialcuna is a good spot to sleep on a pine-needle bed if you've got a tent, and the view of the valley and the steep green hills to the east is well worth spending the night (look for a trail on your right side just after you pass Sialcuna).

Accommodations and Services

A mainstay in the village for decades, the **Pensión Baldovinos** (south side of the park, tel. 505/715-2393, $2 s with shared bath) also offers meals. Expect one of the three mothers who run the kitchen to scold you that "breakfast is the most important meal of the day!" if you try to leave without eating. Next door, **Hospedaje Framar** is new and clean (tel. 505/715-2222, $2 s with shared bath; doors close at 10 P.M.) and the owner scrupulously weeds out the shady elements (or young couples sporting no luggage), so be presentable. The newest of Condega's lodging facilities, **Rincón Criollo La Gualca** (tel. 505/715-2431, $5s with shared bath, $13 d with private bath), is owned by a Belgian-Nicaraguan couple.

Look for the small Internet café in front of the park ($.75 per hour).

Getting There

Any bus that travels between Ocotal, Somoto, or Jalapa and Managua or Estelí can drop you off on the highway in front of Condega, a two-block walk from the center of town. Or take the Yalí/La Rica buses from Estelí (5 A.M.–4:10 P.M.). Make sure to ask if the bus goes through Condega, as there are two routes to Yalí. Express buses will let you off on the highway by the cemetery; *ordinarios* will let you off in front of the park. From Condega, walk out to the Instituto on the highway to try to catch north- or south-bound *expresos*, or wait for slow buses at the park.

PALACAGÜINA AND COFFEE COOPERATIVE

The town of Palacagüina is widely known as the setting for Carlos Mejía Godoy's revolutionary and religious anthem, *"Cristo de Palacagüina,"* in which Jesus is born *"en el cerro de la iguana, montaña dentro de la Segovia"* (in the iguana hill, deep within the Segovia mountains). In the song, the Christ child's *campesino* parents, Jose and María, are dismayed when, instead of becoming a carpenter like his father, he wants to be a guerrilla fighter.

One of Nicaragua's largest fair trade coffee cooperatives, **PRODECOOP** (office in Estelí 75 meters west of the *esquina de los bancos,* tel. 505/713-3268, prodecoop@ibw.com.ni, www .prodecoop.com, reservations required, about $20) is the centerpiece of town, on its own compound between Palacagüina and the northern exit to the highway. Composed of some 2,000

grower families, PRODECOOP exports as much as 30,000 *quintales* (100-pound bags) a year. PRODECOOP can house and feed up to six guests in brand-new accommodations atop the cupping lab and overlooking the vast drying beds, which bustle with activity during the harvest. There is also a swimming pool and a 360-degree view of the surrounding hills.

Getting There

Most *ordinario* buses (not *expresos*) traveling between Estelí and Somoto or Ocotal pass through Palacagüina. Check before the bus departs the station. If you take an *expreso,* the walk from the highway into town will be long and dusty.

PUEBLO NUEVO

First inhabited in 1652, Pueblo Nuevo is one of the few northern towns that was not affected much by the Contra war. There are about 3,000 urban inhabitants and another 19,000 living off the land in the surrounding countryside. Doña Selina will rent you a room in her house, feed you, and should be able to help you find a local guide to go hiking in the surrounding hills or to view some of the organic agriculture by the river. One nice hike is to the community of Pencal, across the river and about 1.5 hours each way. You can also stay in the farmhouse/*hospedaje* Finca La Virgen. While in Pueblo Nuevo, take a look at the infrequently visited **Museo Arqueologico** (next to the phone office, tel. 505/719-2512, open 8 A.M.–noon and 2–5 P.M. Mon.–Fri.) in the Casa de Cultura, exhibiting pottery, old farm implements, and archaeological pieces found in the area.

Twelve kilometers west of town on the road to Limay, you'll find **El Bosque,** an archaeological dig site where the bones of several mastodons, glyptodons (predecessors to modern armadillos), and early ancestors of the horse species have been uncovered. At 18,000–32,000 years old, the bones are considered one of the oldest archaeological sites in the Americas. Closer to the surface, remnants of Paleolithic weapons were discovered on an upper stratum of soil.

Pueblo Nuevo honors San Rafael Arcángel during the week leading up to October 24.

Estelí

© JOSHUA BERMAN

soapstone sculpture of San Juan de Limay

Getting There

Buses leave Estelí twice a day at 11:45 A.M. and 3:10 P.M., leaving Pueblo Nuevo at 6:30 A.M. and 8:30 A.M.; ask in the park about transportation that continues farther west into the country.

N SAN JUAN DE LIMAY

Since 1972, Limay's claim to fame has been its *marmolina* (soapstone) sculptors, trained by a priest named Eduardo Mejía so they could improve their living conditions. Padre Mejía helped the new artists mine the soapstone from nearby Mt. Tipiscayán (Ulúa-Matagalpa for mountain of the toucan), develop their talent, and market their beautifully polished long-necked birds, kissing swans, iguanas, and Rubenesque women. After the revolution, minister of culture, Ernesto Cardenal, helped the sculptors organize a short-lived cooperative. A core of local carvers still lives

and works in Limay, and you can watch them work and purchase some pieces with little effort. In town, just ask for the *artesanos de piedra*.

Nearby Río Los Quesos meanders outside the city limit. Ask a local kid to show you Poza La Bruja swimming hole, ringed with pre-Columbian petroglyphs. Find a place to bed down for the night at **Pensión Guerrero** (warrior pensione; a pink corner building located one block north of the Catholic church, $2.50 s). Limay is part of a sister-city program with Baltimore, Maryland.

Getting There

San Juan de Limay is a 40-kilometer bus ride from Estelí that traverses a 1000-meter mountain pass through coffee fields. Buses follow two routes to Limay (via la Shell y via El Pino) and leave Estelí's COTRAN Norte at 8:45 A.M., 9:15 A.M., 12:15 P.M., and 2 P.M.

Ocotal

Built on a thick bed of red sand and surrounded on all sides by rugged mountains draped with soft green Ocote pines, Ocotal is the last major settlement before the Honduran border at Las Manos and the enormous wilderness that stretches eastward to the Caribbean. Only a couple of streets are paved. Sedate and understated, Ocotal may be nothing more than a place to sleep before hitting the border, but for many coffee growers and subsistence farmers, Ocotal is still "the big city" for supplies and business. To the east, the settlements grow smaller and more dispersed.

ORIENTATION AND GETTING AROUND

Buses will deposit you at the COTRAN bus station, about 10 blocks south of the main plaza. Two main *entradas* (entrances) to the city, one from the south, and another from the highway to the west, lead straight into the town center. If you enter from the west, pause at the top of the monument to San Francisco to appreciate the lay-

© RANDY WOOD

Saint Francis looks over the northern city of Ocotal.

out of the city before continuing into town. Most of the commercial activity occurs between the park, the market, and around the Shell station on the highway. Ocotal is walkable but has numerous taxis anyway, plus a fleet of *ciclo*-taxi rickshaws.

SIGHTS AND ATTRACTIONS

M Iglesia de Nuestra Señora de la Asunción

Start with the three-naved church in the center of town. Construction began in 1804, and the northern bell tower (the left one) wasn't completed until the 21st century! Two centuries of inhabitants have taken the liberty of scratching their names into its soft adobe walls, including U.S. Marines in the 1930s. The church looks out over Ocotal's **central plaza,** one of Nicaragua's most gorgeous. Shady and green, it fills up in the evenings with sparrows and gossiping *campesinos.* Half a block west of the park's southwest corner (across the street from Restaurante Llamaradas del Bosque), the **Casa de Cultura** boasts an impressive collection of photos of gringo military defeat and General Sandino's resistance. Yes, "boast" is the right word there. Ironically, the Marines lodged their troops in the Casa de Cultura as well as most buildings surrounding the park during their stay in Ocotal.

Take a dip at Las Tres Señoritas and their two swimming holes (known as Las Pozas la Ladosa y Salterín) by walking west (or grabbing a taxi) on El Nuevo Almanecer road, and then crossing the river. Explore on your own, or ask locals for more specific directions, but be careful—the rivers here are said to be **encantada** (enchanted). To the south of Ocotal, stout Cerro Picudo bristles with trails and allegedly contains a hidden lagoon on top, not to mention the "Caves of the Dwarf." Find a guide in town.

ENTERTAINMENT

Ocotal's two discos compete for crowds Friday–Sunday. **Discoteca Infinito** (four blocks north of the cathedral) currently has the advantage

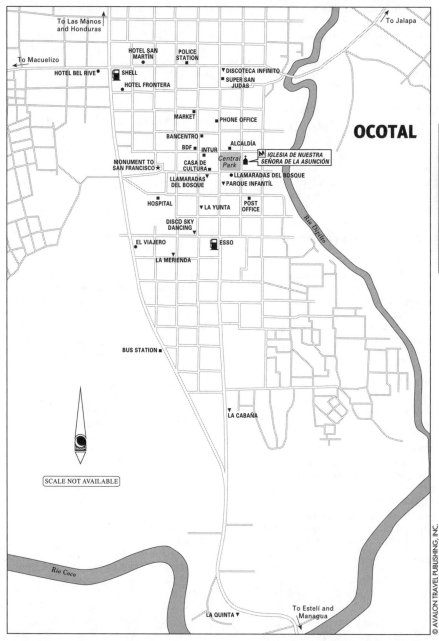

To Las Manos
and Honduras

To Jalapa

To Macuelizo

HOTEL SAN
MARTÍN

POLICE
STATION

HOTEL BEL RIVE

SHELL

DISCOTECA INFINITO
SUPER SAN
JUDAS

HOTEL FRONTERA

OCOTAL

Estelí

MARKET

PHONE OFFICE

BANCENTRO

ALCALDÍA

BDF

INTUR

MONUMENT TO
SAN FRANCISCO

CASA DE
CULTURA

Central
Park

IGLESIA DE NUESTRA
SEÑORA DE LA ASUNCIÓN

LLAMARADAS
DEL BOSQUE

LLAMARADAS DEL BOSQUE
PARQUE INFANTÍL

HOSPITAL

LA YUNTA

POST
OFFICE

DISCO SKY
DANCING

EL VIAJERO

ESSO

LA MERIENDA

Río Dipilto

BUS STATION

MOON

LA CABAÑA

SCALE NOT AVAILABLE

Río Coco

To Estelí and
Managua

LA QUINTA

over **Disco Sky Dancing** (one block west of the Esso). Ocotal celebrates its *fiestas patronales* on the 14th and 15th of August, when you can expect to find Ocotaleños blowing their hard-earned cash on horse shows, live music, gaming tables, and the like. Feel free to join in.

SHOPPING

The municipal market is one block north and one west of the park. The San Judas supermarket is 3.5 blocks north of the cathedral but you can do just as well in the countless smaller *distribuidoras* and the like in the market area. You can browse Mozonte ceramic handicrafts at the INTUR office.

ACCOMMODATIONS

Under $10

Ocotal has nearly a dozen cheap and Spartan *hospedajes*. A favorite among travelers, **Μ Llamaradas del Bosque** (south side of the park, tel. 505/732-2643, $9 s, $16 d) is good value for the money. Backpackers will do fine in quiet, secluded **El Viajero** (3.5 blocks west of the Esso, tel. 505/732-2954, $4 s, $7 d, $11 t, TV and private bath). Although still in the low-cost category, **Hotel Bel Rive** (west side of the highway across from the Shell, tel. 505/732-2146 or 505/732-3249, $7/11 s/d, private bath, phone, TV, fan, and parking) is a big step up in quality.

$10–25

Ocotal's finest is **Hotel Frontera** (on the east side of the highway just south of the Shell station, tel. 505/732-2668, $35/45/55 s/d/t, private bath, phone, TV), with its poolside bar, conference room, parking, Internet, restaurant, and pleasant airy porches overlooking the city and mountains.

FOOD

The menu in these parts is chicken, steak, and fish, and let's just say high up in these mountains you should avoid the fish. **Μ Llamaradas del Bosque** (on the south side of the park, 6:30 A.M.–8 P.M.) is a favorite, serving three meals

buffet-style for around $2. **La Merienda** (one block east and one south of Hotel El Viajero) serves it up in a would-be disco atmosphere. At **La Yunta** (one block east and one south of Hospedaje El Viajero), you'll find higher quality and higher prices: If you've got the time, it's worth the money.

INFORMATION AND SERVICES

The Ocotal **INTUR** office (half a block west of the park's northwest corner, tel. 505/732-3429, open 7:30 A.M.–4:30 P.M. Mon.–Fri., 8:30 A.M.–12:30 P.M. Sat.), is better than most and works locally, training waiters and hoteliers, and organizing cultural exchanges with other parts of Nicaragua. Equally impressive is the Alcaldía's **Center of Documentation** on the northwest corner of the park. Bancentro and other **banks** are located one block west and one north of the park. The **post office** is one block south of the cathedral and one east (open 8 A.M.–noon and 2–5 P.M. Mon.–Sat.). **ENITEL** is two blocks north of the park (open 7 A.M.–5 P.M.). Find a **cyber café** across from the police station, or a block and a half north of the Super San Judas. In either you'll pay about $.75 per hour for dog-slow connections.

GETTING THERE

At least 11 express buses leave Managua's Mayoreo terminal for Ocotal, stopping along the highway in Estelí to pick up additional passengers. Sixteen buses ply the route between Somoto and Ocotal daily, 5:45 A.M.–6:30 P.M. If you miss the *expreso* buses, there are countless additional, painfully slow ordinary buses from Mayoreo.

NEAR OCOTAL

Mozonte

An easy 60-minute walk from Ocotal, the largely indigenous-descendant community of Mozonte is most notable for its workshops of potters who produce ceramics from a particularly fine clay. You can spend the better part of a morning (start walking early to avoid the heat) in Mozonte admiring the craftsmanship of these potters. Both the

Centro de Artesanías and the Centro de Artesanía Ojos de Mujer exhibit a variety of ceramic pieces for sale.

Ciudad Antigua

Ciudad Antigua was the second Spanish attempt to settle Nueva Segovia (the remnants of the first settlement, built in 1543 at the bequest of then-governor Rodrigo de Contreras, are called Ciudad Vieja, and can still be seen near Quilalí at the junction of the Jícaro and Coco Rivers). The wooden church doors still bear the scorch marks of one attempted sacking of the city by pirates. You can pore over some well-loved religious pieces and a few historic documents and other colonial structures that survived the onslaughts of the 19th century at the **Museo Religioso de Ciudad Antigua** (next to the Iglesia Señor de los Milagros, open 8 A.M.–4 P.M. Mon.–Fri.). Two buses a day depart from Ocotal at 7 A.M. and noon.

Macuelizo

If sitting in a completely undeveloped, natural hot spring appeals to you, grab a *camión* at the Shell station and settle in for the 90-minute ride for a day trip to **Macuelizo Termales.** Find a guide in town.

San Fernando and Pico Mogotón

San Fernando is a notably picturesque village of thick adobe-walled homes set around the town park and **Templo Parroquial.** Its 7,000 inhabitants live on more than 200 individual coffee farms and produce an estimated 25,000 *quintales* of coffee annually. More famous than its coffee, however, are its inhabitants, who since the colonial days have been a little lighter-skinned and a little more Spanish-looking. Many have blue or light brown eyes. How do they do it? Well, just don't ask about those last name combinations: Herrera-Herrera, Urbina-Urbina, and Ortez-Ortez, though many attribute the blue eyes to the town's occupation by the U.S. Marines from 1927 to 1931. Life revolves around coffee in San Fernando, and many homes double as coffee-processing mills (*beneficios.*)

You can stage a hike to **Pico Mogotón,** Nicaragua's highest point (2,106 meters) from San Fernando, but even from there, Mogotón is 20 kilometers away. A better hike is to the **Salto San José,** where water rushing off the Dipilto mountain range cascades into a small pool. Take a bus to the community of Santa Clara and get off across from the ball field, turn left (north), and walk the 6–8 kilometers to the river. To be sure of the trail, hire a local kid for some food and a couple *córdobas* to take you. They all know the way and might even jump in for a swim with you.

CROSSING THE BORDER AT LAS MANOS

The Honduran border is 24 kilometers north of Ocotal, open 24 hours. You will be charged $2 to leave Nicaragua and $7 to enter (or $4/$9 after normal business hours or on weekends). There are several small eating booths, two places to change money, and not much else. Fill out the immigration form at the little grey building and walk 100 meters farther down the road to the immigration building to pay and get your exit stamp. Honduran buses to Danlí stop running after 4:30 P.M., so get there early unless your hitchin' thumb feels lucky. To get to the border from Ocotal, buses leave from 5 A.M.–4 P.M. ($.50), or take a cab (around $4–6, depending on how hard you bargain).

JALAPA

Tucked back in one of Nicaragua's farthest corners, fertile, moist Jalapa enjoys a microclimate suitable for the production of tobacco and vegetables its drought-stricken neighbors could only hope for. Jalapa is practically a country apart, only four kilometers from the border and separated from the rest of Nicaragua by 60 kilometers of rutted, disintegrating, nearly impassible road. Surrounded on three sides by Honduras and only surpassed in its remoteness by nearby border outpost Teotecacinte, Jalapa struggles to remain integrated with the rest of Nicaragua.

Throughout the 1980s, that isolation made Jalapa prime stalking ground for Contra incursions from three nearby bases in Honduran territory—Pino-I, Ariel, and Yamales. The city of

Jalapa was flooded with refugees from farming communities farther afield in response to Contra attacks like that of November 16, 1982, when a Contra unit kidnapped 60 *campesinos* at Río Arriba. Jalapa is a peaceful and laid-back place these days, most concerned with good tobacco harvests and the repair of the road that connects it to Ocotal. The whole town comes to life every year at the end of September for the **Festival de Maíz** (the Corn Festival).

Another form of *artesanía* appeared in the mid-1990s: baskets and small containers made of coiled and lashed pine needles. The folks from the Ocotal area and the Atlantic coast battle it out for who had the idea first. **Grupo Pinar del Norte** has lots of fine examples of this unique craft.

QUILALÍ

Starting in the 1930s when Sandino dug into the area of El Chipote and held off the U.S. Marines, Quilalí has been bloodied by decades of battle. You won't find a family in town that didn't lose a loved one to the struggle between Sandinistas and Contras in the 1980s; in fact, the town remains steadfastly Contra to this day and is home to both El Chacál (José Angel Talavera) and El Chacalín (Alex Talavera), the leaders of the Resistance Party (made up of ex-Contras). Upon entering town, you'll notice Quilalí is surprisingly well developed, courtesy of international

aid money destined to support the Sandinista government's opponents. Rumor has it Quilalí's main street was used as a secret airstrip during the 1980s. Many of the Contras here were trained for battle in the United States or in secret bases with locations unknown even to the participants. Their mementos from the U.S. military are treasured today: Look for U.S. Army tin cups, knives, and mosquito nets—not to mention secret stashes of large weaponry that weren't turned in to Doña Violeta's government. The area is also well known for its marijuana production.

The road to Colina La Gloría offers beautiful views of surrounding mountains and passes at least two swimming holes, one each in the Río Jícaro and Río Coco.

Accommodations, Food, and Services
Hospedaje Tere (on main street) costs $4 a night and is the cleanest place in town. Several informal, family establishments, including Comedor Jackson and Sholla, serve typical food for about $3 a plate. Quilalí has a very good hospital supported by Médicos sin Fronteras, and standard services like ENITEL and Correos.

Getting There and Away
Four buses a day leave Ocotal via Santa Clara. The first one is at 5 A.M. From Estelí, five buses depart (5:45 A.M.–1:40 P.M.) for a five hour bonecruncher through San Juan del Río Coco and onward to Wiwilí.

Somoto

Located on the south side of the Pan-American Highway as it veers westward toward the Honduran border at El Espino, Somoto is an average-sized city of 15,000 and capital of the department of Madriz. Tucked into the Cordillera de Somoto at 700 meters above sea level (the highest point of this range is Cerro Tépec-Xomotl at 1,730 meters), Somoto enjoys a fresh climate most of the year. A tributary of the Río Coco traverses the city.

Originally named Tépec-Xomotl, or Valley of the Turkeys, Somoto is known today more for its donkeys, *rosquillas* (baked corn cookies), and blowout carnival each November. Although the *Ciudad de Burros* has less-obvious attractions than nearby Ocotal, you can enjoy a quiet evening in its quaint and friendly park, admiring its church, and enjoying the warmth of the townsfolk. U.S. Marines built the airstrip three blocks south of the park to try out a novel new military technique: the air strike. They bombed nearby Ocotal in the 1930s in a failed attempt to root out General Sandino.

ORIENTATION AND GETTING AROUND

Shiny and new, the COTRAN bus station sits along the north side of the highway, and hosts several noisy and musical families of sparrows in its roof. From the COTRAN, cross the highway (being careful not to get run over by cattle or a run-away wagon, and walk the five blocks directly into the center of town.

SIGHTS AND EVENTS

La Parroquia Santiago de Somoto, is one of Nicaragua's oldest churches. Construction began in 1661, some 86 years before León's great cathedral. If you're around Somoto on the eighth of any month, consider joining the religious masses on their pilgrimage to the tiny community of **Cacaulí,** all hoping for a glimpse of the Virgin Mary. Ever since she appeared to a young farmer named Francisco in the late 1980s, thousands of people have arrived to try to repeat the miracle. They each carry a clear bottle of holy water, which they hold up to the sun at exactly 4 P.M. The Virgin—not parasites—should appear in the water. Whenever the eighth falls on a Sunday, the believers turn out in larger numbers.

Somoto's *fiestas patronales* fall on July 15–25, but the town is more famous for the Carnival of November 11 (or the second Saturday of the month), when it celebrates the creation of the department of Madriz in 1936. All of Nicaragua's best party bands make the trip north, each setting up on one of seven stages—plus mariachis, dance parties, and the standard bull and cockfighting. As for nightlife, try the **Hotel Bambú,** on the highway just east of the bus terminal.

Somoto can be a quiet, pleasant place to pass an afternoon on your way to the border.

ROSQUILLAS SOMOTEÑAS

Although *rosquillas* are baked in adobe wood-burning ovens all over Nicaragua, Somoto is particularly renowned throughout the country for the quality of this baked treat. The *rosquilla* is a crunchy ring of salted corn-dough baked with cheese. When they're not baked the traditional way, you'll find them as flat, molasses-topped *ojaldras* or thick nugget-pockets called *pupusas*. Serve 'em up with a cup of steaming hot, black coffee, still fragrant with smoke from the wood fire, and enjoy: The two tastes naturally complement each other. The two main producers in town are **La Rosquilla Somoteña Betty Espinoza** and **Rosquilla Garcia,** both two blocks west of the COTRAN on either side of the street. If you're traveling anywhere else in the country, *somoteñas* make a cheap, simple gift, greatly appreciated by any Nicaraguan.

Time to make the rosquillas...Somoto is famous for its baked corn treats.

ACCOMMODATIONS

The **Hotel Panamericano** (on the north side of the park, tel. 505/722-2355, $6/8 s/d, hot water and additional amenities in rooms that begin at $15) has a variety of rooms and services, a small zoo, and occasionally cold cans of Milwaukee's Best beer for $.70: It doesn't get any better than this. But the nicest accommodation in Somoto is no doubt the **Hotel Colonial** (half-block south of the church, tel. 505/722-2040, $20/25 s/d, private bath, cable TV, and parking, breakfast included).

FOOD

Comedor Soya (on the plaza) serves a limited soy-based menu, um, with a smile. For excellent *frescos* and fries, check out **Café Santiaguito** (1.5 blocks south of the church). Other options can be found in the market area, as long as you like things fried.

The **Almendro** (across from the Colonial) was mentioned in a Mejía Godoy song ("*el almendro de donde la Tere*" and has nicer meals from $5 (open 10 A.M.–9 P.M.).

INFORMATION, SERVICES, AND GETTING THERE

There is a **bank** across the street from the Alcaldía. The **post office** is across from the Hotel Colonial, and **ENITEL** is behind the church (open until 5 P.M.). A professional and modern health clinic, **Profamilia,** is two blocks south of

COTRAN and open 24 hours a day. **Buses** to Somoto from Estelí run every hour 5:30 A.M.–5:20 P.M. There are also regular express buses from Mayoreo in Managua.

EL ESPINO BORDER CROSSING

The least-used border crossing in Nicaragua, even El Espino is open 24 hours a day (nice work, if you can get it). To get there, take one of the regular buses ($.50) that head toward El Espino, or chip in for a cab (about $4). It's a 40-minute ride from Somoto. At the crossing, you first receive and fill out an immigration form at the booth next to the steel railroad crossing–style gate, then proceed 100 meters up to the little building on the right where you'll pay $2 to exit ($4 after hours) or $7 to enter ($9 after hours). Continuing bus service into Honduras is just over the hill and runs until 4:30 P.M.

The Matagalpa and Jinotega Highlands

Nicaragua's cool, central highlands of rolling blue-green mountains are speckled with small farms, clay-tiled adobe houses, and shady forest streams. It gets chilly up here in *la montaña,* and if the clouds blow through, your exploration from one enchanted valley to the next may feel like a foray into a lost land. This is a country of caves, legends, myths, fresh produce, and above all, Nicaraguan black gold: coffee.

Both Jinotega and Matagalpa paid heavily in blood and destruction during the revolution and

the Contra war that followed, but today's Norteños work their farms without the fear of war and bend their backs instead in the struggle against rural poverty, drought, and devastatingly low prices in the coffee market. The whole region is rich with corn, beans, flowers, and vegetables, and the warmth and friendliness of the hardy people that live in this tough land will astonish you as much as the fresh beauty of the rolling, rocky countryside. Entrepreneur-minded *campesinos* are organizing local eco-tourism initiatives in more than one

ust-Sees

THE MATAGALPA AND JINOTEGA HIGHLANDS

HONDURAS

San Rafael del Norte

Hotel de Montaña Selva Negra

Finca Esperanza Verde

Parque Darío

Grupo Venancia

La Catedral de San Pedro de Matagalpa

Lago Xolotlán

Lago Cocibolca

Salto Santa Emilia

M Grupo Venancia: Rub shoulders with Matagalpa's enlightened citizens and visitors while you enjoy stimulating theater and great music (page 228).

M Finca Esperanza Verde: Call ahead to reserve space at this award-winning eco-tourism effort in the hills above San Ramón, with hiking trails through area coffee farms and deep, fertile valleys (page 237).

M Parque Darío: End your self-guided walking tour of Matagalpa City here, in this shady plaza where you can watch the world go by and listen to the deafening calls of the birds in the treetops (page 227).

M La Catedral de San Pedro de Matagalpa: One of the north's finest structures, this gorgeous cathedral can be spotted from anywhere in town (page 227).

M Hotel de Montaña Selva Negra: A hotel quite unlike any other, Selva Negra has enough farm tours, mountain hikes, good food, and quiet, peaceful relaxation to rest any weary soul (page 240).

M San Rafael del Norte: Visit this cool and historical village in the hills west of Jinotega for a unique taste of the north country; poke through the Sandino Museum and hike to several waterfalls (page 250).

Matagalpa

© SUTAY BERMAN

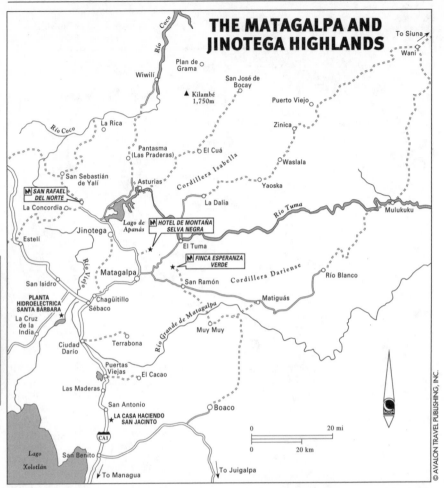

THE MATAGALPA AND JINOTEGA HIGHLANDS

To Siuna
Wani

Río Coco

Plan de Grama

Wiwilí

San José de Bocay

▲ Kilambé 1,750m

Puerto Viejo

Zinica

La Rica

Río Coco

Pantasma (Las Praderas)

El Cuá

Cordillera Isabella

Waslala

San Sebastián de Yalí

Asturias

Yaoska

Río Tuma

M SAN RAFAEL DEL NORTE

La Concordia

La Dalia

Mulukuku

Lago de Apanás

M HOTEL DE MONTAÑA SELVA NEGRA

Jinotega

Estelí

El Tuma

M FINCA ESPERANZA VERDE

Matagalpa

San Ramón

Cordillera Dariense

Río Blanco

San Isidro

Matiguás

PLANTA HIDROELECTRICA SANTA BÁRBARA

Chagüitillo

Sébaco

La Cruz de la India

Río Grande de Matagalpa

Muy Muy

Ciudad Darío

Terrabona

Puertas Viejas

El Cacao

Las Maderas

San Antonio

Boaco

LA CASA HACIENDA SAN JACINTO

CA1

Lago Xolotlán

San Benito

To Managua

To Juigalpa

0   20 mi
0   20 km

© AVALON TRAVEL PUBLISHING, INC.

mountain village, and curious travelers who aren't afraid of using a latrine will discover firsthand the humble hospitality that has also made Matagalpa and Jinotega famous.

PLANNING YOUR TIME

Two or three nights is sufficient for visiting the cities of Matagalpa and Jinotega, but allow an extra day or two if you plan to explore any of the surrounding countryside. Those looking for a peaceful mountain retreat often spend 2–3 nights

at either Hotel Selva Negra, Finca Esperanza Verde, or with a homestay program run by a coffee cooperative. Combining such a trip with a night or two in town can easily consume five or six days, or more if you visit the more remote communities.

HISTORY

Periods of tremendous violence and warfare have wracked the mountainous north for more than a century. In the early 1930s, Augusto César Sandino fought U.S. Marines and the

National Guard here; 40 years later, young revolutionary Sandinistas faced Somoza's National Guard in several bloody battles, particularly between San José de Bocay, Matiguás, and Bilampi. Far more devastating than either of those conflicts, however, were the 1980s, when Matagalpa and Jinotega, (along with the RAAN, or North Atlantic Autonomous Region) experienced the worst of the war between the Sandinista military and Contra troops. Travelers along the region's few roads were frequently ambushed and soldiers from both sides raided villages as a matter of course. Farmers learned to tend their crops with rifles slung over their shoulders, just in case.

Peace swept the region at the start of the 1990s and the past decade has transformed the region into an agricultural powerhouse. Gone are the thousands of cold, wet, and hungry guerrilla soldiers that marched muddily through these hills. Those same rugged trails are now popular with intrepid travelers intent on visiting coffee cooperatives, climbing mountains, and swimming in waterfalls.

The Road to Matagalpa

The ride north from Managua is an intensely visual experience. The road climbs from the verdant plains of sugarcane and rice up through a series of plateaus with long horizons and broad panoramas before reaching the long mountain valleys that characterize the north. Most travelers take an express bus straight through most of the landscape and beeline for the mountains, but Matagalpa's dry lowlands hide a few interesting places of their own.

ROADSIDE ATTRACTIONS
La Casa-Hacienda San Jacinto

A must-see on the high school curriculum of all Nicaraguan history students, the Casa-Hacienda San Jacinto, located about 35 kilometers north of Managua along the Pan-American Highway, merits its own roadside statue. The monument guards the turnoff to the battlefield of San Jacinto and depicts a defiant Andrés Castro standing atop a pile of rocks. This is the site where, in 1856, the Liberals—supported by William Walker and his band of filibusters—and Conservatives battled fiercely. Conservative Andrés Castro, out of ammunition, picked up a rock and hurled it at the enemy, killing a Yankee with a blow to the head. Today, Castro represents the fighting spirit of Nicaraguan nationalism that refuses to bow to foreign authorities.

Three kilometers east of the highway (a flat, 20-minute walk), the museum at the restored San Jacinto ranch house is run-down and little visited except by occasional hordes of high school students. But for $1 admission, you can explore the period relics and admire the displays. If no one's manning the ticket window, just shout until the caretaker rides her bike down from the main building. Bring water: There are no facilities at the site itself, and just one mediocre restaurant at the highway turnoff.

Artesanía El Caminante In El Madroño

As the highway begins its windy ascent, keep an eye out for clusters of painted wooden figures, particularly flamingos, herons, and egrets. This is the fresh air gallery of Asención Zeledón, self-taught woodcarver and sculptor (and several copycat neighbors). He's been carving his creations for nearly 25 years and selling them at the side of the highway, attracting crowds from around the country. The hillsides of El Madroño and north to the Sébaco Valley were once lined with valuable trees like brazilwood, the majority of which were harvested and sold over the past 150 years. Today, the hillsides are mostly bare except for low-value species like escobillo, guacimo, and miligüiiste. Zeledón binds their branches with strong vines to produce original furniture and sculpture. He's a civil war veteran with the shrapnel scars to prove it, fighting now to earn a decent living after having been economically abandoned by the army at the end of the 1980s. El Madroño is located about 75 kilometers north of Managua and about 40

BLACK GOLD: THE STORY OF NICARAGUAN COFFEE

In 1852, Germans Ludwig Elster and his wife Katherina Braun were passing through Nicaragua on their way to the California gold rush. They never made it to California, but they did find gold. Rather, Katherina did.

While crossing Nicaragua, Ludwig met many disheartened travelers returning home from failure in California. He and Katherina decided to cut their journey short and look for gold in the mines of San Ramón, Matagalpa. While Ludwig worked the taxed gold deposits of Matagalpa, Katherina Braun established a home garden and planted some of the coffee beans they'd picked up in Managua. Her discovery—that Matagalpa's climate and soils were just right for the cultivation of the bitter but full-bodied arabica coffee bean—dwarfed the importance of San Ramón's gold mines and changed the course of Nicaragua's history.

Coffee fever gripped Matagalpa in the 1880s, and the Nicaraguan government, eager to capitalize on the crop that neighbor-states Costa Rica and Guatemala had already been growing for 40 years, threw its weight behind the Germans. Laws were passed encouraging young Germans to immigrate to Nicaragua. One such law gave them free land to work; many of these family farms are still operating today.

At first, coffee was shipped in bean (parchment) form through the port of Corinto, around Cape Horn to European importers in Bremen and Hamburg. By 1912, though, the Nicaraguan German community had established their own processing plants where they milled and processed the coffee beans. They used a new "wet" method that stripped the beans of their pulp over grated steel cylinders. Today, Nicaragua is home to more than 40 wet coffee mills, plus the thousands of micro-mills on individual farms.

From Matagalpa to Mochaccino:
How Nicaraguan Coffee is Processed

One of the truly unique aspects of Nicaraguan coffee, besides its exceptional quality, is how much of the process is performed on the farm, before the product is shipped elsewhere. This is a significant difference from the routine adopted by Costa Rican coffee growers, most of whom send off their harvest immediately after picking.

Also, an increasing number of small-scale Nicaraguan coffee farmers are learning to recognize and judge the quality of their product and eliminate the middlemen, or *coyotes,* who have traditionally taken the lion's share of coffee profits. One tool that allows them to do this is the "cupping lab," a specially equipped kitchen where Nicaraguan cooperative members are trained to grind, brew, and rate their own coffee using internationally recognized criteria. One of the key figures in the cupping lab project was Paul Katzeff, CEO and Roastmaster of California-based Thanksgiving Coffee Company (there are wonderful stories about exchanges with Nicaraguan coffee farmers and a whole lot more at www.thanksgivingcoffee.com).

But before you cup it, you must grow, harvest, and process it. Following are the steps involved:

1. Coffee berries are picked during the harvest months from December to February. The fleshy berries are red and yellow and called *café en uva* (meaning grape or cherry coffee).
2. The berries are de-pulped, i.e., the fleshy covering is removed. This is done the same day they're picked to prevent fermenting, which would affect the flavor. This is either done dry or while they're suspended in water ("wet processing").
3. The coffee beans at this stage still have a mucilaginous coating on them. The beans are allowed to sit for 24 hours to allow the coating to ferment, facilitating the removal of the mucilage.
4. After 24 hours, the beans are soaked in water and stirred with wooden paddles. The mucilaginous coating dissolves. During this stage, the good beans sink to the bottom of the vessel, and the bad beans float to the surface, where they're removed.
5. The beans are now called *café en pergamino* (parchment coffee). Small growers sell their beans to the coffee cooperatives at this point. They still have a hard shell around them.
6. The beans are laid out in the sun on broad concrete slabs to dry and raked continuously to prevent burning.
7. When the beans reach 12 percent humidity, they are stored for around one month in a cool,

semi-dark building. During this time, the coffee beans' flavor is enhanced.

8. When ready for shipping, the beans are milled to remove the hard shell. What is left after milling is the familiar coffee bean, in two halves. At this stage, the coffee is considered *café oro* (gold or green coffee).

9. The beans are sorted. All broken, burned, or blackened beans are removed by hand.

10. The beans are packed in 150-pound burlap sacks and sent to the port of Corinto for shipments to the western United States and Asia, or Puerto Cortéz, Honduras for shipments to the eastern United States and Europe.

11. The green coffee beans are roasted, ground, bagged, and brewed into the beverage so many people can't do without. A few cooperatives and companies in Nicaragua roast and package their coffee for distribution in country—you can find these at co-op headquarters or any local supermarket.

Good Beans: What Makes "Gourmet" Coffee
As much as 80 percent of Nicaraguan cooperative–produced coffee can be considered "quality coffee" because it fills the following internationally recognized requirements:

• They are arabica beans (not robusta) grown at an altitude of 900 meters or higher.

• Consisting of big beans, the lots are aromatic, well sorted, and free from broken or burned beans and small stones.

• Beans are given one month to sit during processing and are not de-hulled until just before shipping.

• Beans are transported in sealed containers.

• Beans are adequately stored by the purchaser.

• Upon toasting, the beans are sealed immediately in special one-pound vacuum-packed bags that prevent the introduction of light, air, and moisture, but permit carbon dioxide to escape.

• The consumer can buy the coffee in whole-bean form, not ground.

The forest canopy remains lush and full of life over this small, shade-grown coffee farm.

kilometers south of Sébaco, just south of the Laguna de Moyoá, which makes a good landmark.

La Laguna de Moyoá and Las Playitas

After conquering the first big climb on the highway from Managua (known as Cuesta del Coyol), you'll be greeted by the Laguna Moyoá (Nahuatl for place of the small mosquitoes) on the west side of the highway and the swampy Laguna Tecomapa to the east (unless it is a dry year, when both disappear). Geologists believe they are the remnants of the ancient Lake of Sébaco, a giant reservoir that formed the heavy clay soils of today's Sébaco Valley. A tectonic shift ages ago sent the Río Grande de Matagalpa flowing eastward toward the Atlantic instead of into Lake Xolotlán through Moyoá, and the lake gradually disappeared. It experienced a brief revival during Hurricane Mitch, when Lake Moyoá rose to the edge of the highway and Tecomapa became a legitimate lake through which wading cattle grazed.

Moyoá was once home to the Chontaleña people, and it is possible that they had a fixed settlement on the island in the lake. Some clay pottery has been uncovered from the A.D. 500–1500 period, which would indicate they at least frequented the site, probably to fish and hunt.

The locals do a good business catching fish out of Moyoá—mostly mojarra and guapote—both very good for eating, and both of which you'll see held up on strings along the side of the road. To visit the lake, stop in at Comedor Treminio and ask for Anita Vega or Humberto Treminio, the owners of the land that borders the lake. You can eat your meals at their establishment, and strike a deal with them for the right to camp out on their land. Try the shady grove down at the end of the road that leads to the lake. Birds you might see at Moyoá include *playeritos, piches, zambullidores,* and several types of heron.

CIUDAD DARÍO

Named after the prized poet of Castilian literature, Ciudad Darío was known by the indigenous name of Metapa in 1867 when Rubén Darío was born. Today, a handsome brass statue of the author stands at the southern approach to the city.

Sights

The primary attraction is the unassuming **Casa Natal Rubén Darío** (along the main street in front of the ENITEL building, 8 A.M.–12:30 P.M. and 2–5 P.M. Mon.–Fri.). Darío was born here and then moved to the city of León shortly afterward to live with relatives. The east part of the house has been converted into a small amphitheater for the presentation of cultural shows.

For a tasty meal, try **Comedor Clementina** (from the mayor's office, two blocks north and half a block west) for a hearty beef soup or her famous chicken and *ayote* (a type of squash). There are plenty of fresh fruit juices to sip while you wait for your meal and try to talk with her pet parrot, who speaks Italian (so she claims!). A half a block east from Clementina's is a big *fritanga* (street-side food vendor) that opens up around 6 P.M., $1–2 a plate.

El Coctel (from the Pulpería Masaya, go west one block and north a half block) likes to serve crowds coming out of the museum, and specializes in *carne a la plancha* (grilled steaks); a bit pricier than the other options in town—you can pay more than $7.50 for some things—but it's one of the few restaurants with a real ceiling overhead. The favorite restaurant among the NGO and businessperson crowd is **Doña Conchi's** (a block north of the Shell station toward the north end of town), a relatively upscale place with a full menu ranging from $1.50–7.50 per dish.

Express buses between Managua and points north save an hour off the trip by not entering Ciudad Darío. So, if you're headed there by bus (from Managua's Mayoreo Terminal), make sure to take an *ordinario.* Any local bus leaving Matagalpa or Estelí headed to Managua will go by way of Darío.

Near Ciudad Darío

Anyone between the ages of 7 and 15 will know exactly how to help you find the following historical and geological destinations in the Darío neighborhood of Santa Clara, located about one kilometer east from the town's park (not far from the Carlos Santí baseball stadium).

To get to the **petroglyphs,** start at Darío's mayor's office in the park and head east toward the stadium at the top of a hill (.5 km). On the other side of the stadium is a school for deaf children. Beyond that, the paved road will turn to dirt as you enter Barrio España. There is a *pulpería* (market) on the corner where you can get directions to the petroglyphs, less than a 30-minute walk.

La Posa de Las Yeguas (The Mare's Pool) is a deep spot in the creek where, supposedly, women who weren't faithful to their husbands were turned into mares and went to live. Several rocks there bear petroglyphs and more modern graffiti. It is said the friars of old would go to meditate at **La Cueva del Fraile** (The Friar's Cave), not far from La Posa de Las Yeguas.

SÉBACO

No matter where you travel in the north of Nicaragua, at some point you'll probably find yourself in Sébaco, whether passing through or waiting for a bus or a ride. Located right where the highway splits to take travelers to either Estelí and the Segovias (fork left) or Matagalpa, Jinotega, and the northeast (fork right), Sébaco, a.k.a. *La Ciudad de Cebollas* (the City of Onions) is known throughout the region for its lively roadside commerce. If you're traveling at night, Sébaco is a sudden blast of street lights, traffic, and bustle.

While travelers are more typically interested in the Texaco station's clean restrooms, you can also pick up fresh produce—carrots, beets, and of course, onions—without leaving your bus or vehicle. Sébaco's aggressive roadside vendors will scale the side of your bus and display their goods through your window—Nicaragua's version of a drive-thru. If you have a long bus ride ahead of you, this is a good place to pick up bags of fruit juice, snacks, or freshly harvested gifts for whomever it is you are on your way to visit.

If you need to get out and stretch your legs, or

THE LEGEND OF CIHUACOATL

At the edge of the Río Viejo, there was once a powerful community ruled by a mighty cacique. His wife was considered the most beautiful woman in the country, but she made regular suspicious trips down to the river with great quantities of carefully prepared foods: beverages of seeds and berries, and birds prepared with spices and grains. One day, one of the cacique's men decided to follow the woman down to the river to see what she did. There, he watched as the woman sat calmly on a rock at the river's edge and struck the palm of her hand against the water's surface several times with a sharp smacking sound. From out of the ripples on the water's surface emerged a giant snake, which rose halfway out of the water and placed its head on the woman's beautiful smooth thighs. She fed the snake, its head resting on her lap, and afterwards the two made love at the water's edge. Then the serpent slithered back into the river, down to its underwater cave, and the woman gathered her things to leave.

The cacique's servant ran quickly back to tell the story, trembling as he related the infidelity to the cacique. When the woman returned home, her husband, in a jealous rage, killed the woman with a single stroke of his knife. The snake, upon realizing his lover had been slain, agitated the river with its tail, causing it to rise up violently and destroy the entire community. The goddess Cihuacoatl (the Snake Woman) has been worshiped ever since by the Nahuatl people in the area.

have urgent errands, Sébaco also has several banks, a telephone office, and a well-equipped private health clinic.

History and Sights

The name Sébaco comes from the Nahuatl name Cihuacoatl (the snake-woman). In 1527, the Spanish founded the city they called Santiago de Cihuacoatl on the banks of the Río Viejo alongside the Native American settlement of Cihuacoatl, capital of the Chontales people. But when a major flood put the town under water in 1833, Sébaco was moved to the hill just east of town, where the remnants of Sébaco Viejo can still be found: The **Templo Viejo** houses a simple collection of archaeological artifacts, including pieces of pottery and ceramics, some small statues, and a wooden carving of the deity Cihuacoatl. When they moved, the residents of Sébaco packed up their buildings piece by piece and transported the materials to the new location, where they reconstructed the buildings to approximately their original form. Since then, the houses slowly crept down the hill and back to the water's edge, waiting for history to repeat itself.

And that's exactly what happened. In 1998, Sébaco was hit so hard by Hurricane Mitch it became one of the primary obstacles separating Managua from the north. The large bridge at the south end of town resisted the floods of the Río Grande de Matagalpa, but the river overflowed its banks just south of the bridge and sliced a new channel through the road several hundred meters wide. Some of the flood waters wound up flowing into the watershed of the Río Viejo (which flows south from Jinotega). The combined torrent swelled into a deadly wall of water that ripped through Ciudad Darío.

For an adventure, track down the house of Carlos Miranda, known popularly as Borbollón. On his property is an ancient tamarind tree that's the pride of the city—they call it **El Tamarindo de Oro** (golden tamarind tree) in memory of the golden gifts given to Spanish conquistador Gabriel de Rojas. Said to be 500 years old, its powerful branches arch down to the ground, then turn upward again, forming a verdant leafy cave inside. Borbollón himself is an ebullient character who will tell you stories and raunchy jokes as he shows you the tree, his beautiful farm, and a stone known as the **Piedra de la Mocuana.**

Services

Although there are a few cheap, seedy places to crash in town, you'd be much wiser to continue on to Matagalpa or Estelí, each no more than an hour away. The dozens of decent roadside restaurants offer similar menus of chicken, tacos, beef, and sandwiches. **El Sesteo** is the best sit-down lunch spot in town, with uniformed waiters, an air-conditioned *sala,* and the nod of the expat community, which has been enjoying lunches there since it opened. On the east side of the intersection across from the triangle, the cheaper **Sorbetería Mac-et** serves sandwiches, hot dogs, light lunches, fruit juices, and ice cream.

Sébaco's several banks operate on a standard 8:30–5 schedule. The clean and modern **Profamilia Health Clinic** (located just outside of town along the road that leads to Matagalpa, open 8 A.M.–noon and 1:30–5 P.M. Mon.–Fri.) was built in 2001 and is an easy walk from the center of town. The ENITEL phone office is located just south of the triangle on the west side of the street, open 7:30 A.M.–9 P.M.

Chagüitillo

About two kilometers north of Sébaco along the highway to Matagalpa, Chagüitillo is a small community with access to several dozen pre-Columbian petroglyphs scratched into the stone walls of a canyon just outside the village. The site is named *Apamico* (Nahuatl for Place of the Monkeys). Additional relics depicting monkeys, shamans carrying human heads, and hunting scenes line the banks of the Aranca Burba stream. The locals can easily help you find the two streambeds and show you the petroglyphs; both sites are an easy walk from the center of town. Particularly good guides are Orlando Dávila (tel. 505/775-2149) and Melvin Rizo, who speaks some English (tel. 505/775-2546). Dávila lives in front of the school whose tall green wall is painted with representations of the petroglyphs; Rizo lives a block or two closer to the highway.

In town, find the *pulpería* run by Bernabe Rayo (located on a side street off the main road through town). Chagüitillo is the source of a water project for the city of Matagalpa, and engineers digging the trenches for the pipelines have unearthed many additional artifacts. Some are scattered amongst the many houses of the community, but Rayo has done an admirable job of collecting some of them and trying to form a small community museum out of the pieces. You can support him by purchasing something from his store. He's got an interesting collection of old ceramic pots, cups, and small statues, plus some larger pieces he's reconstructed from the shards.

El Atajo de Guayacán

About 25 kilometers west of the city of Mata-galpa, *El Atajo de Guayacán* (the Guayacán Short-cut) is a dirt road leading north along the west side of a pretty mountain valley to the city of Jinotega. Drivers headed from Sébaco to Jinotega can bypass the city of Matagalpa completely and save an hour's drive. Hikers (use the Matagalpa, Sébaco, and Jinotega INETER quad maps) can use it to penetrate some fantastic mountain valleys. Your first hike should be Cerro Los Chiles, a peak that forms a half-basin along the side of the Atajo de Guayacán.

Matagalpa City

The department of Matagalpa is the most mountainous in Nicaragua, and its capital city remains true to form. As you walk up and down the steep streets, you'll realize the city is draped like a blanket over the rolling valley floor beneath it. Nicknamed *La Perla del Septentrión* (The Pearl of the North), Matagalpa's true precious stone is a ripe, red coffee bean, the production and harvest of which is essential to the region's—and the nation's—economy. Matagalpa enjoys clean, mountain air, but water is another story. Radically depleted by deforestation and human contamination, clean water

is in dreadfully short supply here. During the driest times, city officials cope with the problem by implementing draconian rationing schemes. The surrounding mountains have been mostly scraped clean of trees, but during the wet season, they turn emerald green and remain so throughout the Christmas season, when the coffee harvest turns the city of Matagalpa into a lively center of coffee pickers, prospectors, packers, and processors.

Nahuatl influence is more prominent in Matagalpa than elsewhere, particularly in regional vocabulary, which retains much pre-Columbian vocabulary. The Nahuatl word *chüisle*, for example, is used instead of the Castilian *quebrada* for stream. The city's central office for the region's indigenous community settles land disputes and other issues. Modern-day Nicaraguan politicians prize Matagalpa because its high population can often swing the vote, but tourists will prize Matagalpa as a welcome respite from the heat of the lowlands, plus a chance to sip the best coffee in the world while plotting their forays deeper into the mountains. Ignore the inflated population sign as you enter the valley—the latest figures still put Matagalpa's urban population at less than 100,000.

HISTORY

Matagalpa has been settled for as long as anyone can remember. The beautiful valley where the city of Matagalpa now sits was already a cluster of Nahuatl communities—including Solingalpa

© JOSHUA BERMAN

Matagalpa's streets are San Francisco steep.

Matagalpa

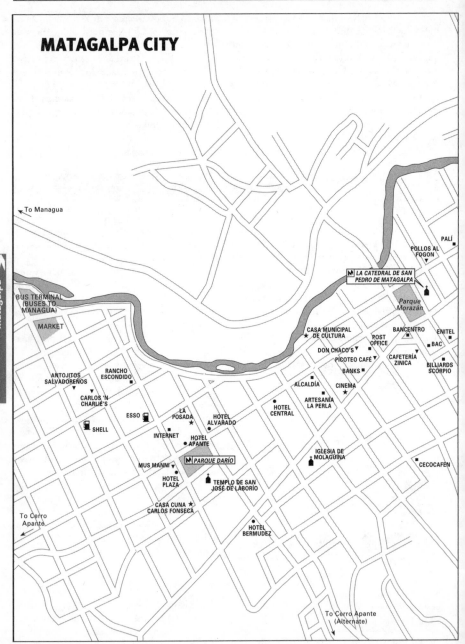

MATAGALPA CITY

To Managua

PALÍ

POLLOS AL
FOGON

LA CATEDRAL DE SAN
PEDRO DE MATAGALPA

BUS TERMINAL
(BUSES TO
MANAGUA)

Parque
Morazán

MARKET

CASA MUNICIPAL
DE CULTURA

BANCENTRO

ENITEL

POST
OFFICE

DON CHACO'S

BAC

PICOTEO CAFÉ

CAFETERÍA
ZINICA

BILLIARDS
SCORPIO

BANKS

ANTOJITOS
SALVADOREÑOS

RANCHO
ESCONDIDO

ALCALDÍA

CINEMA

CARLOS 'N
CHARLIE'S

ARTESANÍA
LA PERLA

ESSO

LA
POSADA

HOTEL
ALVARADO

HOTEL
CENTRAL

SHELL

INTERNET

HOTEL
APANTE

MUS MANNI

PARQUE DARÍO

IGLESIA DE
MOLAGUINA

HOTEL
PLAZA

TEMPLO DE SAN
JOSÉ DE LABORÍO

CECOCAFÉN

To Cerro
Apante

CASA CUNA
CARLOS FONSECA

HOTEL
BERMUDEZ

To Cerro Apante
(Alternate)

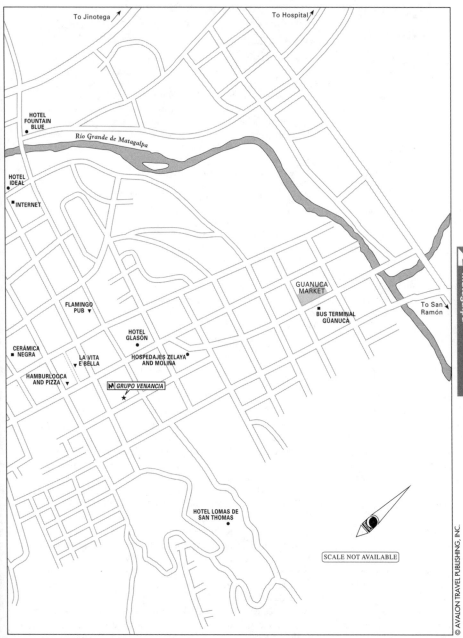

To Jinotega

To Hospital

HOTEL
FOUNTAIN
BLUE

Río Grande de Matagalpa

HOTEL
IDEAL

INTERNET

GUANUCA
MARKET

BUS TERMINAL
GÜANUCA

To San
Ramón

FLAMINGO
PUB ▼

HOTEL
GLASÓN

CERÁMICA
NEGRA

LA VITA
E BELLA

HOSPEDAJES ZELAYA
AND MOLINA

HAMBURLOOCA
AND PIZZA ▼

GRUPO VENANCIA
★

HOTEL LOMAS DE
SAN THOMAS

SCALE NOT AVAILABLE

Matagalpa

© AVALON TRAVEL PUBLISHING, INC.

MATAGALPA, WATER, AND THE LEGEND OF THE SERPENT

Matagalpa is a water-stressed city. In some neighborhoods, the water pressure is only turned on once a day; in others, Matagalpinos are forced to walk to distribution points to fill up containers from tanker trucks. You may see these trucks along the city streets in the early mornings, when everyone comes out with buckets and pans to get what water they can.

At the same time, there's more water in Matagalpa than some people know what to do with. Time and time again, shallow excavations in the city for routine projects have turned up a moist layer of earth just several meters below the surface. When a well-loved priest died in the 1990s, his tomb was dug underneath the floor of the cathedral. Before they had finished digging, the hole had begun to flood. Studies have determined the water under the city of Matagalpa isn't exploitable in quantities great enough to supply the city, and so other alternatives are being developed.

Much of Matagalpa's limited water supply comes from the forested hillsides that surround the city, hillsides that are rapidly being stripped of their timber. Matagalpinos speak of an old legend: The hill known as Apante, just southeast of the city, was said to be an enormous upwelling of water trapped within a pocket of soil and rock. Within the water lived a great snake. One day the snake began to shake, and the hillside began to crumble, threatening to unleash a massive landslide upon the residents of the city. In despair, they turned to the Virgin Mary for protection. Mary fought the snake and subdued it by planting its tail underneath the foundation of the church of Molagüina in the center of the city.

But the snake grows stronger each day. . . when it finally has enough strength to break free, it will shake its tail again, causing the hills to crumble and collapse upon the city. If the deforestation of the hillsides surrounding Matagalpa continue, this prophecy may very well come true.

and Molagüina, which still exist today—when the Spanish first set eyes on it. Nahuatl traditional histories don't include any stories of their people having arrived in this valley—as if they have always been here. Long before it was called the Pearl of the North, Matagalpa was known as the City of Ten in Nahuatl, in reference to the ten small settlements that made up the valley. The name is also attributed to the powerful cacique Atahualpa, who governed the area during the time of colonization (Solingalpa was his wife).

The Spanish established a camp alongside the Nahuatls around 1680. Some powerful Spanish families made up the first settlers; their last names are still common in the region: Alvarado, Castañeda, Reyes, Rizo, Escoto. They set up extensive cattle ranches and planted fields before coffee was even a dream. In 1838, the area was named Departamento del Septentrión, and in 1862, Matagalpa was elevated to the status of city. Even with that status, the city of Matagalpa was of far less economic importance to the nation than Sébaco.

That changed in the second half of the 19th century when Matagalpa became the focus of a sizeable immigration of Germans. They had not arrived in Nicaragua to plant coffee, as is commonly believed, but to develop the gold mines in the east. Once established in Nicaragua, however, they quickly realized how perfect the climate was for the cultivation of coffee and their interest switched to the crop that would define Nicaragua's economy for more than 100 years. Matagalpa had developed a new reason for being, and coffee has been the focus of Matagalpa ever since.

Today, several problems constrain Matagalpa from the prosperity it enjoyed in the 19th century. Most critical is the lack of potable water—even the Chagüitillo water project may provide water for no more than 10 years—but developing rural roads and dealing with the growing solid waste problem will both be necessary before Matagalpa returns to its status as a pearl.

SIGHTS
⛰ Parque Darío
You shouldn't pass through Matagalpa without spending some time in **Parque Darío.** Buy a crushed ice *raspado* and spend some time people-watching. There are probably more trees jammed into the park's tiny confines than any other park in Nicaragua, and come sunset the branches fill with the chatter of thousands of birds. A permanent fixture in the park is a vendor with rows and rows of handmade ceramic piggy-banks for sale, none of which costs more than $1.

Churches and Museums
El Templo de San José de Laborío sits at the edge of the Parque Darío at the south end of town. It's probably as old as the colonial presence in Matagalpa, but no one is quite sure exactly when it was built. It was rebuilt in 1917 on top of its old foundation, but underneath that foundation are the ruins of another that date to at least 1751, and possibly a bit earlier. In 1881, an indigenous uprising used the church as its garrison.

Matagalpa was the birthplace of the founder of the FSLN, Carlos Fonseca. The house he was born in has been converted into a museum. Known as **La Casa Cuna Carlos Fonseca** (one block east of Parque Darío's south side, tel. 505/772-3665, 8 A.M.–noon and 2–5 P.M. Mon.–Fri.), the tiny corner building has the original brick floors, mud walls, and tile roof, and has an interesting assortment of documents, photos, and memorabilia, including Carlos's typewriter and his gear from military training in Korea.

The history of **La Iglesia de Molagüina,** found in the center of the city, has been forgotten. It was probably constructed between 1751 and 1873, though those dates have been questioned by historians. Simple and monastic, it is a well-used and well-loved church: Molagüina is home to a Catholic order of nuns and the College of San José.

The new **Museo de Café** (located on the main street two blocks east of the mayor's office, across from Teatro Perla, open 8 A.M.–5 P.M. Mon.–Fri., closed for lunch, open Sat. mornings) displays some interesting murals and photographs from Matagalpa's history, plus a small collection of indigenous artifacts. Entrance is free and local coffee is available for sale.

⛰ La Catedral de San Pedro de Matagalpa
At the northeastern end of town, **La Catedral de San Pedro de Matagalpa** was a disproportionately large cathedral—the third largest in the nation—when it was built in 1874, reflecting the opulence of Matagalpa at the time. The cathedral is built in the baroque style, with heavy bell towers set at both sides and an airy, spacious interior. It's the most prominent building in town and is easily visible from the hillsides north of town on the road to Jinotega. The cathedral's interior is crisp and cool, tastefully adorned with bas- and medium-relief sculpture, carved wood, and paintings. Mass is held nightly at 6 P.M.

There are two adjacent cemeteries on the hillside east of the city, about a 30-minute walk from town. One is for locals, and one is for foreigners, a rare arrangement in Nicaragua. Both contain headstones hand carved from dark rock, something seen only in Matagalpa. Buried in the cemetery higher up on the hill in the local section is one of the most famous casualties of the 1980s war: Benjamin Linder. An American, Linder was an avid juggler and unicyclist, and his headstone reflects those passions, along with some doves, the symbol of the peace he never lived to see. Burying Linder in the locals section was the highest honor they could give him.

Opportunities to Volunteer
Matagalpa is home to at least 16 organizations that occasionally accept volunteer help if you'd like to make Matagalpa your home for awhile. The **Movimiento Comunal** (tel. 505/772-3200) deals with indigenous issues and supports the fight against water privatization, and rumor has it they sometimes provide Spanish lessons. **La Casa de la Mujer Nora Hawkins** (tel. 505/772-3047) promotes social programs that benefit women. The

Comunidad Indígena (tel. 505/772-2692) is rather disorganized but well-intentioned and could certainly use your assistance: Find a way to make yourself useful. **Habitat for Humanity** (located two blocks east and half a block north of the Deportiva Brigadista, tel. 505/772-6121) has built several housing settlements in the area and continues to be active. Ask about volunteer opportunities at **Centro Girasol** (tel. 505/772-6030), a bright yellow corner building right across the first bridge as you enter Matagalpa from Managua.

ENTERTAINMENT AND EVENTS

Matagalpans celebrate their *fiestas patronales* on September 24th, and the anniversary of their becoming a city on February 14. Every September there is a rowdy country fair that brings in crowds from the north and east, and cattle traders from all over the country. This is the best time of year to catch Matagalpa's traditional music of polkas, mazurkas, and *jamaquelos,* performed by the roving street bands that play at restaurants. *Noches Matagalpinas* are held the last weekend of every month in Parque Darío; the weekend typically involves a street stage with live music and stands set up by the local restaurants.

In 2001, a new dance academy started up, under the able direction of Marcos Valle, who studied modern dance in Spain. The **Academía de la Danza de Matagalpa** puts on dance presentations several times a year. If there's going to be a show, they advertise it at the Casa Municipal de Cultura, next to the fire station.

Local radio stations include Radio Norteña, FM 94.1; Radio Stereo Apante, FM 94.9; and Radio Yes, FM 90.1. The latter has several programs for a rural audience, including impersonations, jokes, and news commentary. Their morning news program is worth a listen in the early hours of the day while you're taking a cold-water mountain shower. A women's cooperative runs the show at FM 101.7.

The two screens at **Metrocinema Matagalpa** (tel. 505/772-2752) feature mostly Hollywood films just a few months after they're shown in the United States. It's clean, modern, and cheap; tickets $2.

Grupo Venancia

A wonderful, low-key cultural space awaits at Grupo Venancia (tel. 505/772-3562, venancia@ibw.com.ni, Thu.–Sat.), where you'll find a convivial open-air bar surrounding a stage and sometimes dance floor. They host music, dance, theater, artsy international film, and both local and global activism. The place is renowned for its free shows every Saturday night. Depending on the event, the crowd at Venancia flows easily between Matagalpa's young Bohemian set and the city's upper crust, and the vibe is always tolerant and respectful, especially for women. Grupo Venancia is, in fact, a non-profit women's group that can probably accurately be called ground zero of Nicaragua's feminist movement. It was founded in 1990 and is constantly conducting both urban and rural workshops on women's rights and domestic violence. Ask about their published materials, ways to volunteer, and try to catch their Saturday morning radio show, "La Hora Lila," on Radio Yes (90.1) at 8:30 A.M.

Nightlife

There's no doubt that the Matagalpinos like to shake their cowboy boots as much as other Nicaraguans, although they prefer ranchera, merengue, and reggetón music over salsa. Matagalpa's various *discotecas* may be open Thursday through Sunday, in general, but the only consistently happening night—with guaranteed crowded and electric dance floors—is Saturday. On the highway toward Managua, look for **Las Tequilas,** just past the Hora del Taco restaurant on the left if heading out of town ($2 or less taxi ride from downtown). **El Rancho Escondido** (open Thurs.–Sun. nights, *corriente* meals for less than $2) and the newer **Hot Dance** are usually popular among a younger crowd. More mature revelers and couples enjoy the hassle-free dance floor at **Rincón Paraíso.**

Although open all week for mediocre lunch and dinner, **La Casona** rules Matagalpa's Friday-night party, with live music in a crowded, open-air back patio. **Carlos 'n Charlie's** (open Thurs.–Sat.) is also popular, offering a standard

Latin DJ mix and generally well-to-do and internationally flavored crowd.

For a relatively safe and friendly, but still testosterone-filled cantina atmosphere, order a few liters of brew at **El Rincón Nica,** sometimes with live music on Fridays, located near Rancho Escondido.

SHOPPING

Both Matagalpa and Jinotega are famous for a particular brand of black pottery produced by the very small-scale artisan community. Black pottery—made black by a particular firing technique—is unique in Nicaragua, whose pottery is typically a natural reddish-orange color. Find it for sale throughout the city. Try the aptly named **Cerámica Negra** (near the Parque Darío), **Artesanía La Perla** (next to the mayor's office), **La Casa de la Cerámica Negra,** or the other Cerámica Negra located two blocks due east of Parque Moraza's north side. Even La Vita e Bella offers an excellent variety of ceramics and jewelry.

You'll find a great selection of local crafts at **Centro Girasol** (a bright yellow corner building right across the first bridge as you enter Matagalpa from Managua, tel. 505/772-6030). They've also got local jams, honey, coffee, and yogurt.

SPORTS AND RECREATION

Unless it is baseball season, the principal recreation activity is hiking through the hills that cradle Matagalpa.

Guides, Tours, and Hiking Information

Start by picking up a map at the **Centro Girasol** (a bright yellow corner building right across the first bridge as you enter Matagalpa from Managua or two blocks south and one west from the COTRAN Sur, tel. 505/772-6030). The "Treasures of Matagalpa" map of the area costs less than $2, benefits local disabled children, and outlines a number of walks, offering guide service as well. If you hear the mountains calling your name but aren't sure where to start, lace up your hiking boots and

call Dutch immigrant Arien Roersma (on the north side of La Casa Materna, in the Barrio 5 de Julio, tel. 505/772-4581, info@matagalpatours.com, www.matagalpatours.com); Arien has intimately explored, hiked, and camped throughout the Matagalpan countryside and has even drawn a number of trail maps.

Check with **CANIMET** (across from the post office, tel. 505/772-6000), a group of small, local business owners that has established an information and tour-operator desk for tourists; ask about local walking tours or hacienda and homestay opportunities.

Hiking Cerro Apante (1,442 meters)

Green, forested Cerro Apante—immediately recognizable by the cluster of antennas on its peak—towers above Matagalpa. Officially, it is a natural reserve whose steep flanks are covered by thick vegetation and a handful of small farms. Apante is a well-preserved piece of tropical humid forest that still contains decent stands of oak and pine, as well as several hundred types of wildflowers, and serves to protect an important source of water for the city (apante is Nahuatl for running water). It is crisscrossed with many small trails that lead to its streams and lagoons, all of which are easily accessed by walking from anywhere in the city.

The two routes to the top both begin by standing at the northwest corner of Parque Darío (in front of Hotel Alvarado). Walking south on the *calle principal* (main street) will take you up to the Apante neighborhood on the edge of town (also serviced by the Chispa–Apante Rapibuses). Continue up the road, keeping the summit to your left and continually asking if you're on the right track to *el cerro*. From the same corner in town, travel due east up a road that climbs steeply, eventually deteriorating into a rutted road. The road switches back a few times, ending at a hacienda atop a saddle in the Apante ridgeline. From there, find a footpath to the top. The actual summit is off limits, and is guarded by a caretaker and his dog, but the nearby ridge enjoys a breathtaking view of its own. You can link the two hikes into a three-hour loop; bring lots of water for the trail.

Matagalpa

ACCOMMODATIONS

Under $10

Matagalpa's numerous spartan, dirt-cheap options at the north end of town are all grungy and cost less than $2 a night, serving mainly *campesinos* and cowboys traveling in from Muy Muy and Mulukuku. You're better off choosing from the many options along the *calle principal* and in particular the establishments around the Parque Darío, the most desirable of which are listed below.

Hotel Plaza (on the south side of Parque Darío, tel. 505/772-2380, 18 rooms range from $2.50 cubby holes with shared bath to $10 doubles with private bath, TV, and fan) has been a stalwart in the Matagalpa lodging scene for decades. On the west side of Parque Darío, **Hotel Apante** (tel. 505/772-6890, $7.50 s with shared bath, fan, and TV) has bright, clean rooms.

One of the best, safest budget options is **Ⲙ Hotel Alvarado** (across from the Parque Darío's northwest corner, tel. 505/772-2830 or 505/772-2252, about $6 pp), run by a friendly Christian doctor couple who run a pharmacy downstairs. Ask for one of the top-floor rooms, which boast private bathrooms, a breeze, and views of the city and mountains from the small balconies. If their eight rooms are full, ask about their other location across town. North along the *calle principal,* you'll find **Hotel Central** (across from the Supermarket Matagalpa, tel. 505/772-3140, $6 d with shared bath, $10 with private bath and fan). The rooms are secure and clean, but a bit musty in the rainy season.

$10–25

Ⲙ Hotel Fountain Blue, a.k.a. *Fuente Azul* (third entrance to Matagalpa just west of the bridge, or from Salomón López 1.5 blocks west, tel. 505 /772-2733, 12 rooms at $19 s with private bath, hot water, TV, fan, $10 s for smaller, box-like rooms with shared bath) is quiet and comfortable, with a pay phone, Internet, free coffee, continental breakfast, and guarded parking.

Hotel Ideal (two blocks north and one west of the cathedral, tel. 505/772-2483, 19 rooms, $8 for small basic rooms with shared bath, or $23 for

fancier rooms with a/c, private bath with hot water) has secure parking available.

$25–50

Hotel Lomas de San Thomas (350 meters east of Escuela Guanuca, tel. 505/772-4189, fax 505 /772-3539, 25 rooms with private bath, hot water, cable TV and telephone, $30 s/$35 d plus tax, on-site bar and restaurant) is a mustard-colored, three-story establishment set on a breezy hill just east of town. Reopened after two years, it is once again the fanciest establishment in the city of Matagalpa. You might enjoy it just for the sense of peace and the breathtaking view of the city, especially at night under a full moon. It gears itself for business conventions and the NGO crew, offering secretarial services, huge conference rooms, fax, Internet, and a tennis court. To get there, leave the highway at the third entrance to Matagalpa and pass straight through town following the signs (about 800 meters from the highway). At the eastern edge of town, turn left and climb the hill on a cobblestone road to the hotel. For similar lodging, see the Hotel de Montaña Selva Negra in the North of Matagalpa section.

FOOD

As always, there's food in both parks, and as always, it's *vigorón* or *chancho con yucca* (both dishes served on banana leaves). If that's not what you had in mind, don't fret; Matagalpa has a wealth of excellent, low-priced eateries and a couple of nicer options as well.

Bakeries

Sniff around just east of Bancentro, and you will surely catch a whiff of warm, fresh breads and pastries wafting out from the **Panadería Belén** (open 8 A.M.–6 P.M. Mon.–Sat.). On the corner of Parque Darío, **Mus Manni** also has great bread and pastries, open seven days 6 A.M.–8 P.M.

Comida Típica

One of the friendliest and most famous *comedores* is **Ⲙ Don Chaco's** (1.5 blocks east of the Alcaldía, open 7:30 A.M.–9 P.M. Sun.–Thu., 7:30 A.M.– 5 P.M. Fri.), where in addition to heaping plates of *comida típica* (with great veggie options), you'll find a delicious *batido* (smoothie) menu of fruits, vegetables, and even soy milk. If you prefer buffet, lunch-line style, with a smorgasbord of Nica food lined up in front of you, the ragingly popular **Mana del Cielo** (located between the banks and cinema) will satisfy;; it's owned by a retired baseball player who played in Nica's pro leagues for a number of years.

To taste the sweet goodness of Matagalpa's best *güiríla* (a sweet-corn pancake wrapped around a hunk of salty *cuajada* cheese, about $.35), you'll have to brave the chaos of the crowds that cluster around the smoky stands across the street from Palí. For *pupusas* and fruit drinks, seek out the cute **Antojitos Salvadoreños** (1.5 blocks south of El Rancho Escondido, open 11 A.M.–9:30 P.M. Tues.–Sun.), where three deliciously greasy, stuffed pancakes cost $1.50. For ridiculously delicious roasted chicken, look for the flames in the window of **Pollos el Fogón** (on the corner across from the Catedral's northwest corner, delivery: tel. 505/772-6004, open 10 A.M.–10 P.M. daily, $3 a plate).

Travelers love the locally famous Don Tano's **Picoteo Café** (located just east of the post office, open 7:30 A.M.–10 P.M. daily), serving chicken, burgers, pizza, and lots of beer. The walls are covered with platitudes painted on wooden plaques; most dishes run around $2.

Pique's (not far from the Parque Morazán) is a stylish Mexican joint, with dishes in the $2.75–4 range. Their *chalupas* and *mole* are especially good, and the atmosphere is relaxing.

La Casona (on the main drag, across from the mayor's office) offers a lunch buffet and a variety of bar-type foods for $3–4 (open 9 A.M.–11 P.M., later on weekends when it turns into a popular bar). Look for the big 7-Up sign outside. **Cafetería Zinica:** in the words of the proprietress herself, "We don't have a menu. We just serve hamburgers—the best damn hamburgers in the country." Actually, they do have a menu and serve several other things, including fresh fruit juices. Super-clean, the place is named after the Matagalpa town where Carlos Fonseca, founder of the FSLN, was killed by Somoza's National Guard.

On the sidewalk just off the northwest cor-ner of Parque Darío, enjoy the country music, chaps-wearin' waitresses, and Tex-Mex menu of **Tombstone Restaurante y Bar,** open daily 10 A.M.–1 A.M.; meals run around $4 and include lots of bar food like wings, onion rings, and cheese fries.

Finer Dining

One of the cornerstones of Matagalpa's dining scene, **M La Vita e Bella** (tel. 505/772-5476, vitabell@ibw.com.ni, 12:30 P.M.–10:30 P.M. Tues.–Sun.) is tucked into an alley in the Colonia Lainez, serving Italian and vegetarian dishes, and desserts that will make you glad you found the place. This is possibly the best restaurant in the city for non-chicken and non-beef dishes; entrées under $4, large pizza $6, excellent wine selection.

There are two notable restaurants on the highway to Managua, both on the right-hand side, a few kilometers south of the first entrance to Matagalpa. **La Hora del Taco** (open 11 A.M.–11 P.M. daily) offers the same finger-licking Mexican menu as its Managua counterpart, with an added outdoor balcony looking out into the Valle Las Tejas; margaritas are less than $2, and the $4 fajita plate is to-die-for.

Around the next bend in the highway, **M El Pullazo** just might serve you the best piece of beef tenderloin you'll taste in Nicaragua, but they won't tell you what their secret recipe is. They have a few other beef dishes too, but no one orders them. Your *"pullazo"* of meat (a vulgar play on the word for "injection") is accompanied by a sweet *güiríla* pancake and hunk of *cuajada* cheese. Wash it down with a beer and you're only $4 in the hole; open for lunch and dinner.

There's also the **Sacuanjoche Restaurant and Bar** at the Hotel Lomas de San Thomas, offering standard fare like steaks, fajitas, shrimp dishes and salads (entrées $4–9), a ceramic shop, and taxi service ($1 to or from the town center).

SERVICES

Emergencies

Note these numbers: Fire tel. 505/772-3167, Police tel. 505/772-3870, Hospital tel. 505/772-2081. The hospital is located at the north end of town on the highway to San Ramón. But you'll get better medical treatment at the Clínica Maya Flores.

Banks

There are a half-dozen banks in Matagalpa—BAC, Banpro, Banexpo, Banco Caley Dagnall, Bancentro, and Banco Mercantíl—and a fistful of money changers that hang out around the southeast corner of Parque Morazán. The banks are mostly clustered in a three-block strip, but the BAC—with the downtown area's only ATM—is on its own, half a block east of the southeast corner of Parque Morazán.

Internet

CyberCafe Downtown (a half block west of the southwest corner of the Parque Darío, open 8:30 A.M.–8 P.M. Mon.–Sat., 10 A.M.–7 P.M. Sun.) is popular and fast. Walking north on the *calle principal,* about halfway to Parque Morazán, you'll find **NetCom** just past La Casona; decent service, open 8 A.M.–9 P.M., closing a bit earlier on Saturday and Sunday (8 P.M. and 7 P.M. respectively). One of the fastest servers in town is at **Cybercafe Matagalpa** (half a block north, one block west from the Palí supermarket, across the street from the Mi Favorita store; open 9 A.M.–9 P.M. daily, closing 7 P.M. on Sundays, about $2 an hour), with cheap membership deals available.

Post Office and Telephones

Correos de Nicaragua Matagalpa (tel. 505/772-4317) is located one block west of Parque Morazán, tucked into a side street that runs south from the main drag, open 8 A.M.–12:30 P.M. and 2 P.M.–5:30 P.M. Mon.–Fri., 8 A.M.–1 P.M.Sat. Fax, phone, and mailbox services are available.

There are a number of card-based public phones and BellSouth posts all over town, especially along the main *calle principal,* and the main ENITEL building is located to the east of Parque Morazán (look for the big antenna jutting out from the city skyline); open 7 A.M.–9 P.M. Cheap, web-based international call service is available at all three Internet places above.

Groceries

If you plan to do some adventuring out east, it's worth your while to stock up at one of Matagalpa's two grocery stores. A block north of the cathedral is an enormous **Palí** (open 8 A.M.–8 P.M. all week, Sundays closed at 6 P.M.), or try the **Supermercado La Matagalpa** (2.5 blocks north of Parque Darío, open 8 A.M.–9 P.M. Mon.–Sat., 8 A.M.–8 P.M. Sun.). For a more colorful experience, check out either of the municipal markets, across from both bus terminals.

Laundry

A block and a half east of the Cancha Brigadista is a washer and dryer for rent, open 8:30 A.M.–5 P.M. Mon.–Sat. $4 a load, including wash, dry, and fold.

Haircuts

The male hairdressers at Max Salon (across from the cinema) are proud, flamboyant, and terribly excited to give you a makeover; let them pamper you with a new 'do, pedicure, and manicure, as they chat away and laugh; expect U.S./European quality ($8 for a cut and dry, more for coloring and highlights). For a simpler, more old-fashioned cut, try the barber shop across from the police station, where a cut and straight-edge shave costs under $4.

Car Rental

Budget (tel. 505/772-3041 or 505/266-6226, reserve@budget.com.ni) has a small lot at the La Virgen Shell Station, just as you enter town from the south. Prices are standard, around $60/24 hours for the cheapest vehicles.

GETTING THERE AND AWAY

Direct Buses to Matagalpa

Express buses from Managua leave the Mayoreo bus terminal every hour from 5:30 A.M. to 5:30 P.M. The ride takes two hours and costs about $2.50. If heading north from Granada or Masaya, you can bypass Managua by grabbing one of two direct buses from the Masaya bus terminal, leaving at 5 A.M. and 6 A.M. and taking less than three hours (these are full-size buses and run every day except Thursday and Sunday). From León, there are two daily expresses, leaving at 4:30 A.M. and 2:45 P.M.; this ride takes less

LA RUTA DE CAFE

Today, coffee merchants and tourists alike can travel a circuit of small coffee cooperatives scattered throughout the mountains of Jinotega, Matagalpa, and the Segovias. As a participant in this "Ruta de Cafe," not only will you sample coffee in special cupping labs, you'll also visit coffee-growing families and their farms, which are often magical cloud forests shrouded in cool mists; you can stay for a couple of hours or a couple of days, living with the families, eating meals with them,

FAIR TRADE

CERTIFIED

You'll find more than coffee when you visit small farms as a *café-turista*. Back home, look for this label to ensure the grower was paid a just price.

picking coffee, and learning about all stages of the process. As a *café-turista*, you'll experience the communities of real people who have been behind every sip of coffee you've ever taken. What's more, you will learn why the quality of a coffee is inextricably tied to the quality of life of those that produce it, as well as the quality of the environment in which they live. Finally, you will learn what Organic, Bird Friendly, and Fair Trade–certified coffees are (visit www.transfairusa.org and www.globalexchange.org for details).

To experience the most activity, be sure to arrange your visit during the peak of the harvest, usually from mid-December through February. Make your arrangements in advance. Start your tour at **CECOCAFEN** (Center of Northern Coffee Cooperatives, tel. 505/772-6353, turismo @cecocafen .com), whose main office in Matagalpa city is located two blocks east of Banco Uno. They can arrange anything from an afternoon coffee cupping at their Sol Café *beneficio* (coffee processing mill) to a day trip, visiting some of their farmers, to a multi-night excursion, staying in *campesino* homes and touring their farms (or even putting some work in during the harvest). Trips include transportation and food, and hikes (with pickups) can be arranged between towns. Prices fully depend on the trip. Or consider a stay at **Finca Esperanza Verde** (www.fincaesperanzaverde .org), anacclaimed accommodation and working organic coffee farm, located outside San Ramón (see the Near Matagalpa section).

In Jinotega, **SOPPEXCA** (Society of Small Coffee Producers, Exporters, and Buyers, tel./fax 505/782-2617, soppexcc @tmx.com.ni) is eager to serve as your tour guide of the region, arranging any number of hikes, trips, and homestays among its growers in the surrounding hills. Their office and cupping lab is located in Jinotega, one block west of the Ferretería Blandón.

There are also several welcoming coffee cooperatives in the hills north of Estelí with similar tours available, notably **PRODECOOP** in Palacagüina and **Venecia** near Condega (see those city sections for more information).

Once your tour is complete, purchasing fair-trade coffee back home is a good way to continue making a difference in the lives of the farmers you've met.

Matagalpa

than three hours and costs about $2.50 pp. Matagalpa-bound buses leave every half hour, starting about 5 A.M. from both Estelí (last bus leaves 5:45 P.M.) and Jinotega (last bus leaves 7 P.M.). There is one direct bus from Chinandega to Matagalpa, leaving at 5 A.M.

Leaving Matagalpa

Matagalpa has two bus terminals—which one you head to depends on your destination. At the south end of town, the **COTRAN Sur** (tel. 505/772-4659 or 505/603-0909) services Managua, Estelí, León, Masaya, and Jinotega. There's a public bathroom there ($.10) and several small eateries.

Express buses to Managua depart every hour from 5:20 A.M.–5:20 P.M. Non-express Managua-bound buses leave every half-hour from 3:35 A.M. –5:50 P.M. Direct buses to Masaya leave twice a day at 2 P.M. and 3:30 P.M. (daily except Thursday and Sunday).

To León via San Isidro and Telíca, there are two daily expresses, leaving at 6 A.M. and 3 P.M. There are also *interlocales* minivans that leave whenever they fill up; or take any bus bound for Estelí, get off at the Empalme León, and catch a bus to León (departing just about every 20–30 minutes).

There is a constant flow of buses to Estelí and Jinotega, leaving every half hour from 5 A.M. till 5:45 P.M. (Estelí) and till 7 P.M. (Jinotega). One daily direct bus to Chinandega leaves Matagalpa at 2 P.M.

At the north end of town, the **COTRAN de Guanuca** services the interior of Matagalpa, including El Tuma–La Dália, San Ramón, Río Blanco, Muy Muy, and Bocana de Paíwas. Road conditions in these areas are bad in the dry season, horrible in the rainy season when bus service sometimes slackens. Buses to points east depart approximately every 45 minutes to an hour until around 4:30 P.M.

GETTING AROUND

Matagalpa is a perfectly good city for walking, except for all those hills, where you'll sweat out all that *fritanga* grease; the taxi fare within town is $.35. City buses ply three different routes back and forth across town, and cost about $.10. Particularly useful is the *Chispa*.

Near Matagalpa

The sparsely populated and mostly undeveloped hillsides that stretch from Matagalpa to the Honduran border encompass the gold-mining triangle set between Rosita, Siuna, and Bonanza, and vary from dense tropical jungle to pine forest to shallow, bushy hillsides. Segmented by dozens of rivers—some of which are impassible in the wet season—and bereft of roads throughout much of the area, the lands east of Matagalpa made good training grounds for the guerrillas that followed Fonseca into battle against Somoza's troops in the 1970s. Thirty years later, the *campesino* population has grown but the wild and rugged landscape is as impenetrable as ever.

EAST OF MATAGALPA

Heading into the geographic heart of the nation, the traveler encounters broad hillsides of shiny coffee bushes beneath shady canopies, plots of corn and beans, and small communities of tile-roofed adobe houses sitting among the rugged mountains that are the eastern reaches of the Cordillera Dariense. The *campesinos* in the folds of these mountains live much the way they have for centuries, even as governments, revolutions, and natural disasters have swirled violently around them.

The major communities of the east, Río Blanco, Matiguás, and Muy Muy, serve as commercial and transportation centers for the region, and they offer rudimentary accommodations for the traveler. But don't expect any luxury rides here: The roads east of Matagalpa are some of the most neglected in the country, notably the stretch between Siuna and Mulukuku, which is practically impassable during the wettest months of the year. That said, you will be traveling through some of the most beautiful—and least visited—parts of an already under-touristed

© JOSHUA BERMAN

Lazy are the days in the *campo*, especially in the rainy season.

Ruins of the Leonesa gold mine are off the beaten track outside San Ramón.

nation. Except for some fledgling ventures in San Ramón, traditional tourist facilities are non-existent in the entire region. That shouldn't stop the more adventurous traveler from seeking out some of the following destinations.

THE SAN RAMÓN–MULUKUKU ROAD

San Ramón

Only 12 kilometers from Matagalpa, the village of San Ramón is nestled in a lovely valley at the base of several steep hills. Founded in the late 1800s, San Ramón got its start around the La Leonesa and La Reina gold mines, and today is a peaceful, friendly hamlet, about five blocks square and surrounded on all sides by green farms and forests penetrated by a number of roads and trails. San Ramón has two parks, a health clinic, a gas station, and a number of non-profit and coffee-related administrative offices. Because of sister-city rela-

tionships with Catalan (Spain), Henniker (New Hampshire), and Durham (North Carolina), small groups of wandering foreigners are not uncommon and San Ramón adeptly hosts both foreign groups and individuals in one of several guesthouse and homestay programs.

Use San Ramón as a more rural alternative to Matagalpa (travel to and from the city is a cinch), or sample one of the short local excursions, such as the walk to the La Pita coffee cooperative. On the way, you'll pass the 100-year-old ruins of the Leonesa mine, overtaken by moss, ferns, and giant ceiba trees.

San Ramón boasts a relatively upscale bed-and-breakfast, the **Albergue Campestre** (tel. 505/772-5003, herma@ibw.com.ni, $17/27 s/d, reservations required) where you can enjoy modern, screened rooms with private baths, and a beautiful garden. Find the Albergue (which is also the office of Finca Esperanza Verde) by walking east from the Shell station, past the police station, and through a small gate at the dead end. This is also the place to inquire about the **Club de Guías** (trained young guides, $10/day, some with English) and the **Casa de Huespedes** (Guest House) system (U.S. tel. 919/489-1656, www.durham-sanramon.org), which offers a secure room, private bath, and three meals for $15 a day.

There are no restaurants in San Ramón, but you won't starve here: Several tasty *comedores* monopolize the sidewalk across the highway from the Shell Station. **Doña Nelys Arauz** and friends serve heaping plates of originally styled Nica food for under $2.

Buses to and from San Ramón are frequent, leaving the Guanuca Terminal every hour 6 A.M.–7 P.M., in addition to the many other eastbound buses that pass through San Ramón on their way elsewhere. A cab from Matagalpa costs about $3 pp, if you're interested in day (or night) tripping into the city of Matagalpa.

Finca Esperanza Verde

Although its office and many of the community programs it supports are in the village of San Ramón, Finca Esperanza Verde (FEV, tel. 505/772-5003, herma@ibw.com.ni, www.fincaesperanza verde.org, reservations required) is very much its own destination, a cool, green getaway 18 km east of San Ramón and 1,180 meters above sea level. Travelers will find a range of peaceful accommodations, as well as beautiful sunsets, delicious food, and a wonderful menu of educational and recreational activities. FEV is a fine example of eco-tourism, conceived of by an ex-Peace Corps couple from North Carolina and closely associated with the Durham, NC–San Ramón Sister City Project; in 2004 it won first place in a *Smithsonian Magazine* Sustainable Tourism contest.

The open air lodge and cabanas, with wide, west-facing vistas, are surrounded by shade-grown, organic coffee plantations, as well as preserved second-generation cloud forest, through which winds an impressive and varied trail system; hike it on your own or, to see more of the 150 species of birds, howler monkeys, numerous orchids, and medicinal plants, hire one of the finca's guides ($4 per hour, per group, well worth it if you speak Spanish). FEV also features several waterfalls, a

butterfly house and breeding project (tours $5 pp), and a delicious spring-fed, potable water supply. From November through February, pick, process, and sort the coffee beans, then follow the coffee to Matagalpa where it is sun dried, sorted, graded, cupped, and exported. The farm's all-Nicaraguan staff enjoy teaching visitors about coffee and are proud that their care of the farm makes it a home to hundreds of species of birds, butterflies, mammals, trees and orchids.

The lodge and cabins, built of hand made brick and other local materials, can accommodate up to 22 people and are equipped with solar electricity, flush toilets, sinks and warm sun showers. Bunks cost $12 pp, and a private cabin for two with a view, $45, all with shared toilet (the bigger your group, the better the deal). Meals ($5–6) include fresh juices, fruits, vegetables and eggs from neighboring farms, and of course, homegrown organic coffee. A gorgeous camping area that features tentsites and a roofed picnic table in the middle of a coffee and banana grove ($6 pp, bring your own gear).

If you have a vehicle with moderate clearance (and 4WD in the rainy season), FEV is a 40-minute drive from San Ramón. Follow the road to Yucúl, then turn left and follow the signs to the finca. By bus, take the Pancasan/ El Jobo bus from the COTRAN Guanuca Terminal in Matagalpa, and get off in Yucúl; then follow the signs to FEV, a beautiful 3.5 km uphill walk that should take under an hour. Don't forget a long sleeve shirt and a rain jacket.

Río Blanco and Cerro Musún

Cerro Musún, one of Nicaragua's youngest and least-visited parks, encompasses the 1,460 meter peak of the same name and is still the haunt of some of Central America's more elusive mammals, like the puma. In 2004, however, Musín (Water Mountain in Nahuatl) lived up to its name when heavy rains caused several of its lower slopes to collapse, destroying several hillside communities in a massive mudslide.

The town of Río Blanco is your jumping-off point for hikes in this tremendous reserve area. Rest up at **Hotel Bosawas** or **Hotel Nicarao** (both $15 s, a/c, TV) before tackling hikes up to the seven waterfalls or the peak itself. Your hikes start at the FUNDENIC guide station (about 1 km out of town), where you can hire a guide to lead you through the reserve (about $6/day).

While you're in town, check out the statues in the Catholic church, artifacts from the pre-Columbian civilizations that occupied these lands. They left behind some petroglyphs at the river's edge (visible only during the dry season). Start searching near the red hanging bridge on the exit to Barrio Martin Centeno.

Two express buses leave for Río Blanco from Managua's Mayoreo terminal around noon; additional service is available from the COTRAN Guanuca in Matagalpa.

Bocana de Paíwas

Bocana de Paíwas has an *hospedaje* and several restaurants, including the well-liked **Restaurante Mirador,** located on a long peninsula overlooking the Río Grande de Matagalpa. This is also the site of some pre-Columbian petroglyphs, tucked into the rocks alongside the Río Grande de Matagalpa.

Mulukuku

Founded primarily to support a Sandinista military base in the 1980s, Mulukuku quickly became a refugee center for those fleeing battles farther north; today's descendants of that time live in a humble but vivacious village on the edge of the mighty Río Tuma.

Mulukuku is well known for one of its expat residents, Doña Dorotea, a 70-year-old nurse who's lived and worked in the community for two decades. Because of her work with Sandinista charities, she became a target for former president Alemán's political mischief and blind personal vengeance—he even ordered her deported after falsely accusing her of performing abortions. Over a period of several weeks in 2001, Dorotea's fellow townspeople rallied behind her as Alemán continued threatening to throw her out of Nicaragua and she pleaded that she had nowhere else to go. Though she was never deported, she spent several frustrating years hassling with her residency permit and is finally back in Mulukuku and continuing her work; Alemán was never asked to explain.

THE EL TUMA–LA DÁLIA ROAD

This paved, patched-together road, usually in a sore state of disrepair, heads due east from the north end of Matagalpa, then curves north, crosses the Río Tuma, and continues to the town of La Dália. From there, it stumbles along as the northern route to Wani and Siuna, first passing through Waslala, which used to be the most populated pueblo east of Matagalpa.

A few kilometers east of the turnoff to San Ramón, look on the left for the **Madre Tierra Panadería** (Mother Earth Bakery; Km 37.5 Carreterra La Dalia, next to CESESMA and La Praga coffee farm, open 8 A.M.–5 P.M. Mon.–Fri.). In the shaded bamboo hut, you'll find mouth-watering home-baked wheat bread, plus yogurt, coffee, and an array of local medicinal herbs and remedies. Under construction at press time, an adjoining bamboo structure plans to house **Tonantzin,** a natural healing, massage, acupuncture, and reflexology center. The Center for Health and Environmental Educational Services, CESESMA (tel. 505/772-5842, cesesma@ibw.com.ni), is a non-profit that provides educational opportunities (theater, dance, crafts, gardening, etc.) for youths in the rural coffee sectors. They accept qualified, long-term (a year or more) volunteers.

Santa Emilia and Salto El Cebollál

The farming community of Santa Emilia is marked by a left turn at about Km 145; a bit further, you'll find a 15-meter waterfall spilling impressively into a wide hole flanked by thick vegetation and a dark, alluring rock overhang. The falls are known alternately as Salto de Santa Emilia and Salto el Cebollál. Before jumping in, consider that the stream flows through at least one upstream community and may be contaminated. Still, the spray from the falls is refreshing and the site is gorgeous in a romantic, popping-the-question kind of way (if she can hear you over the water's roar, that is). Access is just beyond the Puente Yasica, a bridge at about Km 149; look for a small house and parking area on the right, where a soft-drink sign reads Balneario El Salto de Santa Emilia. You'll be asked to pay a $1 parking fee unless you're just jumping off the

This tank marks the entrance to Selva Negra.

Matagalpa

Tuma–Dália bus. From there, walk down the steep trail, following the sound of the falls—and don't forget the ring.

Piedra Luna

About 10 kilometers (15 minutes) southwest of the mountain town of La Dália is a top-notch swimming hole called Piedra Luna by the locals. This makes a great day trip from Matagalpa and will give you a chance to appreciate some of the remaining monster trees in the area. Ask your bus driver to let you off at Piedra Luna and descend the steep hillside down to the river's edge. The swimming hole was formed by the waters of the Río Tuma as they swirled around a several-ton rock sitting midstream. The swimming hole is easily seven meters deep, and local kids come from all over to dive off the rock into the pool. How did the rock get there? Ask the locals, who will relate the fantastic legend of the spirits that carried it there from someplace far away. To get there, take any bus from the north terminal at Matagalpa bound for Waslala or El Tuma–La Dália and ask to be let off at Piedra Luna (approximately a one-hour trip from Matagalpa and a 30-minute walk down to the river).

Peñas Blancas (1,445 Meters)

Located on the road that leads between El Tuma–La Dália and El Cuá, the cliffs of Peñas Blancas are several hundred meters high and carved out of the top of a massive hillside. This is unquestionably one of the most stunning natural sights in northern Nicaragua. At the top of the cliff is a copious waterfall, gorgeous and little known, even by Nicaraguans who live outside of the immediate area. The cliffs and waterfall are easily visible from the highway, next to property owned by Alan Ball. He's currently developing hikes and tours to the waterfall, but you can be proactive and get there yourself by asking around.

Getting there requires some effort, more so if you're using public transportation. By bus, leave Matagalpa bound for Waslala, and pass through El Tuma–La Dália on the road to Waslala. Ask to be let off at the *empalme* of the road to El Cuá–Bocay. Ask for "Isla de Peñas Blancas." From the intersection, walk 15 minutes north to where you will find a sign that says Centro de Entendimiento con la Naturaleza. From there, ask for the best route to the falls. The hike is only possible in the dry season, and there is no well-established trail to the falls. The walk is worth it, as you'll pass through a series of humid forest ecosystems of orchids and mossy trees. Near the falls, the wind is full of spray. The hike up and down can be done in two hours but expect to get extremely muddy and wet.

NORTH OF MATAGALPA

🅼 Hotel de Montaña Selva Negra

This cloud forest retreat has been an anchor in Nicaragua's tourism network for a long time and remains popular for people looking to hike, dine, monkey-watch, or even tie the knot. Hotel de Montaña Selva Negra (Km 140 on the highway between Matagalpa and Jinotega, tel. 505/772-3883, resort@selvanegra.com, www.selvanegra .com) is, at its heart, a coffee farm by the name of La Hammonia, owned and run by Eddy Kühl and Mausi Hayn, third- and fourth-generation German immigrants and members of the founding families of the country's coffee industry. The farm—considered one of the most diversified in Central America—has been built up into an enchanting resort in the German tradition of wooden chalets set around a peaceful (artificial) pond with access to short hiking trails up the adjoining 120 hectare hillside and along its ridge. The main restaurant serves hearty, home-cooked meals using ingredients produced entirely on the farm, on a gorgeous outdoor patio overlooking the water. The environs are wonderfully peaceful. Needless to say, the coffee—internationally renowned—is superb and fresh.

Try to spot some of the 200 species of birds that have been identified here or go tour the coffee farm, flower plantations, and the cattle and livestock. You can easily rent a horse for the day. In 2000, the Kühls built a gorgeous, orchid-adorned stone chapel for the wedding of their daughter, and they now rent out the facilities—chapel, horse-drawn carriage, and fresh-cut flowers—for guests who come to get hitched.

Expect to have a chat with the owners while you're there—Eddy is a wealth of knowledge, a prolific writer, and a well-loved amateur anthropologist; many of the family's ideas have come from the suggestions and talent of the guests who visit them. Prices run from $10 for a spot in

the youth hostel to $30 for a double overlooking the lake to $50 for a private bungalow. To get to Selva Negra, take any bus from Matagalpa heading to Jinotega. They'll let you off at the entrance to the hotel, where an old ruined military tank marks the entrance to the farm.

THE MATAGALPA–JINOTEGA HIGHWAY

The sinuous mountain road between Matagalpa and Jinotega is considered one of the most scenic roads in all of Nicaragua. The road was first opened around 1920 by the English immigrant and coffee farmer Charles Potter for use by mules and wagons taking coffee from his farm to Matagalpa. No small feat of engineering, the road had to negotiate over 100 curves, the worst of which was the Disparate de Potter (still legendary; see below). A stubborn old man, Potter built his road in spite of the naysayers, and it's said he used the road to carry a piano—strung atop two mules—all the way to his farm.

The long valley panoramas are often breathtaking: Momotombo and the Maribio Volcanoes are visible when the sky is clear. You'll pass neatly arranged coffee plantations shaded by windrows of cedar and pine, banana trees, and canopies of precious hardwoods. There is also an endless succession of vegetable and flower fields, and roadside stands that sell farm-fresh goods. Should you take the express bus, you'll miss the opportunity to stop and take photographs, buy fresh vegetables, and hike into the coffee plantations. But if you drive, you may need to concentrate on the road so much that you'll miss the scenery. The best alternative is to take it easy: Hop on and off passing buses and offered rides over the course of an afternoon, enjoying the following sights until you get to Jinotega.

Mirador de La Chispa (Km 133)

Just three kilometers outside of the city of Matagalpa, La Chispa is an impressive overlook on the right side of the highway, with a view of the city.

Hotel Selva Negra (Km 140)

The entrance to Selva Negra is marked by an

old tank on the side of the road, a relic from the revolution and painted over with the rainbows of Doña Violeta's UNO coalition in the early 1990s.

Disparate de Potter (Km 143)

This was the worst, rockiest curve of all the obstacles that Charles Potter faced when building the road between Matagalpa and his farm La Fundadora. There was no way around the rock that made up that part of the mountain, so he stubbornly blasted his way straight through it. The hill's two pieces remain exactly as he left them, with the single addition of a lookout platform on the needle of rock left standing on the outside of the curve. At the side of the road is a well-liked restaurant serving traditional Nicaraguan food, open seven days from 8:30 A.M.–8 P.M., meals in the $4–6 range, also snacks and beverages to accompany the amazing vista from the dining room. Climbing the stairs to the platform is well worth the small fee ($.30 pp). Ask about the

country house for rent at the Finca Peor es Nada, a fully furnished ranch with private bedrooms for up to three couples, $200 per weekend (tel. 505/772-2553, speak with Delia Pérez)

Santa Lastenia (Km 148)

At 1,555 meters above sea level, Santa Lastenia is the highest point along the road, after which one drops rather precipitously into the valley of Jinotega.

Vegetable Stands (Km 152)

Jinotega and Matagalpa are the two most copious producers of vegetables in Nicaragua, and a set of small farm stands along the road are evidence of the rich harvests of this area. Whether you want to eat them or just photograph them, the stacks of fresh cabbage, carrots, broccoli, radishes, beets, lettuce, squash, and greens are a culinary feast for the eyes. The stands are typically run by the family's older children, who might just sweet-talk you into making a purchase.

Matagalpa

© SUTAY BERMAN

Roadside vegetables are kept fresh by the mountain mist.

Jinotega City

When walking the cobbled streets of Jinotega, you can't help but feel you're at the edge of the world, with all kinds of unknowns in the hills to the north and east. Medieval mapmakers would have emblazoned the valley of Jinotega with "Beyond Here Lie Dragons," referring to the hundreds of kilometers of wild, lush mountain country that beckon to the east. East of the city the pavement stops, the roads turn rutted and bumpy, bus service is less frequent, and the accommodations dwindle—at least the kind where they leave a mint on your pillow and fold the edge of the toilet paper into a little triangle. But the immense department of Jinotega is home to hundreds of small communities and thousands of farmers who make their livelihood in the hills around them—including many who have barely ever traveled beyond this land in their lives. Jinotega is replete with fragrant valleys of orange groves, white corn, plantains, sweet vegetables, and a whole lot of cattle. But in-between the small farms, Jinotega is open space— virgin forest, small freshwater lagoons, stately mountain ranges, and some of the loveliest rivers in Nicaragua, including the mighty Río Coco (which forms the northern border of the Jinotega department) and the Río Bocay, one of the Coco's most important tributaries.

Jinotega, or *La Ciudad de las Brumas* (The City of Mists), is the watering hole and commercial center for the department of the same name. Farmers from the north and east inevitably find their way here to do their business and trading, and Jinotega City has built itself into a clean, prosperous community around the business needs of those farmers. It's a working town whose streets are lined with cobblers, tailors, barbers, blacksmiths, watch repairmen, and merchants that deal in housewares, veterinary supplies, saddles, cowboy hats, firearms, auto parts, and an endless stock of farming tools. It's a town very much in tune with the rugged and self-sufficient life of the Nicaraguan *campesino,* and you will learn much just by wandering its streets among such hardy characters. Jinotega, your gateway to the

wide-open expanses of the east, is at once charming and thrilling. As late as the mid-1960s, it wasn't uncommon to find wild monkeys in the old-growth park canopy of *lechito* trees.

Travelers enjoy Jinotega because its high elevation (a full kilometer above sea level) gives it a pleasant climate, especially nice in the picturesque setting. Jinoteganos themselves are at once friendly and aloof—they might leave you to your own, but if you make the effort to talk to them, you'll find them warm, open, and full of country hospitality.

HISTORY

The name Jinotega is said to come from the Nahuatl name Xilotl-Tecatl, (Place of the Jiñocuabo Trees; also translated as The Place of the Eternal Men and Women). Indeed, the natives who lived in this peaceful valley enjoyed healthy and prosperous existences and were known to live to more than 100 years of age. Today's department of Jinotega was in those days the border between two diverse indigenous peoples: to the north, in the Bocay region, lived the Chontales (Kiribie) people, and near the present-day city of Jinotega, the Chorotega. They were an agricultural people who lived off small plots of corn, beans, cacao, roots, tubers, and fruit orchards. They wove their own clothing from wood and cotton fiber, as well as animal skins tinted with plant extracts. In the late 18th century, the Spanish chose to inhabit the southern part of Jinotega, forcing the indigenous peoples to move north. The community of Jinotega was officially recategorized as The Valley of Jinotega in 1851, and as a city in 1883.

For better or for worse, nearly every major armed uprising in recent Nicaraguan history began in the Jinotega department. The young Sandinistas first took to the hills here to battle squadrons of the National Guard in the 1960s, and when the Sandinistas took power, the first groups of Contras took to the hills, again in Jinotega. At the end of the Contra war, the two

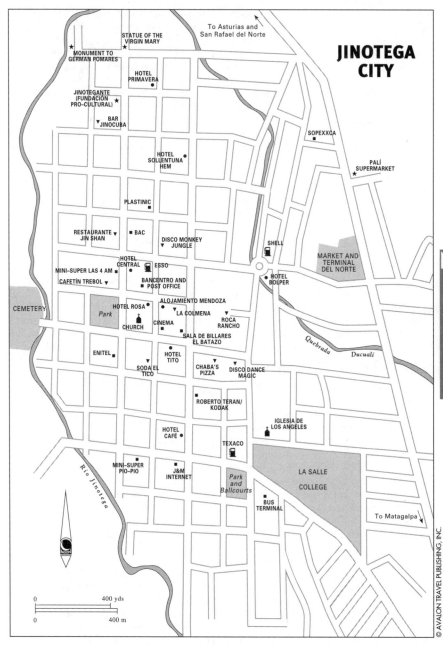

JINOTEGA
CITY

To Asturias and
San Rafael del Norte

★ MONUMENT TO
GERMAN POMARES

STATUE OF THE
VIRGIN MARY

HOTEL
PRIMAVERA

JINOTEGANTE
(FUNDACIÓN
PRO-CULTURAL) ★

BAR
JINOCUBA ▼

SOPEXXCA ■

PALÍ
SUPERMARKET

HOTEL
SOLLENTUNA
HEM ●

PLASTINIC ■

SHELL

MARKET AND
TERMINAL
DEL NORTE

RESTAURANTE ▼
JIN SHAN

■ BAC

DISCO MONKEY
JUNGLE ▼

HOTEL
CENTRAL ● ESSO

MINI–SUPER LAS 4 AM ■

CAFETÍN TREBOL ▼

HOTEL
BOLPER ■

BANCENTRO AND
POST OFFICE ■

CEMETERY

Park

HOTEL ROSA ● ◆
CHURCH

ALOJAMIENTO MENDOZA ●
▼ LA COLMENA

CINEMA ▼

ROCA ▼
RANCHO

SALA DE BILLARES
EL BATAZO ■

Quebrada

Ducualí

ENITEL ■

HOTEL
TITO ■

SODA EL ▼
TICO

CHABA'S ▼
PIZZA

DISCO DANCE ▼
MAGIC

ROBERTO TERAN/
KODAK ■

IGLESIA DE
LOS ANGELES ■

HOTEL
CAFÉ ●

TEXACO

Río Jinotega

MINI–SUPER
PIO–PIO ■

J&M ■
INTERNET

Park
and
Ballcourts

LA SALLE

COLLEGE

■ BUS
TERMINAL

To Matagalpa

0   400 yds

0   400 m

Matagalpa

groups that refused to lay down their weapons and accept the peace treaty (the Recompas and Recontras) fled back into the mountains of Jinotega to keep up their fight.

For most of the 1990s, remnants of fighting groups, like FUAC, plagued certain wilder areas of northeastern Jinotega, hassling the peace-loving Jinotegan farmers trying to raise crops and their families at the same time. Jinotega was possibly the worst affected department in Nicaragua during the 1980s, as Contras and Sandinistas fought each other on the mountain roads and the deep valleys. In those days, there was only one bus per day between the city of Jinotega and Managua (as compared to one every hour now), and travelers intent on driving their own vehicles ran the daily risk of being ambushed, robbed, raped, or killed. Since the 1980s, Jinotega has voted steadfastly against the Sandinistas, who they claim are responsible for 10 years of devastation. The survivors of the generation that was marched off to the mountains as machine-gun fodder are resentful and frustrated now, robbed of their adolescence, and desperately trying to make a decent, honest living off the land.

SIGHTS AND ATTRACTIONS

There are few traditional tourist sights in Jinotega, but lots to see and do. Jinotega was the scene of a few ferocious battles during the revolution years, and it was down by the riverside in Jinotega where much-loved Sandinista commander German Pomares (a.k.a. El Danto) was killed in battle. Pomares and his troops had fought many battles against Somoza's National Guard and had been instrumental in the operation that led to political prisoner Daniel Ortega's release from jail. His sacrifice has not been forgotten, and a very carefully maintained red-and-black memorial marks the spot where he was killed.

Don Pilo is a second-generation medicine man who lives in an unknown location in the mountains west of Jinotega city. Twice weekly, he climbs down out of the mountains with his bags of herbs and potions and sets up camp at the cemetery to sell them. He's a well-loved town character who some put off as a charlatan, and

others consider a true magician and physician. Regardless, both rich and poor wait for him Tuesdays and Fridays to see if he can cure their ills, from intestinal parasites and coughs to bad marriages, naughty children, and spurned lovers. And you don't need a prescription, just a strong stomach. The cures are all natural and brewed out of the stronger medicinal plants of the region, plus bark, moss, and sometimes even soil.

The town cemetery is an interesting place to wander. The graves started at the entrance to the cemetery and have worked their way south over time. The victims of the war in the 1980s are located at the south end of the plot. Some of the older gravestones are particularly ornate and well crafted in stone.

Festivals and Celebrations
Jinotega's *fiestas patronales* begin on May 1 and continue through May 15. You can expect to see folks from all over the north of Nicaragua showing up for the occasion. The *fiestas patronales* of San Juan de Jinotega are June 24. In addition (perhaps just to round out the year with parties), the Aniversario de la Creación del Departamento de Jinotega is celebrated on October 15.

ENTERTAINMENT AND NIGHTLIFE

For friendly bars, start with **Roca Rancho** (a couple blocks east of the park across from the Beneficio Ducalí, tel. 505/782-3730, open noon–midnight daily); Byron and Amelia Molina are your proud hosts and have created a unique space where the Victoria flows smoothly and you are the master of your domain in a kingly, high-backed bar stool.

There's a small movie theater that opens up just before the show and closes down just after— a good place to lick your wounds if you need a rest from walking and/or hiking. There are two small discos in town, but Jinotegans do even less dancing than Matagalpans do. Nonetheless, they're both enjoyable places to spend a Saturday evening. Check out the tried-and-true **Dance Magic,** not far from the center of town. It was formerly a house but was converted into a dance floor, so it's got a cozy feel. Newer and more modern, and attempting to throw a little style into the Nicaraguan disco scene, is **Monkey Jungle** (out on the highway, just north of the northern bus terminal; look for the bamboo walls on the outside and the stuffed-animal monkeys on the inside).

The radio programs of Jinotega are particularly delightful, as their audience, the hardworking *campesinos* of the north, likes its news spicy and its jokes raunchy. Check out Radio La Dinámica (FM 103.7), Radio Estereo Libre (FM 95.3), and Radio Family Estereo (FM 90.7).

Sports and Recreation

Basketball is the game of choice in Jinotega, and there are pickup games most evenings on the *cancha* (town court). Jinotega has an active youth league and both women's and men's teams; the players are better than you'd expect, if you're thinking about getting in a game.

HIKES FROM THE CITY OF JINOTEGA

The western wall of the Jinotega valley makes a popular climb for a Saturday morning. Start at the cemetery and work your way upward to Peña de la Cruz, where the cross is planted. Depending on how ambitious you are, the hike is 30–90 minutes, and you'll be rewarded with an impressive view of the city and the verdant valley of Jinotega. The cross isn't the original—locals say its predecessor was bigger and "better"—but the modern cross is illuminated, thanks to an electric cable that climbs the same steep hillside you just did. Look for the shining beacon of Christianity at night from the city. During misty nights, it's particularly eerie, emitting a diffuse white glow through the mists.

The eastern wall of the valley is steeper and longer, and there are no trails. That doesn't stop many locals from making their way to the top for a look around. Plan on two hours for this one. The easiest way to do it is the steep, windy dirt road that climbs abruptly out of the city and snakes its way to the top of the ridge. By road, it's around an hour on foot, but it's still not an easy walk, as the road is exceptionally steep. Watch your step on loose gravel.

ACCOMMODATIONS

Keep in mind that Jinotega's chief clientele are the small-scale farmers of the east who come in for weekends at a time to see a dentist, sell some corn, and have their boots fixed. They don't require many luxuries and don't want to waste too many *córdobas* while they're in town, as evidenced by all the under-$2 *hospedajes* that spot the neighborhood around the market. The following are some more "upscale" option. As you choose your lodging, remember to ask about hot water, which you will appreciate here more than in other parts of the country—Jinotega is chilly.

Under $10

Hotel Rosa (tel. 505/782-2472) is the oldest gig in town, and a hundred years ago, when it first opened its doors, it was the only gig in town. Its 19th-century feel remains in massive wooden beams, simple rustic rooms, and a laid-back atmosphere. Somewhat dark and dingy, the 30 rooms cost $2 pp.

El Hotelito (just east of the park, next to Sopas Coyote's Bar, tel. 505/782-2079) has 10 rooms with tiled floors, comfy-looking beds, and shared baths for about $4 pp. It closes its doors at 10 P.M.; knock to be let in after-hours. **Hotel Central** (only a block from the park, tel. 505/782-2063) is indeed central and features a massive lobby leading back to 17 cell-like rooms not much larger than their beds ($2.50 each for a shared bath with no hot water). There are three nice rooms upstairs with cable TV, private bath, and hot water, $10 s/d; meals are available at the dining room for around $2 each. Both the hotel and restaurant are closed Sundays.

Toward the north end of town, but still in a quiet residential area, **M Hotel Primavera** (tel. 505/782-2400) is run by a family that expects you to behave; 19 small rooms set around a courtyard are nothing special, but they're clean, simple, and cheap—$3 pp. There's an additional room with its own private bath for a relatively steep $10. Inside the family's living room, there's a pay phone available. The doors close at 10 P.M. and don't open until morning—make sure you're on the right side of the door and mind the sign: "No Women of Bad or Dubious Conduct."

$10–25

Hotel Bolper (located on the south side of the El Carmen Shell station, tel. 505/782-2966) has 13 clean but loudly-furnished rooms with old art deco furniture, private baths, hot water, and TV for $12 s/d. The owner tries very hard (there's even a suggestion box in the hallway!).

Ⓜ Hotel Sollentuna Hem is owned by a Swedish-Nica woman (the name is Swedish for home of the green valley). In business since 1988, the hotel has 17 different rooms (Scandinavian clean, with a unique, mismatched style) with private baths and hot water for $10–18, and special backpacker prices of $5 pp. Complete laundry service is available, as are tours of her farm on the outskirts of town.

$25–50

Jinotega's classiest accommodations, the **Ⓜ Hotel Café** (one block west, 0.5 block north of the Texaco station, tel. 505/782-2710, fax 632-3249, cafehtl@ibw.com.ni, www.hotelcafejinotega.com) stands heads and shoulders above the rest with its 16 tidy, comfortable, and tastefully decorated rooms, taking up two stories and surrounding a lush garden and spiral staircase. The rooms feature private baths, hot water, cable TV, telephones, desks, and a/c; $35/45 s/d plus tax, with mini-suites for $55, continental breakfast included. You'll also find valet parking and laundry service. Hotel Café accommodates groups and has a conference room, business center, and some great views of the surrounding city and countryside, as well as Jinotega's nicest restaurant and bar. Hotel staff can assist in planning your visit and tours of the area.

Restaurante La Colmena (tel. 505/782-2017, $25) has three spacious rooms upstairs that sleep up to three and feature private baths, fans, tiled floors, and plenty of space and air.

FOOD

Street Food

Meals are simple and inexpensive in this neck of the woods. After dark, the streets fill with *fritangas,* and families open their front doors to create cheap eateries in their living rooms and front parlors.

You can eat your way to greasy happiness for under $2 with no effort at all. Start at the southeast corner of the park and troll the two main streets through a sea of enchiladas, *papas rellenas,* (stuffed and fried potatoes) and *gallo pinto* (the national dish of rice and beans).

Restaurants

Soda El Tico is a local favorite, with two locations, one as you enter town from Matagalpa (look for the corner building on your left before you get to the Texaco), the other more central, just east of the park and boasting a clean and inexpensive lunch buffet and simple menu. Meals go for around $2. **Cafetería Trebol** is a popular, charming option with a simple menu of burgers, chicken, and sandwiches; located on the north side of the park, this is a great place to enjoy a hot chocolate or *café con leche* with a plate of French toast; opens for breakfast at 8:30 A.M., 11 A.M. on Sundays.

Look for **Chaba's Pizza** (2.5 blocks east of the park, next door to Dance Magic, tel. 505/782-2692, open 11 A.M.–10:30 P.M. Tues.–Sun.), serving a variety of thin-crust pies for $7–11, delivery service anywhere in town. You'll find excellent, reasonably priced meals and a friendly open-air atmosphere at **Ⓜ Roca Rancho** (tel. 505/782-3730, open noon–midnight daily); local volunteers rave about the jalapeño steak here.

Restaurante La Colmena ("The Beehive") is one of the nicest restaurant in town with a menu of beef, chicken, and fish ($5–9), good service, and a pleasant atmosphere. But a close second is the **Ⓜ Restaurante Borbón** at the Hotel Café, with sandwiches and meals from $4–$10, and a full wine and foreign drink list at the bar; the chicken cordon bleu is spectacular.

SHOPPING

Jinotega is not geared to foreign tourism yet. You won't find postcards or handicrafts for sale here. Instead, Jinotega is a town well prepared to equip you for your adventures north and east of the city. There are several mini-supers with a wide variety of canned goods, breads, and staples to take on the road with you. Mini-super Pio-Pio (named after the sound hungry little chicks make) has the best selection of wine in town. You can also do your shopping at Mini-Super Las 4 A.M., which is big enough to have outgrown the moniker "mini." Mini-Super El Conejo, located more centrally, is smaller but still has more canned and dried foods than you'll ever be able to eat.

Jinotega is also your last chance to load up on car parts if you happen to be driving into the mountains. Elsewhere, this isn't important, but travelers heading north and east of the city should travel prepared with everything necessary to repair their vehicles (and be prepared for at least two flat tires). On some of the beat-up roads that lead out from Jinotega, being prepared can mean the difference between adventure and disaster. (Or at least a long wait; maybe you should stock up on reading material, too). Stop by Repuestos El Pistón for supplies.

INFORMATION AND SERVICES

Jinotega offers one of the more useless regional INTUR offices (near the southeast corner of the park, tel. 505/782-4552), with a paltry display of some local handiwork and a messy basket of outdated brochures. Still, they may be able to answer some of your questions about the area, and they occasionally host cultural events.

Guide Services

Not only does Luis Lautaro Ruiz seemingly know all there is to know about his native Jinotega and the surrounding mountains, he speaks some English and is a professional writer, film producer, musician, and clown. He is a flexible freelance tour guide and will charge comparable prices to guides in Managua ($15–20 a day). He also claims his house, located a half-block north of the Escuela Mistral, is a museum (tel. 505/782-4460, lautaror@ibw.com.ni).

Banks

There's a bank on practically every corner in Jinotega. All the major players are present—Banpro, Bancentro, Banexpo, Banic, BAC, and more. Bank hours are standard; check your firearm at the door, please. The most reliable ATM is found at BanPro, off the northeast corner of the park.

Internet

J&M Internet Café (a few blocks south of the park) has five machines for $3 per hour. A scanner and CD burner are also available, as are soft drinks and snacks. **NetCafe** (across the street from Restaurante/Disco Jun Shan, open 8 A.M.–10 P.M. daily) has cheap, speedy service.

Phone Office and Mail

The **ENITEL** office is located just north of the park along the main street. It's open 7 A.M.–9 P.M. daily. The **post office** is a bit hard to find: It's tucked into a business complex behind Bancentro. As you're facing the front door of the bank, look for a sidewalk that leads behind the building to the offices that are part of the same complex. Open 8 A.M.–4 P.M. A fax machine is available.

OPPORTUNITIES TO VOLUNTEER

One of the most active organizations in Jinotega is **Habitat for Humanity** (tel. 505/772-6121). To work with them, you'll have to arrange the trip before coming down. Still, if you'd like to be useful and plan to spend some time in Jinotega, consider stopping by the following organizations to volunteer your time and services: **Club Infantíl de Niños Trabajadores de Jinotega** (tel. 505/782-3435) offers classes and workshops in trades like carpentry to disadvantaged children and orphans of Jinotega. **Associación de Voluntarios para el Desarrollo Comunitario—AVODEC** (tel. 505/782-2885) works with *campesino* groups in several areas, including agriculture and social development.

GETTING THERE AND AWAY

Buses at the Terminal del Sur head south to Matagalpa and Managua, including several express buses that make one stop along the highway at Matagalpa without entering the city itself, then continue straight on to Managua. Express buses to Managua ($3) leave every hour, and more express buses are being put into service every day, so ask ahead of time to find out what your options are. These buses may or may not make a brief stop along the highway and Matagalpa before continuing straight on to Managua (3–4 hours).

To Points South

The bus terminal (actually, just a parking lot) is located across from La Salle (a Catholic high school). Several eateries line the road behind the station, where you can relax and wait for the bus to leave, as the terminal doesn't have any facilities for passengers. Buses to Matagalpa leave every half-hour from 4 A.M. to 6 P.M. (the trip takes one hour). Buses to Estelí are in "trial stage" at present. There's a direct bus to Estelí every two hours, and if there's enough demand, more will be put in service to run this route. But getting to Estelí is easy even if you don't take one of these *expresos*. Simply take any Managua bus to Sébaco, and transfer to a northbound bus heading to Estelí, Ocotal, Somoto, or Jalapa.

To Points North and East

Buses at the Terminal del Norte go to points inland in Jinotega and beyond, including El Cuá, San José de Bocay, San Rafael del Norte, and Wiwilí. This is where the adventures start, and the rugged conditions at the terminal should prepare you mentally for what awaits you inland: mud, livestock, and a lot of friendly people moving sacks of produce, selling grains and cheap merchandise, and laughing. There is one *expreso* to Wiwilí each day (five hours), but regular buses leave about every hour (seven hours). There are two expresses per day to El Cuá–Bocay (three hours) and regular service about once per hour (four hours). There are two expresses to Pantasma (three hours) and regular service about once per hour (4.5 hours). Pantasma buses go past Asturias and the dam at Lago Apanás.

The north terminal also has regular bus service to San Sebastián de Yalí and La Rica, via San Rafael del Norte and La Concordia, from where you can get back-road bus service to Estelí—a fun way to make a loop through some really beautiful country.

ORIENTATION AND GETTING AROUND

Jinotega occupies the bottom of the steep-walled bowl formed by the mountains that surround it on all sides. The highway passes along its east side, and the cemetery is at the western edge. It's a city with a pleasant, cool climate and not too much vehicular traffic, both of which make it a pleasurable city for walking. There are no city buses, nor is there need for them.

There are several taxi cooperatives that circulate the city streets and that will take you across town for $.80. But Jinotega isn't a big place, and the temperature never gets hot enough to be unpleasant. You should be able to walk anywhere you need to go.

NORTH AND EAST OF JINOTEGA

El Valle de Tomatoya

Located just north of the city of Jinotega on the road to San Rafael del Norte, this is the home of a women's cooperative that produces the region's famous black pottery. Although few like to admit it, the cities of Matagalpa and Jinotega vie with each other for recognition as home of the black pottery. Check in at **Grupo de Mujeres de Las Cureñas** to see their work. The production of black pottery is a little more intricate than other types of ceramic arts, and these women have produced some very beautiful pieces of art, including faithful replicas of some pre-Columbian designs.

Right along the highway is El Centro Recreativo de Tomatoya, a bathing area created by damming up the San Gabriel stream. The owner, Blanca Dalla Torre, has gotten special permission from the Ministry of Health to run the swimming hole, on the condition she regularly empties out the pool and lets it refill with fresh water. Drinks and snacks are available, as well as a complete selection of beer.

Lago de Apanás and the Mancotal Dam

Lake Apanás is the largest man-made body of water in Nicaragua. Luís Somoza Debayle's ad-

© RANDY WOOD

the Morning Glory Spillway, Lago de Apanás

ministration created it in 1964 by damming up the waters of Río El Tuma and flooding the broad valley just north of the city of Jinotega, which until that time was pasture, small farms, and an airstrip that serviced the north of Nicaragua. Today, Lake Apanás is a long, irregularly shaped lake. It feeds the twin turbines at the Planta Hidroelectrica Centroamérica, which produces 15 percent of the nation's hydropower (downstream along the Río Viejo, the same water passes through the turbines at Santa Bárbara and Lago La Virgen, which produce an additional 15 percent of the nation's hydropower). Apanás is not a typical reservoir; unlike many hydropower plants that are located at the dam itself, the Planta Centroamérica is located at the upstream end of the lake, so keeping the lake full is essential. The water passes underneath the highway through massive steel pipes where it drops and passes through the turbines. The hydropower project actually forces the water to change watersheds: Water from the Río El Tuma watershed is discharged into the tributaries of the Río Viejo, where it flows south to Lake Xolotlán (Managua) instead of the Atlantic coast.

Hurricane Mitch nearly sent the whole works downstream in 1998, when waters overtopping the round Morning Glory Spillway (the concrete structure that looks like a flying saucer on its head in the middle of the lake), flowed through the secondary spillway channel, under the bridge, and down a long stair-step energy dissipater. The volume of water rushing through the channel quickly eroded it away along with all of its concrete, nearly destroying the dam itself and nearly causing a wall of water that would have raged for hundreds of kilometers downstream. The loss of the lake would have been economically catastrophic, affecting irrigation, fishing, and hydropower production, not to mention the loss of life and property downstream on the Río El Tuma. The government has been negotiating since 1999 to find a way to repair the spillway and return the dam's safety structures to normal, while the IMF and the World Bank have been trying to privatize the whole system.

To get to the dam, take any bus headed toward Pantasma and get off at Asturias (60–90 minutes from Jinotega). The highway crosses the dam, so you'll know when you've arrived. The lake itself is picturesque, but equally impressive are the remains of the damaged spillway. On the lake side of the road are the remains of an old military base built in the 1980s to prevent Contra troops from destroying the dam. (The Planta Centroamérica was a highly sought Contra target in the 1980s and was similarly tightly guarded to prevent its destruction. Some land mines still litter the hills around the hydropower plant.)

Don't miss the opportunity to cast a line and do some fishing (for giant tilapia and guapote) or swimming. There are several grassy areas at the lake's edge where you can jump in for a refreshing dip in the surprisingly cold waters of Apanás. From the dam, walk along the highway in either direction and choose your place. The lake is safe—there are no underwater structures or water intakes to be afraid of, and the water is quite deep and refreshing. Obviously, stay away from the spillover drain.

Lago Asturias and the El Dorado Dam

The El Dorado dam was completed in 1984 and filled in 1985 as a supplement to the Mancotal Dam. Water is captured in Asturias and pumped up to Apanás, where it flows through the turbines for energy production. Fishermen in the know realize that Asturias is home to some monster freshwater fish. To get there from the Mancotal Dam, walk back toward the city of Jinotega about one kilometer to the first major intersection. That road descends quickly past a few coffee farms and small farming communities to the El Dorado Dam.

El Dorado also experienced severe damage during Hurricane Mitch. As you look at the lake, imagine that the same massive deluge that destroyed Mancotal's spillway also flowed through that placid little lake and out the other side—then appreciate how fortunate it is to have withstood the hurricane.

There's a little grassy hill on the upstream side of the dam where you can pitch a tent and do some fishing. If you'd like to try to hitch a ride with all your catch, occasional vehicles transit this road—mostly old IFAs and pickup trucks—bound for the communities east of El Dorado.

ⓜ San Rafael del Norte

This remote and misty mountain town has a cool climate and is surrounded by eternally green hills. Perched at the top of the watershed, the country around San Rafael is thick with clean swimming holes, the easiest of which to access are in the two creeks that meet at the Los Encuentros restaurant, located a 10-minute walk out of town on the road toward Yalí. The more adventurous should hike down into the gorge that runs on the north edge of town, descend from the Hospedaje Rolinmar, and then start upstream to where cold water rushes through a narrow canyon, shady and thick with green vegetation.

To know San Rafael is to know history. A visit to the **General Augusto César Sandino Museum** (right off the park) gives you a sample of the small town's pride at having served as the proving grounds for the general's legendary battles with the U.S. Marines in the 1930s. Sandino's wife was a San Rafaelina, and Nicaraguan folk musician Carlos Mejía Godoy wrote moving lyrics about love and war in Sandino's hills there.

The surprisingly spacious **La Iglesia de San Rafael del Norte** is more impressive than you'd expect for such an out-of-the-way town; some call it the most beautiful church in all of Nicaragua. Pastel-colored windows admit a calming light in which to view the many bright murals, reliefs, and shrines. Locals distinguish between Sandino the man and Sandinismo as practiced by Daniel Ortega et al. Look closely at the inside left wall of the church, where a painting of the devil bears a remarkable resemblance to Daniel Ortega, implying that Ortega has betrayed the ideals of Sandino.

The community has the Italian priest Odorico d'Andrea to thank for their church—and a whole lot more. From his arrival in 1953 to his death in 1996, Father Odorico achieved virtual sainthood among the people of San Rafael and the surrounding communities. His image, a smiling, warm, obviously kind man in plain brown robes, can be seen in nearly every home, business, and vehicle in the town. Among his achievements are a formidable health clinic, a library, several neighborhoods for the poor, and the renovation of the church. Odorico's fame has multiplied posthumously; many believe he performed miracles and that his body has not decomposed. You can check for yourself at its resting place, called the **Tepeac,** on the hill overlooking the town. Ascending the stairs, you'll pass the 12 stations of the cross until you reach the shrine on top where the tomb lies—as well as gorgeous views of the town and surrounding hills. An impressive stand of old trees shades the hilltop. Virgin pine forests carpet the countryside.

There are great eats at Doña Chepita's, and there are two places to stay: **Hotel Rolinmar** (near the gas station and the nicer of the two) and **Comedor y Hospedaje Aura** (on main street east of church). Buses pass through San Rafael del Norte regularly on the route between Jinotega and San Sebastián de Yalí/La Rica. There is also one express bus to Managua that leaves at 4:30 A.M., passes through Jinotega at 5:30 A.M., and continues south through Matagalpa to Managua. The same bus leaves Managua at 3 P.M. and retraces the route to San Rafael del Norte, arriving sometime after 7 P.M.

El Cuá and San José de Bocay

El Cuá is best known for Benjamin Linder, the only known American casualty of the Contra war. Both towns are now illuminated by mini-hydroelectric power plants he helped design and implement. Both towns were completely enveloped in conflict during the 1980s, overrun first by Contras and then by the FSLN. El Cuá has three *hospedajes,* a gas station, and several places to eat. There's one *hospedaje* in Bocay, a few small eateries, and a gas station.

Ayapal

Ayapal is a small community on the banks of the Río Bocay. From here, you can hire boats to take you downstream to several Miskito communities (not cheap).

Wiwilí

The upstream capital of the Río Coco region lies snug near the Honduran border and a long, bumpy, five-hour slog north of Jinotega. Wiwilí is a mestizo town, meaning it's of Spanish, not indigenous origin. Waspám, 550 kilometers downstream at Waspám, is the other anchor at river's end, and is mostly indigenous.

Matagalpa

© RANDY WOOD

boat traffic on the Río Bocay

Wiwilí is a town split by the Río Coco, which runs broadly through the middle of town. Several hundred inhabitants of Wiwilí lost their lives to the river during Hurricane Mitch, but the political strife outlasted the storm. Post-Mitch, the two sides of the community went their own separate ways to find international aid, and subsequently decided to become independent. While they retained the same name, Wiwilí on the north side of the river is now part of the department of Madriz, while Wiwilí on the south bank remains part of Jinotega. Both are important port towns with access to the deep waters of the Río Coco.

Local coffee cooperative members can lead individuals or groups on community-led tours to nearby Kilambé National Park and other surrounding treasures. This is some truly wild country and we've only heard of a couple of souls who have attempted the epic six-day trip downstream to Waspám, braving crocodiles, bandits, and drug smugglers; there are reportedly guides that will take you on rafts, camping along the river, and hanging out with wandering, dugout canoe–paddling fishermen, known as *nomados,* by locals.

There are a few decent *comedores* and two accommodations in Wiwilí: **Hotel Central,** $3 for a bed with shared bath, or $19 double with private bath. **El Hotelito** has standard singles with shared bath for less than $4.

Wamblán

Wamblán saw some ferocious battles during the 1980s. The last part of the drive to Wamblán is notable for a stunning descent into the city along a mountain ridge. If your trip happens to coincide with the end of the day, the long mountain shadows falling into the ridges will ensure you never forget the moment you entered Wamblán. Those pleasant memories will hopefully outlast your memory of the town's one unpleasant *hospedaje.*

Bosawás Biosphere Reserve

Feel like going deep? We suggest an expedition into Nicaragua's first, largest, muddiest, and least accessible national reserve. Check out a map of Central America, notably the blank space in north-central Nicaragua—that's where you're headed. There are few roads here, but many cruddy trails and powerful rivers, the banks of which are inhabited by nobody at all or by clumps of indigenes living as they have for centuries.

Located 350 kilometers north of Managua, the 730,000 hectares of forest, mountains, and rivers collectively known as Bosawás are located within the municipalities of Waspám, Bonanza, Siuna, El Cuá–Bocay, Wiwilí, and Waslala. Although inhabited by some 40,000 widely dispersed people (more than half of which are Mayangna and Miskito), most of Bosawás remains unexplored, unmapped, and untamed. Its name is derived from the region's three most salient features: the Río Bocay (BO), Cerro Saslaya (SA), and the Río Waspuk (WAS).

Besides unequaled stretches of cloud forest, Bosawás contains tropical humid forest, rainforest, and a wealth of disparate ecosystems that vary in altitude from 30 meters above sea level at the mouth of the Waspuk River to the 1,650-meter peak of Cerro Saslaya. Bosawás is a Central American treasure, an immense genetic reserve of species that have vanished elsewhere in Mesoamerica, including jaguars, rare small mammals, 12 kinds of poisonous snakes, and many bird species, including the gorgeous scarlet macaw and 34 boreal migratory species.

Bosawás was designated a protected reserve in 1997, but where there is no money, there is little enforcement and few rangers—there are many more desperately poor who continue to make a living from this ancient land. In many cases, this translates into slash-and-burn clearing of the forests and the continual push of the agricultural frontier, mostly for subsistence. The 1.8 million acres of protected area was declared a part of the Nature Conservancy's international Parks in Peril program in 2001.

Siuna

If Nicaragua is the wild west of Central America, then Siuna, the primary entry town to Bosawás visitors, is Tombstone in its heyday. Siuna's main gold mine shut down in 1968, leaving its workers isolated and without work. Folks sling their guns like they sling their liquor. The scene in the market is a mix of cowboys and settlers who cut a living out of wild lands that only a few years ago were an immense jungle and now are a patchwork of deforested, steamy tropical pasturelands. While this place is currently at peace, you cannot forget that the law here is the law of man and the law of nature, no more and no less. Only a few years ago, police and military forces staged a series of gun battles with scattered groups of ex-soldiers living the life of guerilla bandits in the hills.

Visiting the Reserve

To do anything in Bosawás, you *must* receive permission (at time of printing, free). Contact Pedro Lopez in Siuna (tel. 505/794-2036, office at central park) or the MARENA office in Managua (tel. or 505/233-1594; the park's principal web-page is www.tmx.com.ni/~bosawas). These offices will also help set you up with reliable guides for your trip; guides are absolutely necessary and cost about $7 per day plus food. You may be convinced to hire two guides for your trip, a recommended safety and comfort precaution.

Unless you have months to explore the reserve, you'll have to pick and choose from various possible destinations. Get off the bus at Casa Roja (1.5 hours from Siuna) to stage an ascent of Cerro Saslaya (4–5 days); or continue to Santa Rosita (2.5-hour bus ride) for a two-hour hike to the river or trailhead to Cerro El Torro (4–5 days). Waslala is a 4–5 hour ride from Siuna and home to the original tomb of Carlos Fonseca (his remains were moved to Managua after the revolution's victory).

Be advised: Any trip in Bosawás is a serious backcountry undertaking and should not be attempted without proper supplies, some wilderness experience, a tolerance for dampness and discomfort, and a basic survival instinct. You should already have supplies like water bottles, a mosquito net, and some kind of pump or purifying tablets for water (start your hike with at least three liters in your bag; a fresh source is available in the park), a brimmed hat, sunscreen, sturdy shoes, and a med kit. Additional supplies that can be purchased in Siuna include rubber boots (for snakes and knee-level mud), four yards of heavy black plastic for a roof in the jungle, a piece of plastic/waterproof cover for your backpack, a machete, hammock, extra rope, and food.

Getting There and Away

To reach Bosawás, you must adjust your previously held notions of "road" to what most people who have driven in this area refer to as the *pegadero* (or place where you get stuck). Siuna lies on the route from Managua to Puerto Cabezas, a drive that can take from 30 hours in the dry season to 30 days in the wet, depending on your mode of transport (please see Getting There in the Puerto Cabezas section for more details on buses). Alternatively, and much quicker, there are domestic flights available from Managua to the towns of Siuna and Bonanza.

Buses to the Bosawás Reserve leave from the northern bus stop of Siuna in the direction of Waslala, with the closest town called Wili.

Matagalpa

Boaco, Chontales, and the Road to El Rama

As you fork east out of Managua at the roadside community of San Benito and rumble into Nicaragua's interior, a world very much unlike Nicaragua's other regions unfolds before you. Less volcanic than León, drier than the south, and more open and accessible than the deep mountains of Jinotega and Matagalpa, the cattle-dominated landscape of Boaco and Chontales has a flavor all its own.

That flavor is cheese. More than 60 percent of Nicaragua's dairy products, including dozens of varieties of cheese and millions of gallons of fresh milk, originate along the east side of Lake Cocibolca. East of the lake, towns are smaller and set farther apart, separated by broad cattle farms—ranches of sometimes thousands of hectares of land. In spite of the extended lakeshore, Boaco

© RANDY WOOD

Must-Sees

Look for **M** to find the sights and activities you can't miss and **N** for the best dining and lodging.

M **The Hot Springs of Aguas Claras:** Nicaragua's premier jacuzzi is powered by the volcanic energy of a land on fire. Soak away your troubles in a pleasant and casual environment (page 261).

M **San José de los Remates:** The newest endeavor in the least-traveled part of the country, this provides a great opportunity to hike, ride horses, see petroglyphs, and cool your heels in a waterfall (page 263).

M **Santa Lucía:** The most charming and picturesque of Boaco's mountain villages, Santa Lucía is rife with gorgeous mountains, river valleys, and opportunities to hike (page 263).

M **Museo Arqueológico Gregorio Aguilar Barea:** This warehouse of statuary burgeons with treasures the Chontales carved long before Columbus (page 268).

N **Juigalpa Fiestas Patronales:** Juigalpa throws a cowboy party unsurpassed in the nation. Join Juigalpans for rodeo, mechanical bull–riding contests, and down-on-the-farm good times (page 270).

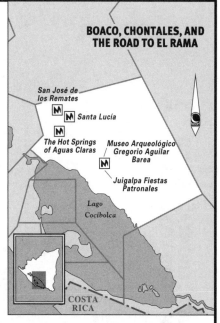

BOACO, CHONTALES, AND THE ROAD TO EL RAMA

San José de los Remates

Santa Lucía

The Hot Springs of Aguas Claras

Museo Arqueológico Gregorio Aguilar Barea

Juigalpa Fiestas Patronales

Lago Cocibolca

COSTA RICA

Boaco

Aguas Claras hot springs

© RANDY WOOD

BOACO, CHONTALES, AND THE ROAD TO EL RAMA

Boaco

El Río Escondido

El Rama

La Esperanza

Nueva Guinea

Cara de Mono

Muelle de los Bueyes

La Gateada

El Ayote

Río Mico

Villa Sandino

Muhan

San Miguelito

Cordillera Chontaleña

Santo Domingo

San Pedro de Lóvago

Santo Tomás

Acoyapa

La Libertad

Juigalpa

M JUIGALPA FIESTAS PATRONALES

Serranía Amerrisque

Cuapa

Puerto Díaz

Camoapa

Comalapa

San Lorenzo

CARRETERA A RAMA

Isla Grande

Isla Muerto

Lago Cocibolca

Altagracia

La Calamidad

M SANTA LUCÍA

M SAN JOSÉ DE LOS REMATES

Muy Muy

Boaco

Teustepe

Empalme de Boaco

M THE HOT SPRINGS OF AGUAS CLARAS

Isla Redonda

Moyogalpa

Granada

Rivas

San Benito

PAN-AMERICAN HWY

To Estelí

To Managua

PAN-AMERICAN HWY

CA1

CA1

CA1

20 mi

20 km

0

0

© AVALON TRAVEL PUBLISHING, INC.

and Chontales's fishing communities are few: Here, the emphasis is on the land.

The cattle ranchers of the east are often well-to-do by Nicaraguan standards, and their wealth is apparent in towns like the clean and well-laid-out city of Juigalpa. Juigalpa's patron saint celebrations are among the best in Nicaragua, involving elaborate bull-riding competitions, horsemanship contests, and festivals. But in true Nicaraguan spirit, even the disadvantaged communities haven't lost their sense of humor. The Boaco town of La Calamidad (The Calamity) retains its name in spite of two government attempts to rename it something less frightful. The locals insist that with poor land, little fresh water, and few opportunities for productive farming, their little town is a calamity and should be named accordingly.

PLANNING YOUR TIME

Neither Boaco nor Chontales is a regular feature on the well-traveled tourist trail, and traditional "sights" are few and far between. That makes this region a ball of soft clay out of which the intrepid and adventurous traveler can sculpt any manner of adventure. You could easily spend a day in one of many quiet cattle towns and back-country agrarian communities like Boaco, Camoapa, or Cuapa. Add an additional day if the rock climbing and hiking opportunities at Cuisaltepe or Cuapa whet your appetite, and another to spend a day horseback at San José de los Remates. Of all the cities in this region, Juigalpa is the most interesting and engaging; its *fiestas patronales* in mid-August should not be missed, as they draw a crowd from all over the country. Too many travelers zip straight through this quiet corner of Nicaragua on a fast bus to El Rama. Two or three days here may convince you there's more to Nicaragua than Granada and San Juan del Sur.

HISTORY

The lands now known as Boaco and Chontales were first settled by the Chontal people (not their own name for themselves; the word is Nahuatl for the mountain people they called savages or foreigners). The Chontals were responsible for many of the statuary and stone monuments unearthed in the Amerrisque mountain range.

In their infancy, the first Spanish settlements of what was then called El Corregimiento de Chontales suffered greatly at the hands of aggressive Miskitos and Zambos, whose frequent attacks devastated 7 of 12 Spanish settlements. In 1749, Camoapa, Boaco (today known as Boaco Viejo), and Juigalpa were attacked; the towns were nearly destroyed and the churches burned to the ground. Boaco's then-governor, Alonso Fernández de Heredia, returned the aggression, leading an excursion that returned with more than a hundred Miskito prisoners. The settlers reestablished their communities eight kilometers to the south, and nothing remains of Boaco Viejo to this day. From 1750 to 1760, the same indigenous groups attacked Juigalpa, Camoapa, Lóvago, Lovigüisca, Yasica, Guabale, Santa Rosa, and nine other communities. In 1762, Boaco was reestablished by Father Cáceres, who was killed shortly thereafter by yet another Miskito attack. In 1782, the church in Juigalpa was—you guessed it—burned to the ground.

When the threat of attack from indigenous peoples diminished, the lands east of Lake Cocibolca were developed into extensive cattle ranches. Coffee was introduced around the Boaco area, but before long its production had been pushed up into the better lands in northern Boaco and southern Matagalpa. Cattle ranching soon became the economic mainstay of the area, followed by the extraction of gold from the mines at La Libertad and Santo Domingo.

The social and economic reorganization of the Sandinista years earned the unbridled antipathy of the people of Chontales and Boaco, who were generally frontier-minded people uninterested in government regulation. As their lands were confiscated and reorganized, they naturally had more sympathy for the Contra forces, whom they clandestinely supported throughout much of the 1980s. Much of the violence of the 1980s occurred in the towns that border both sides of the highway and inland. Since the 1990s, both departments voted against the Sandinista party with overwhelming margins.

Boaco

Boaco

Nestled snugly in a 379-meter-high notch in the Amerrisque mountains, Boaco is a paradox: a departmental capital set back in the hillsides like a common country villa, an agriculture center whose hillsides struggle to produce cattle and corn, and a commercial center beset with poverty. Modern Boaco (the city's name is a combination of Aztec and Sumu words that mean Land of the Sorcerers) is the third city to bear the name: In the 18th and 19th century, two previous Boacos were built and destroyed in the same place. In 1749, an expedition of Zumos, Miskitos, and Zambos armed with English rifles sacked the original Boaco, killed the priest, took several females hostage, and burned the town to the ground. The settlers started over along the edge of the Río Malacatoya in what's now the town of Boaquito, and in 1763, due to a brutal outbreak of cholera and the difficulties the land presented for agriculture, moved to the present site of Boaco. By the 19th century, Boaco was a cow town, though residents raised several crops (such as *cabuya,* for making rope) to sell in the markets of Masaya, a four-day mule-drawn wagon trip. William Walker and his men made an appearance in the 1860s, confiscating haciendas and cattle.

The modern city of Boaco began on a hilltop and crept down the hillside into a valley as it grew, earning the nickname The City of Two Floors. But the two levels are rapidly multiplying into more as Boaco—once a cattle town of nine families—expands up and over the adjacent hilltops. During the Contra war, Boaco was spared from direct battles, but in the hillsides that surrounded the city, Contras and Sandinistas fought numerous skirmishes in Muy Muy, San José de los Remates, and San Francisco. The violence dislodged countless *campesinos,* all of whom eventually found their way to the city of Boaco seeking refuge. Many decided to stay, and Boaco has swelled over the past 20 years, faster than it can provide for its new inhabitants, most of whom occupy neighborhoods of small concrete homes around the outskirts of the city.

Regardless of Boaco's challenges, it's been an inspiration to several notable Nicaraguan authors and scholars, four of whom—Diego Sequeira, Antonio Barquero, Hernan Robleto, and Julian N. Guerrero—have won the Nicaraguan Rubén Darío prize for literature. A monument in their honor, just east and north of the park, overlooks the city from a sort of balcony in the city.

Most travelers visit Boaco after a dip in the hot springs of Aguas Claras and are surprised to find they need a day or two more to check out the area. The hills and valleys around the city are home to charming country towns and small communities of farmers and ranchers who like to claim that their hills are made of cheese and their rivers of milk. They're home as well to lots of mystery: petroglyphs, waterfalls, and hilltops for climbing.

SIGHTS AND ATTRACTIONS

Boaco's patron saint is Santiago Apóstol, and the *fiestas patronales* in his honor are particularly interesting and historic. The festival lasts the entire month of July, during which time the saint's statue is paraded daily from one neighborhood to the next. The crux of the ceremony is from the 23rd to 25th, when the procession is accompanied by dancers whose performance tells an elaborate tale of the expulsion of the Moors from Spain.

A statue located one block east of the church represents a dancer, complete with snake stick in one hand and brass knuckles in the other (he's been repainted several times in order to get the skin tone just right—from 1999 to 2001, he went from pink to brown to an off shade of yellow).

Boaco's two churches neatly serve the residents of Boaco's two levels without their having to traipse up and down the hill. In the lower half, the unmistakable **Capilla de la Santísima Sacramento** is an elaborate and untraditional church whose architecture is nearly Greek Orthodox. A statue of the Virgin Mary stands and keeps watch over the earth from its starched white rooftop. Inside, statues of Jesus and the Virgin Mary line up side by side with the carved stone statuary of Boaco's Chontal and Sumu

BOACO

To Santa Lucía

RESTAURANTE LOS COCOS ▼

RESTAURANTE EL BORBON ▼

MONUMENT TO WRITERS ★

Parque Cerro El Faro

MINISUPER LA DISPENSA ▼

RESTAURANTE ALPINO ▼

FUNDACIÓN NIEBROWSKI ★

POST OFFICE ■

KODAK ■

"BAILANTE" STATUE ★

ENITEL ■

LA PARROQUIA DE SANTIAGO APÓSTOL

RASPADOS EL BAILANTE

ENITEL BARRIO OLAMA ■

Central Park

HOSPEDAJE ALMA ●

BAR/DISCO LA CUEVA ▼

ESKIMO ▼

HOTEL SOBALVARRO ●

DIVERSIÓN 2000

BANPRO ■

CAPILLA DE SANTISIMA SACRAMENTO ✝

BANCENTRO ■

CEMETERY

BUS TERMINAL

SCALE NOT AVAILABLE

MOON

N Boaco

To Ranchón de Peter Carbonaro, Matiguás, and Río Blanco

To Empalme de Boaco

© AVALON TRAVEL PUBLISHING, INC.

FATHER NIEBROWSKI, FATHER OF A CITY

Far more instrumental in the development of modern Boaco than any mayor was a man of the cloth, Father Niebrowski of Poland, who arrived in 1916. While preaching to an underserved community, Niebrowski took it upon himself to better their lot in life and used his determination and practical know-how to bring Boaco into the modern world.

Niebrowski built a cinema, a brick factory whose bricks he used to rebuild the church, and a small hydropower plant on the Río Fonseca, which provided electric light to the city for the first time. Niebrowski also established the first hospital, the first community music band, and countless other things that contributed to Boaco's social welfare. To this day, the Niebrowski Foundation is active in the city and provides for small programs in the Boaco area.

ancestors, an intriguing compromise between the religions of new and old.

La Parroquia de Santiago Apóstol, located at the top of the hill, is a Boaco landmark unchanged since it was designed and built in the mid-1800s. There is a mass every day, and several on the weekends, when the ringing of the church bells fills the town square and scatters the pigeons.

Boaco's highest point is **Cerro El Faro,** the lighthouse without a sea. A concrete pedestal and tower, the Faro offers a good view of the city and the valley of the Río Mayales. Technically, the tower is open all week, but the caretaker closes it when he pleases. Underneath is the town convention center and a popular gymnasium. Evenings, the Faro is one of Boaco's more popular places to steal a few kisses.

ENTERTAINMENT AND NIGHTLIFE

Boaco has two discos, and a very different crowd in each one. In town, just 10 meters down the hill from the park, **La Cueva** is popular among a younger crowd that just wants to dance to modern music: Backstreet Boys, Britney Spears, and the like. Newer and more popular, **El Ranchón de Peter Carbonaro** is a kilometer or two out of town along the highway to Muy Muy, just far enough to weed out the teens. Its relaxing atmosphere is perfect for a drink and some traditional Latin music: salsa, cumbia, and merengue (and the occasional ranchero). By 10 P.M., though, its dance floor is just as packed as La Cueva's, especially when there's live music—even Dimensión Costeüa has played there. Take a taxi there for about $1 per couple.

You can kill an hour or two while you wait for buses at Diversión 2000, a video-game hall of Sony PlayStations and Nintendos that's usually mobbed with 10-year-olds waiting to play Mario Brothers. Games are priced for the budget of a 10-year-old, so you'll be hard-pressed to spend $2 while you're there. Same goes for the ENITEL in Barrio Olama, which has a few Nintendo machines of its own.

ACCOMMODATIONS

There are really only two places to stay in the city, which doesn't matter as most foreign travelers prefer the hot springs at Aguas Claras outside of town. Located at the south edge of the park, **Hotel Sobalvarro** (tel. 505/842-2515, 10 rooms, $5 s) is a remnant of Boaco's history, a once grandiose building of wooden rooms set around a courtyard with a balcony overlooking the lower half of Boaco. It's none too fancy, but it's clean and well cared for. Just where the already steep road turns nearly vertical, **Hospedaje Alma** (6 rooms, $4 s with shared bath) is even more unassuming. The lower half of Boaco has several *pensiónes* along the main road and near the terminal that do a brisk trade in prostitution and quick romantic getaways for young couples; not recommended for travelers.

FOOD

Several restaurants on the top floor of Boaco serve traditional Nicaraguan dishes, burgers, sandwiches, and other foods. One of the least expensive places to have a meal is **Restaurante Maraíta,** which doubles as a popular drinking hole. A little pricier than the others but still well within the budget of economizing travelers, **Restaurante Alpino** is considered the best (the name is a result of the owner's former business selling Christmas trees in Tipitapa). The burgers are good, but the beef *churrasco* steak is fantastic at a measly $4.50. Locals and NGO workers like **Restaurante Borbon,** which is known for its *pollo al vino* and pork chops, among other classics, for around $2.50 a dish, plus huge glasses of *fresco* served on a breezy balcony overlooking the hills. Having a meal at **Restaurante Los Cocos** (a block farther north on the same street) is like eating lunch in someone's living room, and the food is quite good.

Pastries and snacks are for sale in the park; wash 'em down with ice cream at **Eskimo,** adjacent to Hotel Sobalvarro—where you can also enjoy shakes, sandwiches, and burgers, all served on the best front porch in the city. A block east of the park near the statue of the dancer is **Raspados El Bailante,** selling crushed-ices in a half-dozen flavors at $.35 each.

Boaco market

SHOPPING

The best supermarket in town is the well-stocked and well-run **Minisuper La Dispensa,** which has a selection of breads, cheeses, canned and dry goods, wines, and liquors. During the day, a woman sets up shop on the sidewalk outside La Dispensa to sell fresh fruits and vegetables. Of course, no one can beat the prices in the market in the lower half of town.

SERVICES

In the lower part of Boaco along the main strip are two **banks:** Banpro and, 1.5 blocks farther south, Bancentro. **Western Union** is near the market, open 8 A.M.–4:30 P.M. Monday–Saturday. Check your email at the rather slow connection in the **ENITEL** office in Barrio Olama, 1.5 blocks west of the park. It charges $8.50 per hour, and is open 8 A.M.–10 P.M. daily. The **post office** is 1.5 blocks north of the church on the left side. There's a pay phone out front (open 8 A.M.–5 P.M. Mon.–Fri., until noon Sat.). ENITEL is located across from the cathedral's northeast corner (open

8 A.M.–9 P.M. Mon.–Fri.). **Kodak Express** is one block north of the church (open 8 A.M.–6 P.M. Mon.–Sat.).

GETTING THERE AND AWAY

Buses to Boaco leave every 30–40 minutes from Managua. From Boaco, the most comfortable way to travel to Managua is by microbus. Two leave each day from the terminal, at 6:30 a.m. and 12:30 P.M. ($2). Regular buses leave every 30 minutes for Managua until 5:40 P.M.

Five buses leave each day for Santa Lucía, 10:30 A.M.–5 P.M. (one hour). Buses leave from 5:50 A.M. until 5 P.M. bound for Río Blanco (three hours) and Muy Muy. Or for the travel masochist, there's the 12-hour Boaco–Siuna kidney-bruiser over some of the worst dirt roads in the nation.

NEAR BOACO
The Hot Springs of Aguas Claras

The *Aguas Termales* (Hot Waters) located seven kilometers west of the Empalme de Boaco are one of the best reasons to visit the Boaco area. The area is called Aguas Claras, where out of a

Boaco's hilly streets require ingenuity.

crack in the ground bubbles a hot spring heated by an uninvestigated geothermal source (the locals will tell you it's an underground volcano, which probably isn't too far from the truth). Around 2000, an entrepreneur channeled the geothermally-heated waters into pipes and from there into a series of pools protected by palm-thatch roofs. The whole place is now a hotel and resort complex boasting three large pools and two small ones for children. All five are spotlessly clean and more professionally maintained than you'd expect. The water isn't boiling hot, the way you find in similar establishments in Scandinavia, but it's extraordinarily warm, and you can try all the pools until you find one with a temperature that suits you. While you lounge in the pool, you can order food from an extensive menu of traditional Nicaraguan food (chicken, fish, beef) and a wide selection of alcohol. Under the palm thatch are several soft hammocks, and in the lobby of the hotel are a pair of good billiards tables.

There's a high-class hotel on the premises with 17 rooms—6 inside the main building and 11

more in private cabins set around the back. Fancy, modern rooms with air-conditioning and hot-water baths (they're not quite hot tubs, but that was the idea) cost $25 each. Two simple rooms upstairs have a shared bath (no hot tub), fan instead of a/c, and cost $15. It's well worth the extra money to go for the better-quality accommodation. Day-use fees vary during the week, but are never more than $1.50, cheaper for kids; credit cards are accepted for hotel and restaurant expenses, not the entrance fee.

During Semana Santa and weekends in the dry season, the hotel can fill up quickly. Call the office in Managua to make reservations, tel. 505/244-2916. There is no phone on the premises, but the Managua office communicates via a radio.

The Baseball Field at Empalme de Boaco

Years ago, a North American traveler named Jake Scheideman fell ill during an ambitious bicycle tour of Central America and was taken in by a family at Empalme de Boaco. Over several days, they nursed him—a complete stranger—back to health. In 1998 after Hurricane Mitch, Scheideman returned to Nicaragua after many years of having been away, wanting to do something for the community that had taken care of him when he was ill. He asked what they would like, and they chose a ballpark.

The ballpark, constructed in Empalme de Boaco (the intersection of the road to Boaco) took more than two years to complete but is now the best of its kind east of Lake Cocibolca; games are Saturday and Sunday afternoons in season. The construction team moved on to begin a community housing program that has provided new lodging for dozens of families, and they plan to continue. Contact Jake and friends to participate, donate, or learn more, at his bike shop in Northern California: jake@sthelenacyclery.com.

La Cebadilla

Around the turn of the 20th century, a farmer from the mountain town of Cebadilla was surprised to see the Virgin Mary appear before him amongst the rocks where he was tending his cattle. The site has been treasured by the locals ever since.

La Cebadilla is no easier to get to than it ever was, and if you're interested in a hike through an out-of-the-way corner of Nicaragua, try walking up the mountain to La Cebadilla. At one time a small chapel was erected in honor of the Virgin, and there was a small well where it was said the water was blessed. Today, the chapel has mostly fallen to bits.

The hike starts 1.6 kilometers east of Empalme Boaco, where on the south side of the highway there's a dirt road leading south to the community of Asedades and a steel sign with a picture of the Virgin Mary and the words La Cebadilla. The road leads south one kilometer to Asedades, a poor community of adobe houses, flower gardens, and awful, rocky fields. Asedades is surprisingly clean in spite of its poverty and is an interesting look at how resourceful *campesinos* can eke out an existence even when the land is more rock than soil. It's imperative that you find a guide in Asedades to take you up the mountain to La Cebadilla. There are many small footpaths that lead up the hill, but they intertwine and none is well-enough used to be more obvious than the others. The walk up the hill will take you between three and four hours—take water and food along with you and make sure you have something to share with your guide. The walk back to Asedades can take 2–3 hours. Your guide will recommend that you stay at the top of the hill through midday and do your walking in the cool of the afternoon.

At La Cebadilla, you may or may not have visions of the Virgin Mary, but you will certainly have a fantastic view of the valley below and the hills of Boaco to the east, sometimes all the way to the big lake.

ⓜ San José de los Remates

This picturesque cowboy town beckons the explorer and outdoor enthusiast with adventures-in-the-making, like guided horse tours and hikes to waterfalls (Cascada La Chorrera is particularly beautiful in October) and to the impressive collection of pre-Columbian petroglyphs that line the Malacatoya River. You can also access the Cerro Cumaica Natural Reserve from here. The view from the Cruz del Milenio is impressive: On a clear evening, you can see the lights of Granada and Cerro Negro in León.

You may consider visiting San José de los Remates as part of a little-traveled route to San Ramón, Matagalpa. But plan ahead with a phone call to Jorge Isaac (tel. 505/842-2359) to make reservations. Four direct buses leave Teustepe daily and a direct bus from Managua's Mayoreo terminal leaves daily at 12:30 P.M. ($2). Jorge will help you find accommodations in the 10-room town hostel (hot water) or with a local family. If you wander into town on your own, look for Doña Rosinda (from ENITEL, half a block east), who is involved in the town tourism committee and can help you get horses, guides, or maps.

ⓜ Santa Lucía

The town of Santa Lucía was created in 1904 by the decree of president José Santos Zelaya in an effort to concentrate the dispersed and poorly administrated farming communities of the hillsides north of Boaco. Its well-planned and organized beginning boded well for Santa Lucía, which, a century later, remains a picturesque and enchanting mountain village in a valley ringed with green mountains.

Santa Lucía itself doesn't have hotel rooms or fancy restaurants. Nevertheless, travelers should consider a trip to Santa Lucía for three reasons: the beautiful scenery around Cerro Santo Domingo, the long rocky precipice of Peña La Brada, and the indigenous artifacts along the road. Various petroglyphs and other remnants of past cultures are untouched in the wilds around Santa Lucía, including some just 20 meters off the highway: Keep your eyes peeled. Adventurers looking for a challenge should peruse the valley of the Río Fonseca for an archeological wonder called **Las Máscaras.** Those hillsides north of Boaco also cradle the **Paso Las Lajas,** whose petroglyphs show indigenous peoples sitting with the Spanish and their dogs. These carvings were seen several times earlier in the century, but were subsequently lost and passed into the lore of the people of Boaco. Sharpen your machete; they're waiting to be rediscovered.

Two additional hikes in the Santa Lucía area include a gorgeous waterfall, called the **Salto de los Americas.** To get to the waterfall, either ask your bus driver to let you off near it as you travel between Boaco and Santa Lucía, or from Santa Lucía, hike five kilometers (one hour) back down the road south toward Boaco. Look for a *gancho* opening (a V-shaped tree branch through which you can step to avoid the barbed wire) in the wooden fence on the east (left-hand) side. Go through the fence and down the hill to the Río Fonseca. Hike up the river five minutes to a seven-meter waterfall. The pool beneath the falls is deep enough to swan dive off the top, and you can crawl to the cave behind it. There are also several families of monkeys that live in the area.

To get to **Peña La Brada,** hike up the road past the Instituto out of town for an hour along the steep path that leads to the top of the ridge. When you get to the road, walk to your right along it until you reach a little wood shack; just past the shack is a small trail that leads away from the road. Follow it through the forest and

across the fields until you reach a big open pasture with a big farmhouse (as a courtesy, you should introduce yourself before proceeding). The residents will tell you how to find the cliff from there. It's a simple matter of crossing several barbed-wire fences to get to the cliff edge, where the view from the top will thrill you. In addition to a panoramic view of Boaco, you'll be able to see all the way out to the highway and the mountains that rise on its south side.

On the direct road from the highway to Santa Lucía (not the road that leads from Boaco), keep your eyes peeled for **La Roca del Tigre,** a rock emblazoned with a petroglyph of a tiger, located practically at roadside.

For any hikes in the Santa Lucía area, Osmin is the right gentleman to ask to accompany you. He can be found in the ENITEL office, where he works—he's a fun tour guide and trip leader for expeditions into the wild hillsides.

Technically, there are no lodging establishments in Santa Lucía, but should you find yourself stuck there, the **Comedor Santa Lucía** will put you up and feed you. More good food can be found in the *comedor* in the park, which specializes in grilled meat. A direct bus leaves from Managua for Santa Lucía at 10:30 A.M. ($1.50), bypassing Boaco entirely. The same bus leaves Santa Lucía for Managua at 4 A.M. and 5 A.M.

Camoapa

A cow town of 13,000 people set in the mountains east of Boaco, Camoapa got its name from a Nahuatl phrase that can be translated as either Place of the Parrots, Place of the Dark Rocks, or Place of the Yams (how's that for precision?). Once an indigenous community ruled by the cacique Taisiwa, it was later absorbed by the Spanish settlers and incorporated under the name San Francisco de Camoapán.

Today, besides the abundant commerce in dairy products, Camoapa is best known to Nicaraguans for its production of woven straw hats. In the 1960s, a school for promoting the art of weaving was formed, and the art passed through several generations; today, there are reportedly several hundred weavers in Camoapa. The hats they are known best for are created from intricately and

PITA HATS

Pita is a thick-leaved succulent plant in the *amarilidácea* family, originally from Mexico. Its leaves, which can reach one meter in length, gather at the center of the plant around yellow flowers. In the Americas, *pita* is known by various names: *toquilla* in Ecuador, *cogollo* in Venezuela, and *jipijapa* or *pita* in Nicaragua.

The Masigue area, just north of Camoapa, produces the lion's share of *pita* in Nicaragua, and is the natural base for a mini-economy of area hatmakers. Weaving a *pita* hat is a time-consuming process that can last as long as three months if the fiber and weaving are fine. The smoothness of the fabric and the number of weaves per inch determine the quality and thus the price of a hat.

One door up the hill from Restaurante Camfel is the home of a family that works with *pita.* They can show

© RANDY WOOD

you, in addition to hats, several kinds of baskets, bags, and other products they weave by hand in their home. *Pita* artisans take up their work in a number of Camoapa neighborhoods, including Mombachito, Las Lajas, and Laguna Negra.

tightly woven strips of fibrous white *pita* and are sold all over Nicaragua's craft markets.

Camoapa's economy is largely dependent on three dairy cooperatives, the workers of which like to have a good time on the weekends when they return from their farms and ranches outside of town to party and relax. Camoapa's *fiestas patronales* begin on October 2 in honor of San Francisco de Asís, with bull riding, cattle contests, and the like. Camoapans boast that they have the toughest bulls and best horses around. Other weekends, the disco at **Ñ Atenas** is the place to be, unless you're a hat-wearing cowboy, in which case the party is at **La Asociación** (Asogacam) out by the ball field. You'll find beer, mariachi music, and the occasional brawl—just like the old days.

In Camoapa, stay at **Ñ Hotel Las Estrellas** (seven blocks east of the church's north side—six

paved blocks and one more along the dirt road— tel. 505/849-2240, 15 rooms, $7 s/$10 d without a/c, $10 s/$13 d for a/c, TV; credit cards accepted), a former auto-hotel turned honest. Smaller but closer to town along the main road, **Hotel Taisiwa** (tel. 505/849-2304, 11 rooms, $4.25 pp with shared bath, $5 pp with private bath), is named after the former cacique.

Camoapa has several good restaurants, including, again, **Atenas** (one block east of the church's south side), **Camfel** (one block west of the church's north side), a clean place run by seven women who will gladly prepare special orders like chicken salad if you get tired of steak and fried foods, and **Bosquecito** (just down the road that leads to Comalapa), a restaurant filled with potted plants and flowers. A few blocks farther west of Camfel is **Chupi,** with sandwiches, chicken, and ice cream.

Services

Locate the **ENITEL** phone office by its imposing tower planted on the premises. The **post office** is on the south side of the church. The **Miscelanea Urbina** (one block north of the park's northeast corner) is a good place to pick up snacks or supplies, especially if you're gearing up to hike Cuisaltepe.

If you bust your head climbing Cuisaltepe, check in at Camoapa's **Centro de Salud,** where a doctor is always on call, or the **Clínica San Francisco de Asís** (a half-block east and a half-block north from the Colegio San Francisco).

Getting There and Away

Buses from Managua to Camoapa depart Mayoreo Monday–Saturday, starting at 4:30 A.M. and running through 4:10 P.M. There's a reduced schedule on Sundays, but still adequate transportation.

Buses to Managua depart from the shady side of the church (whichever side that is as the day progresses), Monday–Saturday beginning at 6:25 A.M. and running through 5 P.M. The reduced Sunday schedule begins at 5:25 A.M., leaving roughly every two hours until 5 P.M. There

is a minibus that shuttles between the Empalme del Camoapa (San Francisco) and Camoapa, but it's irregular. A ride between the two points will cost you $.50.

Hiking Cuisaltepe

Unless you breezed by it on the midnight bus to El Rama, Cuisaltepe inevitably caught your eye: a massive, rocky promontory that juts out of the hillside between San Lorenzo and the entrance to Camoapa. Approaching it from the west, its silhouette resembles the tip of an upturned thumb, pointing in the direction of the highway. In Nahuatl, Cuisaltepe means Place of the Grinding Stone; it was a good source of the volcanic rock the indigenous peoples used for making long, round stone implements with which to grind corn into dough. Cuisaltepe was the home of the last cacique of the region, Taisigüe.

Hiking Cuisaltepe is no casual endeavor. More than 300 meters high, much of the south side of the rock is a series of vertical crevasses and overhangs and much of the rest of it is prohibitively steep. However, there is one summit approach—from the north side of the rock—

Cuisaltepe

© RANDY WOOD

which you can reach from Camoapa. Hike with much caution: This rock is an easy place to hurt yourself. The climb takes around six hours round-trip, but adjust that estimate according to your own climbing ability. You should have good shoes, as much of the route is loose, slippery gravel.

Your point of entrance is the road to Camoapa. Any bus traveling between Managua or Boaco and the east will take you there, leaving you at Empalme de Camoapa (also called San Francisco) along the highway. A better option is to take a direct bus to Camoapa, 10 of which leave per day from Managua (five on Sundays). From the highway, the road that leads to Camoapa climbs 25 kilometers to the city. Get off the bus before you reach Camoapa at kilometer marker 99, where a small turnoff to the west leads to the community of Barrio Cebollín with a little red bus stop at the entrance. Walk down that road and watch to your left, where you'll see a turnoff that goes south, over the hills to the base of Cuisaltepe. It would be far wiser to pick up a guide in Cebollín, though, as the access to the top of the rock is neither obvious nor easy, and it involves climbing partway up, crossing the small forest located in a notch in the hillside, then climbing the ridge to the summit. There's a crevice or two to avoid en route. You can find guides in Barrio Cebollín in the first house on the left after you pass the school (the house nearest the utility pole). Euclídes and brothers know the mountain well and climb it periodically and would make good guides for those who want to climb.

A good alternative to messing around with early-morning buses from elsewhere is to arrive the evening before your hike and spend the night in Camoapa; the next day, leave on an early-morning bus that can drop you off at Barrio Cebollín on its way out of town.

Hiking Mombacho

In the early 1900s, Nicaraguans from the Granada area transferred their homes and possessions to the Camoapa area to try growing coffee on the area's hillsides. They chose the slopes of one mountain in particular because of its rich soils and named the peak Mombacho, in memory of their Granada homeland. Camoapa's Mombacho is a forested mountain with a rocky protuberance jutting out of the top. It is home to several coffee plantations and a handful of radio towers and makes a pleasant day hike from Camoapa. Long ago, Mombacho was the site of a moonshine distillery, the products of which were sold under the name Mombachito.

Hiking the hill is significantly easier than hiking the Cuisaltepe and offers a beautiful bird's-eye view of Camoapa's open ranges. From Camoapa, the road to Mombacho can be accessed by the Salida de Sangre de Cristo (Sangre de Cristo is the name of a church found along the first part of that road). From ENITEL in the center of Camoapa, walk approximately six blocks west, crossing over a small bridge and arriving at the public school. Turn right at the school and head north until you see the Iglesia de Sangre de Cristo. Continue on that road until you reach Mombacho. The hike from town takes between three and four hours. There's a dirt road that leads up Mombacho from Camoapa to the radio towers. In Nahuatl, mombacho means steep, so be prepared.

Hiking Peña la Jarquína

At the entrance to Camoapa on the southeast side of the highway (to your right as you head toward Camoapa) is a broad, rocky cliff face at whose base nestles a hardwood forest. This is Peña la Jarquína, named after the Jarquíns, a prominent local family. It's an easy 90-minute hike from the entrance to Camoapa, around the back side of the hill to the top. Skilled climbers might find it makes a suitable technical ascent; the rock is solid and has plenty of cracks—and is almost assuredly unclimbed.

Comalapa

Over the hill from Camoapa, the even tinier village of Comalapa has remained almost completely unchanged through the passing centuries and is worth a look if you're interested in seeing what Central American villages of the 18th and 19th centuries looked like (just ignore the concrete slide in the center of the park). In 1752, Friar Morel de Santa Cruz visited Comalapa and described it as follows: "This is a town of Indians located in a land that's stony, mountainous, and fenced in by hills. Its church is of straw, reduced and indecent, lacking a vestry, but possessing an altar. . . 100 families and 484 persons both Indian and Ladino." Comalapa is largely the same 250 years later, though the church is now a quaint stone structure.

Access to Comalapa is through Camoapa. There is one bus per day, leaving Camoapa at 6:30 A.M. The same bus leaves Comalapa at 4 P.M. At other times of the day, hitch a ride with pickups traveling between the communities, or try hiking a piece of the road. The distance between Camoapa and Comalapa is more than 20 kilometers, too far to walk from end to end, but the entire road is shady and has some vantage points for good panoramic views of the surrounding hillsides.

Juigalpa

The last big settlement on the road southeast to El Rama, Juigalpa is a prosperous city of cattle ranchers and farmers whose *fiestas patronales* are considered some of the best in the country, drawing visitors from all over Nicaragua and elsewhere. Juigalpa still strongly bears the traces of its indigenous roots in elaborate statuary and other archaeological pieces still being discovered in the mountains east of town. *Juigalpan* in the languages of Aztec origin means Great City or Spawning Grounds of the Black Snails. Its first inhabitants were likely the Chontal people, who had been displaced in the Rivas area by the stronger Nicaraos. They resisted the Spanish occupation fiercely in the 16th century, rising up no fewer than 14 times to attack the installations of the colonial government.

Upon Nicaragua's independence, the land that comprised Chontales and Boaco was controlled by Granada. In 1858, the Department of Chontales was formed, of which Boaco and part of the Río San Juan remained a part. Juigalpa and the now desolate Acoyapa were the departmental heads at different times. In the 18th and 19th centuries, travelers bound for the gold mines of Santo Domingo and La Libertad crossed Lake Cocibolca, landed in Puerto Díaz, and spent a night in Juigalpa before proceeding.

SIGHTS AND ATTRACTIONS
Ⓜ Museo Arqueológico Gregorio Aguilar Barea
Juigalpa's most interesting attraction is the **Museo Arqueológico Gregorio Aguilar Barea,** an air-plane-hangar-like building housing a collection of more than a hundred examples of pre-Columbian statuary uncovered in the folds of the Amerrisque mountain range. Ranging from one meter to seven meters tall, the pieces are reminiscent of totem poles, elaborately carved in high- and low-relief, with representations of zoomorphic figures and humans (the latter often clutching knives or axes in their hands, or presenting their arms folded across their chests). The statues, thought to be 1,000 years old, were the work of the Chontal people, driven to the east side of Lake Cocibolca by the more powerful Nicaraos some 1,500 years ago.

In contrast to the indigenous cultures of the Pacific region, relatively little is known about the Chontal culture and its statues, more of which are continually being discovered in the Amerrisque range. The museum was built in 1952 by the well-loved former mayor of Juigalpa, Gregorio Aguilar Barea. It also exhibits Nicaraguan coins from across two centuries, gold figurines, original paintings by the museum's namesake, and several historical paintings and photographs. Although supposedly open 9 A.M.–noon and 2–5 P.M. Monday–Friday, the museum's hours more frequently follow the whims of the caretaker. The building has an open front, so even if the gate to the museum is locked, all the statues can be seen from the street.

Parque Palo Solo
The view from the park at the north end of town, **Parque Palo Solo,** is unforgettable and unsurpassed elsewhere in the region. To the north, the

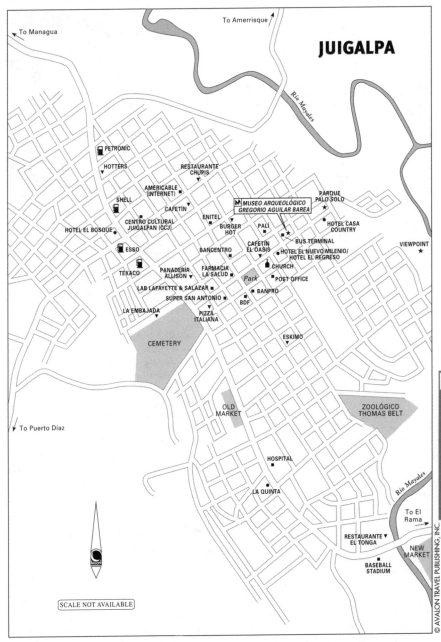

To Managua

To Amerrisque

JUIGALPA

Río Mayales

PETRONIC

HOTTERS

RESTAURANTE CHUPIS

AMERICABLE (INTERNET)

SHELL

CAFETÍN

CENTRO CULTURAL JUIGALPAN (CCJ)

HOTEL EL BOSQUE

ENITEL

BURGER HOT

PALÍ

MUSEO ARQUEOLÓGICO GREGORIO AGUILAR BAREA

PARQUE PALO SOLO

HOTEL CASA COUNTRY

BUS TERMINAL

VIEWPOINT

ESSO

BANCENTRO

CAFETÍN EL OASIS

HOTEL EL NUEVO MILENIO/ HOTEL EL REGRESO

TEXACO

PANADERÍA ALLISON

FARMACIA LA SALUD

Park

CHURCH

POST OFFICE

LAB LAFAYETTE & SALAZAR

SUPER SAN ANTONIO

BANPRO

BDF

LA EMBAJADA

PIZZA ITALIANA

CEMETERY

ESKIMO

OLD MARKET

ZOOLÓGICO THOMAS BELT

To Puerto Díaz

HOSPITAL

LA QUINTA

Río Mayales

To El Rama

RESTAURANTE EL TONGA

NEW MARKET

BASEBALL STADIUM

MOON

SCALE NOT AVAILABLE

Boaco

© AVALON TRAVEL PUBLISHING, INC.

the bull ring in Juigalpa

Amerrisque range sits at the far end of several kilometers of broad tropical savanna. The park is elevated above the surrounding streets, located at the very edge of the hill Juigalpa was built on, and giving the impression of looking over the bulwark of a fortress. The fortress feeling isn't entirely accidental: Juigalpa was built at the top of the hill to offer it some means of defense from the Miskito and Zambo peoples who once raided it from those same mountains 200 years ago. The park was built by Mayor Aguilar Barea in the 1960s and named after the one tall tree that dominated its center. The tree has since been replaced by a fountain adorned with images of the mainstays of the Chontales economy: corn and cattle. A restaurant at the edge of the park serves fancy lunches and dinners.

Juigalpa's other park, in the center of town, is an orderly and clean place, whose statue of a boy shining shoes is unique in Nicaragua. Made by a former mayor who spent his early years earning money as a shoe-shine boy, the statue bears the inscription: "Hard work dignifies a man." It very much captures the spirit of this town.

The Zoo

Juigalpa is well known among Nicaraguans for its zoo, the **Zoológico Thomas Belt** (seven blocks south of the church's southwest corner, open 8 A.M.–6 P.M. daily, entrance fee is $.25), named for the British mining engineer and naturalist who surveyed parts of Santo Domingo, Chontales between 1868 and 1872. Like most zoos in developing countries, however, the Thomas Belt is a depressing collection of large animals—monkeys, snakes, even a few African species—in small cages. From the highway, follow the signs for the Profamilia clinic and then continue another block past Profamilia.

Juigalpa Fiestas Patronales

Juigalpa's *fiestas patronales*, August 11–18, attract visitors from the entire nation and even Honduras and Costa Rica. Much of the festivities takes place on the north side of town, in Juigalpa's Plaza de Toros, but you'll find parties all over. It's a rowdy cowboy festival of bull riding, rodeo competitions, and horseback games. In one of these, called the *carrera de cinta,* mounted riders gallop underneath a wire from which is suspended a small ring. If a rider successfully puts a pencil through the ring at full gallop, he can present it—and a kiss—to the woman of his choice from among the contestants vying to be queen of the festival. The woman who receives the most rings is crowned the queen.

During the rest of the year, you can test your merit as a cowboy on Nicaragua's only mechanical bull at **La Quinta** for $1.50. It's not always available for public use, so you should stop in and ask while you have a meal.

NIGHTLIFE AND ENTERTAINMENT

The best disco in town is **La Quinta** (out on the highway, entrance $1 most nights, $1.75 Saturday night). On weekend nights—and particularly Saturdays—the dance floor tends to collect the young people of the city. Second best is **Hotters** (a half-block south of the Petronic station along the highway), which, with its ripped off "Hooters" logo, picks up the slack on Sunday night and appeals to the cowboy crowd more so than La Quinta. Toward the center of town, **Casa Bravo Club** is an upscale pool hall behind tinted glass and in the comfort of an air-conditioned hall. The baseball field is located down by the river at the south end of town in Barrio Paimuca, and games are played Sundays.

ACCOMMODATIONS

In a city lacking auto-hotels, Juigalpans looking for romance employ the town's plethora of *hospedajes*. The city is littered with inexpensive accommodations, but the trouble is that many of those rooms are intended to be occupied for one hour at a time. Two otherwise obvious places to the west of the park, Hospedaje Angelita and Hospedaje Central, fall into that category and should be avoided.

Stay to the east (rear) side of the church instead. **Hotel El Regreso** (the one-story establishment, tel. 505/812-2068, $3.50 s, $5.75 d with shared bath) has 14 clean rooms. Immediately next door, **Hotel El Nuevo Milenio** ($3.50 s with shared bath, $7 s with private bath, $10 d with

tel. 505/812-0646) has 16 rooms. For a bit more coin, **Hotel Casa Country** (located a block from the Parque Palo Solo at the north end of town, $10.75 d without a/c, $14.25 d with a/c; all rooms have cable TV and private bath) has five luxury rooms on the second story of a gorgeous colonial-style house. The views are easily worth the extra money (across the street is the sometimes-functioning **La Casita Country,** a dining establishment related to the hotel).

La Quinta, farther east along the highway (almost directly across from the hospital) also has 38 rooms ($10 d with fan, $14 with a/c).

FOOD

Juigalpa has a variety of food—often at reasonable prices—naturally, with massive quantities of beef and dairy on the menu. Case in point: **La Embajada** (difficult to find, but everyone knows it, just ask around). The only thing on the menu at this hole in the wall is meat, ordered by the pound (about $4.50). The "Meat Lady" has a secret marinade recipe she learned from her grandmother and is currently passing down to her granddaughter. It's served with salty *cuajada* cheese and tortillas. Daniel Ortega has been known to make an appearance here, and it is also frequented by the big wigs of Chontales.

La Cazuelita (three blocks east and two north from the Esso) is home to a remarkable barbecue-chicken sandwich (less than $3 with fries). This newly remodeled, air-conditioned restaurant is popular with Peace Corps Volunteers and well-off Juigalpans for its excellent Nicaraguan food. The *surtido* ($11, serves 2–3) is a great choice if you'd like to sample the typical meats of Nicaragua.

Right across from the cathedral is **7/24 Casa de Queso,** offering cheeseburgers and Nica-China food. There are a few more places in and near the park, and for good, fresh bread and pastries, stop by **Panadería Allison** (open 5 A.M.–7 P.M. daily). They have a refrigerator full of cold milk to wash it all down.

On the highway in front of the Esso station, **Restaurante Tacho** has great chicken and steak at moderate prices ($2–3.50) in a pleasant atmosphere. Roving bands of mariachis frequent the

BOACO

place, which has a mostly male crowd. For more upscale dining, try **Restaurante La Tonga,** with plates from $5 and up, and, of course, Juigalpa's favorite, **La Quinta,** with a juicy *churrasco.* There's also a new Italian restaurant located two blocks east of the Esso, owned by an Italian.

SERVICES

For Internet, check the new place with a/c behind the Texaco station, less than $2 an hour; also, the local cable company, **Americable,** has machines for under $4 an hour (open 8 A.M.–7 P.M. Mon.–Fri.). The **Centro Cultural Juigalpan** (CCJ, located near the highway a block from the Esso station, open 8 A.M.–8 P.M. Mon.–Sat.) is a bit cheaper, with seven machines for $1.75 per hour.

The only ATM in town is located off of the central park outside the BANPRO. The **post office** is located around the corner from the church, **ENITEL** is four blocks north of the park, open 8 A.M.–noon and 1:30–5:30 P.M. Monday–Saturday, closed Sundays.

There are several pharmacies in town. One of the better ones is **Farmacia La Salud** (at the northwest corner of the park, tel. 505/812-0932). **Hospital La Asunción** (on the southeast side of town along the highway) doesn't have very good facilities by international standards. A better option for travelers is the **Lab Lafayette & Salazar** (two blocks west of the park, tel. 505/812-2292), a private clinic and doctor's office.

The old movie theater is now a Pali grocery store, but Supermercado San Antonio has a better selection and is locally owned.

GETTING THERE AND AWAY

With the exception of express microbuses to Managua, which depart from the north or east side of the church at 6 A.M. and one at 1:40 P.M. (2.5 hours), all buses depart Juigalpa from the cramped bus terminal in the market, leaving hourly for El Rama, from 4:30 A.M.–1:30 P.M. and every half-hour to Managua, from 4 A.M.–5 P.M. You'll also find daily service to Nueva Guinea until 3:20 P.M., to Boaco (via Camoapa and Comalapa), and other local destinations.

NEAR JUIGALPA

Balneario el Salto

Juigalpa's favorite swimming hole is located an easy two kilometers out of town on the highway to Managua. Look for the big blue sign on the northeast side of the highway; the falls are located a scant 100 meters from the highway. El Salto is formed by a concrete dam that causes water to pool up in a natural reservoir. In the dry season, there's no waterfall at all, though the swimming hole remains quite deep. In the rainy season, the water from the Río Mayales tumbles first over the concrete dam and then through a gorge of enormous boulders carved into fantastic shapes by the flowing water. The near shore gets littered with the remains of old picnics after major holidays (like Semana Santa, when the place is packed), but the far shore is tree-lined and grassy. Consider swimming across to the far side and watching the local kids turn somersaults off the wooden-plank diving boards. There is supposedly a $1 fee to get in, but the locals have skirted the fee for so long by entering downstream and walking up the streambed that, with the exception of Semana Santa, no one seems to try to charge any more.

Puerto Díaz

It's a short and uncomfortable ride from Juigalpa down to the village of Puerto Díaz, a sleepy lakeside town of fishing families that pretty much live off what they catch. Puerto Díaz doesn't have any facilities for travelers but is worth a day trip on a lazy Saturday to see how the "far" side of the lake (i.e., the world across the lake from Granada) lives. Buses leave from Juigalpa three times a day at 5 A.M., 2 P.M., and 5 P.M. From the bus terminal, they cross the highway at the Esso station before working their way slowly down to the shoreline.

Cuapa and El Monolito de Cuapa

Tiny, isolated, lonely Cuapa, once just another anonymous farming town in the foothills of the Amerrisque mountain range, gained an awful sort of notoriety during the 1980s, when it came to represent the worst of what the Contra war had become.

In 1985, Contras attacked and took control of

Balneario el Salto

Cuapa, holding it for several hours. They captured the Sandinista mayor Hollman Martínez but later released him when the townspeople pleaded for his life. Twelve other Sandinista activists, sent from the capital to work in Cuapa, weren't so fortunate: The Contras marched them out of town and executed them at the roadside. When the Sandinista military got wind that Contras occupied the town of Cuapa, they dispatched a truckload of 40 soldiers to defend the town. Contras ambushed the vehicle along the road to Cuapa, killing nearly all of them. A small roadside monument bearing the Sandinista flag commemorates both the civil servants and the soldiers killed during the war.

Cuapa is also famous among devout Catholics. In late 1980 and early 1981, the Virgin Mary appeared several times—bathed in radiant light and dressed in pure white—to local farmer Bernardo Martínez. She told Martínez she had a message for the world and for Nicaragua: "Don't preach the kingdom of God unless you are building it on earth. The world is threatened by great danger." She later asked for prayers for unbelievers and for peace on earth. Devout Catholics were overjoyed at the appearance of the Virgin,

but even that moment became rapidly politicized in the toxic climate of the 1980s. Some claimed her message was a coded recrimination of the Sandinista government, and the Sandinistas responded by clamping down on all press coverage of miracles not previously accepted by the Vatican. An elaborate and well-maintained statue and sign greet you at the entrance to Cuapa with *Bienvenido a la Tierra de María* (Welcome to Mary's Land). Believers from all over eastern Nicaragua flock to Cuapa on May 8, the anniversary of the day the Virgin first appeared.

El Monolito de Cuapa (the Cuapa Monolith) is a 75-meter-high chunk of granite that projects like a giant needle out of a field, as though it dropped from the sky and pierced the ground; it's first visible on the bus ride to Cuapa.

Climbing El Monolito isn't easy, but it isn't impossible either. It's a hike, not a technical rock-climb. The locals in Cuapa know all the trails that lead there, and any young *campesino* will be glad to show you the way to the top to see the cross. From the town of Cuapa, it's a 2.5-hour hike to the top, including several extremely steep sections. Hike with good shoes; locals recommend not climbing it on particularly windy days. Ask around for

Boaco

Nicolas, an English-speaking resident of Cuapa (originally from Bluefields), who can be a guide. He runs a tire repair shop next to Parque Zapera.

Whether you've come to see the shrine to Mary or to climb the monolith, Cuapa isn't a bad place to spend the night. One option for the climb is to arrive in the evening, spend the night at Cuapa, and set off to climb the monolith the following morning. You can find accommodations and meals at Restaurante Hospedaje La Maravilla, with rooms in the $1.50–3.50 range. The menu is traditional Nicaraguan food. The hotel fills up the week of June 19–27, when Cuapa celebrates its patron saint, San José.

Six buses leave Juigalpa for Cuapa every day, starting at 6 A.M. and the last departing at 6 P.M. Buses from Cuapa to Juigalpa leave from the town center every day, 6 A.M.–4:30 P.M.

Serranía Amerrisque

A powerful backdrop to the city, the Amerrisque mountain range forms a rocky backbone to the history of the city. Most of the archaeological pieces in the Juigalpa museum were unearthed in the Amerrisques, and countless other sites have yet to be discovered and explored. Although the area is undeveloped for tourists, the rocky peaks make a tempting hike and the locals claim the east side of the range contains several caves.

Your starting point is the road called the Camino de la Vaticana, built by Rome and Holland in the late 1990s. It will lead you nine kilometers east toward the range and the tiny farming community of Piedra Grande. From there, you can strike into the hills to explore. You can try hitching a ride out there to trim down the flat, boring part of the hike, but it won't be easy, as traffic along the road is sparse at best. There are few communities along its length. Consider hiring a pickup truck in town; a group of five travelers offering $15–20 might be able to convince someone to drive them out there. Try to swing a deal for the ride back while you're at it.

Daniel Molina can serve as a guide (tel. 505/812-2940). He is a young man who speaks English and can help you arrange a trip out to the mountains, where he'll help you find a local guide to show you the trails.

Thermal Vents at Agua Caliente

When they're hot they're hot, but when they're

Amerrisque mountains

© RANDY WOOD

THE ROAD TO EL RAMA

During the 1980s, the highway from San Benito (Managua) to Rama, known as the Rama Highway, was a hotly contested military prize. At stake was control of the port at Rama, through which Managua received much of its oil and supplies from the Baltic states and the Soviet Union. The town of La Gateada (The Crawl), perched on a steep hillside on the Rama Highway, was the site of several major battles. After five years of failed attempts, the Contras finally succeeded in capturing the highway in 1987. In a massive offensive, 2,500 Contras captured four towns, including Santo Tomás and San Pedro de Lóvago. In all four, they burned down Sandinista government buildings, the phone office, the courts, fuel depots, and military garrisons. The Contras also demolished five bridges, all but the crown jewel—the bridge at Muelle de los Bueyes—which, standing 150 meters high

over the Río Mico, was easily the most irreplaceable bridge in the nation. The Sandinista military successfully defended the bridge with 400 troops, and it stands today, still one of the highest bridges in Nicaragua.

But by 2000, old age and neglect had all but destroyed the vital highway, skewering the entire length of its thin veneer of asphalt with axle-breaking holes. The legendarily uncomfortable bus trip between Managua and Rama was a twelve-hour endurance test, where battered vehicles lurched along in first gear, swerving madly to avoid the worst of the craters. So when the Alemán administration undertook its reparation, the public was overjoyed. The new road is pleasant to drive on and the trip to Rama is much shortened, but the scandals of corruption and crony capitalism that rocked the project will live on in infamy.

not they're not—a trip out to the hot springs at Agua Caliente is a gamble because their activity is cyclical. On the down side of the cycle, they're nothing more than a trickle of hot water seeping out of the side of the creek bed. When they're active, however, expect to see torrents of bubbles gushing out of the creek bed in water too hot to touch. While eastern Nicaragua lacks the volcanoes of the Pacific horizon, it too was formed volcanically and the hot springs are evidence that under the surface, even quiet old Chontales is bubbling and tectonically active.

To get there, take the Camino de la Vaticana as though you were going to the Amerrisque mountains, but take the first major left-hand turn instead; Aguas Calientes is 4.8 kilometers down the road. You'll know you've reached the site when you get to a relatively new school building followed immediately by a streambed. The hot

springs are located about 100 meters upstream from where the road crosses the stream.

La Libertad and Santo Domingo

These two pueblos have been the site of small-scale gold mining for well over a hundred years. British mining engineer Thomas Belt was surveying in the Santo Domingo area when he wrote his famous book, *A Naturalist in Nicaragua,* in 1874. The mines were, until recently, run by a Canadian organization that ceased activities around 2000. The curious may be interested in poking around either town, both of which, though run-down and slightly decrepit, still very distinctly bear the traces of a gold-rush boom-town atmosphere. La Libertad is the birthplace of former president Daniel Ortega as well as Nicaragua's outspoken and politicized Catholic archbishop Miguel Obando y Bravo.

Boaco

Nueva Guinea

Nueva Guinea was founded as part of U.S. President John F. Kennedy's Alliance for Progress, a program meant to defuse demands for land reform across Latin America in the wake of the Cuban revolution and the postcolonial struggles in the rest of the world. Original settlers were given one *manzana* of land (about one hectare) in the urban center, and 60 in the countryside. The same program was applied to help victims of natural disasters—victims of both the Managua earthquake of 1972 and the eruption of Cerro Negro near León in 1973 were shipped out to Nueva Guinea. In the 1980s, the area was a hot spot of Contra activity under the command of Edén Pastora's group, ARDE, based across the Costa Rica border.

Technically, Nueva Guinea is part of the RAAS (Región Autónoma Atlántica del Sur or the Southern Atlantic Autonomous Region), but it is more easily accessed from the Rama Highway and Juigalpa than Bluefields and the Río Escondido. A full 293 kilometers southeast of Managua, Nueva Guinea lies in the tropical, humid, rolling lowlands that stretch toward the Caribbean. It's one of the rainiest corners of Nicaragua, receiving an average of 8,000 millimeters (yes, that's eight meters) of rainfall each year, but that varies from town to town, based on the forest cover of the area. In terms of population, it is the second largest municipality in Nicaragua, with a de facto population of 120,000 people, many of whom technically live in the municipality of Bluefields but whose transport and public services come from Nueva Guinea.

In the 1960s, Nueva Guinea was a rich, dense, tropical rainforest with a wide variety of animal life, but since then, due to poor public policy, misguided development projects, and inadequate agricultural practices, much of the territory has been transformed into barren, useless pasture. Forested areas include the land that borders the Reserva Indio-Maíz and the Reserva Natural Punta Gorda. Even that land is in the process of being slowly and illegally colonized and exploited, and poor farmers in desperate need of land overwhelm the capacity of the Nicaraguan government to prevent their homesteading.

These days, farmers in the area of Nueva Guinea live in some 140 neighborhoods and dedicate their labor to the production of basic grains—corn, beans, and rice—as well as ginger. Nueva Guinea is a wild place, a town that could easily have been part of the western United States, with horses parked outside of bars and people walking their pigs or herding cattle down main street. The town of Nueva Guinea has few facilities that lend themselves to travelers, but the truly adventurous or curious may appreciate visiting a place so out of the way and so full of history and emotion.

ACCOMMODATIONS

There are three options in Nueva Guinea. **Hotel Nueva Guinea** (on the main drag, 285-0090, $10–25 s), has a variety of rooms, some with a/c, cable, and bath, and others only offering the basics. Newer, quiet **Hotel Miraflores** (300 meters south of URACCAN, 505/285-0039, $10 s) has good mattresses. Backpackers tend to settle into **Las 24 Horas Hospedaje** (municipal market 1.5 blocks north, across from the police station, $2.50 s).

FOOD

Llamas del Bosque (next to the Esso station) serves the best meal in town for about $5. Sit poolside at **Ranchón Kristofer** (three blocks north of the park) or join the crowd on the dance floor. **Comedoría Dalili** (across from the mayor's office) is the least expensive *comedor* in town: Spend less than $1 for a meal.

SIGHTS AND ATTRACTIONS

For the extreme wilderness adventurer, Nueva Guinea is your base for exploration of two of Nicaragua's most pristine nature reserves— **Punta Gorda** and **Indio Maíz**. Retrace the steps of colonial Spanish Captains, Calero and Machuca, who sought the best route to the

Caribbean coast from the west through the small communities of Puerto Prinicipe, Atlanta, and others, concluding in the coastal community of Punta Gorda. Arrange for a guide through the mayor's office. Less demanding is the one hour hike to the gorgeous falls at **Salto Esperanza:** Take the bus to the community of Esperanza and ask around.

At **Finca La Esperanzita,** you can glimpse a good organic agriculture project where small farmers are growing cacao, vanilla, pepper, and several species of tropical hardwoods. They'll gladly provide you with a tour of the facilities, including a coffee-, cacao-, and cinnamon-processing plant run by World Relief one block south and one block east of the hospital.

GETTING THERE AND AWAY

Buses leave for Nueva Guinea from Managua's Mayoreo terminal approximately every hour (eight-hour trip) until 10 A.M.

Boaco

The Atlantic Coast

[Nicaragua's] Atlantic Coast is perhaps best understood if one imagines it as a Caribbean island that, by some geological catastrophe, drifted toward Central America and found itself part of a foreign nation.

Stephen Kinzer

More than a getaway to the white-sand, coconut palm beaches traditional to the Caribbean, Nicaragua's Atlantic coast is a swim through a cultural ocean unlike any other in the world, a fascinating conglomeration of history in the very blood, skin, and language of the people. The vast majority of Nicaragua's 450 kilometers of Atlantic coastline are unexplored, undeveloped, and unapproachable. Edward Marriot calls it "Nicaragua's jungle coast. Not the 'Caribbean'— despite cartographers' insistences—but, deliberately, the 'Atlantic.' No one here spoke of this ocean, with its broken, unlovely shoreline, as the Caribbean: that would have been too misleading,

The Atlantic Coast 279

Must-Sees

Look for **M** to find the sights and activities you can't miss and **N** for the best dining and lodging.

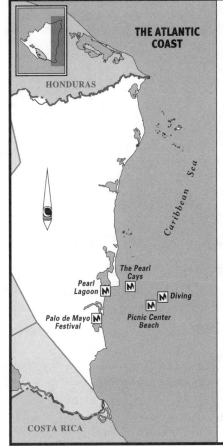

THE ATLANTIC COAST

HONDURAS

Caribbean Sea

The Pearl Cays

Pearl Lagoon

Diving

Picnic Center Beach

Palo de Mayo Festival

COSTA RICA

© JOSHUA BERMAN

An old relic protects the municipal offices in "downtown" Pearl Lagoon.

M Palo de Mayo Festival: Sensual and rhythmic, Bluefield's joyous Maypole celebration is one of the flashiest shows in the country (page 291).

M Pearl Lagoon: The quiet lanes of this waterside village beg to be explored. Follow them all the way out to the beach (page 297).

N The Pearl Cays: No sounds here but the creak of your swinging hammock and the waves lapping on the shoreline (page 300).

M Picnic Center Beach: This Corn Island classic is an uninterrupted crescent of white-sand hedonism; a wonderful beach, a bed, and great food await (page 302).

M Diving: Snorkel, swim, or scuba to visit the reefs and marine life just offshore Little Corn Island (page 306).

THE ATLANTIC COAST

HONDURAS

Río Coco (Wangki)

SEE DETAIL

Santa Fé
El Carmen
San Jerónimo
La Tronquera
Wisconsin
Wawa
Slilmalila
Awalka Tingni
Suahura
Ulang
Cabo Viejo
Laguna Bismuna
Isla Sunbeam
Cabo Gracias a Dios
Barra de Tukrung

To Siuna and Managua
Susun
Wasminona
Sahsa
Sumu Bila
Kukalaya
Saklin
Tungla
Auas Tingni
Wiwas
Sangni Laya
Santa Marta
Auya Pihni
Siksikwas
Mani Watla
Akawas
Likus
Slim
Leimus
Nina Yari
Tuara
Pahra
Laguna Li–Dakura
Barra Sandy Bay
Laguna Dakura
Dakura
Auastara
Miskitos Cays

El Empalme
Bambana
Klingna
Yulú
Tuapí
Krukira
Laguna Pahra
Tingni Tara
Kukalaya

Alamikamba
Layasiksa
Bambana
Laguna Karatá
Lamlaya
Barra de Sahnawala
Puerto Cabezas (Bilwi)

Prinzapolka
San Francisco
Makantaca
Walpasiksa
Laguna Wouhnta
Wouhnta

Barrera
Río Grande de Matagalpa
Prinzapolka
Prinzapolka

HONDURAS
Lakun Tara
Bilwaskarma
Río Coco (Wangki)
Kiwas Tara
Living Creek
Kisalaya
Waspam
Saklin
Tuskru Sirpe
Kum
Anris
Kampa
Boom
Kurmog
Twimaya
Kasau Wita
Siilmasia
Kiahara
Yulnata
Ullang
Iban Tara
Kuyu Tingni
Bismuna Tara

Bratara
Río Kurinwas
Pauta Dimon
Karawala
Kara
Sandy Bay Sirpe
Guerrero Cays
Barra de Río Grande
Tyara Cays
Río Wawasang

Orinoco
Tasbapauni
King Pequeño Cays
Caribbean Sea
La Fe
Bahía de Perlas
Marshall Point
Set Net
Laguna Grande

To Rama
Río Escondido
San Antonio
Bluefields
Kukra Hill
Laguna Smokey Lane
Ⓜ PEARL LAGOON
Ⓜ THE PEARL CAYS

Ⓜ PALO DE MAYO FESTIVAL
El Bluff
Isla del Venado
Ⓜ DIVING
Little Corn Island
Guano Cay
Ⓜ PICNIC CENTER BEACH
Corn Island
Rama Cay
Pigeon Cay
Río Kukra
French Man Cay
Monkey Point

0   30 mi
0   30 km

© AVALON TRAVEL PUBLISHING, INC.

too obvious a misrepresentation. No, this was the Atlantic coast, with its mangrove swamps and alligators, hurricanes and stiff westers that washed up bales of high-grade cocaine, shrink-wrapped for export."

The Atlantic coast is languid and lazy, but it's got an edge, too, and just a shadow of danger. In its entirety, Nicaragua's Caribbean will absorb you. Walking the noisy streets of Bluefields, riding a *panga* up a twisting, jungle river, or sunning yourself on Corn Island, you may start to wonder if the rest of Nicaragua even exists. Welcome to La Costa, where residents have lived this isolation for their entire history. Fill your belly with fresh fish and rum, your ears with reggae and country music, and your journal with a new collection of rich adventures.

PLANNING YOUR TIME

If you lay in a good stack of books, a bottle or two, and a jug of sunscreen, you could spend weeks on Nicaragua's Caribbean coast, exploring the islands, reefs, bays, and broad pine savannahs along the coastline. More realistically, your desire to languish on these sandy shores will outlast your funds (everything except seafood is more expensive here; expect to pay 2–3 times more than you would on the Pacific side for lodging, beef, beer, and soft drinks). If you're traveling overland from Managua, schedule in one day for the trip and another to recover in Bluefields. Otherwise, take an afternoon flight to Bluefields and spend the rest of the day poking around the city. Day trips and overnights beckon to you from all directions at that point: Start with an overnight in Pearl Lagoon followed by a day trip out to the desolate archipelago of the Pearl Cays, or hire a *panga* to Rama Cay. Corn Island is worth a night or two unless you really crave remoteness, in which case you should beeline to Little Corn, the more rustic of the pair, where 2–4 days will provide ample opportunity to dive and explore the reefs, or melt your worries away on the beach.

Stretch your Atlantic coast adventure into a week by jetting up to Bilwi and Waspan, or toss your passport and shoes into the surf, sell your belongings back home, and spend the rest of your life here. Hey—it's happened.

When to Come

The Atlantic coast receives between 3,000 and 6,000 millimeters of rain annually (with the higher levels falling in southern RAAS), making it among the wettest places in the world. The rainy season is punctuated by hurricanes in September and October, and can extend well into December, sometimes longer. The end of December is marked by cool, "Christmas" winds. Most visitors come during the period between late January and April when things are generally dry, sunny, and ideal. The biggest crowds arrive for Christmas, Semana Santa, and during various regional fiestas, when making reservations is a good idea.

Safety Issues

Nicaragua's drug trade is becoming an increasing problem in some areas of the country, particularly on the Atlantic coast and to a lesser degree, Managua. South American drug runners ply the islands and cays of the Caribbean, where they stash fuel supplies and make deals. When traveling in these areas don't let the undercurrent of illicit activity make you paranoid, but do stay alert. While Little Corn Island still offers lots of undisturbed beach time, a spate of robberies in early 2005 means you can't throw caution to the wind. As anywhere else, travel in groups, be aware of your surroundings, and listen to the locals' warnings. Even in paradise you've got to watch your back. And under no circumstances should you agree to transport wrapped packages for strangers, much less make a purchase. Be aware of "fishermen" driving particularly luxurious boats ("catch any white lobster today, amigo?"). Foreigners caught with narcotics can anticipate a long and uncomfortable stay in one of Nicaragua's prisons.

HISTORY

The Atlantic coast of Nicaragua was originally populated primarily by the native Miskito, Mayangna (Sumu), and Rama people, who settled along the rivers and coastline and lived on fishing and small-scale agriculture. Columbus described the coast when he cruised by in 1502, but throughout the 16th century, its reputation for being totally inhospitable—unbearably rainy, riven with insect-drenched jungles, and home to aggressive

YATAMA AND THE STRUGGLE FOR INDIGENOUS SELF-DETERMINATION

Fraught with frequent reversals and setbacks, the struggle of Nicaragua's indigenous people for human rights, electoral privileges, and autonomy has never been easy. The Somoza government was popular in the Atlantic coast primarily because Anastasio and his sons largely ignored non-Spanish speaking Nicaragua. The Miskito people of Puerto Cabezas fondly recall the days when Tacho would fly into the northeast for a visit, accompanied by tons of fresh meat he would distribute. To this day, Tacho is popularly associated with summer barbecues and relative isolation. The Sandinistas, however, paid quite a bit of attention to the Atlantic coast.

The FSLN came to power just when a sense of unity and independence was growing among the Miskito people. The new government gave the native peoples a unique opportunity to press for their own interests and historic demands. The Sandinistas moved quickly to attempt to incorporate the indigenous movement into their own organizational structure, but soon learned the Miskito people were not even remotely interested in being a part of any group led from Managua. The indigenous peoples of the Atlantic coast instead organized themselves into the political group Misurasata and renewed their fight for self-determination.

The Sandinistas blundered badly in their early years on the Atlantic coast. Attempts to break up indigenous patterns of life and form state-sponsored cooperatives, mandates on which crops were to be planted and for how much they would be sold,

and expropriations of foreign-owned companies alienated the indigenous peoples of the Atlantic coast from the start.

The Sandinistas met the growing resistance with violence and repression. Labor strikes and other organized disruptions led to a massive increase in government military presence, and, in 1981, more than 30 Miskito leaders were rounded up and arrested on the grounds that they were inciting the indigenous peoples to rise up against the Nicaraguan state. Whether the charges were true or not, the arrests cemented the Miskito's mistrust of the new government into hatred and many communities packed up and moved across the Río Coco to Honduras, where the Contras tried to win them over. The rancor was mutual: The Sandinista government broke ties with Misurasata, forcefully relocated the remaining Miskito villages to refugee camps outside of Puerto Cabezas, and burned the old villages to make sure roving bands of Contras couldn't make use of them.

Against insurmountable odds, Misurasata leaders, like the controversial Brooklyn Rivera, hoped to convert the entire Atlantic region into an autonomous, self-governing reserve for indigenous peoples. Sandinista minister of state Tomás Borge offered them instead a few concessions that, when accepted, eventually helped to restabilize the region: a limited form of autonomy and self-policing and the chance to return to their ancient homelands. In 1987, after two and a half years of consulting with the Atlantic coast communities, the

and warring Native American tribes—kept settlers away.

Spanish friars Esteban Verdelete and Cristóbal Martíez represented Spain's first two exploratory forays into the coast. While attempting to Christianize the Mayangna and Tawaka (a subtribe) along the Río Coco and the Miskito (Guanae) peoples living in the Caratasca and Wani (Bismuna) lagoons, respectively, both missionaries were killed, and Spain subsequently lost interest in the Caribbean coast. That made it attractive to English and Dutch pirates, who haunted the labyrinthine bays and channels and preyed on Spanish ships traveling to and

from the European mainland. One of these was the Dutch pirate Abraham Blauveldt in the 1630s, whose name in English, Bluefields, came to represent the bay and later the coastal city.

In the 1700s, the English organized the Atlantic coast into a protectorate, giving the British Crown its first "legal" colonial presence along the Caribbean coast. The protectorate established "Miskito Kings" whom the British educated and maintained in power. Under the pretext of protecting the rights of indigenous peoples, England armed the Miskito and Sambo people (the offspring of indigenous people and African slaves fol-

government went a step further in reaching out to the indigenous peoples of the coast: They signed into law an autonomy statute.

The statute reshaped the Atlantic coast like nothing else had since the days of the British. It guaranteed self-rule and first-class citizenship for all minority groups on the Atlantic coast without sacrificing their cultural roots or identities. The statute permitted them to use their own languages, common land, and have a say in the development of the Atlantic coast's natural resources. The statute called for two 45-member coastal governments to be formed, one each for the northern and southern regions, responsible for governing trade, the distribution of goods, and the administration of health and education. The statute's one weakness was its flexibility, which opened the door for internecine feuds and leadership rivalries among the Atlantic peoples.

The Miskitos, who eventually found their way into the ranks of the Contras during the 1980s, organized themselves into a group called Yatama (Yapti Tasba Masraka Nanih Aslatakanka, or Sons of the Mother Earth). With the advent of the Chamorro government, the Yatama Contras generally disbanded and turned in some of their weapons in exchange for land to farm. Yatama made the conversion from armed movement to political party. Chamorro's effort to stabilize the region, plus her government's respect for the newly created Autonomous Regions earned her the respect of the indigenous peoples.

In contrast, the government of Arnoldo Alemán has apparently tried to set the indigenous move-

ment back a hundred years, causing the entire political climate in Puerto Cabezas and the Atlantic to become more tense as a result. Not lost on the indigenous peoples of the Atlantic coast is the auspicious fact that Alemán is of the same political party as Zelaya, who integrated the Atlantic coast at gunpoint a century ago. The now infamous "Pact," in which the Sandinista and Liberal parties essentially divided the government between themselves, imposed election criteria that makes it nearly impossible for small or new parties to get a foothold in the elections.

During the departmental elections of 2000, violence erupted when Yatama was completely excluded from appearing on the ballot or taking part in the elections. Representatives of Yatama vowed that unless they were permitted to participate in the municipal elections, there would be no elections. The military was sent to Puerto Cabezas and bullets flew in armed confrontations with protesters. Several people were killed. During the elections, there was significant Miskito abstention, resulting in the election of a Sandinista mayor.

Outspoken supporters of Yatama accused Alemán of trying to politically eradicate the indigenous community, leaving the Miskito, Mayangna, and Rama peoples to continued poverty and exploitation. Since many of the raw materials Nicaragua exports (such as wood, fish, and gold) are located in areas where the indigenous population has some claim to the land, the threat of political extinction is a real one. The struggle continues.

---

lowing a shipwrecked slave ship in the 1600s), and encouraged them to raid the lands of nearby tribes. They spirited away prisoners of war to Jamaican sugar plantations where they were indentured. But the locals, emboldened with British fire arms, also made aggressive and successful forays into the Spanish territories of Nicaragua, reaching as far inland as Nueva Segovia and Chontales. Sparring between England and Spain didn't conclude until 1790, when nations drew up a peace accord that created a Miskito Reserve between the Ulang River and Punta Gorda.

German Moravian missionaries integrated with

the communities beginning in the early 1800s and are responsible for the coast's largely protestant population today. Their clean, simple churches are characteristic of the Atlantic coast. When the British departed in 1860, the void they left behind was filled by big businesses from the United States, which established timber and banana company camps all along the Atlantic coast. Bluefields became a thriving commercial center with a brass band, small industry, an English-language daily newspaper, and regular steamship connections to New Orleans, Baltimore, Philadelphia, and New York.

Such was the state of Bluefields and the Atlantic coast when President José Santos Zelaya ordered its military occupation in 1894. Zelaya's most trusted general, Rigoberto Cabezas, carried out the orders: His troops sailed down the Río Escondido in February, deposed the Miskito government, and officially united Nicaragua from Atlantic to Pacific for the first time. But "integrating" the Atlantic coast was more a show of strength than an effort to include the Atlantic in Nicaragua's more populous and powerful Spanish-influenced regions. The Managua government showed little respect for Miskito customs and used taxes collected there to strengthen the capital, not the Atlantic coast, in spite of promises. They declared Spanish the official language and granted to foreign companies lumber concessions that extended deep into tribal territories.

As the inland mineral deposits were depleted and the soils of the banana plantations were impoverished, the foreign companies began to withdraw from Bluefields and the Atlantic coast, and Sandino and his anti-imperialist troops brutally attacked those tempted to linger. In the aftermath and right up to the present, the Atlantic coast has decayed into a state of corruption, financial mismanagement, and ruin.

The 1980s

Costeños were decidedly uninterested in their supposed "liberation" in 1979. Somoza had largely left the Atlantic coast to its own devices and Costeños generally viewed the goings-on in Managua as news from a foreign country. And the Moravian church's teaching that "the kingdom of God is pure and the kingdom of politics is profane" also contributed to the Atlantic coast's apolitical tendencies. What followed was arguably one of the Sandinista regime's greatest misjudgments and internationally condemned disgraces.

The revolution collided with a growing sense of Native American autonomy worldwide, which included Nicaragua's Atlantic coast. Miskito and Creole leaders up and down the coast formed a political group called MISURASATA, a concatenation of the words Miskito, Sumu, Rama, Sandinista, and the Miskito word for together. The group's original intent was to work with the new government in Managua, but it found itself instead at odds with the Sandinistas and subsequently disputed their authority to rule the Atlantic coast.

In 1981, Sandinista authorities, pushed to their breaking point by indigenous resistance in the Atlantic and Miskito support for the Contras— especially along the Río Coco—ordered the forced relocation of entire Miskito communities. They burned the empty villages, machine-gunned the cattle, and razed the orchards, presumably to deny support to Contra soldiers operating in the area. Ten thousand Miskito villagers resettled in refugee camps, while more than 40,000 Miskitos and Mayangna escaped over the Río Coco to Honduras. Increasing numbers of Miskitos joined the enemy of their enemy, i.e. the Contras, and escalated the warfare. In 1985, Minister of the Interior Tomás Borge came to a compromise with the Miskito people: In exchange for laying down their arms, they would be permitted to return to the sites of their original villages along the Río Coco to rebuild and begin anew. Many accepted, and since the mid-1980s the Río Coco communities have slowly rebuilt in the delicate autonomy now granted to the two departments of the Atlantic coast.

In 1988, Hurricane Joan leveled and submerged Bluefields and other Atlantic coast communities, killing 148 people and causing $1 billion worth of damage, including the destruction of Big Corn Island's prosperous coconut industry and much of its coral reefs. 100,000 hectares of tropical swamp forest were destroyed, which provoked forest fires the following dry season. The region continues to recover economically to this day.

The 1990s

In recent years, a large immigration of Pacific-side (and mostly Catholic) Nicaraguans has tipped the demographics of most major Atlantic coast communities, putting the black and indigenous populations in the minority for the first time in their history. Considering their long-held isolation and resistance to the Managuan government, this is no small change. For the most part, everybody gets along, but there are undoubtedly rising tensions as the "Spaniards" (as Costeños have always referred to mestizos) seek housing and employment, and at the same time, attempt to import their language, music, food, and other cultural aspects to their new home.

El Rama

At the eastern terminus of the highway from Managua, El Rama straddles the frontier between Atlantic and Pacific more perceptibly than any other Nicaraguan town. A longtime riverine port and trader town, El Rama is a melting pot, where mestizo cattle traders meet Caribbean steamer captains, and dark-skinned Creoles mix with "Spaniards" from the Pacific.

The name Rama is a tribute to the Rama people who once inhabited the shores of the Siquia, Rama, Escondido, and Mico Rivers. The inhabitants of today's El Rama, however, are the progeny of immigrants from Chontales, Boaco, and Granada, all of whom swarmed here in the late 18th century to take advantage of the boom in the wood, rubber, and banana trade. Before 1880, the original port of El Rama was located on the southwest shore of the Río Siquia but was relocated to the present location due to the unbearable mud, floods, and swamps that plagued the original location.

While Nicaraguans from all over the country resented the stringent rationing of food and basic goods during the war years of the 1980s, no one was more indignant than the people of El Rama, whose international port was where the millions of metric tons of military hardware were brought on shore from Eastern-bloc freighters to be shipped up the Rama Highway to military bases around the nation. In the 1980s, while locals were forming lines to receive a half-bar of soap and one pound of rice, they watched steel-armored convoys of tanks, fighter planes, and trucks full of rifles, grenades, and antipersonnel land mines pass through their town bound for the battle lines. Short of the trenches of the front line, nowhere was the military buildup—and the irony of the shortage of basic goods—more obvious.

© RANDY WOOD

Rama's international port

El Rama, though wholly dependent on the river, is also at the mercy of it. El Rama has been under water several times, including during Hurricane Joan, when for three days the only thing seen above the surface of the boiling, muddy waters of the swollen Río Escondido was the church steeple. Deforestation upstream means the river floods more and more frequently these days, and with less advance warning. An electronic system of flood warning devices installed along the river in 2000 will hopefully give residents a chance to evacuate.

The typical traveler spends no more than 15 minutes in Rama between the time he or she gets off the bus and onto a boat to Bluefields. But should you find yourself stuck here (let's face it, few travelers will brave the nine-hour bus ride just to go to Rama), you may find El Rama to be worth a second look, and even useful as the base for an expedition or two.

ACCOMMODATIONS

Not recommended are the two sketchy places down by the port, Hotel Amy and Hotel Manantial, where for $7 you get nasty bathroom facilities, questionable security, and probably prostitutes and their company for your neighbors. The locals direct foreign travelers to **Hotel Johana** (tel. 505/517-0066, $2 a person), which is simple and safe and has more than 30 rooms in a large wooden building. A bit cleaner and far quieter is **Hospedaje García,** with singles for $2.75, double beds for $5, and fancier rooms on the second floor with a/c and a view of the river for $10.50.

FOOD AND SERVICES

Without a doubt, the best place in town for a meal is **Restaurante El Expreso,** whose name has no relation to the speed of the service; lots of seafood, soups, chicken, and steak. Across from the market, **Antojitos Mexicanos** is popular with the locals for Mexican dishes and beer. The **Eskimo** sells sandwiches in addition to ice cream. A good fritanga sets up shop evenings near the market (approximately across from Antojitos Mexicanos).

The **ENITEL** and **post office** are located across the street from each other. ENITEL is open

7 A.M.–9 P.M. Monday–Saturday. For late-night phone calls, try the Pepsi booth on the street that leads to the municipal pier (i.e., the pier with boats for Bluefields). There's a phone there that the owner will let you use. **Farmacia El Carmen,** open 8 A.M.–1 P.M. and 2–6:30 P.M. Monday–Saturday is well stocked with medicines, sanitary supplies, and more.

GETTING THERE AND AWAY

The drive between Managua and El Rama can take up to nine hours, not because of distance but because of the vast expanses of ruined road, which buses are forced to traverse at a crawl. Once the pavement gives way to dirt, it deteriorates rapidly into fields of rainwater-filled potholes that carpet the road from one side to the other; Rama is approximately six hours from Juigalpa. Buses from Managua's Mayoreo terminal depart at 5 A.M., 6 A.M., and 7:30 A.M. From Juigalpa, buses leave from the market every hour until 1:30 P.M.

Many travelers choose to travel by overnight bus, both to experience the early-morning *panga* ride, and so as not to arrive in Bluefields in the dark. Night buses to El Rama are owned by two companies. The first is **Transporte Vargas Peñas** (tel. 505/280-4561 in Managua, tel. 505/572-1510 on the dock in Bluefields), leaving from the bus terminal Ivan Montenegro in Managua at 9 P.M., arriving in El Rama around 7 A.M. The same company owns the fleet of Rama–Bluefields *pangas* and can sell you the boat ticket in Managua, ensuring that you don't get stranded on the dock. The second company, **Transporte Aguilar** (tel. 505/248-3005 or 505/244-2255), leaves Managua's Mayoreo at 9 P.M. and 10 P.M., arriving in El Rama at 5 A.M. and 6 A.M. It's a quicker ride, but you'll have to fend for yourself to get a place on a departing *panga*. With both companies, the ride costs $6. The return journey begins at 5:30 A.M. on the docks of Bluefields, putting you in Managua about 12 hours later.

By Bus to Managua

Five buses for Managua leave from the market from 3–9 A.M.; an express bus leaves from the wharf road (approximately a block east of Hotel

NICARAGUAN BOAT LINGO

As you explore both the Atlantic Coast and Río San Juan regions, you will encounter and employ a variety of watercraft. They're loved, relied-upon, and beaten to splinters over the long years they ply the waves, overburdened with domestic animals, tightly wrapped bags, and their owners, not to mention the occasional sunburned foreign traveler with a plastic garbage bag over her backpack. Familiarity with the names of the various watercraft will ease the process of finding the right boat at the dock.

Pangas refer to the open water taxis. On the Atlantic Coast, they are 7–10-meter-long fiberglass crafts with wooden benches that seat 16–20 people and are the chief means of transport between, for example, the Corn Islands. On the Río San Juan, however, they carry only 6–10 passengers, are rented privately, and are quite expensive.

Lanchas usually refer to smaller motorboats or fishing vessels. They are frequently the cheapest public transportation between towns and occasionally carry up to 60 passengers.

Pipantes are particularly long and skinny *lanchas*.

Colectivos are public *lanchas*.

Planas are motorless, flat-bottom mini-barges, towed by *lanchas*.

Canoas are wooden dugout canoes. They are also called **botecitas, cayucos,** or **botes de canalete.**

Barcos are bigger, slower ships for fishing, cargo, and sometimes passengers. On the Río San Juan, the *barco* generally means the ship that provides service between San Carlos and Granada. They are also called **botes,** but this is a general word that could mean anything.

A cautionary notes about *pangas:* The best seats are in the center of the boat. Elsewhere, you may get wet or—depending on your captain—soaked. You will probably be charged for extra luggage—which will also get soaked. Also, boats (like buses) break down, which can lead to a lengthy wait on the water until the next one comes. Watch for drunk drivers and step back onto the dock if you'd rather not put your life in that person's hands.

All kinds of sturdy—and not so sturdy—craft ply Nicaragua's waters.

The Atlantic Coast

Amy) at noon, 7 P.M., and 10 P.M. Saturday, Sunday, and Tuesday. Express buses don't linger in Juigalpa or stop along the road, shaving two hours off the trip.

By Boat to Bluefields

All transportation is found at the municipal wharf: *Pangas* cast off from the dock as they fill up, from 6 A.M. to 4 P.M. (1.5-hour trip to Bluefields, approximately $10 per person). There's a bigger ship that carries freight and passengers, but it is much slower than the nimble *pangas*. It leaves every Tuesday and Saturday at 11 A.M. (five hours, approximately $5 per person).

NEAR EL RAMA

The folks at El Rama are interested in developing a tourism infrastructure; they just don't know how to do it yet. Any adventuring you do in the region will require ingenuity and patience. Divided by rivers and swamps, the lands around El Rama are teeming with places to explore and look for wildlife. **Los Humedales de Mahogany** is a wetlands reserve important for the reproduction of local species. It's a 4–5 hour trip by boat downstream in the direction of Bluefields along the Mahogany River near the entrance to the Caño Negro (Black Creek). **Cerro Silva** was declared protected in 1997; it's located 2.5 hours along the Río Rama in the direction of San Jerónimo. Once you disembark from your boat, it's a 2.5-hour hike from the river's edge to the park; find a guide in San Jerónimo to lead you there.

The falls of **Salto Mataka** are found along the Río Siquia, 2.5 hours from La Esperanza (the town with the big bridge, just west of El Rama). Also located near La Esperanza is **El Recreo,** a popular swimming hole three kilometers north of town.

Bluefields

A rich waterfront melting pot of nearly 50,000 souls who make a living extracting lobster, fish, shrimp, oysters, and several species of endangered turtles from the sea, as well as logging the coastal forests, Bluefields has never been connected to Nicaragua's highway system and is reached only by water or air. European pirates appreciated its deep, protected harbor in the 1600s and 1700s, and today Bluefields Bay remains an important Atlantic port for a (mostly) more legitimate maritime crowd. The city itself is the capital of the RAAS and hosts both the University of the Autonomous Regions of the Atlantic coast of Nicaragua (URACCAN, the other campuses are in Puerto Cabezas, Siuna, and Nueva Guinea) and the Bluefields Indian and Caribbean University (BICU). Despite all the activity, unemployment—alleviated only by

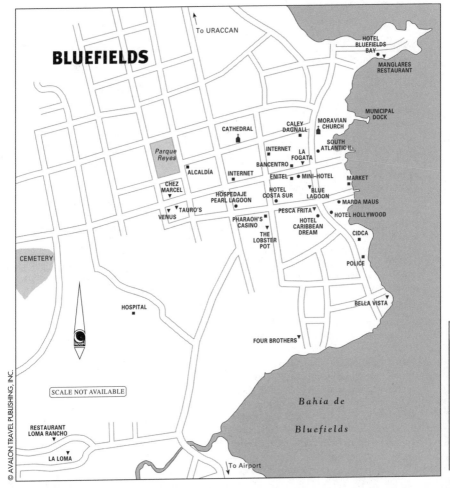

The Atlantic Coast

PALO DE MAYO

Deep root, lofty trunk, dense foliage: from the center of the world rises a thornless tree, one of those trees that know how to give themselves to the birds. Around the tree whirl dancing couples, navel to navel, undulating to a music that wakens stones and sets fire to ice. As they dance, they dress and undress the tree with streaming ribbons of every color. On this tormented, continuously invaded, continuously bombarded coast of Nicaragua, the Maypole fiesta is celebrated as usual.

The tree of life knows that, whatever happens, the warm music spinning around it will never stop. However much death may come, however much blood may flow, the music will dance men and women as long as the air breathes them and the land plows and loves them.

Eduardo Galeano

Celebrated every day in the month of May, the Palo de Mayo, or Maypole dance, is the most well-known and colorful feature of Nicaragua's vibrant cultural Caribbean stew. In English and Nordic tradition of the 19th century, on the first of May young men and women would collect freshly cut flowers. This was known as "going-a-maying." A long, straight pole was set in the center of town and decorated with the fresh flowers and colored ribbons anchored to the top of the pole. The celebration ushered in the spring and expressed hopes for happiness and a good harvest.

How the Palo de Mayo got to Bluefields and the Atlantic coast of Nicaragua remains a mystery, though it very probably passed directly from England during the years the Atlantic coast was an English protectorate, or possibly by way of Jamaica, where it evolved into something more Caribbean and erotic. To date, the Palo de Mayo is celebrated, thanks to the old English Empire, in such disparate locales as Austria, Spain, and amongst the Wenda and Galla people of Africa.

The Palo de Mayo refers to two things: a massive celebration and outpouring of joy held the first of May every year in Bluefields, Pearl Lagoon, and the Corn Islands, and also the name of a dance and style of music. The dance has gotten progressively more sensual in recent decades—sometimes appearing as simulated sex on the dance floor—and the more conservative Costeños have started a movement to return the dance to its more respectable origins.

Most cultural presentations on the Atlantic coast and elsewhere in Nicaragua include a version of the Palo de Mayo that you should make an effort to see, if possible. Set typically to the tropical rhythms of Dimensión Costeña, the popular Bluefields party band, dancers in brightly colored satin costumes go through a series of provocative routines of gyrating hips and shimmying chests.

cruise ship companies that keep hundreds of locals on the payroll—is acute, and increasing penetration of narcotics (including crack, which is grievously cheap) makes Bluefields an increasingly difficult place in which to live.

Bluefield's attraction is its Creole culture, which will become apparent as soon as you enter town. Do not miss the Palo de Mayo celebrations, an exuberant and erotic calypso-tinted dance and music event, unique to the city and celebrated fervently throughout the month of May. At other times during the year, use Bluefields as a stopover for excursions to Pearl Lagoon, various river villages and cays, and of course, the Corn Islands.

SIGHTS AND ATTRACTIONS

Bluefields' principal attraction is its Caribbean feel and the contrast it makes with the rest of "Spanish" Nicaragua. The red-roofed **Moravian church** was the first of its kind on the Central American Atlantic coast. Built in 1848 with English and French—and a touch of Caribbean—design elements, the cut wood is reminiscent of

floating into Bluefields

New Orleans in the 1800s. About a block and a half west, the whitewashed wood and stained glass **cathedral** is the Catholic response. Services can be very atmospheric inside the airy structure.

You can walk up to the **water tower** with a local tour guide. The end of the trail near the URACCAN offers a good view of the harbor; take a bottle of rum and pretend you're an English pirate. Bluefields is also a good place to take in an amateur game of baseball, soccer, or volleyball. Ask at the fields or ball courts (in Parque Reyes) for game times.

FESTIVALS

Bluefields exuberantly honors its **patron saint,** San Jerónimo, on September 30, and then rolls right into its birthday celebrations throughout the month of October.

Palo de Mayo Festival

Also known as the *¡Mayo Ya!* festival, Bluefields's May Day celebration is unique in Central America. In North America, this pagan-rooted party is about springtime, fertility, and the reawakening

of the earth after a long winter. In Bluefields, May falls on the cusp of the rainy season, and the entire month is a bright burst of colors, parades, costumes, feasting, and, most importantly, dancing around the Maypole. Every night is a party, and the festival comes to a rip-roaring peak at the end of the month. Look for it every evening May 1–31 (see the Palo de Mayo special topic).

NIGHTLIFE AND ENTERTAINMENT

Bluefields likes its music loud. You'll hear the reggae bumping wherever you go, and in all its different versions: dance hall, roots, *soka,* punta, Palo de Mayo, reggae *romantica,* and of course, long sets of the eternal king, Mr. Marley. Interestingly enough, the Atlantic coast's second favorite is country music from the United States. We're talking roots country like George Jones, Tammy Wynette, and Merle Haggard—real "tear in yer beer" twangers that residents proudly claim as their own "coastal music."

Discos

Four Brothers (six blocks south of the park) is

still the center of the Creole social scene: a hot, damp juke joint with a wooden-plank dance floor and ice cold beer. You'll need that beer before you can master the "hug up," a sensual Caribbean grind that starts at the hips and goes downward. It can be a rough crowd, so keep your wits about you and take a cab. At the other end of town, and a current favorite among the townies, **Fresh Point** is similar in texture. Look for it just past Hotel Bluefields Bay, and don't miss Saturday nights when the place really starts to rumble. **Disco Bacchus** (half a block south of the central park), and **Venus** (one block south and one west of the park) are more laid back, and the music is a cheerful mix of Latin and Island rhythms.

If dancing is not for you, do what the locals do: Whittle your hours away in the air-conditioned luxury of **Pharoah's Casino.** More than three dozen one-armed bandits will make short shrift of your beer money, but when the humidity outside's at 100 percent, it seems well worth it. Or,

drop in on an amateur **boxing match** at Bluefields' old cinema.

Radio

Bluefields is home to nine (count 'em) radio stations! Check out programs like "Roots Rap Reggae" (9 A.M. on Radio Zinica, 95.9 FM), "Energía Volumen" (4–6 P.M. on Radio La Morenita, 102.1 FM), and "Caribbean Breeze" (1 P.M. on Radio Punto Tres, 90.7 FM). Radio La Costeñísima plays regular sets of Miskito tunes. Hear the "Voice of America" daily at 6 A.M. on Radio Bluefields Estereo (96.5 FM), followed by—what else?—a country music show.

SHOPPING

If you want to take home some local *artesanía,* then look for hand-carved wooden statuettes in uniquely-Caribbean forms in the South Atlantic II, Carribean Dream, and Marda-Maus hotels. For anything else, particularly seafood, head down

---

FROM SEA TO SOUP: ATLANTIC COAST COOKIN'

Atlantic coast cuisine will enchant you with its sheer simplicity and unsurpassed freshness. That lobster on your plate was probably picked off the ocean floor this morning; the fish were swimming laps hours ago. The only way you'll get fresher fish is by cooking it on the ship. Seafood on the Nicaraguan Atlantic is cheap by international standards, delicious by anyone's standards, and well worth the wait (since restaurants are slow, even by Nicaraguan standards). If your travel complaints don't evaporate in the garlicky steam of lobster under your nose, then you obviously are going to need to spend another couple of days.

Start off with **yellowfin, snapper, or sea bass,** grilled with vegetables in a coconut curry. **Conch meat,** when tenderized correctly, is soft and delicate, less briny than other seafood but with a soft texture. Or enjoy a lobster *al vapor,* bulging with delicate, white meat you can pull from the shell with your fingers, drenched in butter and lime.

Mixed soup is served in a helmet-sized bowl choked with crab, lobster, conch, and fish. Not hearty enough? Then reach for **Rondon,** a corruption of "run down" and a thick stew of fish (or sometimes turtle—please avoid this one), vegetables, and coconut milk thickened with starchy tubers and plantains as well. In August, don't miss the **Corn Island Crab Soup festival,** when Costeños cook tons of soft fibrous crabmeat into a festival you won't forget. Atlantic coast crab meat is particularly soft, with a delicate flavor unique to the tropics.

You don't have to stick to seafood to eat well on the Atlantic coast. Even the *gallo pinto* tastes better on here: That's because it's cooked up in sweet coconut oil. In between meals, fill up with **coco bread**—football-sized loaves of soft, rich wheat flour cooked up with coconut and served hot out of the oven. And akin to cinnamon rolls but without the cinnamon, hot coconut **buns** are sweet and sticky, best enjoyed on the dock as you watch the gulls wheel circles around the incoming catch.

to the Municipal Market by the waterfront and start bargaining. Or whet your appetite with fresh coconut milk, which starts at less than $1.

ACCOMMODATIONS

Bluefields is more dangerous than most cities, and certainly less sanitary in general—just get an eyeful of all the dirty water and mangy mutts slithering down the roads. This is one place where the traveler ought to loosen the purse strings a bit for something a little safer and cleaner. Those who try to maintain their rock-bottom travel budget will find themselves in hotels where the neighbors are rotating in and out on a 45 minute schedule, or worse. If you do decide to go for one of the budget hotels, assess both its security measures and the kind of people hanging around it before clinching the deal.

Under $10

You don't get many creature comforts or much privacy in this category. Check out **Lobster Pot** (a half block south of Pharoah's Casino and run by a friendly Cayman Islander), **Hospedaje Pearl Lagoon** (tel. 505/572-2411), and **Hotel Dorado** (tel. 505/572-2365) for basic, cramped accommodations, usually with shared bath and no frills. Steer clear of **Pension Lopez,** which charges by the hour.

$10–25

Right on the main drag, ℕ **Hotel Caribbean Dream** (tel. 505/572-0107, $17) is secure, spotless, and home to one of the better balconies in town. Across from Bancentro, **Mini-Hotel Central** (tel. 505/572-2362, $10 s, tv, a/c) is clean and run by great people; and on the street to the dockside municipal market, **Hotel Marda Maus** (tel. 505/572-2429, $10–19 with TV) is clean and safe enough, but not much more. Next door, **Hotel Claudia** (tel. 505/572-2376, $10–16) is about the same.

$25–50

Just west of the Municipal Market, ℕ **Hotel South Atlantic II** (its predecessor no longer exists; tel. 505/572-1022 or 505/822-2265, $32–58 with private bath, a/c, TV, and phone) has a bar, restaurant, and travel agent on premises. **Hotel Bluefields Bay** (tel. 505/572-0120, kriol@ibw

.com.ni, $35) is an elegant waterside bed-and-breakfast at the north side of town.

FOOD

Bluefields will seem like a much more interesting place once you've eaten a meal: Seafood is one of Bluefields's fortes, so dig in! Carnivores, don't worry: There's lots of beef and chicken as well (including the ever-present chicken chop suey), but you'll find it's a bit more expensive than you're used to in western Nicaragua. But why miss out on lobster fresh from the sea served with lemon and steamed veggies?

Cheaper Meals

Keep your eyes peeled for cheaper fare in the hotel area. The **Paladar Costeño** serves buffet-style meals for under $4 and fresh juices as well. You can also get well-prepared meals in the **Mini-Hotel Central** café. Otherwise ask around for the *fritanga*—there's sometimes one by the Lotería building. One block south of the park and one block west, you'll find a cluster of local restaurants, starting with **Tauro's,** a good choice to sample the famous *rondon* (or "rundown") soup, and across the street and a little farther up hill, there's the inexpensive **Martin Luz Pizzeria** ("Well, it will at least remind you of pizza, anyway," says one local). At the high end of "less expensive" is the surprisingly good restaurant on the second floor of the **Hotel South Atlantic II,** offering seafood and beef for around $4–8 plus drinks.

More Expensive Options

There are two decent options for waterside dining, the nicest of which is found at the ℕ **Manglares Restaurant,** located beneath the Hotel Bluefields Bay and extending over the water on its own dock. Watch the sun set over your dish of fresh lobster. At the other end of town just south of the police station, the **Bella Vista** is less fancy and less crowded. The best place in town overlooks the water from atop the biggest hill west of town. Take a cab to ℕ **Restaurante Loma Rancho** across the street from the BICU (Bluefields Indian Caribbean University). Finally, **Chez Marcel** (open noon–3 P.M. and 6–10 P.M., tel.

ℕ The Atlantic Coast

ATLANTIC COAST FLIGHT SCHEDULE

Airlines
Atlantic Airlines

Managua:	tel. 505/222-5787 or 505/222-3037, fax 505/228-5614
Bluefields:	tel. 505/572-1299 or 505/572-0259
Corn Island:	tel. 505/575-5055 or 505/575-5151
Email:	reservaciones@atlanticairlines.com.ni

La Costeña

Managua:	tel. 505/263-1228 or 505/263-2142, fax 505/263-1281
Bluefields:	tel. 505/572-2500
Corn Island:	tel. 505/575-5131

Flights
Managua–Bluefields

La Costeña	6:30 A.M., 10 A.M. (except Sun.)
Atlantic	6:45 A.M., 10:30 A.M., 2:10 P.M.

Bluefields–Managua

La Costeña	7:40 A.M., 8:40 A.M., 11:20 A.M. (except Sun.), 4:10 P.M.

Atlantic	9:10 A.M., 11:45 A.M., 4:35 P.M.

Managua–Corn Island

La Costeña	6:30 A.M., 2 P.M.
Atlantic	6:45 A.M., 10:30 A.M., 2:10 P.M.

Corn Island–Managua

La Costeña	8:10 A.M., 3:40 P.M.
Atlantic	8:35 A.M., 4 P.M.

Managua–Puerto Cabezas

La Costeña	6:30 A.M., 10:30 A.M., 2:30 P.M.
Atlantic	6:30 A.M., 10:30 A.M.

Bluefields–Puerto Cabezas

La Costeña	12:10 P.M.

Puerto Cabezas–Bluefields

La Costeña	11:10 A.M.

505/572-2347) remains the most exquisite dining experience in Bluefields; this means tuxedoed waitstaff and folded cloth napkins; fresh fish and lobster run around $11–15 in air-conditioned splendor.

INFORMATION

Skip the drowsy personnel at the INTUR office (tel. 505/572-1111) and head instead to **CIDCA** (50 meters north of the police station, open 8 A.M.–5:30 P.M. Mon.–Fri., with a break for lunch), the Research and Documentation center for the Atlantic coast (affiliated with the UCA). They make available to the public a wide selection of materials about Caribbean cultures and languages, including several Miskito-only publications. For the lowdown on the throwdown, check www.bluefieldspulse.com.

SERVICES

Emergency
The fire department is just north of the Moravian church, tel. 505/572-2050; the police are on the same side of the street, three blocks south, tel. 505/572-2333 or 505/822-2432; and the Red Cross can be found in Barrio Fatima at tel. 505/572-2582. Bluefields's Hospital Ernesto Sequeira is located about five blocks south and west of the park, tel. 505/572-2391 or 822-2621.

Phones and Mail
The ENITEL phone office is located in fancy new digs across the street from Bancentro (open 8 A.M.–5 P.M. Mon.–Fri., 8 A.M.–noon Sat.). The post office is a half-block west of the Lotería building, and the Western Union is located a block east of the park.

© RANDY WOOD

Nicaraguan puddle-jumpers fly daily between Managua and the Atlantic Coast.

Banks

Banco Caley Dagnall is the older of the two banks on the Atlantic coast, located in front of the Moravian church. Bancentro is around the corner on Calle Cabezas. Both are open 8:30 A.M.–4:30 P.M. Monday–Friday, 8 A.M.–noon Saturday. And the money changers on the corner opposite Bancentro will find you before you find them.

Internet

Bluefields has its own server and faster Internet access than some other cities. Unless you're already at the URACCAN, your two most convenient cyber cafés are the Copicentro (just west of the abandoned cinema) or Central Computer Service (one block west, half-block south of the Moravian church), both offering Internet access for about $.90 per hour.

Film

The Kodak store is located catty-corner from Pharoah's Casino, open 8 A.M.–6 P.M. Mon.–Fri., 8 A.M.–2 P.M. Sat. Bluefields is so humid, your negatives will seal themselves to each other the instant you carry them out of the shop.

GETTING THERE AND AWAY

By Land

The overland route is no longer the heroic journey it was before they repaved the highway to El Rama in 2002–2003, but you'll need some stamina anyway. Leave Managua for El Rama, where you board an early-morning *panga* and soak up two hours of fresh air, sunrise, and a beautiful trip down the Río Escondido to Bluefields. While this route will stretch out your travel budget, its real appeal is your newfound appreciation for both Nicaragua's massive girth, and the Atlantic coast's geographical isolation (see the El Rama section for more detailed bus information).

By Air

Both La Costeña and Atlantic Airlines offer regular, daily flights between Bluefields, Managua, and Corn Island. The trip to and from

The Atlantic Coast

Managua takes about one hour and costs $45 each way. It is easy to buy a Managua–Corn Island ticket with a stopover in Bluefields. Buy an "open" ticket, which means no dates are fixed, then arrange your onward flight with either of the two airlines by calling or visiting the airport, or by dealing with one of their many ticket brokers around town—(Hotel South Atlantic II is a good one, or look for the Costeña and Atlantic signs elsewhere in town). See the Atlantic Coast Flight Schedule special topic for flight times and contact information.

By Boat

Passenger-boat traffic to Rama Cay, El Bluff, and Pearl Lagoon all originates from the main municipal dock behind the market. Pay a $.10 entrance fee at the first window (pays for the cable-TV connection). Every Wednesday, the trusty old diesel-belching ship *Captain D* leaves the dock at El Bluff bound for Corn Island, making the return trip on Sunday (4 hours, $10 each way). Take lots of water, sun protection, and your sense of humor: The trip eastward is definitely more prone to barf-bag swells.

ORIENTATION AND GETTING AROUND

From the Bluefields airport, it's a boring walk several kilometers north into town; take a taxi instead for the fixed price of $.75. *Pangas* arriving from El Rama land at the municipal docks; walking half a block puts you on the main waterfront drag and within a stone's throw of most of Bluefields's hotels. The central park, also known as Parque Reyes, is located three blocks west of the waterfront road. Bluefields is small enough that you should need a taxi only to go to the extremes of town—the URACCAN campus at the north and the airport at the south. Two nearly identical bus routes run from 6 A.M.–7:30 P.M. Get on and off where you like for $.25.

Near Bluefields

EL BLUFF

El Bluff sprawls over the spit of land that separates Bluefields Bay from the ocean, and before Hurricane Joan breached the bar, it was connected to Bluefields by land. Essentially an industrial park, the inland side of El Bluff houses nearly all of Bluefields's major port and fish-packing facilities. Its harbor was built by Bulgarian engineers in the 1980s with hopes of creating a supertanker port. Wander around the docks and check out the enormous steel ships of Nicaragua's Atlantic fishing fleet, or take a peek at the abandoned airstrip, a remnant from the revolution years. *Pangas* leave for El Bluff all day from the municipal dock in Bluefields, embarking as soon as they fill up with 12 passengers. The last return boat is 4 P.M.

RAMA CAY

Ten kilometers south of Bluefields in the middle of the bay, is the ancestral home of the Rama people. From an unknown tribal origin, the Ramas came to inhabit Rama Cay centuries ago, where they remained largely unaffected by the political turbulence that surrounded them. Then, in July of 1984, Sandinista troops hunting down indigenous supporters of the Contras strafed the island in a vicious air attack that devastated an island on which not a soul was found (the Ramas had gotten word of the attack and scampered off before the air strike). Today, the 1,000 Rama fisherman and oyster harvesters live pretty much the way they always have. Getting to Rama Cay is an easy, $6 *panga* ride from Bluefields and about an hour crossing the bay. Can't get enough Rama? Ask the pastor's family, the McReas, who live across from the Moravian church if they'll rent you a room for the night.

GREENFIELDS NATURE RESERVE

On the outskirts of Kukra Hill, Greenfields (tel. 505/268-1897, info@greenfields.com.ni, www.greenfields.com.ni) is a publicly protected wildland, privately managed as an ecotourism business by a Swiss couple who have been in Nicaragua for more than 25 years. You can hike more than 25 kilometers of trails, canoe through jungle watercourses, and arrange group excursions to the coast. The prices are steep, but they include lodging, meals, and guided tours. You will be isolated in a silent wilderness, surrounded by wildlife and lush vegetation. You can make this a day trip (no lodging, no meals) for $15 pp or $50/group (up to 6 persons), and enjoy excursions with guides by foot or canoe, the botanical park, bathing pier, and more. Arrange your visit in advance by phone.

KARAWALA AND SANDY BAY

Sandy Bay, located three hours north along the Caribbean coast, is one of the only Miskito communities accessible from Bluefields, and nearby Karawala is the last indigenous Ulwa site in the world (the Ulwa are related to the Mayangna but have distinct cultural characteristics and lan-

guage). The boat to both places leaves the *muelle* (dock) in Bluefields on Wednesdays and Fridays at 10:30 A.M. and returns Mondays and Thursdays. There's not much to do in Sandy Bay for non-anthropologists, although the beach is nice. Karawala, however, is situated between pine forest and mangrove swamps and offers world-class tarpon fly-fishing. In town, you'll find basic accommodations and simple, unremarkable meals.

M PEARL LAGOON

Tucked away in the next lagoon north of Bluefields, Pearl Lagoon is a quiet, clean, and safe Caribbean community washed in morning sunlight whose quiet lanes are easily explored on foot. The natural, green splendor of Pearl Lagoon makes a welcome respite from Bluefields, and the little village gives access to local Miskito communities and the enchanting Pearl Cays. The locals earn their living from the water—you'll see boats of the five companies that deal in

© RANDY WOOD

the Moravian church in Pearl Lagoon

The Atlantic Coast

fish and fish processing tied up along the docks or moored in the lagoon. Denmark and Norway have been active in the economic development of the region, constructing municipal piers in Pearl Lagoon, Haulover, Tasbapauni, Kakabila, Brown Bank, and Marshall Point to assist local fishermen in getting their catch to market.

Sights

Of interest in town is the **iron cannon** (the locals lovingly call it "the great gun") mounted in front of the ENITEL building. It is embossed with the seal of the lion and unicorn (symbol of the British Empire) and a date: 1803. The rest is a long-lost mystery. The clean architectural style of the most eye-catching building in town, the whitewashed **Moravian church,** was typical of the period. Attending an evening service there is a memorable experience (dress appropriately), reminiscent of oil-lantern and prayer-book services in the 1800s elsewhere. To the south of town is a small branch of URACCAN.

If you visit Pearl Lagoon over a weekend, don't miss a night of reggae at one of Pearl Lagoon's several small **clubs,** like Carivibes, Cherrylandia, or the 1st Stop Bar. The area's four baseball teams—Sweet Pearly, First Stop, The Young Brave, and the Haulover Tigers—battle it out on Sundays during the dry season.

Accommodations

The **Green Lodge** (tel. 505/572-0507, $4 s) is a pleasant and inexpensive place right on the main drag, with a nice patio area and pleasant owners. Right on the main drag in front of the dock, the **Sweet Pearly** ($6.50 s with shared bath, $9.50 s with private bath) *hospedaje* and restaurant is another standby, with 11 small, clean rooms with fans. The restaurant downstairs is worth giving a miss, though.

Pearl Lagoon's first, nicest, and most successful tourist operation is the **M Casa Blanca Hotelito y Restaurante** (tel. 505/572-0508, $10–30), owned and run by Danish immigrant Svend Friberg and his Nica wife, Dell. Svend runs a clean shop and, with the resolute gaze of a Nordic mariner, will look you straight in the eye and inform you that his restaurant serves the best food

MODERN PIRATES AND THE PEARL CAYS

According to Nicaragua's autonomy laws, all 18 Pearl Cays off the coast north of Pearl Lagoon belong, in perpetuity, to the Nicaraguan government for the collective use of indigenous peoples of the region. Local residents and indigenous leaders have found it curious, then, how seven of these islands ended up "belonging" to a Greek-American real-estate investor named Peter Tsoskos, who tried to sell them off at extraordinary (we're talking tens of millions of dollars) markups on the Internet.

The Pearl Cays possess important turtle-nesting beaches, unspoiled coral-reef systems, and drinking-water supplies, which have been used by Miskitos from the nearby mainland village of Set Net for hundreds of years. The islands are important base camps for local fishermen.

With these new real estate actions, however, locals were prevented from landing on some of the islands by armed squads of Nicaraguan police officers, allegedly hired as private guards by the new "owners." Official suits against Tsoskos, the Bluefields police chief, and the Pearl Lagoon municipal chief by leaders of indigenous groups resulted in the national government's environment branch, MARENA, stepping in. In April 2001, MARENA ordered the sales and resales reversed and all development activity stopped immediately. The imbroglio that ensued left several dead, including a judge. While all is quiet for the moment, political and ethnic tensions continue to broil under the surface. Our suggestion? If enjoying a beautiful picnic on one of the islands, don't ask if it's for sale.

on the Atlantic coast. He and Dell can arrange fishing and snorkeling trips, as well as boat or horseback excursions to nearby communities. **Bella Vista** ($10–15, tel. 505/572-0512) is decent and offers private or shared baths, fans, and mosquito nets. Up the block along the waterfront, set back between the street and the river (near a noisy woodshop), **Hospedaje Estrella** ($10 d) has small, clean rooms, each with a fan, desk, and shared bath.

Food

The **Green Lodge** serves good food, prepared cleanly. Their plate of the day will cost you about $2. **Miss Betty's Bread Shop** is the place to go for pastries, juices, and sweets. The **Casa Blanca** has the best menu in town, served in a pleasant ambience. Shrimp dishes start at about $5 and lobster at $6.50.

Services

The ENITEL office and a police post are in the center of "town" by the wharf. The health clinic is a few blocks south, to the right of the church. At least four pharmacies—Pearl Lagoon Pharmacy, SOS Farmacy, and the Health Center—can take care of basic medical needs. For more serious medical emergencies, you will be strapped into a *panga* and rocketed off to Bluefields. With that in mind, be safe.

Getting There and Away

The *panga* trip up the Río Escondido and then north through a complex network of waterways is a thrilling, beautiful ride that takes under an hour and costs $5 each way. On the way, you'll pass several shipwrecks, and also the active dock at Kukra Hill, named after a cannibalistic indigenous tribe once common in the area. Go to the municipal dock in Bluefields as early as possible—7 A.M. is good—and sign up for the Pearl Lagoon *panga.* Boats leave as soon as they have 20 passengers; after 3 P.M. no additional *pangas* leave the dock. The trip costs $5.50 one way ($6.25 after noon—*just because*). The last boat back from Pearl Lagoon leaves between noon and 3 P.M. if enough passengers have signed up for it.

NEAR PEARL LAGOON

The town of Pearl Lagoon actually sits on the southeast side of a small prominence jutting out into the bay. Walk west from the town to get to the broad, shallow Caribbean beach community of Awas. It's reportedly no more than a half-hour walk down a flat, sandy road that crosses a saltwater estuary and a small footbridge. When you get to the Miskito community of Raitipura (Miskito for on top of the cemetery), turn left and follow the road to Awas. Rent a small palm-thatch hut from one of the locals for $2–4, kick

the Pearl Cays

© RANDY WOOD

The Atlantic Coast

back, and relax. You can also take a *panga* ride up into the Laguna de Perlas (the water body, not the town), and visit the communities of Orinoco and Marshall Point.

Farther up the coast, on the Caribbean side of the land, are the communities of Tasbapauni (two hours from Pearl Lagoon, no lodging) and the Man of War Cays.

ⓜ THE PEARL CAYS

Despite the current controversy over their ownership and development by outside investors, most of the 18 utopian desert islands that make up the Pearl Cays are still untouched and accessible (for now). They are located six kilometers east of a small Miskito village called Set Net.

Hire a boat from Pearl Lagoon and enjoy the ride through the harbor, into the open Caribbean, then up the empty coastline to the cays.

The cays have zero tourist facilities (except for one high-priced, fully serviced "eco-lodge" that is wrapped up in scandal). Be sure to bring drinking water, basic first-aid supplies, and snorkel gear, plus a hammock if you plan on spending the night. Make a deal with your boatman—but pay the bill when he picks you up, not when he drops you off. A round-trip *panga* ride to the Pearl Cays can cost $150, so the more people chipping in, the cheaper it'll be. If you find yourself sharing one of the islets with local fishermen, you may find them cutting down coconuts and telling fishing stories over a fire on the beach; strike up a deal for some fresh fish.

Corn Island

Eighty-three kilometers due east of Bluefields Bay's brackish, brown water, the Corn Islands are a pair of Tertiary period volcanic basalt bumps in a rainbow-blue Caribbean Sea, tempting you to take a taste of Eden. Indeed, tourism is the hope for the islands' sustainability, say many. Ever since local fish and lobster populations began to be stressed by the steadily growing human community on both islands, poverty has risen. Of course, Hurricane Joan didn't help matters in 1988 when she flattened the islands' thriving coconut industry, forcing a greater portion of Isleños to attempt to pull a living from the sea (or from Colombia, whose nearby San Andrés island is part of a major drug-trafficking route). Today, the Corn Islands' seasoned batch of hotels and restaurants are hunkered down and awaiting your arrival.

Corn Island is 10 square kilometers of forested hills, mangrove swamps, and stretches of white coral beaches. The mangrove swamps and estuaries that line several stretches of coastline are crucial to the island's water supply, and the islanders have fiercely resisted attempts by foreign investors to drain or fill them; one group of Italian investors was essentially run off the island. The highest points are Queen Hill, Little Hill

(55 and 57 meters above sea level, respectively), and Mount Pleasant (97 meters).

Three distinct layers of reef, composed of more than 40 species of coral, protect the north side of the island. Though the snorkeling is still impressive, the reefs have deteriorated over the past decades. Overfishing, damaging algae (which grow as a result of increased nutrient levels in the water from sewage runoff), and sedimentation from the poorly managed hillsides of the island—not to mention the worldwide coral die-off due to global warming—have all contributed to this deterioration. Of the six sea turtle species swimming off Nicaragua's shores, four live in Caribbean waters. On land, Corn Island boasts three endemic species of reptiles and amphibians, all threatened by the continued swamp draining.

HISTORY

Pirates on their way to maraud the coast of Central America and Nicaragua's Río San Juan first visited here in the 16th century, sometimes by accident after the reefs tore the bottom of their ships open. But Corn Island was inhabited long before that by the Kukras, a subtribe of the Mayangnas whose

CORN ISLAND

Caribbean Sea

HOTEL BEACH VIEW

MINI-HOTEL MORGAN

CHURCH

BAYSIDE HOTEL

DOS MILLAS

DORSEY CAMPBELL'S YELLOWTAIL HOUSE

MARCOS GOMEZ

NAUTILUS ECO-TOURS

POLICE

ENITEL

Little Hill 54m

TOWN DOCK

FISHER'S CAVE

GUEST HOUSE RUPPIE

SALLY PEACHES

BRIG BAY

RESTAURANTE CESTEO

CASA BLANCA

AIRPORT

ALCALDÍA

Mt Pleasant Hill 90m

HOSPEDAJE TROPICAL DREAMS

POST OFFICE

SANDRA'S COCO BREAD

BASEBALL STADIUM

ENJOYMENT OF LIFE

HOTEL CLUB PARAISO

SOUTH END

BANK

PICNIC CENTER BEACH

Southwest Bay

PICNIC CENTER

Long Beach

Queen Hill 50m

Barracuda Point

0   1 mi

0   1 km

MOON

The Atlantic Coast

penchant for consuming the bodies of their enemies (in a light coconut sauce, we're sure) inspired the first English visitors to call them the Skeleton Islands. The Kukra were eventually assimilated into the Miskitos. Nowadays, the native Creole population shares the island with an increasing number of menial laborers from the mainland, who have overtaken the Creoles in number and have increased the island's total population to nearly 9,000 people. Some scientists estimate that the island's fragile aquifer can only sustain half that.

Native islanders are direct descendants from several of the more infamous European pirates, as well as English royalty and plantation owners—don't be surprised if you meet people with names like Kennington.

SIGHTS AND ENTERTAINMENT

There aren't any museums, but that's not why you came.

Ⓜ Picnic Center Beach

The most popular swimming beach, Picnic Center is a long, golden crescent of soft sand and turquoise water, with a smattering of cheap restaurants and hotels. Or go to **Long Beach,** just as pretty, but a bit rougher and with fewer services.

Other Sights and Events

For good walking adventure, tackle the shore between Enjoyment of Life and Sally Peaches, or break a sweat on the hike up Mount Pleasant or Little Hill—ask at Nautilus for details.

Weekends, the islanders dance to island rhythms at **Reggae Place,** just south of the docks in Brig Bay. Corn Islanders are serious about their **baseball:** A league of eight teams (including two from the Little Island) play in the quite-nice stadium east of the airport.

Be here at the end of August (27–28) for the age-old **Crab Soup Festival.** This is a happy remembrance of the islanders' emancipation from British slavery in 1841 and the freed slaves' spontaneous celebration around a big pot of crab soup on the beach. Be sure to catch the crowning of Miss Corn Island, Miss Coconut, and Miss Photogenic.

DIVING

The island's only dive shop, **Dive Nautilus** (tel. 505/575-5077, www.nautilus-dive-nicaragua.com) offers weathered equipment and the Divemaster services of "Chema" Ruiz, a jolly Guatemalan with a wall full of framed scuba diplomas and an air compressor in his living room. He offers various dive packages and PADI courses for all levels, $15 for an introduction, $45 for a two-tank dive, $250 for open water certification. Chema also rents snorkel gear, bicycles, and can get you a guide to hike or bike the island's high points. Most importantly, his wife, Regina, makes the best cup of coffee on the entire Atlantic coast (no kidding), not to mention a mean lemonade, pizza, and wheat bread upon request. Nautilus also has a fully-equipped house for rent, with a porch, kitchen, and seven beds for $50 a night.

SHOPPING

There are a few *pulperías* (corner stores) in Brig Bay, plus some "commercial center" mini-supermarkets scattered around the island. Local artists work in shell and black coral, but you'll be hard pressed to find any of it for sale. Try the park, for starters. If you're in the market for souvenirs, you're better off taking home some coco bread.

ACCOMMODATIONS

Traditionally more expensive than elsewhere in Nicaragua, Corn Island has been experiencing a price war between hoteliers, making accommodation a bit more reasonably priced, though you'll still drop a few more bones than back west. Hotels with restaurant service will make your stay a lot more pleasant, as eateries elsewhere on the island are few and far between.

Under $10

For less than $10, you can stay with a well-respected family on the north side of the island. Accommodations are simple, clean, safe, and out of the way, and a fun way to gain insight on island culture. **Marcos and Jeanette Gomez** (tel. 505/575-5187, $9 s) rent rooms out of their house or additional buildings out back facing the beach, and **Dorsey Campbell's Yellowtail House** offers a private cabin, plus boat trips out to the reefs. No meals, but Seva's Dos Millas is conveniently right around the corner. Behind the airport, **Hospedaje Angela** (tel. 505/575-5134 $7 s) is a long way from the water.

$10–25

Ⓜ Mini-Hotel Morgan (tel. 505/575-5052) on the north side boasts individual cabins with simple rooms at $15 s, $35 with a/c, fridge, TV, and private bath. They serve three meals a day in the restaurant, or climb the stairs to the open-air balcony for drinks and a top-notch view.

Hotel Beach View (tel. 505/575-5062, $15 s) is run-down, less fancy, and cheaper, with a nice second-story balcony overlooking the water. **Bayside Hotel** (tel. 505/575-5001, $15 s) is simple and pleasant, and their restaurant on stilts over the water is a fun experience. **Ⓜ The Enjoyment of Life Bungalows** (tel. 505/575-5005, $25 s), the most pleasant budget option, are on the island's breezy east coast on their own isolated, sunrise-facing beach. You'll find six nice cabins with private baths and double beds, a bar, restaurant, and camping in the dry season.

$25–50

The **Ⓜ Centro Turistico Picnic Center** (tel. 505/575-5204, verhodgson@yahoo.com, $40 d with a/c, TV, queen-sized beds, and private baths) enjoys not only the best uninterrupted crescent of white sand on the island but knows how to make the most of it. Vernon, the manager, has been in the tourism business for two decades and he runs a class act. Start with the best-stocked bar on the Atlantic coast, and an enormous palm-thatched, open-air patio on which to enjoy it. Then add classic Tosh and Marley tunes in the background, a first-class menu offering fresh-squeezed juices, organic vegetables, and specialties, like ginger lobster. Throw in volleyball pitches, and a party atmosphere to boot.

Hotel Club Paraíso, (tel. 505/575-5111) tucked away on its own grounds in Barrio Brig Bay, has 13 *cabaña*-style rooms with private baths, and fan or a/c for $33–55; laundry service and

---

"DROP YO BOOKA TO DA BENCH!" A FEW CREOLE EXPRESSIONS

Put your Spanish dictionary away in Bluefields—you're in Creole country! At times, the unique rhythms of the costeño tongue are quite difficult to understand, but not so tough to speak. Try some of these local expressions and see if you agree:

"How you mean?"
Explain that.

"No feel, no way."
Don't worry.

"I no vex."
I'm not angry.

"Do you manage what time?"
Do you know what time?

"That ain't nothing."
Thank you.

"Check you then."
Goodbye.

"Drop yo booka to da bench."
Sit down.

"Make I get tree o dem."
Give me three of those.

"She feelin to eat some."
She was in the mood to eat some.

"He own"
His.

"It molest we."
It bothers us.

"She done reach Raitipura."
She arrived at Raitpura.

"Every'ing nice, mon."
It's all good.

THE ATLANTIC COAST DRUG TRADE

Long the territory of pirates plying the waves in tall-sailed wooden vessels, Nicaragua's Atlantic coastline of sparsely populated rivers, cays, and hidden lagoons is now the haunt of drug merchants passing through with their cargo of refined South American cocaine bound for the United States. Nicaragua is increasingly finding itself part of the shadowy and violent world of narco-trafficking that threatens to unravel the social fabric of the entire Atlantic coast.

During the 1980s, each Atlantic coast community had a Sandinista police force and a boat to patrol the coastal waters and estuaries. The governments that have succeeded the Sandinistas have done away with that police presence for lack of the resources to sustain it; in the vacuum of power, the Atlantic coast has become a lawless and virtually unpatrolled haven that plays easily into the hands of drug runners who land to reconsolidate, divide, or distribute their merchandise. The government and military's meager resources are no match for the well-equipped "Go-fast" drug boats sporting 250–500 horsepower engines with the latest in GPS, radar, and weaponry.

It's a well-known fact that many drug boats pass through the wilds of the Miskito Cays, an archipelago of islets, mangrove swamps, and trackless lagoons where the police have found stashes of gasoline used by drug boats headed north to the States. Other points of entry to Nicaragua include Cabo Gracias a Dios and the Río Coco, the city of Rama and the Río Escondido, the northern half of the Pearl Lagoon, and the community of Sandy Bay. Some of these traffickers purchase gasoline from willing locals, paying with bales of high grade, uncut product.

Other drugs come to shore when Colombian traffickers transiting Nicaraguan waters jettison their cargo into the sea when threatened with boarding or capture, either abandoning it or circling back later, using their ample knowledge of the Atlantic currents to predict where the packages will turn up on the beach.

Whether recovered off the beach by the locals or traded offshore by Nicaraguan traffickers, some of the Colombian cocaine inevitably makes it to the communities of the Atlantic coast, where its resale value is irresistible in a region so rampant with unemployment and a rapidly declining quality of life. No one knows for sure just how much coke is passing through Nicaragua's Atlantic coast, though the unofficial word on the street is that 10 kilos change hands every day in Puerto Cabezas alone.

At present, the issue of drug trafficking is far more serious than that of drug use. Even the local ministers have given up exhorting locals not to touch drugs, conceding it's all right to sell or transport drugs (but not use them) if it benefits the community. The reality of the area's poverty is too hard to overcome. But the situation is turning dangerous. In early 2001, three Colombians turned up dead in the coastal community of Sandy Bay, with no explanations; supposedly, they were assassinated by Yatama for having tried to hook the locals on their product, which they were offering at ridiculously low prices. In 2004, hired gunmen burst into the police station at Bluefields, blowing away six officers in a carefully-planned hit. But even just aiding in the trafficking of drugs has deteriorated the coastal societies, which find themselves suddenly caught in the kind of turf wars and gun battles that South Americans and the residents of inner cities of the United States know too well.

Because of drug trafficking crackdowns, you can expect police to thoroughly inspect your bags at every dock and airport

snorkel gear are also available. The restaurant here is not cheap, but the variety and food are alright (from $4 breakfasts and $5 burgers, all the way up to the $17 surf and turf). Snorkel rental and a half-block walk to the beach make snorkeling simple. More traditional rooms are available at **Hotel Restaurante Puerta del Sol** (tel. 505/575-5135, $30/50 s/d), immediately adjacent to the airport with no view.

FOOD

Outside the hotels, there are very few restaurants. The most obvious is **Fisher's Cave**, adjacent to the docks, with a breezy deck over the water of the bay. **N Seva's Dos Millas** (Two Miles) however is the undisputed champion of the island, serving top-notch seafood and ice-cold beer. A meal at **Bayside Hotel** will convince you lobster tastes best next to the sea. Meals are served in a building on stilts directly over the water. Fifty meters north of the airport, **Comedor La Rotonda** makes a mean *gallo pinto* with toasted coco bread for $2.

But for a real happy belly, fill up on **coconut bread,** which usually comes out around midday. Sandra, 50 meters south of the airport (look for a small roadside sign), has followed her mother's tradition of baking the best coco bread on the island.

INFORMATION AND SERVICES

INTUR staff occupy a corner of the airport and may give you a map of the island: Take it with a grain of salt. Every hotel on the island seems to have a slightly different version of this map (in which the competition isn't listed); the INTUR bulletin board is a better source of local goings-on.

The post office is 50 meters south of the airport. There is no Internet on the island, but there is a fax machine at the Acopio across from Fisher's Cave for a steep fee. ENITEL (the phone office) is north of the docks and around the corner. Caley Dagnall is the only bank on the island, occupying a windowless, grim concrete block building on the road south of the airport. You need a passport to

exchange cash or traveler's checks, and there are no credit-card cash advances.

GETTING THERE AND AWAY
By Air
Both Atlantic Airlines and La Costeña airlines offer daily flights to Corn Island (see the Atlantic Coast Flight Schedule special topic).

By Sea
The *Captain D* leaves Bluefields (El Bluff, actually) bound for Corn Island on Wednesdays and returns on Sundays. It's a four-hour, sun-baked trip. Contact the Emusepci office just inside the gates of the municipal dock for current ship schedules (open 7 A.M.–5:30 P.M., tel. 505/575-5193). The same ship may be able to take you all the way upriver to El Rama. To travel in relative luxury, look into the *Ferry 1,* a weekly freighter between El Rama and Corn Island, which will actually arrange your entire overland journey from Granada or Managua. The timing of the trip (it involves several overnights on the boat) is strange, as is the price, which is nearly as expensive as a roundtrip plane ticket, but feel free to look into it (tel. 505/277-0970, ferry1@ibw.com.ni, semarflu@ibw.com.ni).

ORIENTATION AND GETTING AROUND

From the airport, it's a five-minute westward walk to the waterfront, town park (a thin strip of grass and benches), and municipal docks with *panga* service to Little Corn. This "downtown" area is known as Brig Bay. The concrete road, paved since 2003, traces a loop around the northern part of the island as far south as the airport. The nicest beaches on the island are in the southern half: Both South West Bay and Long Beach are gorgeous. The north half of the island tends to be rocky with sharp coral formations.

Taxis cost under $.75 to go anywhere on the island, prices double at night. Minibuses circumnavigate the island twice an hour and cost $.35.

Little Corn Island

A humble, wilder version of its big brother, Little Corn is a mere three square kilometers of tropical desert island laced with footpaths and surrounded on three sides by nine kilometers of coral reef burgeoning with marine life. "La Islita" or "Little Island," as the locals know it, is a delicate paradise, visited by an ever-increasing number of travelers. Although there are accommodations for several ranges of budgets here, the rough ride across 30 kilometers of open ocean should serve to hold destructively large crowds at bay. Little Corn is unpoliced (and a bit of money in the right hands is keeping it that way), edgy, and a little wild. Take a flashlight, your snorkel gear, and a good book. But get here quick: Thick yellow folders sitting on the desks of land developers everywhere ensure this island won't be rustic for long.

SPORTS AND RECREATION

There is plenty to do on La Islita. In between meals, plan for beach hikes, snorkel excursions, and lots of time reading and swinging in your hammock. The Casa Iguana offers fishing, snorkeling, and picnic trips, and most of the beachfront hotels have snorkel gear for rent. For a rewarding hike, walk to the school, turn right and follow the sidewalk to its end; then follow the foot path up and to the left to reach the **lighthouse** (about 20 minutes from the waterfront), perched on Little Corn's highest peak.

Diving

The island's sole scuba shop is also Nicaragua's most developed and professional operation: **Dive Little Corn** (www.divelittlecorn.com, info@divelittlecorn.com) is the first thing you'll see as you get off the *panga,* right on the beach next to the Happy Hut. Services include daily morning and afternoon dives for novice through advanced divers, night dives by appointment, hourly and all-day snorkel trips, PADI certification courses, and kayak rentals. Most dives around the island are shallow (less than 60 feet), but there are a few deeper dives that are more than 100 feet. Little Corn's reef system is unique not only for its healthy abundance of wildlife, but also for its coral formations, which include

The Atlantic Coast

© RANDY WOOD

Little Corn Island: the view from Casa Iguana

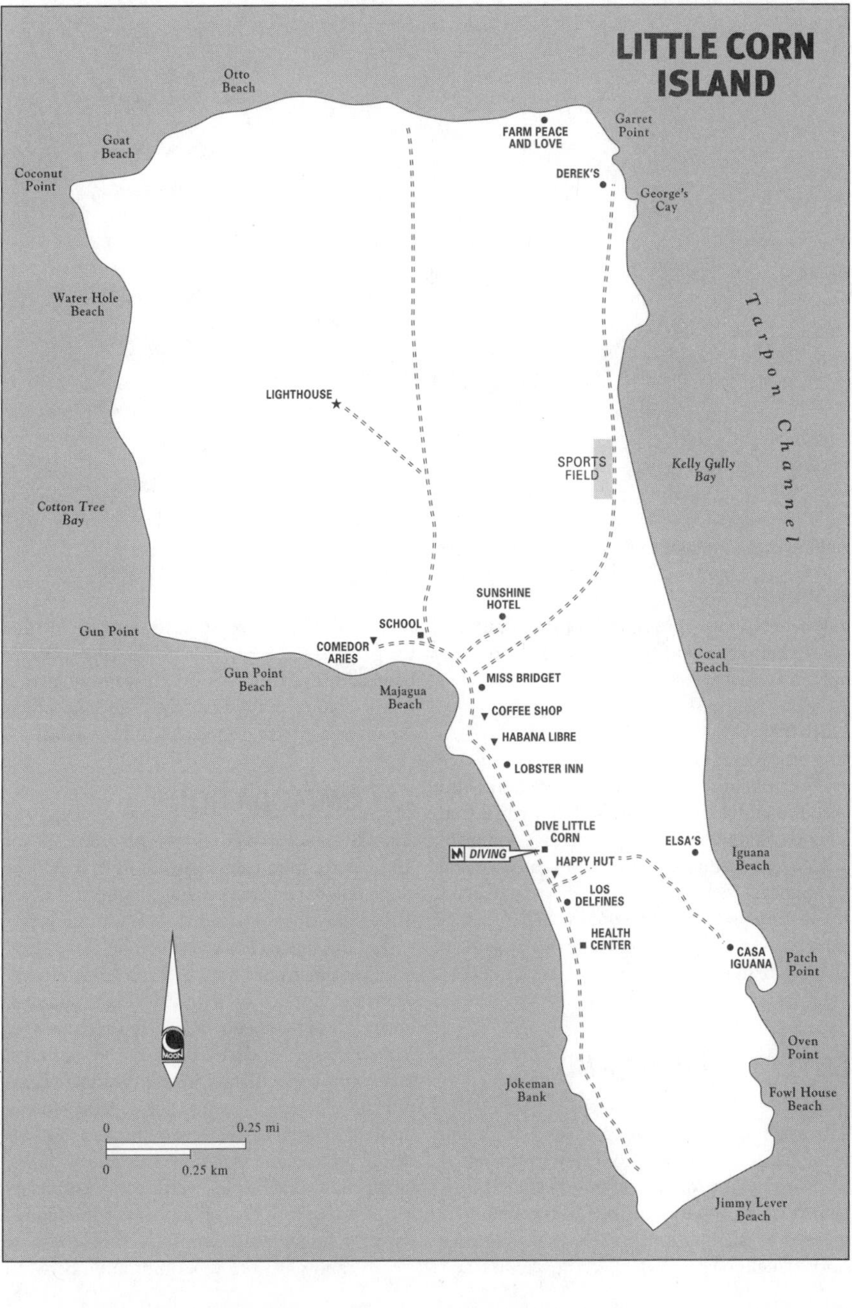

LITTLE CORN ISLAND

Otto Beach

Goat Beach

Coconut Point

FARM PEACE AND LOVE

Garret Point

DEREK'S

George's Cay

Water Hole Beach

Tarpon Channel

LIGHTHOUSE ★

SPORTS FIELD

Kelly Gully Bay

Cotton Tree Bay

Gun Point

SUNSHINE HOTEL

SCHOOL

COMEDOR ARIES

Cocal Beach

Gun Point Beach

Majagua Beach

MISS BRIDGET

COFFEE SHOP

HABANA LIBRE

LOBSTER INN

DIVE LITTLE CORN

DIVING

ELSA'S

Iguana Beach

HAPPY HUT

LOS DELFINES

HEALTH CENTER

CASA IGUANA

Patch Point

Oven Point

Jokeman Bank

Fowl House Beach

0   0.25 mi

0   0.25 km

Jimmy Lever Beach

MOON

The Atlantic Coast

Fishing is the mainstay of the Atlantic coast economy.

overhangs, swim-throughs, and the infamous shark cave. For up-to-date prices and more details, visit their website.

Fishing

The fishing is "good" around Little Corn. There are lobsters and sea urchins everywhere, and within a couple kilometers of shore, you'll find schools of kingfish, dolphin, amber jack, red snapper, and barracuda. Fly fishers can catch tarpon and bonefish right from the beach, or hire Grant at Casa Iguana to take you out for $35 a person. Boat trips can also be arranged with a number of locals, or at the Hotel Delfines—ask around on the front side for a good deal.

ENTERTAINMENT AND NIGHTLIFE

The best place on the island to sip a drink and enjoy the gorgeous waterfront view of the big island on the horizon is certainly Habana Libre, owned by a Cuban transplant to the island ("I married an islander. Everyone here has the same story," laughs owner Ronaldo). The offer the best

mojito on the east coast, with mint fresh from the garden, and home base for the Island Braves baseball team. Or check out the **Happy Hut,** a reggae-colored building on the front side, which organizes a grinding good time on weekends.

ACCOMMODATIONS

A variety of accommodations is now available on Little Corn, from palm-thatch huts to cozy traveler cabins to conventional hotel rooms with color TVs. How close to nature do you want to be?

Ⅿ Casa Iguana (casaiguana@mindspring.com, www.casaiguana.net, from $25 s) is a cinch to recommend: Located on the cliffs of the southeast, breezy side of the island, the Casa Iguana consists of a dozen raised, wooden cabins on the southeast, breezy side of the island, clustered around a communal, hilltop lodge where guests gather to eat, drink, and listen to the waves. The compound is run by two southerners from the United States, Grant and Cathy Peeples, whose native hospitality is matched only by their effort to live harmoniously with the fragile ecosystem of Little Corn. The eleven cabins are a clever compromise between

COMMON FISH FOUND ALONG THE ATLANTIC COAST

Queen triggerfish	Pejepuerco cachuo	Balistes vetula
Blue tang surgeonfish	Navajón azul	Acanthurus coerelus
Squirrelfish	Candil gallito	Holocentrus ascensionis
Atlantic spadefish	Paguara	Chaetodipterus faber
Yellowtail snapper	Rabirrubia	Ocyurus chrisurus
Puddingwife wrasse	Doncella arco iris	Halichoeres radiatus
Blue parrotfish	Pez loro	Scarus coeruleus
Chub mackerel	Estornino	Scomber japonicus
Bar jack	Cojinua carbonera	Caranz rubber
Hogfish	Doncella de pluma	Lachnolaimus maximus
Caesar grunt	Ronco carbonero	Haemulon carbonarium
Red grouper	Mero rojo	Epinephelus morio
Great barracuda	Picuda barracuda	Sphyraena barracuda
French angelfish	Cachama negra	Pomacanthus arcuatus

rustic simplicity and comfort, and include soft mattresses, outdoor showers, private, breezy porches with hammocks, and shelves full of books. Join the other guests each morning for breakfast and each evening for a jovial happy hour and family-style dinner, frequently the day's catch. Casa Iguana provides a host of services, such as snorkel gear rental, picnic excursions to Goat Beach, fishing trips ($45 a person, $10 each additional person), and satellite email. Grant and Cathy know the island better than anybody—above and below the waterline—and are always willing to help you plan your days.

There are two conventional hotels that offer modern rooms with private baths and all the amenities. **Hotel Los Delfines** (tel. 505/892-0186 or 285-5239, hotellosdelfines@hotmail.com, $20–60 s) is the larger, with individual, air-conditioned concrete and glass cabins. They'll be glad to arrange trips for you. Local-owned **Sunshine Hotel** (tel. 505/883-9870, $45 d) is the other, and is rather quiet. A bit simpler but still breezy and clean, **Hotel Lobster Inn** ($20 s) has basic rooms with no a/c, but a full menu in the restaurant downstairs.

There are several cheap *hospedajes* offering not-so-special accommodations: Check out the **Guess House** [sic] Sweet Dreams, for example ($15 s). Otherwise it's back to nature: **Derek's Place** ($4 pp camping, $14 thatch hut, $20 raised cabin) is a long hike to the north end of the island, and from his place to the west you'll find **Ensueños, Wichos,** and **Casa Sunrise** ($20 s), all of which offer bare-bones accommodations in palm-thatch huts or similar. Derek's offers a single meal a day Monday–Friday, and Ensueños makes breakfast but otherwise you'll have to hike back into town for a meal or carry your provisions with you. The easiest way to the north shore is to strike a deal with your *panga* driver. The next easiest is to follow the coast. Cut to the east side of the island as though you were heading to the Casa Iguana and then strike north along the beach. It's about a 45-minute walk: When you reach a rocky, difficult-to-pass point, you're about half way. For the intrepid, try going overland: Follow the track from Miss Bridgit's east and northward, crossing a rugged, muddy ball field, bearing left at the coconut swamp, and keeping the concrete fence-post line to your right. If you have a compass, follow that track for as long as you're headed NNE. Good walking shoes are a must.

Hard to find but worth the effort, **Farm Peace Love** (farmpeacelove@hotmail.com) has a guest room for $40 a couple including breakfast, and a gorgeous fully-equipped (washer, drier, full kitchen) guesthouse for four people ($65/night; 5 night minimum). Unless you get dropped off on their beach, count on a 45-minute trek to get there.

Food

Nearly every accommodation offers meals, but feel free to get out and about to discover some other options. **Elsa's Great Food and Drinks** offers just that, but slowly, in a beachside barbecue setting on the east side of the island. On front side, **Bridgett's First Stop Comedor** is a good choice for home cookin'. **Hotel Lobster Inn** is more formal and offers chicken and steak as well. Knock on the door at the blue house past the school to inquire about coconut bread.

Italian native Paola Carminiani will cook a legitimate three-course Italian meal for $12 a person at her place, **Farm Peace Love.** Have the dive shop radio her at least one day in advance.

Services

The ENITEL (open 8 A.M.–5 P.M. Mon.–Fri.) is the yellow building with the satellite dish, across from the big blue *acopio;* you can find a wimpy health clinic just south of the Hotel Delfines. Anything more complicated than that requires a *panga* ride back to the big island, or even Bluefields.

Getting There and Away

Sometimes one, sometimes two *pangas* ply the route between Corn Island and Little Corn Island ($6 each way, 40 minutes) and are coordinated with the departure and arrival of the two rounds of daily flights. Boats depart from Big Corn Island (pay a $.20 harbor tax) at about 9 A.M. and 4 P.M.; boats depart Little Corn Island at 7 A.M. and 2 P.M.

The trip to Little Corn is often choppy and rough, especially when the seas are up. You can expect to get wet no matter what the weather. Both *panga* drivers enjoy racing their friends,

tipping a cold one before getting behind the wheel, and pushing for mad air. Seats in the front afford a more violent bashing; seats in the back are prone to more frequent splashes of spray. Since it's inevitable, wear your bathing suit and enjoy the ride. The *pulperías* across from the dock on Big Corn sell heavy, blue plastic bags that fit over a backpack for less than $1—an essential investment for keeping your gear dry. Alternatively, rent your own boat and driver, which runs $70–90 each way. Smooth-drivin' Charlie, on Little Corn, provides this service; he can be contacted through any of the hotels there.

A number of larger fishing boats travel between the islands, and these may agree to take on a paying passenger. See Miss Bridgett for the day's schedule. Also, coming soon: boat service for up to 50 passengers between Bluefields and the Corn Islands on Captain Emíldo's ship, *The Adventurer.*

ORIENTATION AND GETTING AROUND

Unless you make special arrangements with your *panga* driver to take you elsewhere, you will be let off at the southwestern-facing beach, where you'll find a cement sidewalk that runs the length of the village. This is called the "front side" by islanders and is the center of most social activity.

Walk north along that sidewalk to the school, baseball field, and phone office before the road deposits you in the unsavory barrios where miserable migrant workers camp out in huts of black plastic and corrugated steel. Turn right at the school for the walk up to the lighthouse and the north side of the island, or follow the red muddy track from Miss Bridget's place through forests and swamps to the north beach and Derek's place. Just south of the dive shop is another muddy track that leads across to the "breezy side" of the island and the Casa Iguana.

Circumnavigating the island on the beach is ill-advised, as the sandy shoreline is interrupted by long, rocky, impassible sections, both at Goat Beach and the southern tip of the island. Elsewhere, there are long sandy stretches of beach to enjoy and explore.

Puerto Cabezas (Bilwi)

Far away from everything, in the northeastern corner of Nicaragua, Puerto Cabezas (or just "Puerto," or even "Port" as it is affectionately known) is hard enough to get to that it may just as well be an island. Because it's only marginally connected to the rest of Pacific Nicaragua by semi-passable roads that turn marshy and unusable during most of the rainy season, most travelers prefer to fly to this outpost city. Puerto is connected to Bluefields by common heritage and history, but nothing more; no roads have ever linked the two major communities of the Atlantic coast.

It is entirely possible that you'll be the only traveler in this town of 56,000 inhabitants, but enough foreign volunteers and missionaries have passed through that you won't draw too much attention. In Puerto, most streets are nothing more

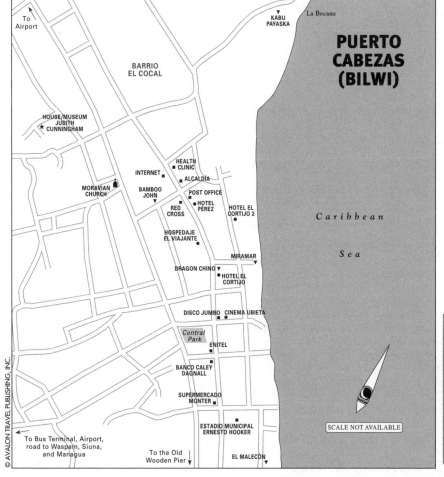

The Atlantic Coast

MAYANGNA LEGENDS

The Origin of the Sun and Moon

In the beginning of time there were, in addition to the humans, two great gods: Uhubaput, the creator of the world, and his companion Udo. One day, the two gods came down to earth disguised as humans suffering from a horrid skin disease that caused blemishes and oozing sores. All the humans who came across Uhubaput and Udo insulted them. The men tried to run them out of town, while the women scolded Uhubaput and Udo and refused to offer them glasses of *chicha* or *wasbul* (traditional, grain-based beverages) to drink. Finally, the townspeople captured the two and "killed" them. Of course, they had no idea Uhubaput and Udo were gods, and, of course, the two gods came back to life immediately.

Uhubaput and Udo returned to town and the first thing they did was to steal all the *wasbul* and drink it. They then began to attack the town. Cutting small saplings, they made a great quantity of arrows. As they shot each arrow, they called out the name of an animal. The arrow, in mid-flight, was converted into the animal and ran through the town causing great damage. Uhubaput and Udo then transformed themselves into strong, handsome humans, and reentered the town. This time, they were received gladly by the women of the town, who were attracted to Uhubaput's and Udo's good looks, and who offered to become their wives.

Uhubaput and Udo were enraged that the women who had been so unfriendly to them when they had appeared sickly were now so eager to marry them. In their fury, they cast divine spells on the women of the town, turning them into different types of small animals. Only two women were spared—the most beautiful and light-skinned. These, Uhubaput and Udo took to be their wives.

When they were done, Uhubaput and Udo danced on the campfire like *Sukias* (priests), raising their arms and fingertips upwards to rise into heaven. Udo began first, but had no luck in rising. Uhubaput then tried. He rose slowly into the heavens where he became the sun. When Udo tried again, he too rose upwards into the heavens, where he became the moon.

The Origin of the Rocks of Kiawa

The god Papangh sent his servant Alwana (Thunder) to earth to teach the people how to be farmers and create baskets and pots with their hands, as well as other things humans would need to prosper. One day when Alwana wasn't home, a *walasa* (evil spirit) by the name of Kiawa entered Alwana's home and stole his wife.

But a parrot had seen what happened and flew to Alwana to tell what had happened in his absence. Alwana was in the fields at the time, planting pine trees in a rocky area known as Alwana

than streaks of bare red earth connecting neighborhoods of humble wooden homes set on stilts. It's a glimpse of many worlds, with Miskitos sailing wooden canoes that they tie up to the old dock alongside steel fishing boats. Puerto is homely and accessible, and it's an easy walk from anywhere in town to the water's edge for a swim in the Caribbean.

This is one of the most important economic centers for the Miskito communities of the northern Atlantic coast and the Río Coco. Outside of Waspám and the communities of the Río Coco, it's one of very few places in Nicaragua where you're less likely to hear Spanish than Miskito—or even Mayangna—spoken on the street.

HISTORY

The Mayangna inhabitants that settled in Puerto Cabezas gave it the name Bilwi, in reference to the great quantity of *wi* (leaves) and the equally great number of snakes hidden in the foliage ("Bil"). Renamed after the general that President Zelaya sent out to the Atlantic coast to unify the nation, Puerto Cabezas—like much of Nicaragua's Atlantic coast—has seen more glorious days. Its zenith was probably at the start of the 20th century, when Puerto was the center for exportation of Atlantic coast lumber and mineral products, including gold from the mining triangle. Its airstrip was, in 1964, the longest in Central America. Testimony to the wealth of Puerto Cabezas during

kumani umhna (a place that really exists: It's found on the Kiwaska River and is a rocky area covered in pine trees). Alwana immediately stopped what he was doing to search for his wife and recapture her. After much searching, he found Kiawa and the woman far upstream in a tributary of the Río Tuma called Río Iyas. But even though Kiawa was drunk, he was an immense and powerful giant, and Alwana was unable to defeat him.

As they fought, Kiawa transformed himself into a giant boa constrictor and devoured the woman so she wouldn't run to Alwana. Alwana grew bigger to try to topple Kiawa, but Kiawa continued growing. The two grew larger and larger until finally Alwana was taller than the clouds. Hidden by the clouds, he took out his machete and cut Kiawa into many pieces. As the pieces fell to earth, the many people Kiawa had devoured were released and returned to life. The pieces of Kiawa became rocks, which can be seen today at the headwaters of the Río Iyas in an area now known as Kiawa. The locals say these rocks are known to bleed from time to time, and certain pieces of Kiawa's body, like his navel and his head, can be spotted very easily.

The Great Flood
Two brothers by the names of Suku and Kuru went out fishing on the Kwahliwah creek, a small tributary of the Río Ukungwas. They caught many fish, especially the Sirik. But, suddenly, a huge fish by the name of Susum took the hook and Suku reeled it in. Suku wanted to roast and eat the fish immediately, but Kuru was opposed to the idea, thinking suspiciously that Susum was really an evil demon. But Suku stubbornly cut a piece of the fish, roasted it and ate it. Immediately, Suku was consumed by a terrible thirst. He had eaten quite a bit and felt too full to get up to get water, so he asked his brother Kuru to bring him water from the river to drink. But no matter how much water Kuru brought him, Suku couldn't slake his thirst. Finally, Kuru grew tired of making so many trips to the river for water and helped drag Suku to the river's edge so he could drink his fill. But as Suku bent down to drink from the river's edge his body lengthened and grew slippery and he began to change into an anaconda with a human face. Kuru grew frightened and ran alone back to town, where he told people Suku had stayed behind to fish. But people were suspicious and finally everyone went down to the river's edge to find Suku—now an immense anaconda—at the top of a ceiba tree. As everyone looked up at Suku in the tree, a massive wave rose out of the river, drowning the entire nation with the exception of Suku and his offspring.

---

the lumber boom is the enormous wooden dock that juts into the Atlantic, built in the mid-1940s out of locally cut hardwoods.

Somoza was well liked in Puerto and the northeast because he largely left the area alone. Puerto locals fondly recall the times Tacho would arrive on the Atlantic coast in his private plane, barbecuing with the locals and telling jokes. Their fondness for Somoza made the Sandinista years even more bitter for the Miskito people. During the 1980s, Puerto absorbed the brunt of the refugee flow out of the Río Coco area when Contra and Sandinista incursions made day-to-day existence miserable and/or impossible for the Miskitos.

Today, with the war behind them and the people back in their ancestral homes, Puerto Cabezas is largely a coastal backwater and commercial hub for the northeast. Its small economy is based on commerce—particularly of wood, fish, and transport. The Nicaraguan military maintains a naval base here, from which it patrols the northern Atlantic coast and Miskito Cays. There are scattered jobs in the timber and fishing industries, and a lot of people looking for a legitimate way to earn a living. While a significant number of Puerteños work in government jobs—Puerto is not only the departmental capital, but also the center of the indigenous community's government—several thousand workers were laid off when the Chamorro government replaced the FSLN, and the city has never quite recovered.

The Atlantic Coast

Another mainstay is "red gold," as lobsters caught off the Miskito coast are referred to; lobster fishing has become, in only the last two decades, a $50-million export industry comprising 10 percent of Nicaragua's foreign trade—but at an enormous cost. In the last couple of years, the international press began reporting that a horrific number of Miskito lobster divers were being crippled and killed as they dove deeper and deeper in search of lobster, usually with faulty equipment and a dangerous lack of safety training. Former Miskito divers in wheelchairs outnumber tourists on many white-sand beaches and untold hundreds have died from the bends. One World Bank report stated that close to 100 percent of (Miskito) divers show symptoms of neurological damage—"presumably due to inadequate decompression."

As area divers kill themselves in order to put lobster on American and Canadian dinner tables, life struggles on in Puerto and the surrounding villages, with a wary eye on the future. Tankers from Venezuela and Curaçao periodically pull up at the dock to replenish the town's supply of petroleum, and a Louisiana-based engineering company continues to fuss with plans to build a modernized port complex complete with grain silos, a power plant, container storage, industrial cargo cranes, and facilities for deepwater tankers; but after years of talk, there is still only the decrepit old dock. In the meantime, Puerto Cabezas continues to experience a two-headed wave of immigration: poor Miskito families from the Río Coco area in search of a better life, and wealthy families from Managua who are starting businesses and buying beachfront properties.

GETTING AROUND

Puerto Cabezas has no bus system, though the mayor's office is trying to put a couple of local city buses in place. In the meantime, Puerto has—no joke—500 licensed taxis cruising the streets in search of fares. The price is fixed at about $.50 per person to go anywhere in town, a bit more to go from the airport to the pier or to the bus terminal.

SIGHTS AND ATTRACTIONS

The **old wooden pier** is the mainstay of the town and certainly worth a look. Built in the 1940s of precious woods culled from the nearby forest, the pier has been on its last legs for years due to extensive hurricane damage, saltwater, and old age. Tied up there are usually a motley crew of old fishing freighters, Miskito double-ended sailboats, and small fiberglass *pangas.* The pier is beautiful during the day, but dangerous at night.

Near the center of town is an interesting house/museum commemorating the life and work of **Judith Kain Cunningham,** a local painter who left behind many works of art when she passed away in 2001 (entrance $1). A prolific artist and artisan, her subject matter was the Río Coco and the Miskito communities of the Waspám region, her passion for which shows through in many of her paintings. Also on display are other works of macramé, sculpture, and more.

At the north end of town just past Kabu Payaska

the old Catholic church in Puerto Cabezas

restaurant is **La Bocana,** a sandy Atlantic coast beach. Enjoy a swim or a splash in the surf, or walk north along the beach to explore the shipwreck of an old fishing boat that wandered in too close to shore.

In Barrio El Cocal, in the northern part of town, the **Moravian church** has services in Miskito every Sunday morning. Puerto has several other pretty churches: the Moravian church and school in the center of town, the **Catholic church** with its stained glass, and the remnants of the former Catholic church behind it.

Located a few kilometers away on the road out of town is the local **URACCAN** campus. What's interesting about the Puerto branch is that during the 1980s it was a military base from which soldiers patrolled the northeast corner of the country. These days, its transformation to an institution of higher learning has been so complete you'd never guess its former incarnation. There's a good library, as well as people with a wealth of information about the area.

ENTERTAINMENT AND EVENTS

Just east of the park is a new movie theater, the **Cinema Ubieta,** built in 2001. It shows films as soon as a week or two after the Managua theaters; admission is about $2, and it presents around two movies per week. In light of the sudden stiff competition, Puerto's original theater, on the corner facing the park, has taken to showing only after-hours adult films.

Disco Jumbo, on the east side of the park, is an old classic with a Caribbean feel that hasn't changed in years. Dance to the throbbing beat of *soka* and salsa; Tuesdays and Wednesdays are ladies' nights. The atmosphere at **Miramar** is better, but the crowd is definitely a bit younger than at Jumbo. Tuesdays, Wednesdays, and Thursdays are ladies' nights. At both clubs, the entrance fee Tuesday–Friday is $.75, Saturday $1.50, and $2.25 for special events. The **Malecón** is Puerto's most happening nightlife venue, with inside and outside tables overlooking the beach and two dance floors that start throbbing on the weekends.

Both **Atlantico,** a bar, and the **Midnight** (located right across from the park) have unsavory reputations; Midnight in particular is the favorite hangout of Puerto's late-night underworld.

Semana Santa in Puerto Cabezas is an unforgettable event that all overseas Puerteños try to come home for. The town sets up dozens of thatched-hut ranchos at La Bocana beach, and the party lasts all day and night for at least a week. Food, drink, music, and of course lots of Caribbean-style dancing—it's all here. Stumble back to your hotel room once in a while to rest and refuel.

SPORTS AND RECREATION

Baseball rules in the northeast, and passions can run high during the height of the season. Check out games almost every weekend in **El Estadio Municipal Ernesto Hooker,** two blocks south of the park. A homerun can just about land in the Caribbean.

ACCOMMODATIONS

Under $10

El Viajante Hospedaje (Barrio Revolución, tel. 505/792-2263) is cheap, safe, and central, with 30 rooms from $7 for shared bath and fan to $16/21 s/d for private bath, a/c, and cable TV. Three meals a day are served in the restaurant.

$10–25

El Cortijo (on main drag, a block south of the mayor's office, tel. 505/792-2340) has rooms ranging from $13 singles to $24 doubles with a/c, private bath, and cable TV; laundry service and parking are available. **M El Cortijo 2** is a classy and elegant version of the first, only two blocks away and sitting atop a bluff over the breaking surf, which you'll hear from your room. It boasts stained-hardwood interiors, a wonderful ocean-facing deck, and a semi-private beach at the bottom of the stairs. Six rooms cost $24 s/d for private bath, a/c, and cable TV; breakfasts are also available.

Hotel Pérez (tel. 505/792-2362, $18/21 s/d) has eight different rooms, all set in an old wooden house on the main drag. All rooms have their own bathroom, and several have a/c.

El Cortijo 2 hotel has a gorgeous ocean view from its backyard.

FOOD

There are three excellent restaurants in Puerto Cabezas evenly distributed through town, all offering essentially the same menu of shellfish, fresh fish, soups, beef, and chicken. At the north end of town, the best meal in the city can be had at M **Restaurante Kabu Payaska** (Sea Breeze), serving seafood on a beautiful grassy lawn overlooking the ocean; $6–8 for lobster, shrimp, or fresh fish. More toward the center of town, **Miramar** is a fraction cheaper and has a view just about as good. Meals at night here can be unforgettable, as the moon rises out of the Atlantic in front of you. There's also dancing on weekends—in fact, some people think of it only as a disco. At the south end of town near the dock is **El Malecón,** with very much the same type of environment and menu.

If for some reason you get tired of fresh, cheap, delicious seafood, you can give your palate a break at the **Dragon Chino,** which serves Nicaraguan-influenced versions of chow mein, egg rolls, and stir-fries. The fried wontons are a town favorite (of course, you can get seafood here as well).

INFORMATION

For a taste of life in Puerto and Nicaragua's northeast, tune in one of the local radio stations for news and commentary—even more interesting if you speak Miskito. Radio Miskut (104.1 FM) has lots of Miskito music and other programming; they also present the "Voice of America." Radio Van (90.3 FM) presents itself as "The Voice of the North Atlantic," but it throws in a cheesy *ranchera* song now and again just for good measure.

SHOPPING

Supermercado Monter is a surprisingly good store, offering a full selection of canned and dry goods, fresh foods, and basic housewares. It's a good place to stock up if you're headed north toward the Río Coco. There are several municipal markets on the main commercial drag as well.

SERVICES

The **post office** is located northeast of the park (open 8 A.M.–noon, 1:30–5 p.m. Mon.–Fri., until noon Sat.). **ENITEL** is located a block southeast of the park (open 7 A.M.–9:30 P.M. Mon.–Fri.); **Banco Caley Dagnall** (across from ENITEL, tel. 505/792-2211, open 8 A.M.–4:30 P.M. Mon.–Fri., till noon Sat.) is the only bank in town, so lines can be horrendous—you may easily have to wait an hour to change money. Your best bet is at noon, when everyone else in town goes home for lunch; otherwise, bring a book. Find Internet cafés at **CECOM** (half-block south of El Cortijo 1) and at **Bilwinet** (behind the Pegatel) for about $1.50/hour. There's another Internet place with a/c right across from the mayor's office.

There's a run-down municipal **hospital** a block from the bus terminal. It has well-trained staff but struggles to keep on hand even the most basic supplies, so, while it's adequate for basic treatment, you should probably leave the complicated procedures for elsewhere, preferably Managua.

GETTING THERE AND AWAY
By Air

A quick flight from Managua or Bluefields is the only practical way to get to Puerto Cabezas. From Managua, Atlantic Airlines has flights departing at 6:30 A.M. and 10:30 A.M., and La Costeña at 6:30 A.M., 10:30 A.M., and 2 P.M. (no 2:00 flight on Sunday).

From Puerto, Atlantic flies to Managua 8 A.M. and noon Monday–Saturday (at noon on Sunday). La Costeña has flights to Managua at 8:30 A.M., 12:30 P.M., and 4 P.M. Monday–Saturday and at 8 A.M. and noon on Sunday. The flight from Managua takes about 90 minutes.

the "Be on Time" Diner

© RANDY WOOD

The Atlantic Coast

SPEAKING MISKITO

The Miskito language doesn't use the vowel sounds "e" (as in bread) or "o" (as in boat), which makes it a flowing, rhythmic language of "a," "i," and "u," as in the following sentence, which exhorts the locals not to let the Yellow Coconut Virus infect the coconut plantations: *Coco lalahni taki pruiba sikniska alki takaskayasa.*

Here are a couple of words you might come across during your travels in the northeast:

Hello	Naksa
Goodbye	Aisabi
What is your name?	Ninam dia?
How are you?	Nahki sma?
Fine	Pain
Bad	Saura
Sick	Siknis
Bye-bye	Aisabi
Thank you	Tingki pali
Food	Plun
Toilet	Tailit
Water	Li
Help	Help
Dirty	Taski
Clean	Klin
Meat	Wina
Chicken	Kalila
Rice and Beans	Rais n bins
Fish	Inska
Small boat	Duri
Lagoon	Kabu
River	Awala
Birds	Natnawira nani
Parrot	Rahwa

One flight per day (every day except Sunday) leaves Bluefields at 12:10 P.M., arriving in Puerto at 1 P.M. From Puerto to Bluefields, La Costeña has one flight per day every day except Sunday leaving at 11 A.M. In Puerto Cabezas, the Atlantic Airlines phone numbers are 505/282-2586, 505/282-2255, or 505/282-2523; La Costeña can be reached at 505/282-2255 or 505/282-2586. Always confirm flights beforehand; reservations or advanced ticket purchases are recommended.

By Land

Oh, you are a brave soul, indeed! Two daily buses (9 A.M. and 1 P.M.) make the arduous 24-hour journey through Nicaragua's muddy interior. The municipal bus terminal in Puerto Cabezas is located on the western edge of town.

The overland trip between the Pacific region and Puerto traverses the most poorly maintained roads in the country. Until recently, all foreign embassies in Nicaragua discouraged travel to or through the "mining triangle" (Siuna, Bonanza, and Rosita), occasionally visited by armed bandits looking for trouble and hostages. Increased police presence has helped dramatically, and more than one traveler has passed through the region without incident, but this region remains a sketchy stretch of road.

Puerto buses leave Managua's Mayoreo terminal, or you can piece the trip together from Jinotega's north terminal on a bus bound for Waslala; from there, you board a second bus to Siuna, and then another to Puerto Cabezas. There's an alternate road from Matagalpa to Siuna by way of Río Blanco and Mulukuku. Both roads are largely impassable during the wet season.

Taxis to Lamlaya cost about $3.50, but you can just as easily hop a bus or truck from in front of Hotel El Cortijo 1 for $.50.

By Boat

There is no official boat transport between Puerto and Bluefields, but the adventurous may be able to score a ride with a local fisherman for the right price. Surer rides are to be had to Sandy Bay and other nearby coastal communities—ask around the dock.

NEAR PUERTO CABEZAS

In **Tuapí,** just 10 kilometers north of Puerto, there's a popular swimming hole on the banks of the river by the same name. Buses leave for Tuapí several times a day from the terminal in Puerto. It's also possible to travel by boat north or south along the Atlantic coast to visit Miskito communities. For points north, make arrangements with a boat owner at the old dock in Puerto Cabezas. You'll have better luck in the early mornings when the boats are setting out for a day's fishing. Someday, travelers will

You can catch boats northbound from Puerto Cabezas.

have interesting adventures in the gorgeous beach-front community of Sandy Bay (two hours from Puerto Cabezas) and the Miskito Cays (two hours across the open sea from Sandy Bay), but as of press time, both locations are known rendezvous points for drug runners and other dangerous types.

For points south, take a bus or taxi ($3.50 per person) to the community of Lamlaya. From there, boats leave daily for Wawa and Karata between noon and 1 P.M., charging $3 one way for a *panga*, and $2 for a "punkin" local boat (which takes twice as long). Or hire a boat to Prinzapolka, quite possibly the single hardest destination to reach in Nicaragua and the statistically poorest community in the nation. You should have a basic command of Miskito to visit these communities on your own, both to avoid suspicion and to be able to communicate.

Tours to the Miskito Communities

The best way to visit and experience local indigenous communities is with **AMICA** (Asociación de Mu-

jeres Indígenas de la Costa Atlántica), an organization making an effort to promote the empowerment and development of women along the northern Atlantic coast. AMICA gives training in gender development, reproductive health, leadership, and AIDS, plus the laws that affect indigenous women.

AMICA (tel. 505/792-2219, amicaenlace @nicarao.org.ni) offers tours to the Miskito communities of Haulover, Wawa Bar, and Karata, offering homestays, nature tours, and dance or cultural presentations. The accommodations aren't nearly as rustic as you'd think—the beds even have box spring mattresses, and the organization provides towels and so on. Prices vary but are quite reasonable (less than $15 pp per night, meals around $2, all negotiable depending on number of people). In all cases, it's crucial to call at least three days ahead so the dancers can limber up and the boatmen can tune up the outboards. The office is located 2.5 blocks south of the baseball stadium.

The Atlantic Coast

Waspám and the Río Coco

Waspám, in the far northern reaches of the Miskito pine savanna and at the edge of the mightiest river in Nicaragua, is the gateway, principal port, and economic heart of the Miskito communities that line the banks of the Río Coco. It is, in itself, a difficult place to get to, yet it is really the first step of the voyage to places even farther away still. The communities here would prefer to be left to their own ways, but this has not been the case, and the Miskito peoples of the Río Coco suffered more than most during the 1980s, including a massive relocation that is still cause for resentment.

Adventures along the Río Coco are neither easy nor cheap, and accommodations and travelers' facilities in the traditional sense of the word are practically nonexistent. The chance to visit this frontier—and it is truly frontier—to live and travel amongst the Miskito people, and to feel the spiritual power of the mighty Río Coco should not be missed. For a successful journey, travelers in this region absolutely must speak decent Spanish and make an effort to learn and use at least some rudimentary Miskito.

THE LAND AND PEOPLE

The Miskito people are reserved but friendly—once you've broken the ice, you'll find them helpful and inquisitive. They like to be left alone but they will certainly greet you with a smile if you approach them. They're also more conservative than other Nicaraguans, so leave the short shorts and bikini tops back home. The Miskito people speak Spanish as a second language and practically no English at all (even though some English words have been assimilated into Miskito, like rice and beans). Foreigners who speak languages other than Spanish or Miskito will inevitably be called Miriki (American). Even Nicaraguans from the Pacific region are considered foreigners and are referred to as mestizos. The Miskito people live largely off the river, fishing for small freshwater species, and off their small, neatly tended fields of corn, beans, and even upland rice. Their version of the ubiquitous tortilla is a thick, wheat-flour cake, which is fried in coconut oil. Starch makes up the rest of the diet along the Río Coco, including tubers like *quiquisque* and yuca. *Rondon* is a fish stew (and along the Río Coco it will be made of fish, not turtle, like on the coast), and the *gallo pinto* is cooked in coconut milk—there's no tastier way to clog your arteries. Wild game also finds its way onto the menu; don't be surprised to find boar, deer, and armadillo.

ENTERTAINMENT

Waspám has one small movie theater—if you call a video recorder projected onto a large screen a theater. Shows cost $1. There are two discos in town. Ko Fu is the liveliest and plays a variety of music, including Bryan Adams, the theme song from *Titanic,* and Palo de Mayo—cut a rug, Miskito style.

ACCOMMODATIONS

There are several lodging establishments, mostly offering shared baths consisting of bucket baths and pit latrines. Remember the Río Coco area is particularly prone to malaria and dengue fever. Make sure your *hospedaje* provides you with a mosquito net, or use your own. You can't rely on a fan to keep the mosquitoes away, as the electricity often fails or is cut off during the night.

Located right across from the airport is **Hospedaje Rose.** In the main house, all the rooms have private bathrooms and 24-hour electricity; three meals are available, as well as Internet and satellite TV. Rose also has a small movie theater.

Las Cabañas offers bamboo huts for around $3.50. **El Piloto** is located on the main road, about 2 minutes from Wangki. They have air-conditioned single rooms with private bathrooms and a kitchen area with meals available ($25).

FOOD

There are several small eateries in town, most serving rice and beans accompanied by a hunk of meat, sometimes fish. You can ensure fish—or shrimp—

SPECIAL HEALTH AND SAFETY CONCERNS IN THE RÍO COCO AREA

Due to its lowland and wet geography, The Río Coco area is particularly prone to malaria and dengue fever outbreaks. All travelers here should ensure they're taking chloroquine to prevent malaria, as well as standard precautions to prevent being bitten by mosquitoes: Keep your skin covered, try to stay indoors around 5 P.M., and use repellent and a mosquito net. A major issue is the availability (or lack) of medical facilities and supplies in the region.

At the same time the Río Coco is venerated, it is also the public toilet for most of the communities that line its shores. Don't be surprised to see someone scooping a bucket of river water out for cooking just downstream of someone defecating. Although the water is usually treated with chlorine, you should pay extra attention to the food and beverages you ingest, and especially all water and water-based drinks. Treat all water with iodine pills or a portable water filter before drinking. That goes double any time you are downstream of Waspám. If you are not carrying bottled water from Managua, it is recommended

that you use a good water filter. While it is possible to purchase bottled water in Waspám, the supply is not always guaranteed, so don't rely on it.

Remember, the Río Coco was a heavily mined area in the 1980s. Though the land mines have largely been cleared away, known mined areas still exist and have been cordoned off with ribbon or wire. Ask the locals before you go wandering too far from the road or river bank. Additionally, the locals took care of some land-mine clearing operations themselves, to speed the process of returning to their homes, by scooping up the mines and throwing them into the river. Some of them probably settled down into the mud, and others were carried downstream. Be wary at all times.

Finally, the entire Atlantic coast is experiencing the effect of drug trafficking from Colombia, and the Río Coco area provides particularly good hiding spots. The delta at Cabo Gracias a Dios is a known point of entry for small smugglers who take advantage of the almost total lack of police vigilance there. Watch your back.

---

for dinner by arranging beforehand with the restaurant where you intend to eat later that day. Vegetables are scarce and any salad usually consists of cabbage and some tomatoes in vinegar; eggs are usually available as well. Ask to try some *wabul,* a thick, warm, green banana drink, which has many variations. Coconut bread can usually be found at the market during the evening, when it's still warm from the oven, or in the early morning. The **Restaurant Funes** is well recommended and has a phenomenal view of the river. They serve up traditional fare plus several dishes cooked with *chile cabro,* a spicy bonnet chili pepper grown only along the Atlantic coast. Also try **El Ranchito,** with full plates for less than $3. For cheap late-night eats, pay a visit to the **frito** lady down by Bar Freddy.

SHOPPING

Besides the *pulperías,* there are four larger stores where you can pick up food supplies for trips up or down the river: El Chino, William White,

Ruben Suho, and Chessman. The owners are friendly and can usually provide dependable information about the region.

INFORMATION AND SERVICES

Besides the people on the street, the current mayor and owner of the only gas station is a dependable source of information. After many years of struggle to have service installed, Waspám finally has an ENITEL phone office (open most weekdays 8 A.M.–noon and 1–5 p.m., until noon Sat.). In a real emergency you might be able to look for the manager's house and ask for a favor. There is no Internet. The post office—really just a private home with a Correos de Nicaragua sign posted out front—is along the airstrip.

There is a local, under-equipped police station in town and a health clinic with very basic services. The Catholic church has a private clinic with slightly better service and more resources; in case of an emergency go to the convent and tell the nuns. One of the attending doctors speaks good English. If traveling to the area, it is highly recommended that a preventative chloroquine dose be taken as recommended by your doctor because of the limited health services and the presence of endemic malaria.

GETTING THERE AND AWAY

By Air

La Costeña (tel. 505/263-2814) is the only airline that services the dusty little airstrip at Waspám. Upon approaching the runway, the pilot radios ahead to have someone shoo the cattle off the runway. Daily morning flights leave Managua most of the week; the flight is about 90 minutes long over some of the most exotic scenery in Nicaragua; it costs about $100 round-trip.

By Land from Puerto Cabezas

The trip to Waspám is a chance to experience scenery you won't find anywhere else in Nicaragua—the Miskito pine savanna. White pine species grow well in the poor soils of northeastern Nicaragua, and they're exploited commercially in pine farms along the road from Puerto. This area is about as flat as Nicaragua gets, and in many areas, it is only a few meters above sea level. Spontaneous forest fires are not uncommon. Transportation to Waspám can be arranged in Puerto Cabezas. The grueling bus trip takes five hours when the road is in good condition and it isn't raining; in the rainy season the trip can take as long as 12 hours. Two or three daily Waspám-bound buses leave Puerto at the crack of dawn; get there early for the 6 A.M. bus. The following day, the same buses leave Waspám at the crack of dawn bound for Puerto Cabezas. Because all the buses leave their respective starting points in the morning, it's impossible to go and return in the same day.

Additionally, there's a truck that leaves Puerto Cabezas every morning between 5 and 6 A.M.— a lumbering, diesel-belching IFA—and many opt to travel with El Chino Kung Fu, a local character with a decent pickup truck that makes regular trips between Waspám and Puerto

Cabezas. Ask around and try to form a group to share the costs. Bear in mind that hitchhiking runs the danger of being an unknowing accomplice to transporting narcotics.

RIVER TRIPS FROM WASPÁM

Waspám is your gateway to the Río Coco, and small boats—fiberglass *pangas* and dugout *batu* canoes—are your means of transport. Be aware that as you travel on the river to other communities, you'll find less and less Spanish spoken and a translator may be necessary. One local volunteer recommends the *panga* trip to San Carlos, where you'll find cheap *hospedajes* to stay in, a dance club, and other basic services. In the upriver villages located between Waspám and Leimus, visitors are not common and facilities are somewhere between limited and nonexistent. Don't plan on staying overnight or finding food for sale.

Nothing is easy or cheap, by the standards of travelers accustomed to the prices of the Pacific side. In general, expect to pay $35–100 per person per day for boat transportation along the Río Coco, which includes the boat, the gasoline, and the boatman. The price of fuel is the most critical factor. The dream adventure, of course, is a trip all the way up to Wiwilí, the port at the upstream end of the river. El Bailarín makes the trip from time to time, but charges $1,000 round-trip per person for the extended voyage, which is more than 550 kilometers each direction. Talk to local store owners or the mayor for pointers in selecting a good motorist.

Waterfalls on the Río Yahuk and Río Waspuk

Two tributaries to the Río Coco, the Yahuk and the Waspuk, are both home to waterfalls the locals say are beautiful places to visit, but make for long trips. To visit the Yahuk, for example, you'd have to hire a boat for two days. The first day, you can motor up the Río Coco to the Yahuk and continue upstream to the falls, then spend the night in San Carlos, and return the following day. The Waspuk falls are reportedly a site of religious significance to the Miskito people.

The trip is just upwards of 130 kilometers in each direction.

TRIPS BY LAND FROM WASPÁM

Travel is difficult, transportation infrequent, and food and lodging service nonexistent. If necessary, you can try arranging a meal with a local family, for which you'll pay. There are two local villages that are close to Waspám: Kisalaya (five kilometers) and Ulwas (three kilometers). Locals will point you in the right direction. There are two taxis in town, which might be able to take you to Ulwas, where you might be able to find a small store to buy cookies, crackers, and maybe a warm soda. Bilwaskarma (10 kilometers; approximately a 45-minute walk from Waspám) is a pleasant village with a small health center that was a world-famous nursing school before the conflict of the 1980s.

THE HONDURAN BORDER AT LEIMUS

Though it's technically possible to cross the Nicaraguan-Honduran border at Leimus, it's a little-used corridor and possibly a difficult immigration process. You are sure to be stopped and questioned, especially as crossing involves at least two days of travel after you get your exit stamp from Nicaragua. Bear in mind that immigration issues get expensive fast. Get your exit stamp in Puerto Cabezas (tel. 505/792-2258, only open Mon.–Fri.) beforehand or you will not be permitted to cross. There is no immigration office in Waspám or along the Honduran border. From Waspám, it's a one-hour *panga* ride to Leimus, then a 4–5 hour overland journey to Puerto Lempira, where you can delve deeper into La Mosquitia or catch a flight to Tegucigalpa.

Solentiname and the Río San Juan

The San Juan River carries the waters of Lake Cocibolca gently out to the Caribbean through a green and uniquely lush landscape of cattle ranches interspersed with some of Nicaragua's most extensive nature and wildlife reserves. It's not easy to get here, and thornier still to get around, but if you've got the patience and determination, this lonely corner of Nicaragua may well surprise you. Hop a wooden *panga,* motor through the still waters of the Solentiname archipelago, or watch the sun set over the watery horizon. Wander along the ramparts of a colonial-era fortress, or meet an eclectic community of artists. The southern end of Cocibolca and the Río San Juan offer as many adventures as you're willing to pursue.

Must-Sees

Look for **M** to find the sights and activities you can't miss and **M** for the best dining and lodging.

M La Isla Elvis Chavarría: One of the Solentiname Archipelago's jewels, "La Elvis" features a museum, a hiking trail, an arboretum, and a wonderful host community of farmers, fishers, and artists (page 337).

M Los Guatuzos Wildlife Refuge and Centro Ecológico: One of the best places in the south to get down and dirty with nature; start by identifying a few of the 389 species of tropical birds (page 339).

M Montecristo River Resort: A cushy destination or launch pad to get further downstream (page 342).

M El Castillo: The mighty embattlements of this historic mud-river fortress have watched over the river since the days pirates prowled the Spanish Mainland (page 343).

M Gran Reserva Biológica Río Indio-Maíz: This massive swath of protected virgin rainforest is accessed at various points down the river, starting at the confluence with the Río Bartola (page 345).

© DANIELLE VAUGHN

All three of Nicaragua's primate species have been sighted throughout the Los Guatuzos reserve.

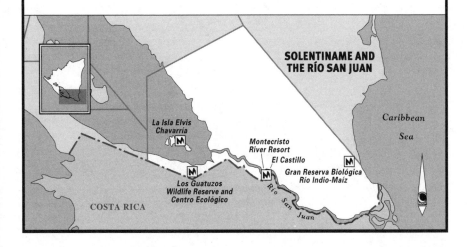

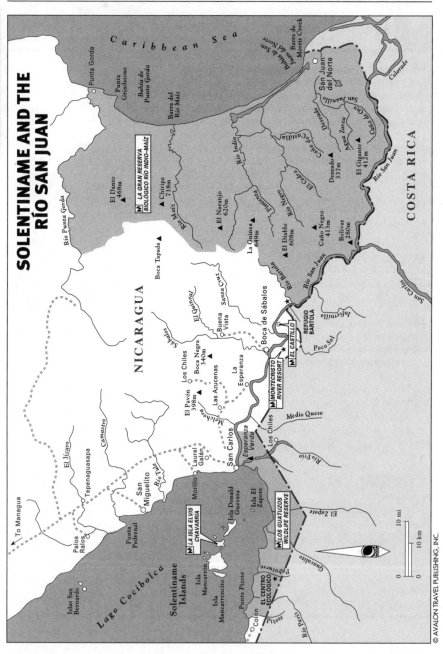

SOLENTINAME AND THE RÍO SAN JUAN

PLANNING YOUR TIME

The San Juan region is challenging, to say the least. Here you've got to have either time or money. If you've got the money, getting around is easy with tour companies or hired *pangas* and drivers, but if you don't you'd better have lots of time. Budget no less than a week in this region, and expect to spend a good portion of that time waiting for boats that operate on maddeningly erratic schedules. While you're at it, budget more for expenses, as well: The region's relative isolation means higher expenses for most items, usually about 25-percent pricier than Managua, and an additional 10-percent higher still on the islands of Solentiname. A final travel tip: The Río San Juan is a border area where any petty bureaucrat can and may demand to see your papers, so play it safe and have them in order and on your person.

HISTORY

The Spanish, intent on piercing the Central American isthmus and navigating to the Pacific, focused intently on the river that nearly reaches the Pacific shore. In 1524, Hernán Cortés wrote King Carlos I of Spain, "He who possesses the Río San Juan could be considered the owner of the World." The strategic and economic importance of this region has not diminished since.

The Spanish founded Granada the same year Cortés was writing the king and set out to explore southern Lake Cocibolca and the Río San Juan afterwards. Not until 1539 was a Spanish expedition sent from Granada to travel downstream in search of the river's outlet to the Caribbean. The mouth of the Río San Juan, choked with labyrinthine estuaries, had eluded explorers for years, including Christopher Columbus, who failed to find it in 1502. When explorers finally reached the Atlantic, Granada became, strangely enough, Spain's first Atlantic port in Central America. To consolidate their hold on the river and protect their interests down to the coast, the Spaniards began a systematic genocide of thousands of indigenous people living in the wilderness along the river and on the islands of Solentiname, the beginning of a 500-year history of blood and power along the San Juan's banks.

In 1567, the first Spanish trade expedition set sail from Granada: three ships laden with agricultural products bound for Panamá. They made it as far as the Caribbean, where English pirates plundered the vessels and fed the surviving sailors to the sharks. Tension and conflict between European nations over the next 300 years led to a virtual state of war between Spain's colonial holdings in Nicaragua and English, Dutch, and French pirates whose respective governments encouraged them to give the Spanish hell. Until the Spanish improved their fortifications along the Río San Juan, the pirates were disastrously successful at sacking and burning Granada, which suffered repeatedly. By 1724, however, fortresses guarded the river at San Carlos, Pocosol, El Castillo, Bartola, El Diamante, Machuca, Río San Carlos, Río San Francisco, Sarapiqui, Concepción Island, and San Juan del Norte, and the heady days of pillaging came to an end.

Throughout the 19th century, the Río San Juan grew in importance for commerce and for its value as a shortcut through the isthmus for travelers bound from New York to California. Cornelius Vanderbilt built up a steamship business that forever changed the region and made San Juan del Norte a major destination. But when the steamship business came to a halt, the river slipped back into bucolic obscurity.

As a sensitive border area during the 1980s, the Río San Juan served as a southern front for Contra forces, particularly for the Alianza Revolucionaria Democrática (ARDE), under the leadership of Edén Pastora, a.k.a. Comandante Cero, who fought on the southern front years after the CIA stopped supporting him. Troops from both sides planted fields of antipersonnel mines, and entire communities evacuated the war zone, fleeing south across the border to Costa Rica or to other points in Nicaragua. The population of the region dropped to fewer than 40,000 until the war ended, then nearly doubled as people returned with their new families, stressing already environmentally sensitive land.

In spite of relentless "the river is ours!" chest

CANAL DREAMS PAST AND PRESENT

After realizing the coveted natural water passage across America was nonexistent, geographers discovered that the lowest point along the entire north-south American divide—from Alaska to Tierra del Fuego—is found in Nicaragua. The fact that it is possible to go no higher than 40 meters above sea level in crossing from the Pacific to the Atlantic Ocean has maintained a fierce interest in the building of an interocean canal there since the early 1500s.

U.S. Army engineer Col. Orville Childs carried out the first systematic study of the canal route in 1852, at the invitation of U.S. millionaire Cornelius Vanderbilt, who, three years earlier, had set up a trans-isthmus transit route across Nicaragua to carry gold prospectors between California and New York.

The original Childs proposal, designed to move sailing ships from ocean to ocean, was followed by another half-dozen U.S. Army and Navy surveys over the next 100 years, with the greatest interest occurring at the turn of the century. At this time, Panamá and Nicaragua were vying for the construction of a U.S.-controlled Pacific–Atlantic canal. After intense lobbying by promoters of both projects, the U.S. Congress finally opted to buy out the bankrupt French company that had already started building the Panama Canal.

The 1914 Bryan-Chamorro treaty, signed by the U.S. and Nicaragua in the year the Panama Canal opened, gave the United States exclusive rights—in perpetuity—to build a canal through Nicaragua. Two further U.S. Army studies for a Nicaraguan canal were commissioned by Congress during the 20th century, one in 1929–1931 for a deep-draft canal similar to that in Panamá, and another in 1939–1940 to build a shallow-draft barge canal. However, despite wartime fears of damage being caused to the Panama Canal, the U.S. Congress never saw sufficient economic merit in either variant to approve construction funds.

The Bryan-Chamorro treaty was abrogated in 1970, at around the same time as containerized cargo traffic began to grow exponentially in international maritime trade. These facts, together with the signing of the Carter-Torrijos treaty in 1979, which would hand over the Panama Canal to Panamá at the end of 1999, spurred renewed interest in the Nicaraguan canal.

During the Sandinista period, a proposal was made by a Japanese consortium to construct a canal that would accommodate ships four times the size of the largest that can squeeze through the locks at Panamá. The Sandinistas were busy fighting the Contra war, with their economy in tatters, and the proposal never prospered.

In the 1990s, two "dry canal" projects surfaced (CINN and SIT-Global), with proposals to build high-speed, trans-isthmus railways connecting ports on both oceans, which would transport containers on specialized railcars between ships berthed at either terminal of the railway. The routes are being proposed as a potential alternative to the Panama Canal and the U.S. transcontinental rail system, both of which are becoming increasingly congested for the east-west container trade between Asia and the East Coast of the United States. The construction cost has been estimated at $1–2 billion.

In 1999, Nicaragua's National Assembly approved a 30-year concession to a private company named EcoCanal for the construction of an inland waterway to permit the navigation of shallow-draft barge traffic along the Río San Juan from Lake Cocibolca to the Caribbean. Although not an interocean project as such, the $50-million waterway could be converted to one with the excavation of the 18-kilometer stretch of land between the Pacific Ocean and Lake Cocibolca—at an additional cost of some $300–400 million.

Politicians from the two leading parties, the Liberals and Sandinistas, have also revived variants of the 1980s Japanese proposal for building a huge, post-Panama canal, with a price tag in excess of $20 billion.

Until now, recent proposals have been paralyzed by a lack of venture capital to finance full feasibility studies, necessary to convert them into bankable projects for construction. Until such studies are completed, doubts will persist over their economic and environmental viability. Nonetheless, the Eco-Canal waterway is generally considered as having the greatest possibility of being undertaken due to its low cost and smaller ecological footprint.

(Contributed by Tim Coone, a journalist by training, who has lived and worked in Nicaragua since the Revolution years.)

thumping up in Managua, the Nicaraguan government has all but abandoned the river, whose lower reaches are neglected and isolated. Many thousands of desperate Nicaraguans still emigrate to Costa Rica, legally or otherwise, in search of work and better living conditions. Even when they stay, Nicaraguans up and down the Río San Juan receive Costa Rican news, radio, and television stations, and sometimes rely on Costa Rican schools and health services. Many towns—especially San Juan del Norte—use the colón in lieu of the *córdoba*. But increased government attention should ensue as wealthy Managua legislators purchase land along the river for their own use and development. The Costa Ricans bristle at being denied the opportunity to promote tourism along the San Juan if Nicaraguans aren't going to do it. Keep your eyes peeled for Costa Rican–run excursions on the river.

San Carlos

Nearly everyone traveling in the Río San Juan region will spend at least some time in San Carlos, whether they wish to or not. Most visitors are disappointed with the port town of 10,000 and try to make their stay here as short as possible. Writer Edward Marriot called it "a place where the air smelled sour as old banknotes; where dead animals lay unremarked in the streets for days; where each day felt hotter than the last; where things of all kinds felt near their end." That may be a little extreme, but there's no denying that the gateway to the San Juan River is decrepit and unimpressive. Until someone decides to invest a little energy, San Carlos's extraordinary tourism potential remains hidden under the grime.

San Carlos is surrounded on three sides by a watery horizon that makes for long, beautiful vistas, often pierced by bright rainbows after the frequent afternoon showers. It is a raucous and spirited hamlet of transients. Many of today's San Carleños were born elsewhere in the country and ended up here on their way to somewhere else. They are field hands on their way to Costa Rican harvests; border soldiers from remote posts in town to blow their meager paychecks; lake

© JOSHUA BERMAN

Solentiname islanders arrive in San Carlos to do some trading.

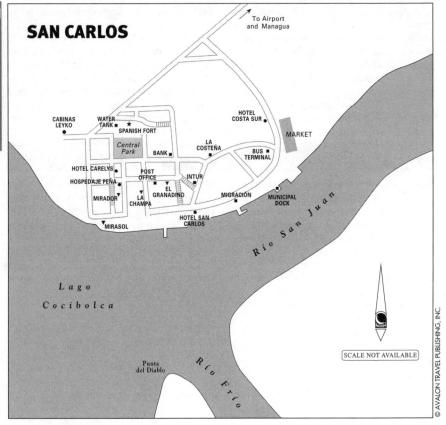

SAN CARLOS

To Airport and Managua

CABINAS LEYKO

WATER TANK

SPANISH FORT

HOTEL COSTA SUR

MARKET

Central Park

BANK

LA COSTEÑA

BUS TERMINAL

HOTEL CARELYS

POST OFFICE

HOSPEDAJE PEÑA

INTUR

EL GRANADINO

MIRADOR

LA CHAMPA

MIGRACIÓN

MUNICIPAL DOCK

MIRASOL

HOTEL SAN CARLOS

Río San Juan

Lago Cocibolca

Punta del Diablo

Río Frío

SCALE NOT AVAILABLE

© AVALON TRAVEL PUBLISHING, INC.

and river merchants trading with Chontales cattlemen, and, of course, international travelers in search of natural beauty and a piece of history.

San Carleños are lively people. They will welcome and embrace you—and then ask you to treat them to a *cervecita* (beer). Some manage to beat the poverty by finding work in the 30-odd NGO offices in San Carlos as *tecnicos,* secretaries, and cleaning staff.

SIGHTS AND ENTERTAINMENT

The old Spanish fort, recently renovated, is worth a look and at present is the only real "sight" in the city, with the exception perhaps of the old cannons on the *mirador* (lookout point)—great for sunsets.

For nightlife, locals make their way to **La Champa** in town (so popular, the name has become a verb: "Let's *champear!*") and **El Bocano,** newer and located just north of the water tower. Bars line most streets throughout town, with the rowdiest ones down by the waterfront; try the Granadino. The annual **sportfishing competition** in September is a big deal for Nicaraguan anglers and attracts crowds from across the nation for prizes like outboard motors and more. Enjoy the **fiesta *patronales*** on November 4; La Purísima is celebrated December 2–8. Most radio stations in the area are Costa Rican and feature Spanglish reggae and *soka.* Radio San Carlos is at 94.9 FM; Radio Trópico Humedo is at 590 AM.

ACCOMMODATIONS

Under $10

San Carlos's half-dozen sleazy *hospedajes*—most on the main drag—charge as little as $2 per person, but you get what you pay for. If you're short on cash, or just into slumming, try **Hospedaje Peña** (a block back from the water, tel. 505/583-0298, $2 s), whose 10 rooms and street-side balcony enjoy a view of the Solentiname Islands. **Hotel San Carlos** ($5/7 s/d) offers about the same quality accommodation, i.e. minimal. **Hotel Costa Sur** (on the road past the bus station, tel. 505/583-0224, $4/6 s/d with shared bath or $7 s with private bath) is clean if a little musty, and far quieter than other options. And **Guest House Yure** (a block south of the park, tel. 505/583-0348, $4 s) has 10 basic rooms.

Find ℕ **Hotel Carelys** (a half-block south of the park, tel. 505/583-0389, $9 d) by asking for "Aquiles" or "Doña Coco." Its 10 rooms are the cleanest and most pleasant in the city, and include private bath, fan, and complimentary soap, drinking water, and old magazines in Spanish.

Another popular choice is the ℕ **Cabinas Leyko** (two blocks west of the church, tel. 505/583-0354). Its 18 rooms start at $6 s but they have some higher-end options with air-conditioning and cable TV for $50 d.

FOOD

You'll find little other than traditional Nicaraguan fare, though prices vary. The dockside *comedores* or market stalls are the best deal. Otherwise, ℕ **El Granadino** serves chicken plates from $2, fish from $5. Its food is the best food in town, and the place has a pleasant vibe, which you can enjoy while you wait and wait and wait for your food. A step up in price and quality is **The Mirador** (near the cannons) where meals start around $5 and are worth it for the pleasant lake views from the outside seating area. Try the jalapeño steak while you're admiring the view. Just below the cannons in the same area is the less impressive **Mirasol,** with similar fare.

INFORMATION AND SERVICES

Tourism Office

INTUR (across the street from the Clínica San Lucas, at the bottom of one of the staircases, tel. 505/583-0301 or 505/583-0363) may be able to help you arrange for special transport and can provide a brochure or two about the region.

Emergency

The police station (tel. 505/583-0350), is located three kilometers from the center of San Carlos on the road to Managua. The fire station is tel. 505/583-2149. Hospital Luis Felipe Moncada is north of town on the highway (tel. 505/583-0238 or 505/583-0244); the Centro de Salud is tel. 505/583-0361. San Carlos's medical services may be okay for minor problems, but for any real emergencies, you're better off chartering a boat south to the hospital in Los Chiles, Costa Rica (one hour or less by boat) or trying to get a flight back to Managua.

Phones and Mail

The newly privatized **ENITEL** (office located up the road toward the hospital) is slowly improving phone service to this overlooked area, but they've got a long way to go. The overloaded circuits frequently shut down, leading to the dreaded *"No hay comunicación."* When there is communication, it is often faint, scratchy, and delayed. Satellite phones—costing a dollar a minute within Nicaragua, $3 to the United States—are more reliable and often your only option (numbers with a 892 exchange are satellite numbers—do not dial zero first).

The San Carlos **post office** (located a block south of the park, tel. 505/583-0276, tel./fax 583-0000, open 8 A.M.–5 P.M., one hour break for lunch Mon.–Fri., 8 A.M.–1 P.M. Sat.) receives and sends mail via the daily La Costeña flight. But Carlos Reyes (near Hospedaje Peña, fax 505/583-0090) can also receive a fax for you.

Banks

Banco de Finanzas (located one block east of the park, tel. 505/583-0144, open 8:30 A.M.–4 P.M. Mon.–Fri., until noon Sat.) will exchange your dollars, but will not deal with traveler's checks, Costa Rican colones, or credit-card cash advances. There are plenty of *coyote* money changers down by the Migración office, trading *córdobas*, dollars, and colones. Otherwise, head for the Western Union just southwest of the church. There is no ATM.

GETTING THERE AND AWAY

You have three choices to get to San Carlos: a bone-crunching nine-hour bus ride from Managua down the east side of the lake, a quick flight from Managua, or the slow boat across the lake from Granada.

By Land

Only the most masochistic and chronically *pinche* (cheap) travelers should attempt the highway from Managua to San Carlos. Past Acoyapa, the road disintegrates entirely and your bus is left to batter its way at walking speed for hours through gulleys, rutted tracks, and mud pits. When the road hasn't been closed entirely, buses leave Managua's Mayoreo Market at 8 A.M. and 11:45 A.M. and occasionally at other times in the morning; the 300-kilometer trip costs $8. If driving on your own, be sure to have a spare tire and jack, plus water and provisions. One obstinate traveler punctured no fewer than seven tires on this road before reaching San Carlos. Buses bound for Managua leave San Carlos throughout the day from the terminal across from the gas station; those bound for Nueva Guinea leave in the afternoon. Ask in advance, as the schedule changes at random.

By Boat

The old **ferry** departs Granada's municipal dock Monday and Thursday at 3 P.M., making stops at Ometepe and San Miguelito and arriving in San Carlos around 6 A.M. the next morning. Be there before 1:30 P.M. to get your ticket—$8 for padded first-class seats with air-conditioning, or $4 down below on the hard wooden benches. The same boat leaves San Carlos bound for Granada on Tuesdays and Thursdays at 3 P.M.; be there before 2 P.M. to get your ticket.

The boat gets crowded at times, especially around Semana Santa, when the hot easterly winds chop the lake into steep swells, and the voyage degenerates into a 16-hour puke-fest. Get there early and be aggressive to stake your territory topside. At other times of the year, the ride is long but pleasant, and sailing west is always easier than sailing east.

For trips down the Río San Juan, go to the Venta de Boletos Transporte Acuático on the main drag toward the gas station (tel. 505/583-0200 or 505/892-0174, 7 A.M.–3 P.M. Mon.–Sat.). Inside the little shack you'll find up-to-date schedules and advance ticket sales for its fleet of *lanchas*. Arrange private boat trips at the Venta, INTUR, or directly with one of a variety of *pangueros* (private boat owners). Ask around the docks or walk the streets looking for signs, such as Armando Ortiz's Viajes Turisticos (near the Western Union, tel. 505/583-0039). Exorbitant gas prices make chartered trips expensive—we're talking hundred of dollars here—but for the convenience, they may be worth it.

A final note: As the demand for transportation continues to grow and shift, so do boat schedules. Always check departure times at the docks well in advance, and be sure to get a second (and third) opinion. For more on boats, see Special Topic on "Boat Lingo," p. 287.

By Air

The daily 50-minute flight from Managua leaves at 9 A.M. Monday, Tuesday, Wednesday, Thursday, and Saturday; at noon on Friday and Sunday. The return flight departs San Carlos around 10 A.M. and 1 P.M., respectively, with the same schedule. The round-trip costs $80. Contact La Costeña in Managua, (tel. 505/263-1228 or 505/263-2142). In San Carlos, the La Costeña office is run by Doña María Amelia Gross out of her home (one block north of the INTUR office, tel. 505/583-0271). Always reserve your spot as far in advance as you can, as flights fill up fast, especially when the buses aren't running due to road conditions; in these cases, every flight can be booked two or three weeks in advance, so plan accordingly.

RÍO FRÍO BORDER CROSSING

Boating south into Costa Rica begins with a visit to the shabby, blue-and-white Migración office

NICARAGUA'S FAMOUS FRESHWATER SHARK

How the *Carcharhinus leucas* became the only shark in the world able to pass between saltwater and freshwater is a fascinating story. After thousands of years of hunting in the brackish outflow of the Río San Juan, Nicaragua's freshwater sharks made their way up the river and formed a healthy population in Lago de Nicaragua. The tale continues with the arrival of humans and their role as both victims and hunters of Nicaragua's bull shark, told in full in Edward Marriott's 2001 book, *Savage Shore*. Indigenous tribes on Ometepe worshiped the shark, sometimes feeding their dead to it. This fear and reverence only faded when the Asian market for shark-fin soup helped to create an industry around harvesting the famous fish, culminating in the late 1960s, when Somoza's processing plant in Granada butchered up to 20,000 sharks a year. Today, the only freshwater shark in the world is seldom seen, although it is still inadvisable to swim in the waters near San Juan del Norte.

on Main Street in San Carlos, recognizable by the long queue that forms before 7 A.M. The office is open 8:30 A.M.–6 P.M. daily. You'll wait in both lines: the first where a very self-important official will curiously scrutinize your passport; the second where you'll pay $2 to be showered with seals, stamps, and signatures. Boats leave from the dock just past the passport window at 10:30 A.M., 12:30 P.M., 3 P.M., and 3:40 P.M. The hour-long chug up the Río Frío to Los Chiles, Costa Rica costs $5 each way.

Once in Los Chiles, there are two more lines:

one to search your bags, another to stamp your passport (Costa Rica Migración is located 200 meters up the road from the dock—be sure to stop and get stamped). If you're entering Nicaragua from Costa Rica, you'll need to buy a Cruz Roja (Red Cross) stamp for about $1, either across the street from Migración, or four blocks away in the Nicaraguan consulate (a half-block north of the church, open 8:30 A.M.–noon and 2–4:30 P.M. Mon.–Fri.). Boats leave regularly for San Carlos through about 5 P.M. Daily direct buses depart for the six-hour trip to San José. (Note: be aware that a second town by the name of Los Chiles is about two hours northeast of San Carlos, in Nicaragua. Be sure to distinguish between the two when asking for directions.)

ORIENTATION AND GETTING AROUND

If you are landing at the "airport," you'll want to grab one of the rickety four-wheel drive taxis to take you the couple of kilometers into town—the five-minute ride costs $.75. The bus station is more or less in the town center, across from the gas station and docks. Coming in by boat puts you in the middle of the action. The main center of San Carlos is only about a dozen city blocks, all south of the central park on the flank of a hill looking south over the water. The waterfront can be a little confusing, especially if you find yourself in one of the narrow market aisles, but all in all, there's not much actual "town" in which to get lost. Main Street would be the one running along the waterfront. The city sprawls northward along the muddy highway to the hospital and airport.

The Solentiname Islands

If you've only seen images of Solentiname as presented by the famous archipelago's primitivist artists, you'd think this was a lush, rainbow-colored fantasy land. You'd be right.

The 36 volcanically formed islands in southern Lake Cocibolca have a long history of habitation, and the signs of its original residents are abundant, including petroglyphs, cave paintings, and artifacts. The inviting name comes from Celentinametl (Nahuatl for Place of Many Guests). Today's Solentiname is home to 750 people belonging to 129 families, as well as an amazing diversity of vegetation, birds, and other wildlife. In addition to its natural beauty and indigenous heritage, Solentiname's most unique and well-known attraction is its current inhabitants' internationally renowned artistic creativity, a talent Padre Ernesto Cardenal discovered in 1966 when he gave brushes and paint to some of the local *jícaro* seed carvers.

The islands are of volcanic origin, and the rich but rocky volcanic ash they're made of is difficult to farm. Nevertheless, *campesinos* manage to harvest beans every January and are now investing in avocados on several islands. Somoza's logging companies deforested most of the archipelago, and rich Boaco cattlemen grazed what was left (well, technically their cows did the grazing). In the last three decades, however, much of the forest has been allowed to regenerate, and the rebirth has attracted artists and biologists from all over the world. Fishing, of course, has always been a mainstay of the islanders' diet, and still is.

Cardenal's arrival occurred shortly after he spent several years at a Trappist monastery in Kentucky. He formed a Christian community in Solentiname in the late 1960s. He stayed on Isla Mancarrón to live, work, and write for the next 10 years. Under his guidance, the simple

© JOSHUA BERMAN

There are 36 islands in the Solentiname Archipelago.

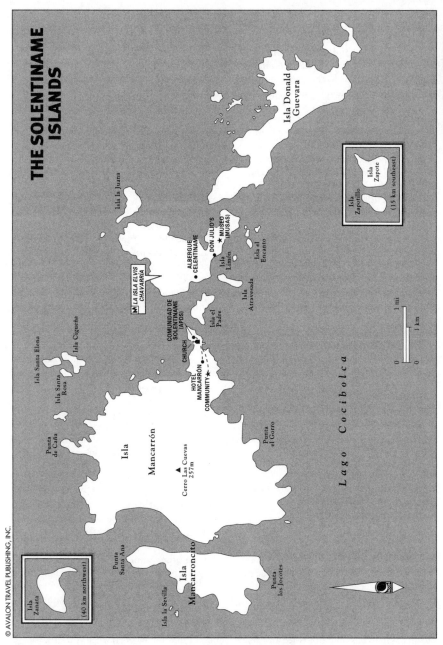

THE SOLENTINAME ISLANDS

© AVALON TRAVEL PUBLISHING, INC.

Isla Zanata
(40 km northwest)

Isla la Sevilla

Punta Santa Ana

Isla Mancarroncito

Punta los Jocotes

Isla Mancarrón

Cerro Las Cuevas 257m

Punta de Caña

Isla Santa Elena

Isla Santa Rosa

Isla Cigüeña

Isla la Juana

Punta el Gorro

Lago Cocibolca

COMMUNITY

HOTEL MANCARRON

CHURCH

COMUNIDAD DE SOLENTINAME (APDS)

Isla el Padre

LA ISLA ELVIS CHAVARRÍA

ALBERGUE CELENTINAME

DON JULIO'S

MUSEO (MUSAS)

Isla Limón

Isla Atravesada

Isla el Encanto

Isla Donald Guevara

Isla Zapotillo

Isla Zapote
(15 km southeast)

0   1 mi
0   1 km

church at Solentiname served as the heart of Nicaragua's Liberation Theology movement, which represented Christ as the revolutionary savior of the poor, and which inspired Carlos Mejía Godoy to write *"La Misa Campesina"* after his visit in 1972. Masses were communal, participatory events, and Cardenal's book, *The Gospels of Solentiname,* is a written record of the phenomenon, with transcriptions of a series of *campesino*-led services throughout the 1970s.

October 13, 1977, a group of anti-Somoza islanders staged a daring and successful assault on the National Guard post in San Carlos. Somoza's vengeance was swift and violent: He burned many of the islands' structures to the ground and forced the evacuation of a large number of their residents.

After becoming the revolution's Minister of Culture in 1979, Cardenal formed the Asociación Para el Desarollo de Solentiname (Solentiname Development Association, or APDS). Under APDS, much of what had been destroyed was rebuilt, and the arts continued to flourish and receive much attention from the rest of the world. Today, there are no less than 50 families who continue to produce Solentiname's unique art of balsa-wood carvings and bright, scenic paintings of the landscape and community.

Interestingly, primitivist painting as a social movement is found in only two other places in the world, each of which was also begun and nourished by a single person. In Haiti, it was a Protestant pastor, and in Yugoslavia, a painter and community leader who persuaded the people to paint on glass.

ORIENTATION AND GETTING AROUND

The four largest of the nearly three dozen islands are essentially the only inhabited ones. They are Isla Mancarrón, Isla Elvis Chavarría (a.k.a. Isla San Fernando), Isla Donald Guevara (a.k.a. Isla la Venada), and Isla Mancarroncito. Only the first two have services for tourists. If you are on a budget, getting around the islands will be your biggest challenge, especially considering that the *colectivo* water taxis only run twice a week, en-suring a minimum stay of three days. To get around, you can either catch a free or discounted ride in someone's *panga,* or you can rent a dugout canoe or rowboat and do some paddling.

MANCARRÓN

The biggest (20 square kilometers) and tallest island, Mancarrón is populated by 34 families—about 200 people. Its 257-meter peak, Cerro las Cuevas, towers over the water. The "town" of Mancarrón, built up in the 1980s, is really nothing more than a cluster of houses, a health center, school, and *pulpería,* five minutes up the muddy path from the dock. Much of the rest of the island is off-limits and has supposedly been purchased by cattle ranchers from Boaco, though conspiracy and corruption theories abound.

Ernesto Cardenal's project began in the 1960s in the church, which was reconstructed and designed by Cardenal. It is unlike any house of worship you've ever seen, featuring children's paintings on the whitewashed adobe walls, a unique crucifix sculpted by Cardenal (who is locally referred to as, simply "El Poeta"), and an altar decorated in pre-Columbian style.

The nearby APDS compound boasts an intriguing library/museum/gallery, a display of indigenous artifacts, and an eclectic collection of books in a variety of languages, including the complete works of Ernesto Cardenal. There are other works on liberation theology, plus the original primitivist painting by local resident Eduardo Arana that helped start the whole project. If you've got the time, ask to see the 1970s BBC video documentary about the Solentiname Islands.

Accommodations

Several families offer simple **homestay accommodations** with three meals for around $10 and up. Reynaldo Urbata comes well-recommended but the other families put a lot of effort into their businesses as well. Just ask around. Up on the hill, **Hotel Mancarrón** (about $50 d) is a fenced-in mini-resort with 15 basic rooms, a bar, restaurant, and a contentious and bitter recent history. As the locals battle for its ownership, it may or may not be open when you visit.

⁊ LA ISLA ELVIS CHAVARRÍA

"La Elvis," as the island is affectionately known owes its name to a young martyr who was captured and killed by the National Guard in 1977 after he attacked the San Carlos National Guard post. The island has a health center, a school (Escuela Mateo Wooten, named after the Peace Corps volunteer who promoted its construction in the mid-1990s), a museum, and a hiking trail.

El Museo Archipiélago de Solentiname (MUSAS) (at the top of the steep path out of town, open 7 A.M.–noon and 2–5 P.M. daily, $1) was built in September 2000 to preserve and display the natural and cultural heritage of the Solentiname Islands and its people. Enjoy the flowers along the path on your way up; they were planted to attract butterflies and hummingbirds. Inside, you'll find depictions of the island's history by local artists, as well as several interesting maps of the area, archaeological information, and a display of traditional fishing techniques and the balsa-wood carving process. Behind the museum are an orchid display, natural medicine garden, arboretum of 42 tree species, a model organic avocado and balsa-wood plantation, a weather station, and a community library.

The Fundación MUSAS (made up of six community leaders, the Italian NGO "ACRA" and several other organizations) also organizes environmental education workshops in the island's school and supports a number of research projects in the area. The museum is open daily, but if you find it closed, speak with the cleaning woman at the bottom of the hill, who will help you find Moncho, the local curator, caretaker, and key master. For more information, swing by the ACRA office (near the hospital in San Carlos, tel. 505/583-0095, or in Managua tel. 505/249-6176, musasni@yahoo.com).

If you find yourself here at the peak of the dry season (March and April), be sure to ask whether or not **La Cueva del Duende** is accessible. The Dwarf Cave, underwater for most of the year, is an important archaeological site that the islands' past inhabitants believed to be the entrance to the underworld. They painted faces to represent their ancestors, whom they believed to reside there, and left other markings as well, including a female fertility figure.

Accommodations

Doña María Guevara has been running the **Albergue Celentiname** (contact her mother, Olivia Silba, in Managua at tel. 505/276-1910, or Berta Rosa in San Carlos at tel. 505/583-0083) since 1984, on a beautiful point at the western edge of the island. She and many of her family members are painters, participating in Cardenal's project since its earliest days. The hotel's eight rooms have capacity for up to 25 people, all with shared bath. There is a picturesque porch, a bar, and a *comedor*. Prices start at around $30 a person and include three meals. Try to make reservations in advance if possible. They can help arrange for transportation when it's available, but expect round-trip transportation from the island to run upwards of $120.

Several hundred meters east, with his own dock on the southern shore of the island, ⁊ **Don Julio** ($10 s including three meals) rents rooms in his rustic and comfortable, lakefront homestead. The kitchen is well-recommended, as are the hammocks at water's edge: a great way to laze away an afternoon. It's a family affair. Don Julio Sequeira Pineda's brother, Chepe, runs transport to and from San Carlos and can arrange any custom trip you desire. Contact their sister, Elena Pineda (tel. 505/277-0939), at her Managua art gallery, Galería Solentiname.

DONALD GUEVARA, MANCARRONCITO, ZAPOTE, AND ZAPOTILLO ISLANDS

Also known as Isla la Venada, or simply, "La Donald," Isla Donald Guevara's namesake was martyred alongside his *compañero* Elvis Chavarría. Mancarroncito is the most well-preserved, wild, and least inhabited of the main islands. Its steep, thickly vegetated hills rise to a 100-meter peak.

Zapote and Zapotillo are the two closest islands to the mainland and are both owned by APDS, which has essentially decided to leave them alone. Zapote is a key nesting area for a variety of birds and turns into a whitewashed, foul-smelling squawk-fest in March and April, when some 10,000 breeding pairs build nests there. Observe the reproductive mayhem from your boat only, as landing there disturbs the birds. Smaller Zapotillo has less bird activity and a more sordid history, involving a fruit farm, an orphanage for boys, and a pedophile Evangelist priest who was eventually chased into Costa Rica, barely escaping with his life.

ISLAS EL PADRE AND LA ATRAVESADA

Located just off the western tip of La Elvis, El Padre island became a howler monkey sanctuary when a single breeding pair introduced in the 1980s subsequently reproduced into a family of some 50 members. The population has never been studied, so write yourself a grant and come on down. Isla la Atravesada, just off La Elvis and to the east of Isla el Padre, is owned by a North American but inhabited by Solentiname's densest crocodile populations.

GETTING THERE AND AWAY

From San Carlos, boats depart on Saturday and Tuesday at 1 P.M. for the two-hour trip to the archipelago (about $2.50 per person). The return trip leaves Solentiname on Monday and Thursday, arriving in San Carlos in time to catch the boat to Managua. Should you want to leave the islands at any other time, be prepared to fork over upwards of $70–100 for a private boat, more if you are traveling in a group.

Tour Packages

The same foundation that runs the museum on Isla Elvis Chavarría has also arranged a fully-guided, four-day exploration of the entire Solentiname Archipelago and the Río Papaturro in Los Guatuzos, including all its natural, archaeological, and cultural attractions. With a group of five people, the price (which includes transportation from San Carlos and around the islands, guide, room, and board) is $134–188 a person, depending on which of the three *hospedajes* you stay in (not available from Hotel Mancarrón). The price per person also goes down as the size of the group increases. Contact the Fundación MUSAS through ACRA (near the hospital in San Carlos, tel. 505/583-0095, or in Managua tel. 505/249-6176, musasni@yahoo .com). Many of the bigger, Managua-based tour companies listed in the Know chapter also have packages to Solentiname.

LOS GUATUZOS WILDLIFE REFUGE AND CENTRO ECOLÓGICO

The 438-square-kilometer strip between Nicaragua's southern border and Lake Cocibolca is a protected wetlands and wildlife reserve replete with myriad species of animals and inhabited by some 1,700 fishermen and subsistence farmers in 11 small communities. The locals are descendants of the Zapote and Guatuzo (or Maleku) peoples as well as the mestizos who arrived in the late 19th century to cultivate rubber. These same *huleros* reverted to the slave trade when the world rubber market crashed, selling Guatuzos for 50 pesos a head to the gold mines of Chontales. Today, only a handful of full-blooded Maleku exist, mostly over the border in Costa Rica.

In the 1930s, settlers introduced cacao to the region, which, because of the crop's need for shade, preserved much of the area's original forest canopy. When plummeting cacao prices and a deadly fungus wiped out the industry in the 1970s, hardwood logging ensued. Only military conflict in the 1980s stopped the logging, but it also drove nearly the entire population of Los Guatuzos into Costa Rica. When families returned in the early 1990s, the area's ecosystem was still largely intact, and the new government quickly acted to protect it from destruction.

Today, residents count on the richness of their natural surroundings to attract visitors and scientists. No fewer than 389 species of birds have been observed here, and between February and April, flocks of migratory species fly through in spectacular concentrations. Los Guatuzos contains dense populations of crocodiles, caimans, feral pigs, jaguars, and howler, white-faced, and spider monkeys. This is also home to a rare, ancient species of fish called the gaspar *(Actractoseus tropicus)*, a living, armored relic of the Jurassic age that uses its snout and fangs to eat other fish, crabs, and even small turtles.

The research center and guest facilities are located 40 kilometers from San Carlos, up the Río Papaturro, which drains the slopes of Costa Rica's northern volcanoes. The narrow river's fauna-rich jungle gradually swallows you as you approach the community of Papaturro. Research station, nature center, and isolated backpacker's hideaway, the Centro Ecólogico offers a full list of activities, including photo/bird-watching safaris, fishing trips, horseback rides through the woods, boat trips in the wetlands and lake, excursions to Solentiname, alligator night hikes, and tours of local villages (all of these activities cost extra, particularly boat trips reliant on gasoline). There is also an orchid display (92 species), butterfly farm, and a turtle nursery (for export to the pet industry).

Accommodations

El Centro (contact FUNDAR in Managua, located from the Vicky, two blocks south, one east, and one south, across from OXFAM, tel. 505/267-8267 or 505/270-5434, centro.ecologico@fundar.org.ni, www.fundar.org.ni) has two eight-bed dorms at $10 a night, plus campgrounds (tents and sleeping pads for rent). Arrange your meals in advance for less than $2 a meal. The center also boasts a conference room, workshop facilities, and support for anyone coming to do field research (GPS equipment, bird nets/traps, and field assistants). They will gladly work out deals for researchers and students. Your hosts and guides, Armando and Aiellen, offer some supplies, like rubber boots for the mud, but bring quick-drying clothes and adequate protection from the sun, rain, and bugs. In San Carlos, FUNDAR works out of the Amigos de la Tierra office (across from the Iglesia del Nazareno, tel. 505/583-0139); they can help arrange transport to Los Guatuzos or down the river to El Castillo.

Getting There and Away

From San Carlos, *colectivos* leave for Papaturro Tuesday, Thursday, and Saturday; the three-hour trip costs $2 a person. Or you can rent a private *panga*—which costs $100, but can take up to 10 people to Guatuzos in only 1.5 hours. You can also arrange for an expensive pickup from

Solentiname

SAN JUAN'S STEAMERS: CORNELIUS VANDERBILT'S NICARAGUAN VENTURE

Entrepreneurs and fortune-hunters heading to California in the famed '49 gold rush found it easier to traverse Central America than to brave the long, perilous overland trek across the United States. American businessman Cornelius Vanderbilt formed the first company that provided passage between New York and San Francisco via Nicaragua. The 45-day trip from New York to California cost $145. Vanderbilt made the first successful voyage himself in 1851. Upon reaching the Nicaraguan shore at Greytown in great, square-rigged clipper ships, passengers boarded side-wheeled *vapores* (riverboats), including the 120-ton iron-hulled *Director* and the smaller *Bulwer*, which worked different stretches of the river (to get around unnavigable rapids, passengers disembarked and transferred to the next upstream ship). The second leg sailed past San Carlos, then traversed the lake to the town of Virgen; there, passengers boarded horse carriages and traveled overland to San Juan del Sur where another clipper ship took them to California.

The route was an immediate success, and by 1853, Vanderbilt's company could scarcely provide enough ships to meet the demand. Vanderbilt's company remained uncontested and by 1854, had transported more than 23,000 passengers between

New York and California. Business was booming along the route, which now included a short railway to avoid the rapids at El Castillo. San Juan del Norte became a rip-roaring port town with 127 foreign consulates and embassies, and a stream of adventuring gringos, foreign investors, and New Orleans whores, prompting U.S. envoy E. G. Squier to remark on the town's "general drunkenness and indiscriminate licentiousness."

The most famous of Vanderbilt's passengers was also one his biggest critics: After Mark Twain made the voyage in 1867, he took Cornelius to task in "An Open Letter to Commodore Vanderbilt." In it, he complained about the wretched quality of the steamship line. More of Twain's comments on Nicaragua are found in a posthumously assembled collection called *Travels with Mr. Brown.*

The boom lasted another half century, fueled after the end of the gold rush by the prospect of an interoceanic canal. The dream all but died when the bid went to Panamá in 1902, and communities up and down the Río San Juan began to wither. Outside San Juan del Norte, the remains of an old iron steam-dredge stand in the shallows of the river where it foundered, testament to the boldest of dreams and the still-unwritten future of transoceanic shipping in Nicaragua.

Solentiname by calling tel. 505/270-5434 or 505/267-8267, or by talking to any of the *pangueros* in Solentiname.

ESPERANZA VERDE

Also a part of the Guatuzos Reserve, this 5,000-hectare protected area 15 minutes from San Carlos is accessible by boat up the Río Frío. The reserve is part of an effort to reforest and protect the overgrazed watershed of the Río Frío and the Río San Juan. At the dock on the river you'll find the **Centro de Interpretación Ambiental Konrad Lorenz,** and a row of six guest rooms with 20 beds ($10 s, plus $12 for three meals, special rates for NGOs, students, and

Nicas). The barren area immediately surrounding the guest facilities is uninteresting, but a 40-minute walk up the road brings you straight into the heart of the rainforest—monkeys, 200 species of birds, giant spiders, mosquitoes, pumas, you name it—and you can spend all day hiking and soaking in the jungle vibe. Take any of the Los Chiles–bound *colectivos,* or arrange for private transport. Contact Leonel Ubau with FUNDE-VERDE in Hotel Cabinas Leyko in San Carlos or at tel. 505/583-0080.

NORTH OF SAN CARLOS

Dozens of small, waterfront fishing villages define the coastline of Cocibolca north of San Carlos, each one at the end of an unimproved spur road from the San Carlos–Managua highway. Given the terrible condition of the road, they're more isolated than you'd expect, but by rented boat you can visit several in a day. The locals don't get many visitors, so you will likely be the only traveler in town.

San Miguelito

A peaceful, lakeside community, San Miguelito boasts an interesting Casa de Cultura, women's

bakery, and access to the island of El Boquete. You can also venture up various rivers, into local wetlands, or over yonder to Solentiname. There are accommodations in the hardwood, Italian-run **Hotel Cocibolca,** with 16 rooms for $6, shared bath, and great sunset views of Ometepe island's silhouette. One daily direct bus leaves Managua's Mayoreo at 7 A.M.; in San Carlos, ask at the bus station. You can also take the slow boat from Granada and get off in San Miguelito before it reaches San Carlos.

Down the Río San Juan

Shove off from the dock, say goodbye to San Carlos, and revel in the excitement of your imminent expedition. The 190-odd-kilometer journey to the sea takes you down the broad, lethargic San Juan through forests and isolated cattle farms. As you float downstream, you'll have the opportunity to stop in several villages, isolated clusters of stilted homes, or in one of several river resorts and research stations. There are a few minor *raudales* (rapids) where the channel suddenly narrows, including the infamous **Raudal el**

Diablo in front of El Castillo. Monstrous *sábalos reales* (tarpon) are often seen rising just upstream from these fast waters, especially when the river is high—their enormous silver hulks break the surface and then mysteriously disappear like some sort of dragon. Downstream of El Castillo, things become decidedly wilder, especially on the Nicaraguan side, where the enormous Gran Reserva Río Indio-Maíz spills over the left bank. Finally, you'll reach San Juan del Norte, with all its ghosts, and a long sandbar, beyond which lies

© JOSHUA BERMAN

panga ride on the Río San Juan

the Caribbean. (Note: In the following section, the terms "river right" and "river left" refer to a boater traveling downstream).

BOCA DE SÁBALOS

A two-hour *lancha* ride brings you to this town long overshadowed by El Castillo and the famous fort just six kilometers downstream. Boca de Sábalos is a working town of about 1,200 souls, located at the mouth of one of Río San Juan's nearly 1,000 tributaries. Boca de Sábalos is not as solidly constructed or as fully developed as El Castillo, but it is more commercially active and has more bars, *hospedajes,* and places to eat than its neighbor. Sábalos is the de facto seat of the El Castillo municipality, which was transferred here temporarily during the war, and then never moved back. There is cheap lodging for the sawmill workers and government employees (many of whom commute each day from El Castillo), and there are facilities for foreign and national aid workers as well, who work with the 11 NGOs in town.

Attractions

The casual tourist is a welcome rarity here. Travelers interested in canoeing up a beautiful river thick with forest and wildlife are sure to be rewarded. To set out exploring, simply negotiate a deal with one of the children near the dock to rent a boat and paddle—feel free to take the kid along for the smiles and knowledge as well. If you don't go up the river, you should at least cross it and check out the other side, even if just for the quick trip. You have surely not lived until you have paid a barefoot five-year-old girl wearing a pink dress and cowboy hat to paddle you across the Río Sábalos in a crude dugout canoe. The trip costs one *córdoba* each way—or whatever you feel like paying. On the other side, you'll find an army post, riverfront bar, and Don Simeón's hotel.

If you prefer to stay on land, hire a vehicle to take you to the massive **African palm plantation,** about a half-hour away. The 2,000-hectare plantation is one of only two such operations in Nicaragua and is also accessed via the Río Santa Cruz. Until recently, the entire operation, including the palm-oil processing factory, was entirely owned by the farmer cooperatives who worked it, employing hundreds of locals. These farmers have struggled ever since they had to sell the factory to the Chamorro family. The long, shady rows of palms are a beautiful background for a daytime walk—just watch out for the snakes.

Or hike down the Río San Juan on the road set back from the river to reach **Yaro's frog and amphibian farm** (he exports them to the pet industry in the United States), or the 100-year-old **steamship wreck**—a rusted hulk half-buried in sand. Ask around for a guide or more detailed directions. To go tarpon fishing, get a permit from the town MARENA office (hook only, no spears), and then hire a guide and boat to take you to just above the Toro Rapids, less than five minutes down the Río San Juan.

Accommodations and Services

Walking up from the dock, you'll first come to **M Hospedaje y Comedor Katiana** ($4.50 s, $10 s with private bath, 14 rooms) on your right, a beautiful hardwood building run by Doña Rosario Manzanares, who is also a great source of local knowledge and unofficial local tourism promoter. Next door is the **Hospedaje Clarica** ($3 pp, 8 rooms, mosquito net, fan, shared bath). Doña Clarica is a wonderful and accommodating cook. Across the street, the **Hotel Central** is cheap and not bad, but not nearly as nice as the other two. Ask around for **Don Simeón Parrales Ulloa's hotel,** located at the confluence of the Río Sábalo and the Río San Juan. Don Simeón is considered the town's historian (and its most successful merchant). The town's sole satellite phone is found in his store on main street, tel. 505/892-0176.

M MONTECRISTO RIVER RESORT

Six kilometers downstream from Sábalo, on river right (only 20 minutes before El Castillo), Montecristo is an upscale tourism complex offering sport fishing, hot tubs, ATVs, hiking trails, and tours of local shrimp and fish farms (tel. 505/266-1694 or 505/276-1119, mca@cablenet.com.ni, www.montecristoriver.com, $35 d, $150 per cabin,

© JOSHUA BERMAN

the Río San Juan seen from the ruins of El Castillo

meals from $3.50). Don Augustín's six *cabañas* are equipped with TV, fridge, and kitchen if you choose not to dine in the bar and restaurant. A fully-equipped boat from Augustín's small fleet, with guide, costs $45–85 a day, plus gas.

Getting There and Away

It's possible to visit Boca de Sábalos (or Montecristo) as a day trip on your way downstream—simply leave San Carlos on the early boat, get off in Sábalos, and then continue to El Castillo when a boat passes in the afternoon (the last one is around 5 P.M.).

N EL CASTILLO

El Castillo is a town of about 1,500 built into the bank of the Río San Juan and named after its principal attraction: **El Castillo de la Inmaculada Concepción de María.** The fortress—dark, moss-covered ruins that still loom above town—was strategically placed with a long view downriver, right in front of the shark- and crocodile-infested Raudal el Diablo (still one of the biggest challenges for upstream vessels). The Fortress of the

Immaculate Conception has more successfully attracted tourists than repelled English pirates, and if you're in the area, this is the one place you should not miss.

The town of El Castillo is a happily isolated river community within earshot of the rapids, and with no roads or cars—reason enough to visit. Its residents work on farms in the surrounding hills, fish the river, commute to the sawmill in Sábalos, the palm oil factory up the Río San Juan, or one of the new resorts up and down the river. In between harvests, a lot of folks cross illegally into Costa Rica—an easy 45-minute walk—and work there.

History

Ruy Díaz, on the first Spanish exploration of the river in 1525, built the first fortificatoin in 1602, on a section of the river he called "The House of the Devil." In 1673, Spain commissioned the building of a new fort, which, when completed two years later, was the largest fortress of its kind in Central America, with 32 cannons and 11,000 weapons. Granada, at long last, felt safe.

In 1762, Spain and Britain began the Seven

Year War, prompting the governor of Jamaica to order an invasion of Nicaragua. An expedition of 2,000 soldiers took all the fortifications until they reached El Castillo, where a massive battle commenced on July 29. Rafaela Herrera, the 19-year-old daughter of the fort's fallen commander, Jose Herrera, seized command of her father's troops and succeeded in driving the British off, who retreated to San Juan del Norte on August 3.

Eighteen years later, 22-year-old Horatio Nelson entered the Río San Juan with a force of 3,500 men. He captured the fortification at Bartola on April 9, and then, two days later, made a surprise attack on El Castillo by circling around on foot and storming it from the land. Nelson's attack was successful, and he took 270 Spanish prisoners. Alas, retaining his new possession proved more difficult than taking it, and in 1781, after nine months in El Castillo without any reinforcement, the soon-to-be Lord Admiral Horatio Nelson and his handful of surviving soldiers—all rotting from sickness—pulled out and went home.

Visiting the Fort

As part of its celebration of 500 years of influence in the Americas, the Spanish government initiated an expensive renovation of the ruins of the old fortress, installed a historical museum and library within the structure, and built the nearby school and Hotel Albergue. The museum costs $1 to enter and is a must-see if you've made it this far. Consider spending some downtime sitting in the surrounding grass fields and contemplating the river. Ask about the Centro de Interpretación and the alleged *mariposario* (butterfly farm).

Fishing, Hikes, and River Tours

Abner Espinoza (better known as Cofal) and his organization, AMEC (see the Information and Services section), can help get you on the water: Local boat rentals go for $10 an hour for two people, rods and lures for $5 a day ($10 to replace a lost lure). Cofal can also find you a more professional rig (probably one of Montecristo's boats) from $140 a day.

Cofal and the AMEC *caseta* can also help you arrange full- or half-day river tours and hikes, in-cluding exploration of several of the area tributaries. For $5 a person, you can hire a local guide to take you on a four-hour hike through the hills and farms behind El Castillo, including visits to one or more of the seven rural communities. Horses cost $10 each per day—remember to patronize those who seem to be caring for their horses. All boat trips are for groups of six, and figure an additional cost of $15 a day for your guide. A four-hour hike in the Gran Reserva Indio-Maíz costs $32, a deeper jungle trip called *Sendero de Agua Fresca* costs $60, and a wildlife tour of the Ríos Santa Cruz (palm plantation), Romerito, and Poposól is $50. Everything is negotiable here, and prices are capricious, so be sure to ask around and know exactly what kind of deal you're striking.

Accommodations

Several *hospedajes* occupy both sides of the main road. They charge around $2 a night and don't offer much. Walking downstream from the dock, look for El Chino's **Hospedaje Nena,** with 14 rooms and a street-side balcony for $4 a night.

Hotel Richarson [sic] (run by Danny Aragón, vice president of AMEC) can host 10 people in six rooms, with private baths and fans; $10 single; $15 couple. It's set off on a side path from the main drag.

The Spanish built 🔛 **Hotel Albergue El Castillo** (tel. 505/892-0174) in 1992 when they refurbished the fort. The Albergue is a two-story wooden lodge with a double balcony overlooking the thin strip of town, the river, and rapids beyond. It sleeps up to 30 people, with shared bath, and the $12 per person price includes an excellent breakfast and bottomless cup of coffee (legitimate coffee, not instant—a rarity in these parts) in the roomy, elegant bar and restaurant. Sit on the porch with your journal and a thermos full of coffee as you watch the tarpons rise above the rapids.

Information and Services

The tourist *caseta* in front of the dock is actually a group operation known as the Asociación Municipal Ecoturismo El Castillo (AMEC) and headed up by a guy named Cofal. AMEC is constantly working on an updated list of local guides, boat services, and has compiled a series of hikes

THE RIVER THAT DIVIDES

If the Nicaraguan government is sure of one thing, the river and its various communities is theirs—and theirs alone...to completely ignore. Nicaraguan sovereignty of the Río San Juan has soured relations with Costa Rica, which were already strained by the thousands of illegal Nica immigrants continually slipping over the border. You'll see the bumper stickers in Managua and elsewhere—"El Río San Juan es 100% Nica," the most visible sign of increasing jingoistic patriotism that has swelled along with border tensions.

In July of 1998, the Costa Rican government began patrolling the river in armed boats, ostensibly to better police a border Nicaragua has made no effort to control. But the international boundary is the southern bank of the river, not the midpoint, and Nicaragua loudly and immediately challenged the Ticos. Costa Rica responded by blockading the Atlantic coastline from the mouth of the Río San Juan south to Barra del Colorado, forcing the fishermen that would have otherwise purchased gasoline for their boats in Costa Rica to travel 30 kilometers north to Greytown. They explained later that the blockade was an endeavor to investigate a supposed black market in tax-free gasoline and was not retaliation for the dispute over the river. The locals disagree.

Since the 1858 Treaty of Jerez-Cañas, Costa Ricans have had the right to use the river for commercial transport but not police it; this has been the starting point for all subsequent negotiation. But Nicaraguans along the Río San Juan distrust armed Ticos on the river. Costa Rica suggested a compromise of joint patrols, which Nicaragua promptly rejected. The situation remains unresolved.

Cooler heads will be needed on both banks to find a solution. The river's watersheds span both sides of the border, and joint ecological management will be essential to stem rapid deforestation and sedimentation currently choking parts of the channel. The river already runs far lower than it did when the Spanish and Cornelius Vanderbilt navigated its broad waters.

and other things to do while in town; contact them via the phone at the Albergue (tel. 505/892-0174). The most reliable phone in town is the satellite phone at the Albergue ($1 a minute within Nicaragua, $3 out of country).

Getting There and Away

Lanchas colectivas depart San Carlos daily at 8 A.M., noon, 2 P.M., and 3 P.M. The 2.5-hour trip to El Castillo costs only $3. Alternatively, a private *panga* costs $110 each way for a group of 10 people and takes less than two hours.

Orientation and Getting Around

Pulling up to the dock on the south side of the river, you'll find a small cement square sitting on the main sidewalk that runs along the river's edge in both directions. It's guarded by twin cannons and a tourism office. The Albergue is above you at the top of the stairs, which also lead to a

second walkway that passes the Castillo, the town school, and more homes.

M GRAN RESERVA BIOLÓGICA RÍO INDIO-MAÍZ

Your first access point to this vast, 3,618-square-kilometer virgin rainforest is just six kilometers downstream of El Castillo (or about three hours by boat from San Carlos). The western border of the reserve is made up by the Río Bartola at its confluence with the Río San Juan. Arrange a hike through the local MARENA post, with AMEC in El Castillo, or at the self-described eco-lodge and research station, **Hotel Refugio Bartola** (tel./fax 505/289-7924 or 505/289-4154, bartola @guises.org, 11 rooms with private bath and mosquito nets). The compound and natural history museum is all surrounded by rainforest and fueled by solar energy but is difficult to contact: You may need to wait until you're in El Castillo.

SAN JUAN DEL NORTE

Located about 100 winding kilometers beyond El Castillo, this stiflingly hot, hugely historic village in Nicaragua's extreme southeast corner is inhabited by about 900 residents. Sir Charles Grey, governor of Jamaica, first seized the land for the English in 1848 and established what was called Greytown. This lonely cluster of eternally damp buildings is, perhaps more than anywhere else in the country, the end of the line.

Present-day San Juan del Norte is not the same place as the rowdy port town of the mid-19th century. San Juan del Norte suffered greatly during the Contra war, and in the 1980s, Hurricane Joan flattened it. In the early 1990s, Comandante Cero returned and burned it to the ground, mostly out of vengeance. (Ten years later, he campaigned for mayor of Managua.) Present-day, rebuilt San Juan del Norte lies hidden in the brackish swamps at the mouth of the Río San Juan, while the original city and its historic cemetery (where segregated burial plots and many English and U.S. graves attest to the town's rich history) lies abandoned and forgotten. Find a guide in town to begin exploring here.

Of the backpackers who have journeyed to San Juan del Norte looking to continue north to Bluefields, most have found themselves stranded in rat-infested rooms, playing dominoes, drinking beer, swatting mosquitoes, and sweating profusely. The few travelers we know who succeeded in reaching Bluefields universally reported near-death experiences and hundreds of dollars in expenses (except one, who found herself speeding north as a personal guest of Comandante Cero himself).

Nevertheless, the trip to San Juan del Norte may be worthwhile, if only for time spent drinking Costa Rican beer with reggae-loving fishermen and outlandish local characters. This trip is not for those afraid of mosquitoes the size of small sparrows and lots of tropical downpours.

Accommodations and Food

Tío Pum offers basic rooms with shared bath for $3, and an early curfew. **Hedley Acton Thomas Barss,** known more commonly as Chalí, also has an *hospedaje* for $3. Chalí is the person in charge of the cemetery and can help you get there. Melvin has clean rooms for $7 a night. For food, try **Doña Angela, Doña Fran,** or **El Ranchón,** and for dancing some *soka,* it's **Disco-Bar de Pulú Fantasía.**

Services

There aren't many. There are some newly installed satellite phones, including one in the mayor's office (tel. 505/273-3055). There is also a MARENA office, army and naval base, and police station.

The Río Indio Lodge

While the Nicaraguan government has steadfastly defended the San Juan River as 100-percent Nica, it's done little to develop this region's massive tourist potential. But on the other side of the river, the Costa Ricans just can't resist doing what they do best, and what's a national border between friends, anyway? Since 2002, the $1.2-million, five-star, **Río Indio Lodge** "ecotourism and sportfishing resort" (tel. 505/273-3082, www.bluwing.com, bluewing@racsa.co.cr), fully Costa-Rican owned and operated, has run fancy sport-fishing trips on this Nicaraguan river. This place is geared to the luxury adventure traveler, not the backpacker: Six-day guided fishing-trip packages start at more than $3000 and include first-class accommodations and luxury services—helicopter, river-boat trips, and a lot more.

Getting There and Away

The easiest way to get to San Juan del Norte is to fork over some major dollars to a tour company. The most realistic way is a long boat ride downriver from San Carlos. The boat leaves there Tuesday and Friday at 6 A.M. (buy tickets the day before), takes at least nine hours, and costs $11 each way. The same vessels leave San Juan del Norte Thursday and Sunday at 4 A.M.

The proposed air strip is still just that—proposed. Nevertheless, with big money investing in the area, regular flights to Managua can't be too far away.

Know
Nicaragua

The Land

The largest and lowest Central American country, Nicaragua is a nation of geographical superlatives. Located at the elbow where the Central American isthmus bends and then plummets southward to Panamá, Nicaragua is almost dead center between North and South America. Part of a biological corridor that for millions of years has allowed plant and animal species from two continents to mingle, it boasts an extraordinary blend of flora and fauna.

In the 16th century, Nicaragua's geographical beauty enchanted the conquistadores, who reported, "The Nicaraguan plains are some of the most beautiful and pleasant lands that can be found in the Indies because they are very fertile with *mahicales* and vegetables, *fesoles* of diverse types, fruits of many kinds and much cacao."

Nicaragua is roughly triangular in shape and dominated by two large lakes in the southwest. The northern border with Honduras is 530 kilometers long, the longest transect across the Central American isthmus. To the south, the southern shore of the Río San Juan defines the better part of the Nicaraguan–Costa Rican border. Wholly within Nicaragua, the San Juan has been a continual source of conflict with Costa Rica, whose attempts to navigate and patrol the river have been met aggressively by the Nicaraguan government. To the east and west lie the Caribbean Sea and the Pacific Ocean, respectively. With 127,849 square kilometers of land area, Nicaragua is approximately the size of Greece or the state of New York. Nicaragua has lost some 50,000 square kilometers to her neighbors over the past several centuries. The eastern third of what is now Honduras, as well as the now–Costa Rican territories of Nicoya and Guanacaste were considered Nicaraguan during colonial times.

Administratively, the nation is divided into 15 units called *departamentos,* and two vast autonomous regions on the Atlantic coast known as the North and South Atlantic Autonomous Regions (RAAN and RAAS). The departments, in turn, are divided into a total of 145 municipalities.

The two autonomous regions elect their own officials on a separate electoral calendar. Nicaragua's three largest cities are Managua, León, and Granada, followed by Estelí, Masaya, and finally the remaining department capitals.

GEOGRAPHY

Rivers run through me
Mountains rise in my body
And the geography of this country
Is taking shape in me
Turning me into lakes, chasms, ravines,
Earth to sow this love
—opening like a furrow—
Filling me with a longing to live
To see it free, beautiful,
Full of smiles
I want to explode with love . . .
      Gioconda Belli (Nicaraguan poet)

Nicaragua's favorite nickname for itself—The Land of Lakes and Volcanoes—is indication enough of its geography, which is indeed dominated by two great lakes and a chain of striking volcanoes. Nicaragua's water and volcanic resources have had an enormous effect on its human history, from the day the first Nahuatl people concluded their migration south and settled on the forested shores of Lake Cocibolca (Lake Nicaragua) to the first Spanish settlements along the lakes to the many as yet unrealized plans to build a trans-isthmus canal (see the Canal Dreams Past and Present special topic in the Solentiname and the Río San Juan chapter).

Geologic History and Formation

The earth that comprises Nicaragua, like all of Central America, took shape 60 million years ago (MYA) when the isthmus formed. Geologically speaking, the land that makes up Nicaragua's northern third is the most ancient. In the area of Telpaneca and Quilalí, rocks dated at 200 million years old are thought to have once been part of a small Jurassic-Cretaceous continent that included

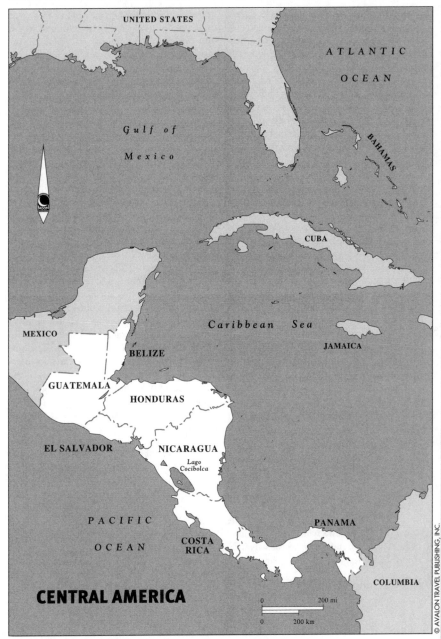

UNITED STATES

ATLANTIC

OCEAN

Gulf of

Mexico

BAHAMAS

MOON

CUBA

Caribbean Sea

MEXICO

BELIZE

JAMAICA

GUATEMALA

HONDURAS

EL SALVADOR

NICARAGUA

Lago
Cocibolca

PACIFIC

OCEAN

PANAMA

COSTA
RICA

COLUMBIA

CENTRAL AMERICA

0   200 mi

0   200 km

© AVALON TRAVEL PUBLISHING, INC.

the modern-day Yucatán Peninsula in Mexico and the Antilles Islands. To the south, what are now Costa Rica's Talamanca Mountains formed an archipelago of isolated volcanoes. During the Tertiary period (65–1.7 MYA), intense volcanic activity and erosion produced large amounts of sediment and volcanic flows that accumulated underwater.

There were at least two periods of intense volcanic activity: one in the Eocenic-Oligocenic period (55–25 MYA) when the lesser features of Nicaragua's central highlands were formed, and a second in the Miocene (25–13 MYA) that produced the larger mountains in Matagalpa and Jinotega. Eleven MYA later, the Pacific region formed when shifting tectonic plates in the Pacific and Caribbean lifted the seabed.

When the so-called Cocos plate slid under the Caribbean plate, the main volcanic mountain range that runs northwest-southeast across the Pacific plains blistered to the surface. Ocean water from the Atlantic rushed in along a broad sunken valley of the Pacific plate now known as the Nicaraguan Depression, and pooled, forming the lakes. Some geologists believe the Atlantic and Pacific actually connected at this point in time and were later cut off by volcanic sedimentation. Erosion began pulling material from the landmass outward to the sea, building up Nicaragua's Pacific region and gradually forming the Atlantic coast.

Plate tectonics theory, in spite of being widely accepted since the 1960s, is most frequently criticized for its failure to adequately explain the geology and geography of several regions of the world, including Central America. It is highly probable that our concept of the geological events that formed Central America will change as geologic science progresses. Regardless of the mechanism, however, the convergence of the plates ensures crustal instability, which manifests itself in frequent volcanic and earthquake activity in all of Central America, and especially Nicaragua.

Volcanoes and Mountain Ranges

Nicaragua has some 40 volcanoes, 6 of which are active. All six can be climbed. Running roughly parallel to the Pacific shore, Nicaragua's volcanoes form part of the "Ring of Fire" that encompasses most of the western coast of the Americas and wraps around, by way of the Aleutian Islands of Alaska, into Japan and Indonesia. The Maribio (Nahuatl for the giant men) and Dirian mountain ranges stretch nearly 300 kilometers from the volcanic peaks of Concepción and Maderas in the middle of Lake Nicaragua (on Isla de Ometepe) to Cosigüina, which juts into the Gulf of Fonseca.

Volcanic activity is central to Nicaragua's history. The first volcanic event in recorded history was the eruption of Volcán Masaya in the early 1500s. The lava flow from this eruption helped form the present-day lagoon at the base of the mountain. Another great lava flow occurred in the year 1772, leaving behind a black, barren path still visible today where the Managua–Masaya highway crosses it. In 1609, the first Spanish settlers abandoned the city of León when Momotombo erupted. And in January of 1835, Volcán Cosigüina violently blew its top, hurling ash as far away as Jamaica and Mexico, covering the area for 250 kilometers around the volcano in ash and burning pumice and forcing the entire peninsula into three days of darkness. This volcanic activity is responsible for the exceptional fertility of Nicaragua's soils, most notably the agricultural plains on the Pacific coast near Chinandega and León.

Today, the most active volcanoes are Momotombo, San Cristóbal, and Telica, all of which tremble in turn and emit plumes of poisonous gases, smoke, and occasionally lava. But climbing these peaks is reason enough to visit Nicaragua! San Cristóbal is the highest, at 1,745 meters. A smaller peak adjacent to San Cristóbal, Volcán Casita still bears the immense scar of the landslide that buried thousands in an avalanche of rock and mud during Hurricane Mitch and trembled briefly again in January of 2002.

Less prominent but more regularly violent, Volcán Telica, just north of León, erupts approximately every five years. Gas vents at its base churn out boiling mud and sulfur. Neighboring Cerro Negro is one of the youngest volcanoes on the planet: It protruded through a farmer's field in the middle of the 1800s and has since grown in size steadily and violently to a height of 400 meters. Cerro Negro's last three eruptions have been increasingly powerful, culminating in 1992 when it belched up a cloud of burning gases and ash seven kilometers high, burying the city of León under 15 centimeters of ash and dust. Eight thousand inhabitants were evacuated as the weight of the ash caused several homes to collapse. Volcán Momotombo's (Nahuatl for great burning peak) perfect conical peak is visible from great distances across the Pacific plains, as far away as Matagalpa. One particularly striking vantage point is from the Managua–Masaya highway as you enter Managua. Momotombo is responsible for approximately 10 percent of Nicaragua's electricity via a geothermal plant located at its base. It hasn't erupted since 1905, but Momotombo's menace has in no way diminished. Increased seismic activity and rumbling in April 2000 caused Managua residents great concern until the mountain eventually quieted back down.

Volcán Masaya is the most easily accessed of Nicaragua's volcanoes and boasts a paved road leading right to the lip of the crater. Volcán Masaya is actually formed of three craters, the largest of which, Santiago, is the only crater in the Americas that contains a visible pool of incandescent liquid lava in its center. The visibility of this lava fluctuates on a 30-year cycle and was best seen from 1965 to 1979.

Ometepe and Zapatera are the two principal islands that occupy the center of Lake Cocibolca. Both are volcanic. Zapatera (625 meters), home to Nicaragua's first inhabitants, is the remnant of an ancient and collapsed volcano. Ometepe (Nahuatl for two peaks) is composed of the volcanoes Concepción (1,610 meters) and Maderas (1,394 meters). While Concepción is still quite active and has erupted as recently as 1956, Maderas sleeps, its crater now drowned in a deep pool of rainwater.

Also accessible and host to a protected cloud forest and system of coffee plantations, Volcán Mombacho (1,345 meters) is a dormant volcano whose explosion and self-destruction is thought to have formed the archipelago of islets in Lake Cocibolca that huddle near the shore of Granada. Mombacho took its modern shape in 1570 when a major avalanche on the south slope buried an indigenous village of 400 inhabitants and left the crater open and exposed.

The central and northern areas of Nicaragua are dominated by three lesser mountain ranges: the Cordilleras Isabelia, Huapi, and Chontaleña. These three ranges radiate northeast, east, and southeast, respectively, from the center of the country, gradually melting into the lowland jungle and swamps of the Atlantic coast. These mountains include a half-dozen prominent peaks and were the scene of intense fighting during several conflicts in Nicaraguan history. Nicaragua's highest point, Cerro Mogotón, at 2,107 meters, is located along the Honduran border in Nueva Segovia.

Lakes and Lagoons

Two great lakes, Cocibolca (Lake Nicaragua) and Xolotlán (Lake Managua) dominate Nicaragua's geography, occupying together nearly 10 percent of the country's surface area.

Lake Xolotlán, although broad (1,025 square kilometers), is surprisingly shallow with an average depth of only seven meters. It reaches its deepest—26 meters—near the island of Momotombito. But look out across the water from Managua's shoreline and take note that no one is fishing. Lake Managua is biologically dead, victim of a century of untreated human waste from the city of Managua and the extensive dumping of industrial wastes during the 1970s, including dangerous levels of lead, cyanide, benzene, mercury, and arsenic. The tremendous opportunities for tourism, recreation, and potable water for human consumption that a clean lake would facilitate have led to an ambitious plan to detoxify Xolotlán. Backed by loans from Japan and the World Bank, the project entails collecting and treating Managua's sewage, and gradually cleansing the lake itself in water treatment plants to be built on the lakeshore.

Lake Cocibolca is the larger of Nicaragua's two lakes and is one of Nicaragua's greatest natural treasures. At 8,264 square kilometers and 160 kilometers long along its axis, Lake Cocibolca is just smaller than the island of Puerto Rico and lies a

HURRICANE MITCH

It was late October 1998, and the rainy season had been reduced to sporadic drizzle, just right for the red beans that were slowly gathering strength in the fields. The newspapers mentioned a hurricane forming in the Atlantic, but Nicaragua seemed spared when the storm, called "Mitch" shifted to the north instead of making landfall on the Caribbean coast.

Instead, on October 28, rain began to fall steadily from a leaden sky over most of Nicaragua. Mitch had come to a near complete stop off the north coast of Honduras, and thick gray arms of clouds swept in long spirals across the entire Central American isthmus, greedily gathering strength from both the Caribbean and Pacific Ocean, while winds around the eye of the hurricane reached 290 kilometers per hour. The rains fell day and night for seven days. The country roads of red earth turned muddy, then became dangerous rivers of coffee-colored water coursing through the center of towns, while cattle that had been left in the fields found high ground or were drowned and swept away. Swollen to 10 times their normal size, Nicaraguan rivers flared over their banks, tearing out trees, snatching away homes, and breaking apart (or just tearing around) every bridge in their path. On October 29, the electricity failed in most of the north as power lines fell and poles were swept away. In Sébaco, the Río Viejo and the Río Grande de Mata-

galpa, which normally pass within a kilometer of each other, rose and combined before tearing through Ciudad Darío.

The waters of Lake Xolotlán rose three meters over the course of three days. Overtopping the basin, the waters barreled through the old, dry channel of the once-intermittent Río Tipitapa, raising the level of Lake Cocibolca and the Río San Juan; the town of Tipitapa, built in the low saddle between the two lakes, was completely inundated. On the Pan-American Highway, the enormous bridge that crossed over the Tipitapa River was damaged, then destroyed, and finally carried away completely. By the 30th, the entire northern half of the country was isolated: Major bridges had been demolished in Sébaco and Tipitapa, and every bridge without exception between León and Managua had been destroyed.

But Mitch was cruelest in Posoltega, Chinandega, where the equivalent of a full year's rainfall came down in under four days. The intense rains filled the crater of Volcán Casita with rainwater, and at 2 P.M. on October 30, the southwest edge of the crater lip tore away, unleashing a deadly avalanche of mud, water, and rock 1.5 kilometers wide and three meters high on the three small communities below. Thousands died immediately, as the mudflow poured southwest more than four kilometers to the highway, crossed it, and continued

---

scant 31 meters above sea level. It's also deep—up to 60 meters in some places, and relatively clean. The prevailing winds, which blow from the east across the farmlands of Chontales, make the eastern part of Cocibolca relatively calm and the western half choppy and rough. A massive pipe system is presently being designed, which, if built, will carry drinking water from Cocibolca to the city of Managua to meet the needs of the capital's rapidly growing population and industrial sector.

Nearly a dozen stunning lagoons mark the gaping maws of ancient volcanic craters. Around Managua alone are the Nejapa, Tiscapa, and Asososca lagoons. West of Managua, the picturesque twin craters of Xiloá and Apoyeque form the

Chiltepe peninsula; near Masaya, the 200-meter-deep Laguna de Apoyo was formed sometime in the Quaternary period (1.6 MYA) by what is thought to be the most violent volcanic event in Nicaragua's prehistory. Not far away is Laguna de Masaya, at the base of the volcano of the same name. Other gorgeous lagoons flank Volcán Momotombo and occupy the craters of the volcanoes Maderas and Cosigüina.

Rivers

To the original Spanish settlers in Granada, the Río San Juan was the elusive "drain" of Lake Cocibolca; since then, the possibility of traveling up the Río San Juan, across Lake Cocibolca, and

southwest into the town of Posoltega. In the aftermath, there was no hope of recovering or even identifying victims.

By the time the rains finally stopped, Hurricane Mitch had reduced Nicaragua's GDP by half and destroyed more than 70 percent of the country's physical infrastructure. Hundreds of health clinics and more than 20,000 homes were carried away, and arable farmland was reduced by 11,550 hectares. Overall, economic losses sustained by this already poor nation were around $1.5 billion. Mitch also opened up political and social scars less obvious than deforested hillsides. Under duress, political divisions reopened as relief money poured in and politicians—particularly President Alemán—struggled to divert it for their own interests.

Though the press called Mitch "the storm of the century," scientists estimate it was much more severe even than that and declared it the most deadly storm event in at least 200 years. However, the hundreds of millions of dollars of aid money that poured into Nicaragua in the aftermath have provided Nicaragua with a much-needed opportunity to strengthen and rebuild, and much effort has gone into ensuring that the Nicaraguan government and people are more capable of dealing with future disasters through training programs, flood-warning detection systems, computer models, and more. These are crucial to Nicaragua's future well-being, because Hurricane Mitch will surely not be the last storm to wreak havoc in Nicaragua.

© JOSHUA BERMAN

then by land to the Pacific Ocean has made the San Juan the most historically important river in Nicaragua. In the years of the gold rush, thousands of prospectors navigated up the Río San Juan en route to California; some made the return trip laden with riches, others with nothing. These days, several sets of rapids and decades of sedimentation reduce its navigability, exacerbated by shifts in the riverbed from occasional earthquakes. Cattle ranches and small farms primarily producing basic grains line both shores (farmers on the southern shore identify more closely with Costa Rica and even use its currency).

Formed by the confluence of three major rivers—the Siquia, Mico, and Rama—the Río Escondido is the principal link in the transportation corridor from Managua to Bluefields and the Atlantic coast. Produce and merchandise (and busloads of travelers) reach El Rama and then proceed down the Escondido. The Escondido and its tributaries are important to the cattle industry in Chontales, but massive deforestation along its banks have unleashed dangerous floods that frequently put the river port of El Rama under water.

The 680-kilometer-long Río Coco is the longest river in Central America, fed by headwaters in both Nicaragua and Honduras. Also known as the Río Segovia or by its indigenous name Wanki, the Coco traverses varied terrains

© JOSHUA BERMAN

There's only one way to float: downstream on the Río San Juan.

that include several minor canyons and vast stretches of virgin forest. Small communities of the indigenous Miskito people, for whom the river bears great spiritual significance, make their homes along its shores.

The Estero Real (The Royal Estuary), at 137 kilometers in length, is the most consequential body of water on the Pacific coast and is one of Nicaragua's best places to spot waterfowl. It drains most of northwestern Nicaragua through extensive mangroves and wetlands to the Gulf of Fonseca and is the nucleus of extensive shrimp-farming operations.

Soils

In the Pacific region, the soils are typically of volcanic origin, highly fertile, and rich with minerals.

The mountainous north and central regions of Nicaragua are less fertile basalt, andesite, and granite-based soils, and their steeper slopes are prone to erosion and soil degradation. The better soils are usually found alongside rivers where deforestation and fierce storms such as Hurricane Mitch haven't carried it away, stripped it of its nutrient value, or buried it under thick layers of sand. In the north and northeast of Nicaragua, the soils are quartz-based and mostly useless for farming, though they typically bear thin stands of white pine. The Sébaco Valley is thought to have once been the bed of an immense lake. The clay-like black soils there retain moisture, which impedes the production of corn or beans but greatly facilitates wet rice farming. Nicaragua's rice industry centers around the city of Sébaco.

Flora and Fauna

Nicaragua's variety of ecosystems, and its position at the biological crossroads between North and South America and between the Atlantic and Pacific Oceans have blessed it with an astonishingly broad assortment of vegetation and wildlife.

FLORA

Of the world's known 250,000 species of flowering plants, an estimated 15,000–17,000 are found in Central America. It is estimated Nicaragua is home to some 9,000 species of vascular plants, many of which are thought to be of medicinal value. But while a few areas are relatively well protected, little effort has been made to protect the rest, where the majority of the land set aside by the government continues to experience intense pressure from the agricultural frontier and the scattered human settlements within the confines of the reserves.

Trees

The *madroño (Calycophyllum candidissimum)* is the national tree of Nicaragua. The hills south of Sébaco form the southern limit of the pine family found on the continent; south of Nicaragua, the pines are out-competed by other species. As of 2002, Nicaragua had a forest area of 5.5 million hectares, the majority of which is broadleaf forest, followed by pine forest *(Pinus caribea* and *P. oocarpa)*. At altitudes greater than 1,200 meters, the forests also include *P. maximinoi* and *P. tecunumanii.* A full 2.5 million hectares of forest are considered commercial timber forest. Though often privately owned, the exploitation of forest products is under the control of the Nicaraguan government.

Principal Ecosystems

Nicaragua's varied topography and uneven rainfall distribution, not to mention the presence of tropical reefs, volcanoes, and volcanic crater lakes, result in a phenomenal diversity of terrain and ecosystems. This can be easily appreciated during

any road trip through Nicaragua, as you watch prairie grasslands melt into rolling hills into near-desert into craggy mountain ranges whose peaks are draped in cloud forest. You can burn your feet on an active volcano's peak and cool your heels in ocean surf the same day. Nicaragua's higher peaks are isolated ecosystems in their own right and home to several endangered as well as endemic species, and the streams, rivers, and two very different coastlines furnish myriad other distinct ecosystems. In general, the land can be divided into the following ecological zones:

Pacific Dry Forest: The lowlands of the Pacific coast, specifically the broad, flat strip that borders the Pacific Ocean from sea level to approximately 800 meters in altitude, are a rain-stressed region dominated by thorny, rubbery species. The region typically receives less than 2,000 millimeters of rain per year. Both trees and non-cactus-like plants in this ecosystem shed their leaves in the middle of the dry season in preparation for the rain to come, and often burst into flower in April or May.

Upland Pine Forest: With the exception of the slopes of several Pacific mountains, namely San Cristóbal and Las Casitas in Chinandega and Güisisíl in Matagalpa, the majority of Nicaragua's pine forests are found in the north near Jalapa and Ocotal. Pines particularly thrive on poor, acidic soils, which erode easily if the area is logged.

Lower Mountainous Broadleaf Forest: Nicaragua's higher peaks are cloud covered for most of the year and home to a cool, moist biosphere, rich in flora and fauna. Most of these areas are the more remote peaks of Matagalpa and Jinotega, like Kilambé, Peñas Blancas, Saslaya, and Musún. It's easier to enjoy this ecosystem on the beautiful and easily visited peaks of Volcán Mombacho near Granada, and Volcán Maderas on Ometepe.

Caribbean Rainy Zone: The Atlantic coast receives rain throughout nearly 10 months of the year and the humidity hovers around 90 percent year-round. Most of the Atlantic coast is covered with tropical forest or even lowland rainforest, with trees that often reach 30 or 40 meters in height. In the north along the Río Coco are the remains of Nicaragua's last extensive pine forests *(Pinus caribaea),* presently subject to intensive logging by national and international concessions.

FAUNA

Nicaragua is home to a great deal of exotic wildlife, much of which—unfortunately—you'll only see for sale on the sides of the highways and at intersections in Managua, where barefoot merchants peddle toucans, reptiles, ocelots, parrots, and macaws. This is a considerable, largely unchecked problem, more so because, of the animals that are captured for sale or export in Nicaragua, 80 percent die before reaching their final destination. To view fauna in their natural habitat involves getting out there, being very, very quiet, and looking and listening. Most critters are shy and many are nocturnal, but they're out there. To date, 1,804 vertebrate species, including 21 species endemic to Nicaragua, and approximately 14,000 invertebrate species have been defined. However, Nicaragua remains the least-studied country in the region, and it is thought that excursions into the relatively unexplored reserves of the north and northeast will uncover previously undiscovered residents of the planet.

Mammals

There are 176 mammal species (including sea life) known to exist in Nicaragua, more than half of which are bats or small mammals, including rodents. Nicaragua has at least three endemic mammal species, two of which are associated with the Caribbean town of El Rama—the Rama squirrel *(Sciurus richmondi),* considered the tropical world's most endangered squirrel due to reduced habitat, and the Rama rice mouse *(Oryzomis dimidiatus).*

Nicaragua is also home to six big cat species, but there's no guarantee they'll be around for long. All six are listed as endangered, most seriously of all the jaguar and puma. Both were once common, but require vast amounts of wildland on which to hunt. The Pacific region of Nicaragua,

home to extensive agriculture for so many consecutive years now, is most likely devoid of big felines, with the possible exception of isolated communities on the higher slopes of some forested volcanoes like Mombacho. In the Atlantic region, small communities of cats eke out their survival in the dense forests of the southeast side of the Bosawás reserve. These species are unstudied and untracked, and are presumably preyed upon by local communities. Better off than the pumas and jaguars are smaller felines like ocelots and *tigrillos* trapped in the central forests, the latter of which are notorious chicken killers in rural farming communities.

There are three kinds of monkeys in Nicaragua: the mantled howler monkey *(Alouata palliata),* known popularly in Nicaragua as the *mono congo;* the Central American spider monkey *(Ateles geoffroyii);* and the white-faced capuchin *(Cebus capucinus).* Of the monkeys, the congo is the most common. One thousand individuals roam the slopes of Mombacho alone. You can also find them (or at least hear their throaty, haunting cries)

Pizotes are playful and curious.

on La Isla de Ometepe and the mountains of Matagalpa, particularly Selva Negra. Howler monkeys are able to project their voices an incredible distance; you can easily hear them several kilometers away. They eat fruits and leaves and spend most of their time in high tree branches. The white-faced capuchin is most frequently found in the forests in southeastern Nicaragua and parts of the Atlantic coast. It is a threatened species, but more so is the spider monkey, whose population has nearly been eliminated.

The Baird's tapir is present in very small numbers in eastern Nicaragua; it is estimated that several communities of this three-toed ungulate inhabit Bosawás. Nevertheless, this species is severely threatened with extinction.

The agouti paca (a large, forest-dwelling rodent known in Nicaragua as the painted rabbit), the white-tailed deer *(Odocoileus virginianus),* and the collared peccary *(Tayassu tajacu),* a stocky pig-like creature with coarse, spiky fur, though abundant, are under much pressure from hunters throughout northeastern Nicaragua. You may still see an agouti or peccary in Jinotega and to the east, if you're lucky.

Aquatic Life

Nicaragua is home to a wide variety of both saltwater and freshwater species of fish, due to its two large lakes, two ocean coastlines, and numerous isolated crater lakes. Among Nicaragua's many saltwater species are flat needlefish *(Ablennes hians),* wahoo *(Acanthocybium solandri),* three kinds of sole, spotted eagle rays *(Aetobatus narinari),* the Gill's sand lance *(Ammodytoides gilli),* two kinds of moray *(Anarchias sp.),* croakers *(Bairdiella sp.),* triggerfish *(Balistes sp.),* hogfish *(Bodianus sp.),* eight kinds of perch *(Diplectrum sp.),* sea bass *(Diplectrum sp.),* and a dozen kinds of shark, including blacktip *(Carcharias. limbatus),* great white *(C. carcharias),* silky *(C. falciformis),* and spinner *(C. brevipinna).*

Among the freshwater species are needlefish *(Strongylura sp.),* grunts *(Pomadasys sp.),* introduced tilapia *(Oreochromis aureus),* catfish *(Hexanematichthys sp.),* mojarra *(Eucinostomus sp.),* and snook *(Centropomus sp.).* Some species of cichlid

(Amphilophus sp.) found nowhere else in the world swim in Nicaragua's varied crater lakes.

At least 58 different types of marine corals have been identified in the Atlantic, specifically in the Miskito Cays, Corn Island, and the Pearl Cays. Nicaragua's most common coral species include *Acropora pamata, A. cervicornis,* and *Montastrea anularis.* Brain coral *(Colypophylia natans)* and black coral *(Antipathes pennacea)* are common. Studied for the first time in 1977 and 1978, the shallow reefs of the Pearl Cays contain the best coral formations in the nation, but are currently threatened by the enormous sediment load discharged by the Río Grande de Matagalpa.

The manatee *(Trichechus manatus)* is an important species currently protected by international statutes. In Nicaragua, it can occasionally be found in the Caribbean in the mouth of the Río San Juan and in the coastal lagoons, notably in Bluefields Bay. In 1993, the freshwater dolphin *(Sotalia fluviatilis)* was first spotted in Nicaragua and is most commonly sighted in Laguna de Wounta. The northern range for the freshwater dolphin was previously thought to be limited to Panamá.

Birds

As a result of its prime location along the Central American biosphere corridor, many thousands of species migrate through the area. To date, 676 species of birds in 56 families have been observed here, the more exotic of which you'll find in the mountains of the north and east, and along the Atlantic shore. Nicaragua has no endemic bird species of its own, but hosts 87 percent of all bird species known. The most exotic bird species known to reside in Nicaragua is also its most elusive, the quetzal *(Pharomacrus mocinno),* known to inhabit highlands in Bosawás, Jinotega, and Matagalpa, especially along the slopes of Mt. Kilambé, and in Miraflor in Estelí.

Nicaragua's elegant and colorful national bird, the *guardabarranco (Momotus momota),* is more easily found than you'd think. The Guardian of the Stream (as its Spanish name translates) can be found catching small insects in urban gardens in the capital. It is distinguished by its long, oddshaped, iridescent tail, which it carefully preens to catch the eye of the opposite sex. The *urraca* is a bigger, meaner version of the North American blue jay, with a dangly black crest on the top of its head. It's one of the larger of the common birds in Nicaragua and can frequently be found in treetops scolding the humans below. Though the *urraca* are everywhere, a particularly sizeable population patrols the slopes of Ometepe's twin volcanoes and the Isletas by Granada. Also in the Isletas, look for the brightly colored *oropendolas (Psarocolius wagleri)* that hang their elaborate, suspended bag-nests from the treetops around the lakeshore.

Reptiles

Of the 172 reptile species that make their homes in Nicaragua, nearly half are North American species, found in Nicaragua at the southern limit of their habitat, while 15 species are found only in Central America and another five are endemic to Nicaragua.

Nicaragua's several species of marine turtles are all in danger of extinction. The Paslama turtle *(Lepidochelys olivacea)* in the Pacific and the Carey turtle *(Eretmochelys imbricata)* and Green turtle *(Chelonia mydas)* in the Atlantic are protected, and much effort has gone into setting aside habitat for them, particularly nesting beaches. However, the struggle is fierce between those who aim to conserve the turtles and those who'd like to harvest their eggs, meat, and shells. There are approximately 20 beaches in the Pacific that present adequate conditions for the nesting of these turtle species, most of which play host to only occasional nesting events. Two beaches, Chacocente and La Flor on the Pacific coast, are the nesting grounds of the Paslama turtle. Massive annual egg-laying events between July and January (primarily during the first and third quarters of the moon) involve between 57,000 and 100,000 turtles, which crawl up on the moist sand at night to lay eggs. It's a safety-in-numbers approach to survival—only 1 out of 100 hatchlings makes it to adulthood. Armed guards on these beaches do their part to make sure the youngsters make it to the sea instead of the soup.

Frequently seen along the Río San Juan and some larger rivers of Jinotega are alligators, crocodiles *(Crocodilus acutus)*, caimans *(Caiman crocodilus)*, and the *Ñoca* turtle *(Trachemys scripta)*.

crocodile on the Río Waspuk

The *garrobo* is a bush lizard the size of a small house cat you're more likely to see suspended by its tail on the side of the road than in the wild. It is hunted by poor *campesino* children and then sold to passing motorists who take it home and make an aphrodisiac soup from the meat. Similarly, the Cusuco *(Dasypus novemincinctus)* is a type of armadillo with plated sides and sharp-clawed feet, commonly found in drier areas of the countryside. (For info on snakes, please see section on Health and Safety.)

Amphibians

Nicaragua's humid forests and riversides are inhabited by 64 known species of amphibians, four of which are endemic, including the Mombacho salamander *(Bolitoglossa mombachoensis)*, the miadis frog, the Cerro Saslaya frog *(Plectrohyla sp.)*, and the Saslaya salamander *(Nolitron sp.)*.

Insects

Each of Nicaragua's different ecosystems has a distinct insect population. Estimates of the total number of species reach as high as 250,000, only 1 percent of which have been identified. Notable species to seek out are several gigantic species of beetles, including *Dynastes hercules* (found in cloud forests); several species of brilliant green and golden Plusiotis, (found in Cerro Saslaya and Cerro Kilambé); the iridescent blue butterfly *Morpho peleides,* common all over the country, and its less common cousin, *M. amathonte,* found at altitudes of 300–700 meters, especially in the forests of Bosawás. Nocturnal moths like the Rothschildia, Eacles, and others are common. For more information about bug hunting in Nicaragua, you'll want to contact Belgian entomologist Jean-Michel Maes (jmmaes@ibw.com.ni), who, with nearly 20 years of research experience in Nicaragua, knows his stuff. He runs the entomological museum in León (normally closed to the public), and sells a CD-ROM entitled *Butterflies of Nicaragua* ($30). There is an increasing number of *mariposarios,* (butterfly farms) in Nicaragua, notably in Los Guatuzos, Papaturro, and El Castillo (Río San Juan), and San Ramón (Matagalpa).

National Parks and Reserves

Nicaragua's complex system of parks and reserves encompasses more than two million hectares. The Sistema Nacional de Areas Protegidas (SINAP) is made up of 76 parks, reserves, and refuges classified as "protected" by the Ministerio del Ambiente y los Recursos Naturales (Ministry of the Environment and Natural Resources, or MARENA). Of these, many are composed of privately owned land, making enforcement of their protected status difficult. That, combined with MARENA's paltry resource base and budget, has led to the decentralization of park management. Since 2001, MARENA has been experimenting with the "co-management" model in six natural reserves, handing natural-resource management responsibilities over to local NGOs who work with the communities within the areas to create sustainable alternatives to natural resource use and eco-tourism infrastructure. Co-management is a novel, ongoing experiment,

and while it has been surprisingly successful in some areas, the great majority of protected lands in Nicaragua remain unmanaged, unguarded, and completely undeveloped for tourism. They are sometimes referred to as "paper parks," existing only in legislation and studies, not in reality. The Río Estero Real, a wetlands preserve in the northwest corner of the country, is one of those, where half of the "protected" territory has been granted to private shrimp farmers who have eliminated most of the mangrove swamps and lagoons where shrimp once bred naturally, replacing them with artificial breeding pools.

Occasionally, being left alone results in untouched, virgin forests and wetlands protected by their own remoteness and natural tropical hostility. More commonly, however, it means that some of Nicaragua's richest treasures continue to be plundered by foreign and national cattle, logging, and mining interests, as well as destructively

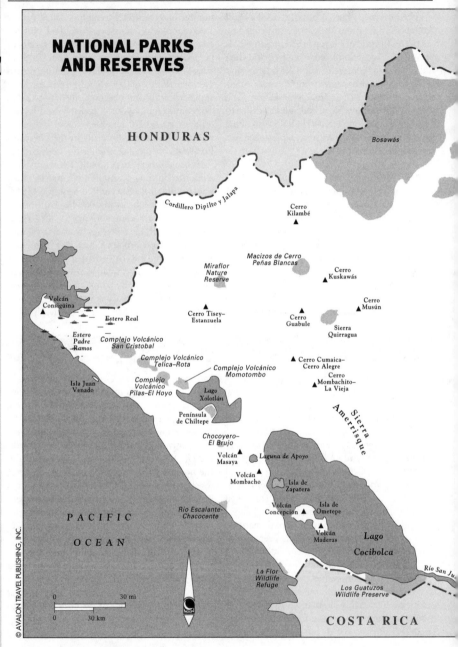

NATIONAL PARKS AND RESERVES

HONDURAS

Bosawás

Cordillero Dipilto y Jalapa

Cerro Kilambé ▲

Macizos de Cerro Peñas Blancas

Miraflor Nature Reserve

Cerro Kuskawás ▲

Cerro Musún ▲

Volcán Consigüina ▲

Estero Real

Cerro Tisey– Estanzuela ▲

Cerro Guabule ▲

Sierra Quirragua

Estero Padre Ramos

Complejo Volcánico San Cristobal

Isla Juan Venado

Complejo Volcánico Telica–Rota

Complejo Volcánico Momotombo

Cerro Cumaica– Cerro Alegre ▲

Cerro Mombachito– La Vieja ▲

Complejo Volcánico Pilas–El Hoyo

Lago Xolotlán

Sierra Amerrisque

Península de Chiltepe

Chocoyero– El Brujo

Volcán Masaya ▲

Laguna de Apoyo

Volcán Mombacho ▲

Isla de Zapatera

PACIFIC

Rio Escalante– Chacocente

Volcán Concepción ▲

Isla de Ometepe

OCEAN

Volcán Maderas ▲

Lago Cocibolca

Río San Ju

0   30 mi

0   30 km

La Flor Wildlife Refuge

Los Guatuzos Wildlife Preserve

COSTA RICA

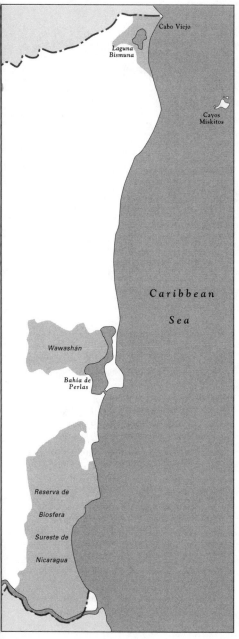

Cabo Viejo

Laguna
Bismuna

Cayos
Miskitos

Caribbean

Sea

Wawashán

Bahía de
Perlas

Reserva de

Biosfera

Sureste de

Nicaragua

managed by *campesino* populations that are given little incentive or education to do otherwise. In the latter case, a typical example is the government's declaring "protected" an area where people have been living traditionally for generations, and who are suddenly expected to drastically alter their fishing, hunting, and planting patterns to protect a "park" that is and always has been their homeland. That has been the experience in the Bosawás Biosphere Reserve, where Mayangna and Miskito people were not consulted during the planning of the reserve and have consequently fought against the new regulations, which interfere with their traditional lifestyle.

Conversely, Fundación Cocibolca, in management of La Flor, has relied heavily on local residents, both for staffing the reserve and for ideas on how to run it. Tourism can go a long way toward bolstering local incentive to protect—rather than consume—the natural world.

The following is a selection of some of the more accessible (or just spectacular) of Nicaragua's protected areas.

NATIONAL PARKS
Volcán Masaya
Nicaragua's best-organized and most easily accessed park features a paved road leading to the crater, a museum, interpretive center, and paid guides to take you through more than 20 kilometers of nature trails. Declaring the 5,100 hectares that surround Volcán Masaya a national park was one of the last things President Anastasio García Somoza did before the revolution took him from power in 1979. The park's extensive lava fields are home to coyotes, garrobo lizards, white-tailed deer, and cusucos. A rare variety of sulfur-tolerant parakeets inhabits the inside of the crater's walls.

Zapatera Archipelago
Comprised of the Zapatera Volcano (629 m) and the eight islets that surround it, the park is located in Lake Cocibolca between the Isla de Ometepe and the city of Granada, 34 kilometers to the north. Although owned by private landholders, the islands were given national-park status

Know Nicaragua

© RANDY WOOD

Volcán Masaya

in the 1980s in recognition of their immense natural, cultural, and historical value, and the government subsequently took control over much of the land. The islands still contain virgin forests and lovely shorelines, but are perhaps most famous for the pre-Columbian statuary that was found there. Many of the statues are observable today in the Convento San Francisco in Granada. Others were sold or plundered, to be spirited off to the far corners of the world. The park and adjacent mainland peninsula served as a massive burial ground for the indigenous people there.

BIOLOGICAL RESERVES
Miraflor

Draped with Spanish moss and carpeted with orchids and lush vegetation, the more than 5,600 hectares of the Reserva Natural Miraflor is a cloud forest, considered one of the most important natural reserves of its type in Nicaragua. The area is privately owned in its entirety, and is managed by several different groups of farmers and *campesino* cooperatives. This is one of the few places in Nicaragua to spot the exotic (and elusive) quetzal and up to a third of the total number of bird species observed in Nicaragua.

Río Indio Maíz

The nearly 264,000 hectares of jungle pressed between the Indio and Maíz Rivers, La Gran Reserva as it is known, abut two additional protected areas, the Punta Gorda Nature Reserve to the north, and the Río San Juan Wildlife Reserve to the south. Together, the reserves are part of the Biósfera del Sureste de Nicaragua, an immense chunk of southeastern Nicaragua dedicated to the preservation of animal and plant species along with their natural ecosystems in the Río San Juan watershed. The reserve is one of the few remaining areas in the Americas where you can experience virgin tropical humid forest as it was 200 years ago (and all the rain, insects, and heat that goes with it). The extent of the wildlife in the reserve has still not been completely determined, but it is, at the very least, one of the last refuges in Nicaragua for ocelots and other big cats.

Cayos Miskitos

Defined as all the cays and small islands found in a 40-kilometer radius from the center of Isla Grande in the Atlantic Ocean off Puerto Cabezas, plus a 20-kilometer swath of shoreline from Cabo Gracias a Dios to the south, the Reserva Biológica Cayos Miskitos has important economic and cultural significance to the Miskito people, who depend on it for fish and shellfish. The Cayos Miskitos are an ecological treasure whose impenetrable lagoons, reefs, mangrove forests, and swamps are home to marine turtles, manatees, dolphins, and several types of endangered coral species. The mangrove forests give shelter to bird species, such as pancho galán, garza rosada, and the brown pelican. Substantial petroleum deposits lie below the continental shelf in the Cayos Miskitos area, so the management of the region will warrant much caution and a careful balance. In the meantime, the cays' most immediate threat is drug traffickers, who use the area as a lair.

WILDLIFE RESERVES

Río Escalante/Chacocente

Named for the peculiar smell of *choco* (rotting turtle egg shells after a hatching), the Refugio de Vida Silvestre Río Escalante/Chacocente encompasses 4,800 hectares of dry tropical forest along the edge of the Pacific Ocean. The area was declared a reserve primarily because of its importance as the nesting ground of the endangered tora and paslama turtles, incredible multitudes of which crawl up on the beach each year to lay eggs in the sand. Exotic orchids, like the *flor de niño* and *huele noche* fill the nocturnal air with a sweet, romantic fragrance. But Chacocente is also home to important forest species, mangrove systems, and the "salt tree." Check the treetops for howler and white-faced monkeys, and keep an eye peeled for the many reptiles, pelicans, white-tailed deer, and *guardabarrancos* that are watching you from the forest edges.

La Flor

This southern Pacific beach, a gorgeous white sandy crescent at the edge of an 800 hectare broad strip of tropical dry forest, is one of the most beautiful beaches in Nicaragua. Thousands of Paslama turtles beach themselves here annually to nest and lay eggs, one of just a handful of beaches in the world that witness such a spectacle. Many *garrobo negro*, iguana *verde*, *lagartijas*, monkeys, coyotes, raccoons, and skunks (some of which prey on the turtle eggs) also make their home in the reserve. The skies at La Flor are full of bird species that make their homes in the relatively intact dry forest: *urracas*, *gavilanes caracoleros*, *chocoyos*, *querques*, *garzas*, and *sonchiches*.

Los Guatuzos Wildlife Preserve

The 43,000 hectares of protected wetlands that separate the southern shore of Lake Cocibolca from the Costa Rican border are a remnant of a Sandinista-era wildlife reserve called Si-a-Paz (a play on words meaning yes to peace). Los Guatuzos preserves both the spirit and the wildlife of the reserve and offers valuable habitat to hundreds of different species, plus several small border settlements of people.

NATURAL RESERVES

Volcán Cosigüina

In the farthest northwestern corner of Nicaragua, more than 12,000 hectares of the Cosigüina peninsula have been declared a natural reserve. The area has been quietly revegetating itself since the volcano's massive eruption in 1835, predominantly as dry tropical forests of *genícero*, *tempisque*, and *guanacaste* trees. Its nearly inaccessible crater has become the home to spider monkeys, coyotes, black iguanas, white-tailed deer, and coatis, but more obvious to the naked eye are the hundreds of bird species, notably the scarlet macaw. Climbing the volcano offers a phenomenal view of the crater lake (which began filling after the eruption 150 years ago), the Gulf of Fonseca, and beyond.

Isla Juan Venado

Much more than a sandy barrier beach island,

Isla Juan Venado contains 4,600 hectares of estuary and coastline along the Pacific coast west of León. Its vegetation is successional, going from mangroves at the water's edge to inland dry tropical forest. Isla Juan Venado is rife with bird species due to the estuary system—its mangroves are home to the nests of thousands of parrots and herons—as well as crabs, mollusks, and more than 50 species of mammals and reptiles.

Volcán Mombacho

A scant 41 kilometers from the lowland heat of Managua is an otherworldly island of cloud forest atop an ancient and dormant volcano. Volcán Mombacho's lower slopes are dedicated to agriculture, cattle raising, and coffee production, but its upper third—above 800 meters—is a spectacular, misty wildlife and cloud-forest reserve. Mombacho is managed by the Fundación Cocibolca, which has done an admirable job of constructing trails and low-impact guest and research facilities. Mombacho is home both to several endemic species of butterflies and the endemic Mombacho salamander.

Chocoyero–El Brujo

The closest natural reserve to Managua, Chocoyero–El Brujo makes up for its small size with the sheer quantity of *chocoyos* (parakeets) that inhabit its cliff caves. There's no excuse for not exploring Chocoyero–El Brujo some lazy afternoon at sundown when the skies fill with the ruckus of thousands of squawking green *chocoyos*. Chocoyero is set in a semi-humid forest of stately *pochote, tigüilote,* and cedar trees, and in addition to its famous birds, provides habitat for several types of owls, monkeys, and squirrels.

Estero Padre Ramos

In the northwest corner of the department of Chinandega, Estero Padre Ramos is home to the most preserved mangrove forest in Nicaragua, more than 150 bird species, and untouched, pristine beaches for as far as the eye can see. The fingers of the estuary are a sea-kayakers dream, or you can try the local *botes* for more adventure.

Other Reserves

There are many more nature reserves, typically

Volcán Mombacho

© RANDY WOOD

small and designated as such in an attempt to protect a very specific resource. In addition to those mentioned previously, there are 11 reserves that protect volcanic or coastal lagoons, 16 that protect specific peaks, such as Kilambé and Pancasán, six that protect volcanic complexes, such as San Cristóbal or Pilas–El Hoyo, plus dozens of others.

BIOSPHERE RESERVES

Nicaragua's two biosphere reserves were indirectly based on a model proposed for protecting several vast areas in the southeast United States. The strategy is to create a central "nucleus zone," with wilderness status totally preventing human activity. The nucleus is then surrounded by various levels of buffer zones with increasing, but still regulated, resource exploitation permitted as the distance increases from the center. That's the intention, anyway. The virgin lands of Bosawás and the Río San Juan areas have long served as "safety valves" for Nicaragua's expanding population, accommodating *campesinos* as they look for new forestland to clear and farm. Several hundred *campesino* families currently inhabit the Bosawás reserve, and in the absence of regulation, more will surely follow.

Located in the remote north-central wilds of Nicaragua, Bosawás is the largest continuous expanse of virgin cloud forest in Central America. In the extreme southeast of Nicaragua, the Refugio de Vida Silvestre Río San Juan stretches from El Castillo southeast to the Atlantic Ocean along the north edge of the Río San Juan. In addition to the river itself, an important part of the reserve are the four interconnected lagoons at the river's mouth and their related pools, all of which are important habitat for manatees and several other mammals.

PRIVATE RESERVES

Nicaragua's newest category of protected areas are called Reservas Silvestres Privadas (Wild Private Reserves). These are entirely private landholdings whose owners have applied to MARENA to become officially declared as part of SINAP. The landowners must meet a number of criteria as well as present a management plan to be classified as protected. At present, there are a handful of approved private reserves and more pending. The areas are usually near other parks or reserves, contain substantial vegetation and wildlife, and are often a part of some biological corridor. At this early point in the game, they are in varying stages of developing their tourism infrastructures. The original six private reserves are Montibelli near Chocoyero, Domitila outside Nandaime, La Maquina on the road to the coast from Diriamba, Toromixcal in San Juan del Sur, César Augusto in Jinotega, and Greenfields near Pearl Lagoon. Look for them in the appropriate regional chapters.

Environmental Issues

Nicaragua's ability to resolve its environmental issues will almost certainly determine the course of its immediate economic growth and social well-being. However, those environmental issues are complex and entangled in a rat's nest of bigger issues, including politics, land rights, population pressure, war, and frequent natural disasters. The remedies are anything but simple.

Chief among Nicaragua's immediate environmental problems is the rapid loss of its once-extensive forests at the rate of 150,000 hectares harvested per year. Some analyses indicate Nicaragua's timber reserves will be completely depleted by the year 2015. The full extent of the problem is not entirely clear, as the calculations of remaining forest are based on figures collected in the 1970s.

The great majority of families in the countryside use *leña* (firewood) as their prime fuel source for cooking, which has put tremendous pressure on forest resources as Nicaragua's increasing population expands into previously unsettled lands. Population pressure and the swelling cattle industry have caused a progression of the agricultural frontier from both the Atlantic and Pacific sides of the country, reducing Nicaragua's forests by 4.6 million hectares from 1950 to

WHAT DOES ECO-TOURISM MEAN TO YOU?

The word "eco-tourism" was created in the 1980s with the best of intentions—ostensibly, to describe anything having to do with environmentally sound and culturally sustainable tourism, the "business" of both preventing tourism from spoiling the environment and using tourism as an economic alternative to spoiling the environment for some other reason.

The success of the concept—and its marketing value—led directly to a worldwide boom in the usage of that prefix that we know so well, even if its actual practice has sometimes fallen short of original intentions. For sure, "eco" has been used, abused, prostituted, and bastardized all over the world, and Nicaragua is no exception. Surely, anything "eco" has something to do with the outdoors, but that's about all we can promise. We've limited our eco-writing, not because we don't believe in its precepts, but because we're wary of what it means in this day, age, and place. When we do use it, we are more likely referring to a program's connection with its community as well as the environment. Some word-savvy tourism marketers have tried to freshen things up by using "alternative" or "adventure tourism," but, when describing an operation that practices the original definition of eco-tourism mentioned above, we prefer "sustainable," "responsible," "ethical," or even "fair trade" tourism.

Semantics aside, as a visitor, you should never forget how choices you make can have a variety of both immediate and long-term effects on how well Nicaraguan natural areas remain preserved in their natural state. The concept of protected areas is still relatively new in Nicaragua and is at times viewed with skepticism—especially by rural folk who live near (or sometimes actually within) these areas. Left to their own devices, poor *campesinos* use the wilderness to supplement their paltry incomes, by chopping wood for fuel, cutting out badly needed farmland, or hunting wild game. MARENA, the government ministry charged with protecting Nicaragua's vast system of parks and refuges, has scant resources to prevent such activities.

That's where you come in. By spending money among the people who live near these protected areas, nature-loving visitors give Nicaraguans a vi-able incentive not to cut into the forest. This means hiring a local guide, buying a meal from a family, or paying a few *córdobas* to pitch a tent or hang a hammock outside a farmer's hut.

Those going on a trip with a tour company are not exempt from any of this—be sure that the company you choose leaves some benefit behind, rather than using only their own guides, transportation, food, etc. Nicaraguans are well aware of the irony of wealthy northerners enjoying forest resources they are not supposed to touch. Help support them.

Guide to Good-Karma Traveling

The North American Center for Responsible Tourism suggests that travelers keep the following guidelines in mind during their trip:

- Travel with a spirit of humility and a genuine desire to meet and talk with local people.
- Be aware of the feelings of others. Act respectfully and avoid offensive behavior, particularly when taking photographs.
- Cultivate the habit of actively listening and observing rather than merely hearing and seeing. Avoid the temptation to "know all the answers."
- Realize that others may have concepts of time and attitudes that are different from—not inferior to—those you inherited from your own culture.
- Instead of looking only for the exotic, discover the richness of another culture and way of life.
- Learn local customs and respect them.
- Remember that you are only one of many visitors. Do not expect special privileges.
- When bargaining with merchants, remember that the poorest one may give up a profit rather than his or her personal dignity. Don't take advantage of the desperately poor. Pay a fair price.
- Keep your promises to people you meet. If you cannot, do not make the promise.
- Spend time each day reflecting on your experiences in order to deepen your understanding. Is your enrichment beneficial for all involved?
- Be aware of why you are traveling in the first place. If you truly want a "home away from home," why travel?

1995. On the Atlantic coast, much of the hardwood logging is happening at the hands of U.S., Canadian, and Asian companies that have negotiated fat timber concessions with Nicaragua's successive cash-strapped governments.

As if forest depletion due to humans hasn't been enough, the remaining pine forests in Nueva Segovia were further devastated by a massive outbreak of the pine bark beetle that began in October 1999 in Teotecacinte, Nueva Segovia. By March 2001, an estimated 6,000 hectares were destroyed in the seven departments that make up north and northwest Nicaragua, with the area around Jalapa being the most hard hit. The beetle attacks both young and mature pine forests weakened by fires, resin harvesting, and poor management, boring through the bark of the tree to feed on the resin that lies between the wood and the bark. At the start of each rainy season, young beetles disperse and fly longer distances. The infestation can spread up to 20 meters per day, spreading a full kilometer in just under two months. As of 2002, the outbreak had still not been completely contained. Further devastated by a massive outbreak of the pine bark beetle that began in October 1999 and continued

through about 2002. The damage done—by both the beetle and the salvage loggers—is still being assessed and recovery will take years.

By whatever mechanism, deforestation leaves the fragile tropical soils exposed to rainfall and the ensuing erosion leads directly to the contamination and elimination of water sources, and even outright microclimate changes. This is the case in much of Nicaragua, where within one human generation, rivers and streams that were once perennial now flow only sporadically, if at all. On the Pacific coast, several decades of intensive agriculture and wind erosion have caused the loss of once-rich volcanic soils as well. In general, the entire Pacific, central, and northern regions of the country are at immediate risk of sustained soil erosion.

Massive efforts are underway to attack the problem from all sides, from environmental education of the youngest children in order to change cultural habits, to the active replanting of hillsides via tree-nursery projects, to the teaching and implementation of less-destructive agricultural techniques. Much of the effort is coming through international funding and expertise, since the beleaguered government ministries have traditionally lacked even the most basic of resources.

History

For the past 135 years, Nicaragua has been a kind of geopolitical mind-altering substance. American politicians and journalists go there, sample the local politics, and immediately start babbling in tongues. It began with William Walker, the nineteenth-century adventurer who declared himself president of Nicaragua, and it continues right up through this morning's newspaper.

Glenn Garvin, Everybody Had His Own Gringo, 1992

PRE-COLONIAL YEARS

Even older than the famous 6,000-year-old footprints baked into the mud in a quiet corner of Managua are the remnants of a Caribbean people

known as *Los Concheros* (the shell collectors), who inhabited—or frequently visited—the Atlantic coast around 2,000 years earlier. Deposits of shells from their fishing and collecting forays have been discovered in several locations, but little else is known about Nicaragua's first inhabitants. Agriculture began around 5,000 years ago with the cultivation of corn. Pottery making followed 2,000 years later.

Sometime in the 13th century, the Chorotega and Nicarao people, under pressure from the aggressive Aztecs in Mexico, fled south through the Central American isthmus, led by a vision of a land dominated by a great lake. The Chorotegas settled on the shores of Lake Cocibolca and around the volcanic craters of Masaya and Apoyo, and the Nicaraos farther south.

© JOSHUA BERMAN

Nicas love a parade; Independence Day (Sept. 15) is celebrated in even the smallest towns.

COLONIALISM

Christopher Columbus, known in the Spanish world as Cristóbal Colón, first set eyes on Nicaragua in July of 1502, on his fourth and final trip to the Americas. Searching for a navigable passage through the land mass, Columbus skirted Nicaragua's Mosquito Coast, then continued on to South America without noticing the outlet of the San Juan. Seventeen years later, the conquistador Pedro Arias Dávila returned under orders from the Spanish crown to explore the land bridge of Nicaragua. During his brief foray, another Spanish explorer, González, encountered the caciques (tribal leaders) Nicarao and Diriangén, who engaged González's men in a brief battle. This gave the Spanish a hint of the warrior spirit of the original Nicaragüenses—a warning that went unheeded amongst the Europeans who would frequently face the same rebelliousness over the next few centuries.

Francisco Hernández de Córdoba arrived not long after González, entrusted with the duty of establishing Spain's first settlements in the new land. Córdoba settled Granada alongside the Chorotega communities on the banks of Lake Cocibolca, and, pushing farther inland and up the Tipitapa River, the settlement of León on the western shores of Lake Xolotlán. Nicaragua remained a part of Spain's overseas possessions for the next 300 years under the governance of the colonial capital in Guatemala.

INDEPENDENCE

Central America won its independence from Spain in 1821, and for a short time remained united as the five provinces of the Central American Federation. The belief that Europe would act militarily to return the former colonies to Spain forced the United States to issue the Monroe Doctrine in 1823, declaring the New World off limits to further European colonization and interference. It was the first step in two centuries of political domination in Latin America. The Central American Federation was a short-lived pipe dream, however: When Nicaragua withdrew from the federation in 1838, the remaining states opted to become individual republics as well and the federation dissolved. Reunion of any form remains nearly impossible.

The Birth of a Rivalry

Newly independent, Nicaragua underwent several years of complete anarchy. The two primary cities, León and Granada, operated as independent city-states until a national government was finally agreed upon in 1845.

The conflict between León and Granada in the 1800s is noteworthy because it established political rivalries that endure to this day. In the early 19th century, Nicaragua's principal exports were cacao, indigo, and cattle, the sale of which allowed the landed and merchant classes to accumulate considerable wealth—on the backs of the Native Americans and landless farmers, of course, who worked the farms and ranches essentially as indentured servants. At the same time, the aspiring bourgeoisie, influenced by the Liberal teachings of the universities in León and by the American and French Revolutions, sought to liberate the poor working classes of their feudal labor obligations, thus making their labor available to all at market prices. The landed class, mostly based in Granada and loyal to the aristocratic system that favored them, resisted. The León Liberals–Granada Conservatives split was responsible for more than 100 years of civil war and continues into modern political-party rivalries.

The Canal, William Walker, and the U.S. Marines

Nicaragua's unique geography has resulted in an uninterrupted history of unrealized transcontinental-canal plans, some of which continue through the present. During the California gold rush (1849–1856), the Central American isthmus served as the route for many a prospector bound for California—and not a few impoverished ones headed back east. Steamship baron and businessman Cornelius Vanderbilt established a cross-isthmus transport company to challenge the Pacific Steamship Company then operating in Panamá. Travelers bound for California sailed up the Río San Juan and across Lake Nicaragua to the small port at San Jorge. There, they were taken by horse cart 18 kilometers across the narrow isthmus through Rivas to the bay of San Juan del Sur. Ships waiting in the harbor then carried the travelers north along the Pacific coastline to California. Vanderbilt dredged the channel of the Río San Juan and built roads, railroads, and docks on both coasts to accommodate the traffic. At about that time, the Leoneses, embroiled in a bitter battle with the Conservatives of Granada, enlisted the help of William Walker, an American filibuster who eventually installed himself as president of Nicaragua, razed the city of Granada, and caused a whole lot of trouble (see the Granada chapter).

Though the relative peace of the Conservative period fostered many advances in infrastructure and technology—including the train from Granada to Corinto and the introduction of the telegraph—the famous "Thirty Years" were also a time of economic stagnation that kept Nicaragua several decades behind its neighbors in coffee exportation. Under the leadership of Liberal General José Santos Zelaya, the bourgeoisie rebelled, and Zelaya became president. He was a fierce nationalist who, among other things, marched troops to the Atlantic coast in order to refute Britain's territorial claims and officially incorporate the Atlantic region into the nation. (The two administrative units of the Atlantic coast bore Zelaya's name until the 1990s.) As a staunch nationalist, he promptly raised the ire of the United States, who arranged his ouster. Zelaya rejected Washington's proposals to build a cross-isthmus canal through Nicaraguan territory while at the same time courting Great Britain to finance the construction of a transcontinental railway.

The United States, which had been constructing the Panama canal since 1904, was threatened by the idea of a nationalist dictator encouraging a competing transport mechanism and in 1909, forced Zelaya out with pressure from the U.S. Marines. The U.S. intervention reestablished the Conservatives in power, but in 1912, the Liberal and nationalist Benjamin

A BRIEF HISTORY OF U.S. INTERVENTION IN NICARAGUA

In President Teddy Roosevelt's addition to the Monroe Doctrine of regional dominance, he proclaimed that the United States, by virtue of its status as a "civilized nation," had the right to stop "chronic wrongdoing" throughout the Western Hemisphere. Subsequently, the so-called Roosevelt Corollary was used to justify troop deployment to Latin America 32 times between the end of the Spanish-American War and the years of the Great Depression. President William Howard Taft provided further rationalization for aggressively dominating Latin America with his "Dollar Diplomacy," an unabashed strategy to advance and protect U.S. businesses in other countries. Nicaragua, which had been host to U.S. fruit, mining, and transportation interests since the 1850s, was a frequent recipient of such foreign policy.

U.S. Marines landed at least seven times during the aforementioned period, and spent a total of 21 years occupying Nicaragua. Official reasons for these visits included "pacification of Nicaragua," "prevention of rebellion," and, of course, "protection of U.S. interests and property." It would be unfair to call these visits uninvited, since nearly all were ostensibly serving the purpose of one or more Nicaraguan parties, usually the Conservatives.

The following is a more detailed list of gringo interventions:

1853: Washington sends U.S. Navy commander George H. Hollins to Greytown to extract an apology from local British officials for having insulted U.S. diplomat Solon Borland. Those responsible were nowhere to be found, so, reports a U.S. Marine Corps historical website, "Hollins' only alternative was to bombard the town, and this he tried to do in the most humane manner possible." Hollins allowed 24 hours for evacuation, then commenced firing. "At 0900 on 13 July, 177 shells plowed into Greytown. That afternoon a landing party of Marines and seamen completed the destruction of the town." Humanely, of course.

1853–1856: U.S. citizen William Walker usurps power and declares himself president of Nicaragua; he is briefly recognized by Washington before the other Central American nations briefly unite, drive him out, and eventually execute him by firing squad.

1894: The U.S. Marines under Lieutenant Franklin J. Moses have a month-long occupation of Bluefields.

Zeledón led a rebellion that provoked the United States to step in again. This time, the invasion was on a much larger scale; 2,700 marines landed at Corinto and took immediate control of the railways, ports, and major cities.

Military aggression aside, the U.S. government was subtly gaining control over Nicaragua in other ways. Following the 1912 attack, U.S. financial institutions began to quietly acquire coffee-export businesses and railway and steamship companies, forcing Nicaragua into a credit noose. Under the watchful eye of the U.S. Marines, governmental control was handed over to the Conservatives, whom Washington thought would more faithfully represent U.S. interests. But the Liberals resisted, staging 10 uprisings between 1913 and 1924, all of which the U.S. military quelled.

In 1924, Conservative President Bartolomé Martínez instituted a novel form of government—a power-sharing arrangement between the Liberals and the Conservatives at the local level. The United States withdrew Marines in 1925 but they were back within the year. No sooner had power sharing begun than ambitious Conservative Emilio Chamorro staged a coup d'etat, seized power, and sparked the Constitutional War. The United States stepped in to prevent the imminent takeover by the Liberals, but because the Conservatives had discredited themselves, the United States was unable to simply hand the power back to them. The deal they worked out was known as the Espino Negro Pact (named after the town where it was signed; Spanish for Black Thorn). It was a crucial

1896: From May 2–4, when fighting near Corinto "endangers American holdings," 15 Marines, under 1st Sergeant Frederick W. M. Poppe, and 19 seamen land in Corinto and stand guard in a "show of force."

1898: As President Zelaya extends his tenure for still another term, the local U.S. consular agent requests the U.S.S. *Alert,* at anchor in the harbor of Bluefields, to stand by in case of an attack on the city. On the morning of February 7, the U.S. flag on shore rises "union downward" over the consulate, signaling a force of 14 Marines and 19 seamen to land; they withdraw the following day.

1899: Another display of force lands, this time with a Colt automatic gun "to prevent both rebels and government troops from destroying American property."

1910: Marines and navy vessels concentrate in Nicaraguan waters and land in Bluefields and Corinto on May 19 "to guard American property."

1912: Nicaraguan president Adolfo Díaz requests the support of U.S. forces. The United States complies when the U.S.S. *Annapolis* arrives in Corinto, deploying a contingent of naval officers to Managua on August 4. Three companies of marine infantry also land and are transported to Managua by train.

1927–1933: President Coolidge sends Marines to find Sandino and "gun the bandit down." They fail.

1981–1990: The CIA runs a secret command operation directing and financing Contra forces in their attempt to topple the Sandinista government. U.S operatives carry out supply and intelligence activities, train commanders and soldiers, plant harbor mines, and sabotage Sandinista holdings.

Note: all citations from "Marine Corps Historical Reference Series, The United States Marines in Nicaragua," by Bernard C. Nalty, Historical Branch, G-3 Division, Headquarters, U.S. Marine Corps, Washington, D.C. 1968. Historical Branch, G-3 Division, Headquarters, U. S. Marine Corps, Washington, D. C. 20380

moment for the Liberals. One of their generals, Augusto C. Sandino, was opposed to the pact, and fled with his men to the northern mountains to start a guerrilla war in opposition of the continued presence of the United States in Nicaragua. The leader of the Constitutional Army was forced to declare, "All my men surrender except one."

The U.S. military tried unsuccessfully to flush Sandino from the mountains in spite of drastic measures, which included the aerial bombing of the city of Ocotal, so in 1933, Washington tried a new approach. Withdrawing U.S. troops from Nicaragua, the United States formed a new military unit called the National Guard, placed young Anastasio Somoza García at its head, and handed the power over to them and the new president, Juan Bautista Sacasa. Sandino enjoyed overwhelming support in Nicaragua's northern mountains and had achieved two of his goals—the removal of both U.S. armed forces and the Conservative oligarchy from power. Sandino represented a major threat to Somoza's political and military ambitions. So in February of 1934, Sandino went to Managua at Sacasa's invitation to negotiate, and when he left the presidential palace that night, several National Guard members ambushed and assassinated him on the streets of Managua. Sandino's assassination was quickly followed by a government-sponsored reign of terror in the northern countryside, destroying cooperatives, returning lands to their previous owners, and hunting down, exiling, imprisoning, or killing Sandino's supporters.

THE SOMOZA ERA

The formation of the National Guard paved the way for its leader, General Anastasio Somoza García, to seize control of Nicaragua in 1937 and begin an enormously wealthy and powerful family dynasty that would permanently reorient and completely control Nicaraguan politics for the following 42 years. So formidable was the rule of the Somoza family that many Nicaraguans and foreigners alike refer to the nearly continuous succession of three Somoza presidents as one all-powerful "Somoza." The Somozas were wily politicians with a near-genius for using existing political conflicts to their personal advantage; they were also expert practitioners of a favorite trick of Latin American dictators, *continuismo*, in which a puppet leader would be elected but resign shortly afterward, handing the power back to the Somozas. Five such "presidents" were elected during the 42-year reign of the Somozas, not one of which lasted longer than three years. The Somozas maintained a strong foothold in the national economy as well (much to the dismay of merchants in Granada) by manipulating the government licensing mechanisms and importing contraband for local markets with the complicity of the National Guard. If there was money to be made anywhere in Nicaragua, the Somozas took notice and squeezed out the competition. They extracted personal income from public utilities and the financial sector, monopolized the cotton industry when it surged in the 1950s and, later, meat, shrimp, and lobster export in the 1960s and 1970s. They owned the nation's prime food-processing industries, sugar refining, cement production, the cardboard, tobacco, and recording industries, and sea and air transport. In fact, it is said that by the late 1970s, the Somoza family owned everything in Nicaragua worth owning.

Anastasio Somoza García

(Presidencies: January 1, 1937–May 1, 1947; May 6, 1950–September 21, 1956)
Born in San Marcos, Carazo, and educated in Philadelphia, Somoza García employed his command of the English language and his sharp business sense to ascend rapidly through his military and political career. One of the first things he did upon taking power was build a mansion on a hill overlooking Managua and give it to the U.S. ambassador for his home (today, it's called the Casa Grande, and it still belongs to the U.S. Embassy). The Roosevelt administration in America saw Somoza as a good businessman and a source of much-needed stability for the country and was willing to overlook his rapacious greed, questionable politics, and strong-handed military tactics in exchange for a Central American leader they could rely on. Through World War II, Nicaragua remained a reliable provider of raw goods, like cotton, timber, minerals, and rubber, to feed the U.S. war machine. World War II was an economic windfall for Somoza in other ways as well: Taking advantage of the political situation, he declared war on Germany and Japan, then confiscated the valuable coffee land of most German citizens living in Nicaragua.

In spite of Somoza García's greed, he is remembered fondly for several public works projects, including the railway from Chinandega to Puerto Morazán, Managua's city water system, the Managua International Airport (originally named Aeropuerto Las Mercedes) and perhaps most importantly, the Pan-American Highway, which began in 1942 (and which not coincidentally happened to pass along the edge of several of his personal farms). Under increasing political pressure to step down from the presidency, Somoza García handed power over to a series of puppet governments and then stepped back into power in 1951, maintaining his presidency through a series of constitutional reforms that eliminated the need for elections. Popular frustration grew until 1956, when, at a celebratory ball in the Social Club of León, he was assassinated by the poet, political idealist, and frustrated nationalist Rigoberto López Pérez.

Luís Somoza Debayle

(Presidency: September 21, 1956–May 1, 1963)
Upon his father's assassination, Luís Somoza Debayle, a.k.a. Tacho, took the reins. An agronomist by training, he showed great political skill at

keeping the nation stable despite political agitation that filled the years of his presidency. Some of the tension was due to his younger brother Anastasio Somoza Debayle's political aspirations, but there were several attempts on Tacho's life as well, including one in 1959, when 100 young men, inspired by Fidel Castro's success in Cuba, attempted to spark a popular uprising. The operation was a military failure that led to their surrender after only two weeks. Meanwhile, Tacho continued his father's legacy of large public works projects, including the hydropower plant and reservoir of Lake Apanás in Jinotega; the improved port facilities at Corinto; the highway from San Benito to El Rama, which helped unite the Atlantic and Pacific coasts; and the nation's first social security system (INSS). The United States continued to support the Somoza political dynasty, and in return, Luís Somoza Debayle allowed the Kennedy administration to stage the disastrous Bay of Pigs operation from Nicaragua's Atlantic coast. In 1963, Tacho lost in popular elections to the Liberal candidate Renée Schick. He never sought another political office but dedicated himself instead to his many businesses until a massive heart attack felled him in 1967.

Anastasio Somoza Debayle

(Presidencies: May 1, 1967–May 1, 1972; December 1, 1974–July 16, 1979)

"Tachito" was the third and most avaricious president of the Somoza dynasty and a graduate of the West Point Military Academy (1946). At the time Tachito became president, the nascent Sandinista (FSLN) movement was gaining attention in the north through attacks and kidnappings; over the next decade, they would prod Tachito into becoming the most relentless and cruel president the nation had ever seen.

The earthquake of December 1972 provided Tachito a unique opportunity: Appointing himself head of the Emergency Committee, he did little more to rebuild the country than funnel aid money into his own bank accounts. He was reelected in 1974, but the Carter administration in Washington refused to countenance Tachito's (Somoza's) flagrant human rights violations. The

assassination of journalist Pedro Joaquín Chamorro, and Tachito's increasingly violent responses to FSLN attacks earned him much international opprobrium. When the FSLN finally ousted him on July 16, 1979, he fled to Miami, and then to Paraguay, where on September 17, 1980, an anti-tank rocket demolished his limousine, killing him instantly. The Sandinista government denied all responsibility for the attack, but it was clear regardless of who fired the rocket, the Somoza dynasty had finally come to an end.

THE SANDINISTA REVOLUTION

Guerrilla groups opposed to the Somoza dynasty and inspired by Fidel Castro began training in clandestine camps in the northern mountains in the early 1950s and coalesced a decade later when Carlos Fonseca Amador, Silvio Mayorga, and Tomás Borge formed the **Frente Sandinista de Liberación Nacional (FSLN).** They shared the belief that dictatorships could never be reformed—only overthrown. Fonseca had studied law in León and was captivated by Marxist theory, which he experienced firsthand during a trip to Moscow in 1958 and a meeting with Che Guevara in 1962. Fonseca's ideas, an inspired combination of Marxism and the nationalist, anti-imperialist beliefs of Augusto Sandino, made up the ideological framework of Sandinismo and dictated the economic and social reforms that followed thereafter.

The first Sandinista insurrections in the Ríos Coco and Bocay (1963) and Pancasán (1967) regions were quickly crushed but legitimized the FSLN among radical university students and citydwellers. As a result, the Sandinistas' military strength and daring escalated rapidly through the 1970s in spite of several bitter defeats at the hands of the National Guard. Tachito's heavy-handed attempts to silence the growing opposition to his government only served to stoke the fire growing beneath him. He overstepped the limits on many occasions. In January 1978, Pedro Joaquín Chamorro, the editor of *La Prensa,* was assassinated in the streets of Managua as he drove to work. Chamorro had attacked Tachito relentlessly

AUGUSTO CÉSAR SANDINO (1893–1934)

The term "Sandinista" is easily associated with Nicaragua, but less well known is the story of the man, who, through his fight against imperialism, became a legend in Nicaragua and the world, and is recognized today by just the merest rendering of his famous broad-brimmed hat.

Augusto C. Sandino was born in Niquinohomo (Nahuatl for Valley of Warriors), the bastard son of a wealthy, landed judge and one of his servant women. But while the judge lived well in town, Sandino's family was so poor they often resorted to stealing crops to eat. Sandino grew disgusted at Nicaraguan society, which engendered such inequity, and questioned both civil society and the Catholic church, which he believed was guilty of propping up the aristocracy. At the age of 17, Sandino witnessed the U.S. Marines' invasion of Nicaragua to prop up Adolfo Díaz's failing conservative presidency. When they crushed a rebellion led by General Benjamin Zeledón, their parading of Zeledón's dead body through the streets of Masaya affected Sandino deeply. Nine years later, Sandino fled to Mexico, where he was inspired by Tampico laborers struggling to unionize in spite of resistance from the U.S.-owned oil companies. Sandino returned to Nicaragua with a new sense of purpose and a strong self-identity shaped by anarchy, socialism, and armed conflict.

He became a renegade general from the Liberals and set up his camp in the mountains outside San Rafael del Norte, Jinotega, where he became one of the first to practice guerrilla warfare, staging effective hit-and-run raids against U.S. Marine installations in Ocotal and the north. Sandino's men, who grew to number nearly 1,800 by 1933, attacked some mining and lumber companies with enough force to drive them away from the Atlantic coast.

Sandino and his troops were brutal—they sometimes killed prisoners of war or slit the throats of the dead and pulled the tongue out and down through the gash, like a necktie. The U.S. military struggled diligently but fruitlessly for seven years to flush Sandino out of the hills. In the words of one U.S. Army lieutenant, "Sandino poses as the George Washington of Nicaragua but he is only a cutthroat and a bandit, preying upon foreigners and the law-abiding citizens of his country." But he was slippery: In Sandino's advantage was a profound knowledge of the land, vast popular support, the willingness to live poor, and an uncanny ability to vanish into thin air.

While Sandino's struggle was ostensibly to force the U.S. military and business interests out of Nicaragua, he represented much more than brute nationalism. In the Segovias, where Sandino enjoyed massive popular support, he formed agricultural cooperatives of landless peasants, imposing taxes on wealthy ranchers and businessmen to support them. He also fought in support of the exploited timber, banana plantation, and mine workers.

During the Great Depression, the Marines eventually left Nicaragua, and the new president of Nicaragua, Anastasio Somoza García, had Sandino assasinated in February 1934. Sandino's body was never found.

Thirty years after Sandino's death, a young idealistic student named Carlos Fonseca Amador resurrected Sandino's image and ideals as the basis of a new political and guerrilla movement, which he called the Frente Sandinista de Liberación Nacional (FSLN)—the Sandinista Front for National Liberation. The FSLN greatly exaggerated Sandino's reputation as a peasant who fought righteously against the imperialistic designs of the United States, because it suited their ideology. Contrary to FSLN doctrine, Sandino was no communist. Rather, Sandino's crusade was often against the bourgeois Nicaraguan Conservatives. His ideology was a mix of his own peculiar leftism with a curious indigenous mysticism; he changed his middle name from Calderón to César in honor of the Roman emperor, claimed he could give orders to his troops using silent mental communication, and predicted Nicaragua would be the site of Armageddon, where "armies of angels would do battle alongside more temporal troops."

Nevertheless, to this day, Sandino remains a hero to Nicaraguans and the world's leftist community. He spearheaded a movement that fought for drastic social and political change and sought to make up for centuries of class discontent that continues even today.

in his newspaper, and while the assassin was never found, everyone suspected Tachito was responsible. One month later in response, the largely indigenous population of the Masaya neighborhood of Monimbó rose up. The protest lasted five days, after which the National Guard, in a fit of unprecedented rage, massacred hundreds. The violence only furthered support for the Sandinistas. Trade unions, student organizations, and popular movements, both private and religious, all threw their weight behind the insurgency, and by May 1979, the Sandinista command offensive, encouraged by an increasingly militant popular attitude, was ready for the next, victorious phase.

The final insurrection lasted 52 days. Combat erupted almost spontaneously and simultaneously around Chinandega, León, and Chichigalpa in the Pacific, and in the mining triangle in the northeast. At the same time, Sandinista troops began pressing north from the border with Costa Rica. They entered León, capturing the city after a two-day battle. The rest of the nation began a massive general labor strike.

On June 8, 1979, Sandinista soldiers and supporters began marching from Carazo, just south of Managua, into the capital itself. The National Guard responded by shelling Managua. Most of the fighting in Managua took place in the lower-middle-class neighborhoods of Bello Horizonte and El Dorado, where extensive networks of concrete drainage ditches made easy battle trenches. On the streets, the people tore up the concrete *adoquines* (paving stones) of the streets and erected barricades (Somoza's own factories produced the *adoquines,* a much-loved irony to this day). The world watched, appalled, as Somoza's aircraft indiscriminately strafed the capital.

Meanwhile, in the north, Matagalpa fell to the FSLN on July 2, 1979, and the strategic town of Sébaco fell the day after, leaving the entire north in the hands of the Sandinistas. The military barracks in Estelí—the last and most important barracks outside of the capital—fell on July 16; FSLN forces surrounded the capital. Trapped by the Sandinistas and abandoned by the United States, Somoza fled Nicaragua in the predawn hours of July 17, leaving Francisco Urcuyo Malianos behind as interim president, whose single responsibility was to hand power over to the Sandinistas. Instead, Urcuyo decided he'd hang on as Nicaragua's new president, serving out the rest of Somoza's term, a brilliant idea that lasted exactly two days. The Sandinistas had won.

The FSLN Government

The exuberance of military victory quickly faded as the new leaders struggled to convert the revolutionary fervor into support for the new nation they wanted to build. They were starting from scratch: Somoza had run Nicaragua as his own personal farm, and overthrowing him had meant obliterating the entire institutional infrastructure of a nation—including the economic, financial, and legislative framework. The sweeping economic, political, and social reforms of the Sandinista revolution made Nicaragua a real-time social experiment, and the entire world—particularly the United States—looked on with both fascination and fear.

Politically, Nicaragua *Libre* (Free Nicaragua) in its infancy was a seething battleground of different social classes' competing interests exacerbated by the dire need to reactivate the economy. But politics took precedent. The Conservative alliance that had been promised a role in the new government found itself nudged off the ruling platform, as the "Group of Nine" fatigue-clad FSLN *comandantes* took full control of the government and made their Marxist tendencies known to the world. Their road map was elucidated in the legendary "Plan 80," which formulated Nicaragua's economy as a delicate balance between private ownership and steadily increasing state control. The nation's commercial sector wanted nothing of the sort, and many private industries balked at joining the new economy; thousands boarded planes for Miami and have only recently returned to Nicaragua. Their refusal to cooperate in the mixed economy eventually contributed to the collapse of the Nicaraguan economy by the late 1980s.

True to their word, the Sandinistas began their land reform policy almost immediately. Two million acres of Somoza's holdings were

OF BEANS AND BULLETS: WHO WERE THE CONTRAS?

The Contras remain one of the most powerful, divisive, and enigmatic elements of Nicaragua's recent history. They owe their name to the Sandinista leaders who christened them contra-revolucionarios. The Contras preferred to call themselves La Resistencia, and others called them "freedom fighters," "bandits," "heroes," and "outlaws."

Not long after the Sandinistas took power in 1979 and long before the Contra movement even had a name, discontent was already swelling among some groups of *campesinos,* who sensed that the Sandinista revolution had gone wrong: Small farmers were being forced to join collectives or were jailed; political meetings were frequent; government propaganda smacked of atheism (or dubious support for the Catholic church); the government was full of Cuban advisors; price controls were making it hard to turn a profit in agriculture; and a lot of people were incarcerated, including many indigenous Miskito people, who had never wanted much more than to be left alone. The revolution was supposed to have made the lives of the poor farmers easier, not harder.

As the first *campesinos* picked up arms and slipped across the northern border into Honduras, they encountered another group eager to see the Sandinistas return to where they had come from: former members of Somoza's National Guard, professional military personnel who longed for their former positions of power and prestige and thirsted for one more battle.

Though they received some early training and organizational help from Argentine military advisers, the Contras weren't an organized force per se until late in the game. Even then, they were composed of numerous factions rife with internal divisions, petty grudges, and ambition among and within their units. Many were simple farm boys looking for fame and fortune at the end of a rifle; others were would-be warlords who used the armed maneuvers to settle old civil disputes or have some vengeance on former drinking buddies. The Contras survived on limited supplies, donations from sympathizers in Miami, and whatever they could take at gunpoint.

The only thing that united the various Contra groups was the feeling that the Sandinista revolution had been a step in the wrong direction. That group included U.S. President Ronald Reagan, who in March 1986, said, "I guess in a way they are counter-revolutionary, and God bless them for being that way. And I guess that makes them Contras, and so it makes me a Contra, too." At various points in the 1980s, the U.S. government played a critical part in the financing and arming of the Contras, in violation of its own laws and without the knowledge of the public.

Based out of camps along the Honduran border, the Fuerza Democrática Nicaragüense (FDN) staged raids in Jinotega, Matagalpa, and Chinandega, and was led primarily by ex–National Guard officers and groups of farmers who called themselves Milicia Popular Anti-Somoza (MILPA, a play on the Spanish word for corn patch). Fighting a completely separate battle along the Río San Juan from camps over the Costa Rican border

---

confiscated and nationalized with the aim of distributing the land among the poor. This was a first in Central America, socially significant, but also environmentally negligent, as previously unexploited and delicate hillsides were soon cleared and planted, unleashing massive deforestation and erosion problems. Worse, in the years after the revolution, critics point out that many of the best pieces of land were distributed not to needy *campesinos* but to the Sandinista elite.

A massive and world-acclaimed literacy campaign to combat Nicaragua's abominably high illiteracy rate followed not long after. The year 1980 was proclaimed "The Year of Literacy" and thousands of volunteers—typically zealous university students—marched out to the rural corners of Nicaragua to teach reading, writing, and basic math skills. It was an overwhelming success that brought the literacy rate to nearly 90 percent, but its Cuban-style incorporation of Sandinista propaganda into the teaching ma-was the Alianza Revolucionaria Democrática (ARDE), led by the infamous Edén Pastora, a.k.a. Comandante Cero (Zero), former Sandinista militant turned Contra. ARDE was a military disaster from the start, so thoroughly riddled with Sandinista spies it never had any hope of victory. Pastora was a would-be *caudillo* who hated organization, refused to delegate authority, and kept his own men divided to prevent any claims to his throne. His macho posturing and reputation for womanizing made him an easy target for sexy female Sandinista spies, a half dozen of whom coaxed him to pillow-talk away just about every military secret he had. Pastora's own men feared he was really a Sandinista sympathizer sent to lead them into military devastation.

Though the Sandinista military committed its share of mistakes and atrocities, the Contras' propensity for brutality and terror is well documented and undeniable. Militarily, they were best at short, sharp raids and random ambushes of military and civilian vehicles. Complicated operations that required timing or planning nearly always went awry, and communication and coordination problems plagued them throughout the war. What they were best at was seeding terror in the hillsides. Their tactics were barbaric: Reagan's "Freedom Fighters" regularly disemboweled victims, chopped their limbs off, and tore bones out of bodies which they shook at the victims' family members. Columns of hungry Contra troops didn't think twice about taking at gunpoint anything they needed from local *campesinos,* from cattle to liquor to boots. On the way, many young women and girls were taken away to be raped and killed, sometimes by decapitation. Young boys and men were routinely castrated and mutilated before being killed.

The Contras commonly targeted suspected Sandinista sympathizers, including government workers in nonmilitary organizations. They brutalized and killed mayors, doctors, nurses, judges, schoolteachers, clergy, policemen, even the staff of utility offices and wealthy townspeople suspected of supporting the new government. Often, those victims who escaped death at the hands of the Contras were forced into the mountains at gunpoint to become soldiers. Intent on derailing the Sandinista economy by preventing the harvest, Contras frequently burned the installations of agricultural cooperatives and massacred anyone who stayed to defend them.

The Contras never had the satisfaction of a military victory. Rather, when the Sandinistas lost public elections and handed power over to the Chamorro government, the incentive to be a Contra vanished. Though some Contras rejected the peace accords and slipped back into the mountains to continue fighting, most disarmed and went back to farming their beans and corn. In the end, though foreign powers had helped the Nicaraguans to nearly destroy themselves over ideology and geopolitics, the Contras who returned to the land knew the struggle to defeat the Sandinista government was simple—the right to a piece of land, to be left alone to work it, and to sell their crops at a fair price.

terials meant many a *campesino*'s first reading lessons taught revolutionary dogma, and the math exercises frequently involved counting items like rifles and tanks. Still, teaching otherwise unlearned country folk how to read was no small accomplishment, and the literacy campaign encouraged young idealistic urbanites to go out into the countryside and learn about their own country and culture. An unprecedented nationalism still palpable today arose from the movement.

Opposition to the FSLN

In their zeal to "defend the revolution at all costs," the Sandinista leaders ran into opposition from all sides—from the business community (represented by the business organization COSEP, led by future president Enrique Bolaños); from Somoza's former cronies who missed their days of wealth and privilege and were enraged by the policy of confiscation; from the former members of the National Guard, many of whom regrouped outside of Nicaragua and became the nucleus of the military *contra-revolucionarios* (Contras); and lastly, from the United States. President Ronald Reagan, upon taking office in 1981, immediately seized on the Communist tendencies of the Sandinista leadership and made Nicaragua the "backyard" focal point of his Cold War policy; he launched a political, economic, and military program designed to strangle the Sandinistas out of power and replace them with something more amenable to the economic interests of North America.

Central America in the 1980s was a hotbed of civil and political unrest, and the Sandinistas were not only openly collaborating with Cuba and the Soviet Union but also exporting their revolution to El Salvador by supporting the FMLN. Sensing a shift in the geopolitical balance of the hemisphere in the context of heightened Cold War tensions, the United States stopped all aid to Nicaragua in 1981, and imposed an economic embargo in 1985. But the desire and the ambition to remove the Sandinistas was not North America's alone—many moderate Nicaraguans felt betrayed by the Sandinistas, who, they felt, had imposed a Marxist-Leninist regime on the nation without their approval and had simply replaced one political elite with another. The land confiscation didn't end with Somoza's land; the Sandinistas confiscated the land of any Nicaraguan that opposed them, and in many cases, kept the best properties for themselves. Thus the U.S.-financed Contras became just the military arm of a multifaceted opposition that soon led to yet another Nicaraguan regime's downfall.

State-led Sandinismo, gross economic mismanagement, and the U.S economic embargo caused production to fall in all sectors. By 1985, export earnings had plummeted to half their pre-revolution figures, and much of the confiscated agricultural land converted into cooperatives remained unproductive and was administered at great expense. The business class, in fear of further expropriations, refused to invest, and many of Nicaragua's skilled laborers fled the country in search of profitable employment elsewhere. In order to combat the Contras, the Sandinistas increased military spending at the cost of social

programs, and sent much of the country's productive labor force into battle. Austerity measures didn't earn the Sandinista government many friends either, as previously common goods, like toothpaste and rice, were parsimoniously rationed, while shoddy Eastern-bloc goods replaced imports of better quality.

By far the most hated Sandinista policy was the military draft. While a necessary measure in light of the increasingly violent Contra attacks in Matagalpa, Jinotega, and much of the east, for most Nicaraguans the draft meant sending their sons and brothers off to be cannon fodder in order to defend a revolution in which they were rapidly losing faith. *Servicio militar patriotico* (patriotic military service), or SMP, was parodied by young men as *Seremos Muertos Prontos* (soon we will be dead).

The Sandinistas called for elections in 1984 as promised, and won easily. Most of the world conceded the elections had been fair and transparent, but Washington was unconvinced and increased funding to the Contras. Congress limited the aid for nonmilitary purposes only, but Reagan sidestepped the rule by declaring the Contra soldiers "refugees."

By the close of the 1980s, both the Contras and the Sandinista government were exhausted and broke. The ruined Sandinista economy could no longer support a prolonged war of attrition, while the collapse of the Soviet Union had decimated their primary source of funding. The Contras had suffered severe military setbacks, mixed messages from their patrons, and had little hope of a military victory. The Iran-Contra scandal in the United States, in which arms were secretly and illegally sold in the Middle East to raise money for Contras, ended all further funding for Reagan's "Freedom Fighters," and their biggest supporter, former CIA director William Casey, died in May 1987. The moment was propitious for a peace initiative, and Costa Rican president Oscar Arías supplied it. In 1987, five Central American presidents attended talks at Esquipulas, Guatemala, and emerged with a radical peace accord (which the United States opposed). The five governments pledged to permit full freedom for political parties, hold periodic elections monitored by external agencies, and commence healing dialogues with opposition groups. The United States and other extra-regional governments were told, in no uncertain terms, to stop open or covert aid to insurrection movements, and those movements in turn were declared illegitimate. Finally, the Sandinistas organized elections in 1990 to show the world that their government was committed to democratic principles and to give Nicaraguans the chance to reaffirm their support for the FSLN. To their surprise, the Nicaraguan people overwhelmingly voted them out of office. The revolution had ended.

THE NEW DEMOCRACY

Violeta Chamorro

Upon losing the elections, the Sandinistas handed power over to Violeta Barrios de Chamorro, widow of the slain journalist Pedro Joaquín Chamorro and center of a ragtag coalition of a Sandinista opposition called the Unión Nacional Opositora (UNO).

Doña Violeta (as she is affectionately known) had no formal political affiliations or training, but her charismatic ability to reconcile and unite ushered Nicaragua into its new era. She attempted to rebuild the nation as though it were a shattered family, which to some degree, it was. Her administration made great gains in reestablishing diplomatic and economic ties with the rest of the world. Chamorro ended the draft, reduced the army, and brought both the army and the police force under civil control. She then began the lengthy and arduous process of demobilizing and disarming the Contras. As a peace offering, Doña Violeta offered them 1,600 square kilometers of land, including much of the Río San Juan area, to resettle and enter the agrarian labor force. Other Contra communities can be found in Jinotega and Matagalpa. Her administration also initiated a new protocol of agrarian reform, which aimed to reassign formerly expropriated lands. More than 15 years later, the issue of land ownership is bitter and contested in several regions.

In the first few years of her government, Doña

Violeta was able to successfully woo the international-aid community back to Nicaragua to help with the reconstruction. Unfortunately, the aid did not arrive in the quantity that the government had hoped for. Notably stingy was the U.S. government, which, once assured the Sandinistas would fall from power, forgot about Nicaragua entirely. Nicaragua's economy was anemic through much of the early 1990s. The 1991 economic stabilization plan pegged the *córdoba* to the dollar and established a slow devaluation to offset inflation. The banking market was opened to private banks, legislation was authored that encouraged foreign investment, and much of the accumulated international debt was pardoned, largely due to Doña Violeta's remarkable diplomacy.

The Sandinistas reinvented themselves as a legitimate opposition political party, and have been strong participants in municipal and presidential elections ever since. However, in spite of their continued support from their traditional base—the poor and disenfranchised—they have been unable to place their longtime leader, Daniel Ortega, back in the presidency. Most Nicaraguans still remember all too well the civil war, chronic shortages of basic commercial goods, and the military draft that plagued the 1980s. Also unforgivable for many was an event now known as *La Piñata*, in which a lame-duck Ortega administration in the late 1980s, looted the state of everything it could, from office equipment to fancy Managua homes, keeping the best of it for themselves. FSLN party heads privatized many state companies under anonymous cooperatives and passed a series of decrees ensuring they would retain some power. In the eyes of many Nicaraguans, it was the final abandonment of every ideal the revolution had ever claimed to stand for.

Arnoldo Alemán

The elections of 1996, run without the massive international funding that characterized previous elections, were rife with abnormalities, near-riots, and chronic disorder: Polling places opened hours late, bags of discarded ballots were found afterward in the houses of officials paid to count them, and the communication network failed. Not surprisingly, in the aftermath, all sides had reason to accuse the others of vote-rigging and fraud. Even so, Nicaraguans turned out in record numbers and elected Managua's slippery PLC (Partido Liberal Constitucionalista) mayor, Arnoldo Alemán over Daniel Ortega, by a margin of 49 to 38 percent. It was the scandalous beginning to a scandalous presidency.

A lawyer by training, Alemán was a political conservative and hard-core capitalist with a sworn aversion to all things Sandinista and a professed admiration for the Somozas, whose proclivity for political manipulation and capacity to accumulate personal fortune Alemán imitated. His economic program courted foreign investment and promoted exports at the expense of a social safety net. Alemán oversaw the continued growth of the economy, boosted the development of *zonas francas* (free trade zones) and the construction of *maquiladoras* (export clothing assembly plants). Politics returned to the back room, where endless scandals of kickbacks, insider deals, and frenzied pocket-filling embarrassed and infuriated the nation. He became a larger-than-life figure as the head of the PLC party, negotiated deals with the Sandinistas when it suited him to do so, and made a pretty penny throughout it all. The net worth of this onetime Miami used-car salesman rose from $20,000 when he took office as mayor of Managua, to $250 million, when he was voted out of the presidency in 2001. But as he came under increased political and popular pressure for corruption, he and Ortega engineered the infamous *El Pacto*. The agreement provided them both diplomatic immunity and a lifetime seat in the Assembly, and divided up the government's most important roles between the FSLN and PLC, including the Supreme Court and the Consejo Supremo Electoral (which runs the elections). Together, Nicaragua's top two *caudillos* (political strongmen) had weakened Nicaraguan democracy by an order of magnitude.

Hurricane Mitch

Midway through Alemán's presidency, on October 28, 1998, the worst storm in recorded history struck Nicaragua. Nicaragua's already debilitated physical infrastructure was devastated, thousands lost their homes and migrated to urban centers to look for work or beg on street corners, and the harvest was essentially destroyed. The worst damage occurred at Posoltega, where a horrific mudslide buried and killed thousands. Alemán took time from planning his lavish wedding to berate the Sandinista mayor of Posoltega as a liar when she first reported the disaster. The Nicaraguan people were appalled, but rising popular opposition to his increasingly corrupt administration was unable to touch him.

Enrique Bolaños and Modern Politics

Enrique Geyer Bolaños, Arnoldo Alemán's nondescript vice-president and former head of COSEP (the Nicaraguan private industry association), came to power in 2002 with the PLC party and an anti-corruption platform. His pledge to clean up Nicaraguan government resonated with Nicaraguans fed up with the abuses Alemán had subjected them to, and they elected him over Daniel Ortega with a 56 percent majority. But despite good intentions, even Bolaños was unable to overcome the powerful party dynamics that have maintained the Nicaraguan political elite in power for centuries. The PLC, which had brought Bolaños to power, was bloated with corruption, and by attacking, it Bolaños destroyed the political support he needed to be an effective leader.

Upon entering office, Bolaños moved quickly to bring indictments against high-ranking PLC officials, including Alemán himself. Alemán under other conditions might have been able to muster the support to resist the charges, but, as his allies slipped away, he was stripped of diplomatic immunity. In December 2003, a Nicaraguan judge found him guilty of corruption and money laundering, and sentenced him to 20 years in prison. This was the first time in recent Latin American history that a blatantly corrupt leader has been convicted and punished. But Alemán continued to wield considerable political influence even from house arrest, and the majority of the PLC turned against Bolaños in retribution for attacking one of their own. Since then, Bolaños has had considerable trouble enacting meaningful legislation, as very few members of the Congress, evenly divided between PLC and FSLN members, support him, and the PLC has mounted a vindictive effort to convict him of corruption himself, alleging his 2001 election campaign was financed by government funds. If true, the same politicians who disbursed the illegal funds are the ones who later accused him, feeling slighted that Bolaños would bite the hand that fed him. Ironically, Enrique Bolaños has better political support from the rest of the world and international institutions than he does from his own political party.

The FSLN, meanwhile, has quietly gained in strength. Popular discontent with rising prices and a steadily falling quality of life has played right into the hands of Daniel Ortega, who promises a better life with a return to Sandinismo. Mayoral elections in 2004 went overwhelmingly to the Sandinista party, while Bolaños's new coalition, APRE, suffered significant defeats in most departments. Faced with enemies on all sides, Bolaños fought back with the tools available to him, and in 2004 enacted a law preventing re-election of former presidents, a jab at both Alemán and Ortega.

And the political dance of the *caudillos* continues.

Government and Politics

You will learn more about Nicaraguan government on the streets and in the countryside by engaging the vivacious Nicaraguans in conversation than any book can hope to teach you, including this one. The history of government and politics in Nicaragua is lengthy and convoluted, and made more enticing by Nicaragua's rare distinction of having experienced three radically different systems of government in as many decades. In 1979, the dictatorship fell to Marxism/Leninism, which was itself later replaced by capitalism and a neo-liberal open market. The ramifications of the changes are still being discussed.

The revolution of 1979 gave the Nicaraguan people unparalleled freedom of expression by Latin American standards. Nicaraguans take advantage of their freedom and you should too. If your Spanish is up to it, encourage the people to share their beliefs, opinions, and ideas with you—starting with your taxi driver on the way from the airport. Politics are central to the lives of most Nicaraguans, and everyone has an opinion—and a solution. It is not uncommon to see Nicaraguan friends, neighbors, and family members engaged in heated, and often alcohol-fueled, political debate. But regardless of the ferocity of the discussion, Nicaraguans usually leave the session with smiles, toasts, and handshakes.

ORGANIZATION

The Republic of Nicaragua is a constitutional democracy, which gained its independence from Spain in 1821. In addition to the national government, there is a parallel government responsible for the administration of the two autonomous regions of the Atlantic coast. The government of the autonomous regions elects its own leaders separately from the rest of the nation.

Branches of Government

Nicaragua's government is divided into four branches. The executive branch consists of the president and vice president. The judicial branch includes the Supreme Court, subordinate appeals courts, district courts, and local courts, plus separate labor and administrative tribunals. The Supreme Court oversees the entire judicial system and consists of 12 justices elected by the National Assembly for seven-year terms. Many consider the judicial system ineffective and plagued by party interests and manipulations by the rich, but it does have some points in its favor, including an approach that attempts to reduce crowding in jails by having the aggressor and the aggrieved meet to strike a deal. For minor offenses, this is an effective tactic. There is no capital punishment in Nicaragua, the maximum

Heated debate characterizes much political discourse in Nicaragua, even between friends.

sentence being 30 years (though the abominable conditions of Nicaraguan prisons makes one wonder if the sentence isn't equally harsh).

The legislative branch consists of the Asamblea Nacional (National Assembly), a chamber in which 90 *diputados* (deputies) representing Nicaragua's different geographical regions vote on policy. The *diputados* are elected from party lists provided by the major political parties, though defeated presidential candidates that earn a minimum requirement of votes automatically become lifetime members, and by law, former presidents are also guaranteed a seat.

The fourth branch of Nicaraguan government is unique to Nicaragua: The Consejo Supremo Nacional is in charge of running democratic elections. Politicized since the Pact of 2000, the body is often accused of furthering the interests of Arnoldo Alemán and Daniel Ortega. Ortega has launched an appeal on several occasions to implement a parliamentary system that would weaken the executive and permit a sort of power sharing favorable to the Sandinistas, without success.

Elections

The Nicaraguan people vote for their president and *diputados* every five years. The president cannot run for consecutive terms. Until Bolaños enacted legislation preventing it in 2004, former presidents were eligible to run again. Now they are not. The Consejo Supremo Electoral (Supreme Electoral Council, or CSE) consists of seven magistrates elected by the National Assembly for five-year terms. The CSE has the responsibility of organizing, running, and declaring the winners of elections, referendums, and plebiscites. Electoral reforms put in place in 2000 allowed the FSLN and the PLC the new ability to name political appointees to the Council, politicizing the CSE to the extreme. The international community decried the fact that the entire process of recognizing new political parties, declaring candidates, and managing the mechanics of holding elections could be so easily subverted to ensure the two strongest parties—the PLC and the FSLN—divide the spoils of government between themselves. These "reforms" have led to a perceived reduction in the transparency of the Nicaraguan government as a whole.

It is interesting to note that nearly every Nicaraguan presidential candidate (with the exception of Doña Violeta), has been, at one time or another, jailed by a previous administration. Tachito jailed Ortega, and Ortega in turn jailed at one point or another both Arnoldo Alemán and Enrique Bolaños. Agustín Jarquín, former comptroller-general and FSLN vice-presidential candidate in 2001, was jailed by both the Sandinistas and by Alemán. . . and the cycle of vengeance continues.

THE CONSTITUTION

The present constitution, written in 1987 by the FSLN administration, was amended in 1995 to balance the distribution of power more evenly between the legislative and executive branches. The National Assembly's ability to veto was bolstered and the president's ability to veto reduced. It was revised again in 2000 to increase the power of the Supreme Court and the comptroller-general's office.

Civil Liberties

Among Latin American societies, the people of Nicaragua enjoy unequaled freedom. Most notable is their nearly unparalleled freedom of speech, a right guaranteed by the constitution and exercised with great vigor by Nicaraguans of all persuasions. The repression, censorship, and brutality of Somoza's dictatorship ended within the recent memory of many Nicaraguans, and they do not take the freedom they enjoy in the 21st century for granted. There is no official state censorship of the media in Nicaragua, though there have been occasional governmental attempts to exert influence through subtler means, such as the embargo of government-sponsored ad revenue of newspapers that seem overly critical.

The constitution additionally guarantees freedom of religion, freedom of movement within the country, freedom of foreign travel, emigration, and repatriation, and the right to peacefully assemble and associate. Domestic and international human rights monitors are permitted to operate freely and interview whomever they wish.

The Nicaraguan constitution prohibits discrimination in all forms, including discrimination by birth, nationality, political belief, race, gender, language, religion, opinion, national origin, or economic or social condition. In practice, however, there are many social forms of discrimination, from former president Alemán's public derision of Managua Mayor Herty Lewites as el Judío (the Jew) to the day-to-day behavior of a *machista* society that, in addition to imposing a double standard on women, also associates lighter-skinned people with the aristocracy and darker-skinned people with the labor force, regardless of whether that's the case. As a popular graffito in Managua exhorts, *"No hay democracia posible en una sociedad de clases."* (Democracy is not possible in a society of classes.)

Nicaraguans are permitted to form labor unions. Nearly half of the workforce, including much of the agricultural labor, is unionized. The trade unions receive much international support from labor groups overseas, who often step in on behalf of Nicaraguan laborers in disputes in the free-trade zones, most recently in a failed campaign against union firings of the Taiwanese Chentex corporation. Alemán's administration earned some bad press by preventing one group of union officials from the United States from entering the country.

POLITICAL PARTIES

It's easy to believe that the concept of the political party in Nicaragua is more for organizational convenience than for conviction of principles. Nicaraguan politicians change from one political party to another as necessary to suit their own ambitions. At the same time, smaller parties continually coalesce into alliances that later fracture into new arrangements. Infighting and division have been an integral part of the Nicaraguan political scene for well over a century, starting with the split between the Conservatives and Liberals in the 1800s that defined political disputes for a century. No other major political party came onto the scene until the FSLN took power in the 1980s. By 1990, no fewer than 20 political parties had risen in opposition to the FSLN; Doña Violeta's UNO coalition was formed from 14 of them.

By 1996, the number of parties swelled to 35, all of which participated in the elections on their own or as one of five coalitions. In 2000, new legislation was enacted to prohibit such a free-for-all at the polls and to make entry more difficult for the smaller political parties. The requirements a political party had to meet to become eligible to run in elections were made prohibitively stringent, which prevented many political parties from participating in the national elections. Popular perception was that it was more of the same political maneuvering in an effort to exclude any newcomers from taking a piece of the government pie.

Three parties were represented in the presidential election of 2001: the FSLN, the PLC, and the Partido Conservador Nicaragüense (PCN), the latter being the moderate-right representatives of the Conservative party. The FSLN, which many considered usurped by the egotistical ambitions of its longtime *caudillo* (Latin American strongman), Daniel Ortega, was a stronger contender than many thought possible. Ortega's campaign downplayed the use of the word "Sandinista" and concentrated on his own personality instead: banners read not "FSLN!" but "Daniel!" The Sandinistas (and their anti-PLC coalition, La Convergencia) battled the PLC-dominated Alianza Liberal (Liberal Alliance), which ultimately won the election.

The Pact

Chief among the factors thought to be crucial to the political future of Nicaragua is *El Pacto* (the pact), a set of constitutional reforms harshly criticized by the majority of Nicaraguans. Developed by Arnoldo Alemán and Daniel Ortega in 2000, when the FSLN was politically weak and Alemán was struggling to find a way to retain some form of political power after handing over the presidency to his successor in the 2001 elections, the pact gave the FSLN and PLC parties a virtual monopoly on government. By raising the requirements necessary for new or small political parties to participate in elections, essentially forcing them off the ballot, the reforms allow candidates to win the presidency with as little as 35 percent of the vote. The pact was also personally beneficial to both Alemán and Ortega, who granted themselves political immunity and guaranteed lifetime seats in the National Assembly. The immunity was providential for Ortega, who was facing charges regarding the alleged sexual abuse of his stepdaughter Zoilamerica during the 1980s.

The Economy

Two successive governments have had to jump-start the Nicaraguan economy from an essential stand-still: the Sandinistas, who picked up the shattered remains upon ousting Tachito, and Doña Violeta, who had to recover from the war and a decade of socialism. Her administration made dramatic progress, reducing the foreign debt by more than half, slashing inflation from 13,500 percent to 12 percent, and privatizing several hundred state-run businesses. The new economy began to expand in 1994 and these days is growing at just over 4 percent, despite several major catastrophes, including Hurricane Mitch in 1998, which decimated agricultural production.

Nevertheless, Nicaragua remains the second poorest nation in the Western hemisphere with a per capital GDP of $780 and its external debt ratio—nearly twice the gross national product—is a serious constraint to growth. Unemployment is a pervasive problem: More than half the adult urban population scrapes by in the informal sector (selling water at the roadside, for example), and population growth is probably going to keep it that way. High demand for jobs means employers can essentially ignore the minimum-wage

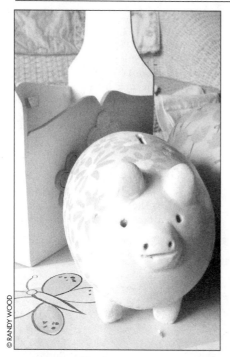

campesino credit union

DEBT, THE HIPC, AND FOREIGN AID

For years, Nicaragua has been one of the most highly indebted nations of the world. When Somoza fled the country, he took the capital reserves of the banks with him, leaving behind $1.6 billion of debt. The Sandinistas, through a combination of gross economic mismanagement, extensive borrowing (primarily from Eastern bloc nations), the U.S. economic embargo, and high defense expenditures augmented the national debt by a factor of 10, nearly half of which was in arrears. By 1994, Nicaragua had the highest ratio of debt to GDP in the world, a challenge every successive administration has had to deal with. Germany, Russia, and Mexico were the first nations to forgive Nicaraguan debt entirely.

Propitious to Nicaragua's future economic growth was its inclusion in the Highly Indebted Poor Countries (HIPC) debt relief initiative in 2000. Inclusion in the initiative means Nicaragua will be exonerated from the majority of its international debt upon compliance with an International Monetary Fund (IMF) and World Bank program, but that program mandates several austerity measures, debt restructuring, and the opening of its economy to foreign markets. More hotly contested is the mandated privatization of public utilities, including the telephone system (privatized in 2002) and municipal water distribution. City water systems have not yet been privatized and the issue is extremely controversial with those who consider water a human right rather than a commodity. Central to the HIPC initiative is Nicaragua's continued effort toward macroeconomic adjustment and structural and social policy reforms, particularly basic health and education.

AGRICULTURE

Nicaragua is, above all, an agricultural nation—a third of its gross domestic product is agriculture-based, and agriculture represents the fastest growing economic sector, at 8 percent growth per year. However, much of the new land put

requirement, especially in the countryside, where agricultural laborers typically earn as little as $1 a day, insufficient for survival even by Nicaraguan standards. Nearly 600,000 people face severe malnutrition.

Nicaragua has an economy almost entirely based on agricultural export of primary material, though in recent years tourism and several nontraditional exports have gained in importance. Export earnings are $700 million and rising: Agricultural programs in 2000 and 2001 that helped increase Nicaragua's ability to export beef and milk give hope that exports will rise in the latter part of the decade. Traditional export products include coffee, beef, and sugar, followed by bananas, shellfish (especially lobster tails and shrimp), and tobacco. New nontraditional exports are on the rise as well, including sesame, onions, melons, and fruit.

into agricultural production is opened at the expense of the forests, the indiscriminate harvesting of which has a negative overall effect on the environment and water supply. Agriculture employs 45 percent of the workforce. Outside of the small, upscale producers who export to international markets, the majority of Nicaraguan agriculture is for domestic consumption, and much of that is subsistence farming. Drought years often require importing of basic grains.

Subsistence farmers typically grow yellow corn and red beans. The choice of red beans over black beans and yellow corn over white corn is cultural and presents additional challenges to farmers, as red beans are more susceptible to drought (and less nutritious) than black or soybeans.

The Sébaco Valley is an agriculturally productive area and the primary source of wet rice for local consumption; it's also widely planted with onions. Extensive irrigation of rice plantations has caused the water table in the Sébaco Valley to drop more than three meters in the 1990s. Jinotega's cool climate is a major source of fruit and vegetable production, including cabbage, peppers, onions, melons, watermelons, squash, and tomatoes.

THE COFFEE ECONOMY

There's no underestimating the importance of coffee to the Nicaraguan economy. Coffee is produced on more than 100,000 hectares of

CAFTA: BOON OR BUGBEAR?

High on the list of policies the Bolaños government has hoped will stimulate the Nicaraguan economy is CAFTA, the Central American Free Trade Agreement (modeled after the similar North American Free Trade Agreement). Talks between CAFTA member nations—Guatemala, El Salvador, Honduras, Nicaragua, and the United States—concluded in 2004 and the agreement is expected to be ratified by late 2005.

While the agreement generated much debate and more than a few anxious farmers, CAFTA's immediate economic provisions appear amenable to Nicaragua. The United States agreed to import a greater quantity of Nicaraguan goods—notably beef and sugar—while permitting Nicaragua to protect domestic farmers from most American foodstuffs. Quotas were raised for most Nicaraguan exports and they are scheduled to increase further over time, giving Nicaraguan farmers a better opportunity to export their crops. But Nicaragua's biggest win was for the textile industry, where Nicaragua negotiated the right to import cloth from Asia, assemble clothing, and sell it duty free in the United States. Nicaragua was the only nation in Central America to receive this concession. Nicaraguan-produced clothing will be even more competitive after 2005, when China's right to do the same expires.

But you've got to give to receive, and not surprisingly, CAFTA comes with a sting. The United States earned the right to export yellow corn for chicken feed, as well as powdered milk. While Nicaraguan farmers produce white (not yellow) corn, they and the cattle ranchers are understandably anxious about the effect corn and milk imports will have on their livelihood.

Opponents of CAFTA bring up other concerns as well. For one, CAFTA promotes the Washington consensus export-economy model, where Nicaragua exports cash crops and imports basic foodstuffs. With little leverage in the marketplace, that increases Nicaragua's vulnerability to prices. The textile provisions will certainly promote job creation, but because the Nicaraguan government has taken few steps to protect its workers, women working in the Free Trade Zones are subject to abuse and are often not permitted to freely form unions. Finally, studies of CAFTA's predecessor, NAFTA, have failed to show a notable improvement in the lives of the Mexicans it claims to affect. Whether CAFTA will be any more beneficial to the Nicaraguans will largely depend on whether the big shots in Managua are willing to protect their people, and history has shown they are not.

© RANDY WOOD

Nicaraguan subsistence farmers grow primarily corn and beans.

Nicaraguan land, contributes an average of $140 million dollars per year to the economy, and employs more than 200,000 people, nearly a third of the agricultural workforce (13 percent of the national workforce). Nicaragua exports its beans primarily to Europe, North America, and Japan—to the tune of 1 million 100-pound burlap sacks every year. These beans are roasted and ground (usually abroad) to produce 11 billion pounds of java.

Because most Nicaragua growers produce full-bodied Arabica beans at altitudes of 900 meters and higher, the quality of its crop is recognized the world over. The June 2004 issue of *Smithsonian* magazine reported Nicaragua as "the 'hot origin' for gourmet coffee, with its beans winning taste awards and its decent wages for many small farmers a hopeful beacon for a global coffee market under siege." It also declared Nicaragua a country where "the goals of a better cup of joe, social justice and a healthier environment are nowhere more tightly entwined." This is important as Nicaragua struggles

to emerge from the worst crash in the global coffee economy in a century.

The Coffee Crisis

Producing and selling Nicaraguan coffee, challenging even in good times, was dealt a staggering blow in 1997, when low-quality Vietnamese and Brazilian Robusta beans drove world prices downward to 25 percent of 1994 prices, a 100-year low. This was compounded by corporate consolidation in the trading and roasting industries, which dealt coffee farmers a blow while well-off overseas consumers were spared the extra costs. With market prices well below the costs of production, the effect on rural Nicaraguan coffee workers has been devastating.

Conditions bottomed out when hacienda owners could no longer afford to even feed their workers, let alone pay them wages, and thousands of families (called *plantónes*) migrated to the cities, marched and camped along the highways, and demanded assistance from the government, including land, food, education, and temporary work. With the help of the cooperatives and some of the hacienda owners, the farmworkers union finally negotiated most of their demands and now more than 2,000 families are getting the title to their own land. The next step will be to see, if the crisis continues, whether they will be able to keep their small allotments in the face of Neo-liberal national governmental policies.

The Future of Coffee

Discerning North American and European java swillers have created an enormous demand for a superior cup of coffee—and they are willing to pay extra for it, as we all well know. If the Nicaraguan coffee industry is to continue to gain ground, it must maintain its reputation for quality coffee. This requires a government-level effort to address environmental issues, like soil fertility and water contamination, the modernization of processing methods, and the resolution of severe micro-credit and marketing issues. Addressing the coffee crisis may provide the framework for dealing with the social ills inherent in modern coffee production, such as the feudal system of ownership and labor that still exists at many of the larger hacienda-style plantations; on these farms, seasonal pickers and their families are paid the barest survival wages and are sucked into a never-ending debt cycle that keeps them desperate and working.

The future of sustainable coffee production, many agree, is in family-run cooperatives in which small-scale farmers, rather than a single, rich hacienda owner, possess the power to control their product. At present, nearly 10 percent of Nicaraguan coffee is grown by 6,000 small-scale *campesino* producers working as members of nine cooperatives in the country's northlands. As much as 80 percent of their coffee can be marketed as specialty coffee for the gourmet and organic market, making these growers less vulnerable to the extreme price oscillations of conventional coffee.

Nicaragua has a number of other advantages over other similarly struggling coffee-producing nations in the region. First of all, nearly 95 percent

of Nicaraguan coffee is grown under a forest canopy that provides shade for coffee bushes and, at the same time, habitat for migratory birds. This can earn a grower a "Bird Friendly" sticker, which, like organic certification (not using chemicals and properly disposing of waste products), gains a significantly higher market price.

Coffee families and their communities also benefit enormously from the Fair Trade certification program (www.transfairusa.org), in which participating companies must comply with strict economic, social, and environmental criteria, guaranteeing producers a fair price. The small-scale farmers who represent most of the certified-organic producers and those linked to Fair Trade markets recently organized to represent their interests at the national and international level by forming an association of small-scale coffee farming co-ops called Cafenica.

Finally, a number of coffee growers, especially those who own their own land, have diversified their income with various non-coffee crops and activities, including several awesome eco-tourism projects. For information on visiting one of the small-scale coffee cooperative families, please see the Matagalpa and Jinotega chapter.

INDUSTRY

Industrial production in Nicaragua reached its zenith in 1978 under Anastasio Somoza, who encouraged industrial expansion in Managua at the expense of the environment, especially Lake Xolotlán. Investment policies of the time exonerated industries from the need to worry about environmental protection. Industry—even agro-industry—has been underdeveloped in the years following the revolution. There is a small amount of production for domestic and regional markets, including cement processing, petroleum refining, and some production of plastic goods. Another aspect of Nicaragua's export industry is the steadily increasing number of Zonas Francas (free trade zones) near Managua, Sebaco, Masaya, and Granada, where tens of thousands of Nicaraguans are employed in foreign-owned sweatshops.

BUT WHAT *KIND* OF JOBS?

Free trade zones (*zonas francas*)—areas that assemble manufactured goods (usually clothing) for duty-free export—have multiplied like rabbits since the Alemán administration and currently employ somewhere between 50,000 and 70,000 Nicaraguan workers, mostly women. Free trade zones don't generate any tax revenue for the government but provide jobs for a nation that desperately needs them. That desperation has not been overlooked by those who do business there.

Apparel magazine reports that Nicaragua's "disciplined and low-cost work force" make it the newest regional competitor in the free-trade factory frenzy, as evidenced by the Korean, Taiwanese, and North American garment companies raising scores of assembly warehouses in Tipitapa, Sebaco, Ciudad Sandino, and Masaya (the largest free trade zone, Las Mercedes, abuts the airport in Managua and is clearly visible from your plane). These firms scour the globe for the absolute cheapest production sites, and Nicaragua is a prime option. At last count, there were 60 such assembly plants in the aforementioned areas, producing goods for well-known brands like Target, J.C. Penney, Talbots, Polo Ralph Lauren, Levis, Gap, Wal-Mart, Kohl's, K-mart, and Mervyns.

Proponents of this industry argue that in a nation with nearly 70 percent unemployment, *maquila* jobs are better than nothing, regardless of the pay or conditions. But labor activists, human rights monitors, and other critics counter that the mere creation of jobs is unjustifiable if it comes at the cost of conditions that deprive workers of dignity, respect, and basic human rights, like the right to assemble or organize. Someone is making lots of money in these free trade zones (exports grew from $2.9 million in 1992 to $400 million in 2003 at a rate only surpassed by Costa Rica) but it's not the workers: They are paid in continuously-devaluing *córdobas* at a fixed rate that makes their pay worth less every month, halving their monthly earnings over the aforementioned period of export growth.

Critics of free trade zones call it a global "race to the bottom," in which international companies flock to the nations where they can both pay the least and encourage governments like Nicaragua's to overlook fundamental labor rights, i.e. paying a living wage and paying it on time, compensating for overtime, and allowing the workers to form unions. Every one of these abuses has occurred in the *zona francas;* some have been addressed, many have been ignored, and, on more than one occasion, the company has closed its doors and relocated to other nations even more desperate for foreign investment.

Nicaragua's sweatshops pay by the piece, not by the hour, and enforce minimum-piece counts before a worker earns her first *córdoba*. A favorite subterfuge is to raise the minimum whenever it seems the workers are attaining it. *Maquila* workers thus work long (usually 10-hour) shifts and endure frequent verbal, physical and sexual abuse from factory supervisors who, among other things, strip-search them on the way out (to "prevent theft") and monitor bathroom breaks. Workplace injuries are ignored, and attempts to form unions are met with mass firings, trumped-up criminal charges, and use of riot police. The Nicaraguan government has made no effort to protect workers and does not intervene in these cases, fearing mass unemployment would be worse than mistreated workers. Indeed, the Nicaraguan workforce was abused long before the days of foreign investment.

The alternative? One idea is the *Fair* Trade Zone, like that formed by a group of unemployed women in Ciudad Sandino called the **Nueva Vida Womens Sewing Cooperative** (tel. 505/269-7073, jhc@jhc-cdca.org, www.fairtradezone.jhc-cdca.org). As owners of their factory, workers at Nueva Vida decide what hours they work, what salaries they are paid, what their labor policies are, and how they share their business's profits amongst themselves. Contact them directly to place an order for your company or organization, or support them by shopping at Michigan-based **Maggie's Functional Organics** (U.S. tel. 800/609-8593, www.maggiesorganics.com). To learn more about the labor rights movement, check in with Campaign for Labor Rights (www.campaignforlaborrights.org) or Global Exchange (www.globalexchange.org).

TOURISM

The so-called "industry without smokestacks" is widely hoped to be a panacea to Nicaragua's economic ills. At present, tourism represents the third-largest source of foreign exchange. Public Law 306 provides a 10-year tax break to newly constructed tourist facilities that meet certain criteria. Certainly, more legislation of this type will help foster economic growth in this sector. More beneficial still are travelers like you, who spend a little money and hopefully take home a good impression of Nicaragua. Since the mid-1990s, investment in tourism has skyrocketed, notably in Managua, Granada, and San Juan del Sur. During his campaign, President Enrique Bolaños pledged to augment tourism with luxury cruise ships and large international hotel and resort chains up and down the Pacific coast. If realized, the plan would turn low-key beach towns like El Velero, Pochomíl, and San Juan del Sur into five-star resort centers much like Montelimar, symbolically and physically constructing new walls between rich foreigners and Nicaraguan tourists and residents. Time will tell.

The People

POPULATION

Nicaragua's population is fast approaching 6 million, nearly a full third of whom live in Managua. Nicaragua is paradoxically the least populous Central American nation and the fastest growing, at just over 3 percent annually. At this rate, Nicaragua's strained resources will have to support a population of between 9 and 12 million by the year 2030. In addition, well over a million Nicaraguans live outside of the country, particularly in Costa Rica (679,000) and the United States (500,000), not to mention several thousand more living in Mexico and other Central American nations.

ETHNIC GROUPS

While Nicaraguans can trace their ancestry back to many sources, most of the population is a blend of Spanish, Native American, and other European stock. Indigenous blood runs most strongly in the northeast, where the Spanish had less influence, and on the mid-Atlantic coast, where English and African influences were dominant.

In the Pacific region, the native population thinned from nearly 800,000 when the Spanish arrived to less than 60,000 after only a couple centuries of conquistador policy and influence, including war, forced slavery, genocide, and introduced European diseases. The native peoples of the northeast, including Matagalpa and Jinotega, were less affected, and thus retain larger indigenous populations today.

Costeños (coastal inhabitants) on Nicaragua's Atlantic side are more Caribbean than Mestizo.

CORN CULTURE

The planting cycle of *maíz* (corn) has governed the life of Nicaraguans and their Mesoamerican descendants ever since the first yellow kernels were laid in the dark volcanic soil. *Maíz* is as central to the Nicaraguan diet as white rice is to the people of Southeast Asia. Beans are just as critical a staple (and a nutritionally critical complement), but in Nicaragua, corn is prepared with more variety, taste, and frequency.

Corn is prepared and consumed in more than a hundred different ways: hot, cold, cooked, ground, and liquefied, in both food and in beverages. Tortillas are, of course, flat cakes of corn dough softened with water and cooked on a slightly rounded clay pan known as a *comal*. The only place you'll find a flour tortilla is in a Mexican restaurant in Managua; Nica corn tortillas are thick, heavy, and (hopefully) hot off the wood stove and slightly toasted. When the same dough is fortified with sugar and lard, then rolled into small lumps and boiled while wrapped in yellow corn husks, the result is a *tamal*, steaming heavy bowls of which market women balance on their heads and loudly vend in the streets. *Nacatamales*, a Nicaraguan classic, are similar but with meat—often spiced pork—in the middle. *Atol* is corn pudding, and *güirila* is a sweet tortilla of young corn, always served with a hunk of *cuajada* (salty white cheese).

Elote is corn on the cob, especially tasty when roasted directly over open coals until the kernels are dry, hot, and a little chewy. When harvested young, the ears of corn are called *chilotes* and are served in soup or with fresh cream. Corn is also oven-baked into hard, molasses-sweetened cookie rings called *rosquillas*, flat cookies called *ojaldras*, and many other shapes. The same dough is also combined with cheese, lard, and spices to produce dozens more items, including *perrerreques, cosas de horno,* and *gofios*.

What do you wash it down with? More corn, of course. *Pinol*, drunk so frequently in Nicaragua the Nicaraguans proudly call themselves *pinoleros*, is toasted and ground corn meal mixed with water. *Pinolillo* is *pinol* mixed with cacao, pepper, and cloves; *tiste* is similar. *Pozol* is a ground corn-meal drink prepared from a variety of corn with a pinkish hue. The ultra-sweet, pink baggies of *chicha* are made from slightly fermented corn-meal (especially strong batches are called *chicha brava*). Then, of course, there is crystal clear, Nicaraguan corn tequila, or *la cususa*.

Corn: It's what's for breakfast, lunch, and dinner.

Elote, **or corn on the cob, is a common streetside snack.**

Mestizos

The term mestizo refers to any mixture of Spanish and indigenous blood and describes the majority of Nicaraguan citizens, whose Spanish colonial ancestors began intermingling with the locals about as soon as they got off the boat. A second wave of *mestizaje* (mixing) occurred from the 1860s through the 1890s, during the wave of rubber and banana production along the Atlantic coast, and again in the 1950s as Pacific farmers moved eastward in search of new agricultural lands at the expense of the Sumu-Ulúa and Miskito peoples.

Note: Mestizo Nicaraguans sometimes use the term "Indio" as a pejorative label for anyone with Native American features, like high cheekbones, straight black hair, short eyelashes, and dark brown skin.

Creoles

After decimating the indigenous peoples of the New World, the Spanish realized they lacked laborers and were thus forced to import African slaves to their colonies in the Americas. Beginning in 1562, English slave traders, and later Dutch, Spanish, and others, supplied the colonies with their human cargo. Along the Atlantic coast of Nicaragua, African slaves intermingled with Miskitos, giving birth to the Zambo (or Sambo) people. They also bred with the Spanish and English, forming the Creoles, primarily found today in Bluefields and San Juan del Norte. Creoles speak a form of English that still bears traces of 19th-century Queen's English, as well as Caribbean and Spanish traits. Their culture includes distinct African elements, including the belief in a form of African witchcraft called *obeah* or *sontín,* the latter a corruption of the English "something," or "something special."

Miskitos

The modern-day Miskitos are really a mixture of several races, and include traces of English and African blood. The Native American Bawihka people, whose territory extended from the Río Coco (Wangki) at Cabo Gracias a Dios south to Prinzapolka, mixed with the African-slave refugees of a Portuguese ship that wrecked on the Miskito Cays in 1642. They later mixed with the English during their long occupation of the Atlantic coast. Over the centuries, the word "Miskito" has been written many other ways, including "Mosquito," "Mosca," "Mískitu," and others. The name derives not from the insect but from the Spanish word *mosquete* (musket), a firearm the British provided the locals to ensure a tactical advantage over their neighbors.

The Miskitos' warlike nature and superior fire power helped them subdue nearly 20 other Native American tribes along the Atlantic coast of Central America. They were valuable allies to the English, who used them in raids against inland Spanish settlements. The Miskitos also absorbed the Prinsu tribe (located along the Bambana and Prinzapolka Rivers) and the Kukra tribe.

Today the Miskitos inhabit much of the Atlantic coast of Nicaragua, from Bluefields northward and all along the Río Coco, which they consider their spiritual home. There are additional Miskito settlements on both Corn Islands, but their two principal centers are Bilwi (Puerto Cabezas) and Waspám. Their language, Miskito, is the old indigenous Tawira language enriched with English and African vocabulary.

The Kukra

The Kukra people were assimilated by the Miskitos over the last two centuries and no longer exist as a tribe. Of unknown but reportedly cannibalistic Caribbean origin, they once inhabited Bluefields, the Corn Islands, and the area around Pearl Lagoon. Today, the only trace of them is the name of the small Pearl Lagoon community of Kukra Hill.

The Garífuna (Black Caribs)

The Garífuna, as a race, are relative newcomers to the world. Their history began on the Lesser Antillean island of San Vicente (Saint Vincent), which in the 1700s had become a refuge for escaped slaves from the sugar plantations of the Caribbean, including Jamaica. These displaced Africans were accepted by the native Carib (Arawak) islanders, with whom they freely intermingled. As the French and English settled the island, the Garífunas (as they had become known), established a worldwide reputation as expert canoe navigators and fierce warriors, resisting the newcomers. The English finally got the upper hand in the conflict after tricking and killing the Garífuna leader, and in 1797, they forcefully evacuated the Garífunas from San Vicente to the Honduran Bay Island of Roatán. From there, many of the Garífunas migrated to the mainland communities of Trujillo, Honduras and Dangriga, Belize. Today, they exist up and down most of the Central American Caribbean coast, with a small but distinct presence in Nicaragua, primarily around Pearl Lagoon. Orinoco (originally Urunugu) is the largest settlement of Garífunas in Nicaragua, established in 1912 by the Garífuna John Sambola. The communities of San Vicente and Justo Point are both Garífuna as well. During the 1980s, the Contra war forced many Garífunas out of their communities and into Bluefields, Puerto Limón (Costa Rica), and Honduras.

The Mayangna (Sumu)

"Sumu" is a derogatory word the Miskito people used to describe all other peoples of Ulúa descent, and as such the word has fallen out of favor. (It means stupid; the Mayangna name for the Miskito people was *Wayas*, meaning stinky.) The Mayangna people, as they are now known, are really a combination of several Ulúa tribes, including the Twahka, Panamka, and Ulwa, which once settled the Kurinwas, Siquia, Mico, Rama, and Grande Rivers of the Atlantic coast. Mayangna tradition has it that in the 9th and 10th centuries they were the inhabitants of a territory that extended from the Atlantic coast and Río Coco to the Pacific, but they were forced off the Atlantic coastal lands by the more aggressive and warring Miskito people and out of the Pacific by the Nahuatls, Maribios, and Chorotegas. The Mayangna people are now centered around the mining triangle and the massive forest reserve of Bosawás.

The Rama

The Rama are the least numerous indigenous people in Nicaragua, numbering only several hundred. Their language is distinct from Miskito and Mayangna and is closely related to the ancient tribal languages of Native American tribes of Panamá and Colombia. Today, only several dozen people can still speak Rama and anthropologists are scrambling to document what they can of the language before it disappears entirely. The Rama people inhabit the pleasant bay island of Rama Cay in the Bay of Bluefields, where they fish and collect oysters. They also grow grains and traditional crops on small plots of land on the mainland of Bluefields Bay and along the Kukra River. The Rama people are reserved and keep mostly to their traditional ways, even using traditional tools and implements. They are excellent navigators and fishermen.

Culture, Conduct, and Customs

Nicaraguans are generally open, talkative, and extremely hospitable. They will be curious about you, and they won't be discreet about it. Expect blunt questions right off the bat about your age, marital status, and your opinions about Nicaragua. Most Nicaraguans are easily approached and excited to talk to foreigners—sometimes whether the foreigner in question welcomes the attention or not.

Despite their directness, Nicaraguans are prone to circuitous and indirect behavior associated with the cultural concept of "saving face." When asked something they don't know, people often invent an answer so that neither party is embarrassed (this is especially true about directions and distances; as Allan Weisbecker observed, "no one, *no one*, south of the Mexican border has any idea how long it takes to go from anywhere to anywhere else"). Business contracts are rife with implied obligations neither party wants to discuss openly. To prevent the discomfort brought on by discussing payment details and clarifying the work to be done, Nicaraguans may opt to keep things to a casual handshake, both sides hoping they are not taken advantage of.

Many urbanites, especially in Managua, are, in fact, recently immigrated *campesinos,* and they bring their country ways—and sometimes livestock—with them to the city. The poorest of these people live in sprawling shantytowns outside most cities, with the exception of Managua, where the shanties are spread throughout the city limits among better neighborhoods. It's worth mentioning that if you're in the backwoods of Nicaragua, and if you get in trouble/miss your bus/have an emergency, the typical Nicaraguan *campesino* would not think twice before extending his hospitality to you, sometimes insisting that you sleep in his own bed while he sleeps on the floor or in a hammock. If the family is reluctant to take cash because they have offered you their home out of kindness, you should provide something else—something from the market, for example. This is a case where the transaction is more of a subtle gift exchange than a business deal. In an effort to promote local, grassroots tourism, some areas of Nicaragua have trained residents how to host a foreign guest. Miraflor, Estelí, and San Ramón, Matagalpa are examples, offering a range of rural experiences living with kindhearted *campesino* families.

In most areas of the country, Nicaraguans are accustomed to seeing foreigners, and the reaction is nearly always one of curiosity, hospitality, and friendliness. Nicaraguans are particularly adept at distinguishing between a nation's people and its government's policy—arguably more so than most tourists—so travelers from the United States should not expect to receive any rancor regarding recent history from Sandinista supporters. In addition, because most Nicaraguan families adore cable TV and have at least one relative sending money back from Miami, Houston, or Los Angeles, many are quite fond of the United States and maintain the dream of traveling there one day. The word *gringo* is used often, but as a descriptive, casual term, almost never with negative connotations. Likewise for *chele, chela,* and their diminutives, *chelito* and *chelita,* all of which simply mean pale or light-skinned, and

are in no way disrespectful. In fact, many cries of, *"Oye, chele!"* (Hey, whitey!) are directed at light-skinned Nicaraguans in addition to foreigners.

FAMILY

The Nicaraguan family is the most basic and strongest support structure of society, and, like in most Developing World nations, it is big—rural women have an average of 4–6 children, and families of a dozen or more aren't uncommon. Urban couples, particularly in Managua, typically have no more than three or four children. In addition, extended families—cousins, in-laws, and fictitious kin (a.k.a. godparents)—are all kept in close contact and relied upon during hard times (which, for many, is their whole lives). Families live close together, often in small quarters, and the North American and European concepts of independence and solitude are not well understood, let alone practiced.

Nicaraguans' traditional dependence on large family structures mandates that they take care of stragglers, even foreign visitors. If, for example, you were stranded in a strange country town in the pouring rain, it would not be strange or uncommon for someone to invite you into their home for coffee.

CLOTHING AND NEATNESS

Nicaraguans place a great deal of importance on cleanliness. Even the poorest *campesino* with the most threadbare and patched clothing takes great care to tuck his shirt in and keep his clothes clean and wrinkle-free. City folk are just as conscientious about looking good and smelling clean. Nicaraguans only wear shorts for playing sports or lounging around the house. Nicaraguan women dress the spectrum from long, conservative dresses to unbelievably bright, tight, and revealing outfits.

Unshaven international travelers wearing stained shorts, ripped t-shirts, and natty dreads stand out like sore, malodorous thumbs, even without their trademark backpacks. If you plan on being taken seriously in any kind of day-

OLD WIVES' TALES: NICARAGUAN CREENCIAS

Like any society with a tradition of rural folk culture, Nicaraguans have hundreds of unique beliefs, or *creencias,* which explain mysteries, offer advice, and dictate practices that prevent or cure common health ailments. In general, most behaviors are associated with causing harm to oneself, and Nicaraguan mothers can be heard admonishing their children, *"¡Te va a hacer daño!"* (It will cause you harm!).

Nicaraguans are sensitive to subtle differences in temperature, and many of the *creencias* involve avoiding hot things when you are cold, or vice versa. Conventional wisdom dictates that intense bodily harm can come from drinking a cold beverage after eating something hot, bathing in the evening after a hot day in the sun (or bathing with a fever), and ironing with wet hair. If you come in from the fields on a hot day and you're sweaty, drinking a cold glass of fruit juice or water can make you sick, especially your kidneys. Better is a cup of hot coffee. If you want to walk outside at night after drinking coffee, however, you should protect yourself by draping a cloth over the top of your head, being careful to cover the ears. Dietary rules tie into the same theme and other worries as well: no fish, eggs, or beans while menstruating, no citrus when sick, and no fish soup when *agitado* (worked up or sweaty).

The belief in the *mal de ojo* (evil eye) is not unique to Nicaragua, although the local version states that a drunkard who looks directly into an infant's eye can kill the child or make it evil. A person well versed in the art of applying the evil eye can cause birth defects in newborn babies, stroke, paralysis among the living, and other woes like the loss of a job or bad luck. You'll frequently see children wearing a red bracelet with two small gray beads—this is to protect the child from *mal de ojo.* Similarly, if a sweaty man looks at a baby, the only cure is to wrap the baby up in the man's sweaty clothes. To guard against the risk, many babies are kept well covered when out of the house. Allowing dew to fall on a baby's brow will stunt its growth (look for women holding umbrellas over their children on a clear night), and letting a baby look in a mirror will cause his or her eyes to cross permanently.

If you have trouble with bats, you can keep them away by hanging a red cloth from the rafters. To keep flies off your food, suspend a bag of water over the table. To avoid family fights, don't cook with a knife in the pan.

Some Nica *creencias* coincide with North American and European practices even if the reasoning is different. For example, Nicaraguans recommend you don't walk around barefoot, but not because you run the risk of contracting ringworm; rather, walking barefoot, they claim, is an unhealthy temperature combination (hot feet on cold floor). Foreigners tempted to make fun of the "crazy" Nicaraguan beliefs will do well to remember our own societies' *creencias.* Whether scientifically grounded or not, Nicaraguan beliefs are popular because they have been passed from generation to generation, and should be given proper regard.

to-day business activities, we recommend you put a little effort into your wardrobe and hygiene: Deodorant, ironed clothing, and a clean appearance will open a lot of doors for you (And do away with the question, "Is it true that people in your country don't bathe because it's too cold?"). If, however, you prefer to remain true to your filth, seek out the hip, bohemian population of young Managuans who take well to carefully unkempt foreigners, especially ones wearing Che Guevara t-shirts and creative facial hair.

CONCEPT OF TIME

"Hay más tiempo que vida." (There is more time than life.) So why hurry? The day-to-day approach to living life in Nicaragua may come from the necessity of survival, or it may just be an effect of the hot sun. Probably both. Nicaraguan life, in general, goes according to *La Hora Nica* (Nica Time), which means a meeting scheduled in Managua for 2:30 P.M. might not start until 3 P.M., or an hour later in the countryside. Foreign travelers accustomed to *La Hora Gringa,* in which everything starts and stops exactly when

planned, will spend their days in Nicaragua endlessly frustrated (and consistently early for meetings). Appointments and meetings are loose, and excuses are easy to come by and universally accepted. Gradually, as you experience Nicaragua, this concept of time will win you over; just be careful when you go home.

ALCOHOL

So he sipped the drink, which was cold and clean-tasting, and he watched the broken line of the keys straight ahead and to the westward . . . But over half of the drink was still in the paper-wrapped glass and there was still ice in it . . . I wonder where she is now . . . I could think about her all night. But I won't.

Ernest Hemingway

Forget the girl, think about the drink: For better or worse, alcohol runs clear and copiously through Nicaraguan society. Both plague and pastime, alcohol is everywhere and it goes largely undisputed that Nicaragua makes the best rum in all of Central America. Rum is the drink of choice, more often than not served up in a rocks glass with Coca-Cola and a spurt of lime as a **Nica Libre.** Of all the rum produced in Nicaragua, Flor de Caña is the highest caliber, of which the caramel-colored, seven-year-old Gran Reserva is only surpassed by the 12-year Centenario (which is twice as expensive). Flor de Caña produces a half-dozen varieties of rum, which increase in price and quality as they age. A *media* (half-liter) of seven-year, bucket of ice, bottle of Coke, and plate of limes (called a *servicio completo*) will set you back only $4 or so. Reach, however, for the plastic bottle of Ron Plata, and take a giant step down in price, quality, and social class. Enormously popular in the *campo*, "Rrrrron Plata!" is the proud sponsor of most baseball games and not a few bar brawls.

But wait—you can get drunk for even less! Most street corners and town parks are the backdrop for many a grimacing shot of Tayacán, or its homemade, corn-mash equivalent, often served

"You're never far from a cold beer."

© RANDY WOOD

in clear plastic baggies that look like they should have a goldfish swimming in them. West Virginians call this stuff "that good 'ole mountain dew"; Nicaraguans call it *la cususa, el guaro,* or *la lija,* brought down from the hills by the moonshine man and his mule. *La cususa* is gasoline-clear, potent in smell (including when you sweat it out the next day), and will bore a hole through your liver quicker than a 9-millimeter. It's sold by the gallon for about $4, often in a stained, sloshing, plastic container that used to contain some automobile-related product, and then resold in baggie-size portions.

The national beers—Victoria and Toña—are both light-tasting pilsners and, well, you can't really say anything bad about an ice-cold beer in the tropics. Expect to pay anywhere from $.60 to $1 a beer. Recent additions to the beer selection are Premium, Bufalo, and Brahva, largely indistinguishable from each other. Brahva is the only alcoholic beverage whose production or dis-

CHICKENS, PIGS, AND EARLY BIRDS: POPULAR NICARAGUAN SAYINGS

Nicaraguans in general, and *campesinos* in particular, love to speak using *refranes* (sayings or refrains). They're an easy way to make a point, and both the way they are phrased and the points they make say much about the country folks' way of thinking. If you learn a refrain or two and throw one out once in a while in casual conversation, you will be sure to earn broad smiles.

Hay más tiempo que vida.—There is more time than life. (There's no need to rush things.)

Él que a buen árbol se arrima, buena sombra le cobija.—He who gets close to a good tree will be covered by good shade. (He who seeks protection will find it.)

Perro que ladra no muerde.—Dogs who bark don't bite.

No hay peor sordo que él que no quiere escuchar.—There's no deaf person worse than he who doesn't want to hear.

A cada chancho le llega su sábado.—Every pig gets his Saturday. (Everyone eventually gets what he deserves.)

Indio comido, puesto al camino.—An Indian who has eaten, gets up immediately from the table. (A way of pointing out someone ready to leave as soon as he/she gets what he/she wants.)

Quien da pan a un perro ajeno, pierde el pan y pierde el perro.—If you give bread to someone else's dog, you'll lose the bread and lose the dog.

Él que madruga come pechuga, él que tarda, come albarda.—He who gets up early eats the best piece of chicken, he who gets up late eats the saddle.

Él que no llora no mama.—He who does not cry does not suckle. (If you don't complain, you'll never get any attention.)

Él que anda con lobos, aullar aprende.—He who walks with wolves, learns to howl. (A warning about the company you keep.)

Barriga llena, corazón contento.—Full belly, happy heart. (Lean back and use this one after a big meal.)

Él que tiene más galillo, traga más pinol.—He who has a bigger throat, drinks more *pinol*. (Being aggressive will get you farther.)

tribution isn't controlled by the Pellas family, which produces every other beverage mentioned in this book. Together, Victoria, Toña, and Flor de Caña are known affectionately as "Vickie, Toni, and Flo."

That said, alcohol abuse is rampant in Nicaragua and increasingly acknowledged as a problem. Most towns have an Alcoholics Anonymous chapter, and many churches forbid their members to drink. Nevertheless, many otherwise religious holidays (including Sundays)—in addition to all nonreligious events—serve as excuses to get falling-down drunk. Just about all men drink

and are firm believers in the famous expression "*una es ninguna*" (one is none). Their benders often start before breakfast and end when the liquor does. In small towns, women are socially discouraged from drinking, though they sometimes do so in the privacy of their own homes or with close friends. Bigger towns and cities, of course, are more modern in this regard.

Should you decide to partake in this part of the culture and get drunk (or *borracho, bolo, picado, hasta el culo*), be sure you have a decent understanding of your environment and feel good about your company. Remember that many a traveler's disaster story begins with "Man, I was so wasted. . . " Always take it slow when drinking in a new place, and remember that your hydration level has an enormous impact on how drunk you get.

And oh, by the way, rum does not make you a better dancer, but it may improve your Spanish; and if you are drinking it alone, staring straight ahead over the broken line of the keys, try not to think about the girl.

RELIGION

Officially, the Republic of Nicaragua endorses no religion. In practice, the overwhelming majority of Nicaraguans describe themselves as Catholic, with evangelical Protestant sects (120 of them!) at around 9–15 percent and increasing annually. Beginning in the early 1970s and continuing through the revolution, Nicaragua was the setting for the fascinating phenomenon of Liberation Theology, a school of Christianity and bourgeois movement that equated Jesus's teachings with Marxism. The degree to which biblical parables were equated to the Marxist struggle varied, and the most radical versions placed Sandino as Jesus or Moses, Somoza as the Pharaoh, and the Nicaraguan masses as the Israelites searching for their promised land through revolutionary struggle.

A tiny percentage of Nicaraguans are descendents of one of the several Jewish families that found refuge here during World War II. Some of them still identify themselves as Jewish, but there is no real practicing community, the only synagogue having been dismantled and sold during the 1980s. Their numbers are small, and the vast majority of Nicaraguans have no concept of Judaism as a modern religion, relating the word *Judío* only to the race of Hebrews they read about in the Old Testament.

LANGUAGE

Spanish is, according to the Nicaraguan constitution, the official language of the republic, though indigenous languages are respected and even used officially in certain areas of the At-

lantic coast. Ninety-six percent of Nicaraguans speak Spanish as their first language, 3 percent speak indigenous languages (Miskito, Mayangna and Rama), and 1 percent speak languages of African origin (Criollo and Garífuna). To hear pure Miskito, travel north from Bluefields or visit Puerto Cabezas or any village along the Río Coco; in some of these villages, Spanish is completely unknown.

Nicaraguan Spanish is probably unlike any Spanish you've ever come across. The chameleon-like ability of the Spanish language to adapt to new areas of the world is strong in Nicaragua, where it is spoken rapidly and liquidly, the words flowing smoothly together and eating each other's tails. Central Americans enjoy making fun of how their Latin neighbors talk, and the Honduran nickname for Nicaraguans, *mucos* (bulls whose horns have been chopped off), is a reference to the Nicaraguans' habit of chopping the "s"

© RANDY WOOD

A sign of neither victory nor peace, flashing a *"dos"* mean you vote for the Sandinistas.

A FEW NICARAGUANISMOS

The textbook Spanish you learned back home will be understood without trouble, but Nicaraguans take pride in the fact that their version of the old-country Castilian is decidedly unique. When you try to look up some of the new words you're hearing and realize they're not in the dictionary, you'll see what we mean.

Blame it on *campesino* creativity and the Nicas' propensity for inventing words they need; blame the centuries of educational starvation, during which language evolved on its own; blame the linguistic mishmash of pre-Columbian Central America and the words left behind. Or just get out your pencil and paper and try to write down some of the unique vocabulary and phrases you hear, because you won't hear it anywhere else. Nicaraguan Spanish uses some old, proper Spanish no longer used in the Old World, and has assimilated pre-Columbian words from Nahuatl and Chorotega tongues as well (especially local plant and animal names). Still other words are pure onomatopoeia. Those interested in pursuing the topic should seek out Joaquim Rabella and Chantal Pallais's *Vocabulario Popular Nicaragüense*, available in many bookstores in Managua. Here's an incomplete sampling (with the Castilian in parentheses when possible).

arrecho: extremely angry (*enfurecido*)

bochinche: a fistfight among several people

boludo: lazy, unmotivated (*haragán*)

bullaranga: loud noises, ruckus (*tumulto, alboroto*)

curutaca: diarrhea (*diarrea*)

cususa: country moonshine (*aguardiente*)

chapa: earring (*arete*)

chigüin: little kid (*bebé*)

chinela: sandal (*sandalia*)

chingaste: the granular residue of a drink like coffee (*poso, residuo*)

chunche: any small, nameless object (*cosita*)

chusmón: mediocre

guaro: general term for booze or alcoholic beverages

hamaquear: to rock something rhythmically (*mecer rítmicamente*)

moclín: perverted old man

ñaña: excrement (*excremento*)

panzona: big bellied, implies pregnant (*embarazada*)

pinche: cheap (*tacaño*)

pipilacha: small airplane (*avioneta*)

salvaje: awesome; literally, "savage," fun response to "*¿Como estás?*"

timba: big belly (*barriga*)

Exclamations

¡Chocho!: Holy cow! Dude!

¡A la puchica!: Wow!

¿Ideay? (eedee-EYE?): What was that all about? What do you mean?

Va pué: OK then; see you; I agree; or whatever (short for *va pués*)

Dalepué: OK, I agree, let's do that.

¡Qué barbaridad!: What a barbarity! How rude! What a shame!

¡Sí hombre!: Yeah man!

hijueputa, jueputa: extremely common, short for the vulgarity *hijo de puta* (son of a whore), pronounced hwayPOOtah and used liberally.

Tranquilo como Camilo: Chillin' like Dylan; fun response to "*¿Como estás?*"

PAINTED ROOSTER: A GUIDE TO NICARAGUAN DINING

DESAYUNO

Huevos	
Enteros, Revueltos, Volteados	

BREAKFAST

Eggs	
Hardboiled, scrambled, over-easy	

ALMUERZO Y CENA

LUNCH AND DINNER

ALMUERZO Y CENA	LUNCH AND DINNER
Carne/res	Beef
Desmenuzada	Shredded and stewed
A la plancha	Served on a hot plate
Churrasco	Grilled steak
Filete jalapeño	Steak in a creamy pepper sauce
Puerco/cerdo	Pork
Chuleta	Porkchop
Pollo	Chicken
Empanizado	Breaded
Frito	Fried
Al vino	Wine sauce
Rostizado	Rotisserie
Valenciano	A chicken and rice dish
Mariscos	Seafood
Pescado entero	The whole fish
Langosta al ajillo	Lobster in garlic sauce
Camarones al vapor	Steamed shrimp
Sopa de conchas	Conch soup
Huevos de paslama	Endangered turtle eggs

PLATOS TRADICIONALES

TRADITIONAL DISHES

PLATOS TRADICIONALES	TRADITIONAL DISHES
Baho	Plantain and beef stew
Nacatamales	Meat-filled corn tamal, wrapped and boiled in banana leaves
Indio viejo	Beef, veggie, and cornmeal mush
Caballo bayo	A sampler's plate of traditional dishes
Gallo pinto	Red beans and rice, generously doused in oil and salt
Cuajada	White farmer's cheese
Leche agria	A sour cream–yogurt combo

| Vigorón | Pork rinds with yucca and coleslaw, served on a banana leaf |

BOCADILLAS

Tostones	**APPETIZERS** Thick, fried, green plantain chips
Tajadas	Crunchy, thin strips of green plantain
Maduro sugar	Ripe, sweet plantains fried in their own
Ensalada of lime	Shredded cabbage, tomatoes, and a dash
Tortilla	Heavy, floppy discs of toasted white corn

BEBIDAS Y (RE)FRESCOS

Tiste and cloves	**DRINKS AND FRUIT JUICES** Toasted cooked corn with cacao, pepper,
Pinol	Toasted, milled corn
Pinolillo	Pinol with pepper, cloves, and cacao
Horchata	Toasted and milled rice with spices
Chicha	Rough-milled corn with vanilla and banana flavors, sometimes fermented

POSTRES   DESSERTS

| Flan | Flan |
| Sorbete, Helado | Sherbet, Ice cream |

Reach for the *chilero* to spice up any meal.

off the ends of spoken words. Backcountry *campesino* Nicaraguan Spanish is inevitably less intelligible to the untrained ear than its urban counterpart, but it is also distinctly more melodic, with a cadence and rhythm distinct to the countryside and celebrated in many of Carlos Mejía Godoy's songs.

And then, of course, there are the vulgarities. Ernest Hemingway wrote, "There is no language so filthy as Spanish. There are words for all the vile words in English and there are other words and expressions that are used only in countries where blasphemy keeps pace with the austerity of religion." In Nicaragua, many fruit and vegetable names can cause a room to break out in wild laughter if said in the right tone and context (and if accompanied by the appropriate hand gesture). As with any language, be careful—the degree to which most *vulgaridades* are considered offensive varies depending on the gender of your company, their age, your relationship with them, and a variety of other factors. Swearing can be a fun, complex, and subtle game if you have the patience to learn. . . *y los huevos!*

Body Language

Limber up your wrist and stretch out those lips. You'll need 'em both if you want to communicate like a true native. Watch people interact on the buses, in the markets, and on the streets, and see if you can spot any of the following gestures in action—then try some out yourself.

Probably the single most practical gesture is a rapid side to side wagging of the index finger. It means "no," and increases in strength as you increase the intensity of the wagging and the amount of hand and arm you use in the motion. In some cases, a verbal "no" in the absence of the **Finger Wag** is disregarded as not serious enough. Use this one liberally with pushy vendors, beggars, and would-be Romeos.

To pull off the **Nicaraguan Wrist Snap,** simply join the tips of your thumb and middle finger and let your index finger dangle loosely. Then with a series of rapid wrist flicks, repeatedly let your index finger slap against the middle one, exactly as you would do with a round tin of to-

bacco dip. The resulting snapping noise serves to either emphasize whatever it is you're saying, refer to how hard you've been working, or, when combined with a nod and a smile, infer something like, "Damn, that's good!"

You can ask, "What?" (or "What do you want?") with a quick **Cheek Scrunch,** occasionally performed with a subtle upward chin tilt. Use the **Lip Point** rather than your finger to indicate something by puckering up as if for a kiss and aiming where you want. Or, if you are listening to a friend's dumb story, point to the speaker with your lips while looking at everyone else to imply, "This guy's crazy or drunk."

The gesture North Americans would normally use to shoo something away—the outstretched, waving, down-turned hand—means just the opposite in Nicaragua, where the **Downward Wave** (occasionally combined with the whole arm for emphasis) means "Come here." This one is a favorite with drunks in the park who love to talk at foreigners for as long as they are tolerated. The North American "come here," i.e., the upturned and beckoning index finger, is a vulgar, possibly offensive gesture. Speaking of vulgar, a closed fist atop a rigid forearm indicates the male sex organ, and an upturned, slightly cupped hand with the fingertips pressed together into a point is its female counterpart. Here's one more for the road: Make a fist, lock your elbow into the side of your body, and move your hand up and down; combined with a dramatic grimace, the **Plunger Pump** tells the whole world you have diarrhea.

ETIQUETTE AND TERMS OF ADDRESS

Latin America is not homogenous across state borders when it comes to addressing each other: While Costa Ricans tend to gravitate toward the formal *usted* form of address among themselves, Nicaraguans prefer the friendly *vos* (second person) form with each other, although *tú* is widely understood. For travelers, it's best to use *Usted* until you've really gotten to know someone (or mastered the tricky *vos* form), particularly after a night out or a long drinking session (you'll be surprised how quickly alcohol lubricates friendships at this latitude).

The term *don* for men and *doña* for women is a colonial term of respect usually related to aristocracy or landownership, but in Nicaragua it's far more commonly used than elsewhere in Latin America, and indicates a higher level of respect or affection, particularly for the elderly, the important, or the wealthy. Practitioners of certain careers sometimes drop their names entirely and go by their profession. That is, it's not uncommon to be presented to someone everyone calls simply *"la doctora," "el ingeniero,"* or *"la abogada."* Just go with it and smile.

It's customary to kiss women on the cheek when greeting, but women will provide the signal whether that's appropriate or not by turning their cheek toward you. Men will offer you their hands for a stiff handshake. When someone new enters the room, rise from your seat to greet them, and when you're ready to end a conversation or leave the room, a friendly *"con permiso"* will pave the way to the door.

TABLE MANNERS

Dig in, piggy! Food is for enjoying, not for delicately spearing at the end of a thin fork. Grab that fried chicken between two hands and gnaw at it, shovel down *vigorón* from its banana-leaf wrapper as best as you can without letting all the shaved cabbage spill down your shirt. Chase it with long swigs of a cold drink. Nicaraguans enjoy good food and good times, and if you're too dainty, the signal is all too clear you're not pleased with the meal. There are limits, of course, so keep an eye on your dining companions for what's appropriate and what's not, but while you're picking away at your fried cheese and sweet plantains, the guy next to you has finished his meal, pulled his shirt up with one hand and is happily rubbing his belly with the other. Don't be afraid to enjoy what's on your plate. If you'd like to get a laugh out of your Nicaraguan hosts or waiters, after you've finished your plate, tell them, *"Barriga llena, corazón contenta"* (Belly full, happy heart).

The Arts

Nicaraguans are, by nature, a creative people, and the many countries and cultures that have taken part in their country's history have each left an unmistakable mark on dance, sculpture, painting, writing, and music. There are many opportunities to experience traditional dance and song, but equally vibrant are the artisans, writers, and performers who are creating in the present, helping to form an artistic environment that's very much Nicaragua's own.

LITERATURE

"Nicaragua," wrote the poet Pablo Neruda, "where the highest song of the tongue is raised." José Miguel Oviedo called the writing of Nicaragua, "the richest and most tragic national literary tradition on the continent." Most start the story of Nicaraguan literature with the groundbreaking words of Rubén Darío. It continues with the van-

guardists of the 1950s and 1960s, the subsequent generation of revolutionary poets and novelists, and the current wave of soul-searchers.

Though poverty has placed books out of the economic reach of most Nicaraguans, the Casa de los Tres Mundos art gallery in Managua doubles as ground zero for the Society of Nicaraguan Writers, and is a good place to start if you have questions about readings, book releases, or other events. There are a few bookstores in Managua that carry Nicaraguan and Latin American selections, as well as Spanish translations of foreign works; Estelí and León also boast interesting bookstores to explore.

Poet and author Gioconda Belli was called one of the 100 most important poets of the 20th century. Her work deals with the themes of feminism, mystical realism, and history, all mixed with a breath of sensuality. Her books *Wiwilí, Sofía de los Presagios,* and *El País Bajo Mi Piel*

© RANDY WOOD

Traditional dance performances are found throughout Nicaragua, known as *"bailes folcóricos."*

(The Country Under My Skin) are widely acclaimed.

The writing of Ricardo Pasos Marciacq reflects not only his appreciation for the long and tumultuous history of Nicaragua but for the richness of its society. His books *Maria Manuela Piel de Luna* and *El Burdel de las Pedrarias* are considered modern classics; the former evokes the years when British-armed Miskitos were wreaking havoc on the Spanish settlements of the Pacific.

Rubén Darío is loved throughout the world of Latin American literature and is considered the father of modernism in Spanish literature. A few of the many other books by Nicaraguan writers worth reading if you have the time and the facility of the language include *El Nicaragüense* by Pablo Antonio Cuadra, *Nicaragua, Teatro de lo Grandioso* by Carlos A. Bravo, and *El Estrecho Dudoso* by Ernesto Cardenal.

DANCE AND THEATER

There's plenty of traditional and folk dance—often mixed with a form of theater—to appreciate. There are several dance institutions in Managua that teach folk classics alongside modern dance and ballet, and sponsor frequent performances. The presence of dance schools outside the capital is on the rise, which means fortunate travelers have a good chance of seeing a presentation outside of Managua, especially in Masaya, Diriamba, Matagalpa, León, and Granada. "El Güegüense," for example, is a 19th-century dance of costumed dancers in wooden masks that satirically represents the impression Nicaragua's indigenous people first had of the Spanish and their horses. This dance and others are often featured at *fiestas patronales* (patron saint celebrations), notably in the Masaya and Carazo regions. "El Viejo y La Vieja" (The Old Man and Woman) pokes ribald fun at old age and sexuality. One dancer,

THE POET IS THE HIGH PRIEST

Throughout Nicaraguan culture, the poet is the high priest. The prophet. The maker of visions. The singer of songs. The one who knows and can say it for others the way others feel it but cannot say it for themselves.

Margaret Randall wrote this in her collection of interviews with Nicaraguan writers entitled *Risking a Somersault in the Air,* commenting on the extraordinary role that poetry has played in Nicaraguan society. Salman Rushdie was equally impressed when, during his tour of Nicaragua and the Sandinista government in the mid-1980s, he found himself surrounded by young warrior-poets at all levels of society.

Indeed, an inordinate number of the revolution's leaders were published writers—including Minister of the Interior and Head of State Security Tomás Borge, and President Daniel Ortega, both of whom published poems from Somoza's prisons in the 1970s (Somoza's forces found and destroyed the only manuscript of the book Ortega wrote during the same time period). Ortega once told Rushdie, "In Nicaragua, everybody is considered to be a poet until he proves to the contrary."

Literature (and painting, pottery, theater, music, and crafts) was strongly supported by the Sandinista government, whose Ministry of Culture, Father Ernesto Cardenal, stayed busy instituting poetry workshops and publishing magazines and books. Cardenal's poetry is internationally acclaimed and widely translated. Another revolutionary, Gioconda Belli, whose work evokes the sensuality of her country's land and people, was named one of the 100 most important poets of the 20th century. But Nicaraguan poetry, no matter how entwined with the revolution, goes way back, before the life of Sandino.

Invariably, one must turn to Nicaragua's literary giant, Rubén Darío, who 100 years ago set the stage for his nation's love affair with poetry by producing a style unprecedented in Spanish literature. Darío is called the father of the modernist movement in Spanish poetry, a literary style that shed long, grammatically intricate Spanish phrases for simplicity and directness. His experimentation with verse and rhythm made him one of the most acclaimed Latin American writers of all time. Darío's legacy stands firm, and stories about his drinking bouts and international exploits still abound. Poet, journalist, diplomat, and favorite son of Nicaragua, Rubén Darío has become the icon for all that is artistic or cultural in Nicaragua. Today, his portrait graces the front of the 100 *córdoba* bill, his name is on most of the nation's libraries and bookstores, and his sculpted likeness presides throughout the land. His legacy is incredible, and Randall asks if today's poets owe everything to him or to the fact that they, like their hero, glean their inspiration "from that violent expanse of volcanic strength called Nicaragua."

A hundred years later, the Sandinistas pointed to Darío's anti-imperialist references, including a passage written at the time of the Spanish-American War in which he denounces the North Americans as "buffaloes with silver teeth," and a poem in which he issues a directed warning to the U.S. president:

O men with Saxon eyes and barbarous souls, our America lives. And dreams. And loves. And it is the daughter of the Sun. Be careful. Long live Spanish America! A thousand cubs of the Spanish lion are roaming free. Roosevelt, you must become, by God's own will, the deadly Rifleman and the dreadful Hunter before you can clutch us in your iron claws. And though you have everything, you are lacking one thing: God!

The muse still reigns in today's generation. *Rubén's Orphans* is an anthology of contemporary Nicaraguan poets, with English translations by Marco Morelli, published in 2001 by Painted Rooster Press. Also, seek out Steven F. White's book, *Poets of Nicaragua, a Bilingual Anthology,* which covers the poets following Darío up to the revolution (1983, Unicorn Press).

DENNIS MARTÍNEZ, ROBERTO CLEMENTE, AND NICARAGUAN BASEBALL FEVER

Save your soccer/football commentary for down the road: Decades of North American and Cuban influence have engendered a nation of baseball fanatics unrivalled in Latin America. Soccer's got some fans—especially in the Carazo region—but in Nicaragua, it's *El Beis* that gets people's blood boiling.

One of Nicaragua's favorite sons and well-admired national heroes is Dennis "El Presidente" Martínez, the kid from Granada who left home in 1976 to make it to the big leagues, where he pitched more winning games than any other Latino. In 1991, he pitched the 13th perfect game in major league history against the first-place Dodgers. Nicaraguans followed every detail of his career with avid determination, as he pitched for the Baltimore Orioles ('76–'86), Montreal Expos ('86–'93), Cleveland Indians ('94–'96), Seattle Mariners ('97), and finally the Atlanta Braves ('98). Martínez was a breath of fresh air and a source of much-needed relief throughout the 1980s, when his pitching and hitting stats were the only good news associated with this war-torn nation; talking baseball was a popular respite from the tragedy and destruction. Martínez retired in 1998 and today, his name graces the stadium in Managua, as well as several charitable foundations, like the Dennis Martínez Foundation, www.dennismartinezfoundation.org.

Also liked and respected was Puerto Rican–born Pittsburgh Pirate, Roberto Clemente. Clemente was so moved by the distress in Nicaragua's capital after the earthquake in 1972 that he rounded up a planeload of clothes, blankets, and food, and flew to Managua to personally distribute it. He never arrived. Immediately after taking off from San Juan, Puerto Rico, his DL-7 plane faltered and plunged into the Caribbean. Investigators suggested the unrestrained cargo shifted during flight and threw the plane off balance; five additional people perished trying to rescue him.

In Nicaragua, a bevy of municipal leagues, town leagues, little leagues, competitions between universities, and even between government ministries dominate the public spotlight. Teams from Estelí, León, Chinandega, Masaya (San Fernando), Granada (Los Tiburones—the sharks), Managua (El Boer), Matagalpa, and Rivas make up the national league, and the

Federación Nicaragüense de Beisból Asociado (with offices in the national stadium in Managua, tel. 505/222-2021) oversees the whole thing. The 60-game regular season begins officially in early January, followed by 24 playoff games and a seven-game championship series at the end of May. The games are serious—as are the fans—but the series' charm is its humility: Unlike elsewhere, baseball is a sport and a pastime, not a mega-marketed seven-figure-salary circus. Not that Nicaraguan players don't dream of one day making it big in "The Show" like their onetime fellow players, Vicente Padilla and Marvin Bernard. Padilla is a star pitcher who, at the age of 26, signed a $2.6-million contract with the Philadelphia Phillies in 2004, and his compatriot, Bernard, took $4.2 million from the San Francisco Giants in 2003. Being the only two Nicas playing in the big leagues, they are followed passionately in the Nicaraguan sports pages. Throughout Nicaragua, very few pueblos lack a ball field of some sort, even if the kids put together games with homemade bats and balls of wound twine and tape. The casual traveler is more often than not welcome to join.

Even the smallest country villages have some sort of baseball field.

dressed up as an old gentleman with cane and top hat, and the other, dressed up as a buxom old woman, perform a dance that usually involves the old man trying to dance with young female members of the audience while his wife chases him, beating him with her cane. "Aquella Indita" is a celebration of the Nicaraguan woman and her reputation for being graceful and hardworking. "El Solar de Monimbó" (Monimbó's Backyard) is a traditional dance from the indigenous neighborhood of Masaya, which captures the spirit of community and celebration.

Besides the traditional folk pieces, Nicaraguans love to dance. Period. And there is no occasion (except maybe a funeral) at which it is inappropriate to pump up the music and take to your feet. The ultra-suave, loose-hipped movements associated with merengue, salsa, *cumbia,* and reggae are most commonly seen at discos, street parties, or in living rooms around the nation. The Palo de Mayo is a popular, modern Caribbean dance form featuring flamboyant costumes, vibrating chests, and not-so-subtle sexual simulations. When you see mothers rocking their babies to loud Latin rhythms, and two-year-old girls receiving hip-gyrating lessons, you'll understand why Nicaraguans are able to move so much more fluidly on the dance floor than you are.

VISUAL ARTS

There are a number of Nicaraguan sculptors and painters whose work is displayed at galleries in Managua, Granada, León, and other places. Though the primitivist painters of Solentiname have gotten the lion's share of the press, there is much more in Nicaragua to be seen. In Managua, there are frequent expos of art, often accompanied by buffets or musical performances. More detail is provided in the Managua chapter.

MUSIC

Music, in an infinite variety of forms, is incredibly important in Nicaraguan society. Expect to find loud, blaring radios in most restaurants, bars, vehicles, and homes. It may seem strange at first to find yourself listening to fast, pulsing merengue beats at six in the morning on a rural chicken bus (or in your hotel lobby at midnight for that matter) when the only people listening are sitting calmly in their seats or rocking chairs. Realize, however, that this behavior is seen as a way to inject *alegría* (happiness) into the environment, or alternately, to get rid of the sadness that some Nicaraguans associate with silence.

Radio mixes are eclectic, featuring the latest Dominican merengues, Mexican and Miami pop, cheesy *romanticas,* plus a bizarre U.S. mélange of Backstreet Boys ("Los Back," for those in the know), Air Supply, and Guns N' Roses. Another wildly popular genre is the *ranchera,* which comes in the form of either polka beats or slow, drippy, lost-love, mariachi tearjerkers, performed by one of a handful of supercelebrity Mexican crooners. Old, rootsy, U.S. country music is extremely popular on the Atlantic coast, and in northern Nicaragua, Kenny Rogers (pronounced "Royers") is recognized as the undisputed king of "La Musica Country."

Managua is host to a small, exciting scene of young local bands and solo musicians, most of whom are direct descendants—children, nephews, cousins—of the generation of musicians that brought Nicaraguan folk music to the world. Their acts range from quiet acoustic solo sets to the head-banging throaty screams of a couple of angry, politically minded metal bands. Common venues to catch live music are Café Amatl, Bar La Cavanga, and Guantanamera.

Live music is also found at most *fiestas patronales,* performed by one of several Nicaraguan commercial party bands whose sets imitate the radio mixes of the day. Among the most popular bands is Los Mokuanes (named after the enchanted mountain and its resident witch in La Trinidad, Estelí), who have been around in one form or another for more than three decades. During the war, they were conscripted by the government to don fatigues and perform at army bases throughout the country. Other favorite bands are Macolla and, representing the Palo de Mayo side of things, Sir Anthony and his Dimensión Costeño.

Getting There and Away

BY AIR

All air traffic to Nicaragua (and the rest of Central America) is routed through the cities of San Salvador, Houston, or Miami. American Airlines has two flights a day to Nicaragua via Miami, and Continental Airlines has one flight every evening via Houston. Latin American airlines TACA, LACSA, and Sansa have service between Miami and Nicaragua, as well as to other Central American destinations. Iberia has one flight per day to Miami with connections to European destinations. Be aware of the $30 cash-only exit fee when flying out of Nicaragua.

BY LAND

The three legal northern border posts are (from west to east): Guasale (in Chinandega), El Espino (near Somoto), and Las Manos (near Somoto). While entering Nicaragua from eastern Honduras, north of Puerto Cabezas, is technically possible, it is a guaranteed lengthy series of

INTERNATIONAL BUS DEPARTURES

To San José, Costa Rica (continuing to Panama City, Panamá)

TicaBus	6 A.M., 7 A.M., 12 P.M. ($10)
King Quality	1:30 P.M. ($15)
Central Line	5 A.M.
TransNica	5:30 A.M., 7 A.M., 10 A.M. ($10)
TransNica luxury bus	12 P.M. ($20)

To Tegucigalpa, Honduras

TicaBus	4:45 A.M. ($20)
King Quality	4 A.M., 11 A.M. ($23)

To Guatemala City, Guatemala

King Quality	4 A.M., 11 A.M. ($49)

To San Salvador, El Salvador

TicaBus	6 A.M. ($10)
King Quality	4 A.M., 11 A.M. ($26)
TransNica	5 A.M. via Choluteca, Honduras

The 11 A.M. King Quality bus to Guatemala spends the night in San Salvador and arrives the next morning.

The Ticabus to Panama City, Panamá stops first in San José, Costa Rica, then continues through the night, arriving in Panama City the following morning.

risky and expensive challenges and is not recommended. On the southern border, the legal crossings are Peñas Blancas on the Pan-American Highway, and Los Chiles, reached via an hour-long boat ride from San Carlos. The feasibility of crossing into Costa Rica via the Río Colorado to Tortuguero is undetermined, but would most likely involve convincing the migration officer in San Juan del Norte that you are not trafficking drugs or jaguar pelts.

Crossings by foot, boat, or bus are pretty standard at both the Honduran and Costa Rican borders. Sometimes, you breeze right through; sometimes there are multiple bag and document checks. Remember that you *always* need an exit and an entrance stamp—at some borders, when leaving Nicaragua, it is possible to walk into the neighboring country with your Nicaraguan exit stamp, and then miss the line for the other country's customs; you'll have a lot of explaining to do at your next passport check.

Driving Across the Border

If you are driving your own vehicle, the process to enter Nicaragua is lengthy, but usually not difficult. You must present the vehicle's title, as well as your own driver's license and passport. You will be given a temporary (30-day) permit to drive in

Nicaragua, which will cost $10—should you lose the permit, you will be fined $100.

By International Bus

All bus lines between Managua and other Central American capitals are based out of Barrio Martha Quezada, and have competing schedules and prices (see Bus Schedule special topic). Several have affiliate offices in other Nicaraguan cities, like Rivas and León.

TicaBus (two blocks east of the Antiguo Cine Dorado, tel. 505/222-6094 or 505/222-3031, ticabus@ticabus.com, www.ticabus.com) is the oldest and best-established Central American international bus company, servicing all of Central America with connections all the way to Mexico. Across the street, **King Quality/Cruceros del Golfo** (tel. 505/228-1454) is a more comfortable ride and offers both breakfast and a drink cart, for a slightly higher price. Right next door to King Quality, **Central Line** (tel. 505/254-5431) offers service only to San José, Costa Rica. **TransNica** (Rotonda Metrocentro 300 meters north, 25 meters east, across from DGI, tel. 505/277-2104 or 505/882-7600) services El Salvador and Costa Rica. Their noon bus to Costa Rica costs double but is the most pleasant trip on the market, with meals and drinks included.

Getting Around

BY AIR

Nicaragua's two local carriers, La Costeña and Atlantic Airlines, are both based at the International Airport in Managua and, between them, offer daily flights to Puerto Cabezas, Waspám, and Siuna in the northeast, Bluefields and Corn Island in the east, and San Carlos in the south. Flights are in single- and double-prop planes and may be a little bouncy at times. Don't be surprised if your pilots (who you'll practically be sitting next to) kick back and take a nap or read the morning paper after they gain altitude and throw on the cruise control (we're not kidding). Flights within the country generally cost $50 each way.

BY BUS

Physical discomfort is important only when the mood is wrong. Then you fasten on to whatever thing is uncomfortable and call that the cause. But if the mood is right, then physical discomfort doesn't mean much.

Robert Pirsig

Nicaragua has a massive fleet of old yellow school buses, retired from the First World and customized to transport Nicaraguans to and from the farthest reaches of their country. Each major population center has one or two bus hubs, with regular and express service to nearby cities and to Managua, plus rural routes to the surrounding

"*Expresos*" will save you time when traveling between any major city.

communities. Generally speaking, Nicaragua's bus system is safe, cheap, and sure to be one of the most memorable parts of your travels. Enjoy being a part of the chatting, smiling, sweating crowd, even when you are packed so tightly into the mass of real-life Nicaragua that you confuse your limbs with someone else's.

In theory, *expresos* are buses that do not stop to pick up extra passengers en route to their destination. This is occasionally true and we recommend paying the 25 percent more for an *expreso* ticket, which sometimes gets you a reserved seat and can save you an hour's travel or more. To points west and south from Managua, there is an especially large number of express microbuses (minivans or *interlocales*) that leave every 20 minutes—or whenever they fill up.

Local buses are called *ordinarios* or *ruteados* and take their sweet time, stopping for every Tom, Dick, and Pedro who waves his hand—hell, they'll stop for a chicken if he flaps his wing too close to the highway. *Microbuses,* sometimes

called *interlocales,* are small, express minivans that depart when full.

In some bus terminals, you'll purchase your ticket before boarding, but usually, you'll board the bus, find a seat, and then wait for the *ayudante* (driver's helper) to come around and collect your *pasaje* (fare). Asking the Nica sitting next to you how much the ride should cost will help you avoid being ripped off (very rare). In some cases, if the *ayudante* doesn't have change, he'll write the amount owed to you on your ticket, returning later in the trip to pay you. This is normal. Most buses have overhead racks inside where you can stow your bags. Less desirable, but common, is for the *ayudante* to insist you put your backpack on the roof or in some cargo space in the back of the bus. It is obviously safer to keep your stuff on your lap or at least within sight, but sometimes you don't have much choice but to trust your chauffeurs.

Urbanos

We advise against using the Managua urban bus

system unless you are with a Nicaraguan or another traveler who has experience with it. The routes are long and confusing and you and your fancy backpack are obvious targets for thieves. *Urbanos* are, of course, much cheaper than taxis, but it only comes down to a couple dollars—or less. You can decide how much it's worth to not feel a knifepoint in your side. Actually, urban buses probably aren't too dangerous during the day, but during rush hour and nighttime, the risk shoots up. Most other major cities have a basic *urbano* bus loop and are much safer than Managua.

BOATS

In several regions of Nicaragua—notably Solentiname, Río San Juan, Río Coco, and the entire Atlantic coast—boat travel is the only viable means of transportation. Because gas prices are as high as $3–4 a gallon in these areas, locals get around in public water taxis called *colectivos* that help cut costs. The aforementioned areas have different kinds of water travel and we've provided a boat vocabulary list for each region. Note: See Special Topic on p. 287 for more.

TAXIS

There are new Japanese models slowly joining Nicaragua's taxi fleet, but the vast majority remain the same tin-can Russian Ladas that were imported during the 1980s and, miraculously, are still chugging along. Granted, many windows don't open, windshields are shattered, and the seats are shot—but who cares when the engine works and there's a sound system more powerful than the one you had in your freshman dorm. In every city except Managua, urban taxis operate on a fixed zone rate, usually no more than $.35 within the central city area. In the capital, however, it's a different story, and you should never get into a cab before settling on a price. Strangely, most old Nicaraguan taxis have no handle with which to roll the windows down. If you can't stand the heat, ask the driver for the *manigueta de la ventanilla;* he's probably got it stashed up front.

DRIVING

Renting a Car

Car rental services (including Avis, Budget, Hertz, Econo, and Hyundai) are easily found in Managua at the airport, the fancier hotels, and a number of agency offices and lots. In terms of price, renting a car here is comparable to just about anywhere else, so by Nicaraguan standards, it will be a huge chunk of your travel budget. However, if you have a group of five people or so, it can be a reasonable way to make a road trip to see the turtles, or to go anywhere else with limited public transportation.

Vehicular Safety

The most dangerous thing you will do in Nicaragua, without a doubt, is travel on its highways. Outside the cities, roads are poorly lit, narrow, lacking shoulders, and are often full of axle-breaking potholes, unannounced speed bumps, fallen rocks, and countless other obstacles. Even in Managua, you can expect to find ox carts, abandoned vehicles, and grazing horses wandering the streets. Because there are no shoulders for taxis to use when boarding passengers, they stop in the right lane and let traffic swerve around them. Also expect macho, testosterone-crazed bus drivers trying to pass everything they can on blind, uphill curves. The fact that beer and rum are sold at most gas stations should give you an idea of how many drivers are intoxicated, especially late at night.

When possible, avoid traveling during peak rush hours in the cities, and after dark anywhere. New highway projects since 2000 have improved the situation in many parts of the country, but road and vehicle conditions are still hazardous and many drivers even more so, occasionally taking advantage of the newly repaved straightaways to speed like bats out of hell. Everywhere you drive, keep an eye out for dogs crossing the road. Experienced drivers suspect they canines are specially trained and then released on the roads to test driver reactions.

Getting Pulled Over

So how's that Spanish coming along? This is where your language skills will really pay off—literally. Police in Nicaragua are well known to be fairer and less corrupt than elsewhere in Central America, but with their dismal salaries, they are still often on the lookout for a little baksheesh. Commonly called *la pesca* (a reference to fishing), Nicaragua's finest are often seen in groups at intersections and traffic circles, surrounded by construction cones, flourishing bright orange gloves, and pulling over everything in sight—especially gringo drivers without diplomatic plates. Drivers complain that the cops' definition of *mala maniobra* (moving violation, literally bad driving) is just about any movement of your vehicle within their sight. Have your papers ready when the officer approaches your window, and know that calling him *"compañero"* is likely to double the bribe. The latest method used by police is to confiscate your license and threaten to hold it hostage until you come in the following week to pay the fine—unless, of course, you'd rather take care of the issue right then. Speaking of bribes, slick talk and some quick cash will get you out of some situations; however, honest Nicaraguan cops, who not only won't accept your 100 *córdobas* but will ticket you for the attempt, are known to exist. Also, paying off the police only serves to encourage and perpetuate corruption. You (and your soul) are better off playing by the rules.

In Case of a Traffic Accident

Do not move your vehicle from the scene of the crime until authorized by a police officer, even if it is blocking traffic. For lack of high-tech crime-scene equipment, the Nicaraguan police force will try to understand how the accident occurred based on what they see at the site. Drivers who move their vehicle at the scene of the accident are held legally liable for the incident—even if you just move your vehicle to the side of the road. Any driver in Nicaragua who is party to an accident where injuries are sustained will be taken into custody, even if the driver has insurance and does not seem to be at fault. This custody will be maintained until a judicial decision is reached (sometimes weeks later) or until the injured party signs a waiver releasing the driver of liability. In many cases, to avoid a lengthy court proceeding and horrifying jail stay, it may be worth your while to plead guilty and pay a fine (which will probably not exceed $1,000, even in the case of a death).

TWO WHEELS

If you intend to ride a motorcycle or bicycle in Nicaragua, be sure to bring your own helmet,

Start talkin': knowing some Spanish will ease your travels in Nicaragua.

© RANDY WOOD

© JOSHUA BERMAN

Easy rider: helmets are a rare site on Nicaraguan motorcycle riders.

tains and past smoking volcanoes is one of the most wonderful experiences to be had in Nicaragua. In general, hitchhiking (in Spanish, "*pedir* ride," with the English cognate), is common in Nicaragua and, provided you use common sense, is relatively safe. In most cities, setting yourself up is as easy as taking a taxi or bus to the town's *salida* (exit) and waiting a couple of minutes. We've tried to provide region-specific tips for hitching to and from individual cities. The farther into the countryside you get, the easier it is to score a ride, especially when you get off the paved road and folks start feeling more responsible for each other.

Obvious things to watch out for are drunk drivers, sketchy vehicles, and dangerous cargo. Women should use extra caution; hitchhiking alone is probably ill-advised. Hitchhiking is a main mode of transportation for soldiers and police officers, and standing next to them may be a good way to get a ride (actually, they may do the same to you, thinking that your foreign appearance is more of a ride magnet than their uniform and gun).

Nicaraguan drivers, true to their culture's desire to save face, may pass you by in a cloud of dust, but they nearly always make some attempt to exonerate themselves, usually in the form of an apologetic face and a hand signal. An upraised, rotating index finger signifies they are turning around soon, and a thumb and forefinger measuring out about an inch shows they are only traveling a short distance. Some drivers will use their entire hand to indicate an impending left or right turn, and others will bunch their fingers and thumb together and point the tips upward to tell you their vehicle is full. Some, flustered at how to respond to your request, may point forward or give some incomprehensible sign. Making eye contact, or catching them pulling out of a gas station, may give them enough *pena* (embarrassment) that they will feel obliged to let you in.

Payment for a ride is usually not expected, but you should certainly offer, especially if they have taken you a long way or carried a large group of your friends. Gas is expensive, and your weight on a long trip costs money. If they turn you down, fine—if not, the experience is well worth a couple of dollars.

an item largely ignored by Nicaraguans—even when baby, junior, and grandma are all crammed onto the motorcycle or bike, with dad driving (or peddling). Supplies are not completely unavailable, though; if you need a bicycle, helmet, or other supplies while in Nicaragua, visit **Casa Shannon** (located in Managua 300 meters south of the Semáforos Rubenia, tel. 505/289-4744, shannon7@ibw.com.ni). This is the biggest bike importer in the country, run by an Irish-American who originally came down in the 1980s with **Bikes Not Bombs** (www.bikesnotbombs.org), a Boston-based non-profit that still supports community bicycle projects in Nicaragua and El Salvador. Another organization that can ship your used bike to Nicaragua and other places in need of cheap transport is **Pedals for Progress** (www.p4p.org).

HITCHHIKING

The Zen of walking out to the highway, sticking out your thumb, and ending up in the back of a breezy pickup truck as it speeds through the moun-

Visas and Officialdom

PASSPORT AND VISA REQUIREMENTS

Every traveler to Nicaragua must have a passport valid for at least six months following the date of entry. A visa is required only for citizens of the following countries: Afghanistan, Albania, Bosnia-Herzegovina, Colombia, Cuba, Haiti, India, Iran, Iraq, Jordan, Lebanon, Libya, Nepal, Pakistan, People's Republic of China, People's Republic of Korea, Somalia, Sri Lanka, Vietnam, and Yugoslavia. Everyone else is automatically given a visa good for three months, which can be extended by going to the Office of Immigration (Dirección General de Migración y Extranjería, 1.5 blocks north of the *semaforos* Tenderí, tel. 505/244-0741, 505/244-1320, or 505/244-3960, open 8:30 A.M.–noon and 2–4:30 P.M. Mon.–Fri.); show up at least four days before it expires with your passport, current visa, and $25. There's no guarantee you'll be given an extension. If the gods smile on you, the extensions

will be for one month at a time. Remember to look presentable. If you're traveling on a simple tourist visa, it may be less cumbersome to simply cross into Costa Rica or Honduras and return the same day. Additional requirements exist for those who intend to work, study, reside for an extended period, or engage in non-tourist activities. Contact your nearest Nicaraguan embassy for details about the requirements.

CUSTOMS AND IMMIGRATION

Upon entering Nicaragua, tourists are required to pay a $7 entrance fee. You also must be in possession of an onward/return ticket, a valid passport, and have evidence of sufficient funds. As you pass through the gate, a red light indicates your luggage will be searched, a green light does not. Should they go through your luggage, you can expect to be taxed for carrying items you obviously don't intend to use yourself, especially electronics, jewelry, and perfume. If your Walkman, camera, or laptop computer isn't in its original box or accompanied by several more of the same, you will pass through customs in a flash. When leaving Nicaragua by plane, you must pay an airport tax of $30 in U.S. dollars only (no credit cards).

NICARAGUAN EMBASSIES ABROAD

El Salvador: 71 Avenida Norte y Primera Calle Poniente No. 164, Colonia Escalon, San Salvador, tel. 503/298-6549, fax 223-7201.

Costa Rica: Avenida Central No. 2440, Barrio La California, San Jose, (frente al Pizza Hut), tel. 506/222-2373, fax 221-5481.

Guatemala: 10 Avenida, 14–72, Zona 10, Guatemala, tel. 502/268-0785, fax 337-4264.

Honduras: Colonia Tepeyac, Bloque M-1, No. 1130, Tegucigalpa, tel. 504/232-7224, fax 239-5225.

Panamá: Intersección de Avenida Federico Boyd y calle 50, Apartado 772, Zona 1, Corregimiento Bella Vista, Ciudad de Panamá, tel. 507/223-0981, fax 211-2080.

FOREIGN EMBASSIES AND CONSULATES IN NICARAGUA

All diplomatic missions in Nicaragua are located in Managua, mostly along Carretera Masaya or Carretera Sur. The city of Chinandega additionally hosts consulates from El Salvador, Honduras, and Costa Rica, and the city of Rivas hosts a consulate from Costa Rica.

North and South America

Argentina: First Las Colinas entrance, then 1 block east, tel. 505/276-0857.
Canada: De Los Pipitos, Calle Nogal No. 25, Bolonia, tel. 505/268-0433 or 505/268-3323,

FIESTA GUIDE

Each community's annual *fiestas patronales* revolve around the local saint's birthday, but the actual party may extend days or even weeks before and after. This guide should help you catch (or avoid) *fiestas patronales* as you travel; the events are associated with special masses, processions, alcohol, dancing, carnivals, show horses, contests, and more alcohol.

Year-round weekly events include the following: Thursdays in Masaya are Jueves de Verbena, Fridays in Granada are Noches de Serenata, and Sundays in León are Tertulias Leonesas. Semana Santa (Easter Week) is a particularly big deal—everyone parties like rock stars at the beach and prices skyrocket across the board.

January
1: New Year's Day

18: Fiestas Patronales, El Sauce

Third Sunday: Señor de Esquipulas, El Sauce (León)

Third weekend: Viva León Festival, León

Third weekend: San Sebastían, Acoyapa (Chontales), Diriamba, Carazo (San Sebastián)

Last weekend: La Virgen de Candelaria, La Trinidad (Estelí)

February
Second weekend: Music and Youth Festival, Managua

March
Third weekend: Folklore, Gastronomy, and Handicraft Festival, Granada

April
Semana Santa

First week: Religious Ash Paintings in León

19–21: Fiestas Patronales, San Jorge (Rivas)

May
1: Labor Day

1: Fiestas Patronales, Jinotega

15: San Isidro Labrador, Condega (Estelí)

30: Mother's Day

Third weekend: Palo de Mayo Festival, Bluefields

June
16: Virgen del Carmen, San Juan del Sur (Rivas)

24: St. John the Baptist, San Juan de Oriente (Carazo), San Juan del Sur (Rivas), San Juan de Jinotega (Jinotega)

29: St. Peter the Apostle, Diriá (Masaya)

Last Friday: El Repliegue Sandinista (Managua)

July
Second Saturday: Carnaval, Somoto

15–25: Fiestas Patronales, Somoto

19: National Liberation Day

25: Santiago, Boaco, Jinotepe (Carazo)

26: St. Ana, Nandaime (Granada), Chinandega, Ometepe

August
1–10: Santo Domingo (Noches Agostinas), Managua

10: St. Lorenzo, Somotillo (Chinandega)

14: Gritería Chiquita, León

15: The Assumption, Granada

14–15: Fiestas Patronales, Ocotal

15: The Assumption and Fiesta del Hijo Ausente, Juigalpa

Third weekend: Mariachis and Mazurcas Festival, Estelí

September
10: San Nicolás de Tolentino, La Paz Centro (León)

14: The Battle of San Jacinto

15: Independence Day

14 and 15: Fishing Fair, San Carlos (Río San Juan)

15: Patron Saint Festival of Villa Nueva, Chinandega

20: San Jerónimo, Masaya

24: La Merced, León and Matagalpa

Fourth weekend: Polkas, Mazurcas, and Jamaquellos, Matagalpa; Festival of Corn, Jalapa

October
12: San Diego (Estelí)

continued on next page

FIESTA GUIDE (cont'd)

Second weekend: Norteño Music Festival in
   Jinotega
24: San Rafael Arcángel, Pueblo Nuevo
Penultimate Sunday: Fiesta de los Agüisotes, Masaya
Last Sunday: Toro Venado, Masaya

November
2: All Souls' Day
3–5: Equestrian Rally in Ometepe
4: San Carlos Borromeo, San Carlos (Río San Juan)
12–18: San Diego de Alcalá, Altagracias (Ometepe)
Fourth Sunday: Folkloric Festival, Masaya

December
First Sunday: Procesión de San Jerónimo, Masaya
6: Lavado de La Plata, Virgen del Trono, El Viejo
   (Chinandega)
7: Purísimas (Immaculate Conception Celebrations) in Managua, Granada, Masaya, and León

Diriamba's fiestas are totally unique in
Nicaragua.

fax 505/268-0437, mngua@dfaitmaeci.gc.ca.
The Canadian Embassy in San José has jurisdiction over affairs in Nicaragua.
Colombia: Planes de Altamira, one block south of
the old Motorama, then 1.5 blocks west, casa
#82, tel. 505/278-4405.
Costa Rica: half a block east of Estatua Montoya along Calle 27 de Mayo, tel. 505/268-7460.
Cuba: Carretera Masaya from the third entrance
to Las Colinas, two blocks east, 75 *varas* to the
south, tel. 505/276-2285.
The Dominican Republic: Las Colinas, three
blocks east of the Spanish Embassy, tel. 505/276-
0654.
El Salvador: Las Colinas, Ave. El Campo Pasaje
Los Cerros no. 142, tel. 505/276-0160.
Guatemala: Carretera Masaya Km 11, tel. 505/279-
9834.
Honduras: Carretera Masaya Km 12, 100 meters
toward Cainsa, tel. 505/279-8231.

Panamá: Third entrance to Las Colinas, then 2
blocks east and, 75 meters south, tel. 505/276-
0212.
Panamá: Carretera Masaya 3ra entrada de Las
Colinas 2 cuadras al este, 75 varas al Sur, tel.
505/276-0212.
United States: Carretera Sur Km 4, Barrio Batahola Sur, tel. 505/266-6010, after-hours tel.
505/266-6038.
Venezuela: Carretera Masaya Km 10, tel.
505/276-0267.

Europe
Austria: From the Rotonda El Güegüense, one
block north, tel. 505/266-0171 or 505/268-3756.
Belgium: Consulado de Bélica, Reparto El Car-
men across from the Esso station, Calle 27 de
Mayo, tel. 505/228-2068.
Denmark: Plaza España one block west, two blocks
north, half a block west, tel. 505/268-0253.

Finland: Bolonia, one block north, 1.5 blocks west of the Hospital Militar, tel. 505/266-3415.

France: Reparto El Carmen, 1.5 blocks west of the church, tel. 505/222-6210.

Germany: 1.5 blocks north of the Rotonda El Güegüense, tel. 505/266-3917.

Great Britain: Los Robles, from the old Sandy's on Carretera Masaya, 1 block south, half a block west, tel. 505/278-0014 or 278-0887.

Italy: one block north and half a block west of the Rotonda El Güegüense, tel. 505/266-6486.

The Netherlands (Holland): Bolonia canal 2, half a block north, one block west, tel. 505/266-4392.

Norway: one block west of Plaza España, tel. 505/266-4199.

Russia: Las Colinas, Calle Vista Alegre No. 214, tel. 505/276-0131.

Spain: Las Colinas Avenida Central No. 13, tel. 505/276-0968.

Sweden: one block west, two blocks north, and half a block west of the Rotonda Plaza España, tel. 505/266-8097.

Switzerland: Consulado de Suiza, one block west of the Las Palmas Clinic, tel. 505/266-5719.

Asia

Republic of China: Planes de Altamira, from the Copa office 200 *varas* south across from the tennis courts, tel. 505/267-4024.

Japan: Bolonia, from the Rotonda El Güegüense one block west, one block north, tel. 505/266-1773.

OFFICIAL HOLIDAYS

Expect all public offices to be closed on the following days. Also remember that Nicaraguan holidays are subject to decree, shutting the banks down without warning to suit some politician's inclination.

January 1: New Year's Day

Late March/early April: Semana Santa, including Holy Thursday, Good Friday, and Easter

May 1: Labor Day

May 30: Mother's Day

July 19: National Liberation Day

August 1: Fiesta Day

September 14: Battle of San Jacinto

September 15: Independence Day

November 2: Día de los Muertes (All Souls'Day)

December 8: La Purísima (Immaculate Conception)

December 25: Christmas Day

Like the rest of Latin America, each town and city has its own patron saint whom the residents honor each year with a prolonged party that lasts from one to three weeks. These *fiestas patronales* combine holy religious fervor with a fierce celebration of sin that features alcohol consumption of biblical proportions. Highlights of the celebration include Virgin and Saint parades, special masses, fireworks, cockfighting, rodeos, concerts, gambling, and show-horse parades. Many towns have additional celebrations of specific events in their history.

Semana Santa (or Holy Week) is the biggest celebration of the year, occurring during the week leading up to Easter Sunday. The week-long vacation sends most city folk to the beach for sun and debauchery (and usually a couple of drownings, too) while shops close their doors and everyone takes a breather. Expect lots of trouble traveling during this time period, as many buses stop running and many hotels hike their rates exponentially.

Tips for Travelers

Travel with Children

There's no reason you can't travel with your children. The family unit is strong in Nicaragua and children everywhere are cherished and adored, not seen as a burden. You may find that traveling with your children helps form a new connection between you and the Nicaraguans you meet. That said, be aware that your children will have to endure the same lack of creature comforts, change in diet, and long bumpy bus rides you do.

Nicaraguan children generally grow up with cloth diapers, which are painstakingly washed out and hung to dry in the sun. Disposable diapers are available in most supermarkets, but they're imported from elsewhere, so they're not cheap. If the nature of your trip permits it, consider taking a supply of diapers along, or purchasing the cloth diapers (which are infinitely cheaper). Other necessities available in Nicaragua include powdered milk for formula, rubber pacifiers (*pacificadores* or *chupetas*), and bottles (*pachas*).

Women Travelers

In Nicaragua, as in all of Latin America, women are both adored and harassed to their wits' end by "gentlemen" hoping for attention. Catcalls and whistles are everywhere, often accompanied with an *"Adios, amorrrr,"* or a sleazy, *"Tss-tss!"* More often than not, the perpetrators are harmless, immature young men with struggling moustaches. It will either comfort or disgust you to know that Nicaraguan women are forced to endure the same treatment every day and you should note how they react—most ignore the comments and blown kisses entirely, and some are flattered and smile confidently as they walk by. Acknowledging the comment further is probably ill-advised, as it will only feed the fire. Be prepared for this part of the culture, and decide ahead of time how you plan to react.

Physical harassment, assault, and rape are much less common in Nicaragua than elsewhere in Central America, but certainly not unheard of, especially when alcohol is involved. Take the same precautions you would anywhere else to avoid dangerous situations. For more, download a copy of "Her Own Way: Advice for the Woman Traveller" at the Canadian Consular Affairs website (www.voyage.gc.ca); also find good advice and tips at www.journeywoman.com.

As for feminine hygiene products, tampons can be difficult to find, as almost all Nicaraguan women use pads (*toallas sanitarias*). Most pharmacies and *pulperías* carry pads, usually referred to by the brand name Kotex, regardless of the actual brand. Nicaraguan women favor pads over tampons due to custom as well as social stigma, as tampons are sometimes associated with sexually active or aggressive women.

Gay and Lesbian Travelers

Despite the fact that homosexuality is officially forbidden by the Catholic church and the state, Nicaragua has both a gay population and a society generally tolerant of homosexuality, although it is often misunderstood. For example, many only associate the term with the transvestite prostitutes of Managua or the open crossdressers in some countryside villages. Also, many Nicaraguans consider the *macho* (dominant) partner of a male-male relationship to be straight and reserve the word *maricón* for the submissive partner (similar to prison culture in other countries); and for some reason, lesbian relationships are more socially frowned upon than male homosexuality.

Still, the gay or lesbian traveler should feel neither threatened nor endangered in Nicaragua provided they maintain a modicum of discretion and choose their situations wisely. Managua, as well as some of the larger towns, contains openly gay clubs, and elsewhere same-sex couples may find local gay communities that will help orient you to nearby tolerant clubs and bars. More information on the gay scene in Nicaragua (and other countries) can be found at www.globalgayz.com. Or track down the 25-minute 1993

PEACE CORPS IN NICARAGUA

The Peace Corps *(El Cuerpo de Paz)* is a U.S. government program created by John F. Kennedy in 1961. Its original goal was to improve the image of the United States in the Third World (and thus decrease the temptation for the world's poor to turn to Communism) by sending mostly young, idealistic volunteers deep into the countryside of developing countries.

More than 40 years later, 165,000 Americans have served as Peace Corps Volunteers (PCVs) worldwide; there are currently some 7,000 volunteers serving in more than 90 countries around the world. Participants voluntarily sign up to receive an intensive three-month training in their host country's language and culture, as well as in technical aspects of their assignment, followed by a two-year tour during which they receive a bare-bones living allowance.

The first Peace Corps Volunteers arrived in Nicaragua in 1969. PC-Nica took a hiatus during Sandinista control and was invited back in 1991. About 150 volun-

Peace Corps volunteers are found in the country's most remote corners, where they live for two years.

teers are currently serving in Nicaragua, situated in some of the most remote corners of the country, as well as nearly every major town and city except Managua and the Atlantic Coast (because of safety concerns). PCVs work in one of five sectors: Environment, Agriculture, Small Business Development, Youth at Risk, and Community Health. If you're interested in learning more, visit www.peacecorps.gov.

film, *Sex and the Sandinistas* for a look at homosexuality in revolutionary, *machista* society.

Travelers with Disabilities

Owing to bullets, land mines, and poor health care, Nicaragua has a significant population of *descapacitados* (disabled) who get around with much difficulty because of ruined sidewalks, dirt roads, aggressive crowds, and open manholes. While Nicaraguans agree the disabled have equal rights, no attempt is made to accommodate them, and the foreign traveler with limited mobility will certainly struggle, but will no doubt find ways to get by.

The Los Pipitos organization, based in Managua with 24 chapters around the country, is devoted to providing support, materials, and

physical therapy to Nicaraguan children with disabilities and their families. Los Pipitos is always looking for volunteers and support. The Managua office is located half a block east of the Bolonia Agfa (tel. 505/266-8033).

VOLUNTEERING

Nicaragua, because of its history of poverty and social experimentation, has always attracted non-traditional tourists. Shortly after 1979, hordes of would-be revolutionaries poured in from all over the world to participate in the great experiment—they picked coffee, taught in schools, wrote poetry and editorials of solidarity, put themselves in the line of fire, and protested in front of the U.S.

Embassy (the less ardent, Birkenstock-clad were called *Sandalistas*). Though the waves of idealist volunteers trickled off about the same time the FSLN lost power, Nicaragua is still very much a needy country, and thousands of *internacionalistas* come here to work, study, and volunteer every year. Anyone with an independent head on their shoulders and a couple hundred dollars a month for living expenses can create their own volunteer opportunity. Grants and awards abound for such individuals.

Where possible, we have included regional opportunities to volunteer in the destination chapters of this book. Other organizations (both faith-based and secular) work throughout the country and provide opportunities in construction, education, translation, agriculture, and general solidarity. Following are a few of these.

Habitat for Humanity (www.habitat.org) is active building homes throughout Nicaragua. **Global Exchange** (www.globalexchange.org) is a human rights organization "dedicated to promoting environmental, political, and social justice around the world"; they have a series of "Reality Tours" in which participants can tour fair-trade coffee cooperatives, monitor elections, and have other unique experiences in Nicaragua. **Witness for Peace** (www.witnessforpeace.org) is a politically independent grassroots organization "committed to nonviolence and led by faith and conscience." Based in Managua, Witness for Peace has maintained a permanent presence in this Central American country since 1983; they offer trips that "combine international travel and education with the struggle for peace, economic justice, and sustainable development." The **American Jewish World Service** (www.ajws.com) has a program called the Jewish Volunteer Corps, which provides support for professionals looking to volunteer in Nicaragua and other countries.

If you are interested in setting up a work trip to Nicaragua for a group, several organizations exist to help plan the project and facilitate logistics: **Bridges to Community**(U.S. tel. 914/923-2200, www.bridgestocommunity.org) works with small Nicaraguan communities on construction, health, and environmental projects.

STUDYING

There are many possibilities for spending a summer, semester, or extended internship in Nicaragua. Programs range from biological fieldwork at remote research stations to language training to social justice programs, like the School for International Training's semester program in Managua entitled "Revolution, Transformation, and Civil Society" (U.S. tel. 888/272-7881). **Cloud Forest Adventures** (www.cloudforestadventures.com) offers a co-ed summer program for high school students, blending Spanish-language classes, ecological appreciation, and learning through outdoor adventure, community service, and cultural immersion. You'll find additional listings at **www.studyabroad.com.**

SPANISH-LANGUAGE SCHOOLS

Oh, the rare happiness of comprehending every single word that is said, and knowing that every word one says in return will be understood as well!

Mark Twain

Nicaragua has a strong network of independent Spanish schools, and an increasing number of visitors to the country choose to combine their

---

¿HABLA ESPAÑOL?

You can certainly get along in Nicaragua with a survival level of Spanish, but it should go without saying that the more you know, the more profound an experience you will have. Much of this book is written with the assumption of a basic conversational proficiency of Spanish. We believe that in spite of the astonishing natural beauty of Nicaragua, its greatest charm is its friendly and interesting people. If you don't speak at least some Spanish, you will be missing out on one of the best reasons to visit Nicaragua. If your Spanish isn't up to par, consider visiting one of Nicaragua's inexpensive Spanish schools.

travels with a few days, weeks, or even months of language study. Most schools follow the same basic structure, mixing language instruction with cultural immersion: two–four hours of class in the morning, community service activities or field trips in the afternoon, and optional homestays with Nicaraguan families.

Obviously, some programs are better than others, and keeping track of the quality of each school's teachers and curriculum is beyond the scope of this book, although we've certainly tried our best. To a certain extent, choosing a school is as much a question of geographical preference as anything else. If possible, it's a good idea to come down and personally look into a few options before making a long-term commitment. Get a feel for the teachers (ask about their experience and credentials), the professionalism of the business, and the lesson plan. Do not trust everything you see on the websites.

Once in the classroom, remember that gaining a language takes time—you must learn one word at a time until they start flowing together in sentences. Be patient, do your homework, and be ready to laugh at yourself (along with everyone else) as you make mistakes. *¡Suerte!*

Multiple Cities

You can create your own language tour by studying at several of the schools below, using your class schedule and family homestays as a way to travel throughout Nicaragua. You can also let **Nicaragua Spanish Schools** (NSS, Managua tel. 505/244-1699, nssmga@ibw.com.ni, www.pages .prodigy.net/nss-pmc) handle the logistics of such a tour by choosing their "TransNica" plan, enrolling you in two or more of the three independent schools that make up the network. Choose from León, Granada, and San Juan del Sur (see the regional listings for details). All three NSS schools start at $195 a week, and the price goes down considerably the more time you study; subtract $60 a week for no homestay.

Estelí

You'll find a cool climate and a number of natural excursions available at one of the three schools here, all of which have been around since the early '90s. **Escuela Horizonte Nica** (located two blocks east and half a block north of INISER, tel. 505/713-4117, horizont@ibw.com.ni, www.ibw .com.ni/u/horizont) has one of the longest track records in town and proffers the lofty vision of "promoting peace and social justice for those living in poverty, those struggling against class, race, and gender prejudices, and those fighting for political freedom." It donates part of its profits to local organizations and has an afternoon activity program that includes visits to local cooperatives and community-development programs. One week of class, with 20 hours of intensive study, afternoon activities, and homestay with a family costs $165, discounts for groups.

The **CENAC Spanish School** (Centro Nicaragüense de Aprendizaje Cultural, tel. 505/713-5437, cenac@ibw.com.ni, www.ibw.com.ni/~cenac) has been around since 1990. Room and board plus 20 hours of class cost $140 a week. It's located on the west side of the Pan-American Highway, 150 meters north of the Shell Esquipulas (or half a block south of Bodegas de Enebas).

Spanish School Güegüense (250 meters east of the Shell Esquipulas, tel. 505/713-7172) offers afternoon activities, including trips to Jinotega, Quilalí, San Juan del Río Coco, and local Estelí attractions. Class and homestay cost $120 per week.

Matagalpa

The fresh climate and steep streets remind some visitors to this northern city of a tiny, inland San Francisco. In the middle of it all is the **A & G Language Academy** (located one block east of the Alcaldía, tel. 505/772-5978, languageacademy@yahoo.com), offering a variety of programs for as little as $125/week for 20 hours of instruction plus homestay. Guides and tours in the surrounding coffee country are available as well.

Granada

Granada's status as ground zero for the Nicaragua tourism scene (from backpackers to upscale) makes it a natural choice for many students who love the city's aesthetic as much as its central location on the gringo route. Roger Ramírez's **One-on-One Spanish Tutoring Academy** (tel. 505/552-6771, www.1on1tutoring.net, located on the Calle Calzada, four blocks west of the central park) has received rave reviews and a constant stream of students since its humble, one-room beginnings. A week of 25 hours of instruction costs $95, plus $60 for room and board with a family. Custom, group, and cultural activities can also be arranged, as can shorter lessons, or class by the hour ($7). (Note: at press time, a core group of One-on-One teachers had defected to form their own school, so be sure to research One-on-One's status before making your decision.)

Casa Xalteva (tel. 505/552-2436, www.casa xalteva.com, located across from the church by the same name) offers a similar package, $150/week, with a stress on volunteer activities; it's highly recommended by former students, has a quiet location, and is part of a small group home for boys, which is supported by your tuition.

The **Escuela Palacio de Cultura** (tel. 505 /552-7114) is the Granada chapter of the NSS. Located in a grand building on the west side of Granada's main plaza, it has wonderfully airy class space overlooking the central plaza.

San Juan del Sur

One of the best deals in the country is **Doña Rosa Silva's Spanish School** (located two blocks south of Hotel Villa Isabella, tel. 505/834-2867, Spanish_silva@yahoo.com), offering four hours of daily instruction, up to six days a week for $90—with a free homestay! Several of her students had nothing but good things to say. Also get personal instruction from **Luis Vicente Lira** (next to Cyber Leo's in the middle of town, tel. 505/872-1645, lvl1948@yahoo.es), $65 a week for three hours of daily instruction.

Escuela San Juan del Sur (located in the Casa de Cultura, across the street from the beach, NSS office or local tel. 505/568-2115) has 17 teachers, all university-trained and relatively young, and classes are small: one-on-one, or two students maximum. They also offer a free hour-long sample class every Thursday at 3 P.M. Students rave about the creative activities, like dancing and cooking lessons.

Laguna de Apoyo

If you prefer to study outside the city, the **Proyecto Ecológico** (tel. 505/868-0841 or 505882-3992, eco-nic@guegue.com.ni, www.guegue.com.ni/eco -nic) is the only Spanish school in Nicaragua in a purely natural setting—the lakeside lodge is in the crater of an ancient volcano. The spot is incredible, only an hour from Managua, less to Granada, yet still tucked away in its own green world. Lodging and food are excellent (homestays are possible too), and the organization is not-for-profit. One week costs $190 and includes classes, activities, and room and board in their lodge.

León

Part of the NSS network, **Escuela de Español Leonesa** (located 1.5 blocks west of the Iglesia La Merced, tel. 505/311-2116) is $195/week with homestay (less for more weeks) or $7/hour. There are also private, hourly lessons offered through the Vía Vía Hospedaje.

Managua

Private lessons, tutoring, and guide services are offered by **Raúl Gavarrette** (tel. 505/233-1298, cel 505/776-5702, aige@tmx.com.ni).

WORKING

In light of Nicaragua's exceeding poverty and sky-high unemployment rate, you'll have a tough time finding paying work. Additionally, immigration laws force you to prove your job couldn't have otherwise gone to a Nicaraguan. Still, there are plenty of foreigners who've pulled it off. Start your job search with your embassy and the many NGOs that work in Nicaragua, including CARE, Save the Children, ADRA, Project Concern International, and Catholic Relief Services. If you are a licensed English teacher you might also try the universities in Managua, though your salary will be the same as a Nicaraguan's (i.e., you'll be able to sustain yourself from day to day but you'll wish you had a cousin in Miami sending you checks). Universidad Centroamericana (UCA), Universidad Nacional Autónoma (UNAN), and Universidad Americana (UAM) all have English departments that may be looking for staff. For more ideas, check out the book, *Work Abroad,* edited by Clay Hubbs, available at www.transitionsabroad.com.

RESORT VACATIONS

For the more sedentary traveler content to stay put and be served, Nicaragua has a handful of resort-type destinations. Montelimar, on the Pacific coast, is an all-inclusive beach compound with reasonable rates for what they offer. The Río Indio Lodge in San Juan del Norte is a new installment of plushness, and in the mountains, Selva Negra offers a more rustic, honeymoon-style getaway on a German coffee farm and private wildlife reserve. Morgans Rock Hacienda and Ecolodge is the newest and most unique upscale option in Nicaragua, offering a small-scale luxury experience on a stunning stretch of Pacific beach in the southwest.

Traveling with a local guide will enhance your experience and support the local economy.

© RANDY WOOD

TOUR OPERATORS

Nicaragua's independent tour companies offer a huge variety of trips, from afternoon city tours to weeklong pirate cruises in the farthest reaches of the country, the logistics of which would be nearly impossible for the solo traveler. These adventures cost money, and of course, as part of a group, you lose some independence; but then again, you are provided with security, freedom from making plans, and, with some companies, luxury. For a current list of active tour operators in Nicaragua, go to www.intur.gob.ni.

Tour operators in Nicaragua are numerous enough to undoubtedly cover a wide range in their levels of social and environmental responsibility—surely, in large part, due to their clients' demands. Before choosing a tour company, research it well and ask lots of questions: Will you interact with the communities through which you'll be traveling? If so, are the people of those communities benefiting in some way other than the opportunity to watch you take photographs of their children? Will your tour operator create an environment that allows you to practice the tenets of ethical tourism as listed in this section?

ALTERNATIVE TOUR PROVIDERS

There are several organizations in Nicaragua that work exclusively to promote low-impact, ground-up tourism, using infrastructures and programs designed to benefit those *campesinos* living in and near Nicaragua's overlooked, under-traveled destinations. **COMARCA TURS Nicaragua** (www.comarcaturs.com), initiated by a Canadian NGO, is attempting "to diversify and increase incomes of Nicaraguan families and communities through the development, training, and marketing of sustainable tourism micro-businesses, thus contributing to an enhanced standard of living throughout the country." Their programs are aimed at open-minded, unrushed foreign travelers, or in their words, "Sustainable Tourists who appreciate the time spent with a local family more than the night slept in the bed of a luxury hotel, or the thrill and treasures found in local transportation more than an all-in-one bus tour."

Run by a Californian who has been working with Nicaragua's street children for years, **Chela Personalized Destinations** (U.S. tel. 415/333-4104, www.chelatravel.com) "pro-

motes global awareness through exploration" in the form of small, personalized group tours of Nicaragua. The cost of trips includes everything except airfare. Chela's owner, Birgit Cory, assures that a portion of all tour profits goes to projects dedicated to keeping children off the streets of Nicaragua.

Health and Safety

BEFORE YOU GO

Resources

Staying Healthy in Asia, Africa, and Latin America, by Dirk G. Schroeder, is an excellent and concise guide to preventative medicine in the Developing World and is small enough to fit in your pocket. Consult the "Mexico and Central America" page of the U.S. Centers for Disease Control (CDC) website for up-to-date health recommendations and advice (www.cdc.gov/travel/camerica.htm) or call their International Travelers Hotline (tel. 404/332-4559 and 877/394-8747). You can also contact the Nicaraguan Embassy in your country.

Vaccinations

Required: A certificate of vaccination against yellow fever is required for all travelers over one year of age and arriving from affected areas.

Recommended: Before traveling to Nicaragua, be sure your tetanus, diphtheria, measles, mumps, rubella, and polio vaccines are up-to-date. Protection against hepatitis A and typhoid fever is also recommended for all travelers.

MEDICAL ATTENTION

Medical care is in short supply outside of Managua, and even in the capital city, doctors in public hospitals are underpaid (earning about $200 a month) and brutally overworked. Though there are many qualified medical professionals in Nicaragua, who studied abroad in Mexico, Cuba, or the United States, there are also many practicing doctors and medical staff that have less-than-adequate credentials. Use your best judgment. Hospitals

and medical facilities typically expect immediate payment for services rendered, but their rates are ridiculously cheaper than they are back home. Larger facilities accept credit cards and everyone else demands cash.

Government-run health clinics, called Centros de Salud, exist in most towns throughout the country, usually near the central plaza. They are free—even to you—but often poorly supplied and inadequately staffed.

We've pointed out the main hospital or private clinic in most regional chapters, but we should also mention here that the newest and most modern hospital in the country is Hospital Vivian Pellas, a $23-million private institution seven kilometers south of Managua on the Carreterra Masaya. For **dental emergencies,** or even just a check-up, seek out the bilingual, well-trained services of Dr. Esteban Bendaña McEwan (300 meters south of the Enitel Villa Fontana tel. 505/270-5021 or 505/850-8981, estebanbm@hotmail.com); Dr. Bendaña is accustomed to dealing with foreign patients and his prices are reasonable.

As for natural medicine, many *campesinos* have excellent practical knowledge of herbal remedies that involve teas, tree barks, herbs, and fruits. The first medicines came from the earth, and the Nicaraguans haven't lost that connection. Try crushed and boiled papaya seeds, oil of *apazote* (a small shrub whose seed is crushed for medicinal use), or coconut water to fend off intestinal parasites, *manzanilla* (chamomile) for stress or menstrual discomfort, or *tamarindo* or papaya for constipation. A popular cold remedy involves hot tea mixed with two squeezed limes, *miel de jicote* (honey from the *jicote* bee), and a large shot of cheap rum, drunk right before you go to bed so you sweat out the fever as you sleep.

Medications and Prescriptions

Many modern medicines, produced in Mexico or El Salvador, are sold in Nicaragua. Because of a struggling economy and plenty of competition, some pharmacies may sell you medicine without a prescription. For simple travelers' ailments, like stomach upsets, diarrhea, or analgesics, it's worth going to the local pharmacy and asking what they recommend. Even relatively strong medications like codeine can be purchased over the counter (in Alka-Seltzer tablet form).

Birth Control: Condoms are cheap and easy to find. Any corner pharmacy will have them, even in small towns of just a few thousand people; a three-pack of prophylactics costs less than $2. Female travelers taking contraceptives should know the chemical name for what they use. *Pastillas anticonceptivas* (birth control pills) are easily obtained without prescription in pharmacies in Managua and in larger cities like León, Granada, and Estelí. Other forms of birth control and sexual protection devices, such as IUDs, dental dams, and diaphragms, are neither used nor sold.

STAYING HEALTHY

Ultimately, your health is dependent on the choices you make, and chief among these is what you decide to put in your mouth. One longtime resident says staying healthy in the tropics is more than just possible—it is an "art form." Nevertheless, as you master the art, expect your digestive system to take some time getting accustomed to the new food and microorganisms in the Nicaraguan diet. During this time (and after), use common sense: Wash or sanitize your hands often. Eat food that is well cooked and still hot when served. Avoid dairy products if you're not sure whether they're pasteurized. Be wary of uncooked foods, including *ceviche* and salads. Use the finger wag to turn down food from street vendors and be aware that pork carries the extra danger of trichinosis, not

GETTING IN HOT WATER

In the cooler parts of the country, namely Matagalpa and Jinotega, some hotels and *hospedajes* offer hot water by means of electric water-heating canisters attached to the end of the shower head. Cold water passing through the coils is warmed before falling through the spout. The seemingly obvious drawback to the system is the presence of electric wires in and around a wet (i.e., conducive) environment. While not necessarily the electric deathtraps they appear to be, they should be approached with caution. Before you step into the shower, check for frayed or exposed wires (or the burned carcasses of former hotel occupants on the shower floor). Set the control knob to "II" and, very carefully, turn the water on. Once you're wet and water is flowing through the apparatus, it's in your best interest not to mess with the heater again.

To save you many cold showers trying to figure out how the darned thing works, we'll let you in on the secret: If the water pressure is too low, the heater isn't triggered on, and the water will not be heated, but if the water pressure is too high, it will be forced through the nozzle before it's had sufficient contact with the coils, and the water will not be heated. Open the faucet to a moderate setting, and rub-a-dub-dub, you're taking a hot shower. When you've finished, turn the water off first and dry off, then turn the little knob back to "off."

to mention the disgusting diet of garbage (and worse) on which most country pigs are raised.

Most importantly, be aware of flies as transmitters of food-borne illness. Prevent flies from landing on your food, glass, or table setting. You'll notice Nicaraguans are meticulous about this, and you should be too. If you have to leave the table, cover your food with a napkin or have someone else wave their hand over it slowly. You can fold your drinking straw over and put the mouth end into the neck of the bottle to prevent flies from landing on it, and put napkins on top of the bottle neck and your glass, too. Have the waiter clear the table when you've finished with a dish—and beware the waiter who, in response to your complaints about the flies, comes back and douses you and your dinner in an aerosol cloud of pesticide that's been banned in the United States for decades.

"Don't Drink the Water!"

At least one well-meaning friend or relative told you this before you shipped off to Central America. While most Nicaraguan municipal water systems are well treated and probably safe, there is not much reason to take the chance, especially when purified, bottled water is so widely available. But rather than contribute to the growing solid waste problem in Nicaragua, why not bring a single reusable plastic water bottle? You can refill it with the 5-gallon purified water dispensers found in most hotel lobbies and restaurants.

If you'll be spending time in rural Nicaragua, consider a small water filter for camping. Alternately, six drops of liquid iodine (or three of bleach) will kill everything that needs to be killed in a liter of water, good if you're in a pinch, but not something you'll find yourself practicing on a daily basis.

Standard precautions also include avoiding ice cubes unless you're confident they were made with boiled or purified water. Canned and bottled drinks without ice, including beer, are safe, but should never be used as a substitute for water when trying to stay hydrated.

Oral Rehydration Salts

Probably the single most effective item you can carry in our medical kit are these packets of powdered salt and sugar known in Spanish as *suero oral*. One packet of *suero* mixed with a liter of water, drunk in small sips, is the best immediate treatment for all of the following: diarrhea, sun exposure, fever, infection, or hangovers. Rehydration salts are essential to your recovery as they replace the salts and minerals your body loses from sweating, vomiting, or urinating, thus aiding your body's most basic cellular transfer functions. Whether or not you like the taste (odds are you won't), consuming enough *suero* and water is very often the difference between being just a little sick and feeling really, really awful.

Sport drinks like Gatorade are super-concen-

Beat the heat with an ice-cold *eskímo* in most town parks.

trated *suero* mixtures and should be diluted 3:1 with water to make the most of the active ingredients. If you don't, you'll urinate out the majority of the electrolytes. Gatorade is common in most gas stations and supermarkets but *suero* packets are more widely available and much cheaper, available at any drugstore or health clinic for about $.50 a packet. It can be improvised even more cheaply, according to the following recipe: Mix one-half teaspoon of salt, one-half teaspoon baking soda, and four tablespoons of sugar in one quart of boiled or carbonated water. Drink a full glass of the stuff after each time you use the bathroom. Add a few drops of lemon to make it more palatable.

Sun Exposure

Theo, I want the sun. I want it in its most terrific heat and power. I've been feeling it pull me southward all winter, like a huge magnet. . .

Vincent van Gogh

Nicaragua is located a scant 12 degrees of latitude north of the equator, so the sun's rays strike the

Earth's surface at a more direct angle than in northern countries. The result is that you will burn faster and sweat up to twice as much as you are used to. Did we mention that you should drink lots of water?

Ideally, do like the majority of the locals do, and stay out of the sun between 10 A.M. and 2 P.M. It's a great time to take a nap anyway. Use sunscreen of at least SPF 30 (Bullfrog's alcohol-based SPF 36 is the authors' choice), and wear a hat and pants. Should you overdo it in the sun, make sure to drink lots of fluids—that means water, not beer—and try not to strain any muscles as you kick yourself for being so stupid. Treat sunburns with aloe gel, or better yet—find a fresh *sábila* (aloe) plant to break open and rub over your skin.

DISEASE AND COMMON AILMENTS

Diarrhea and Dysentery

Everyone's body reacts differently to the changes in diet, schedule, and stress that go along with traveling, and many visitors to Nicaragua stay entirely regular throughout their trip. Some don't. Diarrhea is one symptom of amoebic (parasitic) and bacillic (bacterial) dysentery, both caused by some form of fecal-oral contamination. Often accompanied by nausea, vomiting, and a mild fever, dysentery is easily confused with other diseases, so don't try to self-diagnose. *Examenes de heces* (stool-sample examinations) can be performed at most clinics and hospitals and are your first step to getting better (cost is $2–8). Bacillic dysentery is treatable with antibiotics; amoebic is treated with one of a variety of drugs that kill off all the flora in your intestinal tract. Of these, Flagyl is the best known, but other non–FDA approved treatments like Tinedazol are commonly available, cheap, and effective. Do not drink alcohol with these drugs, but do eat something like yogurt or acidophilus pills to re-foliate your tummy.

Generally, simple cases of diarrhea in the absence of other symptoms are nothing more serious than "traveler's diarrhea." If you do get a case of Diriangén's Revenge, your best bet is to let it pass naturally. Diarrhea is your body's way of

¿DONDE ESTÁ EL BAÑO? A GUIDE TO NICARAGUA'S TOILETS

Nicaragua boasts an enormous diversity of bathrooms, from various forms of the *inodoro* (modern toilet) to the full range of dark, infested *letrinas* (outhouses). Despite so many options, there is a general shortage of actual toilet seats, so having to squat over a bare bowl is common. Also important is mastering the manual flush, useful when the normal pump mechanism breaks down or when the city water pressure fails. Use the bucket that should be sitting beside the toilet to dump water into the bowl all at once, forcefully and from high up to ensure maximum turd swirlage.

Additionally, with most flush toilets, always assume that used toilet paper is to be put in the basket next to the toilet, not in the bowl, so as not to clog up the weak plumbing. You'll get used to it. The most commonly encountered toilet paper is pink and made of recycled paper in a plant in Granada. It's not so soft—you'll get used to that, too. If not, pick up some luxury rolls to travel with, available in most supermarkets. Smart travelers carry their own *papel higiénico*, protected in a plastic bag and easily accessible. Otherwise, try the following phrase with your host when their can runs out of paper: *"Fijase que no hay papel en el baño."*

flushing out the bad stuff, so constipating medicines like Imodium-AD are not recommended, as they keep the bacteria (or whatever is causing your intestinal distress) within your system. Save the Imodium (or any other liquid glue) for emergency situations like long bus rides or a date with Miss Nicaragua. Most importantly, drink water! Not replacing the fluids and electrolytes you are losing will make you feel much worse than you need to. If the diarrhea persists for more than 48 hours, is bloody, or is accompanied by a fever, see a health professional immediately.

Malaria

Malaria is present in Nicaragua, and to date, the

newer chloroquine-resistant strains of the disease have not been detected in Nicaragua. Though the risk is higher in rural areas, especially those alongside rivers or marshes, malaria-infected mosquitoes breed anywhere stagnant pools of water (of any size, even in an empty bottle cap) are found, including urban settings.

Malaria works by setting up shop in your liver and then blasting you with attacks of fever, headaches, chills, and fatigue. The onslaughts occur on a 24-hour-sick, 24-hour-feeling-better cycle. If you observe this cycle, seek medical attention. They'll most likely take a blood test and if positive, prescribe you a huge dose of chloroquine that will kill the bug. Allow time to recover your strength. Weekly prophylaxis of chloroquine or an equivalent is recommended, and the CDC specifically recommends travelers to Nicaragua use Aralen-brand pills (500 mg for adults). Begin taking the pills two weeks before you arrive and continue taking them four weeks after leaving the country. A small percentage of people have negative reactions to chloroquine, including nightmares, rashes, or hair loss. Alternative treatments are available, but the best method of all is to not get bit (see the section on mosquitoes).

Dengue Fever

Dengue, or "bone-breaking," fever will put a stop to your fun in Central America like a baseball bat to the head. The symptoms may include any or all of the following: sudden high fever, severe headache (think nails in the back of your eyes), muscle and back pain, nausea or vomiting, and a full-bodied skin rash, which may appear 3–4 days after the onset of the fever. Although the initial pain and fever may only last a few days, you may be out of commission for up to several weeks, possibly bedridden, depressed, and too weak to move. There is no vaccine, but dengue's effects can be successfully minimized with plenty of rest, Tylenol (for the fever and aches), and as much water and *suero* as you can manage. Dengue itself is undetectable in a blood test, but a low platelet (*plaquetas*) count indicates its presence. If you believe you have dengue,

you should get a blood test as soon as possible to make sure it's not the rare hemorrhagic variety, which can be fatal if untreated.

AIDS

Although large numbers of HIV infections have not yet appeared in Nicaragua, especially compared to other Central American countries, health organizations claim that geography, as well as cultural, political, and social factors will soon contribute to an AIDS explosion in Nicaragua. Currently, there are about 1,500 HIV-positive cases registered with MINSA (the Government Health Ministry), but one World Bank official estimated actual cases at 8,000. Exacerbating the spread of AIDS (in Spanish, *La SIDA*) is the promiscuous behavior of many married males, an active sex-worker trade, less than ideal condom-using habits, and growing drug trouble. AIDS is most prevalent in urban populations, mainly Managua and Chinandega, and is primarily transmitted sexually, not through needles or contaminated blood.

That said, blood transfusions are not recommended. Travelers should avoid sexual contact with persons whose HIV status is unknown. If you intend to be sexually active, use a fresh latex condom for every sexual act and every orifice. Condoms are inexpensive and readily available in just about any local pharmacy; in Spanish, a condom is called *condón* or *preservativo*.

Other Diseases

Cholera is present in Nicaragua, with occasional outbreaks, especially in rural areas with contaminated water supplies. Vaccines are not required because they offer incomplete protection. You are better off watching what you put in your mouth. In case you contract cholera (the symptoms are profuse diarrhea the color of rice water accompanied by sharp intestinal cramps, vomiting, and body weakness), see a doctor immediately and drink your *suero*. Cholera kills—by dehydrating you.

Leptospirosis is caused by a bacteria found in water contaminated with the urine of infected animals, especially rodents. Symptoms include high fever and headache, chills, muscle aches, vomiting, and possibly jaundice. Humans become infected through contact with infected food, water, or soil. It is not known to spread from person to person and can be treated with antibiotics in its early stages.

Hepatitis B also lurks in Nicaragua. Avoid contact with bodily fluids or bodily waste. Get vaccinated if you anticipate close contact with the local population or plan to reside in Nicaragua for an extended period of time.

Most towns in Nicaragua, even rural ones, conduct a yearly rabies-vaccination campaign for dogs, but you should still be careful. Get a rabies vaccination if you intend to spend a long time in Nicaragua. Should you be bitten, immediately cleanse the wound with lots of soap, and get prompt medical attention.

Tuberculosis is spread by sneezing or coughing, and the infected person may not know he or she is a carrier. If you are planning to spend more than four weeks in Nicaragua (or plan on spending time in a Nicaraguan jail), consider having a tuberculin skin test performed before and after visiting. Tuberculosis is a serious and possibly fatal disease but can be treated with several medications.

BITES AND STINGS

Mosquitoes

Mosquitoes are most active during the rainy season (June–November) and in areas near stagnant water, like marshes, puddles, or rice fields. They are much more common in the lower, flatter regions of Nicaragua than they are in mountains, though even in the highlands, old tires, cans, and roadside puddles can provide the habitat necessary to produce swarms of *zancudos* (mosquitoes). The mosquito that carries malaria bites during the night and evening hours, and the dengue fever courier is active during the day, from dawn to dusk. They are both relatively simple to combat, and ensuring you don't get bitten is the best prophylaxis for preventing disease.

First and foremost, limit the amount of skin you expose—long sleeves, pants, and socks will do more to prevent bites than the strongest chemical repellent. Choose lodging accommodations with good screens and if this is not possible, use a fan to blow airborne insects away from your body as you sleep. Avoid being outside or unprotected in the hour before sunset, when mosquito activity is heaviest, and use a *mosquitero* (mosquito net) tucked underneath your mattress when you sleep. Hanging-type mosquito nets are available in Nicaragua, or you can purchase *tela de mosquitero* anywhere they sell fabric and have a mosquito net made by a seamstress. Also, many *pulperías* sell *espirales* (mosquito coils), which burn slowly, releasing a mosquito-repelling smoke; they're cheap and convenient, but full of chemicals, so don't breathe in too much smoke.

Spiders, Scorpions, and Snakes

Arachnophobes, beware! The spiders of Nicaragua are dark, hairy, and occasionally capable of devouring small birds. Of note is the *picacaballo,* a kind of tarantula whose name (meaning horse-biter) refers to the power of its flesh-rotting venom to destroy a horse's hoof. Don't worry, though; spiders do not aggressively seek out people, and do way more good than harm by eating things like Chagas bugs. If you'd rather the spiders didn't share your personal space, shake out your bedclothes before going to sleep and check your shoes before putting your feet in them.

Scorpions, or *alacránes,* are common in Nicaragua, especially in dark corners, beaches, and piles of wood. Nicaraguan scorpions look nasty—black and big—but their sting is no more harmful than that of a bee and is described by some as what a cigarette burn feels like. Your lips and tongue may feel a little numb, but the venom is nothing compared to their smaller, translucent cousins in Mexico. For people who are prone to anaphylactic shock, it can be a more serious or life-threatening experience. Be aware, in Nicaragua the Spanish word *escorpión* usually refers not to scorpions but to the harmless little geckos (also called *perros zompopos*) that scurry around walls eating small insects. And in spite of what your *campesino* friends might insist, those little geckos are neither malevolent nor deadly and would never, as you will often hear, intentionally try to kill you by urinating on you.

LANDMINES IN NICARAGUA

"By the way, how do you know when there's a mine in the road?" "There's a big bang," came the straightforward reply.

My breakfast of rice and beans—"gayo pinto," it was called, "painted rooster"—began to crow noisily in my stomach.

Salman Rushdie, The Jaguar's Smile

Nicaragua has the ignominious honor of having had more land mines—more than 135,000 in place and another 136,000 stockpiled in the wilds of the northeast—than any other country in the Western Hemisphere. This is one of the most brutal and pernicious legacies of the conflicts of the 1980s, and the focus of a major de-mining cleanup effort by the Nicaraguan Army and the Organization of American States (OAS). In fact, no other country in the world is making a greater effort than Nicaragua to clear the land of mines.

The de-mining process, though ongoing, can largely be considered a success: Since the beginning of operations, 75 percent of installed antipersonnel mines have been located and destroyed, and more than 3.8 million square meters of minefield have returned to productive use. The de-mining effort takes place in six-month modules that concentrate on known trouble spots, during which specially trained troops and dogs trained to sniff out explosives comb the territory. After every square meter has been checked for explosives, the region is certified mine-free. The weapons, when uncovered in the field, are detonated on-site. Stockpiles are transferred to and destroyed at one of two special detonating zones: the Escuela de Sargentos Andres Castro outside of Managua and the ENABI army base a few kilometers south of Condega, Estelí.

There are currently four areas where OAS troops are actively searching for and destroying land mines: outside of Matagalpa and Jinotega, outside of Murra (Nueva Segovia), and the lands around Jalapa (Nueva Segovia). Both Sandinista and Contra troops mined Nueva Segovia heavily during their repeated confrontations, and, in 1998, flooding and mudslides caused by Hurricane Mitch washed many known minefields downstream, burying other sites under a layer of earth. Since 2002, OAS troops have been combing the Honduran border from Las Sabanas (Madriz, just south of Somoto) through Jalapa to Wamblán, Jinotega, a distance of nearly 150 kilometers. The department of Chinandega and the border with Costa Rica were declared free of mines in late 2001, and the Río San Juan in 2002.

Antipersonnel explosives have crippled nearly a thousand Nicaraguans and injured countless more (to this day, about 20 people per year). More frequent still are losses of cattle, which go unreported but are the subject of many a *campesino* story. For this reason, an intensive education campaign aimed at the *campesinos* in the affected areas employs comic books with a story line discussing the danger of land mines and what to do if you suspect you've found one.

What does the presence of land mines mean to the traveler? That you should ask a lot of questions if you leave the beaten trail, particularly in the north: Nueva Segovia, Jinotega, Matagalpa, and Jalapa, as well as eastern parts of Boaco. Loose mines don't lie scattered randomly in the hillsides; they were placed at strategic locations, like radio towers, bridges, air strips, and known Contra border crossings. The locals are your best sources of information. They'll be able to tell you if there were battles or heavy Contra presence in the area, if there are known minefields, and if the OAS teams have already passed through. In towns like El Cuá and Bocay, you'll find parcels of land in chest-high weeds even though the land on both sides is intensely farmed. Ask around, and look for the yellow "Area Minada" signs, then move on.

Numerous international organizations work both to clear minefields around the world, such as the UN-sponsored Adopt-a-Minefield program (www.landmines.org), and to ban the devices (www.icbl.org).

There are 15 species of poisonous snakes in Nicaragua, but your chance of seeing one is extremely rare, unless you're going deep into the bush. In that case, walk softly and carry a big machete. Keep an eye out for 1 of 11 pit viper species (family *Viperidae*), especially the infamous fer-de-lance *(Bothrops asper)*, or *Barba Amarilla;* the most aggressive and dangerous snake in Central America, the fer-de-lance is mostly confined to the humid central highlands and the Caribbean coast. Less common pit vipers, but occasionally seen in western parts of the country, are the Ponzigua *(Porthidium ophryomegas);* the Central American rattlesnake *(Crotalus durissus),* known in Spanish as *cascabel;* and a relative of the copperhead, the Cantil, or Castellana, *(Agkistrodon bilineatus).* In addition, there are four rarely seen species of the *Elapidae* family (three coral snakes and the pelagic sea snake). Remember, there are many coral mimics out there with various versions of the famous colored markings; the true coral (only one species of which is found on the west side of the country) has ring markings in only this order: red, yellow, black, yellow.

Chagas' Disease

The Chagas bug *(Trypanosoma cruzi)* is a large, recognizable insect, also called the kissing bug, assassin bug, and cone-nose. In Spanish it's known as *chinche,* but this word is also used for many other types of beetle-like creatures. The Chagas bug bites its victim (usually on the face, close to the lips), sucks its fill of blood, and, for the coup de grace, defecates on the newly created wound. Chagas bugs are present in Nicaragua, found mostly in poor *campesino* structures of crumbling adobe. Besides the downright insult of being bitten, sucked, and pooped on, the Chagas bug's biggest menace is the disease it carries of the same name, which manifests itself in 2 percent of its victims. The first symptoms include swollen glands and a fever that appear 1–2 weeks after the bite. The disease then goes into a 5–30-year remission phase. If and when it reappears, Chagas' disease causes the lining of the heart to swell, sometimes resulting in death. There is no cure.

CRIME

Believe it or not, Nicaragua is, for the moment, still considered one of the safest countries in all of Latin America. If you're traveling south from Honduras, El Salvador, or Guatemala, you should feel your anxiety level drop noticeably—Nicaragua has been more successful at preventing the gang violence that has plagued its northern neighbors. You're more likely to be harassed than attacked in Nicaragua, and most physical assaults involve alcohol. Avoid traveling alone at night or while intoxicated, and pay the extra dollar or two for a cab. Women should not take cabs when the driver has a friend riding up front.

Pick-pocketing (or hat/watch/bag snatching) occurs occasionally in crowded places or buses, but again, this is a situation that can usually be avoided by reducing your desirability as a target and paying attention. Try to avoid urban buses in Managua and, whenever possible but especially when visiting the markets, avoid wearing flashy jewelry, watches, or sunglasses. Keep your cash divided up and hidden in a money belt, sock, bra, or underwear.

If you are the victim of a crime, report it to the local police department immediately (dial 118). Remember, if you've insured any of your possessions, you won't be reimbursed without a copy of the official police report. Nicaraguan police have good intentions but few resources, lacking even gasoline for the few patrol cars or motorcycles they have—don't be surprised if you are asked to help fill up a vehicle with gas. This is not uncommon, and remember that a full tank of gas should cost no more than $30. Travelers are often shocked to find that the police occasionally do recover stolen merchandise. While police corruption does exist—Nicaraguan police earn a pitiful $55–60 per month—the Nicaraguan police force is notably more honest and helpful than in some Central American nations.

Bigger cities, like Estelí and Chinandega, have their shady neighborhoods to avoid, and, because of its size and sprawl, Managua is the most dangerous of Nicaraguan cities. Still, it's a pretty simple task to stay out of the unsafe *barrios.* Although still nowhere near the urban violence being experienced in nearby Honduras and El Salvador, worsening poverty and unemployment have led to a surge in gang membership in the Nicaragua's poorer neighborhoods, and drug use—including crack—is also reportedly on the rise. Still, by not entering unknown areas, not walking at night, and sticking with other people, you can reduce the chances of anything bad happening.

In general, the countryside of Nicaragua is peaceful and safe. Until a few years ago, the one exception was El Triangulo Minero, a mountainous northeastern region around the mining towns of La Rosita, Bonanza, and Siuna. The area was home to a loose band of armed ex-soldiers infatuated with the bandit lifestyle and calling themselves FUAC (Frente Unido Andrés Castro). Today, however, most of their members and leaders have been hunted down and picked off by the army and police, notably in a few gun battles in 2001.

There have been no attacks on foreigners with the 1999 exception of Manley Guarducci, a Canadian mining engineer who was kidnapped and held for ransom. He was released five weeks later, unharmed and unshaken in his desire to remain in Nicaragua.

Always check the latest crime and U.S. State Department reports. In general, avoid the wilds outside Quilalí, Waslala, and the entire Triangulo Minero.

Illegal Drugs

Nicaragua is part of the underground highway that transports cocaine and heroin from South America to North America and, as such, is under a lot of pressure from the United States to crack down on drug traffickers passing through in vehicles or in boats off the Atlantic coast. Drug-related crime is rapidly increasing on the Atlantic coast, particularly in Bluefields and Puerto Cabezas. All travelers in Nicaragua are subject to local drug-possession and use laws, which include stiff fines and prison sentences of up to 30 years.

Marijuana, an herb that grows naturally and quite well in the soils and climate of Nicaragua, is known locally as *la mota, el monte,* or, in one remote Matagalpa valley, *pim-pirim-pím.* Marijuana

prohibition is alive and well in Nicaragua, despite regular use of the plant throughout the population. This controversial anti-ganja policy (critics call it a waste of public funds) allows harsh penalties for possession of even tiny quantities of *cannabis sativa,* for both nationals and tourists alike. Canine and bag searches at airports, docks along the Atlantic coast, and at the Honduran and Costa Rican border crossings are the norm, not the exception.

As a foreign, hip-looking tourist, you may be offered pot at some point during your trip, especially on the Atlantic coast and in San Juan del Sur. The proposal may be a harmless invitation to get high on the beach, or it may be from a hustler or stool pigeon who is about to rip you off and/or get you arrested. Use the same common sense you would anywhere in the world, with the added knowledge that Nicaraguan jails are a major bummer.

Prostitution

The world's oldest business is one facet of Nicaragua's economy that has more than tripled in recent years, especially in Managua, Granada, Corinto, and border/trucking towns like Somotillo. Though illegal, *puterías* (whorehouses), thinly disguised as "beauty salons" or "massage parlors," operate with virtual impunity, and every strip club in Managua has a bank of rooms behind the stage, some with an actual cashier stationed at the door. Then there are the commercial sex workers on Carretera Masaya, and the nation's numerous auto-hotels, which rent rooms by the hour. The situation is nowhere near as developed as the sex tourism industries of places like Thailand and Costa Rica, but it is undeniable that foreigners have contributed in no small way to Nicaragua's sex economy. Travelers considering indulging should think seriously about the social impacts that result from perpetuating this institution, and should start by reading the section on AIDS above.

BEGGING

Inevitably, it is assumed that foreigners in Nicaragua have lots and lots of money. You can definitely expect to have poor children and adults ask you for spare change wherever you travel, usually by either a single outstretched index finger or a cupped, empty hand, both accompanied with an insistent, *"Chele, deme un peso."* It's low-key, nothing like the aggressive beggars in countries like India, so don't be worried or afraid. If you are against giving such handouts, employ the finger wag and keep walking. If you want to contribute, one *córdoba* is the traditional amount, and feel free to use the transaction as a way to initiate a conversation.

Another poignant sight, encountered at sidewalk restaurants and market eateries, are wide-eyed, hungry children watching you eat just as eagerly as the skeletal dogs standing behind them. Your leftovers will not go to waste here as they would at home—a small concession. In many cities, however, increasing numbers of adolescents asking for money are *huele-pegas* (glue sniffers) and your money will only go to buy them more of H. B. Fuller's finest. *Huele-pegas* are identified by glazed-over eyes, unkempt appearances, and sometimes a jar of glue tucked under a dirty shirt. Do not give them money, but feel free to give them some time, attention, and maybe a little food.

Information and Services

MONEY

Currency

Since 1912, Nicaragua's currency has been the *córdoba*, named after Francisco Hernández de Córdoba, the Spanish founder of the colony of Nicaragua. It is divided into 100 *centavos* or 10 *reales*. In common usage, the *córdoba* is also referred to as a *peso*. The U.S. dollar is also an official currency in Nicaragua and the only foreign currency you can hope to exchange (although many communities along the Río San Juan also use Costa Rican *colones*). Travelers from nations other than the United States should bring their money to Nicaragua in U.S. dollars. The currencies of neighboring Central American nations can only be exchanged on the borders. Even in Managua, trying to exchange Central American currency is nearly impossible. As of January 2001, one bank—Bancentro—exchanges the euro, but the rate is not favorable.

The runaway inflation of the Sandinista years (as much as 30,000 percent) is now a mere memory, and the currency these days is relatively stable. However, to offset inflation, the *córdoba* has been steadily devalued since its inception at the rate of approximately US$.37 every six months and has led to the introduction in 2003 of a fancy new C$500 bill for larger purchases. You can do the arithmetic yourself before arriving in Nicaragua, or find the latest rates at the Central Bank of Nicaragua's website (www.bcn.gob.ni).

Costs

Nicaragua is still a budget traveler's paradise, as prices for lodging and food are lower than other Central American nations, notably Costa Rica. You can comfortably exist in Nicaragua on $20 per day, less if you're not traveling and have simple needs. Because there's more to do in Managua than other cities, and taxi costs add up, budget a little more ($25–30 per day) while in the capital. Needless to say, you can

travel for less by eating the way the locals do and forgoing the jalapeño steak and beer, but why would you want to? Budget travelers interested in stretching their money to the maximum should eat at *fritangas* and market stalls, take the slow bus, and avoid prolonged stays in the major cities.

Bank Machines

Known in Spanish as *cajeras automáticas,* ATMs are no longer a novelty to Nicaragua—since 1999, they've appeared in dozens of gas stations all over Managua. Any bank card affiliated with the Cirrus logo will work. You will receive your cash in *córdobas,* and you won't get a good exchange rate.

Wiring Money

There's a branch of Western Union in just about every midsize and large city in Nicaragua. Western Union is the most convenient way for someone to wire you cash, but the transaction fee is steep at 25 percent.

Bank Hours

Unless noted otherwise in this book, all bank hours are 8:30 A.M.–4 P.M. Monday–Friday and 8:30–noon Saturday. Nicaraguans receive their pay on the 15th and 30th or 31st of every month. Should you need to go to a bank on those days, you can expect the lines to be extra long. Bide your time by watching businesspeople carry away large sums of cash in brown paper lunch bags.

Traveler's Checks

U.S.-dollar *cheques viajeros* are accepted in some banks, notably Bancentro, one of the only places to cash a non–American Express check. Checks for currencies other than U.S. dollars will not be cashed. You will need to show your passport to cash traveler's checks, and be sure that your signature matches your previous one or you'll convert your precious dollars into a worthless piece of paper. In general, with so many ATMs and money changers around, traveler's checks are probably more hassle than they're worth in Nicaragua.

Credit Cards

Nicaragua is largely a cash society, but in the last couple of years (thanks to a company called Credomatic), hotels and restaurants that accept credit cards (Visa, MasterCard, American Express, or Diners Club) have become more common throughout the country. Always check ahead, though, because credit cards are still not ubiquitous.

Sales Tax

Nicaragua's sales tax (IGV or Impuesto General de Valor) is a whopping 15 percent—the highest in Central America. You'll find it automatically applied to the bill at nicer restaurants, fancy hotels, and upscale shops in major cities. Elsewhere, sales tax is casually dismissed. Should you decide to splurge on a fancy dinner (places where you'd expect to spend more than $6–10 a meal), expect to pay 25 percent of your bill for tax and tip. Prices in this book do not include the IGV.

Tipping

In better restaurants, a 10–15 percent *propina* (tip) will be graciously added on to your bill, even if the food was undercooked, the beer flat, and the service atrocious. You are under no obligation to pay it if it is unmerited. You might want to give a little something after getting your hair cut: 10 percent is appropriate. Skycaps at the International Airport in Managua will jostle to carry your luggage out to a waiting taxi. Tip what you'd like (a few dollars is appropriate) and never accept the services of someone not wearing an official airport identity badge. Taxi drivers and bartenders are rarely tipped and don't expect to be unless they are exceptionally friendly or go out of their way for you. If you accept the offer of children trying to carry your bags, find you a hotel, or anything else, you have entered into an unspoken agreement to give them a *córdoba* or two.

Bargaining

Looking for a good deal is a sport in Nicaragua—half social, half business, and is expected with most outdoor market vendors and taxi drivers. But be warned: Bargaining is *al suave!* Aggressive, prolonged haggling is not cool, won't affect the price, and may leave ill feelings. To start off

CAVEAT EMPTOR:
BUYING REAL ESTATE IN NICARAGUA

For better or worse, Nicaragua is the latest tropical country chosen by international speculators with hopes of carefree retirement and lucrative appreciation on their new plot of Central American soil. A steady stream of aging baby boomers, aspiring financial managers, and alcoholic ne'er-do-wells on the run from ex-spouses and the taxman continue to find their way to southwestern Nicaragua. Healthy foreign investment? Or the new face of Yankee imperialism? You decide.

Potential real estate moguls typically wind up in Granada (and its nearby *isletas*), Rivas, and San Juan del Sur, all of which buzz with both independent and corporate real estate agents of mostly U.S. and Canadian origin. Before signing that check, however, take a breath, open your eyes, and ask a lot of questions. Start by visiting your embassy. The U.S. Embassy (www.usembassy.state.gov/Managua) has made land reform a priority for its relations with the Nicaraguan government; experienced buyers also seek out Pro-Nicaragua (www.pronicaragua.org), an "Investment Promotion Agency" that can help with information and contacts.

Good deals are still found, but not without some risk. Much of the valued property that is up for grabs has two distinct and viable chains of title ownership: one that dates back to the Somoza period, and one that dates to the Sandinista government's failed agrarian reforms in which they confiscated land, Robin Hood–style, and redistributed it to the masses. Some of this land is still owned by cooperatives and *campesino* families, and some was given to powerful supporters (and lead-

ers) of the Sandinistas. In the aftermath of the revolution, many of these seizures have been contested, many still stand, and very frequently two or three people present legitimate claims to the same lot. Make sure you—and your lawyer—know the history of the property back to 1978, and buy title insurance just in case. More than one new land owner has been surprised to have a stranger confront him with an obviously falsified property title. The Nicaraguan court system may or may not back you up. Title insurance is valuable because the companies that offer it not only research and defend your title, they also know their way around the Nicaraguan court system, no small thing. In the case of contested property, your policy may cover fraud and forgery. Florida-based First American Title Insurance Company is at present the only option (U.S. toll-free 877/641-6767).

Don't completely entrust the job to others—do your own research on the region, the lot, community relations, year-round road conditions, etc. Was an environmental-impact statement done, as is required by law? If so, what did it conclude? Does your new piece of paradise have a fresh-water supply? Lastly, watch out for the word "beachfront." Under Nicaraguan law, land 30–80 meters from the high tide line (depending on who you ask) cannot be bought or sold, but only leased from either the national government or the local municipality as a "concession." Newly elected municipal governments (i.e. small town mayors with grudges) often change policies on concessions, frustrating many a would-be gringo beach bum.

---

the process, after you are given the initial price, act surprised and use one of the following phrases: *"¿Cuánto es lo menos?"* (What is your lowest price?) or *"¿Nada menos?"* (Nothing less?).

Remember these guidelines when bargaining:

• You can't bargain for everything; this includes small items for less than $1, all bus fares, and most lodging expenses.

• Bargaining is social and friendly, or at least courteous. Keep your temper under wraps and always smile.

• Go back and forth a maximum of two or three times, and then either agree or walk away. Remember that some Nicaraguans, to save face, may lose a profit.

• Once you make a deal, it's done. If you think you've been ripped off, remember the $5 you got overcharged is still less than you'd pay for a

Know Nicaragua

double-tall mocha latte back home. Keep it in perspective and be a good sport.

•When bargaining with taxi drivers in Managua, bargain hard, but agree on a price before you enter the cab—once the vehicle is moving, your leverage has vanished in a puff of acrid, black exhaust.

MAPS

The overall champion map of Nicaragua is published by International Travel Map (ITM, Canada tel. 604/687-3320, www.itmb.com), scaled at 1:750,000, colored to show relief, and with good road and river detail. They also offer an excellent Central America regional map. It's easily found in many bookstores and travel shops as well, but not so easily in Nicaragua.

Nelles Maps' Central America map (1:1,750,000) offers a quality overview of the region (plus more detail on Costa Rica) and is good if you are traveling the whole area and don't intend to venture too far off the beaten track.

INETER, the Nicaraguan Institute of Territorial Studies, produces the only complete series of 1:50,000 maps (or "topo quads") of Nicaragua. Produced in the 1960s and photo-revised in the 1980s with Soviet help, these are the most detailed topographical maps of Nicaragua that exist. They can be purchased from the INETER office in Managua (and occasionally at regional offices) for $3 each. The Managua office is located across from Policlinica Oriental and Immigration, tel. 505/249-2768; open 8 A.M.–4:30 P.M. Monday–Friday.

Tactical Pilotage Charts TPC K-25B and TPC K-25C cover north and south Nicaragua, respectively, with some coverage of Costa Rica, Panamá, and Honduras at 1:500,000 scale. Designed for pilots, these maps have good representation of topography and are useful if you do any adventuring in the eastern parts of the country (far easier than carrying a stack of topo maps). Many smaller towns are shown, but only major roads.

TOURISM INFORMATION

The Instituto Nicaragüense de Turismo (INTUR, one block west and one north of the Crowne Plaza Hotel, tel. 505/222-3333, www.intur.gob.ni), an institution of the national government, is based in Managua, with a number of regional offices around the country. They staff a kiosk in the airport as well, which you'll pass after immigration. How useful INTUR is to you depends on your agenda in Nicaragua; most offices can give you a list of the year's upcoming festivals, a fistful of hotel brochures, and in some places, can help arrange tours with local operators. INTUR's regional offices are small and under-budgeted and there is poor coordination with local governments in Sandinista-run cities. INTUR Managua produces and sells maps as well as local guides and listings, and has a visitor's desk for tourists, located, open 8:30 A.M.–2 P.M. Monday–Friday.

Another good resource is the *Guía Telefónica* (national phone book), with basic tourism information and updated hotel listings; pick up your own free copy of at the Publicar office next to the Plaza España Colonia supermarket.

FILM AND PHOTOGRAPHY
Film Processing and Supplies

Quality film and basic camera supplies are widely available in Nicaragua, and there are modern camera shops in most cities. Film processing is considerably more expensive (up to $20 a roll with no doubles) and often lower quality than back home. The biggest company is Kodak Express with a presence in nearly every major city (see Managua services for info on their largest store). Black-and-white film and slide film are rarely available and processed at great expense. No one will know what to do with your digital camera's card, so come prepared to do your own downloading or with a few backup cards.

Photo Tips and Etiquette

Cameras are by no means foreign objects in Nicaragua, but in many towns and neighborhoods, they are owned only by a few local entrepreneurs who take pictures at weddings, baptisms, graduations, etc. and then sell the print to the subject. Because of this, some Nicaraguans may expect that the photo you are taking is for them, and that you will either charge them for the photo or that you are going to send them a free copy. In general, people love getting their pictures taken, but often insist on dressing up, stiffening their bodies, and wiping all traces of emotion from their faces. The only way to avoid this (apart from making monkey noises to get them to laugh) is to take candid, unsolicited photos, something adults may perceive as bizarre and possibly rude. A solution is to ask first, concede to a few serious poses, and then snap away later when they are more unsuspecting but accustomed to your happy trigger finger. If you promise to send a copy, take down their address and actually do it.

COMMUNICATIONS AND MEDIA

Mail

The national postal system is called Correos de Nicaragua, and it is surprisingly effective and reliable. Every city has at least one post office, often near the central plaza and adjacent to the telephone service (but not always). Legal-size letters

Nicaraguan phone booths are operated with prepaid calling cards.

© RANDY WOOD

and postcards cost about $.50 to the United States, and a little more to Europe. Post offices in many cities have a gorgeous selection of stamps. Correo is open standard business hours (with some variations), is almost always closed during lunch, and is open until noon on Saturday.

To receive packages, have the sender use a padded envelope instead of a box, even if the shipment must be split into several pieces; keep the package as unassuming as possible, and try writing Dios Te Ama (God Loves You) on the envelope for a little help from above. In general, mail service to Nicaragua is excellent and reliable, even to remote areas, provided you use envelopes and keep packages relatively small. Boxes, on the other hand, of whatever size, are routed through the *aduana* (customs). This means traipsing to their office at the airport in Managua and enduring a horrific and uncaring bureaucracy intent on not giving you your package. Most major international courier services have offices all over Nicaragua, including DHL and Federal Express, but they, too are subject to dealing with the *aduana*.

Telephone and Fax

The national phone company, completely privatized in 2003, is ENITEL (Empresa Nicaragüense de Telecomunicaciónes), but it is just as commonly referred to by its old name, TELCOR. Every major city has an ENITEL, as do most small towns. In many villages without an ENITEL office, you'll find a local family renting out their private phone or contracted through ENITEL.

When you enter the ENITEL building, go to the front desk and tell the operator where you'd like to call. The operator will place the call for you, and if it goes through, will then send you to one of several private booths to receive it. When you complete the call, go back up to the front desk to pay. Alternately, look around for ENITEL and Publitel payphones, each requiring a different kind of prepaid card; there are also many Bell South coin-operated phones in corner stores, but these are usually more expensive.

Remember, when making calls within Nicaragua, you must prefix your number with a "0" when dialing out of your municipality or to any cell phone. Cell numbers begin with "88," "86," and "77," and cost extra to call. Satellite phones are wickedly expensive to call, begin with "892," and do not require a "0" beforehand.

Important numbers: information "113," long-distance and collect-call operators "110" and "116," police "118," firefighters "115" and "120," and Red Cross "128." A 24-hour Enitel customer service operator is available by dialing "121," and their main office in Managua is located 300 meters west of the Rotonda Centroamérica, second floor (tel. 505/278-3131, fax 505/278-4012, www.enitel.com.ni)

Most ENITEL offices have fax machines as well. A two-page international fax may cost you $4–5 to send; a local fax will cost about $1. Also check in copy shops, Internet providers, and post offices.

International Calls

Its ease and incredibly low cost have made Internet-based calling all the rage, especially in tourist sites with fast connections, like Granada, where competition drives rates to as low as $6 per hour to call the United States, Canada, or Europe. This phenomenon is sure to expand, the prices sure to fluctuate; always ask at the most modern Internet place in town about *llamadas internacionales.*

To make expensive, old-fashioned direct calls overseas, step up to the nearest Enitel desk and give them the number. You'll need to know your country code: Canada and the United States are "1," Germany is "49," Spain "34," France "33," and Great Britain and Ireland "44." A complete listing of the country codes you'll need is in the phone book.

You can also use of your calling card account from back home; tell the operator to connect you with the international bilingual operator for your company, or dial directly: AT&T tel. 1-800-0164, MCI 1-800-0166, Sprint 1-800-0171. Once you connect with the international operator, tell them your card's 800 number, then enter your card number and place your call as you would back home. In many larger cities, the ENITEL offices will have specially marked booths with direct hookups to international companies like MCI or AT&T, circumventing the need to use an operator.

Internet

The information superhighway came to Nicaragua as early as 1993 but wasn't widely accessible until 1999, when makeshift Internet cafés began appearing in Managua. Today, there are Internet cafés in just about every city in the nation, and even a number of small villages, where the web squeaks by on horrible dial-up lines, or hit-and-miss satellite connections.

If you are staying a significant time in Nicaragua, have your own computer, and would rather not use web-mail (web-based email accounts like Yahoo or Hotmail), there are several options for opening your own account, which you can access by dial-up anywhere in the country. IBW Communications (tel. 505/278-6328, www.ibw.com.ni) has reasonable monthly rates, including options with or without Internet access ($10 a month for an email account). For your own ibw.com.ni address, visit IBW's Managua office (200 meters north of the Semaforos ENITEL Villa Fontana), or one of its regional offices around the country. They will install the necessary software and configure your computer, as well as provide reliable tech support as long as you are a customer. Other options are Enitel or Cablenet (tel. 505/255-7280, www.cablenet.com.ni).

Macintosh

Most of Nicaragua is PC, but for Mac devotees and those who enjoy surfing with the best hardware on earth, the **iMac Center** (in Managua one block east and half-block south of the Semáforo UCA, tel. 505/270-5918) is a certified dealer and service provider, with all kinds of Macintosh-related services, repairs, and products (including iPods), plus cheap Internet service.

Newspapers and Magazines

Street vendors are out before 6 A.M. every day hawking the various daily papers, but you can often pick one up in most corner stores. *La Prensa* offers fairly conservative coverage and the front page contains a list of events for the week. *La Prensa* was so anti-Somoza in the 1970s, the dictator allegedly had the editor, Pedro Joaquín Chamorro, bumped off. Needless to say, it didn't help his press. Not long after the revolution, *La Prensa* turned anti-Sandinista and has remained so to this day. During election campaigns, *La Prensa* typically runs a regular series of "flashback" articles recalling the atrocities of the Contra war in the 1980s and dredging up every unresolved Sandinista scandal available. *El Nuevo Diario* is more blue-collar and sensationalist—its coverage of popular scandals is often hilarious.

International papers and magazines are sold in Managua at the Casa de Café, a kiosk on the first floor of the MetroCentro mall, and in the lobbies of the major hotels.

Between the Waves is a free English-language magazine, available in the airport, bookstores, and hotels.

WEIGHTS AND MEASURES
Time
Nicaragua is in standard time zone GMT-6, i.e., six hours earlier than London. Daylight saving time is not observed, which means that during standard time, Nicaragua is in Chicago's time zone, and during daylight saving time, it is one hour behind Chicago. Don't forget, no matter what your watch says, you're always on "Nica Time"—everything starts late, and your whining can't change it.

Electricity
Nicaragua uses the same electrical standards as the United States and Canada: 110V, 60 Hz. The shape of the electrical socket is the same as well. Travelers from Europe and Asia should consider bringing a power adapter if they want to make extensive use of electrical appliances brought from home. Laptop-computer users should bring a portable surge protector with them, as the electrical current in Nicaragua is highly variable. Spikes, brownouts, and outages are commonplace.

Measurements
Distances are almost exclusively in kilometers, although for smaller lengths, you'll occasionally hear feet, inches, yards, and the colonial Spanish *vara* (about a meter). The most commonly used land-area term is the *manzana*, another old measure, equal to 1.74 acres. Weights and volumes are a mix of metric and non-metric: Buy your gasoline in gallons, your chicken in pounds, and so on.

Know Nicaragua

Glossary

alcaldía: mayor's office
arroyo: stream or gully
artesanía: crafts
ayudante: "helper"—the guy on the bus who collects your fee after you find a seat
barrio: neighborhood
beneficio: coffee mill
bombero: firefighter
bravo: rough, strong, wild
cabo: cape
cafetín: light-food eatery
calle: street
cama matrimonial: "marriage bed"—motels and hotels use this term to refer to a double, queen, or king-sized bed; a bed meant for two people.
camión: truck
campesino: country folk
campo: countryside
carretera: highway, road
cayo: cay
centro de salud: public MINSA-run health clinic; there's one in most towns
centro recreativo: public recreation center
cerro: hill or mountain
cerveza, cervecita: beer
chele, chela: gringo, whitey
chinelas: rubber flip-flops
ciudad: city
colectivo: a shared taxi or passenger boat
colonía: neighborhood
comedor: cheap lunch counter
comida corriente: plate of the day
complejo: complex (of buildings)
cooperitiva: cooperative
cordillera: mountain range
córdoba: Nicaraguan currency
corriente: standard, base
coyote: illegal-immigrant smuggler; or profit-cutting middleman
cuajada: white, homemade, salty cheese
departamentos: subsection of Nicaragua, akin to states or counties
empalme: intersection of two roads
entrada: entrance

estero: estuary or marsh
expreso: express bus
farmacia: pharmacy, drugstore
fiestas patronales: Saint's Day parties held annually in every town and city
fresco: natural fruit drink
fritanga: street-side barbecue and fry-fest
gallo pinto: national mix of rice íní beans
gancho: gap in a fence
gaseosa: carbonated beverage
gringo: North American, or any foreigner
guaro: booze
guitarra: guitar
guitarrón: mariachi bass guitar
hospedaje: hostel, budget hotel
iglesia: church
isla: island
laguna: lake
lancha: small passenger boat
lanchero: lancha driver
malecón: waterfront
manzana: besides an apple, this is also a measure of land equal to 100 square varas, or 1.74 acres
mar: sea or ocean
mariachi: Mexican country/polka music
mercado: market
mesa/meseta: geographical plateau
mosquitero: mosquito net
muelle: dock, wharf
museo: museum
ordinario: local bus (also *ruteado*)
panga: small passenger boat
panguero: *panga* driver
pinche: stingy, cheap
playa: beach
pueblo: small town or village
pulpería: corner store
puro: cigar
quintal: 100-pound sack
rancheras: Mexican drinking songs
rancho: thatch-roofed restaurant or hut
rato: a short period of time
reserva: reserve or preserve
río: river

sala: living room
salida: exit, road out of town
salon: large living room, gallery
salto: waterfall
sierra: mountain range
suave: soft, easy, quiet
tope: a dead-end, or "T" intersection
tranquilo: mellow
urbano: public urban bus
vara: colonial unit of distance equal to roughly one meter
volcán: volcano

ABBREVIATIONS

ENEL: Empresa Nicaragüense de Electricidad (electric company)
ENITEL: Empresa Nicaragüense de Telecomunicaciónes (telephone company)
FSLN: Frente Sandinista de Liberación Nacional (Sandinista party)
IFA: (EEH-fa) East German troop transport, used commonly in Nicaraguan public transportation system; it probably stands for something in German, but in Nicaragua, it means *imposible frenar a tiempo* (impossible to brake on time).
INETER: Instituto Nicaragüense de Estudios Territoriales (government geography/geology institute)
MARENA: Ministerio del Ambiente y los Recursos Naturales (Ministry of Natural Resources and the Environment), administers Nicaragua's protected areas
MYA: Million Years Ago
NGO: Nongovernmental Organization
PCV: Peace Corps Volunteer
PLC: Partido Liberal Constitucionalista, the conservative anti-Sandinista party
SINAP: Sistema Nacional de Areas Protegidas (National System of Protected Areas)
UCA: Universidad de Centroamerica
UN: United Nations
UNAN: Universidad Nacional Autónoma de Nicaragua
USAID: United States Agency for International Development, channels congressionally approved foreign aid

Spanish Phrasebook

PRONUNCIATION GUIDE

Spanish pronunciation is much more regular than that of English, but there are still occasional variations.

Consonants

c — as "c" in "cat," before "a," "o," or "u"; like "s" before "e" or "i"
d — as "d" in "dog," except between vowels, then like "th" in "that"
g — before "e" or "i," like the "ch" in Scottish "loch"; elsewhere like "g" in "get"
h — always silent
j — like the English "h" in "hotel," but stronger
ll — like the "y" in "yellow"
ñ — like the "ni" in "onion"
r — always pronounced as strong "r"
rr — trilled "r"
v — similar to the "b" in "boy" (not as English "v")
y — similar to English, but with a slight "j" sound. When standing alone, it's pronounced like the "e" in "me".
z — like "s" in "same"
b, f, k, l, m, n, p, q, s, t, w, x — as in English

Vowels

a — as in "father," but shorter
e — as in "hen"
i — as in "machine"
o — as in "phone"
u — usually as in "rule"; when it follows a "q," the "u" is silent; when it follows an "h" or "g," it's pronounced like "w," except when it comes between "g" and "e" or "i," when it's also silent (unless it has an umlaut, when it is again pronounced as English "w")

Stress

Native English speakers frequently make errors of pronunciation by ignoring stress. All Spanish vowels—a, e, i, o, and u—carry accents that determine which syllable of a word gets emphasis. Often, stress seems unnatural to nonnative speakers—the surname Chávez, for instance, is stressed on the first syllable—but failure to observe this rule may mean that native speakers may not understand you.

NUMBERS

0 — cero
1 — uno (masculine)
1 — una (feminine)
2 — dos
3 — tres
4 — cuatro
5 — cinco
6 — seis
7 — siete
8 — ocho
9 — nueve
10 — diez
11 — once
12 — doce
13 — trece
14 — catorce
15 — quince
16 — dieciseis
17 — diecisiete
18 — dieciocho
19 — diecinueve
20 — veinte
21 — veintiuno
30 — treinta
40 — cuarenta
50 — cincuenta
60 — sesenta
70 — setenta
80 — ochenta
90 — noventa
100 — cien
101 — ciento y uno
200 — doscientos

1,000 — mil
10,000 — diez mil
1,000,000 — un millón

DAYS OF THE WEEK

Sunday — domingo
Monday — lunes
Tuesday — martes
Wednesday — miércoles
Thursday — jueves
Friday — viernes
Saturday — sábado

TIME

While Nicaraguans mostly use the 12-hour clock, in some instances, usually associated with plane or bus schedules, they may use the 24-hour military clock. Under the 24-hour clock, for example, *las nueve de la noche* (9 P.M.) would be *las 21 horas* (2100 hours).

What time is it? — ¿Qué hora es?
It's one o'clock — Es la una.
It's two o'clock — Son las dos.
At two o'clock — A las dos.
It's ten to three — Son las tres menos diez.
It's ten past three — Son las tres y diez.
It's three fifteen — Son las tres y cuarto.
It's two forty-five — Son las tres menos cuarto.
It's two thirty — Son las dos y media.
It's six A.M. — Son las seis de la mañana.
It's six P.M. — Son las seis de la tarde.
It's ten P.M. — Son las diez de la noche.
Today — hoy
Tomorrow — mañana
Morning — la mañana
Tomorrow morning — mañana por la mañana
Yesterday — ayer
Week — la semana
Month — mes
Year — año
Last night — anoche
The next day — el día siguiente

USEFUL WORDS AND PHRASES

Nicaraguans and other Spanish-speaking people consider formalities important. Whenever approaching anyone for information or some other reason, do not forget the appropriate salutation—good morning, good evening, etc. Standing alone, the greeting *hola* (hello) can sound brusque.

Hello. — Hola.
Good morning. — Buenos días.
Good afternoon. — Buenas tardes.
Good evening. — Buenas noches.
How are you? — ¿Cómo está?
Fine. — Muy bien.
And you? — ¿Y usted?
So-so. — Más o menos.
Thank you. — Gracias.
Thank you very much. — Muchas gracias.
You're very kind. — Muy amable.
You're welcome. — De nada (literally, "It's nothing.").
Yes — sí
No — no
I don't know. — No sé.
It's fine; okay — Está bien.
Good; okay — Bueno.
Please — por favor
Pleased to meet you. — Mucho gusto.
Excuse me (physical) — Perdóneme.
Excuse me (speech) — Discúlpeme.
I'm sorry. — Lo siento.
Goodbye. — Adiós.
See you later. — Hasta luego (literally, "until later").
More — más
Less — menos
Better — mejor
Much, a lot — mucho
A little — un poco
Large — grande
Small — pequeño, chico
Quick, fast — rápido
Slowly — despacio
Bad — malo

Difficult — difícil
Easy — fácil
He/She/It is gone; as in "She left" or "he's gone." — Ya se fue.
I don't speak Spanish well. — No hablo bien el español.
I don't understand. — No entiendo.
How do you say . . . in Spanish? — ¿Cómo se dice . . . en español?
Do you understand English? — ¿Entiende el inglés?
Is English spoken here? (Does anyone here speak English?) — ¿Se habla inglés aquí?

TERMS OF ADDRESS

When in doubt, use the formal *usted* (you) as a form of address. If you wish to dispense with formality and feel that the desire is mutual, you can say, *"Me puedes tutear"* ("You can call me "tu").

I — yo
You (formal) — usted
you (familiar) — tú
He/him — él
She/her — ella
We/us — nosotros
You (plural) — ustedes
They/them (all males or mixed gender) — ellos
They/them (all females) — ellas
Mr., sir — señor
Mrs., madam — señora
Miss, young lady — señorita
Wife — esposa
Husband — marido or esposo
Friend — amigo (male), amiga (female)
Sweetheart — novio (male), novia (female)
Son, daughter — hijo, hija
Brother, sister — hermano, hermana
Father, mother — padre, madre
Grandfather, grandmother — abuelo, abuela

GETTING AROUND

Where is . . . ? — ¿Dónde está . . . ?
How far is it to . . . ? — ¿A cuanto está . . . ?

from . . . to . . . — de . . . a . . .
Highway — la carretera
Road — el camino
Street — la calle
Block — la cuadra
Kilometer — kilómetro
North — norte
South — sur
West — oeste; poniente
East — este; oriente
Straight ahead — al derecho; adelante
To the right — a la derecha
To the left — a la izquierda

ACCOMMODATIONS

Is there a room? — ¿Hay cuarto?
May I (we) see it? — ¿Puedo (podemos) verlo?
What is the rate? — ¿Cuál es el precio?
Is that your best rate? — ¿Es su mejor precio?
Is there something cheaper? — ¿Hay algo más económico?
Single room — un sencillo
Double room — un doble
Room for a couple — matrimonial
Key — llave
With private bath — con baño
With shared bath — con baño general; con baño compartido
Hot water — agua caliente
Cold water — agua fría
Shower — ducha
Electric shower — ducha eléctrica
Towel — toalla
Soap — jabón
Toilet paper — papel higiénico
Air conditioning — aire acondicionado
Fan — abanico; ventilador
Blanket — frazada; manta
Sheets — sábanas

PUBLIC TRANSPORT

Bus stop — la parada
Bus terminal — terminal de buses
Airport — el aeropuerto
Launch — lancha; tiburonera
Dock — muelle
I want a ticket to . . . — Quiero un pasaje a . . .
I want to get off at . . . — Quiero bajar en . . .
Here, please. — Aquí, por favor.
Where is this bus going? — ¿Adónde va este autobús?
Round-trip — ida y vuelta
What do I owe? — ¿Cuánto le debo?

FOOD

Menu — la carta, el menú
Glass — taza
Fork — tenedor
Knife — cuchillo
Spoon — cuchara
Napkin — servilleta
Soft drink — agua fresca
Coffee — café
Cream — crema
Tea — té
Sugar — azúcar
Drinking water — agua pura, agua potable
Bottled carbonated water — agua mineral con gas
Bottled uncarbonated water — agua sin gas
Beer — cerveza
Wine — vino
Milk — leche
Juice — jugo
Eggs — huevos
Bread — pan
Watermelon — sandía
Banana — banano
Plantain — plátano
Apple — manzana
Orange — naranja
Meat (without) — carne (sin)
Beef — carne de res
Chicken — pollo; gallina
Fish — pescado
Shellfish — mariscos
Shrimp — camarones
Fried — frito
Roasted — asado
Barbecued — a la parrilla

Breakfast — desayuno
Lunch — almuerzo
Dinner (often eaten in late afternoon) — comida
Dinner, or a late-night snack — cena
The check, or bill — la cuenta

MAKING PURCHASES

I need . . . — Necesito . . .
I want . . . — Deseo . . . or Quiero . . .
I would like . . . (more polite) — Quisiera . . .
How much does it cost? — ¿Cuánto cuesta?
What's the exchange rate? — ¿Cuál es el tipo de cambio?
May I see . . . ? — ¿Puedo ver . . . ?
This one — ésta/ésto
Expensive — caro
Cheap — barato

Cheaper — más barato
Too much — demasiado

HEALTH

Help me please. — Ayúdeme por favor.
I am ill. — Estoy enfermo.
Pain — dolor
Fever — fiebre
Stomach ache — dolor de estómago
Vomiting — vomitar
Diarrhea — diarrea
Drugstore — farmacia
Medicine — medicina
Pill, tablet — pastilla
Birth-control pills — pastillas anticonceptivas
Condom — condón, preservativo

Further Study

BOOKS

A prodigious amount of literature emerged from the Revolutionary years, when Nicaragua was the hemisphere's most celebrated and criticized Socialist experiment of the century. Because of this, you'll find a great deal more resources on Nicaragua in the used-book section, even as Nicaraguan authors, such as Ernesto Cardenal, Gioconda Belli, and Ricardo Pasos Marciaq, continue to publish and be celebrated the world over.

The Revolution

Probably 98 percent of all books ever written about Nicaragua deal with the Sandinista revolution and ensuing civil war. Of these, many were written by journalists assigned to the country in the 1980s—their books are often unique hybrids of history, novel, travelogue, ethnography, and political-science text. Also, being the literary people they are, participants in the revolution wrote a great deal of books, and readers with some time on their hands can experience some fascinating inside perspectives on what has been called "one of the great contemporary events of the Western Hemisphere."

Babb, Florence. *After Revolution: Mapping Gender and Cultural Politics in Neoliberal Nicaragua.* Austin, Texas: University of Texas Press, 2001. Professor of Anthropology and Women's Studies at the University of Iowa, Babb has also published scores of academic papers on Nicaragua, mainly on issues of gender and sexuality.

Barrios de Chamorro, Violeta. *Dreams of the Heart.* Simon & Schuster, 1996. A very readable and human history of Nicaragua from the Somoza years through Doña Violeta's electoral triumph in 1990.

Belli, Gioconda. *The Country Under My Skin: A Memoir of Love and War.* Anchor Books, 2003. Stephen Kinzer writes, "Belli's memoir shows us a side of the Sandinista revolution we have not seen. It also introduces us to an astute veteran of two eternal wars, one between the sexes and one that pits the world's poor against its rich. But it is not really an insider's account of the Sandinista regime. No woman will ever be able to write such an account, because no woman was ever admitted to the Sandinista elite. Belli and other Sandinista women failed utterly in their attempt to penetrate the all-male core of revolutionary power."

Cabezas, Omar. *Fire from the Mountain (La Montaña es Algo Más que una Grán Estapa Verde)*. Crown, 1985. A ribald, vernacular account of what it's like to be a guerrilla soldier in the mountains of Nicaragua; one of the few books about the early stages of the revolution.

Cardenal, Ernesto; Walsh, Donald D. (translator). *The Gospel in Solentiname*. Orbis Books, 1979. These are the transcripts of the masses on Solentiname that helped spawn the Liberation Theology movement.

Chomsky, Noam. *Turning the Tide: U.S. Intervention in Central America and the Struggle for Peace*. South End Press, 1985. Succinctly and powerfully shows how U.S. Central American policies implement broader U.S. economic, military, and social aims.

Davis, Peter. *Where is Nicaragua?* Simon & Schuster, 1987. Davis breaks down the revolution and Contra war, and ties it all into the country's history; he articulates the complexity of the situation in a graspable manner.

Dickey, Christopher. *With the Contras*. Simon & Schuster, 1985. Dickey was the *Washington Post* correspondent in Honduras, and his book makes an excellent complement to Kinzer, who spent much more time with the Sandinistas.

Gentile, William Frank. *Nicaragua: Photographs by William Frank Gentile;* Introduction by William M. LeoGrande; An Interview with Sergio Ramírez Mercado. W. W. Norton & Company, 1989. These are some of the deepest, most powerful photos you'll ever see, with fantastic juxtapositions of Contra and FSLN soldiers.

Kinzer, Stephen. *Blood of Brothers: Life and War in Nicaragua*. G. P. Putnam's Sons, 1991. If you're only going to read one book, this is the one.

Kinzer, the *New York Times* Managua bureau chief during the war, sensed that Nicaragua was "a country with more to tell the world than it had been able to articulate, a country with a message both political and spiritual."

Kunzle, David. *The Murals of Revolutionary Nicaragua 1979–1992*. University of California Press, 1995. Many murals were strictly political, but most intertwined the revolutionary process with cultural, historical, and literary themes. All are celebrated in Kunzle's book; 83-page introduction and 100 color plates.

Randall, Margaret. *Risking a Somersault in the Air: Conversations with Nicaraguan Writers*. San Francisco: Solidarity Publications, 1984. Just as much about Nicaraguan literature as it is about the revolution, this is a fascinating series of interviews with Nicaraguan authors and poets, most of whom were part of the FSLN revolution and government.

Randall, Margaret. *Sandino's Daughters: Testimonies of Nicaraguan Women in Struggle*. New Star Books, 1981. Randall's book explores the role of feminism in the Sandinista revolution, via a series of interviews with participants.

Rushdie, Salman. *The Jaguar Smile*. Elisabeth Sifton Books, 1987. Representing the pro-Sandinista Nicaragua Solidarity Campaign in London, Rushdie takes readers on a poetic, passionate jaunt through Nicaragua as part of a government cultural campaign; he offers a careful (if short) examination of their policies.

Sklar, Holly. *Washington's War on Nicaragua*. South End Press, 1988. Sklar offers an inspection of the Washington politics behind the Contra war.

Zimmerman, Matilde. *Sandinista: Carlos Fonseca and the Nicaraguan Revolution*. Duke University Press, 2001. This is the first English-language biography of the legendary leader of the FSLN and arguably the most important and influential figure of the post-1959 revolutionary generation in Latin America.

Nicaraguans

Lancaster, Roger N. *Life Is Hard: Machismo, Danger, and the Intimacy of Power in Nicaragua.* University of California Press, 1992. Lancaster is an anthropologist and this is an ethnography studying not current events, but their effect on the Nicaraguan individual and family. It is intimate and offers details about Nicaraguan life that one can only get living with the people in their very homes. Also, Lancaster pays attention to issues often passed over, like homosexuality, domestic violence, broken families, and the roots of machismo.

Plunkett, Hazel. *In Focus Nicaragua: A Guide to the People, Politics and Culture.* Interlink Books, 1999. This 100-page overview to Nicaragua also includes Nicaraguans in the 1990s.

Squier, Ephraim George. *Nicaragua: Its People, Scenery, Monuments, and the Proposed Interoceanic Canal.* D. Appleton, 1852. Squier remains one of Nicaragua's most prolific writers; this massive, multivolume tome is available for hundreds of dollars in rare bookstores. The discussion is divided into five parts in which he describes geography and topography; the events during the author's residence, including accounts of his explorations; observations on the proposed canal; notes on the indigenous of the country, including information regarding geographical distribution, languages, institutions, religions, and customs; and the political history of the country since its independence from Spain.

Poetry, Language, and Literature

Morelli, Marco. *Rubén's Orphans.* Painted Rooster Press, 2001. An anthology of contemporary Nicaraguan poets, with English translations.

Rabella, Joaquim and Pallais, Chantal. *Vocabulario Popular Nicaragüense.* This big, red linguistic bible is a wonderful, celebratory dictionary of Nicaraguan

Spanish, complete with regional usages, sayings, and plenty of profanities; available in many bookstores in Managua.

White, Steven, translator. *Poets of Nicaragua: A Bilingual Anthology 1918–1970.* Unicorn Press, 1983.

Miscellaneous

Hulme, Krekel, and O'Reilly. *Not Just Another Nicaragua Travel Guide.* Mango Publications, 1990. An ebullient and fascinating guidebook for traveling Sandinista Nicaragua in the 1980s. Get it if you can find it; only 1,000 copies were printed.

Marriot, Edward. *Savage Shore: Life and Death with Nicaragua's Last Shark Hunters.* Owl Books, 2001. A curious and descriptive journey up the Río San Juan and beyond.

FILM

The World Stopped Watching, a 2003 Canadian film by Peter Raymont and Harold Crooks, was shot in 56 mm. Nicaragua dropped from the spotlight after the end of the Contra war. This documentary, shot in late 2002 and early 2003, picks up the pieces of what happened next. Essentially, this is a sequel to *The World is Watching,* a critically acclaimed documentary from the 1980s, involving many of the same characters.

Walker, a 1987 anachronistic biography of the infamous soldier-of-fortune from Tennessee, stars Ed Harris. Filmmaker Alex Cox (of *Sid & Nancy* fame), wanted to show that "nothing had changed in the 140-odd years between William Walker's genocidal campaign and that of Oliver North and his goons." One reviewer wrote, "What is so amazing about *Walker* is that it got made at all. It's a film condemning capitalism funded by a capitalist studio. Since it was filmed on location, its production money went straight into a country that the United States was currently at war with." Critics mostly panned the film as "sophomoric black comedy," but confirmed Nicaphiles will surely get a kick out of it.

Carla's Song, a 1996 drama by Ken Loach, stars Robert Carlyle and Oyanka Cabezas. Set in 1987, Scottish bus driver George Lennox meets Carla, a Nicaraguan exile living a precarious, profoundly sad life in Glasgow. George takes her back to her village in northern Nicaragua to find out what has happened to her family, boyfriend, and country. Notable for its real and gritty location shots, in both Scotland and Nicaragua, *Carla's Song* is enjoyable and touching and, notes its writer, Paul Laverty, "is just one of thousands of statistics, hopefully reminding the viewer that everyone in this war had a story." Carla's Song was awarded a gold medal at the Italian Film Festival in Venice.

Internet Resources

Moon Handbooks and the Authors
Moon Handbooks: www.moon.com
Randy Wood: www.therandymon.com
Joshua Berman: www.stonegrooves.net

Portals
The Internet is loaded with pages concerning Nicaragua, and long, eclectic lists of links abound. Following are a few central sites to get you started.

www.ibw.com.ni
IBW Internet Gateway is a vast portal to all things Nicaraguan, including services (tourism and otherwise), publications, organizations, and general information (mostly in Spanish).

www.lanic.utexas.edu/la/ca/nicaragua
University of Texas provides a complete list of academic institutions, more Nica portals, nongovernmental organizations, and government ministries in Nicaragua.

Official
www.usembassy.state.gov/Managua
The official U.S. embassy page.

www.state.gov
Site of the U.S. State Departmentís Nicaragua background notes and travel warnings.

www.cia.gov/cia/publications/factbook/geos/nu.html
CIA World Factbook provides current factoids on Nicaraguan geography, people, government, economy, etc., courtesy of the folks who brought you the Contra war.

www.pronicaragua.org
Pro-Nicaragua is an "Investment Promotion Agency" that will help you research that beach home, hotel, or running-shoe factory youíve always wanted to build.

www.intur.gob.ni
Visit the official Nicaraguan government tourism agency's page for a current list of active tour operators in Nicaragua.

www.marena.gob.ni
Providing information on specific parks and reserves, this is the Natural Resources Ministry home page.

www.ncdc.noaa.gov/ol/reports/mitch/mitch.html
This is the U.S. National Oceanic Atmospheric Administrationís fact page on Hurricane Mitch, with information on how it affected Nicaragua.

Political/Solidarity
www.nicanet.org
For more than 20 years, The Nicaragua Network, a coalition of U.S.-based non-profits, many of them regional sister-city organizations, has been committed to social and economic justice for the people of Nicaragua.

www.witnessforpeace.org
Witness for Peace is a politically independent, grassroots organization whose mission is to support peace, justice, and sustainable economies in the Americas by changing U.S. policies and corporate practices that contribute to poverty and oppression in Latin America and the Caribbean. Join a delegation or work brigade in Nicaragua and beyond.

www.globalexchange.org
Global Exchange is a human rights organization dedicated to promoting environmental, political, and social justice around the world. It has long had a focus on Nicaraguan issues and sends delegations there.

www.amigosdenicaragua.org
Amigos de Nicaragua is the official site for Returned Peace Corps Volunteers of Nicaragua.

www.buildingnewhope.com
Building New Hope supports a number of good projects, mostly in the Granada area.

Coffee and Fair Trade
www.transfairusa.org
Transfair USA is the place to start your fair trade research and offers Nicaragua-specific information.

www.nicaraguancoffees.com
Specialty Coffee Association of Nicaragua offers the latest international "Cup of Excellence" winners.

www.thanksgivingcoffee.com
CEO Paul Katzeff has done more for small-scale Nicaraguan coffee farmers than we have room to describe; read about California-based Thanskgiving Coffee Company's latest exchange with Nicaraguan farmers here, then buy a few pounds of beans.

www.pachamamaworld.com
Go shopping: Pachamama features international Fair Trade cooperatives and tours "to show firsthand how people are building sustainable futures for themselves in Nicaragua."

Traveling and Tourism
www.planeta.com
Planeta provides a lively public space devoted to "the development of conscientious tourism that benefits travelers and locals alike" with a full section on Nicaragua.

www.comarcaturs.com
COMARCA TURS Nicaragua is a program to develop sustainable tourism throughout the country.

www.journeywoman.com
For tips, independent women travelers should visit this site. Also download a copy of "Her Own Way: Advice for the Woman Traveller" at the Canadian Consular Affairs website (www.voyage.gc.ca).

www.bacanalnica.com
Go here for a Managua (and beyond) party and events guide; also check www.2night.com.

www.bluefieldspulse.com
For the lowdown on the Bluefields throwdown; events and parties on the Atlantic Coast.

www.sanjuandelsur.org.ni
This site provides an extensive network of local businesses in the southwestern corner of Nicaragua.

www.transitionsabroad.com
Check here for listings of work, volunteer, and study opportunities in Nicaragua and beyond.

Photographers
www.agstar.com.ni
Tomás Stargardter is a Nicaragua-based photojournalist whose website features a wide range of Nicaraguan images, from the natural to the extreme to the political.

Index

Crafts

general discussion: 64–65
basket weaving: 70
black pottery: 229, 248
cowboy boots: 191
Estelí: 193
Masatepe carpentry: 71
Mozonte pottery: 208
National Handicrafts Market: 60
pita hats: 265
pottery: 70, 229, 248
soapstone sculptures: 205
Taller de Cerámica Ducualí Grande: 203
woodcarving: 217
see also specific place

Hiking

Wildlife Viewing

Acknowledgments

We are grateful to the more than 500 readers who wrote to us with hard-won information and suggestions on how to improve this book; we read every one of your communications in the making of this edition and we wish you all many happy travels—hopefully you'll come back to Nicaragua and continue to keep us informed. Field agent Ryan Lamberg went deep into Siuna and Bosawas and authored part of that section in the Matagalpa chapter. Rich "El Gringuito Pelón" Castillo was our invaluable go-to man in Managua; thanks also to Vikki Stein, to Donna Tabor in Granada, Jim Russell in San Juan del Sur, Chris Bacon in Coffee Country, Olin Cohan in León, and Benjamin "Chico Laaargo" Letton in the Charco Verde Lagoon.

A number of still-active Peace Corps Volunteers generously fed us information about their far-flung sites and helped us check facts: thanks to Brian Forde, Charles Ferguson, Nadine Bridges, Kurt Krahn, Kevin Youngman, David Zambrano, Tracy Dickinson, Julie Gilgoff, Sarah Romorini, Justin Lee, David Cook, Mike Gerba, Brian Nash, Brook and Eli Meyer, Audra Teague, Michael Knowles, Luke Schtele, Kate Ashby, Raysun Goergen, Sierra Schroeder, Tania Elliot, Dustin Johnson, Mike Vanderwood, Jeff Mora, Brian Vaughn, Mark Hamel, Laura Willard, Katie Delahunty, and Cosigüina Mateo.

An *abrazo* to the Matagalpa *pelota* for undying *cariño* and first-rate fieldwork throughout the country: Erick, Heather Putman, Daniel Ulloa Chavarría, Felicity Butler, and famed Nicaraguan Gallopintologist Noel Montoya; also Shayna Harris and Isaac Grody-Patinkin.

In San Juan del Sur, thanks to Jane Mirandette, Richard "El Futuro Alcalde de San Juan del Sur" Morales, Paul Phelan, Marie Mendel, and Paige Penland; also Biologist Shaya Honarvar, who we found furiously measuring turtle nests one night at La Flor. On La Isla de Ometepe, thanks to Alvaro Molina and the Spanish Sisters Sofía and Concha Criado. Fellow Nicaphile and scribe, David Gullette provided some choice facts—look for his historical novel, Gringo Pinolero, set along the Río San Juan.

Also, thanks to Timoteo Jeffries, Beth Merrill, Leslie Anne Sullivan, Sergio Zepeda, Terry Halpin, Katherine Stecher, Barbara Larcom, Turalu Murdock, Shannon O'Reilly, Jan Jorg Strik, Joost Guttinger, Samantha Goldstein, and Michael Walfish.

Many thanks to Juan Carlos Martinez, Gianantonio Ricci, and Jordi Pascual Sala and also to Tim Coone, who gave us "Canal Dreams" and a whole lot of history. Several other generous friends made important contributions to the first edition of this book; their work and our gratitude remain.

Words are insufficient to express gratitude for the affection, hospitality, and *gallo pinto* of the Escoto family in La Trinidad (Darwin, Karla, Darling, and Karling) and the familia Ortiz-Jimenez in Pio XII (Mama Mercedes, Don Julio, Lastenia, Mardis, Neyda, and Edén). And this book wouldn't be what it is today without the love and encouragement of the Parra Blandón family (who also provided lots of support for the logistics of all this groundwork and research), and thanks to Ericka Briceño, for her love, insight, and boundless patience.

Thanks to Caprice Olsthoorn for hotels in Granada and animal treatment, Erin Van Rheenen for highlights in Granada, and Carrie Hirsch for tips in Managua. Thanks as well to Lisa Brunetti, Tom from the Bearded Monkey, Merrill Levy for surf stuff, Walter and Heidi Gostner from Italy for kind wishes and detailed notes, Debby Durham for info on Ometepe, M.J. Tolan and Mary Umonzar for miscellaneous tips, and Jonathan Fischer for comments on music and the Centro Cultural Nicaragüense Norteamericana/CCNN.

Back in the field, thanks to Mike Guterbock and Andrea Von der Ohe, Miriam Brodersen, Michael Locke, Jennifer Course, Silvia Rey, Ernest Dubois, Gerald and Bonnie Gantz, Seekey Cacciatore, David, Christopher Lupoli, and Justin "Scuba Buffalo" Lee.

Finally, thank you to our editing squad in Emeryville: Chris Jones, Tabitha Lahr, Kat Smith, and all the rest who made this book what it is and who helped get it into your hands.

ALSO AVAILABLE FROM

 MOON HANDBOOKS®
The Cure for the Common Trip

USA

Acadia National Park
Alaska
Arizona
Big Island of Hawai`i
Boston
California
Cape Cod, Martha's
  Vineyard & Nantucket
Charleston & Savannah
Chesapeake Bay
Coastal California
Coastal Carolinas
Coastal Maine
Coastal Oregon
Colorado
Columbia River Gorge
Connecticut
Florida Gulf Coast
Four Corners
Georgia
Grand Canyon
Hawaii
Hudson River Valley
Idaho
Kaua`i
Maine
Maryland & Delaware
Massachusetts
Maui
Michigan
Minnesota
Montana
Monterey & Carmel
Nevada
New Hampshire
New Mexico
New Orleans
New York State
North Carolina
Northern California

O`ahu
Ohio
Oregon
Pennsylvania
Rhode Island
San Juan Islands
Santa Fe-Taos
Silicon Valley
Smoky Mountains
South Carolina
Southern California
Tahoe
Tennessee
Texas
Utah
Virginia
Washington
Wisconsin
Wyoming
Yellowstone & Grand
  Teton
Yosemite
Zion & Bryce

THE AMERICAS

Alberta
Atlantic Canada
British Columbia
Canadian Rockies
Vancouver & Victoria
Western Canada

Acapulco
Baja
Cabo
Cancún
Guadalajara
Mexico City
Oaxaca
Pacific Mexico
Puerto Vallarta
Yucatán Peninsula

Argentina
Belize
Brazil
Buenos Aires
Chile
Costa Rica
Cuba
Dominican Republic
Ecuador
Guatemala
Havana
Honduras
Nicaragua
Panama
Patagonia
Peru
Virgin Islands

ASIA & THE PACIFIC

Australia
Fiji
Hong Kong
Micronesia
Nepal
New Zealand
South Korea
South Pacific
Tahiti
Thailand
Tonga-Samoa
Vietnam, Cambodia &
  Laos

www.moon.com

With expert authors, suggested routes and activities, and intuitive organization, Moon Handbooks ensure an uncommon experience—and a few new stories to tell.

U.S.~Metric Conversion

1 inch = 2.54 centimeters (cm)
1 foot = .304 meters (m)
1 yard = 0.914 meters
1 mile = 1.6093 kilometers (km)
1 km = .6214 miles
1 fathom = 1.8288 m
1 chain = 20.1168 m
1 furlong = 201.168 m
1 acre = .4047 hectares
1 sq km = 100 hectares
1 sq mile = 2.59 square km
1 ounce = 28.35 grams
1 pound = .4536 kilograms
1 short ton = .90718 metric ton
1 short ton = 2000 pounds
1 long ton = 1.016 metric tons
1 long ton = 2240 pounds
1 metric ton = 1000 kilograms
1 quart = .94635 liters
1 US gallon = 3.7854 liters
1 Imperial gallon = 4.5459 liters
1 nautical mile = 1.852 km

To compute Celsius temperatures, subtract 32 from Fahrenheit and divide by 1.8. To go the other way, multiply Celsius by 1.8 and add 32.

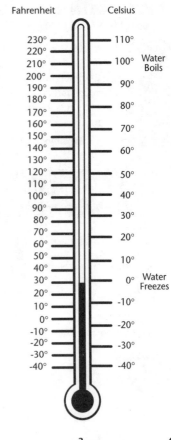

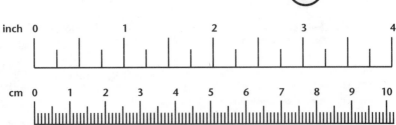

Keeping Current

Although we strive to produce the most up-to-date guidebook humanly possible, change is unavoidable. Between the time this book goes to print and the moment you read it, a handful of the businesses noted in these pages will undoubtedly change prices, move, or even close their doors forever. Other worthy attractions will open for the first time. If you have a favorite gem you'd like to see included in the next edition, or see anything that needs updating, clarification, or correction, please drop us a line. Send your comments via email to atpfeedback@avalonpub.com, or use the address below.

Moon Handbooks Nicaragua
Avalon Travel Publishing
1400 65th Street, Suite 250
Emeryville, CA 94608, USA
www.moon.com

Avalon Travel Publishing
An Imprint of
Avalon Publishing Group, Inc.

Editor: Christopher Jones
Series Manager: Kevin McLain
Acquisitions Manager: Rebecca K. Browning
Copy Editor: Kim Marks
Graphics Coordinator: Tabitha Lahr
Production Coordinator: Tabitha Lahr
Cover Designer: Kari Gim
Interior Designer: Amber Pirker
Map Editor: Kat Smith
Cartographers: Kat Kalamaras, Suzanne Service
Cartography Manager: Mike Morgenfeld
Indexer: Rachel Kuhn

ISBN-10: 1-56691-756-5
ISBN-13: 978-1-56691-756-8
ISSN: 1539-1019

Printing History
1st Edition—2003
2nd Edition—November 2005
5 4 3 2 1

Text © 2005 by Randy Wood and Joshua Berman
Maps © 2005 by Avalon Travel Publishing, Inc.
All rights reserved.

Some photos and illustrations are used by permission and are the property of the original copyright owners.

Front cover photo: © Charles Ferguson

Printed in the USA by Malloy, Inc.

About the Author

Randy Wood

© ERICKA BRICEÑO

Born on the sandy shore of New York's Atlantic coast, Randy Wood spent his childhood in various small sailboats developing a mariner's curiosity for what lies over the horizon. His first opportunity to find out came at the age of 11, when his family ventured from New York to California in a beat-up Volkswagen bus. He has explored ever since, venturing from the salmon boats of Ketchikan, Alaska to the Bolivian Andes, and from the volcanoes of Java to the turquoise seas of Sicily.

He first ventured to Nicaragua in 1998, where he made his home for the next five years while working as an agronomist and engineer. When Hurricane Mitch swept away the only bridge that led to his mountain village, he found himself marooned for several days; his Nica friends still laugh that he was the first one to cross the storm-swollen river because he was the best swimmer and, at 6'2", tall enough to touch bottom. Afterwards he stayed in the country to help with the Hurricane Mitch reconstruction program, also falling in love with and marrying Nicaraguan Ericka Briceño. They returned briefly to the United States, where he completed a Masters' Degree in Development Economics and International Relations at Johns Hopkins SAIS in 2005. He and Ericka continue to live part-time in Nicaragua.

In his limited free time, Randy enjoys playing 12-string folk guitar, swimming and surfing, salsa, , and swing dancing, backpacking, making maps, and fiddling with Linux-based computers. He remains an insufferable gearhead whose challenge to find the perfect backpack and tango its contents continues unabated. His work has appeared in BC Journal of International Relations, Between the Waves Magazine, and SAIS Review.

Randy's website is www.therandymon.com.